The Oxford Handbook of
the Psychology of Working

Editor in Chief PETER E. NATHAN

The Oxford Handbook of the Psychology of Working

Edited by

David L. Blustein

OXFORD
UNIVERSITY PRESS

OXFORD
UNIVERSITY PRESS

Oxford University Press is a department of the University of Oxford.
It furthers the University's objective of excellence in research, scholarship,
and education by publishing worldwide.

Oxford   New York
Auckland   Cape Town   Dar es Salaam   Hong Kong   Karachi
Kuala Lumpur   Madrid   Melbourne   Mexico City   Nairobi
New Delhi   Shanghai   Taipei   Toronto

With offices in
Argentina   Austria   Brazil   Chile   Czech Republic   France   Greece
Guatemala   Hungary   Italy   Japan   Poland   Portugal   Singapore
South Korea   Switzerland   Thailand   Turkey   Ukraine   Vietnam

Oxford is a registered trade mark of Oxford University Press
in the UK and certain other countries.

Published in the United States of America by
Oxford University Press
198 Madison Avenue, New York, NY 10016

Library of Congress Cataloging-in-Publication Data
The Oxford handbook of the psychology of working / edited by David L. Blustein.
    pages cm.—(The Oxford Library of psychology)
  Includes bibliographical references and index.
  ISBN 978–0–19–022749–4 (alk. paper)
  1. Work—Psychological aspects.   2. Work—Social aspects.   3. Vocational guidance.
  4. Psychotherapy—Social aspects.   5. Social policy.   I. Blustein, David Larry, editor.
  BF481.O946 2014
  158.7—dc23
  2014029640

9 7 8 6 5 4 3 2 1

Printed in the United States of America
on acid-free paper

SHORT CONTENTS

OXFORD LIBRARY OF PSYCHOLOGY

The *Oxford Library of Psychology*, a landmark series of handbooks, is published by Oxford University Press, one of the world's oldest and most highly respected publishers, with a tradition of publishing significant books in psychology. The ambitious goal of the *Oxford Library of Psychology* is nothing less than to span a vibrant, wide-ranging field and, in so doing, to fill a clear market need.

Encompassing a comprehensive set of handbooks, organized hierarchically, the *Library* incorporates volumes at different levels, each designed to meet a distinct need. At one level are a set of handbooks designed broadly to survey the major subfields of psychology; at another are numerous handbooks that cover important current focal research and scholarly areas of psychology in depth and detail. Planned as a reflection of the dynamism of psychology, the *Library* will grow and expand as psychology itself develops, thereby highlighting significant new research that will impact on the field. Adding to its accessibility and ease of use, the *Library* will be published in print and, later on, electronically.

The *Library* surveys psychology's principal subfields with a set of handbooks that capture the current status and future prospects of those major subdisciplines. This initial set includes handbooks of social and personality psychology, clinical psychology, counseling psychology, school psychology, educational psychology, industrial and organizational psychology, cognitive psychology, cognitive neuroscience, methods and measurements, history, neuropsychology, personality assessment, developmental psychology, and more. Each handbook undertakes to review one of psychology's major subdisciplines with breadth, comprehensiveness, and exemplary scholarship. In addition to these broadly-conceived volumes, the *Library* also includes a large number of handbooks designed to explore in depth more specialized areas of scholarship and research, such as stress, health and coping, anxiety and related disorders, cognitive development, or child and adolescent assessment. In contrast to the broad coverage of the subfield handbooks, each of these latter volumes focuses on an especially productive, more highly focused line of scholarship and research. Whether at the broadest or most specific level, however, all of the *Library* handbooks offer synthetic coverage that reviews and evaluates the relevant past and present research and anticipates research in the future. Each handbook in the *Library* includes introductory and concluding chapters written by its editor to provide a roadmap to the handbook's table of contents and to offer informed anticipations of significant future developments in that field.

An undertaking of this scope calls for handbook editors and chapter authors who are established scholars in the areas about which they write. Many of the nation's and world's most productive and best-respected psychologists have agreed to edit *Library* handbooks or write authoritative chapters in their areas of expertise.

For whom has the *Oxford Library of Psychology* been written? Because of its breadth, depth, and accessibility, the *Library* serves a diverse audience, including graduate students in psychology and their faculty mentors, scholars, researchers, and practitioners in psychology and related fields. Each will find in the *Library* the information they seek on the subfield or focal area of psychology in which they work or are interested.

Befitting its commitment to accessibility, each handbook includes a comprehensive index, as well as extensive references to help guide research. And because the *Library* was designed from its inception as an online as well as a print resource, its structure and contents will be readily and rationally searchable online. Further, once the *Library* is released online, the handbooks will be regularly and thoroughly updated.

In summary, the *Oxford Library of Psychology* will grow organically to provide a thoroughly informed perspective on the field of psychology, one that reflects both psychology's dynamism and its increasing interdisciplinarity. Once published electronically, the *Library* is also destined to become a uniquely valuable interactive tool, with extended search and browsing capabilities. As you begin to consult this handbook, we sincerely hope you will share our enthusiasm for the more than 500-year tradition of Oxford University Press for excellence, innovation, and quality, as exemplified by the *Oxford Library of Psychology*.

Peter E. Nathan
Editor-in-Chief
Oxford Library of Psychology

David L. Blustein

David L. Blustein is a Professor in the Department of Counseling, Developmental, and Educational Psychology at the Lynch School of Education at Boston College. Professor Blustein is a Fellow of Division 17 (Counseling Psychology) of the American Psychological Association and he has received the Division 17 Early Career Scientist-Practitioner Award, the John Holland Award for Outstanding Achievement in Personality and Career Research, and the Extended Research Award by the American Counseling Association. Professor Blustein is also a Fellow of the American Educational Research Association and of the National Career Development Association. Professor Blustein has published over 90 journal articles and book chapters in career development, work-based transitions, the exploration process, the interface between work and interpersonal functioning, and the psychology of working. He also has published a book entitled *The Psychology of Working: A New Perspective for Career Development, Counseling, and Public Policy*. In addition, Professor Blustein has consulted with state and national government agencies on issues pertaining to career development education and the school-to-work transition process.

CONTRIBUTORS

Saba Rasheed Ali
College of Education
University of Iowa
Iowa City, IA

Mary Z. Anderson
Department of Counselor Education and
    Counseling Psychology
Western Michigan University
Kalamazoo, MI

Tamba-Kuii M. Bailey
Department of Counseling Psychology and
    Community Services
University of North Dakota
Grand Forks, ND

David L. Blustein
Department of Counseling, Developmental,
    and Educational Psychology
Lynch School of Education
Boston College
Chestnut Hill, MA

James M. Croteau
Department of Counselor Education and
    Counseling Psychology
Western Michigan University
Kalamazoo, MI

Ellen Fabian
Department of Counseling & Personnel
    Services
University of Maryland
College Park, MD

Lisa Y. Flores
Department of Educational, School, and
    Counseling Psychology
University of Missouri
Columbia, MO

Anderson J. Franklin
Department of Counseling, Developmental,
    and Educational Psychology
Lynch School of Education
Boston College
Chestnut Hill, MA

Douglas T. Hall
School of Management
Boston University
Boston, MA

Edwin L. Herr
College of Education
The Pennsylvania State University
University Park, PA

Cindy L. Juntunen
Department of Counseling Psychology and
    Community Services
University of North Dakota
Grand Forks, ND

Neeta Kantamneni
Department of Educational Psychology
University of Nebraska-Lincoln
Lincoln, NE

Maureen E. Kenny
Department of Counseling, Developmental,
    and Educational Psychology
Lynch School of Education
Boston College
Chestnut Hill, MA

Mary Beth Medvide
Department of Counseling, Developmental,
    and Educational Psychology
Lynch School of Education
Boston College
Chestnut Hill, MA

Philip H. Mirvis
Global Network for Corporate Citizenship
Ipswich, MA

Spencer G. Niles
College of Education
The Pennsylvania State University
University Park, PA

Isaac Prilleltensky
Department of Educational
    and Psychological Studies
University of Miami
Coral Gables, FL

Mary Sue Richardson
Department of Applied Psychology
New York University
New York, NY

Robin A. Alcala Saner
Department of Educational Psychology
University of Minnesota
Minneapolis, MN

Charles Schaeffer
Department of Applied Psychology
New York University
New York, NY

Graham B. Stead
College of Education and Human Services
Cleveland State University
Cleveland, OH

Anthony A. Sterns
College of Nursing
Kent State University
Kent, OH
Department of Marketing
The University of Akron
Akron, OH
Business, Management, and Leadership
School of Professional Studies
City University of New York
New York, NY

Harvey L. Sterns
Institute for Life-span Development and
    Gerontology
Department of Psychology
The University of Akron
Akron, OH
Department of Family and Community
    Medicine
Northeast Ohio Medical University
Rootstown, OH

Jane L. Swanson
Department of Psychology
Southern Illinois University Carbondale
Carbondale, IL

Sherri L. Turner
Department of Educational Psychology
University of Minnesota
Minneapolis, MN

Michael J. Zickar
Department of Psychology
Bowling Green State University
Bowling Green, OH

Julia L. Conkel Ziebell
Department of Educational Psychology
University of Minnesota
Minneapolis, MN

CONTENTS

PART 1

Theoretical Foundations

The Psychology of Working: A New Perspective for a New Era

David L. Blustein

Abstract

This chapter serves as an introduction to *The Oxford Handbook of the Psychology of Working*. The two foci of the psychology of working, a critique of existing discourses about work and career and a framework for a new perspective for understanding the psychological nature of working, are reviewed. A brief synopsis of each of the sections and chapters in this book is then presented, with a summary of how these contributions function, independently and collectively, to create the foundation for a dignified and inclusive discourse on the role of work in people's lives. The chapter concludes with suggestions for advancing the psychology-of-working perspective.

Key Words: psychology of working, working, career development, organizational psychology, poverty, social justice, career counseling

Working is a central aspect of life, providing a source of structure, a means of survival, connection to others, and optimally a means of self-determination (Blustein, 2006, 2008; Budd, 2011; Juntunen, 2006; Richardson, 1993, 2012). Across the globe, people devote considerable time and effort in preparing for, adjusting to, and managing their work lives. Many of the major crises affecting people and communities have been and continue to be related to working (Clifton, 2011; Wilson, 1996). These crises often affect nations and states at a macro level, and have a profound impact on the course and trajectory of individual lives (Sen, 1999; Wilson, 1996). Wars, famines, and risks to personal safety have all been directly related to access to work (Clifton, 2011; Sachs, 2005); in short, lack of work is a significant cause of social and economic disruptions as well as poverty. At the same time, working, when it is dignified and meaningful, can create the foundation for a satisfying life that allows people to support themselves and their families, and to find an outlet for their values and interests in the world

of work (Lent, Brown, & Hackett, 2002; Savickas, 2011; Super, 1980).

A close review of narratives, memoirs, fiction, and other forms of artistic expression underscores the centrality of work in people's lives (Blustein, 2006; Bowe, Bowe, & Streeter, 2000; Budd, 2011; Terkel, 1974). The importance of working has not escaped the attention of psychologists in their roles as scholars, policy advocates, and practitioners (e.g., Blustein, 2008; Brown, & Lent, 2005; Fassinger, 2008; Fouad & Bynner, 2008; Hall and Associates, 1996; Savickas, 2011). The results of this attention have led to sustained studies of working, careers, and occupational well-being, yielding a rich literature encompassing a wide array of work-related issues and challenges (e.g., Brown & Lent, 2005; Duffy, Diemer, Perry, Laurenzi, & Torrey, 2012; Eggerth, DeLancy, Flynn, & Jacobson, 2012; Flores et al., 2011; Quick & Tetrick, 2010; Walsh & Savickas, 2005). In fact, much of the early work of applied psychologists (the forerunner of clinical, counseling, and industrial/organizational [I/O] psychology) was devoted to helping people sort out their work-based plans and helping organizations select the most appropriate candidates for an ever-increasing range of jobs (Koppes, 2007; Savickas & Baker, 2005). The applied specialties in psychology (with the exception of I/O psychology) soon became infused with a focus on mental health issues, which clearly helped to expand the impact of psychology and to benefit people in need of services.

Following the trend toward increasing specialization within psychology, working, as a context for human behavior, became increasingly compartmentalized throughout most of psychology, ultimately yielding a highly insular view of a portion of our lives that takes up a significant amount of time and energy. For example, with some notable exceptions (e.g., Axelrod, 1999; Lowman, 1993; Richardson, 2012; Socarides & Kramer, 1997), working is not a central part of most psychotherapy and personality theories. Furthermore, within North America (and in many other parts of the globe), psychological practice and scholarship on working increasingly has tended to focus on those with some degree of privilege and choice. These factors, when considered together, have led many scholars to critique existing discourses and to advocate for a more inclusive perspective of the role of work in one's psychological well-being (e.g., Blustein, McWhirter, & Perry, 2005; Harmon & Farmer, 1983; Richardson, 1993).

In this chapter (and in many chapters within this Handbook), the term "psychology of working" is used to capture both the critique of the extant foci and emphases in the work-based psychological disciplines as well as the emerging perspective that seeks to encompass the full range of working experiences for the full range of individuals who work and who want to work. As a means of enacting the inclusive agenda of this movement, I have developed this Handbook project to bring together a community of scholars and practitioners to think carefully and critically about the complex challenges that people face in their work lives across a wide array of contexts and situations.

In this introductory chapter, I describe the foundation that exists for the psychology of working and outline the potential for this Handbook to expand and deepen the emerging discourse about the role of work in people's lives. After presenting the basic premises of the psychology of working, I then review the sections and chapters, with the intention of setting the stage for the contributions that follow. I conclude with some observations culled after reading the chapters, with the intention of highlighting future directions for scholarship, practice, and theory development.

What Is the Psychology of Working?

The psychology of working, as a perspective, can be traced to the beginning of applied psychology, which focused extensively on working, both from individual and organizational perspectives (Koppes, 2007; Savickas & Baker, 2005; Zickar, 2004). Beginning with Parsons in vocational guidance and Munsterberg and others in personnel psychology, nascent psychologists in the early part of the 20th century initiated the study of work with the intention of broadening our understanding of this essential part of life. At the same time, many of the early psychologists who studied working also had an interest in applied practice. Vocational guidance scholars and practitioners were interested in helping people make wise choices about their future with the goal of enhancing the meaning and satisfaction of their working lives. Personnel psychologists were interested in a similar array of questions regarding person–environment fit, but from the perspective of the organization, with the intention of improving productivity, worker tenure, and job satisfaction. By the middle of the 20th century, both fields burgeoned, creating impressive bodies of scholarship, thoughtful theories, and well-respected practices. While the original distinctions of vocational guidance and personnel psychology soon gave way to a plethora of disciplines and subdisciplines, the common theme among these approaches was, and continues to be, the psychological study of working. One of the challenges, however, was in establishing a conceptual framework to integrate these disciplines and reduce the artificial splits that had emerged, separating the various psychological studies of working. In addition, the artificial splits functioned to separate the study of working from that of other domains of life, leading to a circumscribed focus that has adversely affected the entire psychological enterprise.

Prior to a more detailed overview of the psychology of working, it is important to clarify what the psychology of working is not. First and foremost, it is not a theory, *per se*; rather, it is a perspective that grew out of a confluence of trends within psychology and within the broader intellectual world. The psychology-of-working perspective initially emerged from a critique of existing discourses about work and career that have been dominant in applied psychology and career development for the past few decades. The critique levied against traditional studies of career choice and development as well as traditional I/O psychology helped to carve out the contours of a new and more inclusive perspective. The perspective that is emerging is early in its development; however, this Handbook is designed to facilitate the growth of an inclusive, empathic, and just approach to understanding the role of work in people's lives.

A second and equally essential point is that the psychology of working is not attached to any one scholar or group of scholars. The psychology-of-working perspective reflects decades of sustained critique of the traditional array of assumptions and perspectives about work and career. As reflected in this volume, the psychology-of-working perspective has emerged on the shoulders of courageous scholars who have identified the inherent biases in studying and intervening in the work lives of people with a modicum of privilege (e.g., Harmon & Farmer, 1983; Helms & Cook, 1999; Kornhauser, 1957; Richardson, 1993; Smith, 1983; Zickar, 2004). In addition, these critiques continue to emerge with new ideas for the expansion of psychological considerations of working and career, often without an explicitly stated overarching perspective (e.g., Helms &Cook; Szymanksi & Parker, 2003). One of the objectives, therefore, of this Handbook is to provide an opportunity for a sustained synthesis of critiques and new paradigms and perspectives.

In the sections that follow, I introduce the psychology of working by first focusing on its role as a critique of existing discourses. This is followed by a selected review of the most important attributes of the psychology-of-working perspective. When considered collectively, these two sections provide readers with a "briefing" of the major features of the psychology-of-working perspective, thereby setting the stage for the chapters that follow. Embedded in the discussion that follows is the rationale for the present Handbook and an overview of how the psychology of working can transform how psychologists, social scientists, and counseling professionals understand and intervene in the work lives of people across the full spectrum of power, privilege, and social location.

The Psychology of Working as a Critique

One of the trends in the psychological study of working over the course of the 20th century was the move from exploring working for the vast majority of people who worked and who wanted to work to the exploration of the work lives of people with some degree of volition and privilege. With some notable exceptions (e.g., Harmon & Farmer, 1983; Kornhauser, 1957; Richardson, 1993; Smith, 1983), the agendas of contemporary vocational psychology and I/O psychology, over time, have been on understanding and facilitating the work lives of people who tend to have some level of choice in how they will engage in their work lives. Within the sections that follow, I review specific critiques that have emerged from analyses of the impact of external barriers and diverse sources of oppression on human behavior and well-being.

Feminism and gender. One of the most important critiques came from feminist thinkers, who applied new ideas and political perspectives to the established norms about work and career, noting how the field had marginalized the lives of women who often faced daunting challenges in gaining access to training, employment, and dignified work (e.g., Barnett & Hyde, 2001; Betz & Fitzgerald, 1987; Brown, 2009). The feminist critique has generated a broad and more inclusive perspective that has sought to examine the connections and disconnections among various life roles (Fassinger, 2008). For example, feminist scholars highlighted the overt and covert ways that sexism constrained the development of interests and limited upward mobility for women in the workplace (Betz & Fitzgerald, 1987; Fassinger, 2008). The feminist critiques have also evoked thoughtful dialogues on the hegemony of market work over care work (Richardson, 2012). In addition, feminist scholars have creatively explored the complex relationships between personal and political issues (Brown, 2009).

Race and culture. Some of the seminal critiques of career development have emerged from incisive examinations of how race and racism function to constrain opportunities for people of color in many Western cultures (Carter & Cook, 1992; Helms & Cook, 1999; Smith, 1983). In short, the critiques emerging from scholars and practitioners concerned with race and culture have highlighted how access to opportunity is unfairly distributed, in large measure, due to racism and other forms of social oppression. These critiques also have generated a growing interest in how culture frames the discourse about work and careers (Stead, 2004). By examining the impact of race and culture in the psychological study of working, we have been forced to reckon with inherent biases in traditional, Western-based perspectives of work and career, thereby generating an essential foundation for an inclusive and politically embedded psychological study of working.

Sexual orientation. The discrimination that individuals face due to their sexual orientation has generated a necessary critique of the prevailing career choice and development perspectives and assumptions (Chung, 2003; Lidderdale, Croteau, Anderson, Tovar-Murray, & Davis, 2007). The stigma that is evoked by nonheterosexual orientations is particularly pernicious in many education and work-based settings, often resulting in significant challenges for people as they develop work-based plans and adjust to work (Croteau, Anderson, DiStefano, & Kampa-Kokesch, 2000). A key consequence of discrimination and living in fear of psychological and, at times, physical abuse is the constriction of opportunities for a self-determined work life. As such, giving voice to the experiences of LGBT individuals in the workplace also serves to raise concerns about the viability of the traditional career narrative.

Disability. One of the most consistent critiques of the focus on volitional careers and studies of relatively well-educated workers has emerged from the rehabilitation movement (Fabian & Leisner, 2005; Neff, 1985; Szymanski & Parker, 2003). By focusing on the nature of disability and handicapping conditions, scholars and practitioners have had to confront inequities at work and have faced clients who often have had less-than-optimal levels of choice in their work lives. In fact, some of the most articulate calls for an inclusive psychology of working have been advanced by Neff (1985) and others (e.g., Szymanski & Parker, 2003), who have advocated for a contextualized study of working in people's lives. When considering the impact of disabling conditions at the workplace, we are confronted with several issues that are inherent in the contemporary vision of the psychology of working. For example, some disabling conditions constrain one's options, via social barriers that are unrelated to the way in which a given disability may affect one's work performance. In addition, the stigma that is often evoked by disabling conditions influences the ways that individuals make meaning of, and respond to, work-based challenges (Neff, 1985). In effect, the psychology of disability has set the stage for an inclusive and contextualized psychological study of working.

Epistemology. From an epistemological level, critiques of existing psychological discourses, including the discourse about work and careers, have emerged from social constructionist perspectives (Burr, 1995; Gergen, 2009). One of the hallmarks of these critiques is the questioning of existing practices, theories, and underlying assumptions about a given phenomenon or body of knowledge. Beginning with the seminal articles by Savickas

(1993) and Richardson (1993), the assumptions that have formed the basis of much of the study of working, careers, and psychological practice have been identified. The social constructionist critique encourages a more relativistic understanding of knowledge, acknowledging that the assumptions that guide a field of inquiry are shaped by relationships and culture (Burr, 1995; Flum, 2001; Schultheiss, 2003, 2007). In addition, the social constructionist perspectives seek to unpack how knowledge is constructed, identifying the social and political discourses that frame how questions are asked and how they are examined. (Further details on social constructionist analyses can be found in Blustein, Schultheiss, & Flum, 2004, and Chapter 3 in this volume.)

Summary. As reflected in this brief overview, critiques have been raised from multiple vantage points, with a number of common themes. First, the study of careers, *per se*, while creative and substantive in its contributions, has functioned to circumscribe the range and depth of how working is studied in psychology and how individuals and organizations can achieve well-being in their working lives. Second, the prevailing discourse in the study of working and career has resulted in the relative neglect of those without as much choice in their working lives. Third, with notable exceptions, many contemporary perspectives on working and career have tended to marginalize attention to the pervasive role of social barriers in creating unequal access to work. Fourth, again with some notable exceptions (e.g., Richardson, 2012; Savickas, 2011; Super, Savickas, & Super, 1996), the psychological study of working has become increasingly insular, creating ideas and practices that are not consistently embedded in the broader fabric of life. These critiques helped to establish a foundation for the development of a psychology-of-working perspective, as reviewed next.

The Psychology of Working as a Perspective

The development of the contemporary psychology-of-working perspective can be traced directly to the contribution by Richardson (1993), who argued convincingly that psychologists needed to reframe their foci to include (1) an emphasis on working rather than careers; (2) an expansion of prevailing epistemological perspectives to embrace social constructionism; (3) attention to both care work and market work; and (4) an exploration of working from an interdisciplinary perspective. These recommendations served to integrate numerous critiques and established a framework for an expanded and inclusive study of working. While the chapters included in this Handbook will elucidate the full scope of the psychology-of-working perspective, a brief overview of its most salient attributes is warranted in this chapter.

The role of values in the psychology of working. Prilleltensky (1997) published a seminal article arguing that psychologists need to be aware of the values that guide their work. Eschewing the notion that psychological science and practice are value free or value neutral, Prilleltensky noted that values and moral decisions permeate our work. According to Prilleltensky, psychologists ought to articulate their values and moral decisions and should be able to identify ways that these decisions are manifested in their work.

Infusing a focus on values and morals into the psychology-of-working perspective suggests several important implications. Given that working takes place in a social and political context that frames the nature of individuals' experiences, the decisions that scholars and practitioners make about how to study work have vast consequences for individuals, families, and communities. For example, psychologists who are studying the best ways to train leaders in organizations may be asked to provide guidance on how managers can reduce grievances for violations of workers' rights. In addition, studying the career choice and development of middle-class students attending relatively prestigious colleges manifests an inherent set of values. Of course, each of these endeavors is a legitimate expression of the applied aspects of our work, often resulting in significant positive outcomes for clients and communities. However, by ignoring the question of values, we risk making decisions about scholarship and practice that may function to create and/or sustain privileges for some and lack of power for others.

Core assumptions of the psychology of working. The psychology-of-working perspective has several core tenets that are intended to guide the study of working and the development of interventions for individuals, organizations, and communities. The list that follows is not intended to be exhaustive; rather, it summarizes the main points that have been articulated to date in the literature (e.g., Blustein, 2006, 2011; Fassinger, 2008; Fouad & Bynner, 2008; Juntunen, 2006; Richardson, 1993, 2012).

• *Diverse epistemologies, including logical positivism, post-positivism, as well as social constructionism, are viable strategies to use in understanding the nature of working.* Rather than creating an implicit or explicit expectation that scholarship ought to endorse a particular modality of understanding the nature of the world, the psychology-of-working perspective chooses not to reify one vantage point over another. The choice of epistemologies ought to be based on the questions that are posed and the values that are inherent in a project. Recent research on issues of relevance to the broadly inclusive study of working advocated in this Handbook has relied upon diverse epistemologies, ranging from logical positivist (e.g., Duffy et al., 2012; Eggerth, DeLaney, Flynn, & Jacobson, 2012; Kenny, Blustein, Haase, Jackson, & Perry, 2006) to post-positivist (Blustein et al., 2010; Flores et al., 2011), and social constructionist perspectives (Stead & Perry, 2012).

• *Work is a central aspect of life.* While obvious to most readers, the central role that work plays in life, in promoting or inhibiting well-being, and in establishing the basis for healthy, safe, and nurturing communities is clearly affirmed. The argument about the central role of work in life has been constructed around extensive research (Blustein, 2008; Quick & Tetrick, 2010; Richardson, 2012) as well as an examination of narratives, memoirs, bodies of art, literature, and music (Blustein, 2006; Budd, 2011). As reflected in our early evolutionary history, working is a central organizing aspect of life, one that connects people across historical and cultural boundaries (Blustein, 2006; Budd, 2011; Donkin, 2001).

• *Working is central to mental health.* A related assumption that is central to the psychology-of-working perspective is that working has the potential to foster and sustain positive mental health. Considerable scholarship supports this view, including studies of the impact of unemployment and underemployment (e.g., Paul & Moser, 2009), in which mental health problems have been causally linked to the absence of working. In addition, the availability of dignified work has been associated with reductions in mental health problems, antisocial behavior, and other maladaptive behaviors (e.g., Blustein, 2006; Shore, 1998).

• *The psychological study of working includes in its purview the work lives of everyone who works and who wants to work.* As indicated earlier, one of the fundamental assumptions of the psychology of working is the creation of a sufficiently large and welcoming tent to include everyone who works and who wants to work (Richardson, 1993). This assumption does not exclude the traditional focus on career choice and development, career management, or other perspectives that have framed the psychological study of careers to date. Rather, this point is designed to embrace the full scope of working across the globe, including jobs that represent the culmination of planning and significant education as well as jobs that are taken for survival (and all of the jobs that are located between these two poles). In addition, the psychology-of-working perspective includes in its mission issues pertaining to unemployment, underemployment, and adjusting to disabling conditions that adversely affect access to work.

• *Work and nonwork experiences are often seamlessly experienced in the natural course of people's lives.* As noted earlier, psychological theory and practice has become increasingly insular, leading to artificial splits that are not consistent with the lived experience of people. As such, the relatively seamless nature of life ought to be captured in scholarship and practice about working. In contrast to the increasing compartmentalization of psychology, the psychology-of-working perspective strives to reduce or eliminate *a priori* categories that separate psychological discourses. The optimal discourse would be one that examines the lived experience of working, which is conveyed in the language of people talking about their lives. As conveyed in memoirs and narrative excerpts (e.g., Blustein, 2006; Bowe et al., 2000; Terkel, 1974), working is inextricably connected to the rest of our lives. We inhabit multiple roles in life and these roles intersect with each other in organized and random ways, creating a rich tapestry of life experiences (cf. Super, 1980).

• *An experience-near understanding of the role of work in people's lives is integral to the psychological exploration of working.* To understand the complex and nuanced nature of working, psychologists would benefit from developing an empathic approach to the experiences that individuals face in their work-based tasks. Recent qualitative research (e.g., Flores et al., 2011; Fouad, Cotter, Carter, Bernfeld, & Liu, 2011; McIlveen, Beccaria, DuPreez, & Patton, 2010) has revealed deep levels of complexity and nuance in the ways in which people understand and make meaning about their working experiences, underscoring the importance of empathy and relatedness in research. In a broader sense, encouraging an experience-near connection to working has the potential to enhance counseling practice and public policy initiatives about working.

• *The psychology-of-working perspective seeks to identify how social, economic, and political forces influence the distribution of resources and affordances.* By including a focus on macro-level factors, psychologists are able to understand how working serves as one of the most vital playing fields in life, the location of both dreams and disappointments. While traditional studies of working within vocational and I/O psychology have explored and identified social and economic barriers, the psychology-of-working perspective places considerations of these resources and obstacles at the forefront of conceptualizations, research, practice, and policy recommendations.

• *The psychology-of-working perspective embraces the fact that working occurs in various contexts, including the marketplace and caregiving contexts.* As Richardson (1993, 2012) has so compellingly argued, work is not limited to employment for money, goods, or services; a truly comprehensive approach to working necessitates a focus on care work (caring for family members, loved ones, etc.), which is, and has been, a constant across time periods and cultures.

• *The psychology-of-working perspective embeds conceptualizations of working in cultural and relational contexts.* Recent conceptualizations of working that have explicitly infused cultural and relational frameworks have yielded informative perspectives about unemployment (e.g., Stead & Perry, 2012), social class (McIlveen et al., 2010), care work (Richardson, 2012), and poverty (Blustein, 2011b). In these formulations, culture and relationships are seen as the vehicle through which people make sense of, and attach meaning to, their lives.

• *As a framework, the psychology of working has the potential to enrich existing theories.* The broad and inclusive scope of the psychology of working provides an opportunity for existing career choice, career counseling, psychotherapy, organizational psychology, and career management theories to expand their impact and explanatory reach. As a meta-perspective, the psychology of working offers traditional theories with the conceptual rationale and tools to generate new formulations that can expand their relevance as the world of work continues its radical transformation.

• *Optimally, working has the potential to fulfill core human needs.* Numerous scholars have sought to identify the needs that working can fulfill (e.g., Neff, 1985; O'Brien, 1986). When considering these various taxonomies from an integrative perspective, the following three sets of needs have been identified (Blustein, 2006):

• Need for survival and power: Harkening back to our hunter-gatherer roots, working, at its core, is integral to our survival. In addition, working has the potential to enhance one's power in the world, via material acquisition as well as the attainment of status and prestige.

• Need for social connection: For many people, working provides extensive opportunities for relationships (Flum, 2001; Schultheiss, 2003). Furthermore, working serves as one of the major theaters for interactions with others, including relationships that are supportive as well as relationships that are problematic. In addition, working provides an informal connection to the social world via the sense of contribution that people experience in their work (Blustein, 2011a).

• Need for self-determination: At its best, working provides people with opportunities to engage in activities that are interesting, stimulating, and meaningful, thereby fostering a sense of self-determination (Ryan & Deci, 2000). In addition, self-determination can be attained via extrinsically motivating tasks that are useful in helping people attain goals that they value.

Current Status of the Psychology-of-Working Perspective

As reflected in these tenets, the psychology-of-working perspective offers a potentially transformative framework for enhancing and expanding the way in which work is understood in psychological research, practice, and public policy advocacy. At its core, it is an inclusive perspective that seeks to reduce the privileging of affluence in contemporary psychological discourses about working. The initial forays into the psychology-of-working perspective have generated considerable scholarship and program development efforts. While some of these contributions have been linked explicitly to the ideas embedded in the psychology of working, others reflect a more subtle shifting zeitgeist that reflects an intellectual climate that is increasingly welcoming of a critical examination of the traditional career narrative.

The social justice aspects embedded in the critiques of traditional studies of careers have informed considerable shifts across the spectrum of theory, research, and practice. For example,

social justice considerations are now more explicitly infused into new texts (e.g., Hartung & Subich, 2011; Watson & McMahon, 2012), review articles and chapters (e.g., Fassinger, 2008; Fouad, 2007), and theoretical initiatives (Richardson, 2012; Vondracek, Ferreira, & Santos, 2010). In addition, an emerging body of scholarship is exploring how differential access to the opportunity structure creates a domino effect that functions to sustain inequity and injustice (Blustein, McWhirter, & Perry, 2005; Toporek & Chope, 2006).

Other initiatives emerging from the sociopolitical critique inherent in the psychology of working are evident in research on unemployment and dislocated workers (e.g., Blustein, Medvide, & Wan, 2011; Fouad et al., 2011). In addition, a number of incisive articles examining work-based immigration have used a psychology-of-working perspective, yielding important insights about irregular migrant workers (e.g., Marfleet & Blustein, 2011) as well as Latino/a immigrants entering the United States (e.g., Eggerth et al., 2012). While examinations of poverty and social class have been part of the career discourse for decades (cf. Super, 1957), recent initiatives have been more numerous and substantive, including important contributions by Diemer and Ali (2009), Noonan, Hall, and Blustein (2007), and McIlveen et al. (2010).

Furthermore, innovations in counseling practice have been generated from an explicit incorporation of the psychology-of-working perspective. One particularly compelling example is the work by Hees, Rottinghaus, Briddick, and Conrath (2012), who explored the needs of dislocated workers using ideas culled from the psychology of working. In addition, an integrative counseling perspective has been developed using the psychology-of-working framework, providing a conceptual rubric for inclusive psychological practice that integrates the full scope of clients' issues into the counseling process (Blustein, Kenna, Gill, & DeVoy, 2008). Furthermore, Richardson's (2012) recent articulation of a model for counseling for work and relationships, while emerging from a broad array of conceptual and theoretical vantage points, includes many of the salient features of the psychology-of-working perspective.

Psychoeducational interventions that have been developed to intervene with client populations living in at-risk contexts also have been informed by many aspects of the psychology-of-working perspective. For example, a number of new programs that have been developed within urban educational communities have thoughtfully blended a focus on critical consciousness and race and racism along with traditional career development interventions (Ali, Yang, Button, & McCoy, 2012; Blustein et al., 2010; Perry, DeWine, Duffy, & Vance, 2007). Within the assessment world, Duffy and his colleagues have developed a sophisticated psychometric tool designed to measure an individual's experience of work volition (Duffy et al., 2012).

One of the most important trends that have emerged within vocational psychology is the revived use of the terms "work" and "working." Consistent with the advice of Richardson (1993) and supported by traditions within fields as disparate as labor relations and occupational sociology (e.g., Budd, 2011), psychologists, counselors, and scholars are increasingly referring to work to capture a fuller scope of activities in both the market and caregiving contexts (e.g., Bhat, 2010; Duffy et al., 2012; Fouad, 2007; Richardson, 2012; Shen-Miller, McWhirter, & Bartone, 2012). While some may suggest that the precise term that is used is not necessarily central to the inclusiveness and relevance of our work, I believe that care should be exercised not to reify the term "career," which may function to constrain the mission for psychologists, social scientists, and practitioners interested in working (Blustein, 2006).

As this brief review of the conceptual framework and initial research/program development initiatives of the psychology of working has revealed, a groundswell of new ideas, practices, and policy recommendations is emerging from all quarters of psychology and the helping professions. The perspective that has been advanced is now taking shape and is poised to foster important innovations in research, theory, practice, and public policy. To facilitate this growing transformation in how psychologists and related professionals think about and intervene in the work lives of their clients and communities, I have solicited contributions from scholars who have joined this effort to take this perspective to the next level of depth and impact. The chapters of this Handbook, which are summarized next, provide clear, knowledge-based foundations for the continued exploration of the psychological nature of working.

Overview of the Handbook

The Handbook has been structured around five broad themes, based loosely on *a priori* considerations about working and careers derived from the literature as well as my own experience as a practitioner and scholar. The first theme is an exploration of the theoretical and epistemological framework for the psychology of working. The second theme is devoted to the context of working, with a focus on the diverse ways in which race, gender, sexual orientation, poverty, and family frame the entire enterprise of working. The third theme examines the psychology of working from the vantage point of organizational psychology and the management perspective on careers. The fourth theme is devoted to counseling practice and psychotherapy. The fifth theme is focused on public policy and community-based implications.

Theoretical Foundations

The initial section begins with the current chapter, which is designed to create the foundation for the chapters that follow. The next chapter, by Isaac Prilleltensky and Graham Stead, provides a comprehensive overview of critical psychology, which reflects an essential intellectual stream that has contributed to the psychology of working. As detailed earlier in this chapter, the diverse critiques that have stimulated the development of a more inclusive perspective convey an exemplar of critical thought. Prilleltensky and Stead provide an insightful analysis of the critical psychology movement, beginning with a critique of some of the underlying assumptions of psychological discourse. Included in the Prilleltensky and Stead chapter is a critical analysis of individualism, positive psychology, mechanistic approaches, and ethnocentrism, among other traditions, which have shaped the ways in which work is understood in psychology. Prilleltensky and Stead also have raised a number of recommendations for the development of a liberating psychology of working.

The next chapter, also by Graham Stead, furnishes an extensive examination of epistemology and discourse analysis in relation to the psychological study of working. Stead's discussion provides a summary of various streams of ideas that have contributed to a social constructionist perspective, including relational theories, discourse and language analyses, and power. This chapter expands Richardson's (1993) early contribution on the role of work in people's lives, thereby enhancing the utility of careful epistemological analyses of the psychological study of working.

Another critical theoretical foundation is represented in the theories of career choice and development, which have formed the backbone of vocational psychology. In the fourth chapter, Jane Swanson explores these theories via the lens of the psychology of working, reviewing the traditional theories along with emerging theories. Swanson's chapter begins with a comprehensive review of person–environment fit theory, social cognitive career theory, the theory of work adjustment, and lifespan developmental theory. She follows this review by exploring theories that have been informed by the psychology-of-working perspective, social constructionist thought, narrative theory, and other critical perspectives.

The Context of Working

As reflected in the ongoing critiques of traditional vocational and I/O psychology, the context for working is characterized by considerable inequity, racism, sexism, ageism, and heterosexism. In short, the playing field is far from equal. In this section, several scholars explore selected social barriers with an eye toward identifying the complex ways that oppression shapes the nature and trajectory of one's working life.

In the first chapter in this section, Lisa Flores uses multicultural and psychology-of-working perspectives to examine the impact of racism in working. In an expansive analysis, Flores highlights how racism affects work-based disparities, health, well-being, and job satisfaction. Flores builds on a perceptive review of relevant demographic data and a critical appraisal of a wide array of work-related phenomenon in arguing that race is central in considerations of equity, access, social justice, and dignity in the workplace.

Building on one of the earliest critiques of the traditional career discourse, Neeta Kantamneni's chapter discusses the role of gender in preparing for, and adjusting to, the workplace. Kantamneni reviews the complex ways that gender, gender role socialization, sexism, and discrimination affect the experience of working for men and women. Kantamneni highlights some of the notable ways in which gender-related phenomena influence both men and women, noting how socialization and sexism function to constrain the work lives of people. Kantamneni concludes with a number of perceptive recommendations for counseling practice and continued research.

Next, Mary Anderson and James Croteau present an insightful review of the literature on sexual orientation and working. Perhaps the most hidden of the diverse forms of social oppression, heterosexism has adversely shaped working environments in multiple and often insidious ways. As reflected in Anderson and Croteau's work, the infusion of a psychology-of-working perspective has the potential to transform how we think about sexual orientation and the world of work. Their insightful and informative chapter provides a needed roadmap for a psychology of working that embraces and affirms sexual orientation diversity.

A core concern of the psychology of working is the lack of access due to constraints in the opportunity structure and poverty. Following this vantage point, Saba Rasheed Ali describes the role that social class plays in all aspects of education, training, and working. She summarizes compelling data on working and poverty, highlighting the low wages and lack of opportunity that plague the lives of the poor. Ali then reviews the ambivalent relationship that vocational psychology has faced in including social class and poverty in its theories and practices. She concludes with numerous constructive recommendations for practice, public policy work, and research that will expand an inclusive discourse on work and poverty.

Mary Sue Richardson and Charles Schaeffer then explore the literature on family and working, summarizing their ideas about market work and care work in a fully developed dual model of working. Richardson and Schaeffer's contribution makes a compelling case that studies of working have privileged market work over care work, leading to a neglect of this essential mode of working that involves nearly everyone across the globe. The Richardson and Schaeffer argument is that balanced attention to and affirmation of market work, paid care work, and unpaid care work can foster the sorts of theories and practices that can reduce sexism and enhance the quality of life for both men and women.

The aging of the workforce is endemic in many nations around the globe, leading to challenges and transformation among workers and the workplace. Harvey and Anthony Sterns provide an expansive tour of the literature on aging and working, highlighting how an aging workforce can continue to contribute to the social and economic world. They review the literature on working and aging from organizational and self-management perspectives, respectively. In addition, they highlight the importance of creating functional and welcoming workplaces as a means of fostering a dignified and safe work life for older workers.

As indicated at the outset of this introduction, the literature on disability and working has provided one of the key foundations for an inclusive psychology of working. Ellen Fabian's chapter continues this trajectory by providing a contemporary examination of the literature on disability and working. Her chapter examines the complex issues evoked by disabling conditions (including, but not limited to, physical disabilities, psychiatric conditions, and developmental disabilities) from the vantage point of the psychology of working. In addition, Fabian reviews various legislative agendas designed to support people with disabling conditions as they negotiate the world of work. As reflected in Fabian's comprehensive chapter, the strength and vitality of the disabled community's advocacy provides important lessons for an expansive legislative and public policy agenda that will ensure greater equity to the resources that support dignified and meaningful work.

Organizational Implications

In an attempt to reduce artificial splits in the psychological study of working, I have included two chapters from outstanding scholars of management and I/O psychology in this Handbook. In the first chapter, Douglas (Tim) Hall and Phil Mirvis build on the long and storied history of the study of careers within the world of management with a creative application of the psychology of working to a host of challenges that have been evoked by the transformative changes in the world of work. Hall and Mirvis examine three fundamental questions in their chapter: (1) What is my work? (2) What is my work identity? and (3) What is success? Through examining these questions, Hall and Mirvis expand the discourse in career management to include a broad array of problems, populations, and positions.

Building on a critical perspective infused with values about justice and inclusion, Michael Zickar provides an essential chapter that presents a transformative discourse for I/O psychology. By embedding a critical historical perspective into his analysis, Zickar reviews selected aspects of the first century of scholarship and practice in I/O psychology, noting the roots of the profession and the challenges inherent in infusing a workers' perspective into a field that has committed itself, for the most part, to the welfare of employers and their organizations. Zickar concludes with a number of thoughtful recommendations for integrating the psychology-of-working perspective into I/O psychology with the intention of creating an experience-near study of work within organizations that affirms diversity and inclusion.

Counseling and Psychotherapy

The practices of counseling and psychotherapy have been and remain central in efforts to improve the welfare of individuals. Within the working context, counseling and psychotherapy have had a complex history that has resulted in a very rich literature on career counseling and a far less abundant literature on exploring the role of working within traditional mental health counseling and psychotherapy. The two chapters in this sections are designed to reinvigorate both the career counseling and psychotherapy disciplines. The first chapter in this section, by Sherri Turner, Julia Conkel Ziebell, and Robin Alcala Saner, expands the traditional career choice and development counseling model to embrace clients with less-than-optimal levels of volition. Turner and her colleagues initially reviewed the counseling challenges among traditionally disenfranchised client populations, including the poor, homeless, LGBT individuals, and individuals with disabling conditions. Integrating observations from their analyses of best practices with marginalized groups, Turner et al. concluded their chapter with recommendations for working with clients who face less-than-optimal options in the world of work and who may also face oppression in various contexts of their lives.

AJ Franklin and Mary Beth Medvide devote their chapter to tackling the daunting task of considering how to infuse affirming views about work, social justice, and diversity into psychotherapy theory and practice. Based on a masterful synthesis of career development theories, selected psychotherapy theories, and the psychology of working, Franklin and Medvide meet this challenge by developing a foundation for an inclusive paradigm for integrative counseling practice. Their chapter concludes with a detailed case example and recommendations designed to foster needed developments in integrative practice.

Community-Based Interventions and Public Policy

One of the key attributes of the psychology of working has been an expansion of practice outside of the consulting room and a corollary expansion of scholarship outside of the university research lab and library. In short, the social justice ethic that underlies the psychology of working is clearly focused on creating systemic changes in all of the institutions that influence the working lives of people. The first chapter in this section, by Maureen Kenny, is devoted to an exploration of the relationship between education and work. Kenny provides an exhaustive review of the crisis in contemporary education, noting the challenges that exist in infusing work-based learning into the educational enterprise. She then reviews an extensive body of literature examining such issues as career academies, school-to-work research, career development education, and work-based issues inherent in current considerations of educational reform. Kenny concludes with a thoughtful articulation of research agendas and policies that are suggested by her review and by a consideration of the psychology-of-working perspective in relation to the needs of the education community.

The next chapter, by Cindy Juntunen and Tamba-Kuii Bailey, explores the contexts of training and employment. Juntunen and Bailey review the complex work-related transitions that adults face as they negotiate increasingly unstable education, training, and occupational contexts. Juntunen and Bailey highlight the advantages of a comprehensive array of interventions and programs that offer individuals relational support, opportunities for continued training, and broad systemic changes in their resources and affordances. The Juntunen and Bailey contribution is particularly eloquent in its use of a psychology-of-working perspective as a link between traditional vocational psychology scholarship and the real-life challenges of clients and communities.

The role of public policy in creating facilitative and/or inhibiting conditions for the attainment of a meaningful and upwardly mobile working life has received considerable attention in recent years. Spencer Niles and Edwin Herr, two of the leaders in career development and public policy, have prepared a compelling chapter that affirms the importance of a clear and compelling public policy agenda as a means of promoting social change. Niles and Herr summarize some of the most notable exemplars of policy initiatives that have fostered access to counseling services and to humane educational and work-based opportunities. They note as well the challenges that exist in creating the rationale and establishing the research framework to support public policies that will enhance opportunities for the entire array of people seeking meaningful and dignified work.

The Way Forward: Connecting the Dots

As I indicated at the outset of this chapter, I have sought to bring together a community of scholars to consider the challenges that have been raised in the psychology-of-working critique of existing discourses in our field. These chapters, both individually and collectively, articulate a perspective and a point of view that has the real potential to transform psychological studies and interventions regarding working. Moreover, the authors have creatively established the posts for an expanded and inclusive tent for scholars and practitioners interested in promoting fair and dignified work opportunities.

Once we have expanded the tent, what is the way forward for the psychology of working? In the section that follows, I consider the broad and integrative view of this collective body of work, which may help to articulate the lines between the dots.

One of the most tired (yet accurate) clichés in our field is that the world of work is changing rapidly and in unexpected ways. This observation is certainly evident in these chapters, but the impact of the changes is complicated by the growing acknowledgment that the "grand career narrative" (Savickas, 2002) is over for an increasing proportion of working people across the globe. (Indeed, I have argued elsewhere that the grand career narrative was not relevant for most working people, even during the boom period after World War II. See Blustein, 2006, for further details on this position.) So, what will replace the grand career narrative? Some aspects of the new narrative can be derived from the chapters in this Handbook.

Individual Interventions

From an individual perspective, it seems clear that people will need to be well trained, flexible, and highly motivated to manage their work lives in a context of rapid change and, for many working people, a context of shrinking or stagnant opportunities. In addition, the question of career choice volition will continue to be complex and dynamic. The collective perspectives derived from the chapters suggest that we probably need to consider a multidimensional perspective wherein volition will wax and wane based on economic conditions, affordances, labor market availability, individual skill sets, and other social, economic, political, and psychological conditions. Given the movement toward greater instability with respect to unemployment and underemployment, it would seem important to reconceptualize how individuals manage their work lives as well as how people can obtain support for work-based problems.

While the traditional discourses of career counseling, career management, and career development education are relevant for many, there is a need for a new set of ideas and solutions to the problems that people face in finding and sustaining dignified work. Perhaps the most complex question is how psychologists and counselors can help individuals develop the complex and changing sets of skills that they will need to survive and optimally thrive in the new world of work. When considering the observations of many of the chapter authors, success in the world of work will require dexterity, flexibility, creativity, resilience, relational support, and high levels of literacy and numeracy skills. In addition, success at work will require a social world that affirms and creates opportunities for dignity and access in one's work life. In my view, the literature and perspectives conveyed in these chapters suggest that the solutions that were developed for 20th-century work-based problems may not be sufficient for the problems of the 21st century. Therefore, while many will still benefit from career counseling, traditional psychotherapy, and work-based education, other interventions will need to be developed.

The skeleton of 21st-century work-based intervention is taking shape in the new models that have been introduced by Savickas (2005) and Richardson (2012). These two perspectives are constructed around the notions of change, contextualization of work, and agency. In addition, the theories by Lent et al. (2002) and other cognitively based theorists (e.g., Reardon, Lenz, Sampson, & Peterson, 2009) will be essential as counselors and other providers help clients to develop rich and useful constructions about themselves and about their educational and work lives. However, the nature of the counseling interventions will need to continue to evolve and shift as the needs of clients become more complex. For example, integrative interventions that blend work-based counseling and mental health counseling are clearly needed for clients who are caught in the maelstrom of unemployment and underemployment. In addition, counselors and psychologists will need to learn more about job search and skill development strategies as clients increasingly look for ways to become more competitive in the labor market. Although individual efforts are clearly needed, the broadened psychology-of-working perspective that is embedded in these pages points to the need for broad, systemic changes in order to create more opportunities for people, as summarized next.

Public Policy Agendas

In addition to the Niles and Herr chapter, several other contributions in this Handbook have articulated important public policy issues that may be particularly helpful for working people. As articulated in previous publications (e.g., Blustein, 2006; Blustein et al., 2012), a broad and concerted effort to creating full employment is essential to

expand opportunities. In addition, psychologists, other social scientists, and helping professionals need to make a case with local and national leaders about the centrality of work in people's lives (cf. Richardson, 1993). Continued efforts at linking education and work will be helpful in creating schools and educational institutions that prepare people for 21st-century jobs. Improved training and adult education are also critical to enhancing opportunities for all working people, who increasingly face a labor market that expects and rewards lifelong learning.

These ideas are not necessarily new or radical. Scholars have been advocating these policies for decades, with varying degrees of success. So, how will this Handbook help to move forward a more effective public policy agenda? In the sections that follow, I propose some ideas, derived in large measure from these chapters, that may help to strengthen our arguments and impact.

Research Agendas

Critical to the policy enterprise is a need for research that will inform policy challenges. As reflected in many of these chapters, a psychology-of-working agenda has the potential to stimulate more inclusive research that includes diverse epistemologies and objectives. For example, integrative research on the impact of unemployment at the individual and community levels may help to document the broad and pernicious impact of unemployment and underemployment. In addition, research that describes in detail the insidious role of social barriers such as racism, sexism, classism, ageism, and heterosexism in the workplace may help to underscore the need for policies based on values of fairness and justice.

The psychology-of-working perspective that is represented in these chapters provides ideas and assumptions about work that are inherently grounded in a value system that affirms change, justice, and maximizing the well-being of individuals and communities. The traditional discourses in vocational and I/O psychology have generally (although not always) eschewed a research agenda that has an implied or explicated political perspective. In contrast, many of the authors in this Handbook were able to articulate research agendas that embraced an explicit value system. While the values that make up the psychology of working, naturally, will vary considerably, one cohering theme is the endorsement of greater access to education, training, and work opportunities. As such, research that adopts a psychology-of-working perspective may be able to tackle some of the thornier issues facing people at work without the implicit barrier of an elusive objectivity. This is not to suggest that scholars should become journalists or advocates without rootedness in science and scholarship. Rather, the psychology-of-working perspective that is emerging from a collective view of these chapters is constructed around the belief, as articulated by Prilleltensky (1997), that science has the potential to liberate people from oppression and to foster caring communities.

In addition to policy-based research, an integrative review of these chapters suggests the continued importance of exploratory and theory-driven research. While the topics framing this research agenda are expansive, a few themes can be discerned from the contributions herein. One theme is the exploration of the diverse ways that people construct meaning about work and about the contexts of their work lives. Building on a growing line of scholarship in vocational psychology (e.g., Ali et al., 2012; Kenny, Blustein, Chaves, Grossman, & Gallagher, 2003), continued research that identifies the internal and external resources and barriers that people face as they negotiate work-based tasks is warranted. Another theme revolves around the development of theories that are useful, relativistic, yet sufficiently structured to support further scholarship. As an exemplar, recent initiatives emerging from relational theories provide an illustration of the sort of theoretical enterprises that emerge from a more inclusive focus on working (e.g., Blustein, 2011a; Richardson, 2012).

While research and theory development efforts similar to the ones outlined above have been evident in our field for decades, a collective view of the chapters within this Handbook offers some ways of enhancing the impact of these efforts. One of the most important suggestions is to think broadly and critically about the issues and problems that are posed in research. The diverse theoretical and epistemological views articulated in these chapters provide some useful guidelines about how to unpack existing assumptions that guide the intellectual currents in a given line of work.

A hallmark of this Handbook is its disciplinary pluralism. I have explicitly sought the input of scholars interested in working from across the spectrum of psychological specialties. The vision that is conveyed by these Handbook chapters is inherently inclusive; indeed, one of the common elements in the chapters is the inclusion of literature from outside of the author's own specialty. These sorts of integrative analyses have resulted in a body of work that has a wider reach than traditional psychological scholarship about work and careers. Building on the integrative nature of these chapters, it would seem useful for teams of scholars from various specialties within psychology and outside of psychology to collaborate and create new research and practice initiatives. The importance of culture, race, and other social identities emerged here as a central theme that warrants careful consideration in research and theory development. Given the centrality of work in people's lives and in the welfare of communities, I also suggest disseminating results in trade publications and other popular media outlets. The classic publication by Wilson (1996) entitled "When Work Disappears," which was published as a trade book, is an excellent example of a research-oriented contribution that entered the public discourse about work and poverty. With the broad and inclusive vision underlying the psychology-of-working perspective, it may be possible for psychologists who are writing about work to bring research findings of social relevance to the public via academic venues as well as more popular outlets.

Closing Comments

In my view, each of these chapters offers creative, insightful,, and highly informative overviews of a given body of literature within the working context. While each chapter addresses a circumscribed line of work, the collective vision that emerges from this Handbook provides a clear and accessible knowledge base for the continued development of the psychology-of-working perspective. As the Editor of this Handbook, I have been humbled in attracting a roster of major scholars and leaders in their respective fields to contribute to this endeavor. My hope is that readers will be as moved as I have been in reading these stellar contributions. And, hopefully, readers will feel inspired to continue the work of these scholars and of those who preceded them in creating an expansive and socially just vision of working.

Acknowledgments

I would like to thank Alice Connors-Kellgren, Saliha Kozan, and Bailey Rand for their comments on an earlier version of this draft.

References

Ali, S. R., Yang, L. Y., Button, C. J., & McCoy, T. T. H. (2012). Career education programming: A critical psychology-case study research approach. *Journal of Career Development, 39,* 357–385.

Axelrod, S. D. (1999). *Work and the evolving self: Theoretical and clinical considerations*. Hillsdale, NJ: The Analytic Press.

Barnett, R. C., & Hyde, J. S. (2001). Women, men, work, and family: An expansionist theory. *American Psychologist, 56*, 781–796.

Betz, N., & Fitzgerald, L. (1987). *The career psychology of women*. Orlando, FL: Academic Press, Inc.

Bhat, C. S. (2010). Assisting unemployed adults find suitable work: A group intervention embedded in community and grounded in social action. *Journal for Specialists in Group Work, 35*, 246–254.

Blustein, D. L. (2006). *The psychology of working: A new perspective for career development, counseling, and public policy*. Mahwah, NJ: Lawrence Erlbaum Associates.

Blustein, D. L. (2008). The role of work in psychological health and well-being: A conceptual, historical, and public policy perspective. *American Psychologist, 63*, 228–240.

Blustein, D. L. (2011a). A relational theory of working. *Journal of Vocational Behavior, 79*, 1–17.

Blustein, D. L. (2011b). Vocational psychology at the fork in the road: Staying the course or taking the road less traveled. *Journal of Career Assessment, 19*, 316–322.

Blustein, D., Kenna, A., Gill, N., & DeVoy, J. (2008). The psychology of working: A new framework for counseling practice and public policy. *Career Development Quarterly, 56*, 294–308.

Blustein, D. L., McWhirter, E. H., & Perry, J. C. (2005). An emancipatory communitarian approach to vocational development theory, research, and practice. *Counseling Psychologist, 33*, 141–179.

Blustein, D. L., Medvide, M. B., & Wan, C. M. (2012). A critical perspective of contemporary unemployment policy and practices. *Journal of Career Development, 39*, 341–356.

Blustein, D. L., Murphy, K. A., Kenny, M. E., Jernigan, M. Gualdron, L., Connolly, M., Catraio, C., Backus, F., Sullivan, M., Urbano, A., Land, M., & Davis, O. (2010). Exploring urban students' constructions about school, work, race and ethnicity. *Journal of Counseling Psychology, 57*, 248–254.

Blustein, D. L., Schultheiss, D. E. P., & Flum, H. (2004). Toward a relational perspective of the psychology of careers and working: A social constructionist analysis. *Journal of Vocational Behavior, 64*, 423–440.

Bowe, J., Bowe, M., & Streeter, S. (2000). *Gig: Americans talk about their jobs*. New York: Three Rivers Press.

Brown, L. (2009). *Feminist therapy*. Washington, DC: American Psychological Association.

Brown, S. D., & Lent, R. W. (Eds.). (2005). *Career development and counseling: Putting theory and research to work*. Hoboken, NJ: John Wiley & Sons.

Budd, J. W. (2011). *The thought of work*. Ithaca, NY: ILR Press.

Burr, V. (1995). *An introduction to social constructionism*. Florence, KY: Taylor & Frances/Routledge.

Carter, R. T., & Cook, D. A. (1992). A culturally relevant perspective for understanding the career paths of visible racial/ethnic group people. In H. D. Lea & Z. B. Leibowitz (Eds.), *Adult career development: Concepts, issues, and practice* (pp. 192–217). Alexandria, VA: National Career Development Association.

Chung, B. (2003). Career counseling with lesbian, gay, bisexual, and transgendered persons: The next decade. *Career Development Quarterly, 52*, 78–85.

Clifton, J. (2011). *The coming jobs war*. New York: Gallup Press.

Croteau, J. M., Anderson, M. Z., DiStefano, T. M., & Kampa-Kokesch, S. (2000). Lesbian, gay, and bisexual vocational psychology: Reviewing foundations and planning construction. In R. M. Perez, K. A. DeBord, & K. J. Bieschke (Eds.), *Handbook of counseling and psychotherapy with lesbian, gay, and bisexual clients* (pp. 383–408). Washington, DC: American Psychology Association.

Diemer, M. A., & Ali, S. R. (2009). Integrating social class into vocational psychology. *Journal of Career Assessment, 17*, 247–265

Donkin, R. (2001). *Blood, sweat, & tears: The evolution of work*. New York: Texere.

Duffy, R. D., Diemer, M. A., Perry, J. C., Laurenzi, C., & Torrey, C. L. (2012). The construction and initial validation of the work volition scale. *Journal of Vocational Behavior, 80*, 400–411.

Eggerth, D. E., DeLaney, S. C., Flynn, M. A., & Jacobson, C. J. (2012). Work experiences of Latina immigrants: A qualitative study. *Journal of Career Development, 39*(1), 13–30.

Fabian, E., & Liesener, J. (2005). Promoting the career potential of youth and young adults with disabilities. In S. D. Brown & R. W. Lent (Eds.), *Career development and counseling: Putting theory and research to work* (pp. 551–573). Hoboken, NJ: John Wiley & Sons, Inc.

Fassinger, R. E. (2008). Workplace diversity and public policy: Challenges and opportunities for psychology. *American Psychologist, 63*, 252–268.

Flores, L. Y., Mendoza, M. M., Ojeda, L., He, Y., Rosales Meza, R., Medina, V., Wagner Ladehoff, J., & Jordan, S. (2011). A qualitative inquiry of Latino immigrants work experiences in the Midwest. *Journal of Counseling Psychology, 58*, 522–536.

Flum, H. (2001). Relational dimensions in career development. *Journal of Vocational Behavior, 59*, 1–16.

Fouad, N. A. (2007). Work and vocational psychology: Theory, research, and applications. *Annual Review of Psychology, 58*, 543–564.

Fouad, N. A., & Bynner, J. (2008). Work transitions. *American Psychologist, 63*, 241–251.

Fouad, N. A., Cotter, E. W., Carter, L., Bernfeld, S., & Liu, J. P. (2011). A qualitative study of the dislocated working class. *Journal of Career Development, 39*, 287–310.

Gergen, K. J. (2009). *Relational being: Beyond self and community*. New York: Oxford University Press.

Hall, D. T., and Associates (1996). *The career is dead—long live the career: A relational approach to careers*. San Francisco, CA: Jossey-Bass.

Harmon, L. W., & Farmer, H. S. (1983). Current theoretical issues in vocational psychology. In W. B. Walsh & S. H. Osipow (Eds.), *Handbook of vocational psychology* (Vol. 1, pp. 39–77). Hillsdale, NJ: Erlbaum.

Hartung, P. J., & Subich, L. M. (Eds.). (2011). *Developing self in work and career: Concepts, cases, and contexts*. Washington, DC: APA.

Hees, C. K., Rottinghaus, P. J. Briddick, W. C., & Conrath, J.A. (2012). Work-to-school transitions in the age of the displaced worker: A psychology of working perspective. *Career Development Quarterly, 60*, 333–342.

Helms, J. E., & Cook, D. A. (1999). *Using race and culture in counseling and psychotherapy: Theory and process*. Boston: Allyn & Bacon.

Juntunen, C. L. (2006). The psychology of working: The clinical context. *Professional Psychology: Research and Practice, 37*, 342–350.

Kenny, M. E., Blustein, D. L., Chaves, A., Grossman, J., & Gallagher, L. (2003). The role of perceived barriers and relational support in educational and vocational lives of urban high school students. *Journal of Counseling Psychology, 50,* 142–155.

Kenny, M. E., Blustein, D. L., Haase, R. F., Jackson, J., & Perry, J. C. (2006). Setting the stage: Career development and the student engagement process. *Journal of Counseling Psychology, 53,* 272–279.

Koppes, L. (2007). *Historical perspectives in industrial and organizational psychology.* Mahwah, NJ: Lawrence Erlbaum Associates Publishers.

Kornhauser, A. (1957). Democratic values and problems of power in American society. In A. Kornhauser (Ed.), *Problems of power in American democracy* (pp. 184–217). Detroit, MI: Wayne State University Press.

Lent, R. W., Brown, S. D., & Hackett, G. (2002). Social cognitive career theory. In D. Brown (Eds.), *Career choice and development* (pp. 255–311). San Francisco, CA: Jossey-Bass.

Lidderdale, M. A., Croteau, J. M., Anderson, M. Z., Tovar-Murray, D., & Davis, J. M. (2007). Building LGB vocational psychology: A theoretical model of workplace sexual identity management. In K. J. Bieschke, R. M. Perez, & K. A. DeBord (Eds.), *Handbook of counseling and psychotherapy with lesbian, gay, bisexual, and transgender clients* (2nd ed., pp. 245–270). Washington, DC: American Psychological Association.

Lowman, R. (1993). *Counseling and psychotherapy of work dysfunctions.* Washington, DC: American Psychological Association.

Marfleet, P., & Blustein, D. L. (2011). "Needed not wanted": An interdisciplinary examination of the work-related challenges faced by irregular migrants. *Journal of Vocational Behavior, 78*(3), 381–389.

McIlveen, P., Beccaria, G., du Preez, J., & Patton, W. (2010). Autoethnography in vocational psychology: Wearing your class on your sleeve. *Journal of Career Development, 37,* 599–615.

Neff, W. S. (1985). *Work and human behavior* (3rd ed.). New York: Aldine Publishing Company.

Noonan, A. E., Hall, G., & Blustein, D. L. (2007). Urban adolescents' experience of social class in relationships at work. *Journal of Vocational Behavior, 70,* 542–560.

O'Brien, G. E. (1986). *Psychology of work and unemployment.* New York: John Wiley.

Paul, K. I., & Moser, K. (2009). Unemployment impairs mental health: Meta-analyses. *Journal of Vocational Behavior, 74,* 264–282.

Perry, J. C., DeWine, D. B., Duffy, R. D., & Vance, K. S., (2007). The academic self-efficacy of urban youth: A mixed methods study of a school-to-work program. *Journal of Career Development, 34,* 103–126.

Prilleltensky, I. (1997). Values, assumptions, and practices: Assessing the moral implications of psychological discourse and action. *American Psychologist, 52,* 517–535.

Quick, J. C., & Tetrick, L. E. (Eds.). (2010). *Handbook of occupational health psychology* (2nd ed.). Washington, DC: American Psychological Association.

Reardon, R. C., Lenz, J. G., Sampson, J. P., & Peterson, G. W. (2009). *Career development and planning: A comprehensive approach.* Mason, OH: Carnegie Learning.

Richardson, M. S. (1993). Work in people's lives: A location for counseling psychologists. *Journal of Counseling Psychology, 40,* 425–433.

Richardson, M. S. (2012). Counseling for work and relationships. *Counseling Psychologist, 40,* 190–242.

Ryan, R. M., & Deci, E. L. (2000) Self-determination theory and the facilitation of intrinsic motivation, social development and well-being. *American Psychologist, 55,* 68–78.

Sachs, J. D. (2005). *The end of poverty.* New York: Penguin Press.

Savickas, M. L. (1993). Career counseling in the postmodern era. *Journal of Cognitive Psychotherapy, 7,* 205–215.

Savickas, M. L. (2002). Career construction: A developmental theory of vocational behavior. In D. Brown (Eds.), *Career choice and development* (pp. 149–205). San Francisco, CA: Jossey-Bass.

Savickas, M. L. (2005). The theory and practice of career construction. In S. D. Brown & R. W. Lent (Eds.), *Career development and counseling: Putting theory and research to work* (pp. 42–70). Hoboken, NJ: John Wiley & Sons, Inc.

Savickas, M. L. (2011). *Career counseling.* Washington, DC: American Psychological Association.

Savickas, M. L., & Baker, D. B. (2005). The history of vocational psychology: Antecedents, origin, and early development. In W. B. Walsh & M. L. Savickas (Eds.), *Handbook of vocational psychology* (3rd ed., pp. 15–50). Mahwah, NJ: Lawrence Erlbaum Associates.

Schultheiss, D. E. P. (2003). A relational approach to career counseling: Theoretical integration and practical application. *Journal of Counseling and Development, 81,* 301–310.

Schultheiss, D. E. P. (2007). The emergence of a relational cultural paradigm for vocational psychology. *International Journal for Educational and Vocational Guidance, 7,* 191–201.

Sen, A. (1999). *Development as freedom.* Oxford: Oxford University Press.

Shen-Miller, D. S., McWhirter, E. H., & Bartone, A. S. (2012). Historical influences on the evolution of vocational counseling. In D. Capuzzi & M. D. Stauffer (Eds.), *Career counseling: Foundations, perspectives, and applications* (pp. 3–42). New York: Routledge.

Shore, M. (1998). Beyond self-interest: Professional advocacy and the integration of theory, research, and practice. *American Psychologist, 53,* 474–479.

Smith, E. J. (1983). Issues in racial minorities' career behavior. In W. B. Walsh & S. H. Osipow (Eds.), *Handbook of vocational psychology: Vol. 1, Foundations* (pp. 161–222). Hillsdale, NJ: Erlbaum Associates.

Socarides, C. W., & Kramer, S. (1997). *Work and its inhibitions: Psychoanalytic essays.* Madison, CT: International Universities Press.

Stead, G. B. (2004). Culture and career psychology: A social constructionist perspective. *Journal of Vocational Behavior, 64,* 389–406.

Stead, G. B., & Perry, J. C. (2012). Toward critical psychology perspectives of work-based transitions. *Journal of Career Development, 39,* 315–320.

Super, D. E. (1957). *The psychology of careers.* New York: Harper & Row.

Super, D. E. (1980). A life-span, life-space, approach to career development. *Journal of Vocational Behavior, 13,* 282–298.

Super, D. E., Savickas, M. L., & Super, C. M. (1996). The life-span, life-space approach to careers. In D. Brown &

L. Brown (Eds.), *Career choice and development* (3rd ed., pp. 121–178). San Francisco, CA: Jossey-Bass.

Szymanski, E. M., & Parker, R. M. (2003). *Work and disability: Issues and strategies in career development and job placement* (2nd ed.). Austin, TX: Pro-Ed.

Terkel, S. (1974). *Working: People talk about what they do all day and how they feel about what they do.* New York: Pantheon Books.

Toporek, R. L., & Chope, R. C. (2006). Individual, programmatic, and entrepreneurial approaches to social justice: Counseling psychologists in vocational and career counseling. In R. L. Toporek, L. H. Gerstein, N. A. Fouad, G. Roysircar, & T. Israel (Eds.), *Handbook for social justice in counseling psychology: Leadership, vision, and action* (pp. 276–293). Thousand Oaks, CA: Sage Publications.

Vondracek, F. W., Ferreira, J. A. G., & Santos, E. J. (2010). Vocational behavior and development in times of social change: New perspectives for theory and practice. *International Journal of Educational and Vocational Guidance, 10,* 125–138.

Walsh, W. B., & Savickas, M. L. (Eds.) (2005). *Handbook of vocational psychology.* Mahwah, NJ: LEA.

Watson, M., & McMahon, M. (Eds.) (2012). *Career development: Global issues and challenges.* New York: Nova Science Publishers.

Wilson, W. J. (1996). *When work disappears: The world of the new urban poor.* New York: Knopf.

Zickar, M. (2004). An analysis of industrial-organizational psychology's indifference to labor unions in the United States. *Human Relations, 57,* 145–167.

Critical Psychology, Well-Being, and Work

Isaac Prilleltensky *and* Graham B. Stead

Abstract

Critical psychology emerged as a reaction to (a) the oppressive turn in individualism, (b) the negative repercussions of the status quo on large sectors of the population, and (c) psychology's witting or unwitting complicity in upholding the societal status quo. The critical psychology movement questions psychology, and society, on the basis of moral, epistemic, and professional shortcomings. This chapter reviews critical psychology's reservations about dominant assumptions in these three domains, and offers an alternative set of principles designed to advance well-being in persons, communities, psychological science, and professional practice. Following an alternative conception of well-being, this chapter applies it to the world of work. It reviews problematic assumptions pertaining to the moral, epistemic, and professional values impacting the world of work, and offers theoretical and practical recommendations for advancing the well-being of workers, organizations, and communities. Humanitarian work psychology and critical management studies offer valuable avenues for merging critical psychology with the world of work.

Key Words: critical psychology, values, epistemology, professional practice, status quo, oppression, social justice, work

Mens Sana in Corporation Sano—such was the title of a recent article in *The Economist* describing the growing presence of psychologists and mental health counselors in corporations. The piece raises fundamental questions about the role of psychologists in corporations: "Should companies pry into people's emotional lives? Can they be trusted with the information they gather? And should psychologically frail workers put their faith in people who work primarily for their employers rather than in their personal doctors?" (Schumpeter, 2010, p. 65). Good intentions notwithstanding, history shows that psychologists have not always enhanced worker well-being, but rather productivity and managerial control; and while productivity and managerial control do not have to come at the expense of worker well-being, they often do (Baritz, 1974; Islam &

Zyphur, 2009; Ralph, 1983). This is where critical psychologists come in.

Critical psychologists do not take for granted that psychologists' presence in industry is a good thing, even when corporations pay well. Critical psychologists question sacred cows, which does not make us very popular, but which allows us to look in depth at psychological values, assumptions, and practices (Prilleltensky, 1997). This sort of examination leads to three fundamental questions in critical psychology: Whose well-being are we talking about? Whose values and assumptions are being upheld? And who benefits from the status quo? (Fox, Prilleltensky, & Austin, 2009). In tackling these questions, critical psychologists do not just seek answers, but also alternatives (Prilleltensky & Nelson, 2002).

By pretending to talk universally for everybody, psychology often confuses the well-being of management with the well-being of the workforce. By neglecting power differentials, psychology promotes the values and assumptions of dominant groups. And by failing to challenge injustice and the status quo, psychology benefits the privileged. These are no mere provocations or ideological pronouncements (Parker, 2007; Prilleltensky, 1994; Teo, 2005, 2009). The record shows that psychology has sided with the powerful, and has often inflicted pain in vulnerable populations, including children, women, immigrants, Aboriginal peoples, and mental health patients (Chamberlin, 1978, 1984, Clarke & Braun, 2009; Everett, 1994; Fox, Prilleltensky, & Austin, 2009; Huygens, 2009; Olfman, 2006; Parker, 2007; Ussher & Nicolson, 1992).

Critical psychology is concerned with the well-being of four primary entities: persons, communities, the science of psychology, and the profession of psychology. The well-being of individuals and communities is greatly affected by the availability of decent employment (Clark, 2010), the occupational environment (Fullan, 2008; Sisodia, Sheth, & Wolfe, 2007), and the world of work in general (Blustein, 2006; Rath & Harter, 2010). Consequently, the world of work is very fertile ground for critical psychologists, which is why this chapter addresses the intersection among critical psychology, well-being, and work.

The critical psychology movement questions psychology, and society, on the basis of moral, epistemic, and professional shortcomings (Teo, 2005, 2009). In this chapter we review critical psychology's reservations about dominant assumptions in these three domains, and offer an alternative set of principles designed to advance well-being in persons, communities, psychological science, and professional practice. Following an alternative conception of well-being, we apply it to the world of work. We review problematic assumptions pertaining to the moral, epistemic, and professional values impacting the world of work, and offer theoretical and practical recommendations for advancing the well-being of workers, organizations, and communities.

Work encompasses many sectors. Most of our practical and research experience derives from the not-for-profit world. Prior to becoming academics, both of us worked in counseling and mental health services in communities and schools. In our current research, we study not-for-profit organizations and have come to appreciate the struggle of workers in this much unappreciated and undervalued field

(Chetkovich & Kunreuther, 2006; Evans, Hanlin, & Prilleltensky, 2007). We have also come into contact with the teaching workforce, another trying sector (Darling-Hammond, 2010; Farber & Azar, 1999; Hargreaves & Shirley, 2009; Ravitch, 2010). Both human service workers and educators struggle to gain respect from government and the business community, who largely fund them and control their boards (Payne, 2008). In this chapter we are especially sensitive to their plight.

Critical Psychology

Critical psychology emerged in response to twin concerns about the state of society and the state of psychology (Fox, Prilleltensky, & Austin, 2009). While several strands of critical psychology exist, most of them converge in a critique of the moral, epistemic, and professional values of the profession, and their unwitting support for social structures in need of transformation (Teo, 2005, 2009). This section presents the problems. The next presents solutions.

Moral Values

Morality refers to the study and practice of doing what is right (Facione, Scherer, & Attig, 1978). Values, in turn, refer to a set of principles that can guide moral reasoning and action. Values have to be justified by a set of criteria (Kane, 1994, 1998). In our case, a key criterion is the impact of said value or principle on the well-being of the individual, the community, the profession, and the science of psychology. There are different ways to construct a set of morally justifiable values. One way is to witness the outcome of existing values on various segments of the population. Another is to imagine an ideal society and derive from such scenario corresponding values. Critical psychologists have embraced mostly the former, although it is hard to move forward without the latter. In witnessing the deleterious effects of individualism on people, communities, and the world of work, critical psychologists began questioning this Western principle.

Individualism. Historically, individualism was meant to protect the individual from the tight grip of religion and oppressive norms. Organized religion and its normative derivations were used to control, among others, women, peasants, and children. Individual desires were suppressed and conformity reigned supreme. The Freudian revolution greatly enhanced our understanding of repression and its psychological and social sequelae. This sort of individualism was liberating, freeing people from the tyranny of religion, conformity, and oppressive traditions (Taylor, 1991).

Unfortunately, this type of cultural individualism became conflated with economic individualism and capitalism, which thrive on consumerism. The quest for personal elevation, driven by ubiquitous advertising and the allure of fame, often results in disconnection from community and meaninglessness (Sloan, 1997). The relentless pursuit of economic gain, synergistically, leads to exploitation of workers and unprecedented gains for the captains of industry (Chomsky, 1999). Perversely, the cultural individualism that was meant to liberate people from one type of conformity, such as Victorian rigidity, is handmaiden for another type, mindless consumerism to become the best, most admired, talked about, and coveted person (Cushman, 1990).

In North American culture, individualism was not bolstered by capitalism alone, but also by the Protestant ethic of self-reliance and independence. Many British settlers escaped religious persecution in Europe and thrived on the opportunities presented to them by the United States. Their contextually and historically appropriate response—self-reliance and independence from government institutions—would contribute greatly to the prevailing idea in many Western nations that people are solely responsible for their own well-being. If people succeed in life it is due to their own hard work, and if they fail it is due to their own shortcomings (Bellah, Madsen, Sullivan, Swidler, & Tipton, 1985). This is a wonderfully simplistic and seductive narrative on which many books were written, movies made, and political speeches given. "Victim-blaming" was soon to follow as an apologia for the capitalist system. Never mind if children grow up in poverty in communities infested by drug and crime; if they work hard enough, anybody can rise above adversity. This mantra penetrates invisibly every stratum and discourse in society. Blaming the victim became one of the main occupational hazards for medicine, social work, education, social services, counseling, and psychology. Instead of looking at problems holistically, contextually, and ecologically, the gaze focused on the person in front of you (Ryan, 1971).

Thus, the Protestant ethic, capitalism, and the medical model conspired to turn an originally liberating notion—individualism—into an oppressive one, not just for the poor and the marginalized, but for the many consumed with consumerism (Cushman, 1990). It has become abundantly clear since 2008 that individualism, with its attendant qualities of greed and hubris, nearly destroyed the economy. Capitalism, in its present unregulated form, greatly facilitated the financial collapse that took place.

This ever-brief analysis touched only on religion, the economy, and the helping professions, but the impact of individualism can be felt also in educational policies, the media, and popular culture as well. In fact, in North America, and in the United States in particular, it is a form of life (Bellah et al., 1985). Critical psychologists responded to the fact that individualism was becoming noxious for the individual and communities alike. The social and professional obsession with the self, disconnected from social context, turned self-liberation into self-adulation. Self-determination, unrestrained by social justice, easily degenerates into self-absorption. The self supreme, unperturbed by the need to share resources and obligations with others, became the greed monster that now graces our TV screens: Madoff, Lehman Brothers, AIG, Bank of America, Goldman Sachs, Conrad Black, and Silvio Berlusconi.

In its multifarious manifestations, individualism did become a monster. The singular pursuit of the profit motive created handy justifications for what the world witnessed in 2008. Not only was individualism devoid of restraining justice motives, it was bereft of caring, compassion, and any sense of community. Critical psychologists mounted compelling critiques of individualism and the way psychology was unwittingly supporting it by theories and practices that reinforced blame-the-victim discourses (Albee, 1990; Prilleltensky, 1994). Individualism became, in short, bad for the person and bad for the community, which is not to say that many in positions of privilege did not take advantage of it. On the contrary, the gap between rich and poor grew exponentially since the 1960s, with the top 1% of the population becoming enormously rich and the inequality gap growing enormously large (Wilkinson & Pickett, 2009). Critical psychologists aligned themselves with the rest of the population for which quality of life had diminished. To answer the three fundamental questions of critical psychology (whose values, whose well-being, and who benefits): the individualism of the well-to-do benefited primarily their own well-being, though we hasten to add that these are short-term and superficial benefits. For the privileged are not immune to isolation, competition, and the hedonic treadmill that propels them to achieve more and more, never quite achieving a sense of satisfaction (Diener & Biswas-Diener, 2008).

The status quo. The hegemony of individualism prevails through cultural, political, economic, and military power. At times, the status quo is softly maintained by stories of heroes who overcome adversity—"proving" that anybody can make it in "America"—or by derisive portrayals of the poor through victim-blaming definitions. Other times, as in dictatorial regimes, the status quo is harshly upheld by brute force. In either its soft or harsh variety, power is omnipresent in society. Even in the most democratic of societies, money can buy influence and powerful lawyers, lobbyists, and politicians. Corruption for the preservation of the status quo is not the sole province of what we call Third World countries: there is plenty to go around in First World countries as well. But the mere invocation of democracy serves to silence critics, who are portrayed as eternally ungrateful at best or as enemies of the public good at worst (Chesney, 1998). Against legal, economic, and political forces that perpetuate the status quo, critical psychologists hold up a mirror to society, and the picture is not pretty. Whereas in Northern and Western countries critical psychologists can afford to voice discontent, in other places, like El Salvador, critical psychologists are portrayed as subversives and killed by paramilitary troops. That was the fate of Ignacio Martín-Baró (1994), a Spanish psychologist and Jesuit priest who was killed with other colleagues in 1989 at his university. Martín Baró is credited with founding and fostering liberation psychology in Latin America (Quiñones Rosado, 2007; Watkins & Shulman, 2008). He claimed psychologists should work to develop a psychology of emancipation to assist the poor to overcome conditions of oppression. Today, the vision of liberation and critical psychology is advanced in the Southern continent through the work, among many others, of Maritza Montero (2007, 2009) in Venezuela and Ignacio Dobles Oropeza and his colleagues in Costa Rica (Dobles Oropeza, 2009; Dobles Oropeza, Arróliga, & Zúñiga, 2007).

It is no coincidence that critical and liberation theories of psychology have emerged in colonial contexts. In Africa, Frantz Fanon documented the psychological scars of colonization. Originally from the Caribbean isle of Martinique, he lived in Algeria and experienced French domination, with its deleterious effects on the local Black population. Fanon became an early exponent of anticolonial theory (Bulhan, 1985; Fanon, 1965; Hook, 2004; Parker, 2007). Critical psychology is very active today in South Africa and other parts of the continent

(Hook, 2004). But the rebellion against the status quo in psychology did not happen just in colonial contexts.

German intellectuals in the late 1920s, 1930s, and 1940s created the Frankfurt school of critical theory, which sought to blend Marxism with social science. The blend of Marxism and social science became very influential in academic circles for decades to come. The fundamental insight that the means of communication reflect the views of the dominant class originated much critical research in sociology, political science, and psychology (Held, 1980). Erich Fromm, among others, used extensive psychoanalytic theory in his critique of the societal status quo, documenting the pernicious impact of social competition and the drive to have and to own instead of the drive to become (Fromm, 1965). After the Second World War, Klaus Holzkamp developed in Berlin a psychology of emancipation and subjectivity that assumed the official label of critical psychology in Germany (Tolman, 1994).

In other parts of Europe, especially in Great Britain, feminist and anticolonial psychologists in the 1970s and 1980s contributed to discursive critiques of the status quo, revealing the cultural codes that perpetuated racism and the oppression of women. An influential book edited by Henriques, Hollway, Urwin, Venn, and Walkerdine, *Changing the Subject* (1984), did much to advance discursive critical psychology. Ian Parker (2007) and his colleagues in the Discourse Unit at Manchester Metropolitan University continue to explore the ways in which psychology is an accomplice in the perpetuation of injustice.

In an effort to consolidate the various strands of critique of the status quo in psychology, Dennis Fox and Isaac Prilleltensky co-founded the Radical Psychology Network in 1993 and published in 1997 the first edition of *Critical Psychology: An Introduction* (Fox & Prilleltensky, 1997). The book gave voice to voices of discontent within psychology. The second edition, vastly revised, and with a new co-editor, came out in 2009 (Fox, Prilleltensky, & Austin, 2009). Both editions were meant to make critical psychology accessible and applicable to many psychologists who needed a framework to articulate their inchoate dissatisfaction with the societal state of affairs, and with psychology's role in it.

Psychology's role in individualism and the societal status quo. In *The Morals and Politics of Psychology: Psychological Discourse and the Status Quo* (1994), Prilleltensky analyzed how the major theories and fields of applied psychology actually reproduced individualism and maintained the dominant state of affairs. In the preface to the book, George Albee (1994) wrote that psychologists "have accepted uncritically the assignment to preserve the status quo...[through] our identification with management in industrial psychology, or our acceptance of the belief that school failures result from the child's individual defect rather than from problems in the school's social environment" (1994, pp. ix–x). The book detailed the conservative tendencies within psychoanalysis, behaviorism, humanism, and cognitivism, as well as in the practice of therapy, school, and industrial/organizational psychology.

For different reasons, all these fields supported more than they challenged the status quo. Prilleltensky identified four central mechanisms for doing so. In the first instance, "values that benefit dominant segments of society are portrayed as benefiting society as a whole" (Prilleltensky, 1994, p. 35). This is evident in the history of industrial/organizational psychology, in which practices aimed at improving managerial control are propagated as equally beneficial to workers (Baritz, 1974; Islam & Zyphur, 2009; Ralph, 1983; Wells, 1987). Secondly, "social problems that originate in the structure of the socioeconomic system are discussed in terms of psychological maladjustment" (Prilleltensky, 1994, p. 35). This ideological tactic was captured in the title of Ryan's (1971) seminal book *Blaming the Victim*. Misfortune is to be traced back to the individual's maladaptive behaviors, thoughts, and emotions. In a classic study by Caplan and Nelson (1973), 80% of psychological studies dealing with African Americans ascribed their challenges to intrapersonal inadequacies as opposed to socioeconomic circumstances. A vast lexicon of deficiencies was developed in psychology to describe personal ineptitude: weak-ego, maladaptive coping mechanisms, maladjusted personality, cognitive deficiencies, and on and on (Gergen, 1990).

A related and third mechanism for the promotion of the status quo is the abstraction of human realities from their sociohistorical context, attributing socially created phenomena to "human nature" or "genetic predispositions." Thus, gender roles are reified in nature and the intellectual performance of African Americans fixed in genetic makeup. "What has been mediated by sociohistorical process," Sampson (1981) claimed, "is treated as though it were an 'in-itself', a reality independent of these very origins" (p. 738).

A fourth way in which psychology props up the current state of affairs is through *dislocation*, a term suggested by Sullivan as a "process whereby something new is brought into a cultural system and has the ability to mute the partial critical insight of that cultural system" (Sullivan, 1984, p. 165). Family therapy, for example, addressed the lack of context in individual therapy, but it did not go far enough in introducing a truly holistic and contextual approach to mental health. Similarly, forensic psychology was introduced to deal with deviant behavior in ways that prevent the system from looking at the social roots of crime. In the 1960s, a Washington D.C. judge, Bazelon, put it well in an address to forensic psychologists:

> In considering our motives for offering you a role, I think you would do well to consider how much less expensive it is to hire a thousand psychologists than to make even a miniscule change in the social and economic structure. (Caplan & Nelson, 1973, p. 210)

Reform is not to be confused with transformation. For the social system to endure, change is inevitable. As Gross observed, "if the establishment were a mere defender of the status quo, it would be much weaker. While some of its members may resist many changes...the dominant leaders know that change is essential to preserve, let alone, expand power" (1980, p. 58). This was well captured in Lampedusa's *The Leopard*, where the young nephew said to his uncle, the prince, "if we want things to stay as they are, things have got to change" (Gross, 1980, p. 58).

The 1970s and 1980s witnessed a cacophony of voices protesting psychology's support for the system. Sullivan's analysis of behaviorism and psychometric psychology concluded that they function as "legitimators of the status quo, that is, they render interpretations which back up or legitimate a certain socio-political constellation of power" (1984, p. 26). "Because mainstream psychology is embedded in the dominant political, economic, and religious ideologies, professional psychologists have upheld these ideologies rather than examining their impact upon the lives of others" (Braginsky, 1985, p. 881). "Because psychology seems to be unique among the social sciences in its inability to reflect on its place in the social order, it will, in this unreflective stance, function as an apologist for the status quo" (Sullivan, 1984, pp. 131–132). Ingleby claimed in no uncertain terms that psychologists' "unwritten contract is to maintain the status quo" (1974, p. 317).

From traditional victim-blaming ideologies (Prilleltensky, 1994) to the new positive psychology

(Ehrenreich, 2009), psychology still engages in context minimization (Shinn & Toohey, 2003): the neglect of context in accounting for psychosocial problems. The most recent incarnation of that proclivity is positive psychology, which minimizes the role of circumstances (such as social injustice) in people's happiness (see, for example, Lyubomirsky, 2007, or Seligman, 2002). "The real conservatism of positive psychology," writes Barbara Ehrenreich, "lies in its attachment to the status quo with all its inequalities and abuses of power" (2009, p. 170). She rightly assumes that the benefits of positive psychology may be accessible to middle-class people who are not overly bothered by inequality and injustice:

> Like pop positive thinking, positive psychology attends almost solely to the changes a person can make internally by adjusting his or her own outlook .... Positive psychologists' more important contribution to the defense of the status quo has been to assert or "find" that circumstances play only a minor role in determining a person's happiness .... Why advocate for better jobs and schools, safer neighborhoods, universal health insurance, or any other liberal desideratum if these measures will do little to make people happy? Social reformers, political activists, and change-oriented elected officials can all take a much-needed rest.... In the great centuries-long quest for a better world, the baton has passed to the practitioners of "optimism training," the positive psychologists, and the purveyors of pop positive thinking. (Ehrenreich, 2009, pp. 171–172)

Indeed, Seligman (2002) and Lyubomirsky (2007), among others, claim that social circumstances account for only a very small fraction of people's happiness. Most of success or failure in life may be attributed to genetic makeup or motivational factors, as if motivational factors may be solidly detached from the environment in which people grow up. Positive psychologists claim that happiness is determined largely by genetics (50%) and volitional factors (40%) and only moderately by circumstances (10%) (Lyubomirsky, 2007; Seligman, 2002). Although positive psychologists claim that circumstantial factors account for about only 10% of happiness and volitional factors for about 40%, we should keep in mind that the psychological and behavioral variables said to account for the 40% cannot be easily disentangled from the circumstances of people's lives (McGue & Bouchard, 1998; Turkheimer, 1998).

In summary, critical psychology emerged as a reaction to (a) the oppressive turn in individualism, (b) the negative repercussions of the status quo on large sectors of the population, and (c) psychology's witting or unwitting complicity in upholding the societal status quo. We saw that critical psychology scholars and activists started working in earnest in Latin America, Africa, Australia, Europe, and North America in the 1970s, 1980s, and 1990s. Today, critical psychology is a scholarly and social movement dedicated to advance justice and well-being for the people most negatively affected by the dominant social order.

Epistemic Values

Epistemology concerns the study of knowledge. As such, epistemic values are criteria we use to elicit the most reliable portrayal of the object of study. We need to employ methods suitable to the unique nature of phenomena. Giving a career interest inventory written in English to an immigrant newly arrived from a non-English-speaking country would be rather inappropriate. We calibrate our methods to the nature of the experience we wish to explore.

Critical psychology has been concerned mainly with three shortcomings of mainstream psychology's ways of study. According to critics, the main discipline has often engaged in mechanistic, reductionist, and ethnocentric approaches. We describe these problematic assumptions in this section. Alternatives will be offered in the next segment of the chapter.

Mechanistic approaches. Assuming a physics model of causation, psychology diminished the role of self-determination and agency. "It is criticized that the human subject is wrongly conceptualized as a passive and reactive machine, driven by causes, with components that can be added up (such as nature and nurture)" (Teo, 2005, p. 36). The machine metaphor is primordial in behaviorism, which studies human behavior in terms of stimulus and response, largely obviating the mediating effects of subjectivity, reflexivity, and agency (Teo, 2009). Critical psychologists object to this mechanistic approach, claiming that natural science models do not do justice to the subject of study, a much more complicated organism than others studied in laboratory and controlled environments.

Reductionist approaches. Related to the first concern, critical psychologists object to the atomistic approach of mainstream psychology. The totality of the human experience can be ill described by studying isolated pieces of it. Borrowing heavily from the natural sciences, psychology sought to emulate models that could isolate centers of behavior, emotions, or thoughts. This defies the complexity of the human subject, who behaves differently in different contexts, and who makes sense of complex phenomena before responding. As Teo observed,

> It is *reductionist* to assume that the parts sufficiently explain the complexity of human subjectivity.... The idea that studying the parts of a whole is sufficient and that the parts will fit together into a meaningful whole through additive processes is based on a limited worldview. Parts do not add up when it comes to human mental life. Critics have argued that a psychology that does justice to human subjectivity should begin with the nexus of human experience in order to understand the parts and not vice versa. (2009, p. 39)

Mechanistic and reductionist approaches are heavily influenced by methodologism, or methodolatry: the determination of the object of study based on existing measurement techniques (Parker, 2007; Teo, 2005, 2009). We study what we have tools for. Instead of creating tools suitable to the subject of study, we create research questions that suit the tools we have, such as surveys, questionnaires, and contrived social situations (Pancer, 1997).

Ethnocentric approaches. Much of mainstream psychology and career psychology in the last century came to reflect its dominant groups: European White males. Women and people from other cultures had to be measured according to this yardstick. Immigrants to the United States were evaluated, and deemed intellectually incompetent, based on ethnocentric measures (Kamin, 1974). Similar biased procedures were used to assess the "deficient" mental state of women, African Americans, and various colonized groups, like Aboriginal peoples (Prilleltensky, 1994). Examples of male, Euro, White-centric assessments and interventions abound in the history of psychology (Hook, 2004; Moane, 2011; Oliver, 2004). Feminist and anticolonial psychologists describe the pathologization of women and Aboriginal peoples by mental health professionals and the establishment (Durrheim, Hook, & Riggs, 2009; Fox, Austin & Prilleltensky, 2009; Watkins & Shulman, 2008). You cannot universalize the standard of male, White, European psychology, yet this is exactly what happened over the last century (Teo, 2005).

Professional Values

Moral and epistemic values inform professional practice. The moral and epistemological assumptions of psychologists get translated into action and codified in diagnostic rubrics, assessment tools, therapy manuals, and psychological reports. Individualistic, reactive, and alienating approaches developed in the mechanistic and reductionist context described above. Critical psychologists objected to these three applications in psychology.

Individualistic approaches. It follows from individualistic cultures and reductionist approaches that assessments and interventions would be focused mainly on individuals. This is particularly the case in trait-and-factor and related approaches in career psychology. The majority of career psychology theories draw on aspects of trait-and-factor theory, notably Holland's (1997) career theory, Gottfredson's (2002) theory, and work adjustment theory (Dawis, 2005). Few psychologists prior to the arrival of community psychology would venture outside their offices to engage in multilevel interventions; even school and industrial psychologists would work in their own offices within schools or plants. Infused with Protestant notions of self-reliance, conservative invocations of victim blaming, and epistemic legacies of reductionism, it was only too easy for psychologists to focus diagnosis and treatment on the individual, to the exclusion of environmental factors in the workplace, school, church, and community (Fox, Austin, & Prilleltensky, 2009; Gergen, 2009).

Reactive approaches. If physics was the idealized parent of psychological science, then medicine was the desired object of psychological practice. And much of medicine, as we know it, is reactive. The health system, which is probably better called the illness system, operates in wait-and-see mode. Experts wait for patients to knock on their doors, asking for assistance. Preventive and public health approaches, which look at social determinants of health, threaten the medical model, and consequently received limited support among health systems across the world (Albee, 1982, 1996). Psychology followed the medical model, and it also engaged primarily in reactive models.

Alienating approaches. Professional arrogance, especially in psychiatric institutions, came to characterize the mental health system. Horrific cases of abuse in mental institutions told the story of professionals becoming more and more dehumanized. Psychiatric patients became objects of control, as opposed to partners in health (Chamberlin, 1984; McCubbin, 2009). Similar arrogance was practiced with "refrigerator" mothers whose children became autistic (Kanner, 1949), with children who had to be subdued (Olfman, 2006), and with Aboriginal peoples who had to be Westernized (Glover, Dudgeon, & Huygens, 2010). Children, women, psychiatric patients, and minorities in general became the subject of control and domination.

All in all, shortcomings in moral, epistemic, and professional values did not paint a pretty picture of psychology. Critical psychologists looked into these practices and rebelled: they did not want to be part of an oppressive system. And while critique is usually ahead of emancipatory practices, we offer in the next section some concrete alternatives to the dispiriting image.

A Critical Approach to Well-Being

To create a useful, effective, and liberating psychology of work, we offer a set of recommendations corresponding to the concerns of the previous section: moral, epistemic, and professional values.

Critical Approach to Moral Values

We counter the problems of individualism, injustice in the status quo, and psychology's tacit support for the system with interdependence, justice, and solidarity, respectively.

Interdependence. The value proposition of interdependence lies precisely in balancing competing values. The problem is not just with individualism, but with any value, such as collectivism, that is promulgated in extreme form. Pushed to their extremes, self-determination becomes selfishness and collectivism turns into oppression (Prilleltensky, 1997, 2001). We maintain that personal, relational, organizational, and community well-being rely on a set of well-balanced and integrated values (Prilleltensky & Prilleltensky, 2006).

Our first proposition is that the well-being of a person relies on the well-being of his or her relationships, of the organizations with which he or she comes into contact, and of the community at large (Prilleltensky & Prilleltensky, 2006; Rath & Harter, 2010). In turn, the well-being of organizations depends on the well-being of the people who populate it, of the relationships within it, and of the community at large (Fullan, 2008; Sisodia, Sheth, & Wolfe, 2007). The same can be said for the well-being of the community at large. It is hard to imagine community wellness in a place where organizations are dysfunctional and relationships acrimonious (Nelson & Prilleltensky, 2010). As Robert Putnam (2000, 2002) has shown, communities with low levels of social capital, or relational networks, suffer from poor education, health, and welfare and have high crime rates. Similarly, communities with high levels of inequality experience more psychosocial problems such as addictions, teen pregnancy, school dropouts, and child abuse (Wilkinson & Pickett, 2009). Recent research has also drawn connections between levels of economic inequality within states and differences in rates of mortgage delinquency (Brescia, 2010). Going from the macro to the micro level, we can see that people who live in communities with high levels of unemployment experience less satisfaction with life than people in communities with higher levels of employment (Clark, 2010). Children who grow up in poor communities experience more stress in the family and less success in school and are exposed to more risk factors in their neighborhoods (Evans, 2004). Indeed, beyond social capital, unemployment, and child poverty, there are many cases that illustrate the interdependence between personal, relational, organizational, and community well-being. Children who grow up in abusive families develop certain defensive behavioral patterns that predispose them to engage in poor relationships as adults. Lack of trust may lead to interpersonal conflict at work and in the community (Prilleltensky, Nelson, & Peirson, 2001). Lack of control at work may lead to stress that gets manifested in anger at home. Crime in the community leads to isolation, which affects mental health and well-being (Prilleltensky, 2012).

To promote the well-being of each entity (people, relationships, organizations, and communities) as well as their synergistic effects, we need to articulate a set of values. To advance individual well-being, we need to foster self-determination, meaningful engagement in life, optimism, positive relationships, and opportunities for growth (Diener & Biswas Diener, 2008; Lyubomirsky, 2007; Prilleltensky & Prilleltensky, 2006). Relational well-being, in turn, relies on caring, compassion, and mutual support (Blustein, Schultheiss, & Flum, 2004; Gergen, 2009). Organizational well-being rests on values of effectiveness, reflection, and support (Fullan, 2008; Sisodia, Sheth, & Wolfe, 2007). Finally, community well-being requires support for public institutions, respect for diversity, social capital, and most of all, social justice (Nelson & Prilleltensky, 2010). These values must be in balance to achieve the synergy required to foster harmonious relationships, personal growth, and thriving communities (Watkins & Shulman, 2008).

Political geography shows us that countries with totalitarian regimes, such as the former Soviet Union, oppressed their citizens in their quest for collectivism, whereas Western nations, like the United States, foster isolation among its citizens. In their quest for success, citizens of the latter experience loneliness (Putnam, 2000, 2002). In their quest for obedience, the former impose state will. In either case citizens lose. To balance the need for personal emancipation with the need to support other groups and the community at large, we espouse emancipatory communitarianism, or the belief that the well-being of the private citizen must be balanced against the well-being of other entities (Prilleltensky, 1997). Without a well community, or healthy relationships, the well-being of the very individual is in jeopardy. Ours is not a call to abandon personhood or creative individualism. On the contrary, ours is a call to create communities and workplaces where no individual achieves so much that others are left with little. Communitarianism without the emancipation of the individual is oppressive, and emancipation without controls reverts to individualism.

If we think of the person and the community as two poles of an ecological continuum, relationships and organizations serve as mediating mechanisms through which people support each other and foster dialogical bonds for the solution of common problems (Gergen, 2009). It is impossible to look after the community in the abstract if you do not start with relationships and organizations of concern. Workplaces need to embrace the individuality of workers and foster collective responsibility.

Justice. This concept is defined as the fair and equitable allocation of resources, obligations, and bargaining powers (Miller, 1999). Critical psychologists reject the status quo because it fails millions of people, because it is unjust and unfair. The economic and political edifice of unregulated capitalism rests on inequality and injustice. The more unregulated and extreme capitalism becomes, the more the inequality gap widens (Chomsky, 1999).

The main argument for the just nature of the system is that it affords equal opportunities to all. This is patently false: poor children growing up in dilapidated communities with poorly resourced schools have far fewer opportunities to go to a good college, let alone finish high school, than children from well-endowed backgrounds (Darling-Hammond, 2010; Evans, 2004; Ravitch, 2010). Faced with this inconvenient truth, defenders of the status quo point fingers to parents, accusing them of not taking advantage of the opportunities presented to them (Farber & Azar, 1999). But wait a minute, you say, these parents were once children who grew up in drug-infested neighborhoods with teen parents who had no clue how to raise children. At this point you can engage in an infinite regress blaming the parents of the parents of the parents, or you can stop and say: children who grow up in conditions of disadvantage can hardly be blamed for the circumstances of their lives, for they had no control over them.

Injustice fails not only the education of poor children, but also their health. Adler and Stewart (2009) coined the term "behavioral injustice" to address the health consequences of growing up in disadvantage. Addressing the obesity epidemic, they demonstrate that many poor people grow up in "obesogenic" environments that perpetuate the consumption of high-fat foods and limit fitness opportunities. As they note,

> Although some individuals are able to make and maintain change, the medical model largely ignores the forces contributing to the development and maintenance of obesity. Patients walk out of the health care provider's office only to reenter the same environment that led to their weight gain in the first place. The commercial and structural forces in their environment still are powerful. These people thus may be caught in "vicious cycles" of "accelerators" of the obesity epidemic.... resulting from the interaction of an increasingly obese individual with an "obesogenic environment" that encourages an overconsumption of food and discourages physical activity. (Adler & Stewart, 2009, p. 55)

Critical psychologists question the notion that people can improve their health or work opportunities at any time "because they are free to do so." This is to ignore the vast inequities in access to resources that define one's opportunities in life. This is not to say that people are devoid of agency to struggle for social justice. Rather, to ignite that agency, we need to acknowledge first that the environment does not present similar opportunities to all. We agree with Adler and Stewart that it is "unjust to hold people accountable for things over which they have little control .... This places the primary responsibility on society to provide equal opportunities for all people to be able to make the healthier choices, and it reframes the discussion as one of justice rather than blame" (2009, p. 61). Nations and communities that distribute resources more equitably and make access to healthier environments easier achieve better levels of psychosocial health and well-being (Wilkinson & Pickett, 2009).

Stead and Perry (2012a) argued that to assist people with their career choices, there should be less emphasis on individualist and reductionist perspectives and more emphasis on multicultural, multicontextual, and community perspectives to work. In so doing, ethically based social justice perspectives can be employed, such as that of Ali, Liu, Mahmood, and Arguello (2008).

Psychology's role in solidarity and social change. Contrary to mainstream psychology's tacit support for the status quo, critical psychologists actively support solidarity with marginalized groups and foster social change (Huygens, 2007, 2009; Nelson & Prilleltensky, 2010; Prilleltensky & Nelson, 2002). Critical psychologists engage with the poor and marginalized in participatory, collaborative, and emancipatory ways.

Prilleltensky and Nelson (2002) describe in detail how the values of self-determination, empowerment, caring, compassion, respect for diversity, and social justice inform practice in educational, clinical, organizational, health, and community settings. In all cases, critical psychologists honor the process of empowerment and justice as much as the outcome. This means giving voice and choice to the partners with whom we work, respecting their dignity by acknowledging their strengths and power differentials, and seeking avenues to gain control of their lives in ways that enhance reciprocal empowerment and not personal aggrandizement. Two examples illustrate these principles.

Brinton Lykes (Lykes, 1997, 1999; Lykes & Coquillon, 2009), for example, has been working in Guatemala with indigenous women for many years, gaining their trust and finding ways to empower them to gain control of their lives despite great trauma caused by mass killings by paramilitary troops. Many projects have sprung from their work together, including photo voice exhibitions and recovery efforts. In authentic partnerships of solidarity, the women transform their psychosocial reality while gaining recognition of past atrocities and injustice.

Ingrid Huygens (2007), in Aotearoa, New Zealand, studied processes of Pakeha (White inhabitants) change in response to the Treaty of Waitangi. The treaty, signed in 1840 between the British crown and the Maori people, granted the Maori population rights and privileges that were never quite honored by the White colonizers. Huygens documents the process of unlearning colonization and building bonds of solidarity with Maori communities. Her research offers many lessons about the transformation of dominant groups: questioning the legitimacy of White privilege, openness to the challenges of oppressed groups, pursuit of counter-hegemonic accounts of colonization, responsibility for the outcomes of domination, and fair relationships based on recognition of past injustices (2007, p. 247).

Critical Approach to Epistemic Values

To counter mechanistic, reductionist, and ethnocentric approaches to the study of lives, organizations, and communities, we espouse holistic, agentic, and culturally appropriate methods.

Holistic and agentic approaches. Critical psychologists embrace the challenge of studying people in their context, through quantitative and qualitative means that capture their lived experience. They acknowledge that despite great social forces, people exercise autonomy and self-determination. They balance the respect for agency with respect for social forces. Choices are influenced by cultural and social messages and opportunities. As Nussbaum (2006) explains,

> People adjust their preferences to what they think they can achieve, and also to what their society tells them a suitable achievement is for someone like them. Women and other deprived people frequently exhibit such "adaptive preferences," formed under unjust background conditions. These preferences will typically validate the status quo. (p. 73)

Therefore, critical psychologists pay attention to the exercise of self-determination, but in due recognition of the social determinants of health and well-being (Commission on Social Determinants of Health, 2008; Marmot, 2004).

Culturally appropriate approaches. Multiple cultures exist within any particular community: the culture of people with disabilities, the culture of people from Morocco, the culture of LGBT folk. Instead of searching for universals, critical psychologists search for specifics, and attune their modes of help accordingly. There is profound disrespect in expecting your clients to play by your rules and follow your hegemonic notions of decorum, wellness, and happiness. This requires sincere humility and a listening stance. Critical psychologists working with poor people, for example, have developed authentic mechanisms to bridge across cultures (Smith, 2010).

Critical Approach to Professional Values

To counter individualistic, reactive, and alienating orientations, critical psychologists devise interventions that are multilevel, strength-based, empowering, and proactive.

Multilevel culture and community change. Personal well-being is a multilevel phenomenon that requires not just personal adjustments, but also environmental ones (Rath & Harter, 2010). The well-being of a worker in a factory depends not simply on his or her attitude, but also on the climate, level of compensation, fair policies, emotional support, challenging opportunities, and the like (Blustein, 2006). A healthy working environment reflects effective, reflective, and supportive policies and practices that take into account the differential level of power of workers within the organization. While an ecological approach is better than one focusing strictly on the attitudes of the single workers, we should remember that it is possible to devise multilevel interventions that are aimed at enhancing managerial control at the expense of worker well-being.

Strength-based and empowering change. Critical psychology interventions are not just multilevel, they are also empowering. The goal is to provide voice and choice to workers, to recognize their strengths, and to create a working environment where there is mutual respect for the needs of everybody in the enterprise. Instead of defect-finding expeditions, critical psychologists venture to find assets in people, institutions, and communities. This is reflected in the questions we ask our partners and in the interventions we co-create with them. Appreciative inquiry is one example of action research based on strengths (Cooperrider & Srivastva, 1987). Asset Building Community Development (ABCD) is another (Kretzmann & McKnight, 1993). Narrative approaches to therapy (Morgan, 2000) and resilience building in youth (Liebenberg & Ungar, 2008) also work on strengths as opposed to deficits. These approaches acknowledge people's strengths and afford them voice and choice. Strength-based practitioners create partnerships with citizens to build on their assets. They do so by asking questions such as: What have you done to cope well with adversity? How did you achieve what you have? What are some of your strengths and virtues?

Proactive change. Instead of waiting for workers and organizations to develop signs of problems, we espouse a proactive approach based on analyses of risk and protective factors. It is far more humane, and cost-effective, to prevent problems than to cure them. Effective strategies exist for improving organizational climate and worker well-being. Similarly, a great deal is known about policies and practices that optimize satisfaction and fairness in the workplace (Fullan, 2008; Marmot & Feeney, 1996; Maton, 2008; Sisodia, Sheth, & Wolfe, 2007). For the most part, these interventions engage the workforce in visioning and devising a better place, build vertical and horizontal partnerships across the organization, minimize competition, and create a sense of shared responsibility. Proactive interventions do not just seek positive outcomes, but also meaningful processes. A collaborative, inclusive, and effective process can be a powerful outcome in itself, as it builds trust and ownership. In the case of effective school improvement, teachers collaborate with administration, better schools help struggling schools, senior teachers mentor junior teachers, everybody shares data, and parents are invited to be part of the solution (Hargreaves & Shirley, 2009).

Overall, effective preventive interventions are comprehensive, use varied teaching methods, provide sufficient dosage, are theory-driven, promote positive relationships, are appropriately timed, are culturally relevant, use outcome evaluation, and have well-trained staff (Nation et al., 2003). These features should inform school, worksite, and community-level interventions.

Critical Approaches to Work and Career Psychology

To examine critical psychology and the world of work, we need to consider the extent of its application to career psychology. Career psychology is different from the psychology of working in that the former largely employs mainstream approaches to research and counseling, without challenging the prevalent status quo. Furthermore, career psychologists largely study work as hierarchical and as a series of occupational choices (e.g., Brown & Associates, 2002; Brown & Lent, 2005). The focus is primarily on the individual, with some attention to context. The psychology of working, in turn, focuses on work as a central human activity that is both sociocultural in nature and embedded in all domains of life. All aspects of work, including paid and nonpaid work, are studied in the psychology of working. Moreover, the psychology of working focuses on oppression and social barriers to work (Blustein, 2006).

Theories

Theories in career psychology include, among others, person–environment fit (e.g., Dawis, 2005; Holland, 1997), social cognitive career theory (Lent, Brown, & Hackett, 2002), developmental and lifespan perspectives (e.g., Savickas, 2002; Super et al., 1996), sociological approaches (e.g., Johnson & Mortimer, 2002), systems theory (Patton & McMahon, 1999), action theory (Young, Valach, & Collin, 2002), and most recently Blustein's (2011) relational theory of working. Many, but not all, career theories have focused on a logical positivist approach to resolving career problems, in which the emphasis has been on examining the individual's personality and inner thought processes, and aligning these with jobs that suit such characteristics. This is also an essentialist perspective, as the core inner traits of individuals are to be discovered and described. Essentialism focuses on core characteristics of the individual and largely separates the individual from contexts, hence the danger of blaming the victim and minimizing contexts (Burr, 2003). Essentialism is part of every career theory, traditional and recent, with the possible exception of the sociological perspective (Johnson & Mortimer, 2002). This separation is of concern to critical psychologists. There is also an emphasis on work adjustment in career psychology, as evinced in Dawis's (2005) career theory, and there is little focus in career theories on how the world of work, instead of the worker, might be adjusted. Some of the more recent career theories have focused on the importance of context, for example Young, Valach, and Collin's (2002) contextualist career theory, and how micro and macro systems affect individual lives, for example Patton and McMahon's (1999) systems theory of career development. There has been increased reference to career issues of women, culturally diverse people, minorities, people with low socioeconomic status, immigrants, and the disabled in career theories, but little on the importance of social justice and work.

Career and Work Literature

There have been implicit but no explicit references to critical psychology in career theories. Variables such as motivation, self-efficacy, self-concept, career aspirations, career maturity, emotion and cognition (almost all as inner processes), career interventions, and counseling techniques are researched in relation to the career choice process, sometimes within various contexts, such as socioeconomic status, language, race, and country (Brown & Lent, 2005). The focus is on assisting the individual from an individualist perspective.

However, despite these limitations, there has been some critical commentary from within the career literature. The importance of social justice and work has been highlighted by several authors, such as Ali et al. (2008), Blustein, McWhirter, and Perry (2005), Stead and Perry (2012a), and Watson and Stead (2002). For example, McWhirter, Blustein, and Perry (2005), argued for integrating the emancipatory communitarian approach into the psychology of work as useful in assisting people with few or no occupational choices. Watson and Stead queried what the role of practitioners is and who their clients are, arguing for mutual collaboration and power sharing in research and counseling for all people.

McIlveen and Patton (2006) provided a critical review of objective assessment and psychometrics in career development, with special reference to the work of Foucault (1977). Their argument is that through logical positivism, traditional career approaches have resulted in career constructs becoming reified (i.e., terms constructed through language are assumed to be objective and concrete), without consideration that such constructs have been *constructed*. Furthermore, they stated that career psychologists, through corporate sanction, "become legitimized as the controllers of individuality" (p. 23). This is reminiscent of the research of Savage (1998) and McKinlay (2002) showing how employees' selves are managed and controlled in corporate environments, resulting in what McKinlay referred to as "dead selves" (p. 595). McIlveen and Patton believed that counselors should acknowledge their power in the counseling relationship and become critically and reflexively aware of their discourses in the career field.

While career counselors assist many clients, it is through career counseling discourse, in association with psychological discourse, that people become categorized, diagnosed, and documented. Following Foucault (1977), they become "normalized," and these are some of the powerful discourses to which McIlveen and Patton (2006) refer to. What is important to note here is that the traditional, so-called "objective" discourses in the career psychology literature are not the only ones available. There are many other discourses. However, alternative discourses often get marginalized. This is why Foucault (1977) referred to power and knowledge as intimately connected. It is through discourses that knowledge gets accepted, often through respected authors, organizations, and institutions. These are not necessarily the most useful or even most desirable discourses available, and they are not universally factual and objective. They are only deemed so within the regime of truth purveyed within a particular discourse. This is one reason why critical psychologists view knowledge as local and contextualized.

An explicit statement of critical psychology in relation to the psychology of work-based transitions will be published as a special issue of the *Journal of Career Development*. In the special issue, the editors, Stead and Perry (2012b), stated that there has been a paucity of distributive justice and equity in the resources provided to people in work transitions. Furthermore, they claim that the focus in career psychology has been less on structural and societal problems and more on adjustment of personal problems. Prilleltensky and Stead (2012) reflect on the adjust/challenge dilemma in which the following choices are present in the counseling process: (a) adjust and challenge the system, (b) focus on adjustment but do not challenge the system, (c) challenge the system and do not adjust to it, or (d) neither challenge nor adjust to the system. The consequences of each choice are discussed in relation to the well-being of people and communities. Blustein, Medvide, and Wan (2012) argued that traditional discourses in career psychology have served not only to marginalize the unemployed but also to reinforce oppressive practices in public policy, research, and practice in relation to unemployment. They believed that career psychologists have seldom critically examined research on the individual in relation to unemployment or located unemployment within a combination of political, social, and psychological domains. Using a case study methodology, Ali, Yang, Button, and McCoy (2012) conducted a career education program among ninth-grade high school students in rural Iowa. The program was informed by critical psychology approaches in emphasizing collaboration involving the researchers, school personnel, and students in the research process. The program focused on personal and environmental barriers to academic and career planning facing the students. Finally, McWhirter and McWhirter (2012) provided an informative analysis of career guidance in Chile, not only offering a critique but also suggesting ways in which vocational guidance could be transformed to the benefit of Chilean youth living in difficult economic conditions. Additional examples of commentary on political factors in relation to work on a national level may also be found in studies in Portugal (Santos & Ferreira, 1998) and South Africa (Nicholas, Naidoo, & Pretorius, 2006).

Although career psychology is an inherently cultural enterprise, it marginalizes cultural and cross-cultural psychology in its literature (Stead, 2004, 2007). As Stead and Bakker (2010a) argue, theorists need to acknowledge the role cultural beliefs play in their theories' construction and applicability to a diverse range of cultures within and outside the United States. Closely related to social constructionism is discourse analysis, which is emerging as an alternative way to conceptualize career psychology and the psychology of work. Discourse analysis comprises a variety of perspectives, with its critical variant (e.g., Foucault, 1977; Hook, 2004) being anti-essentialist and anti-humanist and focusing on language and power, which are seen as two sides of the same coin, in constructing meaning and realities. The Foucauldian perspective focuses on who is being served and why various people or groups benefit at the expense of others. It is interested in how discourses can be taken for granted and accepted in some contexts but can be oppressive in other contexts (Stead & Bakker, 2010a).Blustein, Schultheiss, and Flum (2004) provided a relational perspective of career and work using social constructionism. They stated that a goal of the relational approach to the psychology of work would be to "construct generative discourses that challenge existing traditions of knowledge and suggest new possibilities for practice and policy" (p. 435). The relationship approach highlights the narrative approach. They claimed that the relational approach would be more integrative of people's diverse life domains than current research on career. The relational approach moves from intrapsychic processes to relationally embedded contextual domains.

Stead and Bakker (2010a, 2010b) argued for discourse analysis as an approach to critically evaluate the epistemological and ontological assumptions in career psychology. Discourse analysis, they argue, can be employed to analyze individual and institutional ways of communicating, and how some bodies of knowledge become marginalized. The emphasis is on how discourses are socially constructed, who benefits from such discourses, and whose approaches are marginalized. One example is the marginalization of qualitative research in favor of quantitative research in the career psychology literature. For example, Stead et al. (2012) content analyzed 3,279 articles from 1990 to 2009 in 11 major international and U.S. journals that published articles on careers and work. They reported that 55.9% of articles provided quantitative methods, 35.5% were theoretical/conceptual, and only 6.3% employed qualitative or mixed-methods research.

The data showed from 1990 to 2009 the number of quantitative empirical articles continued to increase relative to qualitative and mixed-method empirical articles. This is an example of how methodologism is prevalent in career psychology. Discourse analysis can provide the tools to critically evaluate the literature on work and career and provide new alternatives to existing practices in research, counseling, and policy.

Humanitarian Work Psychology

While career psychology concerns itself with the individual in relation to occupations, it has seldom turned its gaze on unemployment and researched how unemployment and poverty can be ameliorated. Humanitarian Work Psychology (HWP) is an international nonpartisan organization that applies the principles of organizational psychology to humanitarianism, especially in relation to poverty reduction and promotion of decent work that includes local stakeholders' needs (see http://www.humworkpsy.org). The focus is on collaboration with communities to develop plans for fostering well-being and work. Berry et al. (2011) argued that poverty reduction is not a subject only for economists, but that organizational psychologists have the skills and social obligation to address this crucial issue. Such activities include data gathering, data analysis and synthesis, conflict resolution, training, partnership building, communication, policy development, implementation of programs, and other skills. The purpose is to turn "what is" to "what might be" by utilizing organizational research in innovative, practical, and effective ways to reduce poverty. There are many excellent resources in this field, including Smith (2010), Blustein (2006), Carr and Sloan (2003), and Owusu-Bempah and Howitt (2000), among many others. Harper (2003) believed that in relation to poverty, psychological research has been largely methodologically inadequate, as a result of experimental designs and response-format questionnaires, and also politically unaware. Poverty and employment are intimately connected, and a critical approach to the psychology of work is well positioned to address these global concerns.

Critical Psychology and Critical Management Studies

In addition to its emancipatory potential in career psychology and the psychology of work, a critical approach can influence management strategies. In fact, the marriage of critical approaches with management studies gave birth to the field of Critical Management Studies (CMS). This field of study applies to management many of the same insights that critical psychology applies to mainstream psychology (Adler, Forbes, & Willmot, 2008). While recognizing the potential of collaborative enterprises in fostering human flourishing, CMS deals with the barriers that contemporary organizations and the theories that support them erect in frustrating human potential.

> What CMS addresses is the needless frustration of this potential that occurs when, instead of enabling human flourishing, organizations incubate and normalize stress and bad health, naturalize subordination and exploitation, demand conformism, inhibit free communication, erode morality, create and reinforce ethnic and gender inequalities, and so on. Instead of being progressive forces for emancipatory change, mainstream theory, as well as the everyday practice of organization and management, become reactionary means of conserving forms of exploitation and oppression institutionalized in the status quo. There is, in this sense, good reason to introduce, develop, and apply critical perspectives on management and organizations. (Alvesson, Bridgman, & Willmott, 2009, p. 8)

Like critical psychology, CMS questions taken-for-granted assumptions in management. Three of these unquestioned assumptions are the naturalization of dominance, the paragon of productivity, and the lack of reflexivity. The first one concerns the unquestioned acceptance of White male-dominated work environments. The second deals with the presumption that all human interaction in the workplace ought to be evaluated on the basis of the bottom line. Relationships are worth it only insofar as they generate money. This instrumental approach to human relations perpetuates the objectification of human beings in the workplace. The final critique, concerning the lack of reflexivity, feeds the previous two: it is precisely the lack of self-reflection that enables dominant groups to proceed with oppressive approaches without guilt or self-recrimination (Alvesson, Bridgman, & Willmott, 2009).

In a series of telling case studies, Wolfram Cox, LeTrent-Jones, Voronov, and Wier (2009) apply critical theory to organizational conflicts and dilemmas. Their collection of case studies demonstrates the usefulness of narrative, discourse, and power analyses in dissecting the often-diverging sets of interests that plague workplaces. The growing literature on CMS promises to open new avenues for studying organizational development and human flourishing.

Conclusion

Critical psychology and critical approaches in general have much to offer to the psychology of work. The main contributions may be divided into deconstruction and reconstruction. The former entails the dismantling of oppressive practices through methodic questioning of assumptions. The latter pertains to building relationships and structures within the workplace and society that foster the values of self-determination, cooperation, respect for diversity, and social justice. To achieve the goals of deconstruction and reconstruction, we need to challenge psychology and allied professions to challenge the societal status quo. The psychology-of-work approach and critical management studies are aligning with emancipatory approaches that put people ahead of profit. Humanistic work psychology promotes the principles of collaboration, service, and social justice. Career psychology, while closely attached with mainstream psychology, is also beginning to question some of its assumptions.

A critical psychology approach to work reminds us that the well-being of employees and community members, not just management and corporate leaders, is important. Furthermore, it brings attention to the values and aspirations of all people, not just dominant groups. If the entire community is to benefit from a psychology of work, we had better make sure that all the voices are heard, that rights and obligations in the world of work are fairly distributed, and that the well-being of workers is not devoid of justice. No wellness without fairness.

References

Adler, N., & Stewart, J. (2009). Reducing obesity: Motivating action while not blaming the victim. *Milbank Quarterly, 87,* 49–70.

Adler, P., Forbes, L., & Willmott, H. (2008). Critical management studies: premises, practices, problems, and prospects. *Academy of Management Annals, 1,* 119–180.

Albee, G. (1994). Preface. In I. Prilleltensky, *The morals and politics of psychology: Psychological discourse and the status quo* (pp. ix–x). Albany, NY: The State University of New York Press.

Albee, G. W. (1982). Preventing psychopathology and promoting human potential. *American Psychologist, 32,* 150–161.

Albee, G. W. (1990). The futility of psychotherapy. *Journal of Mind and Behavior, 11*(3/4), 369–384.

Albee, G. W. (1996). Revolutions and counterrevolutions in prevention. *American Psychologist, 51,* 1130–1133.

Ali, S. R., Liu, W. M., Mahmood, A., & Arguello, J. (2008). Social justice and applied psychology: Practical ideas for training the next generation of psychologists. *Journal for Social Action in Counseling and Psychology, 1,* 1–13.

Ali, S., Yang, L., Button, C. J., & McCoy, T. T. H. (2012). Career education programming in three diverse high schools: A critical psychology—case study research approach. *Journal of Career Development, 39,* 357–385.

Alvesson, M., Bridgman, T., & Willmott, H (2009). Introduction. In M. Alvesson, T. Bridgman, & H. Willmott (Eds.), *The Oxford handbook of critical management studies* (pp. 1–26). New York: Oxford University Press.

Baritz, L. (1974). *The servants of power: A history of the use of social science in American industry.* Westport, CT: Greenwood.

Bellah, R. N., Madsen, W. M., Sullivan, W. M., Swidler, A., & Tipton, S. M. (1985). *Habits of the heart.* Berkeley, CA: University of California Press.

Berry, M. O., Reichman, W., Klobas, J., MacLachlan, M., Hui, H. C., & Carr, S. C. (2011). Humanitarian work psychology: The contributions of organizational psychology to poverty reduction. *Journal of Economic Psychology, 32,* 240–247.

Blustein, D. L. (2006). *The psychology of working.* Mahwah, NJ: Lawrence Erlbaum.

Blustein, D. L. (2011). A relational theory of working. *Journal of Vocational Behavior, 79,* 1–17.

Blustein, D. L., McWhirter, E. H., & Perry, J. C. (2005). An emancipatory communitarian approach to vocational development theory, research, and practice. *Counseling Psychologist, 33,* 141–179.

Blustein, D. L., Medvide, M. B., & Wan, C. M. (2012). A critical perspective of contemporary unemployment policy and practices. *Journal of Career Development, 39,* 341–356.

Blustein, D. L., Schultheiss, D. P., & Flum, H. (2004). Toward a relational perspective of the Braginsky, D. (1985). Handmaiden to society. In S. Koch & D. Leary (Eds.), *A century of psychology as science* (pp. 880–891). New York: McGraw Hill.

Brescia, R. H. (2010), The cost of inequality: Social distance, predatory conduct, and the financial crisis. *NYU Annual Survey of American Law, Vol. 66, Albany Law School Research Paper.* Available at SSRN: http://ssrn.com/abstract=1661746

Brown, D., & Associates. (2002). *Career choice and development* (4th ed.). San Francisco, CA: Jossey-Bass.

Brown, S. D., & Lent, R. W. (Eds., 2005). *Career development and counseling. Putting theory and research to work.* Hoboken, NJ: John Wiley & Sons.

Bulhan, H. A. (1985). *Franz Fanon and the psychology of oppression.* New York: Plenum Press.

Burr, V. (2003). *Social constructionism.* London, England: Routledge.

Caplan, N., & Nelson, S. (1973). On being useful: The nature and consequences of psychological research on social problems. *American Psychologist, 28,* 199–211.

Carr, S. C., & Sloan, T. S. (2003). *Poverty and psychology. From global perspective to local practice.* New York: Kluwer-Plenum.

Chamberlin, J. (1978). *On our own: Patient-controlled alternatives to the mental health system.* New York: McGraw-Hill.

Chamberlin, J. (1984). Speaking for ourselves: An overview of the ex-psychiatric inmates movement. *Psychosocial Rehabilitation Journal, 2,* 56–63.

Chesney, R. (1998). Introduction. In N. Chomsky, *Profit over people: Neoliberalism and global order* (pp. 7–16). New York: Seven Stories Press.

Chetkovich, C., & Kunreuther, F. (2006). *From the ground up: Grassroots organizations making social change.* Ithaca, NY: Cornell University Press.

Chomsky, N. (1999). *Profit over people: Neoliberalism and global order.* New York: Seven Stories Press.

Clark, A. (2010). Work, jobs, and well-being across the millennium. In E. Diener, J. Helliwell, & D. Kahneman (Eds.), *International differences in well-being* (pp. 436–465). New York: Oxford University Press.

Clarke, V., & Braun, V. (2009). Gender. In D. Fox, I. Prilleltensky, & S. Austin (Eds.), *Critical psychology: An introduction* (2nd ed., pp. 232–249). London: Sage.

Commission on Social Determinants of Health. (2008). *Closing the gap in a generation: Health equity through action on the social determinants of health.* Geneva: World Health Organization.

Cooperrider, D. L., & Srivastva, S. (1987). Appreciative inquiry in organizational life. *Research in Organizational Change and Development, 1,* 129–169.

Cushman, P. (1990). Why the self is empty: Toward a historically situated psychology. *American Psychologist, 45,* 599–611.

Darling-Hammond, L. (2010). *The flat world and education: How America's commitment to equity will determine our future.* New York: Teachers College.

Dawis, R. (2005). The Minnesota theory of work adjustment. In S. D. Brown & R. W. Lent (Eds.), *Career development and counseling. Putting theory and research to work* (pp. 3–23). Hoboken, NJ: Wiley.

Diener, E., & Biswas Diener, R. (2008). *Happiness: Unlocking the mysteries of psychological wealth.* Oxford: Blackwell.

Dobles Oropeza, I. (2009). *Memorias del dolor: Consideraciones acerca de las comisiones de la verdad en América Latina.* San José, Costa Rica: Arlekín.

Dobles Oropeza, I., Baltodano Arróliga, S., & Zúñiga, V. (Eds.). (2007). *Psicología de la liberación en el context de la globalización neoliberal.* San José, Costa Rica: Universidad de Costa Rica.

Durrheim, K., Hook, D., & Riggs, D. (2009). Race and racism. In D. Fox, I. Prilleltensky, & S. Austin (Eds.), *Critical psychology: An introduction* (2nd ed., pp. 197–214). London: Sage.

Ehrenreich, B. (2009). *Bright-sided: How the relentless promotion of positive thinking has undermined America.* New York: Metropolitan Books.

Evans, G. (2004). The environment of childhood poverty. *American Psychologist, 59,* 77–92.

Evans, S., Hanlin, C., & Prilleltensky, I. (2007). Blending ameliorative and transformative approaches in human service organizations: A case study. *Journal of Community Psychology, 35*(3), 329–346.

Everett, B. (1994). Something is happening: The contemporary consumer and psychiatric survivor movement in historical context. *Journal of Mind and Behavior, 15,* 55–70.

Facione, P., Scherer, D., & Attig, T. (1978). *Values and society: An introduction to ethics and social philosophy.* Englewood Cliffs, NJ: Prentice Hall.

Fanon, F. (1965). *Los condenados de la tierra [Wretched of the earth].* Mexico City: Fondo de Cultura Economica.

Farber, B. A., & Azar, S. T. (1999). Blaming the helpers: The marginalization of teachers and parents of the urban poor. *American Journal of Orthopsychiatry, 69,* 515–528.

Foucault, M. (1977). *Discipline and punish: The birth of the prison.* New York: Pantheon.

Fox, D., & Prilleltensky, I. (1997). *Critical psychology: An introduction.* London: Sage.

Fox, D., Prilleltensky, I., & Austin, S. (Eds.). (2009). *Critical psychology: An introduction* (2nd ed.). London: Sage.

Fromm, E. (1965). *Escape from freedom.* New York: Avon Books.

Fullan, M. (2008). *The six secrets of change.* San Francisco: Jossey Bass.

Gergen, K. (1990). Therapeutic professions and the diffusion of deficit. *Journal of Mind and Behavior, 11,* 353–368.

Gergen, K. (2009). *Relational being.* New York: Oxford.

Glover, M., Dudgeon, P., & Huygens, I. (2010). Colonization and racism. In G. Nelson & I. Prilleltensky (Eds.), *Community psychology: In pursuit of liberation and well-being* (pp. 353–370). New York: Palgrave Macmillan.

Gottfredson, L. S. (2002). Gottfredson's theory of circumscription, compromise, and self-creation. In D. Brown & Associates (Ed.), *Career choice and development* (4th ed., pp. 85–148). San Francisco, CA: Jossey-Bass.

Gross, B. (1980). *Friendly fascism.* Montreal, Canada: Black Rose.

Hargreaves, A., & Shirley, D. (2009). *The fourth way: The inspiring future for education change.* Thousand Oaks, CA: Corwin.

Harper, D. J. (2003). Poverty and discourse. In S. C. Carr & T. S. Sloan (Eds.), *Poverty and psychology. From global perspective to local practice* (pp. 185–203). New York: Kluwer-Plenum.

Held, D. (1980). *Introduction to critical theory: Horkheimer to Habermas.* Berkeley, CA: University of California Press.

Henriques, J., Hollway, W., Urwin, C., Venn, C., & Walkerdine, V. (Eds.). (1984). *Changing the subject.* London: Methuen.

Holland, J. L. (1997). *Making vocational choices: A theory of vocational personalities and work environments* (3rd ed.). Odessa, FL: PAR.

Hook, D. (Ed.). (2004). *Introduction to critical psychology.* Cape Town: University of Cape Town Press.

Huygens, I. (2007). *Processes of Pakeha change in response to the Treaty of Waitangi.* Hamilton, New Zealand: University of Waikato.

Huygens, I. (2009). From colonization to globalization: continuities in colonial "commonsense." In D. Fox, I. Prilleltensky, & S. Austin (Eds.), *Critical psychology: An introduction* (2nd ed., pp. 267–284). London: Sage.

Ingleby, D. (1974). The job psychologists do. In N. Armistead (Ed.), *Reconstructing social psychology* (pp. 314–328). Harmondsworth, England: Penguin.

Islam, G., & Zyphur, M. (2009). Concepts and directions in critical/organizational psychology. In D. Fox, I. Prilleltensky, & S. Austin (Eds.), *Critical psychology: An introduction* (2nd ed., pp. 110–125). London: Sage.

Johnson, M. K., & Mortimer, J. T. (2002). Career choice and development from a sociological perspective. In D. Brown & Associates (Eds.), *Career choice and development* (4th ed., pp. 37–81). San Francisco, CA: Jossey-Bass.

Kamin, L. (1974). *The science and politics of IQ.* Potomac, MD: Erlbaum.

Kane, R. (1994). *Through the moral maze: Searching for absolute values in a pluralistic world.* New York: Paragon.

Kane, R. (1998). Dimensions of value and the aims of social inquiry. *American Behavioral Scientist, 41,* 578–597.

Kanner, L. (1949). Problems of nosology and psychodynamics in early childhood autism. *American Journal of Orthopsychiatry, 19,* 416–426.

Kretzmann, J. P., & McKnight, J. L. (1993) *Building communities from the inside out: A path toward findings and mobilizing a community's assets.* Chicago, IL: ACTA Publications.

Lent, R. W., Brown, S. D., & Hackett, G. (2002). Social cognitive career theory. In D. Brown & Associates (Eds.), *Career choice and development* (4th ed., pp. 255–311). San Francisco, CA: Jossey-Bass.

Liebenberg, L., & Ungar, M. (Eds.). (2008). *Resilience in action*. Toronto: University of Toronto Press.

Lykes, M. B. (1997). Activist participatory research among the Maya of Guatemala: Constructing meanings from situated knowledge. *Journal of Social Issues, 53*(4), 725–746.

Lykes, M. B. (1999). In collaboration with A. Caba Mateo, J. Chavez Anay, I. A. Laynex Caba, & U. Ruiz. Telling stories—rethreading lives: Community education, women's development and social change among the Maya Ixil. *International Journal of Leadership in Education: Theory and Practice, 2*, 207–227.

Lykes, M. B., & Coquillon, E. D. (2009). Psychosocial trauma, poverty, and human rights in communities emerging from war. In D. Fox, I. Prilleltensky, & S. Austin (Eds.), *Critical psychology: An introduction* (2nd ed., pp. 285–299). London: Sage.

Lyubomirsky, S. (2007). *The how of happiness*. New York: Penguin.

Marmot, M. (2004). *The status syndrome: How social standing affects our health and longevity*. New York: Henry Holt.

Marmot, M., & Feeney, A. (1996). Work and health: Implications for individuals and society. In D. Blane, E. Bruner, & R. Wilkinson (Eds.), *Health and social organization* (pp. 235–254). London: Routledge.

Martín–Baró, I. (1994). *Writings for a liberation psychology*. Cambridge, MA: Harvard University Press.

Maton, K. (2008). Empowering community settings: Agents of individual development, community betterment, and positive social change. *American Journal of Community Psychology, 41*, 4–21.

McCubbin, M. (2009). Oppression and empowerment: The genesis of a critical analysis of mental health. In D. Fox, I. Prilleltensky, & S. Austin (Eds.). *Critical psychology: An introduction* (2nd ed., pp. 300–316). London: Sage.

McGue, M., & Bouchard, T. J. (1998). Genetic and environmental influences on human behavioural differences. *Annual Review of Neuroscience, 21*, 1–24.

McIlveen, P., & Patton, W. (2006). A critical reflection on career development. *International Journal for Educational and Vocational Guidance, 6*, 15–27.

McKinlay, A. (2002). "Dead selves": The birth of the modern career. *Organization, 9*, 595–614.

McWhirter, E. H., Blustein, D. L., & Perry, J. C. (2005). Annunciation: Implementing an emancipatory communitarian approach to vocational psychology. *Counseling Psychologist, 33*, 215–224.

McWhirter, E. H., & McWhirter, B. T. (2012). Critical perspectives on adolescent vocational guidance in Chile. *Journal of Career Development, 39*, 386–404.

Miller, D. (1999). *Principles of social justice*. Cambridge, MA: Harvard University Press.

Moane, G. (2011). *Gender and colonialism: A psychological analysis of oppression and liberation* (2nd ed.). London: Macmillan.

Montero, M. (2007). La problematización como aspecto critico en el proceso de liberación [Problematization as a critical aspect in the process of liberation]. In I. Dobles Oropeza, S. Baltodano Arróliga, & V. Leandro Zúñiga (Eds.), *Psicología de la liberación en el context de la globalización neoliberal* (pp. 216–229). San José, Costa Rica: Universidad de Costa Rica.

Montero, M. (2009). Community psychology's voyage into complexity: On liberation change and politics. In G. Nelson & I. Prilleltensky (Eds.). *Community psychology: In pursuit of liberation and well-being* (pp. 519–530). New York: Palgrave.

Morgan, A. (2000). *What is narrative therapy? An easy-to-read introduction*. Adelaide, South Australia: Dulwich Publications.

Nation, M., Crusto, C., Wandersman, A., Kumpfer, K., Seybolt, D., Morrisey-Kane, E., & Davino, K. (2003). What works in prevention: Principles of effective prevention programs. *American Psychologist, 58*, 449–456.

Nelson, G., & Prilleltensky, I. (2010). *Community psychology: In pursuit of liberation and well-being* (2nd ed.). New York: Palgrave.

Nicholas, L., Naidoo, A. V., & Pretorius, T. B. (2006). A historical perspective of career psychology in South Africa. In G. B. Stead & M. B. Watson (Eds.), *Career psychology in the South African context* (2nd ed., pp. 1–10). Pretoria, South Africa: Van Schaik Publishers.

Nussbaum, M. (2006). *Frontiers of justice: disability, nationality, and species membership*. Cambridge, MA: Harvard University Press.

Olfman, S. (Ed.). (2006). *No child left different*. London: Praeger.

Oliver, K. (2004). *The colonization of psychic space: A psychoanalytic social theory of oppression*. Minneapolis, MN: University of Minnesota Press.

Owusu-Bempah, K., & Howitt, D. (2000). *Psychology beyond western perspectives*. Leicester: BPS.

Pancer, M. (1997). Social psychology: The crisis continues. In D. Fox & I. Prilleltensky (Eds.), *Critical psychology: An introduction* (pp. 150–165). London: Sage.

Parker, I. (2007). *Revolution in psychology: Alienation to emancipation*. London: Pluto Press.

Patton, W., & McMahon, M. (Eds.). (1999). *Career development and systems theory: A new relationship*. Pacific Grove, CA: Brooks/Cole.

Payne, C. (2008). *So much reform, so little change: The persistence of failure in urban schools*. Cambridge, MA: Harvard University Press.

Prilleltensky, I. (1994). *The morals and politics of psychology: Psychological discourse and the status quo*. Albany, NY: The State University of New York Press.

Prilleltensky, I. (1997). Values, assumptions, and practices: Assessing the moral implications of psychological discourse and action. *American Psychologist, 52*(5), 517–535.

Prilleltensky, I. (2001). Value-based praxis in community psychology: Moving toward social justice and social action. *American Journal of Community Psychology, 29*, 747–778.

Prilleltensky, I. (2012). Wellness as fairness. *American Journal of Community Psychology, 49, 1–21*.

Prilleltensky, I., & Nelson, G. (2002). *Doing psychology critically: Making a difference in diverse settings*. London: Palgrave.

Prilleltensky, I., Nelson, G., & Peirson, L. (Eds.). (2001). *Promoting family wellness and preventing child maltreatment: Fundamentals for thinking and action*. Toronto: University of Toronto Press.

Prilleltensky, I., & Prilleltensky, O. (2006). *Promoting well-being: Linking personal, organizational, and community change*. Hoboken, NJ: Wiley.

Prilleltensky, I., & Stead, G. B. (2012). Critical psychology and career development: Unpacking the adjust-challenge dilemma. *Journal of Career Development, 39*, 321–340.

Putnam, R. (2000). *Bowling alone: The collapse and revival of American community*. New York: Simon & Schuster.

Putnam, R. (Ed.). (2002). *Democracies in flux: The evolution of social capital in contemporary society*. New York: Oxford University Press.

Quiñones Rosado, R. (2007). *Consciousness in action: Toward an integral psychology of liberation and transformation*. Caguas, Puerto Rico: ilé Publications.

Ralph, D. (1983). *Work and madness*. Montreal: Black Rose.

Rath, T., & Harter, J. (2010). *Well being: The five essential elements*. New York: Gallup Press.

Ravitch, D. (2010). *The death and life of the great American school system*. New York: Basic Books.

Ryan, W. (1971). *Blaming the victim*. New York: Random House.

Sampson, E. (1981). Cognitive psychology as ideology. *American Psychologist, 36*, 730–743.

Santos, E. J. R., & Ferreira, J. A. (1998). Career counseling and vocational psychology in Portugal: A political perspective. *Journal of Vocational Behavior, 52*, 312–322.

Savage, M. (1998). Discipline, surveillance and the "career": Employment on the Great Western Railway 1833–1914. In A. McKinlay & K. Starkey (Eds.), *Foucault, management and organization theory. From panopticon to technologies of self* (pp. 65–92). London: Sage.

Savickas, M. L. (2002). Career construction: A developmental theory of vocational behavior. In D. Brown & Associates (Eds.), *Career choice and development* (4th ed., pp. 149–205). San Francisco, CA: Jossey-Bass.

Schumpeter (2010, July 10). Mens sana in corporation sano. *The Economist*, p. 65.

Seligman, M. (2002). *Authentic happiness*. New York: Free Press.

Shinn, M., & Toohey, S. M. (2003). Community contexts of human welfare. *Annual Review of Psychology, 54*, 427–459.

Sisodia, R., Sheth, J., & Wolfe, D. (2007). *Firms of endearment*. Upper Saddle River, NJ: Wharton School Publishing.

Sloan, T. (1997). *Damaged life: the crisis of the modern psyche*. London: Routledge.

Smith, L. (2010). *Psychology, poverty, and the end of social exclusion*. New York: Teachers College.

Stead, G. B. (2004). Culture and career psychology: A social constructionist perspective. *Journal of Vocational Behavior, 64*, 389–406.

Stead, G. B. (2007). Cultural psychology as a transformative agent for vocational psychology. *International Journal for Educational and Vocational Guidance, 7*, 181–190.

Stead, G. B., & Bakker, T. M. (2010a). Discourse analysis in career counseling and development. *Career Development Quarterly, 59*, 72–86.

Stead, G. B., & Bakker, T. M. (2010b). Self in career theory and counselling: A discourse analysis perspective. *British Journal of Guidance & Counselling, 38*, 45–60.

Stead, G. B., & Perry, J. C. (2012a). Practice trends, social justice and ethics. In M. Watson & M. McMahon (Eds.), *Career development: Global issues and challenges* (pp. 59–71). New York: Nova Science.

Stead, G. B., & Perry, J. C. (2012b). Toward critical psychology perspectives of work-based transitions. *Journal of Career Development, 39*, 315–320.

Stead, G. B., Perry, J. C., Munka, L. M., Bonnett, H. R., Shiban, A. P., & Care, E. (2012). Qualitative research in career development: Content analysis from 1990 to 2009. *International Journal for Educational and Vocational Guidance, 12*, 105–122.

Sullivan, E. V. (1984). *A critical psychology*. New York: Plenum Press.

Super, D. E., Savickas, M. L., & Super, C. M. (1996). The life-span, life-space approach to careers. In D. Brown & L. Brown (Eds.), *Career choice and development* (3rd ed., pp. 121–178). San Francisco, CA: Jossey-Bass.

Taylor, C. (1991). *The malaise of modernity*. Toronto: CBC Publications.

Teo, T. (2005). *The critique of psychology: From Kant to postcolonial theory*. New York: Springer.

Teo, T. (2009). Philosophical concerns in critical psychology. In D. Fox, I. Prilleltensky, & S. Austin (Eds.), *Critical psychology: An introduction* (2nd ed., pp. 36–53). London: Sage.

Tolman, C. W. (1994). *Psychology, society, and subjectivity: An introduction to German Critical Psychology*. London: Routledge.

Turkheimer, E. (1998). Heritability and biological explanation. *Psychological Review, 105*, 782–791.

Ussher, L., & Nicolson, P. (Eds.) (1992). *Gender issues in clinical psychology*. New York: Routledge.

Watkins, M., & Shulman, H. (2008). *Toward psychologies of liberation*. New York: Palgrave.

Watson, M. B., & Stead, G. B. (2002). Career psychology in South Africa: Moral perspectives on present and future directions. *South African Journal of Psychology, 32*, 26–31.

Wells, D. (1987). *Empty promises: Quality of working life programs and the labor movement*. New York: Monthly Review Press.

Wilkinson, R., & Pickett, K. (2009). *The spirit level: Why more equal societies almost always do better*. New York: Penguin.

Wolfram Cox, J., LeTrent-Jones, T. Voronov, M., & Weir, D. (Eds.) (2009). *Critical management studies at work*. Cheltenham, UK: Edward Elgar.

Young, R. A., Valach, L., & Collin, A. (2002). A contextualist explanation of career. In D. Brown & Associates (Ed.), *Career choice and development* (4th ed., pp. 206–252). San Francisco, CA: Jossey-Bass.

Social Constructionist Thought and Working

Graham B. Stead

Abstract

The psychology of working is examined in relation to social constructionism. Social constructionism focuses on discourse, language, relationships, and culture; in this chapter, social constructionism is related to how the psychology of working might be constructed, not discovered or objectively determined, as a means of offering alternative perspectives to vocational psychology. This chapter reflects on social constructionism, its development and applicability to the psychology of working, epistemology, language and discourse, power/knowledge, the relational self, and narrative, and addresses common criticisms of social constructionism. Possible research directions utilizing social constructionism are provided.

Key Words: social constructionism, work, career, discourse, power

The purpose of this chapter is to describe social constructionism and demonstrate its usefulness to the psychology of working (e.g., Blustein, 2006). This chapter is not a comprehensive overview of social constructionism, but reflects my perspective of what may be useful for the psychology of working. It is difficult to provide a concise explanation or definition of social constructionism as there is no one agreed-upon definition or even summary of what social constructionism comprises. It is not a theory or a perspective linked to one author or one definitive book but a collection of approaches that have more or less similar ways of understanding the social sciences. The following major sections are included: what is social constructionism, historical and recent developments, discourse and language, power/knowledge and normalization, relational self, narrative, criticisms of social constructionism, and possible research directions.

What Is Social Constructionism?

To understand social constructionism, it may be helpful to first explain what views many social constructionists subscribe to and those with which they disagree. Cushman (1995) provided eight of what he called "basic propositions" of social constructionism. In these propositions he emphasized that individuals are socially constructed in culture and history. Specifically, people are embedded in a matrix of language, symbols, rituals, moral understandings, power, and privilege. By "construction" is meant how we describe, categorize, or label people. We draw constructions from, for example, psychological, political, legal, economic, and religious discourses. Constructions occur within discourse. According to Foucault (1972), discourses are not merely words that designate objects, but are "practices that systematically form the objects of which they speak" (p. 49). In this sense, discourse refers to institutionalized ways of communicating in which objects are ordered in a way that makes sense to its practitioners. So the discourses of the psychology of working are different in some ways from the discourses on working found in, for example, organizational psychology, economics, or politics.

Discourses employ their own terminologies and ways of construction, based on whose interests they serve. These discourses are also based on regimes of truth and are useful in that they result in actions on people. Once people are described or labeled, various things may happen to them. Take race, ethnicity, and culture, for example. These terms are constructions, as there is no agreed-upon way to allocate all people to these groups and there is no clear explanation as to how these groups differ from each other (Stead, 2004). However, they are very real in discourses and actions are taken toward people based on these constructions in work environments.

Burr (2003) believed that the following are commonly held beliefs of social constructionists: (a) there is a critical perspective toward taken-for-granted, "obvious," or "innocent" knowledge, (b) our understanding of the world is historically and culturally informed (i.e., knowledge is local and temporal, and universal knowledge claims are suspect), (c) knowledge is created and sustained by social relationships, and (d) knowledge and action are intertwined (i.e., words *do* things). Lock and Strong (2010) listed five general tenets of social constructionism: (a) meaning and understanding are central to human activities, (b) meaning and understanding start with social interaction, (c) ways of meaning-making are embedded in culture, time, and space, and vary in different contexts, (d) people do not possess predefined characteristics or traits, and therefore there is a skeptical view of essentialism (i.e., that individuals have a core nature that can be discovered; Burr, 2003), and (e) a critical perspective.

Gubrium and Holstein (2008) pointed out that social constructionism is not synonymous with qualitative research, phenomenology, grounded theory, ethnomethodology, or constructivism, although there is some overlap with each of these domains. Social constructionism is sometimes assumed to be either a subset of constructivism or a synonym for constructivism, and both assumptions are problematic. While there are similarities between these two approaches, such as their mutual interest in human relationships, as is the case with social constructivism, social constructionists eschew the belief in inner mental processes that continues to be part of constructivism (Sparkes & Smith, 2008). The term "constructionism" is sometimes used in vocational psychology to bridge these positions, but once discourse of the inner mind is present, "social constructivism" may be the underpinning approach. Young and Collin (2004) clarified the similarities and differences between social constructionism and social constructivism in the vocational psychology literature. An understanding of social constructionism's development and current usages may provide a better understanding of what this approach means.

Historical and Recent Developments

To understand social constructionism it will be helpful to briefly trace some of its historical developments. (These developments are provided more comprehensively in Lock and Strong, 2010.) One of the earliest perspectives allied to social constructionism is that of Niccolò Machiavelli (1469–1527), an Italian best known for his 1513 political treatise *The Prince*. He wrote about how rulers might maintain their political power through strategizing and wielding power. He did not view rulers as possessing power, but focused on how they used power in relationships. This was and still is very different to commonsense notions of power, which is assumed to be a possession or trait of some people (Clegg, 1989). The notion of power as situated in networks of relationships, rather than within people, is prominent in the work of Foucault (1980). Another Italian, Giambattista Vico (1668–1774), criticized rationalistic Cartesian perspectives. He questioned knowledge as being timeless and also believed that those who construct things understand what they have constructed in ways that those who did not create them cannot. Vico entertained the notion of phenomena being constructed, which predated an important perspective of social constructionism.

The Age of Enlightenment, also known as the Age of Reason, flowered in the 18th century as a reaction to power invested in royalty and the wealthy and was a critical evaluation of traditional beliefs. The importance of freedom, democracy, rational thinking, reason, science, and individuality was extolled. In this era, empiricism became highly valued, as found in much of vocational psychology today, but the Romantics and Postmodernists later questioned its knowledge claims. The Romantic era of the 19th century was a reaction to the focus on rational thought and emphasized feelings, emotions, and the unconscious, as evinced in psychodynamic approaches and humanism (Gergen, 1991). Empirical observations and measurement were not considered the only ways of understanding, and metaphysical perspectives were valued. Romantic expressions, such as self-fulfilment, self-actualization, and the unconscious, continue to be found in vocational research and counseling.

Reaction to Positivism

Much of the theory and literature of vocational psychology is driven by positivism. One may also safely assume that social constructionism has developed many of its viewpoints as a reaction to positivism and empirical methods. Logical positivism can be traced to the works of Francis Bacon (1561–1626), who problematized Aristotle's deductivism (i.e., theories are first developed and thereafter facts are gathered to fit these theories) and stated that theories should be empirically derived from observable phenomena. Positivism, which is closely linked to Enlightenment thought, became established by the "Vienna Circle" in the 1920s, which comprised academics such as Rudolf Carnap, Otto Neurath, and Hans Hahn, among others. This group rejected metaphysical thought as being meaningful and stated that scientific knowledge is best obtained through rational thought, empirical observation, and experience. They emphasized the importance of objectivity and the value-free nature of scientific inquiry (Mouton, 1993).

The tenets of positivism have been challenged in the physical sciences (e.g., Feyerabend, 2010; Kuhn, 1962) and the social sciences (e.g., Danziger, 1990; Teo, 2005). Both Kuhn and Feyerabend pursued the notion that there is no singular paradigm or method in scientific discourse and argued that science is not entirely bound to logical empiricism and rational inquiry. "We find, then, that there is not a single rule, however plausible, and however firmly grounded in epistemology, that is not violated at some time or other ... [and that this is] both reasonable and *absolutely necessary* for the growth of knowledge" (Feyerabend, 2010, p. 7). While social constructionists believe that positivism is given an inordinate amount of attention in the vocational psychology literature (see Stead et al., 2012) and are mystified by some of its standpoints, most social constructionists do *not* advocate the demise of positivism and quantitative methods. They believe that there should be an ongoing dialogue between different approaches (see Burr, 2003; Gergen, 2009b; Holstein & Gubrium, 2008). To call for the demise of a research tradition would be to advance foundationalism, in which one believes in the secure and definitive position of one's approach and therefore considers other approaches as fundamentally wrong (Gergen, 2001).

Wittgenstein and Derrida

Wittgenstein (1953), a British philosopher, was influential in social constructionism in that he believed that meanings reside in various discourses and contexts and therefore are not definitive and universal. He did not view language as representing reality, but as reality construction in human interaction. Derrida (1976), a French philosopher, argued that the meaning of a sign (e.g., a word) is never fixed but alters depending on the discourse employed and the context. Nothing is fully present in a word, as it is dependent on the meanings of other words *ad infinitum.* Therefore, definitions of terms such as "psychology of working" and "social justice" are dependent on the meanings of each word in that definition, and these meanings are dependent on other meanings, and so on indefinitely. As language is unstable and never fixed, a definable core self (e.g., finding your true self) must therefore be a myth, as people are described through language. One may argue that definitions employed in the psychology of working or vocational psychology are useful within their respective discourses, or their regimes of truth, but they are never unalterable and always open to revisions and various interpretations.

Foucault

The works of Foucault (1972, 1977, 1980) are often allied to social constructionism, owing to Foucault's emphasis on knowledge creation through social discourses in cultural contexts, rather than through internal cognitions (Burr, 2003). Foucault also emphasized how power is ubiquitous in social interactions, rather than internal to a person, and that power and knowledge are two sides of the same coin. He saw knowledge as constructed through power, and thus "regimes of truth" (such as the received perspectives of vocational psychology and the psychology of working) are created rather than being objective and universal truths.

Recent Developments

Social constructionism garnered much attention with Berger and Luckmann's (1966) book *The Social Construction of Reality: A Treatise in the Sociology of Knowledge.* Berger and Luckman were sociologists, but their work spread to psychology and related fields. The focus was on how language and social interaction are employed in knowledge construction. More recently, Russian authors such as Mikhail Bakhtin and Lev Vygotsky have contributed to social constructionism. Vygotsky and Luria (1993) believed that it was through relationships with others that higher mental functioning emerged and that cultural tools are essential to constructing psychological processes. A particularly influential social constructionist in psychology is Kenneth Gergen, whose article "The social constructionist movement in modern psychology" (Gergen, 1985) was seminal in directing psychologists to an alternative approach. He continues to be prolific in the field (e.g., Gergen, 2009a, 2009b).

The vocational psychology literature includes many discussions based on social constructionist thought, such as Blustein, Schultheiss, and Flum (2004), Cohen, Duberley, and Mallon (2004), Coupland (2004), McIlveen and Patton (2006), McIlveen & Schultheiss (2012), Richardson (2004, 2012), Stead (2004, 2007), Stead and Bakker (2010a, 2010b, 2012), and Young and Collin (2004). There have been various foci, such as relational perspectives, culture, assessment, self, and meanings of work. Richardson (1993) provided a relatively early perspective on work in people's lives and argued that diverse methodologies for a multiplicity of work locations should be entertained. She believed that social constructionism is well positioned to research power, race, class, and gender, developmentally and in work contexts. Recently, Richardson (2012) emphasized the role of discourse and language in knowledge creation in work environments.

Social Constructionism and Epistemology

Epistemology is that branch of philosophy that examines the basis and nature of knowledge and how we know what we purport to know. There are many ways to know the psychology of working, such as empirical perspectives (i.e., what we experience with our senses is what we know, and so the mind acts as a mirror to the world), rationalist perspectives (i.e., the experience of the world comes from within a person, who also has innate thoughts to begin with), and poststructuralist perspectives (i.e., what we know is constructed through language and discourse). Social constructionists fall into the latter group as they believe that only through agreement and negotiation can we describe anything. Knowledge is viewed as being in a state of flux and is based on discourses to describe people and things, rather than knowledge being determined objectively. Social constructionism has the capabilities to liberate research from relatively fixed and predetermined ways of knowing and allows dominant discourses to be challenged and alternative discourses to be explored. Thus, a critical reading of taken-for-granted discourses is encouraged and provides a useful means to further explore the psychology of working.

Language and Discourse

Language and discourse are sometimes used synonymously, but they differ. Language may be viewed as the structure, connectedness, and meaningfulness of one's statements. Following Foucault (1972), discourses are systems of rules, practices, and beliefs that determine how people and objects are constructed, defined, and explained. Our perspectives of work, poverty, and oppression depend on the languages and discourses employed, and these may include, for example, positivist, constructivist, and social constructionist languages and discourses. Social constructionists believe that one's language and discourses encourage one to view the world in various ways and emphasize that how we construct the world is closely related to history and culture. Whether work is viewed as paid and unpaid or is anything that requires unwilling or willing effort, or is synonymous with career and job, depends on social interaction and negotiation—that is, how we view work becomes intimately connected to the discourse(s) we employ. In place of an objective, value-neutral study of work, there are negotiated discourses, which are sometimes referred to as the politics of representation, and therein is power in discourse. Power is not only repressive but is also productive; it seduces one by the knowledge it provides. Through the politics of representation, certain perspectives and terminologies are favored and others marginalized or ignored. In this way, discourse produces knowledge (Foucault, 1980). The roles played by discourse and language will be described in relation to meanings of work and metaphors.

Meanings of Work

According to the *Shorter Oxford English Dictionary* (Trumble & Stevenson, 2002), work is anything that is done, as in a deed, an action, or a proceeding. This is a rather broad definition and has resulted in not only differing meanings as to what constitutes work for purposes of research, but also different terms for specificity, such as vocation, career, occupation, and job. Such terms and meanings are negotiated. I am unsure how the terms "vocation," "career," and "work" precisely differ from each other or whether "vocational psychology" is much different from "career psychology," although in my experience editors and reviewers prefer one to use one of these terms consistently or, when using both terms, to provide a definition of what these terms mean. It seems to me that these terms mean whatever a given author wishes them to mean. Researchers allocate their own meanings to the terms as they see fit within the theoretical approaches, cultures, and contexts they are writing. The dominant meanings of these terms proceed from discourses of power and acceptance by others. The subjectivity of such terminology is revealed when the meanings of these terms differ and change.

The fact that this book is not about the psychology of careers or occupations but of the psychology of *working* is testimony to how language and negotiation dictate what we view and how we view it. By using the term "working," this book is more receptive to discussing, for example, work as paid and unpaid, oppression and discrimination in work, unemployment, and the working lives of those from lower socioeconomic environments. It is likely less interested in focusing only on hierarchical career development, commonly known as the "career ladder," and the work trajectories of the wealthy and upper middle class. This does not mean that by referring to the psychology of working and not to career or occupation, one is providing a more accurate or objective account of work, but rather a perspective that may be contextual, useful, and sensitive toward social justice concerns. The psychology of working, as I understand it, is particularly concerned with injustice in relation to work and the well-being of people within work in its broadest meaning. The world does not come with a guidebook on how to interpret it. That is left to us to fashion, and as we cannot transcend the world and view it objectively or in its totality, we are left to our perspectives, which are intimately linked to discourse, history, and culture. Ultimately, I am left with interpreting the psychology of working as you are, and while there are probably many similarities in our interpretations, there are some or perhaps many differences.

Metaphors

The term "work" is often used in relation to *metaphors*, which are not only expressive but commonly used in most discourses. What is interesting about metaphors is that they are hardly pointers to a so-called "objective reality," in that they refer to one thing but ask you to think of something different (Sarup, 1993). They allude to something and are commonly used in research articles on work. For example, we may be asked to examine the *world of work* through a cultural *lens* and use the *building*

blocks of knowledge to create the *scaffolding* for a better understanding of the *glass-ceiling effect* and the *inner* processes of individuals. A common metaphor in psychology and vocational psychology is *discovery*, such as a "discovery-oriented approach." To discover something is to find a foundational truth or something "objective," rather than what is more likely occurring in vocational psychology, namely a construction. Metaphors and other figures of speech cannot be avoided as they are too embedded in everyday language and discourse. Some of the metaphors used in the psychology of working tend to dichotomize (e.g., full-time work/leisure time), or seek to indefinitely build on knowledge for a universal psychology, or focus on inner mental states and the external environment (also a dichotomy) to provide insight into the meanings of work. Social constructionists prefer metaphors in keeping with relationships and connection, or what Bird (2000) refers to as the language for the in-between—a language of movement and activity in contexts. It is a language of not clearly separating terms such as self, family, and work, as if they were isolated entities. It is the language of studying work as activities throughout one's daily life, and not affecting or being affected by discrete domains.

The use of fresh metaphors in understanding work will broaden and enrich our perspectives, rather than us relying on the commonly used metaphors in vocational psychology. This is evinced when reviewers of journal articles require a predetermined scientific language to be employed. Having submitted social constructionist and discourse analysis manuscripts to psychology journals, I am frequently asked to use the language and metaphors of traditional psychology or positivism to describe these perspectives and to employ reductionistic definitions of the many seemingly different terms that I use. How is one to define social constructionism or the self in a sentence or two? This does not permit alternative perspectives to flourish, but limits the proliferation of knowledge and maintains power within the mainstream regime of truth and knowledge.

Power/Knowledge and Normalization

Foucault (1980) provided a perspective of how power and knowledge interact in social relationships. He saw power and knowledge as two sides of the same coin and referred to power/knowledge. Foucault's thesis was that people's characteristics are constructed and subjected to discourse within culture and time. Through their *subjectification* (i.e., the subjective allocation of descriptors to individuals), people become *objects* of knowledge that are described, statistically catalogued, and studied. Foucault (1972, p. 17) famously stated, "Do not ask who I am and do not ask me to remain the same: leave it to our bureaucrats and our police to see that our papers are in order. At least spare us their morality when we write." Perhaps this is a thought that may well be applicable to psychologists' diagnostic dispositions. Considering people as objects of knowledge is vastly different from pre-Enlightenment eras, when ordinary people were below the surveillance radar and were barely described, with only the nobility and wealthy being allocated such privileges. Foucault (1980) acknowledged the realities of hierarchical power but did not view power as situated inside a person. He saw power as manifested through discourses in relationships with others and power becoming visible through resistance. If there is no resistance, it is probably domination but not power, according to Foucault (1980). He did not view power as only negative, as power also produces knowledge. Power produces mainstream perspectives and marginalizes other perspectives in vocational psychology.

Foucault outlined how power can transpire in working environments. In *Discipline and Punish,* Foucault (1972) referred to Bentham's panopticon, a hypothetical tower in which guards could observe prisoners at all times but not vice versa. The guards' continual surveillance results in the self-gaze of each prisoner, thus leading to self-regulation and responsibility. For Foucault, this is how power transpires in society, in schools, prisons, hospitals, workplaces, and so on, namely via institutional surveillance leading to self-surveillance. There have been some management studies reporting on surveillance. Savage (1998) researched management and employee relationships in the Great Western Railway in Britain from 1833 to 1914. He reported that while workers were previously punished and fined, this changed in that the workers in the latter half of the 19th century were motivated and disciplined to work their way up the career ladder through self-monitoring and self-regulation. This proved to be a more "effective" way to improve employee productivity and to develop a modern work culture. Grey (1994) employed case studies of young trainees in an accounting firm. He reported that trainees who conceptualized their selves in terms of their work viewed disciplinary techniques as assisting their progress in the workplace. Job appraisals were viewed as a benevolent way of furthering their career aspirations. Instead of workers viewing employee ratings as intrusive and annoying, they were perceived as an acceptable technique to assist workers to realize their "true potentials." In an analysis of Scottish banking 20 years prior to 1914, McKinlay (2002) found that employee conformity through self-regulation to the banks' cultural expectations facilitated promotion but resulted in what he referred to as the banker's "dead selves." McKinlay viewed this as the enmeshment of bureaucratic and self-regulation to produce a highly controlled working environment.

Through power, knowledge about people and things is created, such as theories about work, categories (e.g., diagnoses), and assessments. Through powerful discourses, certain knowledges become marginalized and other knowledges elevated. This is particularly noticeable in the vocational psychology literature, where Stead et al. (2012) reported that among 11 journals that published 3,279 career- and work-related articles between 1990 and 2009, 55.9% of the articles reflected quantitative research methods and 6.3% qualitative research methods. The remaining articles were conceptual/theoretical.

The role of power/knowledge is underscored when vocational psychologists focus on the individual. It is the individual who is encouraged to adapt, adjust, and find solutions to the presenting problem, be it unemployment, work dissatisfaction, or poverty. For Foucault (1977), counseling can become a normalizing judgment, in which the individual is required to self-regulate in keeping with social norms. This is also noticeable in the assessment process, where test manuals include average scores and norm tables, so that the counselor and client can judge the extent to which the client deviates from the norm. Vocational psychology traditionally focuses on the individual using an array of terminology, discourse, assessments, diagnostics, interventions, psychological associations, regulatory bodies such as ethics committees, and so on, in what Rose (1985) referred to as the "psychological complex." The ultimate effect of disciplinary power is self-regulation, in which people become what Foucault calls "docile bodies." That some people are unemployed or poor is the result of a larger system of societal discourse and culture and not merely reflective of so-called individual weaknesses or shortcomings. To focus solely on the individual and his or her deficits is to uphold the status quo, which runs counter to the psychology of working perspectives.

Relational Self

Theories of vocational psychology have traditionally viewed career decision making as best occurring when there is a suitable fit between one's self and the requirements of a job (e.g., Dawis & Lofquist, 1984; Holland, 1997). It is said that once you understand who you are in terms of various characteristics, such as abilities, interests, self, and personality traits, then you would be best suited to jobs that match these traits. This has its origins in the work of Frank Parsons (1909) and is rooted in trait-factor and person-environment fit theories, including those of Holland and Super (see Brown & Associates, 2002). Social constructionists question essentialism, which emphasizes a unique inner self. This means that they do not view an individual as having an internal, core nature that is waiting to be discovered (Burr, 2003). Essentialism is closely linked to humanism and much of current psychological thought. In contrast, social constructionists view selves as continually being created in and varying between relationships with others over time (e.g., Burkitt, 2008; Gergen, 1991; Stead & Bakker, 2010b). Therefore, the self is not seen as a fixed and stable entity, but as flexible, fragmented, and changing depending on the situation. From a social constructionist perspective, a "fragmented self" does not refer to a psychological disorder but to a self continuously in the process of becoming.

While we cannot literally see a person's self, it is widely assumed that we can infer an inner self from a person's actions. This is a product of Enlightenment thinking and the Protestant work ethic. As Gergen asks (2009b), how do we know that actions do in fact reflect an inner mind or self? It is arguable that commentaries on the "nature" of an inner self are only interpretations. Social constructionists believe that the self is constructed in relationships through discourse. Our thoughts, feelings, and beliefs emanate from language, and discourse in relationships. According to Bauman (2002), the inner thoughts that people are thought to have are no more than recitals of public rhetoric, the discourses commonly found in one's culture(s). When we theorize and think about work, we are inextricably entwined in the discourses on work that we choose to employ, discourses that are culturally and historically bound. Terms like "self-determination" and "agency," as reflecting an inner self that drives the individual to do things, thus become problematic. It may be more appropriate to refer to a person's "selves," as they vary in time and context. A person does not behave in the same way in all situations but in relationships in different contexts.

While social constructionists have long emphasized the relational aspects of the self, vocational psychologists have been promoting relational research as a way to overcome decontextualized research in vocational psychology. Relational research also emphasizes the importance of relationships in developing career awareness, searching for work, functioning productively in the work environment, and managing work-based crises, such as unemployment. The perception of a self-sufficient, self-driven worker whose working life is based on rugged individualism is viewed as outdated, decontextualized, and reductionistic by social constructionists in vocational psychology. Rather, a relational perspective of people co-constructing their work lives with others is underscored. Relational support and networks are important for general psychological health and in work environments with stress and anxiety. Moving the locus of self as inner to a relational domain also relieves the individual of solely taking responsibility for work-related issues or being focused on self-regulation. Such a perspective also situates the psychology of working in relationships in contexts and communities (Blustein, 2006). Richardson (1993) proposed a new discourse for people constructing their lives in market work, personal relationships, and personal care work. She argued for a narrative approach in research and counseling to enable people to co-construct and examine alternative meanings in their lives. In so doing, the landscape for studying work is broadened to include care work and also those with few or no work-related choices (Blustein, 2011).

The Other

One way social constructionists view the construction of meaning is through "the other." While it is useful to explain what someone or something is, we are also aware of what it is not. This is also what Sampson (1993b) refers to as the "absent standard" or the "serviceable other." The "other" is constructed to be serviceable to the dominant group and, according to Sampson, is represented only through the dominant group's discourse. For example, females are often defined through the discourses of males. The poor are frequently defined and described through the discourses of the middle class and the wealthy. Through difference, meaning is constructed and meanings are created within discursive frameworks (Hall, 1997/2001; Sampson, 1993a, Sampson, 1993b). Difference is largely created through the power of certain discourses, in that categories are developed to enhance the one domain at the expense of the other. Few of these categories are "real"; rather, they are constructed to suit a group of people. Such categories commonly found in the psychology of working literature are gender, socioeconomic status, race, ethnic group, work/leisure, and an array of DSM disorders. Selves are also constructed with the other in mind, and the serviceable other serves to sustain a self and give it meaning. Selves are built on their relationships to other selves (Sampson, 1993a), and so hard-working, male, upwardly mobile, financially independent, and confident selves have their contrasts, such as the unemployed, the poor, and those with low confidence, to sustain them and give them meaning. The dominant conception of self becomes constructed through discourses defining the selves of others. A consideration of the construction of the other has implications for unfair and oppressive practices in working environments, in that these constructions often need to be challenged with a relational way of understanding work replacing them. Through relationships, narratives are constructed, as discussed below.

Narrative

Social constructionists generally are deeply suspicious of *meta-narratives*, a term Lyotard (1984) popularized to indicate the search for a universal theory, namely narratives that encompass all narratives by reconfiguring them in one universal language or mode of understanding. Marxism is one example of a meta- or grand narrative. Science in the form of positivism is generally suspicious of local narratives as being too subjective but, as Lyotard points out, science is dependent on the narrative as a starting point to explain its theories and principles. Social constructionists are especially interested in local narratives, the narratives of ordinary people to explain their lives, and in this way the marginalized or "the other" may not be erased through an overriding dominant narrative.

Social constructionism does not endorse a specific counseling therapy or research method. However, it does question therapies linked to the medical model, those that focus on cause and effect, and therapies that emphasize interiority (i.e., one's problems residing inside the mind). This would include psychoanalysis and cognitive therapies, among others. Social constructionists question the taken-for-granted and wonder how else it could be (Gergen, 2009a), and so alternative but rigorous perspectives are sought. Traditional constructions of therapy and research need not necessarily be that

way, and social constructionists wonder how else we might view the client's or research participant's concerns. Narratives can structure seemingly disparate occurrences, simplify events and provide meaning, and legitimize certain narratives and marginalize others (Preuss & Dawson, 2009). In narrative therapy and research, one generally encourages the participant to provide a narrative of the problem or issue at hand. The participant provides a plot; this could, for example, be his or her struggle to find employment or difficulties relating to others in the workplace. As narratives are based on memories, they can be selective, and no narrative is an absolute truth. Therefore, counselors and researchers explore with a client or research participant other ways of constructing the story by examining, for example, "missing links," contradictions, or dichotomies to determine the discourse being used. While interviews are clearly an important part of work narratives, other means of data collection can include archival sources, e-mails, photographs, film, and music.

Narrative approaches are accepting of social constructionist perspectives and social constructionism's emphasis on meaning making, not through truth or an absolute reality but through language and discourse. It is believed that through language and discourses, we constitute and describe our worlds. How we view theories, the literature, research methods, or clients' reflections is conducted through stories. Examples of narrative constructivism in the career literature include Bujold (2004), Guichard and Lenz (2005), and McIlveen and Patton (2007).

It is important to note that narrative constructivism overlaps considerably with narrative constructionism (e.g., see Strong & Paré, 2004; White & Epston, 1990) in its interest in the narrative and social interaction, but there is an important difference between the two. Narrative constructionism avoids references to inner processes or personal scripts while focusing on the narrative through social interaction (Sparkes & Smith, 2008). It eschews narratives as reflecting the deep recesses of one's inner self but examines the relational, sociocultural interactions that make up narratives. Instead of placing the narrative within the individual, it is situated in relationships with others (i.e., co-construction), and so agency, emotions, and memories are performed as social interactions, as performances, and as narratives (Sparkes & Smith, 2008). An example of the narrative in vocational counseling is Campbell and Ungar (2004), and there is also an interesting study on workaholism by Boje and Tyler (2009). There are many references where one may employ narrative constructionism in therapy (e.g., White & Epston, 1990) and in research (e.g., Clandinin, 2007; Riessman, 2008). For example, in a therapeutic context, White and Epston emphasized challenging the client's dominant problem narrative, externalizing this narrative, and separating it from the client to enable an alternative story of the client's problem. This is based on the assumption that a client's problem is never reduced to one narrative of the problem (i.e., the dominant narrative). Regarding research, Riessman offered a variety of analytic methods to interpret texts that can be, for example, pictorial, cinematic, and written. The analytic methods she proposed are thematic analysis, structural analysis, dialogic/performance analysis, and visual analysis.

Criticisms of Social Constructionism

Various misunderstandings and criticisms of social constructionism appear regularly in academic literature, such as the meaning of reality, relativism, moral relativism, and agency, and these are addressed below.

Reality

Critics often state that social constructionists deny that there is a reality out there and that they believe that we cannot be sure that events even happened. This is a misguided criticism. Gergen (2009a) pointed out that to consider reality being "out there" is already based on preconceived notions of an inner and outer world. Indeed, poverty, pollution, unemployment, and death are very real. Once we begin to discuss what these terms mean to us, we provide discourses based on our views, and the terms above do not reside in only one perspective or discourse. To say that there is only one way to view whatever issue you may think about is to close curiosity and dialogue. Using unemployment as an example, who counts as unemployed is a contested point, and what unemployment means and how it should be studied and limited is varied and situated in many discourses such as economics, law, politics, sociology, religion, and psychology. That a person does not have paid work is obvious, but how we define and situate the unemployed in discourses is another matter.

Relativism

Perhaps the most common criticism is the belief that social constructionists view everything as relative and that all ideas are of equal worth. Rather, social constructionists view all ideas as situated in discourses, which in turn are situated in culture, time, and space. There are thus no foundational or fundamental truths on which to compare perspectives. As we cannot transcend this world or offer an objective opinion on it, we remain unable to speak definitively on it. However, within certain discourses in which realities are created, such as the language of statistics, moral discourses, or the language of the psychology of working and vocational psychology, there can be truths, and therein one can perhaps compare and evaluate various perspectives. However, where there are differing paradigms within a subject area, it may be difficult to make comparisons, as would be the case between person-environment fit approaches and social constructionism. But such perspectives are always compared to a criterion that has no absolute foundation, only a regime of truth within a discourse. What is of interest to social constructionists is how powerful discourses contribute to the status or marginalization of perspectives in vocational psychology and how such discourses are acted upon. (See Agger, 2007, for an informative and entertaining discussion on relativism.)

Moral Relativism

Social constructionists are often criticized for being morally relativist. Critics complain that social constructionists do not take moral stands to destroy oppression, eradicate unfair labor practices, eliminate poverty, and fight for the values decent societies should adhere to. This is as if hitting something will destroy it once and for all. As Gergen (2009b) points out, the production of good can create the very conditions for evil, and vice versa. This view has been present in Eastern philosophies for millennia. The short answer to the complex question of moral relativism is that social constructionists encourage dominant views to be vigorously challenged and questioned. Religious, political, and social values, of which there are many, are all important in challenging the status quo and that which compromises people's well-being. Social constructionists are certainly not indifferent to these voices. Social constructionists may individually argue for one perspective, but they will avoid stating the moral superiority of their values. Critics of the "moral shallowness of constructionism are seldom interested in establishing just any value commitment…but typically demand commitment to their particular values" (Gergen, 2009a, p. 169). According to Gergen, social constructionists would prefer to be involved in a mutual exploration of the issues at hand in which dialogue rather than distance is desired. There are many competing voices arguing for ways to solve societal ills, such as unemployment, labor and employment practices, management and worker disagreements, strikes at work, poverty, and so on. To do nothing about these issues is problematic, but to use social constructionism to defend the superiority of one view and the concomitant solutions to the problem is to misunderstand social constructionism. Gergen states that he knows of no one who claims that all moralities are equal. He argues for moral pluralism, rather than moral relativism, in which a preferred morality might be sought but alternative traditions are not eliminated. For example, topics concerning social justice and the psychology of working are of interest to social constructionists. There is thus an acceptance of diverse views and responsible relational dialogue, both characteristic of the psychology of working.

Agency

Another prevalent criticism of social constructionism concerns agency. Agency is found in most career theories and is generally viewed as an internal state. It is believed that people make their own decisions in relation to work, but we are seldom informed about how people use available discourses in making decisions. The notion of agency is grounded in the individualism of the Enlightenment and in Western cultures. We find it in statements such as, "Which occupation do you *intend* to pursue?" From an essentialist perspective, our intentions are internal and we make our own decisions. From a social constructionist perspective, our intentions are about identifying a performance (Gergen, 2009b). Choosing an occupation is a well-known performance. Performances come from a rich and available cultural catalogue of discourses. By seemingly deciding for ourselves to follow a certain occupation or intending to make a work-related decision, we are selecting among a variety of available performances rather than delving into our minds for answers. There are multiple rationales for making decisions, and we draw from these available options. Our intentions are not conceived in our minds but in available discourses. In this way the agency/determinism debate is relinquished with a focus on action and relationships, a focus on culturally available performances. Thus, an emphasis on the interiority of the individual is replaced by a focus on discourses and relationships when utilizing social constructionism in the psychology of working

Possible Research Directions

There are many possibilities for conducting research from a social constructionist perspective,

and a few possibilities are presented. Research could analyze different discourses present in the psychology of working, such as work discourses by academic school of thought, culture, gender, social class, family members, and for what purposes and who benefits from them. Such discourses may be verbal, textual, or image-based. The context in which these discourses occur and the effects of these discourses (i.e., what discourses do) would be important considerations. Social constructionist researchers would be aware that whatever data are obtained, they do not represent the interviewee's individual thoughts; rather, the data are co-constructed by the interviewer and interviewee and situated within the larger societal and cultural discourse arena. An analysis of why certain vocational psychology discourses are accepted and others marginalized would also be informative. In a similar vein, one may examine how power and resistance operate in the discourses of work.

There has been recent research on immigration and work (e.g., Flum & Cinamon, 2011), which lends itself to social constructionist research. The relational aspects of immigration and the social and contextual barriers of this work transition could be studied. For example, how do family and work relationships interact initially and over time, and how is relational support at work enacted?

While discourses and relationships are important areas for social constructionists, documents, pictures, videos, and buildings are also researchable. For example, Durrheim and Dixon (2001) examined racism as spatiotemporal interactions over four historical periods. Possible studies could include the employment of space for interactions in work settings, such as schools, office areas, hospitals, and universities. How we construct others is arguably related to how we construct buildings and spaces, and also with whom and how we interact with others in these places.

Research into unemployment has not been well represented in the vocational psychology literature. A possible line of inquiry could be how discourses on unemployment serve to support the notion that low levels of unemployment are acceptable or even desirable. Another line of research could be how management discourses may preclude unemployed people from being hired.

Conclusion

Social constructionism emphasizes discourse and language and how these function in relationships with others to produce knowledge. Its focus is on connection, interaction, and dialogue. It is interested in the narratives of people in context rather than providing grand narratives in a search for universals. In so doing, it is well positioned to provide useful knowledge to understand marginalized people and communities, such as the poor, the oppressed, the discriminated against, and those whose lifestyles are not indicative of the norm. It is an approach that challenges one to think differently and to imagine situations as they may become. Its perspective is very different from what one encounters in traditional vocational psychology, but its views are liberating and may offer new ways to conceptualize the psychology of working.

References

Agger, B. (2007). Does postmodernism make you mad? Or, did you flunk statistics? In W. Outhwaite & S. P. Turner (Eds.), *The Sage handbook of social science methodology* (pp. 443–460). Los Angeles, CA: Sage.

Bauman, Z. (2002). Identity: Then, now, what for? In M. Kempny & A. Jawlowska (Eds.), *Identity in transformation. Postmodernity, postcommunism, and globalization* (pp. 19–32). Westport, CT: Praeger.

Berger, P. L., & Luckmann, T. (1966). *The social construction of reality: A treatise in the sociology of knowledge*. New York: Doubleday.

Bird, J. (2000). *The heart's narrative: Therapy and navigating life's contradictions*. Auckland, New Zealand: Edge Press.

Blustein, D. L. (2006). *The psychology of working*. Mahwah, NJ: Lawrence Erlbaum.

Blustein, D. L. (2011). Vocational psychology at the fork in the road: Staying the course or taking the road less traveled. *Journal of Career Assessment, 19,* 316–322.

Blustein, D. L., Schultheiss, D. E. P., & Flum, H. (2004). Toward a relational perspective of the psychology of careers and working: A social constructionist analysis. *Journal of Vocational Behavior, 64,* 423–440.

Boje, D., & Tyler, J. A., (2009). Story and narrative noticing: Workaholism autoethnographies. *Journal of Business Ethics, 84,* 173–194.

Brown, D., & Associates. (2002). *Career choice and development* (4th ed.). San Francisco, CA: Jossey-Bass.

Bujold, C. (2004). Constructing career through narrative. *Journal of Vocational Behavior, 64,* 470–484.

Burkitt, I. (2008). *Social selves. Theories of self and society* (2nd ed.). Los Angeles, CA: Sage.

Burr, V. (2003). *Social constructionism*. London, England: Routledge.

Campbell, C., & Ungar, M. (2004). Constructing a life that works: Part 1, Blending postmodern family therapy and career counseling. *Career Development Quarterly, 53,* 16–27.

Clandinin, D. J. (Ed., 2007). *Handbook of narrative inquiry*. Thousand Oaks, CA: Sage.

Clegg, S. R. (1989). *Frameworks of power*. London: Sage.

Cohen, L., Duberley, J., & Mallon, M. (2004). Social constructionism in the study of career: Accessing the parts that other approaches cannot reach. *Journal of Vocational Behavior, 64,* 407–422.

Coupland, C. (2004). Career definition and denial: A discourse analysis of graduate trainees' accounts of career. *Journal of Vocational Behavior, 64,* 515–532.

Cushman, P. (1995). *Constructing the self, constructing America. A cultural history of psychotherapy*. Reading, MA: Da Capo Press.

Danziger, K. (1990). *Constructing the subject. Historical origins of psychological research*. Cambridge, UK: Cambridge University Press.

Dawis, R.V., & Lofquist, L. H. (1984). *A psychological theory of work adjustment*. Minneapolis: University of Minnesota Press.

Derrida, J. (1976). *Of grammatology*. Baltimore, MD: Johns Hopkins University Press.

Durrheim, K., & Dixon, J. (2001). The role of place and metaphor in racial exclusion: South Africa's beaches as sites of shifting racialization. *Ethnic and Racial Studies, 24,* 433–450.

Feyerabend, P. (1975/2010). *Against method* (4th ed.). London: Verso.

Flum, H., & Cinamon, R. G. (2011). Immigration and the interplay among citizenship, identity and career: The case of Ethiopian immigration to Israel. *Journal of Vocational Behavior, 78,* 372–380.

Foucault, M. (1972). *The archaeology of knowledge*. London: Tavistock.

Foucault, M. (1977). *Discipline and punish: The birth of the prison*. New York: Pantheon.

Foucault, M. (1980). *Power/knowledge. Selected interviews and other writings, 1972–1977*. New York: Pantheon Books.

Gergen, K. J. (1985). The social constructionist movement in modern psychology. *American Psychology, 40,* 266–275.

Gergen, K. J. (1991). *The saturated self. Dilemmas of identity in contemporary life*. New York: Basic Books.

Gergen, K. J. (2001). Psychological science in a postmodern context. *American Psychologist, 56,* 803–813.

Gergen, K. J. (2009a). *An invitation to social construction* (2nd ed.). Los Angeles, CA: Sage.

Gergen, K. J. (2009b). *Relational being. Beyond self and community*. New York: Oxford University Press.

Grey, C. (1994). Career as a project of the self and labour process discipline. *Sociology, 28,* 479–497.

Gubrium, J. F., & Holstein, J. A. (2008). The constructionist mosaic. In J. A. Holstein & J. F. Gubrium (Eds.), *Handbook of constructionist research* (pp. 3–10). New York: The Guilford Press.

Guichard, J., & Lenz, J. (2005). Career theory from an international perspective. *Career Development Quarterly, 54,* 17–28.

Hall, S. (1997/2001). The spectacle of the other. In M. Wetherell, S. Taylor, & S. J. Yates (Eds.), *Discourse theory and practice. A reader* (pp. 324–344). London: Sage.

Holland, J. L. (1997). *Making vocational choices: A theory of vocational personalities and work environments* (3rd ed.). Odessa, FL: Psychological Assessment Resources.

Kuhn, T. S. (1962). *The structure of scientific revolutions*. Chicago, IL: The University of Chicago Press.

Lock, A., & Strong, T. (2010). *Social constructionism. Sources and stirrings in theory and practice*. Cambridge, UK: Cambridge University Press.

Lyotard, J. F. (1984). *The postmodern condition*. Minneapolis, MN: University of Minnesota Press.

McIlveen, P., & Patton, W. (2006). A critical reflection on career development. *International Journal for Educational and*

Vocational Guidance, 6, 15–27. doi: 10.1007/s10775-006-0005-1

McIlveen, P., & Patton, W. (2007). Narrative career counselling: Theory and exemplars of practice. *Australian Psychologist, 42*, 226–235.

McIlveen, P., & Schultheiss, D. E. (Eds.) (2012). *Social constructionism in vocational psychology and career development*. Rotterdam: Sense Publishers.

McKinlay, A. (2002). "Dead selves": The birth of the modern career. *Organization, 9*, 595–614.

Mouton, J. (1993). Positivism. In J. Snyman (Ed.), *Conceptions of social inquiry* (pp. 1–28). Pretoria, South Africa: Human Sciences Research Council.

Parsons, F. (1909). *Choosing a vocation*. Boston, MA: Houghton Mifflin.

Preuss, L., & Dawson, D. (2009). On the quality and legitimacy of green narratives in business: A framework for evaluation. *Journal of Business Ethics, 84*, 135–149.

Richardson, M. S. (1993). Work in people's lives: A location for counseling psychologists. *Journal of Counseling Psychology, 40*, 425–433.

Richardson, M. S. (2004). The emergence of new intentions in subjective experience: A social/personal constructionist and relational understanding. *Journal of Vocational Behavior, 64*, 485–498.

Richardson, M. S. (2012). A critique of career discourse practices. In P. McIlveen & D. E. Schultheiss (Eds.), *Social constructionism in vocational psychology and career development* (pp. 87–104). Rotterdam: Sense Publishers.

Riessman, C. K. (2008). *Narrative methods for the human sciences*. Thousand Oaks, CA: Sage.

Rose, N. (1985). *The psychological complex: Psychology, politics and society in England 1869–1939*. London: Routledge & Kegan Paul.

Sampson, E. E. (1993a). *Celebrating the other. A dialogic account of human nature*. Boulder, CO: Westview Press

Sampson, E. E. (1993b). Identity politics. Challenges to psychology's understanding. *American Psychologist, 48*, 1219–1230.

Sarup, M. (1993). *An introductory guide to post-structuralism and postmodernism* (2nd ed.). Athens, GA: University of Georgia Press.

Savage, M. (1998). Discipline, surveillance and the "career": Employment on the Great Western Railway 1833–1914. In A. McKinlay & K. Starkey (Eds.), *Foucault, management*

and organization theory. From panopticon to technologies of self* (pp. 65–92). London: Sage.

Sparkes, A. C., & Smith, B. (2008). Narrative constructionist inquiry. In J. A. Holstein & J. F. Gubrium (Eds.), *Handbook of constructionist research* (pp. 295–314). New York: The Guilford Press.

Stead, G. B. (2004). Culture and career psychology: A social constructionist perspective. *Journal of Vocational Behavior, 64*, 389–406.

Stead, G. B. (2007). Cultural psychology as a transformative agent for vocational psychology. *International Journal for Educational and Vocational Guidance, 7*, 181–190.

Stead, G. B., & Bakker, T. M. (2010a). Discourse analysis in career counseling and development. *Career Development Quarterly, 59*, 72–86

Stead, G. B., & Bakker, T. M. (2010b). Self in career theory and counselling: A discourse analysis perspective. *British Journal of Guidance & Counselling, 38*, 45–60.

Stead, G. B., & Bakker, T. M. (2012). Self in work as a social/cultural construction. In P. McIlveen & D. E. Schultheiss (Eds.), *Social constructionism in vocational psychology and career development* (pp. 29–43). Rotterdam: Sense Publishers.

Stead, G. B., Perry, J. C., Munka, L. M., Bonnett, H. R., Shiban, A. P., & Care, E. (2012). Qualitative research in career development: Content analysis from 1990 to 2009. *International Journal for Educational and Vocational Guidance*. doi: 10.1007/s10775-011-9196-1

Strong, T., & Paré, D. (2004). *Furthering talk. Advances in the discursive therapies*. New York: Kluwer Academic/Plenum Publishers.

Teo, T. (2005). *The critique of psychology. From Kant to postcolonial theory*. New York: Springer.

Trumble, W. R., & Srevenson, A. (2002). *Shorter Oxford English dictionary on historical principles* (5th ed.). Oxford, UK: Oxford University Press.

Vygotsky, L. S., & Luria, A. R. (1993). *Studies on the history of behavior: Ape, primitive, and child*. Hillsdale, NJ: Erlbaum.

White, M., & Epston, D. (1990). *Narrative means to therapeutic ends*. New York: W. W. Norton & Company.

Wittgenstein, L. (1953). *Philosophical investigations*. Oxford, UK: Blackwell.

Young, R. A., & Collin, A. (2004). Introduction: Constructivism and social constructionism in the career field. *Journal of Vocational Behavior, 64*, 373–388.

Traditional and Emerging Career Development Theory and the Psychology of Working

Jane L. Swanson

Abstract

This chapter reviews traditional or foundational theories of career development, as well as recent and emerging theories, using a critical lens informed by psychology of working and other new paradigms. The primary portion of the chapter is a review and critique of the traditional theories, followed by a discussion of the distinction between theories of career development and theories of career counseling, as well as the historical intersection of career and noncareer counseling. Three emerging perspectives are then presented as contemporary approaches to changing views of *career* and *work*.

Key Words: career choice, career counseling, psychology of working, career development theories

Vocational psychology had its origin in the work of Frank Parsons, as documented in his 1909 book *Choosing a Vocation.* Parsons defined the importance of understanding oneself, understanding the occupational world, and using "true reasoning on the relationships of these two groups of facts" (Parsons, 1909, p. 5). Theories of career choice and development emerged from Parsons' work, beginning with trait-and-factor approaches and evolving throughout the 20th century into a number of competing explanations of vocational choice (Swanson & Fouad, 2010). These theories are reviewed in the first portion of the chapter.

Recently, Fouad (2007) outlined five assumptions underlying vocational psychology theory and research, assumptions that are in flux or even nearing extinction. Because these assumptions are relevant to the present chapter, they are discussed here to frame consideration of the traditional theories.

1. Everyone Has the Ability to Make Work Choices

Traditional/foundational theories typically do not question whether or not individuals have

volition regarding any aspect of choice. In fact, these theories developed out of recognition that individuals had increasingly diverse choices and, therefore needed assistance in sorting through the multitude of options available to them in an expanding world of work and a growing economy, such as Parsons' work at the beginning of the 20th century (Zytowski, 2001) or in the education and employment of veterans after World War II (Whiteley, 1984). This is particularly true for theories with their origins up to the late 20th century, including theories proposed by Holland and Super, and the Theory of Work Adjustment (TWA). In contrast, theories developed in the 1980s or later, such as Gottfredson or Social Cognitive Career Theory (SCCT), incorporated constructs that reflected environmental constraints on choice. The question of volition is at the forefront of changes within theories of career choice and development, particularly Blustein's psychology-of-working approach.

2. Work Is a Contained Part of People's Lives

The foundational theories took as their primary aim the world of work, and rarely made connections to the other aspects of individuals' lives. This focus was undoubtedly rooted in the fact that the world of work was dominated by men (specifically middle-class and white men) in the mid-20th century. Work was a male domain, and family and home belonged to women. Questions regarding work/nonwork interface did not begin in earnest until women were evident in the broader sphere of working, and, further, in the pursuit of *careers*. As women entered the working world, their nonwork responsibilities did not change substantially (Hochschild, 1989), thus creating the dual roles that led to study of the intersection of the two domains. Conversely, being male required consideration of work decisions and career choices; being female allowed one to avoid those choices if so desired. The social revolution brought about by women's entry into the world of work required changes in career theories. Super's acknowledgment of a variety of life roles was the first step, and contemporary discussions of market work and personal work provide rich explication of these ideas (Richardson, 2012).

3. The World of Work Is Predictable

The world of work perhaps has never been as predictable as we believe it to be; however, recent changes have radically altered the landscape, locally, nationally, and globally (DeBell, 2001, 2006; Fouad & Bynner, 2008). DeBell (2001) described the "new world economy," characterized by increased globalization, an expanding gulf between the rich and the poor (and a shift in jobs), instability in businesses due to mergers and acquisitions, restructuring of work itself, and rapid and unpredictable technological changes. Theories of vocational choice and development, and their application with clients, must have sufficient flexibility to account for the unpredictability of the future. A similar critique was offered by Savickas et al. (2009), that current theories are "rooted in assumptions of stability of personal characteristics and secure jobs in bounded organizations" and must be "reformulated to fit the postmodern economy" (p. 240).

4. An Individual Will Make One Decision Early in Life

This assumption is clearly no longer sustainable, and it has not been for quite some time. More pertinent to the present discussion, though, is that the traditional/foundational theories have accommodated and explained multiple choice points throughout the lifespan (such as TWA's focus on the process and outcome of work adjustment, and

Super's notion of recycling of stages). However, by focusing on choice points (such as career counseling for choice of academic major in higher education), the *application* of these theories has perpetuated the outdated notion of a single decision early in life. A future direction for the foundational theories is to explicitly address this issue.

5. Career Counseling is Short Term and Focused on Providing Information

While not as directly relevant to a critique of traditional theories (see later section regarding theories of career development vs. theories of career counseling), the continued belief in this assumption prevents counselors and clients from fully engaging in central issues raised within emerging and contemporary theories. As Savickas et al. (2009) noted, "counselors have to face the fact that information about traditional career paths becomes more and more questionable and hazardous" (p. 242).

Fouad's (2007) identification of these five assumptions followed a comprehensive review of recent research in vocational psychology, which she characterized as having a strong tradition of being grounded in theory and a contemporary focus on contextual factors. As these assumptions continue to change, she encouraged theorists and researchers to turn their attention to new questions (Fouad, 2007).

Traditional Theories of Vocational Choice and Career Development

Traditional/foundational theories of career development are typically divided into three broad categories, which also reflect the evolution of these theories during the 20th century: (1) person–environment fit, (2) developmental, and (3) social cognitive. Parsons' (1909) work led to trait-and-factor approaches, which evolved into the person–environment fit theories of Holland and TWA. Super's life-span, life-space theory provided a rich alternative that incorporated developmental concepts, and was shaped by Savickas into career construction theory; Gottfredson also applied developmental concepts in describing circumscription and compromise regarding occupational choice. Social cognitive career theory (Lent, Brown, & Hackett, 1994) applied Bandura's concepts of self-efficacy and outcome expectancy to the prediction of vocational interests, choice, performance, and satisfaction. As will be discussed in a later section, the evolution of these theories throughout the 20th century included greater attention to contextual issues and environmental constraints, leading to the emergence of paradigms, such as the psychology of working, that offer a more inclusive account of individuals' work experiences.

Person–Environment Fit Theories

Two primary theories are considered person–environment fit theories: Holland's vocational personality typology (Holland, 1959, 1997; Nauta, 2013) and the Minnesota TWA (Dawis, 2005; Swanson & Schneider, 2013). Both of these theories evolved from earlier trait-and-factor counseling (Chartrand, 1991; Rounds & Tracey, 1990), which in turn was based on Parsons's (1909) social reform efforts at the turn of the 20th century. Further, both TWA and Holland's theory (as based on Parsons) may be described as "matching models" (Betz, 2008), in which vocational choice is maximized by specifying important characteristics of the individual and the environment, and then attempting to find the best match or fit between individual and environment. These theories are "anchored in the psychology of individual differences" (Juntunen & Even, 2012, p. 6). The specific characteristics of individuals and environments that are considered to be important vary by theory. An additional component of matching models is that the degree of fit is quantified in some manner, and fit may then be used to predict central outcomes, such as the person's satisfaction or tenure (i.e., length of time in the work environment).

Both TWA and Holland's model evolved within the discipline of vocational psychology, yet they share a conceptual foundation with the broader study of *person–environment psychology*. This perspective is built upon the assumption that there is a reciprocal relationship between people and their environments: people influence their environments, and environments influence the people in them (Walsh, Price, & Craik, 1992). Work is but one of many environments in which people interact (others include school, family, intimate relationships, and living environments), all of which influence and are influenced by the individuals in them. Vocational psychology—its science and its practice—has embraced the tenets of person–environment psychology (Swanson & Chu, 2000), as evidenced by the TWA and Holland models of person–environment fit.

Holland's theory has had a profound impact on vocational psychology since its introduction in 1959, in part because of the accessibility of the underlying premises and terminology. The primary premise is that career choice is an expression of one's personality, resulting in members of a given occupation having similar personalities to one another, and, thus, creating a characteristic work environment. Holland defined six broad vocational personality types—Realistic, Investigative, Artistic, Social, Enterprising, and Conventional—each described by prototypic interests, self-concept, values, potential competencies, and preferred work activities and environments (Holland, 1997). Four working assumptions underlie Holland's theory: (a) most individuals can be described by their resemblance to these six types; (b) environments also can be described by their resemblance to these same six types; (c) people search for environments, and environments search for people, that provide a good match; and (d) personality and environment interact to produce behavior. Thus, both persons and environments can be described by one or more types, and these types may be used to quantify the level of person–environment fit, which may then be used to predict important outcomes such as satisfaction and tenure. Types develop as a "product of a characteristic interaction among a variety of cultural and personal forces including peers, biological heredity, parents, social class, culture, and the physical environment" (Holland, 1997, p. 2).

Holland also described several secondary constructs and postulates related to how the types interact to predict behavior, including calculus, congruence, differentiation, consistency, and identity. *Calculus* refers to the structural arrangement of the six types, portrayed as a hexagon with the distance between types inversely proportional to their theoretical interrelations. Adjacent types share more in common than do opposing types. The remaining four secondary constructs describe the relationships between types within people or environments and between persons and environments. *Congruence*, which occupies a central role in Holland's theory, serves as the mechanism for quantifying the match between a person and an environment in terms of the six types and is used to predict important outcomes such as tenure and satisfaction. *Differentiation* refers to the degree of definition of an individual's or environment's types; *consistency* is the "internal coherence" (Spokane, 1996) of an individual's or environment's types; and *identity* refers to the degree of clarity and stability of an individual's or environment's types. These four secondary constructs were hypothesized by Holland as useful in predicting vocational outcomes, such that an individual who is congruent, differentiated, consistent, and high in identity would be predicted to be more satisfied and better adjusted than an individual who is incongruent, undifferentiated, inconsistent, and low in identity.

The hexagonal structure of the six types serves two crucial functions in Holland's theory: defining the degree of consistency in an individual's or environment's types and defining the degree of congruence between an individual and an environment. Moreover, "Holland's hexagon" is well known and frequently used by career practitioners and clients, and serves as the foundation for presenting results of interest inventories and for organizing career information.

TWA, as reflected in its name, has as its primary focus the process of *adjustment* to work environments, including the characteristics of a person that predict his or her satisfaction with the work environment as well as his or her level of satisfactoriness within the work environment (Dawis & Lofquist, 1984). TWA consists of two models—a predictive model and a process model (Dawis, 2005). The *predictive model* focuses on the variables that explain whether or not individuals are satisfied with their work environments, and whether or not they are satisfactory to their work environments, which in turn predicts individuals' tenure in their work environments. The *process model* focuses on how the fit between individuals and their environments is attained and maintained.

The predictive model represents the core of TWA and is focused on predicting whether or not work adjustment occurs. TWA proposes two sets of parallel characteristics: (1) an individual has a set of needs and values that may be met by rewards available in the work environment and (2) the work environment has a set of job requirements that may be met by the skills and abilities that the individual possesses. Each of these intersections of an individual and his or her environment is described by the term *correspondence*, or its lack, *discorrespondence*. If a person's needs are met by his or her work environment, then the person and environment are in correspondence; if not, then they are in discorrespondence. This determines the individual's level of *satisfaction* with the work environment. Likewise, if the work environment's requirements are met by the person, then the person and environment are in correspondence; if not, then they are in discorrespondence, which determines the individual's level of *satisfactoriness* to the work environment. Said another way, an individual has needs and the work environment has rewards; if needs and rewards correspond, then the individual is satisfied. Likewise,

an individual has abilities and the work environment has ability requirements; if abilities and ability requirements correspond, then the individual is considered satisfactory.

If an individual is both satisfied and satisfactory, then the individual and his or her environment are in a state of harmonious equilibrium, and work adjustment has been achieved. If, however, the individual is dissatisfied, unsatisfactory, or both, then a state of disequilibrium exists, which serves as a motivational force propelling some type of change to occur. Thus, dissatisfaction serves a central motivational role in TWA. Adjustment behavior may take one (or more) of four avenues (Dawis, 2002). A dissatisfied individual has two possible choices: attempting to change the environment, in terms of the number or kinds of rewards that it provides, or attempting to change himself or herself, in terms of the number or kind of needs that he or she requires. Ultimately, an individual must decide whether to stay in the current work environment or leave for another environment. If individuals are unsatisfactory, they have two possible choices: increasing their level of skill or expanding their skill repertoire to meet the requirements of the environment, or attempting to change the environment's expectations. Moreover, the environment has several possible actions, with the ultimate outcomes of retaining or terminating the individual. Although TWA focuses on both the individual and the environment, the theory clearly emphasizes what the person experiences: the term *satisfaction* refers to an individual's satisfaction with his or her job, whereas the term *satisfactoriness* refers to an individual with whom the work environment is satisfied. Tenure occurs when an individual is both satisfied and satisfactory (Dawis, 2005).

In addition to these basic predictions, TWA proposes a number of moderating relationships and variables. The twin processes of correspondence, satisfaction and satisfactoriness, influence one another: an individual's level of satisfaction with his or her work environment is predicted to influence his or her level of satisfactoriness to the work environment, and, conversely, an individual's level of satisfactoriness is predicted to influence his or her level of satisfaction. Another type of moderator variable included in TWA is personality style, which describes how an individual characteristically interacts with his or her environment. TWA proposes four styles: *celerity* (the speed with which an individual initiates interaction with the environment), *pace* (the intensity of an individual's response to the environment), *rhythm* (the pattern of an individual's responses, such as steady, cyclical, or erratic), and *endurance* (how persistently an individual responds to the environment). These style variables also can be used to describe the environment.

The process model adds to TWA's ability to predict work adjustment by focusing on *how* adjustment occurs and *how* it is maintained. As noted earlier, discorrespondence between a person and his or her environment serves to motivate behavior; the process portion of TWA defines the parameters and outcomes of that motivational force. TWA proposes that individuals' adjustment styles characterize how they react to the occurrence of discorrespondence. Adjustment style consists of four variables: *flexibility* (the amount of discorrespondence an individual will tolerate before reaching a threshold of dissatisfaction leading to either active or reactive adjustment behavior), *active adjustment* (when an individual acts upon the environment in an effort to decrease discorrespondence), *reactive adjustment* (when an individual acts upon himself or herself to reduce the amount of discorrespondence), and *perseverance* (the length of time that an individual is willing to persist in a discorrespondent environment after engaging in adjustment behavior). Adjustment styles are relevant to the environment too. All four of these adjustment-style variables are hypothesized to vary among individuals and work environments, and they are important factors in predicting adjustment behavior.

Developmental Theories

Developmental theories of career choice focus on the sequential nature of influences on interests and aspirations, as well as the sustained progression of these influences from childhood throughout the lifespan. In contrast to the person–environment theories, developmental theories incorporated a broader set of contextual factors, including the intersection of work and other life roles, and the influence of gender and socioeconomic status on career choices (Swanson & Fouad, 2010). Two such theories were proposed by Super and Gottfredson.

SUPER'S LIFE-SPAN, LIFE-SPACE THEORY

Super "revolutionized the field of vocational psychology" (Betz, 2008, p. 365) by viewing choice of vocation as a developmental process over the lifespan, rather than a single point in time. A hallmark of Super's theory is that vocational development is a process of making a series of decisions, culminating in vocational choices that represent an implementation of one's self-concept. Vocational choices are viewed as successive approximations of a good match between the vocational self and the world of work.

Super's theoretical propositions included a focus on developmental contextualism and social context, as well as an acknowledgment of differences among individuals and among occupations, as explicated in person–environment fit theories. Super proposed five specific stages (Growth, Exploration, Establishment, Maintenance, and Disengagement) of career development, with specific tasks to be mastered at each stage. These five stages were viewed as "maxicycles" that occurred over the course of a lifetime, as well as "minicycles" that recurred during transitions and re-decision points. The *Growth* stage (ages 4 to 13, or childhood to early adolescence) encompasses four tasks: becoming concerned about the future, increasing personal control over one's own life, convincing oneself to achieve in school and at work, and acquiring competent work habits and attitudes (Super et al., 1996). During the *Exploration* stage (ages 14 to 24, or adolescence to early adulthood), the three primary tasks are crystallizing, specifying, and implementing a career choice (Super et al., 1996). The *Establishment* stage (ages 25 to 44, or early to middle adulthood) entails entering and becoming established in one's career and work life; the tasks of this stage include stabilizing, consolidating, and advancing in one's chosen career. *Maintenance* (ages 45 to 65, or middle adulthood to retirement, renamed *Management* by Savickas, 2005) involves maintaining the gains achieved at work; primary tasks are renewal, holding, updating, and innovating. The fifth and final stage, *Disengagement* (over age 65 or during the retirement transition), commences when an individual retires or otherwise disengages from the workforce.

Super characterized the stages as linear and predictable but not invariant; that is, individuals typically go through these stages, but not everyone progresses through them in the same manner or at fixed ages. Each transition between stages is characterized by a "minicycle," or a recycling through the stages of growth, reexploration, and reestablishment. The age ranges are the approximate ages at which most individuals encounter each stage. Within each stage, Super proposed characteristic developmental tasks. Mastery of these tasks allows individuals to function effectively in their life roles within that stage and prepares them for the next task. Super proposed this concept of *career maturity* to describe an individual's readiness or ability to master the developmental tasks and cope with stage-related transitions; the term *career adaptability*, later introduced to more accurately reflect adult career issues (Savickas, 1997; Super & Knasel, 1981), is defined as "readiness to cope with changing work and work conditions" (Savickas, 1994, p. 58).

A fundamental aspect of Super's theory is that vocational choice is an implementation of the self-concept, which includes objective and subjective views of the self. Individuals construct their careers in a continuing self-evaluation within their social context: They begin by considering work roles that fit their self-concepts, their self-concepts are shaped by feedback from the external world (e.g., parents, teachers, employers), and in turn, the evolving self-concept begins to be implemented in different work roles.

Super considered the development of vocational choices within the context of other life roles: "While making a living, people live a life" (Super et al., 1996). Super delineated six specific roles that individuals might hold (child, student, homemaker, worker, citizen, and "leisurite"), often concurrently and interactively. His "life-span, life-space" theory acknowledged that these roles occur at different times and in different combinations throughout an individual's life, and thus the salience of different roles will vary among and within individuals. *Life space* corresponds to the roles that one fulfills at various times in life, and *life span* denotes the stages described earlier; an individual "lives in the intersection of the two dimensions" (Super et al., 1996, p. 128).

GOTTFREDSON'S THEORY OF CIRCUMSCRIPTION AND COMPROMISE

Gottfredson's theory (1996, 2005) focuses on the developmental narrowing of vocational choices through the process of circumscription and compromise. *Circumscription* occurs as the range of considered occupations decreases through the application of sex type, social class/prestige, and finally, interests. *Compromise* then occurs as an individual confronts questions of accessibility to occupational paths, and thus eliminates options. Although Gottfredson's theory has received little independent support, it continues to garner attention among practitioners and is important because of the inclusion of gender roles and social status, thus representing a "link between developmental theories and later theories that included sociocultural influences" (Juntunen & Even, 2012; p. 24). Unique contributions of this theory are the roles of compromise and circumscription, and the resultant self-defined social space (Gottfredson, 2005).

Gottfredson (1996, 2005) developed her theory of circumscription and compromise to explain why individuals' vocational expectations, even when they are children, vary by sex, race, and social class. Gottfredson differs from Super in that she views vocational choice first as an implementation of the social self and only secondarily as an implementation of the psychological self. Inherent in this approach is the circumscription of psychological variables, such as interests or values, by social variables, such as gender or social class. Gottfredson focuses on cognitive development as children grow in awareness of themselves and their social place in the world and begin to eliminate vocational options that are not compatible with their evolving self-image. Gottfredson proposed four development processes to account for the observed reproduction of differences in occupational perceptions and choices by sex, race, and social class: cognitive growth, self-creation, circumscription, and compromise.

Cognitive growth. Over time, children develop increasingly complex cognitive structures that allow them to process occupational information and determine the quality of matches. However, children begin to narrow their options and make other decisions that directly affect their career choices long before they have developed sufficient cognitive complexity to do so satisfactorily.

Self-creation. Gottfredson discussed the concept of self-creation to address the relative influence of genetic factors and environmental influences. Repeated experiences consolidate an individual's genetically based characteristics, turning them into "traits" that gain stability across a variety of situations. However, adolescents rarely have sufficient experiences to draw upon when they are making choices related to education and career.

Circumscription. Circumscription is the process by which children narrow the "zone of acceptable alternatives" or "social space" by progressive elimination of unacceptable alternatives, or those that conflict with one's self-concept. In her four-stage model of circumscription, Gottfredson suggested that elimination of alternatives is progressive and irreversible (except under unusual circumstances) and mostly occurs without conscious awareness. In Stage 1 (ages 3 to 5), children develop an *orientation to size and power* and categorize people in simple ways, such as big versus little. They recognize observable physical differences between men and women, which increases in Stage 2 (ages 6 to

8), when children develop an *orientation to sex roles*. In this stage, children use sex appropriateness to define their vocational aspirations and construct their tolerable-sex-type boundary, in which they rule out occupations that do not conform to their sex-type expectations. Stage 3 (ages 9 to 13) entails *orientation to social valuation*, in which children become aware of occupational status hierarchies and now view the range of occupations along the two dimensions of prestige level and sex type. Children establish their tolerable-level boundary to eliminate occupations that are unacceptably low in prestige and their tolerable-effort boundary to eliminate occupations that they perceive as too difficult to attain. By the end of Stage 3, the full range of occupations has been whittled down to those that are of the appropriate sex type, that have high enough prestige, and that are not too difficult. What remains is a child's zone of acceptable alternatives (or social space). In Stage 4 (ages 14 and older), adolescents become aware of the need to consider their vocational choices, and they develop their *orientation to the internal, unique self*. Here, interests, values, and abilities are clarified, and occupational exploration occurs within the zone of acceptable alternatives as circumscribed in earlier stages. Stages 1 through 3 are focused on rejecting unacceptable alternatives, with greater attention to the social self; Stage 4 is focused on identifying which of the acceptable alternatives are most preferred, with greater attention to the psychological self (Gottfredson, 1996). Stage 4 thus begins the process of compromise.

Compromise. Vocational aspirations can be viewed as the product of accessibility (choices that are most realistic) and compatibility (person–environment fit), and idealistic aspirations may give way to realistic ones. Compromise entails the modification of alternatives due to inaccessibility, leading to the acceptance of less attractive alternatives. Gottfredson (1996) suggests that sex type, prestige, and field of interest are the three dimensions considered in the process of compromise, and in a specific order such that sex type is least likely and field of interest most likely to be compromised. In other words, the dimensions that are established first developmentally, those closest to the core of self-concept, are maintained longer.

Gottfredson's theory explicitly addresses the impact of sex-role socialization and other societal factors that influence the development of occupational aspirations. As such, it offers a complementary perspective to Super's theory. On the other hand, Super's theory was designed to span a much broader scope of career behavior than does Gottfredson's theory and, thus, is a more comprehensive theory of lifespan career development. Gottfredson's theory has received relatively little attention from researchers, despite its intuitive appeal to practitioners. One reason for the minimal attention is likely related to the difficulty in assessing perceptions in early childhood and in measuring the important constructs in the theory (Fassinger, 2005; Swanson & Gore, 2000). Further, the dimensions of sex type, prestige, and interest are difficult to consider separately from one another (Phillips & Jome, 2005). Some support has been shown for the revised theory regarding different degrees of compromise (Blanchard & Lichtenberg, 2003).

Social Cognitive Career Theory

Until recently, SCCT (Lent, Brown, & Hackett, 1994, 2000) would have been classified as an "emerging" theory; however, it has generated a substantial amount of research attention in the 20 years since its introduction and is now considered a stalwart among theories of career choice and development. SCCT grew out of an effort by Hackett and Betz (1981) to apply Bandura's (1986) concept of self-efficacy to the career choice process. Self-efficacy expectations—or "people's judgments of their capabilities to organize and execute courses of action required to attain designated types of performances" (Bandura, 1986, p. 391)—are thought to influence the development of interests, choices, actions, and performance.

Another of Bandura's constructs incorporated into SCCT is outcome expectations, or people's beliefs about the outcomes of consequences of events. In the context of career choice, outcome expectations influence the development of interests, choices, and actions by focusing on what individuals perceive they will gain by pursuing specific career paths. SCCT differs from earlier theories in its focus on the personal constructions that people place on events related to career decision making (Lent, Brown, & Hackett, 2000). Based on Bandura's concepts, as well as early work by Hackett and Betz (1981), Lent et al. (1994, 2002) developed a unified social cognitive framework to explain and predict career behavior. Specifically, their three-part model links interests, choices, and performance based on Bandura's social cognitive model. A recent, fourth, model focuses on work satisfaction (Lent, 2008; Lent & Brown, 2006).

Basic to all of the models, Lent et al. (1994, 2002) propose that performance accomplishments, verbal persuasion, vicarious learning, and physiological states and arousal forge an individual's self-efficacy expectations, which are conceptualized as situation-specific. Lent et al. (1994, 2002) also propose that demographic and individual difference variables (such as sex, race/ethnicity, and socioeconomic status) interact with background and contextual variables to influence learning experiences that play a role in forming self-efficacy beliefs. Those self-efficacy expectations, in turn, are related to outcome expectations that individuals have about the outcomes of behavior.

In the model pertaining to development of *interests*, outcome expectancies and self-efficacy beliefs both predict interests (Lent et al., 2002). Interests (together with self-efficacy beliefs and outcome expectancies) predict goals, which in turn lead to behaviors related to choosing and practicing activities, which then lead to performance attainments.

Lent et al. (2000, 2002) also propose that background and contextual variables, termed *contextual affordances*, help to explain why an individual does not pursue an area in which he or she has strong interest. Background and contextual variables may serve as perceived barriers, or supports, to entry or to outcome expectations. Lent et al. (2000, 2002) conceptualize two types of contextual affordances, those that are much earlier (distal) than the choice and those that are closer in time (proximal) to the choice. Examples of distal influences may be factors that either constrict or facilitate the development of self-efficacy and outcome expectations (e.g., gender-role socialization, impoverished learning environments), while proximal barriers and supports affect the implementation of choices (e.g., anxiety about moving, financial support to go to college). Barriers and supports may be objective or subjective; what is important is an individual's perception of the barrier.

The *choice* model (Lent et al., 2002) proposes that person inputs (e.g., gender, race, disability, personality, and predispositions) and background context together influence learning experiences, which influence self-efficacy beliefs and outcome expectancies. As already described, these influence interests, which influence choice goals; goals influence actions, and actions influence performance attainments. Lent (2005) notes that the process of making a career choice involves choosing a goal (e.g., becoming a scientist), taking action to implement that goal (completing courses in a biology major), and the subsequent consequences of those actions (successful graduation in biology). The *performance*

model predicts the level of performance as well as the persistence an individual has in pursuing goals (Lent et al., 2002). This model proposes that past performance accomplishments influence self-efficacy and outcome expectancies, which in turn influence performance goals; these lead to performance attainment level. In other words, past performance influences self-efficacy beliefs along with the expectations individuals have about the outcomes of their future behavior. These expectations affect the goals that people set for themselves, which then affect the level of performance they attain. The choice and interest models involve the content of career choices, such as the field or specific occupation in which one would like to work, while the performance model predicts the level of performance toward which one aspires within one's chosen field (Lent et al., 2002). Finally, the *satisfaction* model (Lent, 2008; Lent & Brown, 2006) posits the roles of self-efficacy expectations and work conditions/outcomes in predicting an individual's goal-directed activity; all three constructs predict work satisfaction.

Summary and Critique of "Traditional" Theories

The history of the traditional theories in vocational psychology includes evolving conceptualizations: Parsons' work in 1909 led to a trait-and-factor approach, which evolved into person–environment fit. Super proposed life-span, life-space theory as an alternative, which was further shaped by Savickas into career construction theory. We are currently in the midst of another paradigm shift into contextual and relational approaches.

A common criticism of traditional theories is the lack of attention to the larger sociocultural context within the scaffold of the theory. As a consequence, the examination of these contextual factors, including the adequacy of extant theory in explaining vocational behavior for a broad range of individuals, was instigated by scholars other than the original theorists. At times, such efforts were not welcomed by the theorists themselves, perhaps because they distracted from the core concepts and the ability to explain behavior for most people. Generally speaking, these traditional theories have held up to scrutiny (Betz, 2008; Juntunen & Even, 2012), and authors of emerging perspectives recommend continuing to use the contributions of these theories as foundation to the newer approaches (Blustein, 2006; Savickas, 2011).

Despite the initial inattention to contextual factors, the structural elements of the theories themselves do not limit subsequent attention to these factors. For example, person–environment fit theories were built upon the foundation of individual differences (Dawis, 1992), which presumably would be fertile ground for explication of the broad diversity of people's experiences, yet may have been obscured by the task of assessing individual differences, which was accomplished primarily to yield scores for further prediction (Savickas, 2011). Developmental theories focus on the unfolding of self and the interaction of self with career choices, which again presumably would be amenable to description of diversity of individuals' experiences, yet the emphasis has been on describing the universality of developmental paths. SCCT departed from earlier theories by building in distal and proximal contextual variables, in a way that allowed a more complex interplay between individual factors (such as self-efficacy and outcome expectations) with environmental factors (such as supports and barriers, background affordances). For this reason, SCCT has served as a bridge between the traditional theories and the emerging paradigms.

For clients who come to "traditional" practice settings, such as college/university counseling centers, these traditional theories continue to provide utility, because essentially they are the theories designed to explain the work lives of individuals seeking higher education to enter the middle-class occupational and organizational structure. However, structural changes in specific occupations and in the general world of work may undermine the utility of the theories even in these traditional settings. Other theories are necessary to understand broader experience, particularly as the variables of choice or volition, work and life roles, and economic factors depart from the traditional viewpoint. Moreover, traditional theories have had little expansion outside of the traditional bounds, which may be better addressed by newer perspectives such as those offered by Savickas, Richardson, and Blustein. Work by these three scholars is presented in subsequent sections.

Theories of Career Development and Theories of Career Counseling

A discussion of traditional theories of career development is not complete without a related discussion of theories of career counseling; these two sets of theories are not as logically connected as one might think. Theories of career *development* are devised to explain some aspect of vocational behavior, such as initial career choice, work adjustment, or lifespan career progress. Theories of career *counseling*, on the other hand, have the goal of providing counselors with direction for how to work with clients, and are similar to a discussion of theoretical orientation, or one's philosophical stance regarding the nature of personality and of therapeutic change. Most of the prominent theories of career development have relatively little to say about the most effective way to work with clients, although they do provide a guide to what should be considered the most important fodder for work with clients, such as maximizing the fit between individuals and their current or future work environments, or assisting clients in expressing their self-concepts through work and other life roles. On the other hand, many theories of career development have spawned theories of career counseling, such as the Person–Environment Correspondence model, which is an outgrowth of TWA (Eggerth, 2008; Lofquist & Dawis, 1991), or the Career Development and Assessment Counseling model, an application of Super's life-span, life-space theory (Niles, 2001; Super et al., 1992). More recently, Savickas's (2005, 2013) adaptation of Super's theory into Career Construction theory has been further developed into the Life Design theory of career counseling (Savickas, 2011, 2012).

As noted by previous writers (Osipow, 1996; Savickas, 2011; Subich & Simonson, 2001), the evolution of theories of career counseling is relatively recent; the distinction between theories of career development and theories of career counseling has been traced to a conference held in the early 1990s (Savickas & Lent, 1994). Although Parsons' (1909) book *Choosing a Vocation* launched theories of career development as well as the practice of career counseling, theoretical explication of these two tracks developed relatively independently. Other models of career counseling include those proposed by Crites (1981), Yost and Corbishley (1987), Peterson, Sampson, and Reardon (1991), Spokane (1991), and Isaacson and Brown (1993); readers are referred to Subich and Simonson (2001) for more information about each of these models. As they noted, the "call for the development of theories of career counseling has become the anthem of the field" (Subich & Simonson, 2001, p. 258).

Two contemporary models warrant particular mention: Gysbers, Heppner, and Johnston's (2003) career counseling model and Fouad and Bingham's (1995) culturally appropriate career counseling model. The Gysbers et al. (2003) model of career counseling has two major phases: (1) goal or problem identification, clarification, and specification and (2) client goal or problem resolution. At the core of the model is the working alliance between counselor and client, which consists of agreement on the goals and tasks of counseling and formation of a bond between counselor and client (Bordin, 1979). The Fouad and Bingham (1995) model includes assessment of the impact of cultural variables in each of seven steps of career counseling, and examines five spheres of influence of cultural variables on career issues (core, gender, family, racial or ethnic group, and dominant group). These two models have received sustained attention and may provide useful frameworks for emerging theories of career counseling.

"Career" Versus "Personal" Counseling

The artificiality of the schism between "career" and "personal" counseling has been documented by many previous writers (Haverkamp & Moore, 1993; Heppner & Davidson, 2002; Juntunen, 2006; Richardson, 1996; Robitschek & DeBell, 2002; Swanson, 1995, 2002; Whiston & Rahardia, 2008). The origins of this distinction lie in the separate historical traditions underlying career counseling and psychotherapy and have been maintained to the current day, despite efforts to soften the sharp edges that divide these modalities. For example, Haverkamp and Moore (1993) argued that the implicit definition of personal counseling is too broad, consisting of anything not directly related to career, whereas the implicit definition of career counseling is too narrow, consisting primarily of initial career choices of young adults and neglecting adult work adjustment or the intersection of work and nonwork roles.

On the other hand, some authors have warned against what might be called the "over-therapizing" of career counseling (Brown & Krane, 2000). Moreover, Heppner and Davidson (2002) warned that career issues (and career psychology generally) risk becoming "watered down" if too fully integrated with noncareer issues and foci in counseling. Evidence relevant to their warning comes from two sources: related to vocational overshadowing, or the tendency of therapists to overlook career concerns when there are co-occurring personal concerns (Magee & Whiston, 2010; Spengler, 2000; Spengler, Blustein, & Strohmer, 1990), and literature related to negative attitudes toward career counseling by trainees and faculty alike (Gelso et al., 1985; Heppner, O'Brien, Hinkleman, & Flores, 1996). These two phenomena would seem to work in tandem, such that the devaluing of the activity

of counseling that focuses on career issues would increase the likelihood of ignoring those career concerns in favor of other presenting issues, resulting in clients' career concerns not receiving the attention that is warranted.

At least three frameworks or conceptual realignments (Blustein & Spengler, 1995; Richardson, 2003, 2006, 2009; Robitschek & DeBell, 2002) have been proposed to attempt a rapprochement among the "career" versus "personal" dimensions in counseling and training. All three of the frameworks are conceptually intuitive, yet they also represented a profound shift in thinking about work and foreshadowed the later emergence of 21st-century theories (as described in the next section). First, after reviewing what they labeled "substantive distinction versus subtle differences" in the career and personal domains, Blustein and Spengler (1995) proposed "domain-sensitive counseling," in which the two practices of career and personal counseling are integrated into a comprehensive framework that is sensitive to the domain—career or noncareer—in which a client's problems arise (or at least initially present themselves). In this framework, a counselor is capable of intervening across either domain as needed.

The second framework was articulated by Richardson (1993, 1996, 2009) as a paradigm shift for the field of vocational psychology, namely from the study of career development to a study of work in people's lives. She traced the evolutionary progression of the "false split" that has occurred between career and personal counseling, beginning with a "split" between normal and pathological personality functioning, leading to a further split in a consideration of aspects of the self into different domains of functioning, including the occupational domain, which led to the practice of vocational guidance and counseling. A further split then occurred by the shift of focus from "vocation" to "career," as the aspect of self connected to vocation was now situated outside of the self, in the structure of the occupational world. Discussion of "career" was defined less by self and more by occupational alternatives. As Juntunen (2006) paraphrased Richardson's position, "by focusing on career as an activity that is external to the person (because it is regulated by the occupational structure), we negate the central role of work in human experience" (Juntunen, 2006, p. 345). Richardson (1996) also commented on the split between the public (career) and the private (personal)—a distinction that may underlie the greater stigma, and desire for privacy and concealment, associated with "personal" counseling than career counseling (Ludwikowski, Vogel, & Armstrong, 2009).

The third framework was offered by Robitschek and DeBell (2002), who proposed that vocational/career issues be considered as primary issues and contextual factors in counseling. They argued not for a reintegration of vocational psychology into counseling psychology, but, rather, for a larger paradigm shift. In this new paradigm, vocational issues would "provide another facet to understanding the multiple life roles and complex contexts in which we live" (Robitschek & DeBell, 2002, pp. 801–802). Thus, instead of defining counseling *per se* as either "career" or "personal," clients would bring primary issues and contextual factors to counseling; some clients would have primary issues that are vocational in nature, and the counselor would explore other contextual factors relevant to those issues; for other clients, vocational issues would be among a variety of contextual issues surrounding a nonvocational primary issue.

In addition to these paradigm shifts, a number of authors have offered conceptual and practical suggestions regarding the integration of work and personal issues within counseling. For example, Robitschek and DeBell (2002) offered several suggestions for implementing their new paradigm, in order to reduce the artificial distinction between the two domains, and Juntunen (2006) outlined the benefits of integrating work and nonwork (personal) issues in practice settings that are not specifically designated as career counseling. A common theme is the importance of assessing work-related issues with every client, beginning with intake forms and continuing through therapy, and to be attuned to the interaction of work and life roles.

From Traditional to Emerging Theories: 21st-Century Views of Work

In the past decade or more, substantial changes have occurred within the field of vocational psychology (Fouad, 2007; Juntunen & Even, 2012). Theories of career development (or vocational choice) have shifted from a focus on the individual, to an explicit recognition of contextual factors, to a person-in-complex-social-and-economic-systems perspective. Among the newer paradigms, different foci have emerged, including equal valuing and explicit consideration of work and relationship, market and care work; embedding work within a relational context; expanding consideration of the experience of *work* beyond that of *career*; and

attention to co-construction and postmodern perspectives.

These changes have been viewed as paradigm shifting (Richardson, 2012), in the sense of Kuhn's (1962) description of the progress of scientific knowledge. According to Kuhn, these shifts occur in a nonlinear way, represent often-radical departures from previous views, and open up new perspectives to understanding phenomena that previously would not have been considered valid. Generally speaking, a major thrust of the paradigm shift in vocational psychology has been from a positivist epistemology, in which individuals are defined "objectively" as a set of traits that are discoverable and quantifiable through psychometric assessment or other forms of empirical observations, to postmodern epistemologies such as constructionism, in which individuals define their own meaning and construct their own stories.

The history of vocational psychology is strongly tied to the emergence of the psychometric movement in the first half of the 20th century (Dawis, 1992), and measures of vocationally relevant constructs assumed a central role for researchers and practitioners. These measures were built upon and reinforced the positivist epistemology: interests, values, and abilities were viewed as unobservable yet very real traits that could be revealed through the use of well-constructed scales. Used in career counseling, the scores produced by interest and other inventories often were treated as infallible indicators of something to be uncovered and confirmed by the counselor and client (Reed, Patton, & Gold, 1993).

In spite of this apparent paradigmatic shift, there are clear continuities with history. Juntunen and Even (2012) noted the responsiveness to social change that characterizes the history of vocational psychology, beginning with Parsons's (1909) landmark work that launched the field. Parsons responded to contemporary real-world issues resulting from social, political, and economic changes occurring at the outset of the 20th century (Swanson, 1996), and the newly emerging and contemporary perspectives (including the psychology-of-working approach) fit well with that trend.

Blustein (2011) and others have called for new theoretical perspectives that "encompass an expanded vision of working along with an integrative understanding of the complex, reciprocal relationships between work and other life domains ... [and] how people make meaning of their interactions with others and with the broader social world" (p. 2). These newer approaches would seem particularly relevant for those individuals caught in the changing world, perhaps those outside of the traditional practice settings noted earlier.

The current zeitgeist in theories of work/life/career encompass a number of overlapping yet distinct approaches, including relational perspectives (Blustein, Richardson), narrative approaches (Richardson, Savickas), social constructionism epistemologies (Blustein, Savickas), and more expansive definitions of "work" (Blustein, Richardson). These approaches corroborate Fouad's (2007) five assumptions as described at the outset of this chapter and have provided expanded and contemporary views of the role of work in people's lives.

Some of the new perspectives, such as boundaryless or protean careers (Arthur & Rousseau, 1996; Hall, 1996), have decoupled the worker from his or her employing organization, casting the individual as owning his or her career rather than having it owned by the organization. This has led to a view of the individual as agentic and as exerting volitional choice. However, much of this original writing was from the perspective of industrial/organizational psychology, in which a preexisting or ongoing relation between a worker and his or her organization was a given. In other words, discussion of boundaryless or protean careers does no more to include those individuals outside of a traditional career ladder than any other existing theory. These approaches, however, do address issues related to structural changes in the world of work.

On the other hand, writing within the realm of traditional vocational psychology has often suffered from a lack of recognition of the impact of economic and labor market factors. Yet, these factors have considerable bearing on the progression and experience of work/career. Another factor in the emerging perspectives, a welcome addition, is explicit recognition of the role of economic and market influences. Vocational psychology has had as its primary focus the individual, yet has often neglected the economic and social realities in which individuals engage in work and career.

The word "career" has an interesting history (Blustein, 2006). Super introduced it but did not intend to have it supplant "vocational." As Blustein (2006, p. 12) noted, Super "inadvertently placed the notion of work into a context that was embedded deeply in a lifestyle that was, for the most part, characteristic of relatively well-educated and often affluent people within advanced Western countries." Super's intention, however, was to emphasize the range of work-related issues across the lifespan. In common parlance, the term "career" is used to describe a much broader range of occupational paths than that intended by scholars and theorists. For that reason alone, perhaps it is time to either retire the word "career" (much like Richardson's [1996] proposal to retire the term "career counseling") or, alternatively, to reclaim the meaning of the word to denote a narrower and more carefully drawn definition. Reclaiming the word would allow for more precision in research regarding lifespan patterns of working, similar to Savickas's (2002) reminder that much research purporting to focus on "career development" is more accurately described as "vocational behavior."

Three recent conceptualizations represent significant departures from the traditional paradigms: Savickas's (2011, 2013) career construction theory and life design paradigm; Richardson's (2012) model of counseling for work and relationships; and Blustein's psychology of working. These approaches have broadened the scope of discourse and draw upon perspectives outside of vocational psychology, as well as outside of psychology.

A major impetus for these new models is the changing nature, or "new social arrangement," of work (Savickas et al., 2009, p. 239). Recent conceptualizations of "work" have expanded to include unpaid work such as caregiving and volunteer activities, in an attempt to capture the multiple forms that work may take in an individual's life. For example, work has been defined as "an instrumental and purposive activity that produces goods, services, or social relations which have both social and/or personal value" (Richardson, Constantine, & Washburn, 2005, p. 60). Similarly, Blustein (2006, p. 3) defined working as entailing "effort, activity, and human energy in given tasks that contribute to the overall social and economic welfare of a given culture."

How work is conceptualized, perceived, and structured has received much attention in recent years. Individuals' labor force experiences will be substantially affected by current and future societal trends, including globalization and innovations in technology (DeBell, 2006; Niles, Herr, & Hartung, 2002), and changes continue in the nature of "work" itself, with a redefinition of work roles, work/family boundaries, and the general manner in which work occurs. Relatedly, the manner in which "careers" are structured is undergoing conceptual shifts, such as the idea of "boundaryless" or protean careers (Arthur & Rousseau, 1996; Hall, 1996) and changes in the psychological contract between individuals and their employing organizations, away from lifetime employment and mutual commitment. Another factor is that the nature of the workforce itself is undergoing dramatic changes, in terms of increasing diversity in age, race/ethnicity, sex, sexual orientation, disability, and factors that motivate employees (Bobek & Robbins, 2005; DeBell, 2006; Niles, Herr, & Hartung, 2002). Further, the psychological contract that existed between employer and employee has weakened to the point of vanishing, with increasing numbers of part-time, contingent, freelance, and otherwise insecure workers, who are hired for "projects" rather than "jobs" (Savickas, 2011). All of these changes have far-reaching implications for theories of career and work, as well as models for assisting individuals in planning their work lives.

In addition to changes in the nature and structure of work, there are significant changes in the epistemology and discourse concerning working and vocational behavior. Epistemology, or the philosophy of knowledge, concerns questions about how knowledge is defined (How do we come to know? What is our source of knowledge?), which also applies to the methodology or practice of knowledge. Traditional theories of career choice and development rest on a positivist epistemology, which was the prevailing philosophy of science at the time the theories were initially proposed. Positivism holds that the purpose of science is to pursue knowledge by focusing only on what is observable and measurable. Science is the way to uncover the truth, which operates on a deterministic set of laws of cause and effect (Trochim, n.d.). Positivism relies on a base of knowledge that is observable and testable (Blustein et al., 2012). Post-positivist epistemology, in contrast, entails "a wholesale rejection of the central tenets of positivism" (Trochim, n.d.).

Within vocational psychology, postmodern epistemologies have challenged the status quo of the positivist paradigm. A predominant post-positivist approach is social constructionism, which emphasizes the "inherent relativism of knowledge, reality, and human experience" (Blustein et al., 2012, p. 245). In this view, knowledge is created through cognitive processes and social interactions, rather than by individual objective observation, and how an individual understands the world is embedded in culture and history (Gergen, 1999; Juntunen & Even, 2012; Young & Collin, 2004). As Savickas et al. (2009, p. 246) described, "Positivist research on careers concentrates on decision making and declaring a choice. The comparable process for the social constructionist perspective is articulating intentions and anticipations regarding possible selves and life in the future." Thus, the postmodern or post-positivist perspective redirects attention to understanding how people construct meaning about their careers and assisting them in designing meaning (Richardson, Constantine, & Washburn, 2005; Savickas et al., 2009; Young & Collin, 2004). The three emerging frameworks described in the subsequent section have all been influenced by, and contributed to, the postmodern epistemologies such as social constructionism.

Career Construction Theory and the Life Design Paradigm (Savickas)

The origins of career construction theory are found in Super's life-span, life-space theory, and vestiges of Super's theory remain in Savickas's formulation. Career construction theory explains the processes through which "individuals construct themselves, impose direction on their vocational behavior, and make meaning of their careers" (Savickas, 2013, p. 1). The primary concept is *self-construction*, which begins during childhood as individuals are first actors and then become agents, and later authors, of their own lives and careers. Career construction theory draws from McAdams and Olson's (2010) view of personality development, which views individuals as driven by adaptation to their environment, versus by "maturation of inner structures" (Savickas, 2013, p. 2)

Savickas argued for a reconceptualization of how careers are constructed given societal changes in the way that work is structured. In the 20th century, "career" as articulated by Super meant a path through one's work life, which could be objectively defined and was evident to others. In contrast, the 21st-century view is of boundaryless, protean careers, which require subjective construction by the individual and adaptation to changing conditions. Career construction theory "views career as a story that individuals tell about their working life, not progress down a path or up a ladder" (Savickas, 2013, p. 6). Although people have "objective" careers, they also construct subjective careers with which to impose meaning and direction on their behavior. This subjective career story carries an individual throughout transitions.

Savickas (2005, 2013) described the "four Cs" of career concern, control, curiosity, and confidence. *Career concern* refers to a future orientation and recognition of the importance of planning for tomorrow, which is characterized by planfulness and optimism, versus *career indifference*, which is characterized by apathy and pessimism. *Career control* entails the ability to have control over one's own choices (not independence *per se*), versus *career indecision*, which is characterized by confusion, procrastination, and impulsivity. *Career curiosity* follows self-control, as an individual becomes inquisitive about his or her interests and occupational alternatives. The important role of curiosity is reflected in the attention paid to exploration in other theories of career development (Savickas, 2013). A lack of curiosity leads to *unrealism* about self and environment. *Career confidence* reflects self-efficacy or anticipating success regarding education and career. Lack of confidence may lead to career *inhibition*. These four processes have some developmental trajectory, in that it would seem necessary to express concern prior to experiencing control, which would in turn be a necessary condition for curiosity and confidence. Savickas (2013) described these four Cs as dimensions that may progress at different rates, and "disequilibrium between the four developmental lines" could produce problems that would be labeled as indifference, indecision, unrealism, and inhibition.

Savickas (2011, 2012) recently proposed a career counseling model. In discussing the evolution of theories/approaches, Savickas (2011) described distinctions among the three types of interventions (vocational guidance, career education, and career counseling), linking these terms to the three perspectives on the self and to the historical progression of theoretical perspectives in vocational psychology. *Vocational guidance* focuses on scores and traits and is concerned about matching and occupational fit, à la Holland's theory. *Career education* focuses on stages and tasks and is concerned with readiness and vocational development, à la Super's theory. Savickas reserved the term *career counseling* for his own life design paradigm, with a focus on stories and themes, and with designing work life via career construction theory.

Counseling for Work and Relationships (Richardson)

The second emerging framework was articulated by Richardson (1993, 1996, 2009, 2012) as a paradigm shift for the field of vocational psychology, namely from the study of career development to a study of work in people's lives. She traced the evolutionary progression of the "false split" that has occurred between career and personal counseling, beginning with a "split" between normal and pathological personality functioning, leading to a further split in a consideration of aspects of the self into different domains of functioning, including the occupational domain, which led to the practice of vocational guidance and counseling. A further split then occurred by the shift of focus from "vocation" to "career," as the aspect of self connected to vocation was now situated outside of the self, in the structure of the occupational world. Discussion of "career" was defined less by self and more by occupational alternatives. As Juntunen (2006) paraphrased Richardson's position, "by focusing on career as an activity that is external to the person (because it is regulated by the occupational structure), we negate the central role of work in human experience" (Juntunen, 2006, p. 345).

Richardson (2012) has addressed the intersections of work and relationships, most recently describing the four major social contexts of market work, personal care work, personal relationships, and market work relationships. *Market work* is akin to the traditional view of work, defined as the work that people do for pay; Richardson's definition also includes work that people do within educational institutions to prepare for paid work. *Personal care work* is work done in one's personal (nonpaid work) life to care for oneself and others (including care for dependents, relationships, and communities). *Personal relationships* encompass interpersonal relationships outside of work, with family and friends, whereas *market work relationships* include relationships within the market work context, such as supervisors, colleagues, and teachers.

Richardson (2012) traced the two predominant paradigms within vocational psychology: *vocational choice*, as first articulated by Parsons (1909), and *career development*, as epitomized by Super. Both paradigms offered solutions to individuals' work preferences and societal labor market needs at specific times in history. First, Parsons' model "preserved the deeply ingrained individualism of American culture with its belief in free will while at the same time meeting the needs of the labor market during a time of industrial turmoil and economic hardship" (p. 195) and evolved into a scientific matching model that provided a structured mechanism for making a vocational choice. Second, Super's idea of *career* "fit the demands of the maturing industrial economy" (p. 196) and placed vocational choice within a larger developmental sequence, with stages that came before and after that choice.

These extant paradigms were not without limitations, despite their contemporary utility.

The vocational choice paradigm "masked the ways in which 'choice' was, in fact, very limited or even non-existent" for some individuals, who did not have the luxury of choosing among jobs or vocational paths (Richardson, 2012, p. 195). A focus on *choice* thus "perpetuates a belief in free will, that the individual is the master of his or her fate, and that any problems or limitations are the fault of that individual" (p. 196). The career development paradigm kept choice as a central concept and added a "verticality" component by emphasizing the upward progression of careers over time. The concept of "boundaryless" careers (Arthur & Rousseau, 1996) further highlighted the aspect of choice by focusing on individuals' ability to define their own careers regardless of organizational structures. "What is being masked is not only lack of choice but also the deteriorating conditions of market work" (Richardson, 2012, p. 197).

The limits of the extant paradigms are what lead to paradigm shifts; Richardson (2012) argued for a paradigm shift that would reflect and be responsive to changes in the nature of people's lives and in the nature of work. Her view that career counseling "has become overidentified with and trapped in the occupational structure" (Richardson, 1996, p. 356) led her to propose that the label of "career counseling" be retired, and to suggest an alternative label of "counseling/psychotherapy and work, jobs, and careers." More recently, she has discussed the practice of "counseling for work and relationship" as a mechanism for conceptualizing the interrelatedness. She described two central shifts in thinking: a shift from discourse about "career" to discourse about "work," and a shift of focus beyond the occupational domain to a broader consideration of multiple, interrelated social contexts (Richardson, 2009).

Previous scholars have addressed issues related to the complex intersection of work and nonwork roles in people's lives, building models of role spillover, role conflict, and role enhancement. However, the majority of this literature rests firmly in the camp of market work (Blustein, Medvide, & Kozan, 2012)—namely, from an industrial/organizational perspective—which may focus on organizations' perspectives and goals and overlook individuals' perspectives and goals.

Psychology of Working (Blustein)

An understanding of the objective and subjective nature of work and working has been informed by a number of disciplines, both within and outside of psychology. The psychology of working, as described by Blustein (2006, 2008, 2011), represents an expansion of the epistemological lens traditionally evident in vocational psychology, from the study of the psychology of *careers* to a psychology of *working*. "Career" has been defined as "the individually perceived sequence of attitudes and behaviors associated with work-related experiences and activities over the span of the person's life" (Hall, 1976, p. 4). As Blustein (2006, p. 3) noted, however, our concept of "career" is "deeply embedded in a sociocultural framework that is relevant to only a minority of individuals around the globe"—those characterized by status and achievement. A key feature of Blustein's perspective is explicit recognition that not all individuals have choice or volition related to work and careers; in fact, there is considerable variability in individuals' experiences regarding volition, and poor and working-class individuals may experience little choice regarding their working lives (Blustein & Fouad, 2008; Liu & Ali, 2008). "Working" is thus a more universal and inclusive term than "career."

FUNCTIONS OF WORK

Blustein's (2006) perspective focused on three fundamental human needs that are potentially fulfilled by working: need for survival, need for relatedness, and need for self-determination.

Need for Survival (and Power)

Need for survival is attained through work via the power gained through the exchange of work for money or for goods and services. Although this view of work is closely linked to the study of work by economists, Blustein (2006) argued that there are important psychological implications as well. Further, work as a means of fulfilling survival needs may also confer or enhance social status. Prestige, status, and power as functions of work, according to Blustein (2006), have been "woefully neglected in contemporary discussions of careers" (p. 22), although some scholars have included prestige in explaining occupational choice (such as Gottfredson, 2005).

The need for survival becomes increasingly evident in difficult economic times, as access to work becomes even more scarce and the impact of unemployment (and underemployment) on mental health becomes more pervasive (Goldsmith & Diette, 2012; Paul & Moser, 2009; Swanson, 2012). Richardson (2012) commented that the context of market work is one of radical change, but also of "deteriorating conditions"

(p. 193) such as erosion of wages, health insurance and pension benefits, increased income volatility and wage inequality, and poor labor conditions.

Need for Relatedness

Work also provides a means of social connection, both in terms of a link to the "broader social milieu" and in development of interpersonal relationships (Blustein, 2006). Further, the changes in the structure of work, noted earlier, alter the availability and nature of interpersonal relationships (Juntunen & Even, 2012) and warrant further research attention.

Need for Self-Determination

Finally, work provides a mechanism for achieving or implementing self-determination. Self-determination has been explicated in the work of Deci and Ryan (Deci & Ryan, 1985; Ryan & Deci, 2000), which describes the process by which activities that are extrinsically motivating are internalized. Blustein (2006) noted that self-determination offers a broader perspective than existing literature on job satisfaction, which may not capture the experience of poor or working-class individuals.

RELATIONAL THEORY OF WORKING

Blustein (2011) has further explicated the need-for-relatedness function of work into an expanded "relational theory of working." Based on this theory, Blustein outlined a series of research directions, including understanding the experiences of relationships and work, the role of relational support in choice and transitions, and the intersection of "care" or personal work and market work (Richardson, 1996, 2009; Schultheiss, 2006).

Summary

The "traditional" or foundational theories of vocational psychology and career development—represented by person–environment fit, developmental, and social cognitive perspectives—continue to provide useful predictions about vocational behavior as well as practical guidance to practitioners working with individuals seeking career assistance. However, sole reliance on these theories can no longer be justified, given economic and societal changes in the way that work is structured and experienced, and the growing recognition of individuals excluded from the theories' purview. The emerging perspectives of Blustein, Savickas, and Richardson offer great promise and warrant additional study. Moreover, the extent to which concepts from the foundational theories may be retained and integrated

with concepts from the emerging theories is an important avenue for theorists and researchers.

Such future expansion and integration of foundational and emerging theories would benefit from explicit attention to the assumptions noted by Fouad (2007), described at the beginning of this chapter. Identification of these assumptions underlying 20th-century notions of career development also leads to consideration of each assumption's converse—namely, the lack of volition in making work choices, the important connections of work to other arenas of individuals' lives, the unpredictability of the world of work, the multiple career- and work-related decisions an individual will make throughout life, and a revisioning of career counseling as broader and more integrative—which will guide theorists, researchers, and practitioners as they adapt to 21st-century realities of work.

References

Arthur, M. B., & Rousseau, D. (Eds.). (1996). *The boundaryless career*. Oxford, UK: Oxford University Press.

Bandura, A. (1986). *Social foundations of thought and action*. Englewood Cliffs, NJ: Prentice Hall.

Betz, N. E. (2008). Advances in vocational theories. In S. D. Brown & R. W. Lent (Eds.), *Handbook of counseling psychology* (4th ed., pp. 357–374). New York: Wiley.

Blanchard, C. A., & Lichtenberg, J. W. (2003). Compromise in career decision making: A test of Gottfredson's theory. *Journal of Vocational Behavior, 62*, 250–271.

Blustein, D. L. (2006). *The psychology of working: A new perspective for career development, counseling, and public policy*. Mahwah, NJ: Erlbaum.

Blustein, D. L. (2008). The role of work in psychological health and well-being. *American Psychologist, 63*, 228–240.

Blustein, D. L. (2011). A relational theory of working. *Journal of Vocational Behavior, 79*, 1–17.

Blustein, D. L., & Fouad, N. A. (2008). Changing face of vocational psychology: The transforming world of work. In W. B. Walsh (Ed.), *Biennial review of counseling psychology* (pp. 129–155). New York: Routledge/Taylor & Francis.

Blustein, D. L., Medvide, M. B., & Kozan, S. (2012). A tour of a new paradigm: Relationships and work. *Counseling Psychologist, 40*(2), 243–254.

Blustein, D. L., & Spengler, P. M. (1995). Personal adjustment: Career counseling and psychotherapy. In W. B. Walsh & S. H. Osipow (Eds.), *Handbook of vocational psychology* (2nd ed.). Mahwah, NJ: Lawrence Erlbaum.

Bobek, B. L., & Robbins, S. B. (2005). Counseling for career transition: Career pathing, job loss, and reentry. In S. D. Brown & R. W. Lent (Eds.), *Career development and counseling: Putting theory and research to work* (pp. 625–650). New York: Wiley.

Bordin, E. S. (1979). The generalizability of the psychoanalytic concept of the working alliance. *Psychotherapy: Theory, Research and Practice, 16*, 253–260.

Brown, S. D., & Krane, N. R. (2000). Four (or five) sessions and a cloud of dust: Old assumptions and new observations about career counseling. In S. D. Brown & R. W. Lent (Eds.), *Handbook of counseling psychology* (3rd ed., pp. 740–766). New York: Wiley.

Chartrand, J. M. (1991). The evolution of trait-and-factor career counseling: A person × environment fit approach. *Journal of Counseling and Development, 69*, 518–524.

Crites, J. O. (1981). *Career counseling: Models, methods, and materials.* New York: McGraw-Hill.

Dawis, R. V. (1992). The individual differences tradition in counseling psychology. *Journal of Counseling Psychology, 39*, 7–19.

Dawis, R. V. (2002). Person-environment correspondence theory. In D. Brown & Associates (Eds.), *Career choice and development* (4th ed., pp. 427–464). San Francisco: Jossey-Bass.

Dawis, R. V. (2005). The Minnesota theory of work adjustment. In S. D. Brown & R. W. Lent (Eds.), *Career development and counseling: Putting theory and research to work* (pp. 3–23). New York: Wiley.

Dawis, R. V., & Lofquist, L. H. (1984). *A psychological theory of work adjustment.* Minneapolis: University of Minnesota Press.

DeBell, C. (2001). Ninety years in the world of work in America. *Career Development Quarterly, 50*, 77–88.

DeBell, C. (2006). What all applied psychologists should know about work. *Professional Psychology: Research and Practice, 37*, 325–333.

Deci, E. L., & Ryan, R. M. (1985). *Intrinsic motivation and self-determination in human behavior.* New York: Plenum.

Eggerth, D. E. (2008). From Theory of Work Adjustment to Person-Environment Correspondence counseling: Vocational psychology as positive psychology. *Journal of Career Assessment, 16*(1), 60–74.

Fassinger, R. E. (2005). Theoretical issues in the study of women's career development: Building bridges in a brave new world. In W. B. Walsh & M. L. Savickas (Eds.), *Handbook of vocational psychology: Theory, research, and practice* (3rd ed., pp. 84–124). Mahwah, NJ: Lawrence Erlbaum.

Fouad, N. A. (2007). Work and vocational psychology: Theory, research and practice. *Annual Review of Psychology, 58*, 543–564.

Fouad, N. A., & Bingham, R. P. (1995). Career counseling with racial and ethnic minorities. In W. B. Walsh & S. H. Osipow (Eds.), *Handbook of vocational psychology: Theory, research, and practice* (2nd ed., pp. 331–365). Hillsdale, NJ: Lawrence Erlbaum.

Fouad, N. A., & Bynner, J. (2008). Work transitions. *American Psychologist, 63*, 241–251.

Gelso, C. J., Prince, J., Cornfeld, J. L., Payne, A. B., Royalty, G., & Wiley, M. O. (1985). Quality of counselors' intake evaluations for clients with problems that are primarily vocational versus personal. *Journal of Counseling Psychology, 32*, 339–347.

Gergen, K. J. (1999). Agency: Social construction and relational action. *Theory & Psychology, 9*(1), 113–115. doi:10.1177/0959354399091007

Goldstein, A., & Diette, T. (2012). Exploring the link between unemployment and mental health outcomes. Retrieved from http://www.apa.org/pi/ses/resources/indicator/2012/04/unemployment.aspx, April 28, 2012.

Gottfredson, L. S. (1996). A theory of circumscription and compromise. In D. Brown & L. Brooks (Eds.), *Career choice and development: Applying contemporary theories to practice* (3rd ed., pp. 179–232). San Francisco: Jossey-Bass.

Gottfredson, L. S. (2005). Applying Gottfredson's theory of circumscription and compromise in career guidance and counseling. In S. D. Brown & R. W. Lent (Eds.), *Career development and counseling: Putting theory and research to work* (pp. 71–100). Hoboken, NJ: Wiley.

Gysbers, N. C., Heppner, M. J., & Johnston, J. A. (2003). *Career counseling: Process, issues, and techniques* (2nd ed.). Boston: Allyn & Bacon.

Hackett, G., & Betz, N. E. (1981). A self-efficacy approach to the career development of women. *Journal of Vocational Behavior, 18*, 326–339.

Hall, D. T. (1976). *Careers in organizations.* Pacific Palisades, CA: Goodyear.

Hall, D. T. (1996). *The career is dead—Long live the career.* San Francisco, CA: Jossey-Bass.

Haverkamp, B. E., & Moore, D. (1993). The career-personal dichotomy: Perceptual reality, practical illusion, and workplace integration. *Career Development Quarterly, 42*, 154–160.

Heppner, M. J., & Davidson, M. M. (2002). Be careful what we wish for: The integration of career psychology. *Counseling Psychologist, 30*, 878–884.

Heppner, M. J., O'Brien, K. M., Hinkelman, J. M., & Flores, L. Y. (1996). Training counseling psychologists in career development: Are we our own worst enemies? *Counseling Psychologist, 24*, 105–125.

Hochschild, A. R. (1989). *The second shift: Working parents and the revolution at home.* New York: Viking Penguin

Holland, J. L. (1959). A theory of vocational choice. *Journal of Counseling Psychology, 6*, 35–45.

Holland, J. L. (1997). *Making vocational choices: A theory of vocational personalities and work environments* (3rd ed.). Odessa, FL: PAR.

Isaacson, L. E., & Brown, D. (1993). Career information, career counseling, and career development (5th ed., pp. 379–386). Boston, MA: Allyn & Bacon.

Juntunen, C. L. (2006). The psychology of working: The clinical context. *Professional Psychology: Research and Practice, 37*, 342–350.

Juntunen, C. L., & Even, C. E. (2012). Theories of vocational psychology. In N. A. Fouad, J. A. Carter, & L. M. Subich (Eds.), *APA handbook of counseling psychology.* Washington, DC: American Psychological Association.

Kuhn, T. S. (1962). *The structure of scientific revolutions.* Chicago: University of Chicago Press.

Lent, R. W. (2005). A social cognitive view of career development and counseling. In S. D. Brown & R. W. Lent (Eds.), *Career development and counseling: Putting theory and research to work* (pp. 101–130). Hoboken, NJ: Wiley.

Lent, R. W. (2008). Understanding and promoting work satisfaction: An integrative review. In S. D. Brown & R. W. Lent (Eds.), *Handbook of counseling psychology* (4th ed., pp. 462–480). New York: Wiley.

Lent, R. W., & Brown, S. D. (2006). Integrating person and situation perspectives on work satisfaction: A social-cognitive view. *Journal of Vocational Behavior, 69*(2), 236–247.

Lent, R. W., Brown, S. D., & Hackett, G. (1994). Toward a unifying social cognitive theory of career and academic interest, choice, and performance. *Journal of Vocational Behavior, 45*, 79–122.

Lent, R. W., Brown, S. D., & Hackett, G. (2000). Contextual supports and barriers to career choice: A social cognitive analysis. *Journal of Counseling Psychology, 31*, 356–362.

Lent, R. W., Brown, S. D., & Hackett. G. (2002). Social cognitive career theory. In D. Brown (Eds.), *Career choice and development* (4th ed., pp. 255–311). San Francisco: Jossey-Bass.

Liu, W. M., & Ali, S. R. (2008). Social class and classism: Understanding the psychological impact of poverty and inequality. In S. D. Brown & R. W. Lent (Eds.), *Handbook of counseling psychology* (4th ed., pp. 159–175). New York: Wiley.

Lofquist, L. H., & Dawis, R.V. (1991). *Essentials of person-environment correspondence counseling*. Minneapolis: University of Minnesota Press.

Ludwikowski, W. M. A., Vogel, D., & Armstrong, P. I. (2009). Attitudes toward career counseling: The role of public and self-stigma. *Journal of Counseling Psychology, 56*(3), 408–416.

Magee, I. M., & Whiston, S. C. (2010). Casting no shadow: Assessing vocational overshadowing. *Journal of Career Assessment, 18, 239–249.*

McAdams, D. P., & Olson, B. D. (2010). Personality development: Continuity and change over the life course. *Annual Review of Psychology, 61,* 517–542.

Nauta, M. M. (2013). Holland's theory. In S. D. Brown & R. W. Lent (Eds.), *Career development and counseling handbook: Putting theory and research to work* (2nd ed). New York: Wiley.

Niles, S. G. (2001). Using Super's career development assessment and counselling (C-DAC) model to link theory to practice. *International Journal for Educational and Vocational Guidance, 1,* 131–139.

Niles, S. G., Herr, E. L., & Hartung, P. J. (2002). Adult career concerns in contemporary society. In S. G. Niles (Ed.), *Adult career development: Concepts, issues and practices* (3rd ed., pp. 2–18). Columbus, OH: National Career Development Association.

Osipow, S. H. (1996). Does career theory guide practice or does career practice guide theory? In M. L. Savickas & W. B. Walsh (Eds.), *Handbook of career counseling theory and practice* (pp. 403–409). Palo Alto, CA: Davies-Black.

Parsons, F. (1909). *Choosing a vocation.* Garrett Park, MD: Garrett Park Press. (Reissued in 1989).

Paul, K. I., & Moser, K. (2009). Unemployment impairs mental health: Meta-analyses. *Journal of Vocational Behavior, 74*(3), 264–282.

Peterson, G. W., Sampson, J. P., & Reardon, R. C. (1991). *Career development and services: A cognitive approach.* Pacific Grove, CA: Brooks/Cole.

Phillips, S. D., & Jome, L. M. (2005). Vocational choices: What do we know? What do we need to know? In W. B. Walsh & M. L. Savickas (Eds.), *Handbook of vocational psychology* (3rd ed., pp. 127–153). Mahwah, NJ: Lawrence Erlbaum.

Reed, J. R., Patton, M. J., & Gold, P. B. (1993). Effects of turn-taking sequences in vocational test interpretation interviews. *Journal of Counseling Psychology, 40,* 144–155.

Richardson, M. S. (1993). Work in people's lives: A location for counseling psychologists. *Journal of Counseling Psychology, 40,* 425–433.

Richardson, M. S. (1996). From career counseling to counseling/psychotherapy and work, jobs, and career. In M. L. Savickas & W. B. Walsh (Eds.), *Handbook of career counseling theory and practice* (pp. 347–360). Palo Alto, CA: Davies-Black.

Richardson, M. S. (2009). Another way to think about the work we do: Counselling for work and relationship. *International Journal for Educational and Vocational Guidance, 9*(2), 75–84.

Richardson, M. S. (2012). Counseling for work and relationship. *Counseling Psychologist, 40*(2), 190–242.

Richardson, M. S., Constantine, K., & Washburn, M. (2005). New directions for theory development in vocational psychology. In W. B. Walsh & M. L. Savickas (Eds.), *Handbook of vocational psychology* (3rd ed., pp. 51–84). Mahwah, NJ: Lawrence Erlbaum.

Robitschek, C., & DeBell, C. (2002). The reintegration of vocational psychology and counseling psychology: Training issues for a paradigm shift. *Counseling Psychologist, 30,* 801–814.

Rounds, J. B., & Tracey, T. J. (1990). From trait-and-factor to person-environment fit counseling: Theory and process. In W. B. Walsh & S. H. Osipow (Eds.), *Career counseling: Contemporary topics in vocational psychology* (pp. 1–44). Hillsdale, NJ: Lawrence Erlbaum.

Ryan, R. M., & Deci, E. L. (2000). Self-determination theory and the facilitation of intrinsic motivation, social development and well-being. *American Psychologist, 55,* 68–78.

Savickas, M. L. (1997). Career adaptability: An integrative construct for life-span, life-space theory. *Career Development Quarterly, 45,* 247–259.

Savickas, M. L. (2002). Reinvigorating the study of careers. *Journal of Vocational Behavior, 62,* 381–385. doi:10.1006/jvbe.2002.1880

Savickas, M. L. (2005). The theory and practice of career construction. In S. D. Brown & R. W. Lent (Eds.), *Career development and counseling: Putting theory and research to work* (pp. 42–70). New York: Wiley.

Savickas, M. L. (2011). *Career counseling.* Washington, DC: American Psychological Association.

Savickas, M. L. (2012). Life design: A paradigm for career intervention in the 21st century. *Journal of Counseling and Development, 90,* 13–19.

Savickas, M. L. (2013). Career construction theory and practice. In S. D. Brown & R. W. Lent (Eds.), *Career development and counseling handbook: Putting theory and research to work* (2nd ed). New York: Wiley.

Savickas, M. L., & Lent, R. W. (1994). *Convergence in theories of career development: Implications for science and practice.* Palo Alto, CA: Consulting Psychologists Press.

Savickas, M. L., Nota, L., Rossier, J., Dauwalder, J., Duarte, M. E., Guichard, J., et al. (2009). Life designing: A paradigm for career construction in the 21st century. *Journal of Vocational Behavior, 75,* 239–250.

Schultheiss, D. E. P. (2006). The interface of work and family life. *Professional Psychology: Research and Practice, 37,* 334–341.

Spengler, P. M. (2000). Does vocational overshadowing even exist? A test of the robustness of the vocational overshadowing bias. *Journal of Counseling Psychology, 47,* 342–351.

Spengler, P. M., Blustein, D. L., & Strohmer, D. C. (1990). Diagnostic and treatment overshadowing of vocational problems by personal problems. *Journal of Counseling Psychology, 37,* 372–381.

Spokane, A. R. (1991). *Career intervention.* Englewood Cliffs, NJ: Prentice Hall.

Spokane, A. R. (1996). Holland's theory. In D. Brown, L. Brooks, & Associates (Eds.), *Career choice and development* (3rd ed., pp. 33–74). San Francisco: Jossey-Bass.

Subich, L. M., & Simonson, K. (2001). Career counseling: The evolution of theory. In F. T. L. Leong & A. Barak (Eds.), *Contemporary models in vocational psychology* (pp. 257–278). Mahwah, NJ: Erlbaum.

Super, D. E., & Knasel, E. G. (1981). Career development in adulthood: Some theoretical problems and a possible solution. *British Journal of Guidance & Counselling, 9*, 194–201.

Super, D. E., Osborne, W. L., Walsh, D. J., & Brown, S. D. (1992). Developmental career assessment and counseling: The C-DAC model. *Journal of Counseling & Development, 71*(1), 74–80.

Super, D. E., Savickas, M. L., & Super, C. M. (1996). The life-span, life-space approach to careers. In D. Brown, L. Brooks, & Associates (Eds.), *Career choice and development* (3rd ed., pp. 121–178). San Francisco: Jossey-Bass.

Swanson, J. L. (1995). The process and outcome of career counseling. In W. B. Walsh & S. H. Osipow (Eds.), *Handbook of vocational psychology* (2nd ed., pp. 217–259). Mahwah, NJ: Lawrence Erlbaum.

Swanson, J. L. (1996). The theory *is* the practice: Trait-and-factor/person-environment fit counseling. In M. L. Savickas & W. B. Walsh (Eds.), *Handbook of career counseling theory and practice* (pp. 93–108). Palo Alto: Davies-Black.

Swanson, J. L. (2002). Understanding the complexity of clients' lives: Infusing a truly integrative career-personal perspective into graduate training. *Counseling Psychologist, 30*, 815–832.

Swanson, J. L. (2012). Work and psychological health. In N. A. Fouad, J. A. Carter, & L. M. Subich (Eds.), *APA handbook of counseling psychology*. Washington, DC: American Psychological Association.

Swanson, J. L., & Chu, S. P. (2000). Applications of person-environment psychology to the career development and vocational behavior of adolescents and adults. In M. E. Martin Jr., & J. L. Swartz-Kulstad (Eds.), *Person-environment psychology and mental health: Assessment and intervention* (pp. 143–168). Mahwah, NJ: Lawrence Erlbaum.

Swanson, J. L., & Fouad, N. A. (2010). *Career theory and practice: Learning through case studies* (2nd ed.). Thousand Oaks, CA: Sage.

Swanson, J. L., & Gore, P. A. (2000). Advances in vocational psychology theory and research. In *Handbook of counseling psychology (3rd ed.,* pp. 233–269). Hoboken, NJ: Wiley.

Swanson, J. L., & Schneider, M. (2013). Minnesota theory of work adjustment. In S. D. Brown & R. W. Lent (Eds.), *Career development and counseling handbook: Putting theory and research to work* (2nd ed). New York: Wiley.

Trochim, W. M. (n.d.). *The research methods knowledge base* (2nd ed.). Retrieved from http://www.socialresearchmethods.net/kb/ (version current as of October 20, 2006).

Walsh, W. B., Price, R. H., & Craik, K. H. (1992). Person-environment psychology: An introduction. In W. B. Walsh, K. H. Craik, & R. H. Price (Eds.), *Person-environment psychology: Models and perspectives* (pp. vii–xi). Mahwah, NJ: Lawrence Erlbaum.

Whiteley, J. M. (1984). Counseling psychology: A historical perspective. *Counseling Psychologist, 12*, 3–109.

Whiston, S. C., & Rahardja, D. (2008). Vocational counseling process and outcome. In S. D. Brown & R. W. Lent (Eds.), *Handbook of counseling psychology* (4th ed., pp. 444–461). New York: Wiley.

Yost, E. B., & Corbishley, M. A. (1987). *Career counseling: A psychological approach*. San Francisco, CA: Jossey-Bass.

Young, R. A., & Collin, A. (2004). Introduction: Constructivism and social constructionism in the career field. *Journal of Vocational Behavior, 64*, 373–388.

Zytowski, D. G. (2001). Frank Parsons and the Progressive Movement. *Career Development Quarterly, 50*, 57–65.

PART 2

The Context of Working

Race and Working

Lisa Y. Flores

Abstract

The world of work has been one of the key contexts for the manifestation of the pernicious impact of racism. Using a multicultural and psychology of working perspective, this chapter reviews literature across various disciplines on the work experiences of people of color to illuminate their career narratives. The effects of racism on work disparities, psychological and physical health, occupational health, job satisfaction, and other work-related outcomes among workers of color in the United States are explored. In addition, research that has applied cultural and race-based frameworks to understanding the effects of culture on work-related variables among people of color is reviewed. Finally, research with people of color that has addressed the psychology of work's three functions of work—work for survival and power, work for social connection, and work for self-determination—is highlighted. Recommendations regarding future vocational research, practice, and policies that can assist people of color in their journey toward seeking work that fulfills their individual needs are provided.

Key Words: work, career, work discrimination, Latino, Hispanic, African American, Asian American, Native American, racism, people of color

When the practice of career counseling originated in the early 1900s, this marked a major period in the country's history as it transitioned from an agricultural to an industrial society (Pope, 2000; Zytowski, 2001). This period was characterized by the development of new technologies, increasing demand for industry workers, shifting migration to urban settings, and increasing numbers of immigrants moving to the United States. Together, these societal shifts spurred Frank Parsons' work with marginalized groups and gave rise to the practice and study of vocational guidance and counseling (Blustein, 2006; O'Brien, 2001; Zytowski, 2001). Thus, vocational psychology's roots are deeply embedded in social justice and advocacy work with marginalized groups such as the poor, immigrants, and youth.

We live in a much different era today. Much has changed in the labor market over the past 100 years; however, the oppression and social inequalities that were clearly present during Parsons' times continue to be a defining characteristic of our society today (DeBell, 2001). The United States is perceived to be a country of opportunity and wealth, yet a significant portion of people in the United States—many of whom are people of color—live in poverty, struggle to gain access to quality health care, education, and dignified work, and experience institutional barriers that prevent them from achieving their life goals. Scholars have argued that vocational theories, research, and practice are largely geared toward a small, privileged segment of society: middle-class, educated, white-collar workers (Blustein, 2006; Richardson, 1993). Moreover, middle-class cultural values (i.e., individualism, affluence) and beliefs (i.e., open opportunity structure, myth of meritocracy) are reflected in contemporary vocational theories and practice. For these reasons, Blustein (2006) has criticized the field for its almost exclusive focus on those who experience some privilege in selecting careers while overlooking the vocational experiences of members from marginalized groups who do not have access to resources that are vital to developing economic capital, who do not experience a great deal of volition in the world of work, and who are employed in nonprofessional occupations. This chapter focuses on the career narratives of a group of workers whose experiences in the labor force are affected by racism: people of color.

The appraisals by Blustein (2006) and Richardson (1993) of the field are substantiated by empirical data that finds that the existing career counseling and vocational psychology knowledge base regarding the career development of people of color is limited (Byars & McCubbin, 2001; Flores et al., 2006). A recent analysis of career development articles published in the leading U.S. vocational journals from 1969 to 2004 reported that 6.7% (n = 281) of all articles in this period were related to the career development of diverse racial and ethnic groups in the United States (Flores et al., 2006). To date, most of our knowledge about career and work experience is based on studies conducted on White, middle-class individuals. Advancements in the empirical literature are needed with culturally diverse samples to assist in the development of culturally relevant theories and models and culturally effective work interventions for a broad range of individuals in our society.

Work consumes a significant portion of the day-to-day lives of adults and plays a vital role in psychological health (Blustein, 2008). However, for many U.S. racial minorities, it also serves as a central context for the manifestation of racism. Consequently, vocational psychologists and other mental health professionals need to carefully understand the context of work for members of diverse racial groups in order to better meet their psychological and vocational needs. Accordingly, the goal of this chapter is to address the impact of racism on the vocational lives of racially diverse workers in the United States. Using multicultural and psychology-of-working perspectives, this chapter will incorporate research across various disciplines, including psychology, sociology, economics, human resources, and medicine, to better understand the career narratives and work experiences of people of color in the United States. First, I provide an overview of demographic shifts that are occurring in the United States and highlight the educational and work patterns of people of color in the United States. Second, I address how race affects the work-related experiences of racially diverse workers and review research that has examined outcomes of racism in the workplace. Third, I provide an overview of cultural theories that may be fruitful in explaining the work trajectories of people of color and summarize key empirical studies that have incorporated these cultural variables in examinations of work. Fourth, I provide a synopsis of research on workers of color that illuminates the three main work-related needs that serve as the framework for Blustein's (2001, 2006) psychology of working: work for survival, relatedness, and self-determination. Finally, I offer recommendations regarding future research, practice, and policy to assist people of color in their journey toward seeking work that meets their individual needs.

Overview of U.S. Demographics, Educational, and Work Statistics
Defining Terms

It is important to clarify and discuss the terminology that I will be using to address the key racial groups of interest in this chapter. In this chapter, race is understood to be socially constructed and defined within the context of a particular society (Helms, 1990). Social definitions of race often encompass the shared experiences of a group such as common histories, physical characteristics, relationship patterns, beliefs, behaviors, and sociopolitical and economic conditions. In the United States, five major racial groups have been constructed: Native American, Asian American, Black/African American, Latino American, and White American. For the purposes of this chapter, the terms "racial groups," "racially diverse groups," "racial minorities," and "people of color" will be used interchangeably to reference Native American, Asian American, Black/African American, and Latino American workers collectively. Because White Americans experience a range of race-related privileges as members of this group (see Neville, Worthington, & Spanierman, 2001), they are not referenced in this chapter. It is important to acknowledge, however, that White Americans can experience oppression in other forms in the workplace (e.g., sexism, homophobia, classism), and these workers' experiences in the labor force will be highlighted in other chapters.

Demographic Patterns

The demographic landscape in the United States has dramatically changed since the foundation was laid for what would later emerge as vocational psychology. Today, the U.S. population includes over 300 million people (U.S. Census Bureau, 2009), 35% of whom are members of racially diverse groups. Across the racial minority groups, 15.8% are Latino American, 12.4% are African American, 4.6% are Asian American/Pacific Islanders, 0.8% are Native American/American Indian, and 2.6% are multiracial. As the demographic makeup of our society continues to shift and becomes increasingly multicultural, it is imperative that vocational psychologists and other mental health workers are knowledgeable of the professional obligations to provide effective services to racially diverse individuals. The following census statistics illuminate the changing demography in the United States:

- In upcoming decades, the proportion of Whites in the population is expected to decrease in size, while the proportion of other racial groups is projected to grow. Latino Americans and Asian Americans, the fastest-growing groups in the United States, are estimated to represent 30.2% and 8.1% of the population in 2050, respectively (Ortman & Guarneri, 2009). By 2045, it is projected that collectively people of color will constitute the majority population in the United States (Ortman & Guarneri, 2009).

- Social class is intricately linked to race in the United States. That is, the economic inequalities that exist are racialized; a disproportionate number of African Americans, Latinos, and Native Americans are poor, while a disproportionate number of Whites are among the financially elite (Lui, Robles, Leondar-Wright, Brewer, & Adamson, 2006). The poverty rates among African Americans, Latinos, and Native Americans were 22.4%, 20.8%, and 22.7%, respectively (U.S. Census Bureau, 2009). In addition, African Americans have the lowest median household income ($33,463) among all racial groups, followed by Native Americans at $35,381 and Latinos at $39,923 (U.S. Census Bureau, 2009).

Educational and Labor Force Statistics

These current population demographics are mirrored in our social institutions, specifically our educational and work settings. Overall, the National Center for Educational Statistics (Hussar & Bailey, 2009) reports that educational enrollment rates are expected to increase in the next several years across elementary, secondary, and postsecondary levels. However, this trend is more prominent among students of color than White students. Between 2007 and 2018, the enrollment of White college students is projected to increase 4%. In comparison, the number of students of color enrolling in colleges and universities will increase significantly, ranging from a low of 26% among African Americans to a high of 38% for Latinos (Hussar & Bailey, 2009).

Also reflected in our educational and work institutions are disparities in achievement and success that are rooted in race-based discrimination. Although gains have been reported in the number of degrees earned across diverse racial groups since 1997, marked disparities continue to exist in educational completion and dropout rates across racial groups. For example, Whites are more likely than African Americans and Latino Americans to complete high school (90.4% vs. 81.4% and 60.9%) and college (31.1% vs. 17.6% and 12.6%; U.S. Bureau of the Census, 2009), and Black and Latino students drop out of high school at higher rates than White students (Chapman, Laird, & KewalRamani, 2010). In addition, several math- and science-related academic majors, or STEM majors (e.g., architecture, engineering, math and statistics, physical sciences and science technologies)—disciplines that are considered highly lucrative—are dominated by White students. In 2008, the percentage of degrees conferred to Whites in STEM areas was unusually high (close to 70% or higher; Hussar & Bailey, 2009). These well-documented academic gaps need to be reduced as they have direct implications on one's eventual work opportunities, socioeconomic standing, and earning potential.

The labor force growth rate is on the rise and is expected to increase faster for people of color than Whites (U.S. Bureau of Labor Statistics, 2008), with the Latino labor force growing at a faster rate than any other group. While people of color are an important and growing segment of the U.S. labor force, data indicate that they tend to be segregated into certain jobs and significant disparities exist in employment status and earnings. Black and Latino Americans were less likely to be employed in managerial, professional, and related occupations and had lower earnings than Whites and Asians (U.S. Bureau of Labor Statistics, 2010). Further, Blacks (14.8%) and Latinos (12.1%) experienced higher rates of unemployment than Whites (8.5%) and Asians (7.3%) in 2009, even after controlling for educational attainment (U.S. Bureau of Labor Statistics, 2010).

To help people of color better integrate and succeed in schools and workplaces, it is critical that vocational psychologists attend to their experiences in these settings to get a better understanding of their career narratives and the struggles they may encounter. In the next section, I highlight the effects of racism on the work experiences of U.S. racial minorities.

Working and Racism

Collectively, African Americans, Latinos, Asian Americans, and Native Americans have endured a long and painful history in the U.S. labor force. Whether by force or choice, people of color have worked in a U.S. labor system that has exploited their work and inflicted unimaginable human rights violations. These harsh conditions can be found today in the form of sweatshops, indentured servitude, and other violations of labor laws.

Work is situated in a racial and cultural context, and as such, race plays an important role in the work experiences and opportunities of people of color. According to the U.S. Equal Employment Opportunity Commission (2011), race-related discrimination occurs when an employee (or prospective employee) is treated unfavorably because of his or her race or characteristics related to his or her race. This type of discrimination can take a variety of forms that lead to unfair work environments (e.g., unfair recruiting, hiring, and promotion practices, discrimination in compensation and other benefits), harassment (e.g., offensive remarks, ethnic jokes, racial slurs), and employment policies or practices that negatively affect a group of workers.

Today, racism has created a schism in the world of work whereby racial differences are reflected in employment, unemployment, and underemployment rates, representation in low-skilled versus high-skilled jobs, access to resources necessary for accumulating economic capitals, and employment in positions that offer upward mobility and job security. Sociological explanations of labor force inequalities between Whites and other racial groups include the persistent inequality perspective and the cohort explanation perspective (Maume, 2004). The persistent inequality perspective suggests that the institutional, discriminatory barriers in the labor market that people of color encounter persist over their lifetime and contribute to these differences. On the other hand, the cohort perspective holds that employment disparities are the result of generational differences and social forces and policies that affect generations of workers differently. The latter perspective suggests that younger cohorts do not face the same discriminatory behaviors that older cohorts have, and as such, experience a more equitable and open labor market. Further, Baumle and Fosset (2005) contend that while traditional forms of discrimination may not be evident, employers may be engaging in "statistical discrimination," or behaviors that are not rooted in prejudice but are motivated by inferences or generalizations about productivity for groups of workers. Thus, racism can be direct or indirect, or can be embedded in other practices that are considered to be acceptable workplace behaviors.

Researchers have noted that most people believe that bias against racially diverse workers is declining in the workplace as a result of the Civil Rights Movement in the 1960s and the equal opportunity laws and policies that have been implemented since that time (Baumle & Fosset, 2005). However, data consistently indicate that Latino/as and African Americans earn less than their White counterparts (U.S. Bureau of Labor Statistics, 2010). Progress has been made in narrowing the educational and work inequalities experienced by people of color; however, persistent gaps indicate that people of color have not reached parity with their White counterparts. These disparities are consistent when other personal (e.g., gender, educational attainment, generational) and work-related (e.g., work experience) factors are controlled, providing support for the persistent inequality perspective. For example, when compared to White workers, Black and Latino workers experienced persistent and growing wage disparities over time (Alon & Haberfeld, 2007; Browne & Askew, 2005; Maume, 2004). Maume (2004) found that the earning gap was smaller, but still present, among younger cohorts compared to older cohorts, but this gap became stronger over time. In a comparison of labor force participation and earning differences across groups of female workers during the high school-to-work transition, White women had higher starting salaries than Black women and Latinas (Alon & Haberfeld, 2007). This gap persisted over time, but it was more pronounced among those without a college degree. Similarly, White women had higher initial employment rates than their Black and Latina counterparts that also persisted over time, and this gap was more pronounced among those with lower levels of education. These findings highlight that the prominent wage and employment gaps are particularly prominent among Black and Latina women with lower levels of education, the workers who are likely to be employed in low-skilled occupations.

Color discrimination is also a reality that darker-skinned workers encounter in the labor force. Findings from a national database of immigrants indicated that immigrants with lighter skin color earned significantly more than those with darker skin color (Hersch, 2008), and these differences were replicated for their spouses after controlling for a variety of demographic characteristics (e.g., years of residence, education, language proficiency, race, country of origin) and other work-related characteristics (Hersch, 2011). Moreover, Hersch (2011) found that these effects do not decrease over time.

In addition to disparities in employment and earnings, racially diverse workers are more likely to report experiences of racial discrimination at work than their White peers (Krieger et al., 2008; Raver & Nishii, 2010; Shannon, Rospenda, Richman, & Minich, 2009), with Black workers reporting more work discrimination and higher levels of job threat than other groups (Shannon et al., 2009). Other researchers reported that the ethnic harassment experiences of Latinos in the workplace primarily involved verbal ethnic harassment in the form of ethnic slurs, derogatory ethnic comments, or ethnic jokes (Schneider, Hitlan, & Radhakrishnan, 2000).

As members of two oppressed groups, women of color are especially susceptible to workplace harassment in the forms of both racial and gender discrimination. This "double jeopardy" hypothesis has been supported in separate studies that found that women of color reported high levels of sexual and racial harassment in the workplace (Berdahl & Moore, 2006; Gomez et al., 2001; Krieger et al., 2008; Richie et al., 1997). Buchanan and Fitzgerald (2008) found that both sexual and racial harassment interacted to effect supervisor satisfaction and perceived organizational tolerance for harassment. Specifically, in comparison to other interaction combinations, those women who had (a) higher levels of racial harassment (regardless of sexual harassment level) and (b) lower levels of racial harassment and higher levels of sexual harassment also reported higher dissatisfaction with supervisors and perceptions that their work organization was tolerant of harassment. The effects of "double jeopardy" were not substantiated in other studies that reported that harassment in one area was sufficient in predicting low organizational commitment, job dissatisfaction, and high turnover intentions, and that a second form of harassment did not have additive effects on these work outcomes (Raver & Nishii, 2010). This was replicated in a qualitative study of prominent Black women whose reports of the effects of racism

and sexism in the workplace were similar to the outcomes of White women who experienced sexism only (Richie et al., 1997). These researchers found that both groups of women used similar coping mechanisms for dealing with sexism and racism in the workplace, which provides some support for the belief that experience with harassment in one area might elicit coping behaviors that help to buffer the effects of harassment in another area.

Psychological and Physical Health

Race-based work stressors can have a negative effect on the health and well-being of our racially diverse workforce. Indeed, the deleterious effects of racism on the psychological and physical health of people of color have been well documented. Studies with racially diverse samples indicated that racial discrimination was a significant predictor of self-reported psychiatric symptoms (Klonoff, Landrine, & Ullman, 1999), psychological distress and cigarette smoking (Krieger, Smith, Naishadham, Hartman, & Barbeau 2005), posttraumatic stress symptoms (Flores, Tschann, Dimas, Pasch, & de Groat, 2010), hypertension (Din-Dzietham, Nembhard, Collins, & Davis, 2004), stress, suicidal ideation, anxiety, and depression (Hwang & Goto, 2009), and overall psychological well-being (Schneider et al., 2000). In a sample of female African American employees, racial harassment had significant effects on these women's generalized job stress, supervisor and coworker satisfaction, organizational tolerance for harassment, and posttraumatic stress symptoms (Buchanan & Fitzgerald, 2008). A recent meta-analysis of 134 studies found that perceived discrimination had a negative effect on both mental and physical health outcomes (Pascoe & Richman, 2009). Specifically, these researchers reported effects of −.20 and .13 (weighted for sample size) between perceived discrimination and negative mental health outcomes across 110 studies and negative physical health across 36 studies, respectively. Ethnicity and gender did not moderate the relation between perceived discrimination, and mental health and gender did not moderate the effect between perceived discrimination and physical health, meaning that the effects were consistent when compared across groups.

Occupational Health

Another form in which race plays a role in the work lives of people of color is through segregation in jobs in which occupational health risks among workers are especially high. According to the National Institute for Occupational Safety and Health (2009), people of color in the United States are more likely to be employed as low-wage workers, to be employed in low-skilled jobs, and to experience fatal work injuries and diseases than Whites. This occupational segregation among people of color has lead to the coining of the term "brown-collar jobs" to describe their overrepresentation in low-paying, stressful, and demanding jobs (Catanzarite, 2002). Krieger and colleagues (2008) found that a sample of low-income Black and Latino workers reported high exposure to dangerous occupational conditions. Racial discrimination was positively related to workplace abuse among a sample of low-income Black and Latino men and women (Krieger et al., 2008) and to exposure to occupational hazards among a nationally diverse sample (Shannon et al., 2009) and Black and Latino men (Krieger et al., 2008). In a study on the link between racial discrimination and workplace injuries and illnesses, Latino workers were more likely than White workers to experience work-related injuries and illnesses, and this relation was mediated by race-based discrimination experiences (Shannon et al., 2009).

Job Satisfaction

The effects of negative racial work climates on the job satisfaction of racially diverse workers are equivocal. One study found that correspondence between workers' values and workplace values were related to job satisfaction and turnover intentions in a sample of African American workers (Lyons & O'Brien, 2006). Specifically, higher levels of perceived fit were related to higher levels of job satisfaction and lower turnover intentions. Interestingly, the racial climate at the department level in the organization did not moderate these relations, suggesting that the role of work-related values and perceived fit between personal and employer values are more important than racial climate in determining work satisfaction and intentions to stay with the employer. Similarly, Hodson (2002) reported no significant patterns in job satisfaction across groups of workers based on the representation of women and/or racial minorities in work groups. On the other hand, other researchers found that perceived discrimination was significantly related to job satisfaction among racially diverse samples. Specifically, ethnic- and gender-related harassment were negatively related to organizational commitment and job satisfaction, and positively related to turnover intentions among a racially diverse sample of library workers (Raver & Nishii, 2010). Further, Valdivia

and Flores (2012) found that higher levels of perceived discrimination in the community at large were related to lower job satisfaction among a sample of Latino immigrant workers.

Other Work-Related Effects

The effects of institutional racism in educational and work systems are also believed to be manifested in other negative work-related outcomes for people of color. Researchers suggest that racism is related to restricted occupational consideration, high barriers, lack of access to quality educational and training opportunities, and limited role models and mentoring (Constantine, Erickson, Banks, & Timberlake, 1998).

People of color report high aspirations (Adams, Cahill, & Ackerlind, 2005; Kenny et al., 2007) and share similar levels of academic and work aspirations as Whites (Fouad & Byars-Winston, 2005; McWhirter et al., 2007); however, they perceive fewer career opportunities than Whites (Fouad & Byars-Winston, 2005), and their expectations for achieving their career goals are lower than their aspirations (Flores, Navarro, & DeWitz, 2008). In part, this might be explained by beliefs that society has lower expectations for their success (Blustein et al., 2010) and expectations that racist institutions and systems will present external barriers to achieving one's goals. Indeed, a meta-analysis of 16 studies with over 19,000 participants found that people of color anticipated more work barriers than Whites (Fouad & Byars-Winston, 2005).

A sample of Native American adults who did not complete high school identified lack of family support as a key obstacle to their career pursuits, while their counterparts who completed college identified discrimination and alienation from community as major barriers (Juntunen et al., 2001). Mexican American youth anticipated more barriers to attending college related to ability, preparation, motivation, and support and separation from family than their White peers (McWhirter, Torres, Salgado, & Valdez, 2007). Moreover, these students anticipated greater difficulty in overcoming barriers than Whites. Qualitative investigations found that high school and college students of color (a) experience racial discrimination from peers and teachers/ faculty (Constantine, Miville, Warren, Gainor & Lewis-Coles, 2006; Stebleton, 2012), (b) identify a range of barriers to achieving their career goals, with friends, self-discipline, and family being the most common barriers (Kenny et al., 2007), and (c) were aware that society had low expectations because of their racial and ethnic backgrounds that they would succeed in life (Blustein et al., 2010; Constantine et al., 2006).

Attending to educational and occupational barriers, and more importantly, one's belief in one's ability to overcome barriers, is one avenue for improving the vocational outcomes and options of people of color. For example, greater numbers of barriers were related to higher career indecision among a sample of African American youth (Constantine, Wallace & Kindaichi, 2005), consideration of careers with lower occupational prestige among a sample of Mexican American girls (Flores & O'Brien, 2002), consideration of female-dominated occupations among a sample of Latina college students (Rivera, Chen, Flores, Blumberg, & Ponterotto, 2007), lower educational aspirations among a sample of Mexican American youth (Ojeda & Flores, 2008), and lower school engagement and career aspirations among a sample of diverse urban high school students (Kenny, Blustein, Chaves, Grossman, & Gallagher, 2003).

Finally, due to the racial disparities in the U.S. labor market, the limited presence of same-race role models across all career fields and in higher-paying, professional positions is another negative outcome of racism that may affect the career development of people of color. When available, mentors can have an influential effect on the professional development of people of color; however, the presence and availability of mentors and role models in the work lives of people of color varies (Richie et al., 1997). Prior research has indicated a significant relationship between a person's race and the race of his or her role models, such that people tend to identify role models who share their racial backgrounds (Karunanayake & Nauta, 2004). Youth of color identify family members as role models (Flores & Obasi, 2005; Karunanayake & Nauta, 2004); however, these studies found no differences in the number of role models, the influence of role models, or the effects of having a role model on various career indices.

Cultural Theories and the Work Development of People of Color
Racial/Ethnic Identity Development

Racial identity theory describes the racial consciousness, attitudes, feelings, thoughts, and behaviors that individuals experience as they cycle through a series of statuses in constructing their racial identity (Helms, 1990). Researchers have hypothesized a link between racial identity and career development

outcomes, such that higher statuses are believed to be associated with more advanced career development tasks and behaviors (e.g., Helms & Piper, 1994). However, studies have reported mixed findings on the relation between racial worldviews and career outcomes. Some of the research has revealed nonsignificant or small relations between racial identity attitudes and gender-traditional career aspirations (Evans & Herr, 1994) and social cognitive variables (Gainor & Lent, 1998) among samples of African American college students. In the latter study, racial identity attitudes did not moderate the relations between social cognitive variables, suggesting that the relations among these variables were consistent across the different racial identity statuses (Gainor & Lent, 1998). Yet others have found links between racial identity and career self-efficacy, outcome expectations, career interests, and career barriers (Byars-Winston, 2006), career maturity and life role salience (Carter & Constantine, 2000), and hope and vocational identity (Jackson & Neville, 1998). Specifically, in a sample of Black college students, a racial ideology reflective of the shared experiences across racial groups was negatively related to career self-efficacy and positively related to outcome expectations, and an ideology that emphasized a group's unique experiences was positively related to career interests, choice of career barriers, and barriers to performing a job (Byars-Winston, 2006). In another study, racial identity was related to Asian Americans' career maturity and African Americans' life role salience (Carter & Constantine, 2000). Possible explanations for these contradictory findings include the use of different racial identity measures across studies or limitations with racial identity theory (Rowe, 2006) and measurement (Cokley, 2007). Alternatively, these studies have examined different career outcomes, and it is possible that racial identity's effects on career development are not as broad as originally conceptualized by Helms and Piper.

Acculturation and Worldview Models

The sociocultural environment can also influence career development by shaping the messages that one receives about work and providing differential exposure to the world of work. Acculturation is an important variable when studying the career development of people of color as this cultural variable has been linked to work-related beliefs, attitudes, and behaviors (Miller & Kerlow-Myers, 2009). Berry (2003) defines acculturation as the adaptation process to the sociocultural context experienced by minority group members; adaptation is assessed according to the degree of adaptation to one's culture of origin as well as one's adaptation to the dominant culture. Due to the emphasis of dominant cultural values and practices in work settings, acculturation toward the dominant culture is likely to facilitate the work development of people of color. That is, when individuals are able to navigate effectively within the dominant culture or multiple cultures, they are likely to have access to a variety of learning experiences that will lead to the development of vocational identities and occupational considerations.

In a review of acculturation research in the career development literature, Miller and Kerlow-Myers (2009) reported mixed findings on the relation between acculturation on different career outcomes. Acculturation has been linked to a number of career outcomes, including career choices (Tang, Fouad & Smith, 1999), career-related self-efficacy (Flores, Navarro, Smith, & Ploszaj, 2006; Flores, Robitschek, Celebi, Anderson, & Hoang, 2010; Patel, Salahuddin, & O'Brien, 2008; Rivera et al., 2007), job satisfaction (Nguyen, Huynh, & Lonergan-Garwick, 2007; Valdivia & Flores, 2012), job performance (Leong, 2001), career interests (Flores, Navarro et al., 2006; Leong, Kao, & Lee, 2004; Tang et al., 1999), and educational goals (Castillo, López-Arenas, & Saldivar, 2010; Flores, Ojeda, Huang, Gee, & Lee, 2006; Flores et al., 2008; McWhirter, Hackett & Bandalos, 1998).

Another relevant cultural variable that has been examined in relation to the career development of people of color is critical consciousness. Critical consciousness refers to an increased awareness among members of oppressed groups of the sociopolitical nature of their work selves and identities. In addition, critical consciousness describes a heightened awareness of social inequalities, an understanding of the effects of sociopolitical barriers and institutional racism in creating these social disparities, and a belief that one can change the system to lead to better outcomes for members of socially marginalized groups. Investigations of the career experiences of high-achieving women of color revealed that these women have a strong awareness of how gender and race have affected their professional development and opportunities, high levels of engagement in their communities, and a strong desire to advocate for the advancement of others from oppressed groups (e.g., Gomez et al., 2001; Richie et al., 1997). In a series of studies with urban high school adolescents, Diemer and colleagues reported that sociopolitical development had a positive effect on youths' career development. Specifically, these researchers found that sociopolitical development in high school was positively related to work salience (Diemer et al., 2010), higher vocational expectations (Diemer & Hsieh, 2008; Diemer et al., 2010), vocational identity and career commitment (Diemer & Blustein, 2006), and adult occupational attainment (Diemer, 2009).

Psychology of Working and People of Color

The psychology of working (Blustein 2001, 2006) is a relatively new perspective that seeks a more inclusive understanding of working and posits that work meets three main needs: survival, relatedness, and self-determination. This approach assumes that individuals may hold varied perspectives about work and their work identities. In addition, this framework focuses on dimensions of privilege that are relevant to one's access to resources that influence work opportunities and the work experiences of a broad range of individuals in the United States. The psychology of working has served as the foundation for recent studies that have investigated conceptions of work with diverse samples of youth and adults (Blustein et al., 2002, 2010; Chaves et al., 2004; Fouad et al., 2008; Juntunen et al., 2001; Kenny et al., 2007).

One of the core premises of the psychology of working is that our understanding of work should extend to everyone represented in the global workforce, including the working poor, racial minorities, and those workers who are employed in positions that are not a reflection of their personal choices or an expression of their self. Therefore, before reviewing the literature that has addressed psychology-of-working's taxonomy in relation to the work lives of people of color, I first highlight studies that have examined the meaning of work across culturally diverse samples.

Meaning of Work

A number of recent qualitative inquiries have deepened our understanding of the work narratives of racial-minority adults and youths. These examinations advance knowledge through their use of social constructivist approaches to develop a rich description of the perspectives that our racially diverse workforce hold about work and those factors that influence their work decisions. Through these investigations, the work narratives and career development of people of color are illuminated, providing a rich and complex analysis of how personal and cultural backgrounds help to shape work experiences.

People of color endorse a variety of work values beyond compensation and security needs that represent their beliefs about work (Eggerth & Flynn, 2012; Lyons & O'Brien, 2006). An often-held belief is that workers in low-paying jobs characterized by poor working conditions work simply to work and do not derive any meaning or satisfaction from work. While one study found that less meaningful work was related to negative characteristics of the job (Hodson, 2002), another reported that the majority of the sample, consisting of workers employed in jobs with repetitive tasks, experienced positive meaning in work despite the job stress (Eggerth & Flynn, 2012; Isaksen, 2000). These workers expressed pride and responsibility in the work they did and viewed work as a necessary part of a larger purpose.

A sample of racially diverse, predominantly low-socioeconomic-status urban youth was more likely to define work based on outcomes (financial gains, earning a livelihood), tasks (physical and mental dimensions), and the attitudes they held of work (Chaves et al., 2004). Juntunen and colleagues (2001) examined the meaning of career and career-related concepts among a sample of Native American adults. These researchers found that participants viewed career as a lifetime pursuit and as an activity that involved future planning and goal setting. Work was also a means to pass on cultural and tribal traditions to future generations. Finally, people of color also view work as a way to implement their religious and spiritual beliefs (Constantine et al., 2006; Flores et al., 2011).

Work as Survival and Power

Research indicates that racial minorities believe that work serves to meet basic needs and that people work to survive and for financial security (e.g., Chaves et al., 2004; Constantine et al., 2006; Eggerth & Flynn, 2012; Flores et al., 2011; Gomez et al., 2001). A sample of racially diverse, predominantly low-socioeconomic-status urban high school students responded that they viewed work as a means for survival (Chaves et al., 2004). Similarly, adult Latino workers viewed work as a means to make money for basic living needs (Flores et al., 2011; Gomez et al., 2001). Latino immigrant workers sought jobs that would provide living wages for their family, and viewed work as a means to gain power by improving the family's status and advancing their personal development (Flores et al., 2011).

Collectively, the findings described above on how people of color make meaning of work and their approach to work as a means of survival reflect the complexities of career development. While these findings indicate that people of color in low-wage jobs cope with difficult jobs well and make positive and adaptive use of these opportunities, it does not mean that these workers would not benefit from more egalitarian and broader work opportunities or that, if given the choice, might choose to spend their working lives employed in alternative jobs. Until the time comes when all groups of workers are afforded equal power and access to quality education and work opportunities, we must guard against using these findings to support the status quo.

Work for Social Connection and Relations

According to the psychology-of-working perspective, people also work to fulfill relational needs and other life roles. Given the importance of family and the community in the lives of people of color in the United States, the influence of family and the significance of family roles and other life roles in work-related decisions is a critical area of exploration. A number of investigations have provided support for the link between social variables and the career development of youth (e.g., Flores & O'Brien, 2002; Jackson & Nutini, 2002; Kenny et al., 2003), college students (e.g., Constantine & Flores, 2006; Fouad et al., 2008; Tang et al., 1999), and adults (e.g., Gomez et al., 2001; Juntunen et al., 2001; Pearson & Bieshke, 2001; Richie et al., 1997). Family and community influences in the career development of people of color can occur in the form of transmitting values on the role of work and education (Fouad et al., 2008; Pearson & Bieshke, 2001), expectations and involvement in decision making (Fouad et al., 2008; Tang et al., 1999), and support (Flores & O'Brien, 2002; Fouad et al., 2008; Torres & Solberg, 2001). Specifically, family influences have been linked to career aspirations (Constantine & Flores, 2006; Kenny et al., 2003), career choices (Flores & O'Brien, 2002; Tang et al., 1999), career-related self-efficacy (Flores et al., 2010; Torres & Solberg, 2001), career indecision (Constantine & Flores, 2006), and school engagement (Kenny et al., 2003).

A relational orientation, or a tendency to approach career decisions and career development based on one's relationships with others and interactions in the work world (Blustein, 2011), was a common theme in the career narratives of Native Americans (Juntunen et al., 2001), immigrants

(Flores et al., 2011; Stebleton, 2012), and women of color (Gomez et al., 2001; Pearson & Bieschke, 2001; Richie et al., 1997). Juntunen and colleagues (2001) found that, in contrast to traditional career development theories that place interests and skills as key determinants of career decision making, Native Americans' career decisions were influenced by the perceived needs of their communities, and work was an expression of the self within a community. These participants assessed career success according to one's contribution to the family and community, and family support was identified as an important resource in their career development. Women of color addressed balancing roles in their personal and professional lives, described connections with other women and people of color, and credited others in their family and communities for their career accomplishments (Gomez et al., 2001; Pearson & Bieschke, 2001; Richie et al., 1997). The relational context of work was also extended in women's descriptions of feeling supported by family members, partners, friends, teachers, colleagues, and other professional women in their careers and their desire to support and serve as role models for members of their community. Gomez and colleagues (2001) reported that familism values helped Latina women balance family needs with high work demands. Similar results on finding meaning through work connectedness, social relations in the workplace, and fulfilling family obligations have also been extended to samples of youth of color (e.g., Adams et al., 2005), Asian American college students (Fouad et al., 2008), and Latino and African immigrants (Eggerth & Flynn, 2012; Flores et al., 2011; Stebleton, 2012).

Work as Self-Determination

People of color identify a range of internal and external motivations that drive their work-related pursuits. Although a sample of urban youth were more likely to report that people worked for survival needs, they also described work as a means for personal development and an opportunity to implement one's self-concept (Chaves et al., 2004). Other samples of urban youth reported that vocational planning and positive career expectations were associated with school engagement (Kenny et al., 2003) and work hope, career planning, and autonomy support predicted achievement motivations (Kenny et al., 2010).

People of color described a range of motivators in their career paths, including fulfilling one's calling in life, making a difference in the world, working in an area that they felt passionate about, doing something

that makes them happy, or proving they could succeed both to themselves and others (Constantine et al., 2006; Gomez et al., 2001). Another qualitative study of successful women of color indicated that while they received both extrinsic and intrinsic rewards from their career, they tended to emphasize the intrinsic benefits they derived from working, including the value of working and doing work they felt passionate about (Richie et al., 1997). Finally, Latino immigrant workers described a range of external and intrinsic motivations to work, such as a strong work ethic, doing what they like to do, and pursuing personal needs through work (e.g., achievement, autonomy; Eggerth & Flynn, 2012; Flores et al., 2011).

Conclusion

As the United States is moving toward a truly multicultural society with no majority group, it is more important now than ever before in our country's history that professionals interested in the world of work and its occupants heed the imperatives of the psychology of working (Blustein, 2006). This approach to understanding the experiences of workers breaks down existing boundaries in our research and work that have perpetuated a monocultural perspective and provided a biased understanding of work in favor of the experiences of educated, professional workers. A psychology-of-working perspective challenges the status quo in the profession and advocates that we establish a significant body of literature that expands knowledge and practice to all workers regardless of personal and cultural backgrounds and regardless of the jobs they perform.

The extant literature on the work-related experiences of people of color in the United States identifies a range of challenges and stressors that they encounter that help to shape their career narratives and outcomes. In comparison to White workers, people of color are more likely to earn less, to experience negative effects on psychological and physical health due to racism, to be at increased risk for occupational health problems, to perceive more barriers to achieving their goals, and to lack access to resources that can improve their job options. In conjunction with the psychology of working, cultural theories pertaining to racial identity, acculturation, and critical consciousness can advance knowledge and broaden our understanding of the role of work in the lives of people of color in the United States.

Future Directions

The insidious nature of racism that continues to plague the U.S. workplace hurts our society because it limits the potential contributions of people of color and creates unequal outcomes for these workers solely based on their racial status. Major issues that remain to be solved include (a) the limited research on people of color, particularly those who are not college educated and who do not seek professional careers, (b) the high risk of workplace stressors among workers of color, (c) the continued educational (e.g., achievement) and work-related (e.g., differential pay, over- or under-representation in certain occupations, underrepresentation in leadership positions) inequalities between people of color and Whites, and (d) the lack of attention to these issues among the general public. The future research, practice/consultation, and advocacy of vocational psychologists can play an important part in remedying these issues.

First, it is essential that vocational psychologists heed the advice of scholars (Blustein, 2006; Richardson, 1993) to expand our research knowledge to segments of the population that are underrepresented in the literature. As noted earlier, reviews of the vocational research have concluded that the majority of studies are conducted with predominantly White samples (Byars & McCubbin, 2001; Flores et al., 2006). As researchers, we need to make efforts in our own work to diversify our samples and ensure adequate representation of people of color who portray the forms of diversity found in these communities (e.g., educational attainment, social class standing, generational variations). Moreover, while knowledge of high school and college students' career development is important, we need to extend our work to racially diverse young adults who enter the workforce after high school as well as racially diverse adult workers representing other developmental stages. More research is needed on the work experiences of people of color in specific occupational fields, especially nonprofessional jobs, given the differential barriers experienced by workers across work settings. As journal editors and reviewers, we also need to hold others accountable for sampling racially diverse students and workers and should expect researchers to make concerted efforts to target racially diverse participants. Finally, future research can build upon the prior psychology-of-working studies that have demonstrated that people of color hold varied conceptions of work, seek multiple avenues for social connection at work, and have different motivations for working.

Training future vocational psychologists in the areas of consultation and advocacy will help to link our knowledge of research to practice and policy.

Regarding consultation work, vocational psychologists can promote diversity training across all levels of education. Developmentally appropriate educational interventions that raise awareness of both personal and structural and institutional forms of racism can increase attention to these issues among the future members of our country's labor force—the people who will hold the power in the future to change longstanding, discriminatory practices in the workplace. In terms of educational policy, vocational psychologists can advocate for a diversity course requirement for high school and college students as a necessary skill for working effectively with diverse coworkers in the future. In addition, vocational psychologists can consult with business faculty on how diversity awareness and knowledge of diversity issues in the workplace can be incorporated into existing coursework. Vocational psychologists also have unique training and skills to serve as consultants to a wide array of sectors of the labor force. In this role, vocational psychologists can apply their knowledge of disparities in the hiring and promotion processes to help companies diversify the workplace and ensure that they are operating from policies that benefit all of their workers, regardless of racial background. We can help companies assess the general workplace climate for workers of color and assist these companies in developing into multicultural organizations.

References

Adams, E. M., Cahill, B. J., & Ackerlind, S. J. (2005). A qualitative study of Latino lesbian and gay youths' experiences with discrimination and the career development process. *Journal of Vocational Behavior, 66*, 199–218.

Alon, S., & Haberfeld, Y. (2007). Labor force attachment and the evolving wage gap between White, Black, and Hispanic young women. *Work and Occupations, 34*, 369–398.

Baumle, A. K., & Fossett, M. (2005). Statistical discrimination in employment: Its practice, conceptualization, and implications for public policy. *American Behavioral Scientist, 48*, 1250–1274.

Berdahl, J. L., & Moore, C. (2006). Workplace harassment: Double jeopardy for minority women. *Journal of Applied Psychology, 91*, 426–436.

Berry, J. W. (2003). Conceptual approaches to acculturation. In K. M. Chun, P. Balls Organista, & G. Marin (Eds.). *Acculturation: Advances in theory, measurement, and applied research* (pp. 17–37). Washington, DC: American Psychological Association.

Blustein, D. L. (2006). *The psychology of working: A new perspective for career development, counseling, and public policy.* Mahwah, NJ: Lawrence Erlbaum Press.

Blustein, D. L. (2008). The role of work in psychological health and well-being: A conceptual, historical, and public policy perspective. *American Psychologist, 63*, 228–240.

Blustein, D. L. (2011). A relational theory of working. *Journal of Vocational Behavior, 79*, 1–17.

Blustein, D. L., Chaves, A. P., Diemer, M. A., Gallagher, L. A., Marshall, K. G., Sirin, S., & Bhati, K. S. (2002). Voices of the forgotten half: The role of social class in the school-to-work transition. *Journal of Counseling Psychology, 49,* 311–323. doi:10.1037/0022-0167.49.3.311

Blustein, D. L., Kenna, A. C., Gill, N., & DeVoy, J. E. (2008). The psychology of working: A new framework for counseling practice and public policy. *Career Development Quarterly, 56,* 294–308.

Blustein, D. L., Murphy, K. A., Kenny, M. E., Jernigan, M., Perez-Qualdron, L., Castaneda, T., Kpepke, M., Land, M., Urbano, A., & Davis, O. (2010). Exploring urban students' constructions about school, work, race and ethnicity. *Journal of Counseling Psychology, 57,* 248–254.

Browne, I., & Askew, R. (2005). Race, ethnicity, and wage inequality among women: What happened in the 1990s and early 21st century? *American Behavioral Scientist, 48,* 1275–1292.

Buchanan, N. T., & Fitzgerald, L. F. (2008). Effects of racial and sexual harassment on work and the psychological well-being of African American women. *Journal of Occupational Health Psychology, 13,* 137–151.

Byars, A. M., & McCubbin, L. D. (2001). Trends in career development research with racial/ethnic minorities. In J. G. Ponterotto, J. M. Casas, L. A. Suzuki, & C. M. Alexander (Eds.), *Handbook of multicultural counseling* (2nd ed., pp. 633–654). Thousand Oaks, CA: Sage.

Byars-Winston, A. M. (2006). Racial ideology in predicting social cognitive career variables for Black undergraduates. *Journal of Vocational Behavior, 69,* 134–148.

Carter, R. T., & Constantine, M. G. (2000). Career maturity, life role salience, and racial/ethnic identity in Black and Asian American college students. *Journal of Career Assessment, 8,* 173–187.

Castillo, L. G., López-Arenas, A., & Saldivar, I. M. (2010). The influence of acculturation and enculturation on Mexican American high school students' decisions to apply to college. *Journal of Multicultural Counseling and Development, 38,* 88–98.

Catanzarite, L. (2002). Dynamics of segregation and earnings in brown-collar occupations. *Work and Occupations, 29,* 300–345. doi: 10.1177/0730888402029003003

Chapman, C., Laird, J., & KewalRamani, A. (2010). *Trends in high school dropout and completion rates in the United States: 1972–2008 (NCES 2011–012).* National Center for Educational Statistics, Institute of Educational Sciences, U.S. Department of Education. Washington, D.C. Retrieved February 8, 2011, from http://nces.ed.gov/pubsearch.

Chaves, A. P., Diemer, M. A., Blustein, D. L., Gallagher, L. A., DeVoy, J. E., Casares, M. T., & Perry, J. C. (2004). Conceptions of work: The view from urban youth. *Journal of Counseling Psychology, 51,* 275–286.

Cokley, K. (2007). Critical issues in the measurement of ethnic and racial identity: A referendum on the state of the field. *Journal of Counseling Psychology, 54,* 224–234.

Constantine, M. G., Erickson, C. D., Banks, R. W., & Timberlake, T. L. (1998). Challenges to the career development of urban racial and ethnic minority youth: Implications for vocational intervention. *Journal of Multicultural Counseling and Development, 26,* 83–95.

Constantine, M. G., & Flores, L. Y. (2006). Psychological distress, perceived family conflict, and career development issues in college students of color. *Journal of Career Assessment, 14,* 354–369.

Constantine, M. G., Miville, M. L., Warren, A. K., Gainor, K. A., & Lewis-Coles, M. E. L. (2006). Religion, spirituality, and career development in African American college students: A qualitative inquiry. *Career Development Quarterly, 54,* 227–241.

Constantine, M. G., Wallace, B. C., & Kindaichi, M. M. (2005). Examining contextual factors in the career decision status of African American adolescents. *Journal of Career Assessment, 13,* 307–319.

DeBell, C. (2001). Ninety years in the world of work in America. *Career Development Quarterly, 50,* 77–88.

Diemer, M. A. (2009). Pathways to occupational attainment among poor youth of color: The role of sociopolitical development. *Counseling Psychologist, 37,* 6–35.

Diemer, M. A., & Blustein, D. L. (2006). Critical consciousness and career development among urban youth. *Journal of Vocational Behavior, 68,* 220–232.

Diemer, M. A., & Hsieh, C. A. (2008). Sociopolitical development and vocational expectations among lower socioeconomic status adolescents of color. *Career Development Quarterly, 56,* 257–267.

Diemer, M. A., Wang, Q., Moore, T., Gregory, S. R., Hatcher, K. M., & Voight, A. (2010). Sociopolitical development, work salience, and vocational expectations among low socioeconomic status African American, Latin American, and Asian American youth. *Developmental Psychology, 46,* 619–635.

Din-Dzietham, R., Nembhard, W. N., Collins, R., & Davis, S. K. (2004). Perceived stress following race-based discrimination at work is associated with hypertension in African-Americans. The Metro Atlanta Heart Disease Study, 1999–2001. *Social Science & Medicine, 58,* 449–461.

Eggerth, D., & Flynn, M. (2012). Applying the theory of work adjustment to Latino immigrant workers: An exploratory study. *Journal of Career Development, 39,* 76–98.

Evans, K. M., & Herr, E. L, (1994). The influence of racial identity and the perception of discrimination on the career aspirations of African American men and women. *Journal of Vocational Behavior, 44,* 173–184.

Flores, E., Tschann, J. M., Dimas, J. M., Pasch, L. A., & de Groat, C. L. (2010). Perceived racial/ethnic discrimination, posttraumatic stress symptoms, and health risk behaviors among Mexican American adolescents. *Journal of Counseling Psychology, 57,* 264–273.

Flores, L. Y., Berkel, L. A., Nilsson, J. E., Ojeda, L., Jordan, S. E., Lynn, G. L., & Leal, V. M. (2006). Racial/ethnic minority vocational research: A content and trend analysis across thirty-five years. *Career Development Quarterly, 55,* 2–21.

Flores, L. Y., Mendoza, M. M., Ojeda, L., He, Y., Rosales Meza, R., Medina, V., Wagner Ladehoff, J., & Jordan, S. (2011). A qualitative inquiry of Latino immigrants work experiences in the Midwest. *Journal of Counseling Psychology, 58,* 522–536.

Flores, L. Y., Navarro, R. L., & Dewitz, J. (2008). Mexican American high school students' post-secondary educational goals: Applying social cognitive career theory. *Journal of Career Assessment, 16,* 489–501.

Flores, L. Y., Navarro, R. L., Smith, J. L., & Ploszaj, A. M. (2006). Testing a model of nontraditional career choice goals with Mexican American adolescent men. *Journal of Career Assessment, 14,* 214–234.

Flores, L. Y., & Obasi, E. M. (2005). Mentors' influence on Mexican American students' career and educational development. *Journal of Multicultural Counseling and Development, 33,* 146–164.

Flores, L. Y., & O'Brien, K. M. (2002). The career development of Mexican American adolescent women: A test of social cognitive career theory. *Journal of Counseling Psychology, 49*, 14–27.

Flores, L. Y., Ojeda, L., Huang, Y. P., Gee, D., & Lee, S. (2006). Relation of acculturation, problem solving appraisal, and career decision-making self-efficacy to Mexican American high school students' educational goals. *Journal of Counseling Psychology, 53*, 260–266.

Flores, L. Y., Robitschek, C., Celebi, E., Andersen, C., & Hoang, U. (2010). Social cognitive influences on Mexican Americans' career choices across Holland's themes. *Journal of Vocational Psychology, 76*, 198–210.

Fouad, N. A., & Byars-Winston, A. M. (2005). Cultural context of career choice: Meta-analysis of race/ethnicity differences. *Career Development Quarterly, 53*, 223–233.

Fouad, N. A., Kantamneni, N., Smothers, M. K., Chen, Y. L., Fitzpatrick, M., & Terry, S. (2008). Asian American career development: A qualitative analysis. *Journal of Vocational Behavior, 72*, 43–59.

Gainor, K. A., & Lent, R. W. (1998). Social cognitive expectations and racial identity attitudes in predicting the math choice intentions of Black college students. *Journal of Counseling Psychology, 45*, 403–413.

Gomez, M. J., Fassinger, R. E., Prosser, J. C., Cooke, K., Mejia, B., & Luna, J. (2001). Voces abriendo caminos (voices foraging paths): A qualitative study of the career development of notable Latinas. *Journal of Counseling Psychology, 48*, 286–300.

Helms, J. E. (1990). *Black and white racial identity: Theory, research, and practice.* Westport, CT: Greenwood Press.

Helms, J. E., & Piper, R. E. (1994). Implications of racial identity theory for vocational psychology. *Journal of Vocational Behavior, 44*, 124–138.

Hersch, J. (2008). Profiling the new immigrant worker: The effects of skin color and height. *Journal of Labor Economics, 26*, 345–386.

Hersch, J. (2011). The persistence of skin color discrimination for immigrants. *Social Science Research, 40, 1337–1349.*

Hodson, R. (2002). Demography or respect?: Work group demography versus organizational dynamics as determinants of meaning and satisfaction at work. *British Journal of Sociology, 53*, 291–317.

Hussar, W. J., & Bailey, T. M. (2009). *Projections of educational statistics to 2018 (NCES 2009–062).* National Center for Educational Statistics, Institute of Education Sciences, U.S. Department of Education. Washington, D.C.

Hwang, W. C., & Goto, S. (2009). The impact of perceived racial discrimination on the mental health of Asian American and Latino college students. *Asian American Journal of Psychology, S*, 15–28.

Isaksen, J. (2000). Constructing meaning despite the drudgery of repetitive work. *Journal of Humanistic Psychology, 40*, 84–107.

Jackson, C. C., & Neville, H. A. (1998). Influence of racial identity attitudes on African American college students' vocational identity and hope. *Journal of Vocational Behavior, 53*, 97–113.

Jackson, M. A., & Nutini, C. D. (2002). Hidden resources and barriers in career learning assessment with adolescents vulnerable to discrimination. *Career Development Quarterly, 51*, 56–77.

Juntunen, C. L., Barraclough, D. J., Broneck, C. L., Seibel, G. A., Winrow, S. A., & Morin, P. M. (2001). American Indian perspectives on the career journey. *Journal of Counseling Psychology, 48*, 274–285.

Karunanayake, D., & Nauta, M. M. (2004). The relationship between race and students' identified career role models and perceived role model influence. *Career Development Quarterly, 52*, 225–234.

Kenny, M. E., Blustein, D. L., Chaves, A., Grossman, J. M., & Gallagher, L. A., (2003). The role of perceived barriers and relational support in the educational and vocational lives of urban high school students. *Journal of Counseling Psychology, 50*, 142–155.

Kenny, M. E., Gauldron, L., Scanlon, D., Sparks, E., Blustein, D. L., & Jernigan, M. (2007). Urban adolescents' constructions of supports and barriers to educational and career attainment. *Journal of Counseling Psychology, 54*, 336–343. doi: 10.1037/0022–0167.54.3.336

Kenny, M. E., Walsh-Blair, L. Y., Blustein, D. L., Bempechat, J., & Seltzer, J. (2010). Achievement motivation among urban adolescents: Work hope, autonomy support, and achievement-related beliefs. *Journal of Vocational Behavior, 77*, 205–212.

Klonoff, E. A., Landrine, H., & Ullman, J. B. (1999). Racial discrimination and psychiatric symptoms among Blacks. *Cultural Diversity and Ethnic Minority Psychology, 5*, 329–339.

Krieger, N., Chen, J. T., Waterman, P. D., Hartman, C., Stoddard, A. M., Quinn, M. M., Sorensen, G., & Barbeau, E. M. (2008). The inverse hazard law: Blood pressure, sexual harassment, racial discrimination, workplace abuse and occupational exposures in U.S. low-income Black, White and Latino workers. *Social Science & Medicine, 67*, 1970–1982.

Krieger, N., Smith, K., Naishadham, D., Hartman, C., & Barbeau, E. M. (2005). Experiences of discrimination: Validity and reliability of a self-report measure for population health research on racism and health. *Social Science & Medicine, 61*, 1576–1596.

Leong, F. T. L. (2001). The role of acculturation in the career adjustment of Asian American workers: A test of Leong and Chou's (1994) formulations. *Cultural Diversity & Ethnic Minority Psychology, 7*, 262–273.

Leong, F. T. L., Kao, E. M. C., & Lee, S. H. (2004). The relationship between family dynamics and career interests among Chinese Americans and European Americans. *Journal of Career Assessment, 12*, 65–84.

Lui, M., Robles, B., Leondar-Wright, B., Brewer, R., & Adams R., with United for a Fair Economy (2006). *The color of wealth: The story behind the U.S. racial wealth divide.* New York: New Press.

Lyons, H. Z., & O'Brien, K, M. (2006). The role of person-environment fit in the job satisfaction and tenure intentions of African American employees. *Journal of Counseling Psychology, 53*, 387–396.

Maume, D. J., Jr. (2004). Wage discrimination over the life course: A comparison of explanations. *Social Problems, 51*, 505–527.

McWhirter, E. H., Hackett, G., & Bandalos, D. L. (1998). A causal model of the educational plans and career expectations of Mexican American high school girls. *Journal of Counseling Psychology, 45*, 166–181.

McWhirter, E. H., Torres, D. M., Salgado, S., & Valdez, M. (2007). Perceived barriers and postsecondary plans in Mexican American and White adolescents. *Journal of Career Assessment, 15*, 119–138.

Miller, M. J., & Kerlow-Myers, A. E. (2009). A content analysis of acculturation research in the career development literature. *Journal of Career Development, 35,* 352–384.

National Institute for Occupational Safety and Health. (2009). *Work organization and stress-related disorders: Emerging issues.* Retrieved from http://www.cdc.gov/niosh/programs/workorg/emerging.html.

Neville, H. A., Worthington, R. L., & Spanierman, L. B. (2001). Race, power, and multicultural counseling psychology: Understanding White privilege and color-blind racial attitudes. In J. G. Ponterotto, J. M. Casas, L. Suzuki, & C. J. Alexander (Eds.), *Handbook of multicultural counseling* (2nd ed., pp. 257–288). Thousand Oaks, CA: Sage.

Ng, E. S. W. (2010). What women and ethnic minorities want. Work values and labor market confidence: A self-determination perspective. *International Journal of Human Resource Management, 21,* 676–689.

Nguyen. A. M. T. D., Huynh, Q. L., & Lonergan-Garwick, J. (2007). The role of acculturation in the mentoring-career satisfaction model for Asian/Pacific Islander American university faculty. *Cultural Diversity and Ethnic Minority Psychology, 13,* 295–303.

O'Brien, K. M. (2001). The legacy of Frank Parsons: Career counselors and vocational psychologists as agents of social change. *Career Development Quarterly, 50,* 66–76.

Ojeda, L., & Flores, L. Y. (2008). The influence of gender, generation level, parents' education level, and perceived barriers on the educational aspirations of Mexican American high school students. *Career Development Quarterly, 57,* 84–95.

Ortman, J. M., & Guarneri, C. E. (2009). *United States population projections: 2000 to 2050.* Retrieved February 8, 2011, from http://www.census.gov/population/www/projections/analytical-document09.pdf

Patel, S. G., Salahuddin, N. M., & O'Brien, K. M. (2008). Career decision-making self-efficacy of Vietnamese adolescents. *Journal of Career Development, 34,* 218–240.

Pascoe, E. A., & Richman, L. S. (2009). Perceived discrimination and health: A meta-analytic review. *Psychological Bulletin, 135,* 531–554.

Pearson, S. M., & Bieschke, K, J., (2001). Succeeding against the odds: An examination of familial influences on the career development of professional African American women. *Journal of Counseling Psychology, 48,* 301–309.

Pope, M. (2000). A brief history of career counseling in the United States. *Career Development Quarterly, 48,* 194–211.

Raver, J. L., & Nishii, L. H. (2010). Once, twice, or three times as harmful? Ethnic harassment, gender harassment, and generalized workplace harassment. *Journal of Applied Psychology, 95,* 236–254.

Richardson, M. S. (1993). Work in people's lives: A location for counseling psychologists. *Journal of Counseling Psychology, 40,* 425–433.

Richie, B. S., Fassinger, R. E., Linn, S. G., Johnson, J., Prosser, J., & Robinson, S. (1997). Persistence, connection and passion: A qualitative study of the career development of highly achieving African American-Black and White women. *Journal of Counseling Psychology, 44,* 133–148.

Rivera, L. M., Chen, E. C., Flores, L. Y., Blumberg, F., & Ponterotto, J. G. (2007). The effects of perceived barriers, role models, and acculturation on the career self-efficacy and career consideration of Hispanic women. *Career Development Quarterly, 56,* 47–61.

Rowe, W. (2006). White racial identity: Science, faith, and pseudoscience. *Journal of Multicultural Counseling and Development, 34,* 235–243.

Schneider, K. T., Hitlan, R. T., & Radhakrishnan, P. (2000). An examination of the nature and correlates of ethnic harassment experiences in multiple contexts. *Journal of Applied Psychology, 85,* 3–12.

Shannon, C. A., Rospenda, K. M., Richman, J. A., & Minich, L. M. (2009). Race, racial discrimination, and the risk of work-related illness, injury, or assault: Findings from a national study. *Journal of Occupational and Environmental Medicine, 51,* 441–448.

Stebleton, M. J. (2012). The meaning of work for Black African immigrant adult college students. *Journal of Career Development, 39,* 50–75.

Tang, M., Fouad, N. A., & Smith, P. L. (1999). Asian Americans' career choices: A path model to examine factors influencing their career choices. *Journal of Vocational Behavior, 54,* 142–157.

Torres, J. B., & Solberg, V. S. (2001). Role of self-efficacy, stress, social integration, and family support in Latino college student persistence and health. *Journal of Vocational Behavior, 59,* 53–63.

U.S. Bureau of Labor Statistics (2008). *Labor force statistics from the current population survey: Characteristics of the employed.* Retrieved February 8, 2011, from http://www.bls.gov/webapps/legacy/cpsatab2.htm

U.S. Bureau of Labor Statistics (2010). *Labor force characteristics by race and ethnicity, 2009.* Retrieved February 8, 2011, from http://www.bls.gov/cps/cpsrace2009.pdf.

U.S. Census Bureau (2009). *American Community Survey: 1-year estimates.* Retrieved February 8, 2011, from http://www.census.gov/acs/www/.

U.S. Equal Employment Opportunity Commission (2011). *Fact sheet: Race/color discrimination.* Retrieved February 15, 2011 from http://www.eeoc.gov/facts/fs-race.pdf

Valdivia, C., & Flores, L. Y. (2012). Factors affecting the job satisfaction of Latino/a immigrants in the Midwest. *Journal of Career Development, 39,* 31–49.

Zytowski, D. G. (2001). Frank Parsons and the progressive movement. *Career Development Quarterly, 50,* 57–65.

Gender and the Psychology of Working

Neeta Kantamneni

Abstract

Gender and work are intimately interwoven concepts. The gendered context of work, including sexism and discrimination, has historically excluded access to work for women; similarly, gender socialization experiences have influenced how women and men construct meaning around work. The purpose of this chapter is to utilize an inclusive, psychology-of-working framework to examine how work intersects with both female and male gender roles. The complex manner in which working and gender roles interface will be explored, along with an emphasis on understanding how socialization and sexist practices create limitations for individuals seeking and adjusting to work.

Key Words: gender, gender role socialization, sexism, gender discrimination, working and power

Gender and sexism have a rich history of scholarship within vocational psychology, with numerous researchers extensively examining how gender is related to the construction of meaning from work and to one's overall experience of working (Blustein, 2006). Historically, vocational guidance and career development was primarily intended for middle-class men, largely because of the social climate within the United States. During the early 20th century, when vocational psychology emerged as a field, access to occupational choice, employment, and the job market, was, for the most part, available only to White men. Women's employment outside the home was uncommon and their contribution to the paid workforce was minimal at best. In fact, even as late as the 1950s and 1960s, very little attention was given to the career development of women (Farmer, 2006), despite the fact that women were entering the workforce at higher rates. It wasn't until the civil rights and feminist movements and changes to higher education legislation in the early 1970s that interest in the career development of women gained momentum (Farmer,

2006). Several positive events in the United States affected the entrance of women into the labor force, including (a) technological developments that made household chores less time-consuming, (b) greater access to contraception and birth control choice for women, (c) legislative changes related to civil rights, (d) the Cold War energizing a race to increase the scientific competence of Americans in order to beat Russia, (e) the women's rights and feminist movements, and (f) the gay rights movement (Farmer, 2006). Additionally, labor shortages during World War II stimulated the gender shift in the labor force and encouraged women to engage in work outside of the home (Blustein, 2006). After the war ended, many women were expected to return to housework, yet women began to appreciate the benefits of paid work, which propelled them into remaining active within the labor force. By the 1960s, the feminist movement transpired into a social movement that created significant changes in how society viewed women's work both inside and outside the home (Blustein, 2006). It is important to note, however, that much of the traditional discourse examining women's participation in the U.S. labor force has focused primarily on middle-class White women and has disregarded women of color. For example, African American women were working long before the civil rights and feminist movements in the United States, often in underpaid work.

Historically, the career development literature has been male-centered; in 1977, Leona Tyler contended that much of what we know about how an individual prepares for the world of work might be aptly labeled as the vocational development of middle-class men (Heppner & Heppner, 2005). Frank Parsons (1909), the founder of vocational psychology, argued that vocational counseling was necessary to match men to work. Despite the focus on men's work, it wasn't until recently that research has begun to investigate how gender and gender socialization affects men's vocational decision making. Whereas men's career development was studied from a normative perspective that assumed that understanding how men make career decisions allows vocational psychologists and career counselors to work with all individuals, historically research did not examine how men's construction of their gender identity specifically affected their vocational development. For example, until recently very little attention has focused on examining how male gender role socialization, masculine identity, and conflict between traditional and nontraditional gender roles are related to the vocational decision making of men, despite the fact that researchers have examined how gender role socialization has affected women's career development for the past three decades.

Since the 1980s, a plethora of research has emerged examining how gender and career development are related, with a focus specifically on women's career development. Several prominent vocational psychologists (e.g., Betz & Fitzgerald, 1987, Farmer, 1997) have focused primarily on examining the barriers that women experience in entering and maintaining work within the United States. In fact, of all the contextual factors (e.g., race/ethnicity, social class, sexual orientation, ability status) that can and do have an impact on vocational decision making, gender is perhaps the most researched contextual influence. The examination of women's engagement in work is one of the most important and well-known methods of integrating a contextual focus into the psychology of working (Blustein, 2006). Perhaps the heightened emphasis on examining how gender affects women's work is due to the institutional sexism that has systematically limited women's opportunities for employment, advancement, and power within the world of work. Historically women have not had access to the same opportunities as men in terms of work advancement. In fact, the existence and prevalence of sexism in the workforce has been well recognized and established within the field of vocational psychology in both empirical and theoretical work (e.g., Betz & Fitzgerald, 1987; Fitzgerald, 1993a; Norton, 2001). Additionally, recent research and literature (e.g., Heppner & Heppner, 2009; Jome & Toker, 1998; Rochlen, Suizzo, McKelley, & Scaringi, 2008) is beginning to delineate the societal factors that may hinder men from choosing nontraditional career paths. It is vital that we understand how sexism, gender discrimination, and gender socialization affect how both women and men construct meaning around work. This may be particularly important for individuals who experience discrimination that directly interferes with their ability to find gainful and meaningful employment. As the field of vocational psychology moves toward an inclusive psychology-of-working perspective, it is important that psychologists and counselors examine how gender and work intersect for all individuals, even those whose choice and volition around work-related decisions may not be easily available.

The purpose of this chapter is to examine how working interfaces with gender. First, an overview of both women's and men's participation and pay in the workforce will be provided, followed by a discussion of the complex ways that working and gender roles intersect. An emphasis will be placed on how socialization and sexist practices create barriers that limit access to work for women and men. Next, a discussion of gender from a psychology-of-working perspective will be provided, with a focus on how gender influences the meaning of work as a source of survival and power, social connection, and self-determination. Following, two career counseling frameworks, a critical feminist approach and a male socialization approach, will be highlighted. These approaches have specifically integrated gender role socialization and a gendered perspective toward career counseling. The chapter will conclude with suggestions for future directions in moving toward an inclusive, gendered perspective in the psychology of working.

Women's and Men's Participation and Pay in the U.S. Labor Force

Both men and women participate in significant and beneficial ways within the U.S. labor force. Men's participation in the labor force has decreased over the past 50 years, whereas women's participation has increased. In 2010, approximately 71% of men participated in the labor force (Bureau of Labor Statistics [BLS], 2011), a substantial decrease since 1950 and 1970, at which time approximately 86% and 80% of men were employed within the labor force, respectively (BLS, 2007). Numerous factors may have influenced this decline. For example, the Social Security Act was amended in 1950, allowing individuals under the age of 50 to be eligible for disability payments (BLS, 2007). More recently, the world has moved to a global market, which may be creating an economic climate in which the jobs that men have traditionally been employed in, such as manufacturing, have been outsourced to other countries, resulting in less work for men in the United States. Similarly, the economic downturn and recession has had a major impact on men's work, with 10.5% of men unemployed in 2011 (BLS, 2011). The decline in men's participation in the labor force is expected to continue in the future; men are anticipated to participate in the labor force at a rate of 66% by 2050 (BLS, 2007).

While men's participation in the labor force has decreased over the last 50 years, trends in women's participation have considerably increased. In 1950, women participated in the labor force at a rate of approximately 34% (BLS, 2010; Farmer, 2006); this rate increased significantly during the 1970s and 1980s, in part due to the women's rights movement, which advocated for women's right to be gainfully employed in the workforce (Farmer, 2006). Women's labor force participation peaked at the end of the 1990s, when it reached approximately 60%. However, since the beginning of the new millennium, women's participation has decreased; currently 58.6% of women are employed within the United States.

Despite the fact that women now participate in the workforce at a higher rate compared to 50 years ago, women's work tends to be focused in traditionally female occupations (Betz, 2005). For example, women represent greater than 90% of the childcare workers, preschool and kindergarten teachers, registered nurses, dental hygienists, medical assistants, hairdressers, and receptionists (BLS, 2011). Similarly, men are also generally segregated into male-oriented occupations; men represent greater than 90% of construction managers, engineering managers, civil engineers, computer hardware engineers, environmental engineers, miners, firefighters, construction workers, machinists, pilots, motor vehicle operators, and most installation, maintenance,

and repair workers. Although women have made progress in entering male-dominated professions such as medicine and law, gender segregation still exists in many occupational domains. For example, men are employed in engineering fields at a much higher rate when compared to women; only 11.5% of engineers are currently female (National Science Foundation [NSF], 2006).

Even in fields where women are entering male-dominated jobs, occupational segregation still exists. For example, women are now receiving medical degrees at a comparable rate to men. In 2009–2010, women received 48% of the medical degrees awarded, representing the largest number of women entering the medical profession to date (American Association of Medical Colleges [AAMC], 2010). However, female physicians tend to enter subspecialty branches of medicine at differential rates. For example, women make up 77% of the medical residents in obstetrics and gynecology, 73% of the medical residents in pediatrics, 64% of the medical residents in dermatology, and 54% of the medical residents in family medicine. Conversely, men make up 72% of the radiology residents, 69% of the general surgery residents, and 65% of the anesthesiology residents (American Medical Association [AMA], 2008). It is interesting to note that the medical specialties that women are segregated in are more relational in nature and typically pay less than the medical specialties that men are employed in.

Women and men continue to receive differential pay for their work. In 1963, the Equal Pay Act was signed into legislation within the United States and asserted that women and men be paid equally for similar work; essentially this act deemed wage discrimination to be illegal. At that time, women earned 59 cents for every dollar men earned. In 2009, women who were employed full time earned 80 cents to every dollar men earned (BLS, 2011). Although this has increased substantially since 1963, pay equity, or the notion that women and men be paid equally for the same work, still does not truly exist in today's society (Lips, 2010). Even in female-dominated fields, such as teaching and nursing, men continue to receive higher pay. For example, female nurses and elementary and middle school teachers earned 86.5% and 91% of male nurses and teachers' median income, respectively (BLS, 2010). However, when examining women's to men's earnings ratios among racial/ethnic minorities, a different story unfolds. Women's to men's earnings ratios were highest among African Americans (94 cents to every dollar) and Latinos (90 cents to every dollar) when compared to Asians (82 cents) and Whites (79 cents to every dollar; BLS, 2011). Perhaps this is due to the fact that men from racial/ethnic minority backgrounds may already experience wage discrimination and receive lower pay when compared to White men.

It is clear that women and men participate in the labor force in different ways. Despite efforts to decrease occupational segregation, particularly for women, occupational segregation and differential pay continue to exist in both overt and subtle ways. For example, evidence that men receive higher pay even in fields that are traditionally female (i.e., teaching) confirms that wage discrimination still exists. When we unpack trends of women accessing employment in traditionally male occupations (i.e., medicine), subtle trends of occupational segregation surface indicating that women and men continue to differ in the ways they specialize in their careers. Differential specialization, in turn, continues to maintain wage discrepancies between men and women in the world of work, resulting in women continuing to face obstacles that impede their progress toward obtaining equal status as workers in the United States.

Social Factors Related to Labor Force Participation

Social factors can have an influential role on the working lives of both women and men. Gender role socialization, exposure to role models, social messages about work, and harassment and discrimination related to gender may directly and indirectly influence women and men as they make work decisions. The purpose of this section is to provide a gendered analysis on how societal factors have affected the construction of meaning in work for both women and men. This section will highlight various societal factors (i.e., gender role socialization) that obstruct women's and men's willingness to seek nontraditional work as well as institutional and societal barriers (i.e., sexual harassment, undervaluation of women's work) that may impede women from experiencing the privileges associated with work.

Gender Role Socialization

Socialization practices within United States have influenced the occupational and educational decisions that both women and men make. Gender role socialization is the process in which girls and boys, and women and men, are socialized into gender-defined roles based on their biological sex

(Nutt & Brooks, 2008). Gender role socialization can have a powerful impact on how girls and boys learn about appropriate fields of work at a very early age, gain information about the opportunity structure of career options available to them throughout childhood, and construct the vocational aspect of their identities through adolescence and early adulthood.

Gender role socialization may affect exposure to gender stereotypes in the world of work. Early in their lives, girls and boys learn about what types of jobs are more "suitable" for men and women (Betz, 2005). Messages and beliefs that some occupations are more appropriate for either men or women still exist to date. For example, research has found that people consistently rate specific occupations as either more feminine or masculine (Betz, 2005); nurses, receptionists, elementary school teachers, and dietitians are viewed as feminine occupations, whereas engineers, physicists, and heavy equipment operators are judged as highly masculine occupations (Betz, 2005; Shinar, 1975). Girls and boys may see and hear these messages about what types of careers they "should" enter based on their gender identity from parents, schools, and the media (Nutt & Brooks, 2008). These messages may be either overt (hearing others say "Girls can't be pilots" or "Real men aren't nurses") or covert (e.g., hearing others refer to physicians as men and nurses as women regardless of whether gender is known). Children learn gender stereotypes related to occupations at the young age of 2 to 3 and begin to construct their vocational identities and make gender-stereotyped choices for themselves as early as elementary school (Betz, 2006). For example, Mac Kay and Miller (1982) found that third- and fifth-grade girls frequently aspired toward occupations that have higher female representativeness (e.g., nurse, teacher) and boys frequently aspired toward occupations that were stereotypically masculine (e.g., policemen, truck driver, pilot). Even as they get older, girls continued to aspire to female-dominated careers (Miller & Budd, 1999).

Similarly, girls and boys may not be exposed to models of individuals employed in nontraditional careers, which further reinforces the stereotypes that women and men are not allowed or welcome in specific types of careers. Beginning as early as elementary school, both girls and boys are exposed to gender-stereotyped role models (e.g., most elementary teachers are female, whereas a large percentage of principals and administrators are male; Betz, 1994; BLS, 2011). For example, girls may not see any female administrators and thus may foreclose on education administration as a potential occupation choice. However, since many teachers are female, girls may continue to be open to teaching as a possible career. Eccles (1987) suggested that the lack of nontraditional role models for young women may affect the perceived field of work options that girls and women have. Before children even fully understand what it means to possess a gender identity, they may be either consciously or unconsciously constructing vocational identities for themselves that correspond to their gender identity, likely based on these early socialization experiences.

Socialization experiences also may affect how both women and men construct meaning from their vocational lives. Girls and women historically have been socialized to prioritize childrearing and homemaking roles at the expense of other life roles, such as educational and occupational aspirations and pursuits (Betz, 2005). Much of the early scholarship on women's career development has highlighted the complex nature of the career decision-making process for women; women often make work decisions in conjunction with decisions surrounding other life roles, such as their involvement in family caretaking and household responsibilities (Betz & Fitzgerald, 1987; Blustein, 2006). From an early age, girls are generally socialized to engage in caretaking roles; they are encouraged to play with dolls, to be nurturing and sensitive, and to place the needs of others before their own (Betz, 1994). In turn, boys are typically socialized to be independent, strong, and resilient and, later in life, are encouraged to place more importance on their work goals than other aspects of their life (Heppner & Heppner, 2005). Although shifts are currently occurring in regards to men's responsibility for household work and caretaking, socialization within the United States continues to place responsibility for the care of others on women (Blustein, 2006). This socialization process can have a profound impact on how important women perceive their own educational achievements and work goals (Betz, 2005). For example, Farmer (1997) conducted a longitudinal study on the career aspirations of female and male high school students and found that while girls and boys initially start with equally high educational and career aspirations, the aspirations for the girls declined as they matured.

Socialization also can have a profound impact on how men construct their work identities. The traditional view of men as breadwinners has resulted in a societal expectation that men are defined by their work (Heppner & Heppner, 2009). From their first job, men are socialized into a world of work that stresses a lack of separation from "being a man" and "working;" a man's masculinity is often contingent on the degree of career success, achievement, and financial rewards he obtains (Heppner & Heppner, 2009). Further, just as women are highly socialized to be caretakers and nurturers, men are similarly socialized to be workers; if they choose not to work or do not have access to employment, men are generally thought not to have met the societal expectations of masculinity and, therefore, may be shunned and rejected by society (Heppner & Heppner, 2009; Skovholt, 1990).

These socialization experiences can have very direct consequences on the creation and implementation of work identities. Both women and men who engage in nontraditional roles may face discrimination from their work, social, and family lives (Perrone, Wright, & Jackson, 2009). Historically, work occurring within the home, often considered as women's work, has been defined within a patriarchal power structure that devalues women's work in favor of work outside the home, often considered to be men's work (Schultheiss, 2009). Despite the fact that the majority of women are now working, women may continue to experience expectations from family, friends, and their community to take on the primary homemaker and caretaking roles (Betz, 1994), resulting in their accommodating their occupational aspirations to meet their home and family responsibilities (Gilbert & Kearney, 2006). For example, mothering continues to be viewed as more important than fathering within society (Gilbert & Kearney, 2006), perhaps resulting in high expectations being placed upon women to take on a disproportionate share of the childcare and household responsibilities. Women face a unique conundrum in today's world of work; they experience direct and indirect socialization experiences and expectations to engage in childcare and housework while also receiving messages from society that these types of roles are not as prestigious or valued and are not considered "real work." Schultheiss (2009) argues that this challenges women to choose between "mothering or mattering" and often to choose a caretaking role that is both expected and disregarded in patriarchal societies.

Gender role socialization can also have a significant influence on internal views of women's and men's abilities (Gilbert & Kearney, 2006). Research has indicated that women develop perceptions of their abilities based on societal messages on what girls and women are good at. In fact, perhaps one of the most fruitful avenues of research on gender and working emerging from feminist scholars has examined women's beliefs in their abilities, particularly as they relate to participation in math and science fields. For example, Betz and Hackett (1981) established that self-efficacy beliefs are strongly related to women's career aspirations in science and technology fields; self-efficacy beliefs were found to be a stronger predictor than abilities among a sample of undergraduate university students. Research has also found that women possess lower self-efficacy expectations in nontraditional areas such as math, science, technology, engineering, mechanical activities, and outdoor/physical activities but possess higher self-efficacy in gender-traditional activities such as teaching and counseling (Betz & Hackett, 1997). Further, women possessed lower outcome expectations, or beliefs that desired outcomes will result from successful behaviors, related to work (Betz, 2005). This line of research over the past 20 years has been vital in understanding the career development of women because self-efficacy beliefs can serve as a critical filter in circumscribing career and academic pursuits (Blustein, 2006).

Socialization based on gender can have important consequences for men as well. Socialization may lead men to circumscribe their career options based on whether certain work is deemed appropriate for men. Despite possessing interests in particular areas of work, men may foreclose on these areas if they are deemed feminine by society. For example, a male college student may consider nursing as a major, yet may hear messages from friends and the media that nursing is not acceptable work for men. Moreover, men may perceive threats to their masculinity, sexuality, and power as a man if they choose to engage in female-dominated work. For example, in a study of men working in traditionally female-dominated occupations, Lupton (2006) found that men were concerned with preserving their sense of masculinity and heterosexuality. Further, men perceived that traditionally female occupations did not possess the same power and prestige than traditionally male occupations possessed.

Gender role socialization may also impede men's participation in caretaking and nurturing roles; these roles can sometimes be the most rewarding roles that one partakes of in life. Due to socialization influences that suggest work must play a central role in men's lives, and expectations that men should serve as a breadwinner in the family, men may experience discrimination or judgment from family and friends if they choose

to prioritize family roles instead of work roles. For example, Brescoll and Uhlmann (2005) found that stay-at-home fathers and employed mothers were both evaluated more negatively than mothers and fathers who engaged in gender-traditional roles. Surprisingly, stay-at-home fathers received the most negative evaluations regarding their choice. Further, a qualitative investigation by Rochlen, Suizzo, McKelley, and Scaringi (2008) found that stay-at-home fathers acknowledged experiencing stigma related to their roles as primary caretakers. Clearly, men are detrimentally affected by socialization experiences and stigma related to making nontraditional work-related decisions. While women are constricted by narrow gender roles defining them in homemaking and nurturing roles, men are also constricted by narrow gender roles defining them as the primary breadwinner (Perrone, Wright, & Jackson, 2009).

Socialization experiences can have a profound impact in how both women and men perceive their work options, circumscribe and foreclose on potential work choices, and construct meaning out of their vocational identities. Although much of the research examining the effects of gender socialization have focused on the socialization experiences of women, socialization is pertinent to men as well. As the world of work continues to change and become more global, men and women may be required to make work choices that do not correspond with traditional socialization. For example, as manufacturing jobs, a traditional employment area for men, continue to be outsourced to other countries, men may be required to choose work that has been traditionally thought of as "women's work" (i.e., service jobs, nursing). This change can have a profound impact on men's sense of identity, which in turn can affect their psychological well-being. Further, men may experience discrimination and stressors in their environments that devalue them in these types of positions. Women, on the other hand, may also be constricted by narrow gender roles, which can have an even larger impact in today's patriarchal society that continues to value work that men engage in. It is important to think critically about how we socialize both girls and boys in childhood about the role of work in their lives because of the potentially negative impact this may have on their psychological and vocational development. Further, we must continue to examine how we reinforce these messages into adulthood, creating both overt and covert barriers that hinder women and men from making nontraditional choices.

Equity, Sexism, and Work

Various vocational psychologists (e.g., Betz & Fitzgerald, 1987; Blustein, 2006; Fitzgerald, 1993a; Walsh & Osipow, 1994) have recognized that overt and covert sexism exists in the United States. Women and men experience discrimination both within the workplace and from their families, friends, and community. Discrimination can affect the hiring process, the work climate, and wages earned; historically women have experienced intense discrimination for entering what was thought to be a man's domain. Considering that much of the discrimination and sexism within the workforce has predominantly focused on women, this section will primarily focus on how sexism and discrimination impede women from obtaining equity in work.

A longstanding aspect of discrimination against women has been the consistent undervaluing of work completed by women (Lips, 2010). Research has indicated that work completed by men tends to be evaluated more favorably than women (Lips, 2010), job applications and résumés are evaluated more favorably for men when compared to women (Harvie, Marshal-McCaskey, & Johnston, 1998), and success by women is often attributed to "luck" rather than competence (Lips, 2010; Lott, 1985). Further, women who are successful at work are often described as unfeminine and less likeable (Lips, 2010; Lott, 1985). These attributions and evaluations can have a direct impact on the undervaluation of women's work and may be why women receive less credit and less pay for their work.

An indirect form of sexism that impedes women's progress in the world of work is the undervaluation of the type of work that women engage in. Richardson (2012) delineated the difference between market work (i.e., work conducted for pay in society) and personal care work (i.e., work done to care for relationships, such as dependent others and communities). Traditionally, personal care work has been conducted by women whereas market work has been conducted by men. Richardson argued that although personal care work includes vital tasks necessary for the maintenance and growth of society, these tasks are not valued as "work" in traditional discourse about work and career. Conversely, market work, or paid work, has been defined as the only type of work that is valued within American society. With the little value associated with personal care work, not only are women's contributions to society devalued but women are also deemed as not having an occupational identity that is worthy of being respected; in fact, their contribution is simply not thought of as "real" work. As Richardson argued, personal care work and those who engage in it generally have second-class status within American society, perhaps due to patriarchal values that fail to recognize the importance of work related to the care of others.

Further, as discussed earlier, women who choose to participate in market work are socialized to enter traditionally female occupations, which likely generate less pay than traditionally male occupations (Betz, 2005); these occupations tend to be relationally focused. Despite the important role many traditionally female jobs possess, these occupations are not valued as highly in society and therefore are not financially rewarded at the same level as many traditionally male occupations. Further, when women attempt to enter nontraditional careers, they may experience discrimination; they may hear messages in subtle and overt forms that clearly indicate that they are not welcome (Fitzgerald & Harmon, 2001). These messages can include verbal harassment, a lack of social support, discrimination in pay and promotions, lack of involvement in informal and social work-related activities, and unpleasant work environments (Betz, 2005). For example, women may not be invited to social gatherings or sporting events after work by their male colleagues; even though these events are social in nature, official business and informal mentoring may occur at these events, leaving those who are not invited at a disadvantage.

Motherhood has also been a source of discrimination for women in employment and working (Lips, 2010). Until legal proceedings in the 1970s, discrimination based on pregnancy or the potential of pregnancy was legal in the United States (Lips, 2010). In 1991, the Supreme Court ruled against the practice of discriminating in employment based on pregnancy or the potential of pregnancy (Lips, 2010). However, although formal discrimination is now illegal, societal expectations that women are assigned to the bulk of childcare responsibilities create work–family dynamics that directly affect women's work. Further, the socialization for women to engage in caretaking directly influences their work decisions (Fitzgerald, Fassinger, & Betz, 1995). Many women plan their careers in a manner that is mindful of work–family balance and conflict (Betz, 2005). An unfortunate consequence of this planning is that many women may downscale their career aspirations in order to prioritize their family obligations. Additionally, employers may be hesitant to hire women due to fear that they will leave their jobs due to family priorities. This can be particularly damaging when considering that many women do not have the option of choosing to work; rather, engaging in paid work is necessary to obtain basic needs.

Gender-based discrimination in working may also surface in concerns by employers over the work values that women possess. Pratto and her colleagues (1997) proposed a social dominance approach that focuses on perceptions of men's and women's work values to account for the gender gap in occupational attainment; they argue that employers make hiring decisions based on their perceptions of a candidate's value system. Considering that women are fairly new to the world of work, employers and hiring managers assume that women hold values that challenge the system and status quo whereas men possess values that perpetuate existing systems within the employment setting (Lips, 2010). Simply stated, men are perceived to hold values that maintain the status quo whereas women are perceived to serve the interests of oppressed groups. In experimental investigations, Pratto and her colleagues (1997) found that research participants favored women for positions that served the interests of oppressed groups and favored men for positions that preserved the status quo, regardless of whether applicants' résumés violated stereotypes regarding value systems (Lips, 2010). Although Pratto and her colleagues' (1997) research was conducted in an experimental, laboratory setting with college students as participants rather than true hiring managers, this line of research is extremely informative in examining the power structures that may play a role in perpetuating occupational segregation and discrimination of women in the world of work.

Sexual harassment is a longstanding and increasingly visible problem in the workplace for women (Farmer, 2006). Sexual harassment was legally defined in 1980, when the U.S. Equal Employment Opportunity Commission published guidelines on sexual harassment in the workplace (Fitzgerald, 1993a). Defined as behavior that creates a threatening, offensive, or hostile work environment for women and interferes with work performance (Farmer, 2006), sexual harassment has been categorized in two broad categories (Fitzgerald, 1993a). *Quid pro quo* harassment attempts to extort sexual relations by making job-related threats, whereas *hostile environment* harassment occurs when pervasive and unwelcome sex-related verbal or physical conduct is present in the workplace regardless of job-related consequences (Fitzgerald, 1993a).

Fitzgerald (1993a) estimates that approximately half of women employed in the workforce or enrolled in post-secondary education will be harassed during their lifetime; African American and Latina women may have a greater likelihood of workplace harassment (Betz, 2005). Recently, an AAUW report (2006) found two thirds of college students experienced sexual harassment during their college experience; many of these students stated that these experiences damaged their educational experiences in college (Fassinger, 2008). The high rate of likelihood that harassment can occur for many women in the workplace or at educational institutions is even more striking when considering the consequences of harassment. Sexual harassment has been related to job loss, decreased job satisfaction, decreased morale and absenteeism, and damaged interpersonal relationships at work (Fitzgerald, 1993a). Sexual harassment has also been found to be directly related to psychological (i.e., stress-related reactions to harassment, such as depression or anxiety) and work outcomes (i.e., job satisfaction and organizational withdrawal) and indirectly related to health outcomes (i.e., sleep disturbances, headaches; Fitzgerald, Drasgow, Hulin, Gelfand, & Magley, 1997). Women who experienced sexual harassment had higher levels of absenteeism, expressed stronger intentions to leave their employment, and spent more time thinking about leaving their jobs (Fitzgerald, Drasgow, Hulin, Gelfand, & Magley, 1997). While women often receive the most direct negative effects of sexual harassment in the workplace, men too experience adverse effects; hostility toward women in the workplace was related to declines in well-being for both female and male employees, suggesting that all employees suffer when working in environments that are hostile toward women (Fassinger, 2008; Miner-Rubino & Cortino, 2004).

It is also important to examine harassment as a mechanism of social control (Fitzgerald, 1993a). Historically, workplace harassment has been viewed as an expression of hostility for women entering a man's world. Workplace harassment clearly sent the message to women that they should not venture beyond the roles of homemaker and caregiver and were not welcome in the masculine field of paid, outside work. As Fitzgerald (1993a) clearly notes, sexual harassment originated from and currently supports women's subordinate position in society. Women are often expected to accept and deal with harassment and are faced with making decisions that are so aversive that they may not be considered as choice at all; to report harassment and cope with often very negative consequences (i.e., job loss or demotion, stigmatization, social alienation) or to be silent while continuing to live with the negative consequences of being ostracized, at times on a daily basis (Fitzgerald, 1993a).

A consequence of the sexist and discriminatory practices described can be seen in what has been commonly referred to as the glass ceiling in women's employment. The glass ceiling refers to the small number of women at top levels of management. Although women can aspire to high-level positions within organizations and companies, many institutional barriers, such as those described above, often prevent them from advancing within the organization (Lips, 2010). For example, women represent only 3% of the chief executive officers among Fortune 500 companies and hold only 15% of board seats within these companies (Lang, 2010). In the influential book *Opting Out? Why Women Really Quit Career and Head Home*, Stone (2007) argues that women are forced to quit their careers by unwelcoming and hostile workplace climates that are grounded within a competitive framework. Inhospitable workplaces, coupled with sexism and gender-based discrimination, create a societal context in which women may feel unwelcome in the world of work.

Further, the benefits of working for women have been well documented (i.e., source of income, means to implement one's self-concept, source of social support; Betz, 2006), yet the consequences of the gender-based discrimination in working can contribute to mental health and physical concerns for women. For example, working allows women to utilize their abilities, allows them develop their unique talents, and allows them to achieve (Betz, 2006). Working can also be beneficial for women by providing social support, opportunities to experience success, and increase their self-complexity (Barnett & Hyde, 2001). Further, working can provide women with income (Barnett & Hyde, 2001) and an opportunity to gain not only financial independence and security but also wealth, which is highly valued within capitalistic societies such as the United States. For individuals from lower socioeconomic backgrounds and particularly for women living in poverty, the benefits and necessities of working are even greater, since working may provide the only means for basic survival and for accessing basic necessities such as food, shelter, and clothing. These benefits may be particularly salient for single mothers who are solely responsible for the financial support and well-being of their families. In these cases, the consequences of sexist and discriminatory hiring practices and harassment in the workplace can be profound. If women experience great benefits from working and in many cases are required to work for survival but also experience adverse and hostile work environments that discourage, discriminate against, and harass women for entering a man's world, they are often forced into a no-win situation in which they need to develop coping mechanisms to deal with these hostile environments. In essence, this results in placing responsibility for creating individual change (i.e., coping with unhealthy work environments) onto women who often do not have access to power structures that can lead to large-scale, societal changes that could potentially eliminate discrimination in the workplace.

Psychology of Working

It is beyond the scope of this chapter to provide a comprehensive overview of the psychology-of-working framework, but readers are referred to the introductory chapter in this Handbook, Blustein (2006), and Blustein, Kenna, Gill and DeVoy (2008), for a thorough and complete overview. This section will provide a brief overview of the psychology-of-working perspective and present a discussion on how gender can be an influential aspect of the psychology of work. Briefly stated, the psychology-of-working framework operates on the premise that the context of work shapes human lives and that work needs to be explored and understood for all citizens, not simply those who are privileged to have choice and volition in selecting work (Blustein et al., 2008). This perspective emerged from a need to develop an inclusive perspective that examined the role of work in the lives of individuals who may not have volition or choice in their work lives.

Working as Survival and Power

One of the most fundamental purposes of working is to provide people with access to resources that are necessary for survival (Blustein, 2006). Through work, and the financial rewards associated with work, people can access food and water, shelter, clothing, and safety (Blustein et al, 2008). It is only after meeting these basic needs that people can achieve higher-level goals, such as self-actualization (Blustein et al, 2008). Despite influential theorists (e.g., Maslow, 1968) arguing that achieving higher-level goals can occur only after basic needs are met, many traditional career development theories operate on the premise that all individuals have choice and volition to make work decisions that are based on their self-concept and provide them an avenue to implement this self-concept. In an ideal world, working would be a meaningful activity that provides a road toward self-actualization for all individuals; however, this is regrettably not the reality for much of the world's population, including many individuals who live in the United States and other Western nations (Blustein et al., 2008).

In addition to providing a means for survival, work also provides people with ability to meet the human need for economic and social power (Blustein, 2006; Blustein et al., 2008). The act of working provides access to both material and social resources; work provides people with money, status, prestige, and privilege (Blustein et al., 2008). An individual's economic and social power is often directly linked to his or her work and career choices (Schulenberg, Vondracek, & Crouter, 1984). However, the power individuals receive through their work is not equitable for all individuals in the United States, simply because individuals are born with varying levels of access to the opportunity structure (Blustein et al., 2008). One's educational opportunities, exposure to role models, and perceptions of one's opportunity structure are all closely linked to one's social class and affect how one develops meaning related to working (Blustein, 2006; Gysbers, Heppner, & Johnston, 2003). Thus, counselors and psychologists must understand the structural barriers in place that may influence the meaning of work, particularly for individuals who may not possess volition or choice in their work decisions.

Considering that paid work outside the home was largely unattainable for women until the mid-20th century, women were unable to access the financial rewards and privileges associated with work until the past half-century. For example, in 1940, census figures illustrate that only 4% of women with children were employed in the labor market (Farmer, 2006). Not being allowed to and/or being discouraged from earning an income and providing shelter, food, clothing, and other basic necessities has left women in a very vulnerable position within society; they have been forced to be dependent on men (fathers, spouses, or other male family members) for basic necessities required for survival. Even for women who worked outside the home (e.g., African Americans have historically worked outside of the home long before the women's suffrage movement, an offshoot of the work women conducted as slaves

in the United States; Blustein, 2006), the work that was attainable for women typically paid poorly and may not have provided sufficient resources for a comfortable living. Further, women not employed in the workforce also did not have access to many privileges that are linked to paid work, such as access to health insurance and retirement planning.

Even after women consistently began working outside the home, they were often employed in gender-traditional employment that was not valued and paid as highly as men's work. Sex segregation within the occupational landscape and differential pay have critical consequences on women's ability to finance basic necessities and access power within society. For example, women have a higher working poor rate (6.5%) and a higher poverty rate than men (5.6%; BLS, 2011; Farmer, 2006). Devoid of equitable pay, women are at a much higher risk for not being able to find employment that provides adequate financial resources to pay for basic needs. Without access to work, or work that pays comparable wages when compared to men, women are left in a subordinate and disempowered position within society; likewise, obstructing and underpaying women's work maintains a power structure that privileges men (Blustein, 2006).

Additionally, whether partnered or single, many women with children in today's society simply do not have a choice regarding whether to work or not (Schultheiss, 2009). Even if they want to stay at home and care for their children, many women cannot afford this choice and are forced to work for financial reasons. Women from lower social class backgrounds are faced with an even larger dilemma. They are required to work to obtain the financial resources required for basic necessities, yet if they have children, the cost of childcare meets or exceeds the financial benefits of work (Schultheiss, 2009). If they are forced to rely on government assistance to help pay for childcare while they work, they are often judged by society as irresponsible, socially unacceptable, and "bad mothers" (Schultheiss, 2009).

For women from middle-class backgrounds, the aforementioned barriers (i.e., undervaluation of work completed by women, sexism, sexual harassment, and gender-based discrimination) hinder women from entering upper-level positions that are often associated with access to power. Considering that work can often provide individuals with social status, and the power and privileges that come with a high social status, experiencing oppression and discrimination within the workforce maintains the status quo that preserves these privileges solely for men. As Pratto's (1997) social dominance approach asserts, women may be discouraged from entering high-level positions that have access to power due to covert and implicit assumptions that hiring women will disrupt the status quo.

An example of women's lack of representation in positions of power within the world of work can be seen in the number of women employed in upper-level government positions. One could argue that very few positions in society have as much power as those that directly work at creating, expanding, and refining the governances within U.S. society. Yet, when we examine the number of women within these positions, we see a clear lack of representation. Of the 100 senators and 435 members of the House of Representatives in 2011, 17 (17%) senators and 90 (16.8%) representatives were women (Center for American Women and Politics [CAWP], 2011; Women in Congress, 2011); of the 50 states, only 6 had female governors (CAWP, 2011). These very low percentages of representation are even more striking when one considers that women represent 51% of the U.S. population (U.S. Census Bureau, 2011). How can we work toward wage equity, punish discrimination against women, and enable women to gain access to power within society when women do not have representation in the positions that can directly create these laws?

Working and Social Connection

In addition to resources and power, working provides individuals with an opportunity to connect to others in their social environments (Blustein, 2006). Work has the potential to provide supportive and nurturing relationships, which can help individuals cope with challenges as well as provide an avenue for directly relating to others and developing one's identity (Blustein et al., 2008). Additionally, work can help contribute to the larger society, which has the potential to provide individuals with a sense of connection to the greater community (Blustein et al., 2008). Despite the potentially profound impact that social connection can have on work choices, the role of social connection has been somewhat overlooked within the vocational literature. For example, Richardson (2012) recently called upon vocational psychologists to expand their understanding of how various social contexts affect work decisions. In her proposal of a social constructionist perspective, Richardson argued that market work relationships, or relationships with mentors, bosses, supervisors, colleagues, teachers, and students, are an important area in which people construct their lives. Despite its importance, Richardson argued that market work relationships and their influence on vocational identity development have been largely overlooked as a social context that affects work choices.

Working as a means for social connection can be salient for both women and men. Despite the school of thought that argues that relationships may be more important for women due to socialization experiences (Lips, 2010), leading feminist theorists have argued that relationships, and relational perspectives, are just as meaningful for men as they are for women (Jordan & Hartling, 2002). However, men may not be as comfortable or willing to discuss the implications of social connection due to gender role socialization that generally encourages men to be strong, autonomous, and individually focused (Heppner & Heppner, 2009). For example, paid work typically involves working closely with colleagues and coworkers, which has the potential to provide meaningful social connection within people's vocational lives. In particular, for men who may not have been socialized to relationally connect to other men, work can provide a socially acceptable way to relate to men and build meaningful relationships. This is also true for women; work can provide the opportunity to relate to and connect with other women who possess similar vocations and work interests. Further, for women in nontraditional careers, work can provide the potential to build meaningful relationships that facilitate support and encouragement in the workplace. This is particularly important for women of color. In fact, research has documented the important role that family, friends, and mentors, both at work and outside of work, can have on women persisting in the world of work (Betz, 2005). Connection to others can be helpful and supportive for both White women and women of color. For example, in a qualitative investigation of high-achieving African American and Caucasian women, Richie and her colleagues (1997) found that interconnectedness with others was an important factor in continuing toward achievement. Pearson and Bieschke (2001) and Gomez and her colleagues (2001) found that family values and support had a significant influence on African American and Latina women's vocational development.

Another aspect of social connection in working is the interface between working and family life (Blustein, 2006). Since the time that women have entered the workforce, work–family balance has been a continual issue that women face when making work decisions. Although the work–family connection has historically been examined as a woman's issue, the struggle to relate meaningfully to both work and family is not exclusive to women: men, too, struggle with this challenge. In a seminal piece, Barnett and Hyde (2001) argue that multiple roles in regard to work and family responsibilities are beneficial for both women and men. They argue that possessing multiple roles is beneficial for the mental, physical, and relationship health of men and women; further, Barnett and Hyde (2001) argue that multiple roles buffer people from failure in other roles and provide additional income, social support, opportunities to experience success, expanded frames of reference, and adaptive gender role beliefs. Barnett and Hyde (2001) contend that while multiple roles are advantageous to both genders, the benefits of these roles depend on role quality. For example, while providing opportunities for success, multiple roles also provide opportunities for failure, especially in the context of workplace discrimination.

Much of the literature that has paid attention to the interface between work and family has focused on middle-class populations (Blustein, 2006) and has not paid sufficient attention to the portion of the population for whom engaging in paid work is not a choice. For psychologists and counselors to fully understand how both women and men construct identities around work and family, the research and literature must be expanded to represent individuals who are from lower-class backgrounds. This may be particularly important for individuals who experience a larger number of barriers to finding meaningful work or advancing within the workplace, since strong work relationships and connection within the workplace can act as a buffer against the negative effects of these types of barriers. Without strong relationships or a connection to colleagues and peers, individuals who experience significant barriers may have difficulty staying engaged with their work environments and colleagues, may decline advancement opportunities due to lack of support, or may simply choose to withdraw from specific work environments due to the feelings of isolation and dissatisfaction. Further, work often allows people to feel connected with the greater community. Without an avenue to develop this feeling of connection to a greater community, men and women alike are at risk of experiencing a plethora of mental health (i.e., depression, hopelessness) and existential concerns.

Working as Self-Determination

Working provides individuals with the opportunity for self-determination, or to pursue activities that they are intrinsically interested in and that represent an expression of their self-concept (Blustein, 2006; Deci & Ryan, 2000). However, many individuals do not have the privilege of selecting work for self-determination; rather, many individuals have to find to work in jobs that are inherently uninteresting, undignified, and unmotivating (Blustein et al., 2006). In fact, Deci and Ryan (2000) have recognized that many human tasks are neither interesting nor rewarding. Deci and Ryan (2000) identified various contextual factors that may create more comfort and perhaps even more meaning in work that is inherently uninteresting (Blustein et al., 2006). Specifically, Deci and Ryan (2000) argued that work that is pursued for extrinsic reasons, such as financial resources, may become personally meaningful if the work provides opportunities for autonomy, relatedness, and competence (Blustein et al., 2008). Additionally, Blustein (2006) argued that value congruence and access to the opportunity structure might also promote meaning in work. Value congruence is the degree to which individuals' personal goals and values correspond with an organization or an employer's goals and values; access to the opportunity structure reflects people's abilities to access and use resources that will benefit their work experiences and help them perform work-related duties, resulting in successful work experiences (Blustein et al., 2008). Self-determination theory has the potential to enhance employment conditions, particularly for individuals who may not have much choice regarding work and may be forced to take any available job to support themselves.

As articulated thus far, gender role socialization can explicitly and implicitly encourage women and men to enter traditional occupations that fit with their gender, regardless of whether they are interested or passionate about the occupation. For example, a woman may enter nursing because she is encouraged by others, she deems it to be a viable and acceptable career for a woman, she sees others like her being successful in nursing, and she deems it an occupation that may be amenable to juggling work and family responsibilities. However, this woman may not be intrinsically interested in nursing nor is she passionate about working in the healthcare field. Although this woman may not be interested in nursing as a vocation, nursing may provide other benefits that are meaningful to her, resulting in her being motivated to stay in the occupation. For example, she may feel like she's competent at her work, she may enjoy spending time with and gaining support from her colleagues, she may feel like her boss allows her to work autonomously at her job, nursing may correspond with her values, and she may have had access to scholarships specifically designed to recruit students to nursing. All of these factors may influence this woman's motivation to enter the nursing field and to construct meaning around her employment in nursing despite the fact that she is uninterested in the tasks and duties related to nursing.

Access to the opportunity structure is an important aspect of self-determination. Traditional notions of career development have historically emphasized that a structure of opportunity is available to all individuals if they simply work hard enough (Gysbers, Heppner, & Johnston, 2003). This belief coincides with the myth of meritocracy in the United States; meritocracy assumes that societal resources, such as education and career training opportunities, are distributed primarily on the basis of individual merit (Rossides, 1997). Yet, this belief that advancement in the labor market is based on merit alone is an extremely damaging American myth because meritocracy does not truly exist in the United States. The education and training one receives is often based on a combination of access to resources and opportunities and individual efforts. A comprehensive discussion of why people are motivated to work in certain vocations needs to include a discussion of the opportunity structure available to individuals that are not based on merit alone (Blustein, 2006). This includes one's access to housing, supportive family members, a safe neighborhood, effective education, and financial support for education and training (Blustein, 2006). It is commonly thought that people who have greater access to opportunity are more likely to find rewarding work (Blustein, 2006).

Women and men have differential access to the opportunity structure. Women live in poverty at a higher rate than men (Heppner & O'Brien, 2006) and are more likely to be single caretakers of dependent others (U.S. Census Bureau, 2011), and thus are more likely to have less access to housing and financial resources compared to men. This may result in women being forced to make decisions regarding work that are both demeaning and dangerous (i.e., prostitution). Work in these areas can act as a way to further disempower women, although many vocational psychologists have argued that work outside the home can act as an avenue to empower women and achieve equity between the sexes (Betz & Fitzgerald, 1987; Blustein, 2006). Clearly, access to opportunity plays a large role in how work decisions are made, especially for those who may not feel they have a choice at all.

Career Counseling Frameworks that Integrate an Inclusive Gendered Perspective

Implementing a psychology-of-working perspective is vital when examining the role of work in the vocational lives of both female and male clients. To provide effective career counseling that operates from an inclusive framework, it is important to review career counseling frameworks that integrate an inclusive, gendered perspective. Due to space limitations, a comprehensive overview of a multitude of frameworks that highlight the role of gender in making work decisions will not be provided. Instead, this section will highlight two separate frameworks, a critical feminist approach and a male socialization approach, which can be used to provide work-based counseling for both women and men. Each of these approaches specifically integrates gender role socialization and incorporates an inclusive gendered perspective to understand the meaning of work in women's and men's lives.

Critical Feminist Approach

Chronister, McWhirter, and Forrest (2006) developed a critical feminist approach that infuses feminist principles in providing career counseling to women from an empowerment perspective. The critical feminist approach is a framework that allows counselors to systematically examine the influence of larger contextual factors such as gender role socialization and sexism on women's career development. This approach integrates McWhirter's (1994, 1997) five *C*s of empowerment: collaboration, competence, context, critical consciousness, and community.

First, a critical feminist approach emphasizes the need to have a collaborative, dynamic relationship between a counselor and a client; the power differential within this relationship is minimized as much as possible. The second component for counseling for empowerment, competence, focuses on recognizing and emphasizing women's skills, resources, and experiences in a strength-based manner. The third component, context, refers to understanding women and their lives within an ecological perspective that includes families, work environments, sociopolitical histories, cultures, educational environments, and the economic conditions within the home, neighborhood, community, and nation (Chronister, McWhirter, & Forrest, 2006). This includes a close examination of the oppressive power and privilege that women may have experienced within their contexts. The fourth component, critical consciousness, concentrates on identifying how power is manifested in the woman's life and creating awareness of how she can transform the power dynamics within her life (Chronister, McWhirter, & Forrest, 2006). Finally, community, the fifth component of counseling for empowerment, requires women to engage with some form of community to obtain support from others and to contribute to the empowerment of others.

Chronister, McWhirter, and Forrest (2006) argue that a career counseling approach that infuses these principles of counseling for empowerment operates from a feminist perspective by addressing power dynamics related to varying levels of diversity (i.e., gender, race/ethnicity, class, sexual orientation, age, and ability) and across a broad range of contexts (i.e., family, community, and within the larger society). Further, a critical feminist approach incorporates an emphasis on women's strengths and resources as part of the empowerment process (Chronister, McWhirter, & Forrest, 2006). This can be an incredibly powerful aspect of the career counseling process, considering the historical oppression of women within society, particularly the devaluation of qualities and values that are deemed feminine.

Further, a critical feminist approach allows counselors to examine the multiple sociocultural and ecological factors that may be influencing a client's life. This is a critical step in holistically understanding the emotional, physical, mental, economic, career, and spiritual needs of women (Chronister, McWhirter, & Forrest, 2006). Additionally, infusing a critical consciousness framework allows psychologists and counselors to explore power dynamics both within the counseling relationship and within society as a whole. Exploring these power dynamics for women may include an emphasis on examining and understanding family and work dynamics, gender role socialization, sexism, racism, classism, and the school and work contexts of an individual (Chronister, McWhirter, & Forrest, 2006). Finally, encouraging and empowering women to connect with their communities has the potential to provide women with a source of identity, strength, hope, history, resources, and opportunities for support and challenge (Chronister, McWhirter, & Forrest, 2006). This corresponds with the psychology-of-working perspective that argues that work can provide individuals with a sense of connection with the greater community.

Chronister, McWhirter, and Forrest (2006) argue that a critical feminist approach can be empowering for all women. It has the potential to allow women to understand the various contextual influences that affect how they construct their work identities in a manner that is both significant and meaningful to them. The authors argue that this approach does not differ substantially from effective, holistic career counseling; rather, conceptualizing clients from a critical feminist approach allows counselors and female clients to highlight certain processes and dynamics within a framework that guides an empowering career counseling process for women (Chronister, McWhirter, & Forrest, 2006).

Male Socialization Approach

Heppner and Heppner (2005) noted that a curious irony exists within the career development literature of men. Historically, the field of vocational psychology has been male-centered, yet much of the foundational work in career development viewed men as a homogeneous group and did not examine the context of men's career decisions. For example, early vocational research did not examine how gender role socialization affects men's career choices, nor did researchers explore the psychological consequences for men who work in nontraditional fields.

To provide career counseling that is sensitive to the unique factors that affect men's work decisions, Heppner and Heppner (2005) argue that ten issues are critical to address when working with men. First, it is important to examine and understand how early and current gender role socialization has influenced both personal and work choices. When examining gender role socialization, discussions related to how early attitudes about sex-appropriate and sex-inappropriate occupations were formed can be greatly beneficial to understanding the socialization process. Men may not be aware of the early messages they received. A second issue that may be significant for men is socialization related to the role that work should play in men's lives (Heppner & Heppner, 2005). Society typically defines men based on their employment, which in turn may lead men to strongly identify with their work. Men may hear messages that to be a "real" man, they need to be successful in their career, achieve, make money, and afford material possessions (Heppner & Heppner, 2005). It may be beneficial to explore how these socialization experiences have affected how men construct meaning from their vocational lives. Third, to provide effective career counseling to men, vocational psychologists and career counselors should not subscribe to the myth that all men are alike and should embrace the fact that men may differ in various aspects, including but not limited to racial/ethnic background, sexual orientation, development, ability status, and spirituality.

A fourth issue that may be important when providing gender-sensitive career counseling for men is to accurately assess gender and gender-related constructs. Heppner and Heppner (2005) argue that career counselors may want to consider assessing for gender role conflict, gender-related stress, and male roles. Fifth, it is important that career counselors use a holistic approach when working with men and integrate an examination of psychological adjustment within career counseling. Building on a strengths-based perspective, the sixth issue that Heppner and Heppner (2005) highlight is the importance of going beyond the negative aspects of gender role socialization by exploring, recognizing, and affirming the strengths that male socialization can develop. It is important not only to highlight these strengths but also to draw these skills out during the counseling process. A seventh issue that may be important when counseling men is the difficulty of seeking help. The act of seeking counseling can go against male gender role socialization thus men may be resistant to initially seeking help. It may be particularly important to encourage men to seek help when needed.

Eighth, Heppner and Heppner (2005) argue that building a strong working alliance can be very important but also poses some challenges due to male socialization that discourages men from relating to others, particularly other men. Additionally, career counselors need to be aware that men may be socialized to take action rather than process their feelings and emotions during counseling due to socialization experiences that may have discouraged them from talking about their emotions. It may be important to balance problem solving with identifying psychological issues and feelings. Finally, an issue that may be particularly important for men is the changing job market and skills requirements (Heppner & Heppner, 2005). The personal characteristics that have been vital to employment over the past generation, such as competitiveness, hierarchy, longevity, and stability, may not be valued as highly in today's world of work. Men are being asked to adapt to and obtain new work and interpersonal skills in today's workplace, which may result in feelings of discomfort, inadequacy, and stress.

Heppner and Heppner (2005) argue that providing gender-sensitive counseling to men needs to integrate these ten critical issues. It is particularly important to address these constructs as the world of work changes within the United States, as we move toward a global economy, and as economic crises endanger work for men today. For example, if men are traditionally socialized to identify deeply with their work, what happens to that identity when work becomes more difficult to attain? It appears that for both men and women, economic barriers are making it even more difficult to find meaningful work. If unemployed for long periods of time, how are men coping with their masculinity and gender identity? It may be particularly important to discuss gender identity and role socialization with men who are employed in nontraditional work, both paid and unpaid. How does gender role socialization affect men who choose not to engage in paid work or men who cannot find gainful employment? Similarly, how does engaging in nontraditional work, or work considered feminine in nature (i.e., caretaking, nursing), affect men's sense of identity and masculinity as well as their access to power within a patriarchal society? These questions are critical when beginning to implement a psychology-of-working perspective when counseling men.

Conclusion

Considering the gendered context of work and the strict gender role socialization around work-related activities that has permeated American society, it is evident that gender and work are intimately related. This chapter has explored the complex ways that working and gender roles intersect by examining gender role socialization, sexism, discrimination, and equity from an inclusive, psychology-of-working perspective. Access to meaningful paid work has historically been denied to women. As women continue to enter the world of work at increasing rates, remnants of this exclusion continue to exist in the form of both overt and covert sexism and discrimination. Similarly, as women engage in paid work, both for intrinsic reasons to implement self-concept and extrinsic reasons to acquire the financial resources to meet basic survival needs, the role of men in the world of work continues to shift and change. Women and men continue to balance work roles with family roles in a manner that allows them to obtain the resources needed for survival, to gain power and status within society, to relate to others in meaningful ways, and to pursue activities that represent an expression of their self-concepts.

To implement an inclusive approach to understanding the role of gender on working, counselors and psychologists must conceptualize work in a manner that traditional career theories often did not account for. Choice and volition related to work may not be a privilege that all individuals have; clearly, women have been denied access to this privilege for years. Further, individuals from low socioeconomic backgrounds may not have access to opportunity structures that allow them to have choice in their work decisions. These opportunity structures often influence how individuals construct meaning around the intersection of gender and work. We must explore and understand the meaning of work for all individuals, not simply those who are privileged to have what is often referred to as a career. Thus, in conclusion of this chapter, readers are left with some areas that still need to be fully discussed when exploring work from a gendered perspective.

Future Directions

The following questions need to be investigated to fully understand the gendered context of working from an inclusive perspective:

1. How do structural barriers, such as gender role socialization, exposure to role models, limited educational opportunities, the continued existence of sexism, and income inequity and poverty affect how both women and men perceive their opportunities within the world of work? Further, how do these structural barriers circumscribe work choices for women and men?

2. How does gender intermix with other dimensions of identity (i.e., race/ethnicity, social class, sexual orientation, ability status, and spirituality) to create a unique vocational identity for individuals? Specifically, how is meaning constructed around work when gender is fused with other important dimensions of identity? Gender must not be examined alone because the socialization experiences related to gender can be culture-specific.

3. How can we help women develop strategies to augment resistance to sexism and gender role socialization? How can we help men develop strategies to augment gender role socialization and notions of masculinity that may circumscribe their work options? This is particularly important when one considers how pervasive gender role socialization, sexism, and discrimination continue to be within society.

4. How does gender affect work decisions for individuals who may not perceive that they have much choice in the process? For individuals who simply need to find employment to obtain the necessary resources for survival, how does gender affect the meaning they construct out of their work lives? Do women and men differ in the types of work they are willing to engage in for survival?

5. How do sexism and discrimination factor in the types of employment that are available to women? For example, considering the objectification of women's bodies within society and often the high rewards associated with it, do women feel the need to objectify their bodies through prostitution or exotic dancing in order to find employment that provides enough financial resources to survive within the United States? This may be particularly salient for women, considering the wage discrepancies between men and women.

References

American Association of Medical Colleges (AAMC, 2010). U.S. medical school applicants and students 1982–83 to 2010–2011. Retrieved from https://www.aamc.org/.

American Association of University Women. (2006). *Drawing the line: Sexual harassment on campus.* Washington, DC: American Association of University Women Educational Foundation.

American Medical Association. (2008). Women residents by specialty. Statistics history. Retrieved from http://www.ama-assn.org

Barnett, R. C., & Hyde, J. S. (2001). Women, men, work, and family. *American Psychologist, 56,* 781–796.

Betz, N. E. (1994). Basic issues and concepts in career counseling for women. In W. B. Walsh & S. H. Osipow (Eds.), *Career counseling for women* (pp. 45–74). Hillsdale, NJ: Lawrence Erlbaum Associates, Inc.

Betz, N. E. (2005). Women's career development. In S. D. Brown & R. W. Lent (Eds.), *Career development and counseling: Putting theory and research to work* (pp. 253–277). Hoboken, NJ: John Wiley & Sons.

Betz, N. E. (2006). Basic issues and concepts in the career development and counseling of women. In W. B. Walsh & M. J. Heppner (Eds.), *Handbook of career counseling for women* (2nd ed, pp. 45–74). Mahwah, NJ: Lawrence Erlbaum Associates.

Betz, N. E. & Fitzgerald, L. (1987). *The career psychology of women.* Orlando, FL: Academic Press.

Betz, N. E.. & Hackett, G. (1981). The relationship of career-related self-efficacy expectations to perceived career options in college women and men. *Journal of Counseling Psychology, 28,* 399–410.

Betz, N. E.. & Hackett, G. (1997). Applications of self-efficacy theory to the career assessment of women. *Journal of Career Assessment, 5,* 383–402.

Blustein, D. L. (2006). *The psychology of working: A new perspective for career development, counseling, and public policy.* Mahwah, NJ: Lawrence Erlbaum Associates.

Blustein, D. L., Kenna, A. C., Gil, N., & DeVoy, J. E. (2008). The psychology of working: A new framework for counseling practice and public policy. *Career Development Quarterly, 56*, 294–308.

Brescoll, V. L., & Uhlmann, E. L. (2005). Attitudes toward traditional and nontraditional parents. *Psychology of Women Quarterly, 29*, 436–445.

Bureau of Labor Statistics (BLS; 2007). Changes in men's and women's labor force participation rates. Retrieved from http://www.bls.gov

Bureau of Labor Statistics (BLS; 2010). Median weekly earnings of full-time wage and salary workers by detailed occupation and sex. Retrieved from http://www.bls.gov

Bureau of Labor Statistics (BLS; 2011). Employment status of the civilian noninstitutional population 16 years and over by sex, 1973 to date. Retrieved from https://www.bls.gov

Bureau of Labor Statistics (BLS; 2011). Women in the labor force: A databook. Labor force statistics from the Current Population Survey. Retrieved from http://www.bls.gov.

Center for American Women and Politics (CAWP, 2011). Women in elective office. Retrieved from http://www.cawp.rutgers.edu/fast_facts/levels_of_office/documents/elective.pdf

Chronister, K. M., McWhirter, E. H., & Forrest, L. (2006). A critical feminist approach to career counseling with women. In W. B. Walsh & M. J. Heppner (Eds.), *Handbook of career counseling for women* (2nd ed, pp. 167–192) Mahwah, NJ: Lawrence Erlbaum Associates.

Deci, E. L., & Ryan, R. M. (2000). The "what" and "why" of goal pursuits: Human needs and self-determination of behavior. *Psychological Inquiry, 11*, 227–268.

Eccles, J. S. (1987). Gender roles and women's achievement-related decisions. *Psychology of Women Quarterly, 11*, 135–171.

Farmer, H. S. (2006). History of career counseling for women. In W. B. Walsh & M. J. Heppner (Eds.), *Handbook of career counseling for women* (2nd ed, pp. 1–44). Mahwah, NJ: Lawrence Erlbaum Associates.

Farmer, H. S. (1997). *Diversity and women's career development: From adolescence to adulthood.* Thousand Oaks, CA: Sage Publications, Inc.

Fassinger, R. E. (2008). Workplace diversity and public policy: Challenges and opportunities for psychology. *American Psychologist, 63*, 252–268.

Fitzgerald, L. F. (1993a). Sexual harassment: Violence against women in the workplace. *American Psychologist, 48*, 1070–1076.

Fitzgerald, L. F. (1993b). The last great open secret: The sexual harassment of women in academia and the workplace. Washington, DC: Federation of Behavioral, Psychological, and Cognitive Sciences.

Fitzgerald, L. F., Drasgow, F., Hulin, C. L., Gelfand, M. J., & Magley, V. J. (1997). Antecedents and consequences of sexual harassment in organizations: A test of an integrated model. *Journal of Applied Psychology, 82*, 578–589.

Fitzgerald, L. F., Fassinger, R. E., & Betz, N. E. (1995). Theoretical advances in the study of women's career development. In B. W Walsh & S. H. Osipow (Eds.), *Handbook of vocational psychology: Theory, research, and practice* (2nd ed, pp. 67–109). Hillsdale, NJ: Lawrence Erlbaum Associates.

Fitzgerald, L. F., & Harmon, L .W. (2001). Women's career development: A postmodern update. In F. T. L. Leong & A. Barak (Eds.), *Contemporary models in vocational psychology* (pp. 207–230). Mahwah, NJ: Lawrence Erlbaum Associates.

Gilbert, L. A., & Kearney, L. K. (2006). Sex, gender, and dual-earner families: Implications and application for career counseling for women. In W. B. Walsh & M. J. Heppner (Eds.), *Handbook of career counseling for women* (2nd ed, pp. 193–217). Mahwah, NJ: Lawrence Erlbaum Associates.

Gomez, M. J., Fassinger, R. E., Prosser, J., Cooke, K., Mejia, B., & Luna, J. (2001). Voces abriendo caminos (voices foraging paths): A qualitative study of the career development of notable Latinas. *Journal of Counseling Psychology, 48*, 286–300.

Gysbers, N. C., Heppner, M. J., & Johnston, J. A. (2003). *Career counseling: Process, issues and techniques* (2nd ed). Needham Heights, MA: Allyn & Bacon.

Harvie, K., Marshal-McCaskey, J., & Johnston, L. (1998). Gender-based biases in occupational hiring decisions. *Journal of Applied Social Psychology, 28*, 1698–1711.

Heppner, M. J., & Heppner, P. P. (2005). Addressing the implications of male socialization for career counseling. In G. E. Good & G. R. Brooks (Eds.), *The new handbook of psychotherapy and counseling with men: A comprehensive guide to settings, problems, and treatment approaches* (pp. 172–185). San Francisco, CA: Jossey-Bass.

Heppner, M. J., & Heppner, P. P. (2009). On men and work: Taking the road less traveled. *Journal of Career Development, 36*, 49–67.

Heppner, M. J., & O'Brien, K. M. (2006). Women and poverty: A holistic approach to vocational interventions. In W. B. Walsh & M. J. Heppner (Eds.), *Handbook of career counseling for women* (2nd ed, pp. 75–102). Mahwah, NJ: Lawrence Erlbaum Associates.

Hesson-McInnis, H., & Fitzgerald, L. F. (1992, November). *Modeling sexual harassment: A preliminary analysis.* Paper presented at the APA/NIOSH Conference on Stress in the 90's: A Changing Workforce in a Changing Workplace, Washington, DC.

Jome, L. M., & Tokar, D. M. (1998). Dimensions of masculinity and major choice traditionality. *Journal of Vocational Behavior, 52*, 120–134.

Jordan, J. V., & Hartling, L. M. (2002). New developments in relational-cultural theory. In M. Ballou & L. S. Brown (Eds.), *Rethinking mental health and disorder: Feminist perspectives* (pp. 48–70). New York: Guilford Press.

Lang, I. H. (2010, April 14). Have women shattered the glass ceiling? *USA Today.* Retrieved from http://www.usatoday.com

Lips, H. M. (2010). *A new psychology of women: Gender, culture, and ethnicity.* Long Grove, IL: Waveland Press, Inc.

Lott, B. (1985). The devaluation of women's competence. *Journal of Social Issues, 41*, 43–60.

Lupton, B. (2006). Explaining men's entry in female-concentrated occupations: issues of masculinity and social class. *Gender, Work, and Organization, 13*, 103–128.

Maslow, A. (1968). *Toward a psychology of being* (2nd ed). New York: Van Nostrand Reinhold Co.

Mac Kay, W. R., & Miller, C. A. (1982). Relation of socioeconomic status and sex variables to the complexity of worker functions in the occupational choices of elementary school children. *Journal of Vocational Behavior, 20*, 31–39.

McWhirter, E. H. (1994). *Counseling for empowerment.* Alexandria, VA: American Counseling Association Press.

McWhirter, E. H. (1997). Empowerment, social activism, and counseling. *Counseling and Human Development, 29*, 1–11.

Miller, L., & Budd. J. (1999). The development of occupational sex-role stereotypes occupational preferences and academic subject preferences in children at ages 8, 2, and 16. *Educational Psychology, 19*, 17–35.

Miner-Rubino, K., & Cortina, L. M. (2004). Working in a context of hostility toward women: Implications for employees' well-being. *Journal of Occupational Health Psychology, 9*, 107–122.

National Science Foundation (NSF, 2006). Employed scientists and engineers, by occupation, highest degree level, and sex: 2006. Retrieved from http://www.nsf.gov/statistics.

Norton, S. (2001). Women exposed: Sexual harassment and female vulnerability. In L. Diamant & J. Lee (Eds.), *The psychology of sex, gender, and jobs* (pp. 83–102). Westport, CT: Praeger.

Nutt, R. L., & Brooks, G. R. (2008). Psychology of gender. In S. D. Brown & R. W. Lent (Eds.), *Handbook of counseling psychology* (4th ed, pp. 176–193). Hoboken, NJ: John Wiley & Sons.

Parsons, F. (1909). *Choosing a vocation.* Boston: Houghton Mifflin.

Pearson, S. M., & Bieschke, K. J. (2001). Succeeding against the odds: An examination of familial influences on the career development of professional African American women. *Journal of Counseling Psychology, 48*, 301–309.

Perrone, K. M., Wright, S. L., & Jackson, Z. V. (2009). Traditional and nontraditional gender roles and work: Family interfaces for men and women. *Journal of Career Development, 36*, 8–24.

Pratto, F., Sidanius, J., & Siers, B. (1997). The gender gap in occupational role attainment: A social dominance approach. *Journal of Personality and Social Psychology, 72*, 37–53.

Richardson, M. S. (2012). Counseling for work and relationship. *Counseling Psychologist, 40*, 190–242.

Richie, B. S., Fassinger, R. E., Linn, S. G., Johnson, J., Proesser, J., & Robinson, S. (1997). Persistence, connection, and passion: A qualitative study of the career development of highly achieving African Americans- Black and White women. *Journal of Counseling Psychology, 44*, 133–148.

Rochlen, A. B., Suizzo, M. A., McKelley, R. A., & Scaringi, V. (2008). "I'm just providing for my family": A qualitative study of stay-at-home fathers. *Psychology of Men & Masculinity, 94*, 193–206.

Rossides, D. W. (1997). *Social stratification: The interplay of class, race, and gender* (2nd ed). Upper Saddle River, NJ: Prentice Hall.

Schultheiss, D. E. P. (2009). To mother or to matter: Can women do both? *Journal of Career Development, 36*, 25–48.

Schulenberg, J. E., Vondracek, F. W., & Crouter, A. C. (1984). The influence of the family on vocational development. *Journal of Marriage and the Family, 46*, 129–143.

Shinar, E. H. (1975). Sexual stereotypes of occupation. *Journal of Vocational Behavior, 7*, 99–111.

Skovholt, T. M. (1990). Career themes in counseling and psychotherapy with men. In D. Moore & F. Leafgren (Eds.), *Men in conflict* (pp. 39–53). Alexandria, VA: American Association for Counseling and Development.

Stone, P. (2007). *Opting out? Why women really quit career and head home.* Berkeley and Los Angeles, CA: University of California Press.

U.S. Census Bureau. (2011). 2010 census data. Retrieved from http://2010.census.gov/2010census/

U.S. Census Bureau. (2011). America's families and living arrangements: 2011. Retrieved from http://www.census.gov

Walsh, W. B., & Osipow, S. (1994). *Career counseling for women. Contemporary topics in vocational psychology.* Hillsdale, NJ: Lawrence Erlbaum Associates.

Women in Congress (2011). 112th Congress, 2011–2013. Historical data. Retrieved from http://womenincongress.house.gov/historical-data/representatives-senators-by-congress.html?congress=112.

Toward an Inclusive LGBT Psychology of Working

Mary Z. Anderson *and* James M. Croteau

Abstract

This chapter examines LGBT issues in explicit relationship to the psychology of working. It presents an overview of the two most developed areas of LGBT vocational psychology: LGBT workplace discrimination/climate and LGBT workers' management of sexual identity. Within each area, the chapter discusses select recent theoretical and empirical literature that deepens current understandings and promotes movement toward an inclusive LGBT psychology of working. It illustrates and makes recommendations for future scholarship that promotes such movement. Major recommendations include (a) continuing methodologically rigorous study of LGBT workplace climate and sexual identity management, (b) continued focus on the broad context of workplace climate with particular attention to action-oriented identification of factors that contribute to hospitable workplaces, (c) continued scholarly focus on a breadth of workplace sexual identity management constructs, including study that promotes understanding of day-to-day behaviors, ongoing strategies, and motivations underlying expression of sexual identity, and (d) expanding scholarship that interrupts the current predominance of an LGBT vocational psychology that is exclusively focused on, and derived from, the work lives of White, middle- and upper-class, lesbian women and gay men. Accomplishing this last recommendation will require a significant shift in perspective to intentionally prioritize understanding the experiences of workers who are not professionals and/or highly formally educated, workers who are people of color, and workers who are bisexual and transgender. Drawing on the broader LGBT psychology literature, this chapter offers multiple specific suggestions for developing more inclusive scholarship.

Key Words: gay, lesbian, sexual minorities, vocational psychology, work, discrimination

Lesbian, gay, bisexual, and transgender (LGBT) vocational psychology is a relatively recent development within the field of vocational psychology. This body of literature can be seen as having grown out of the second wave of the larger LGBT psychology literature that focused on understanding and affirming the lives of LGBT people, particularly in the context of pervasive societal heterosexism and homophobia (Croteau, Bieschke, Fassinger, & Manning, 2008; Maher et al., 2009). Although isolated studies appeared earlier, a more substantial and integrated body of LGBT vocational psychology literature began to emerge in the late 1980s and the 1990s. In the mid-1990s two special sections of the *Career Development Quarterly* and a special issue of the *Journal of Vocational Behavior* provided foundational descriptions of the core career-related concerns of sexual minority workers (largely lesbian and gay) and offered prescriptions for affirmative practice (e.g., Croteau, 1996; Croteau & Bieschke, 1996; Fassinger, 1995; Milburn, 1993; Pope, 1995). In the past 20 years, LGBT vocational psychology has continued to develop, emphasizing more theory-based understanding, the development of LGB-specific vocational theoretical perspectives, and more rigorous research methods (Badgett, Lau, Sears, & Ho, 2007; Croteau, Anderson, DiStefano, & Kampa-Kokesch, 2000; Croteau, Anderson, & VanderWal, 2008; Lidderdale, Croteau, Anderson, Tovar-Murray, & Davis, 2007).

Psychology of working (POW) is an even more recent development in vocational psychology, the hallmark of which has been a shift from a focus on career choice, interests, and decision making toward a broader view of the entirety of the experience of working (Blustein, 2006; Blustein, Kenna, Gill, & DeVoy, 2008). POW recognizes that framing vocational psychology primarily around traditional notions of career choice necessarily means a focus on the narrow range of people with access to the power and social privileges that allow for the choice of a career based on what is intrinsically fulfilling. In its broadest terms, POW presses vocational psychology to expand its solid but narrow base in the areas of choice, interests, and decision making to address the full scope of work and workers. With this broadening of perspective, POW further highlights functions of work common across people with varied levels of social power; work is described as providing means for survival and access to power, means for social connection, and means for self-determination.

The very notion of LGBT vocational psychology has been consistent with the POW perspective in expanding the "who" of vocational psychology. Prior to the emergence of LGBT vocational psychology as an area of focus, the experiences of workers with a minority sexual orientation were almost entirely invisible to the field. Although reviews of LGBT vocational psychology demonstrate that there has been attention to career choice, interests, decision making, and traditional career choice counseling with this population, the most consistent and developed areas of emphasis within LGBT vocational psychology have been consistent with the POW perspective (Croteau et al., 2000; Lidderdale et al., 2007). The enduring focus has been on workplace experiences, with two themes receiving the most attention: workplace discrimination and climate, and workplace sexual identity management (Croteau, 1996; Croteau et al., 2000; Lidderdale et al., 2007). These themes have clear connections to POW themes of survival and power, social connection, and self-determination.

At one level, LGBT vocational psychology has been quite consistent with the POW perspective; however, deeper examination shows that the POW critique has much to offer LGBT vocational psychology. The most striking limitation of the LGBT workplace literature is the overarching bias that permeates the full breadth of psychological research and scholarship—a bias toward primarily studying, theorizing, and representing experiences of predominantly White, well-educated, middle- and upper-class people. Thus, while the experience of working, particularly in terms of LGBT workplace discrimination and climate and LGBT worker sexual identity management, has been a primary focus of LGBT vocational psychology, the focus has largely been on the working experiences of a racially and economically privileged segment of the LGBT population.

In terms of inclusiveness, it is also important to note our choice of terminology in reference to sexual orientation. Thus far we have been using the term "LGBT" because we have been referring to an overall body of literature (i.e., LGBT vocational psychology). We will also use that term when we allude to the directions in which we hope the literature develops (i.e., LGBT psychology of working). We include lesbians, gay men, bisexual men and women, and transgender people when discussing this overall literature because our intention is to shape the overall effort of scholarship and practice in this area to be inclusive across minority sexual orientation and gender identity groups. In truth, however, much of the existing focus has been on lesbian women, gay men, or both, with some emerging focus on bisexual people and transgender people, particularly in the past 5 to 10 years. As we review specific literature, we will be as precise as we can about who was studied or who was being discussed, and we will limit our terminology accordingly, to recognize extant limits in inclusivity in regard to bisexual and transgender people.

Given our understanding of the history and content of LGBT vocational psychology to date and how that fits with the POW perspective, we have chosen a particular focus and organization for integrating LGBT issues within the POW. First we will give an overview of the two most developed areas of LGBT vocational psychology consistent with the POW perspectives focused on experiences of working: LGBT workplace discrimination and climate, and LGBT workers' management of sexual identity at work. Then within each area we will discuss recent theoretical and empirical literature that deepens current understandings and promotes movement toward a more inclusive LGBT psychology of working. Rather than offering an exhaustive review of recent literature, we have selected a relatively small collection of scholarly contributions to serve as exemplars for advancing understanding and moving scholarly efforts toward the POW perspective. We conclude the chapter with a broad discussion of moving from an LGBT vocational psychology to an LGBT psychology of working.

Workplace Discrimination and Climate

The earliest vocational research focused on sexual minority issues was primarily aimed at describing experiences of workplace discrimination and exploring the impact of discrimination on lesbian and gay workers (Croteau, 1996; Croteau et al., 2000). In this context, a body of practice-focused literature also emerged, providing recommendations for incorporating knowledge of potential discrimination and appreciation for individual differences in sexual identity development in the career counseling process. Career counselors were urged to assist LGB clients in assessing and making choices based on their assessment of workplace climate as part of the career and job search process.

Beginning with this earliest literature, and continuing to the more recent workplace literature, it is clear that experiences of discrimination and fear of future discrimination are pervasive (Badgett et al., 2007; Croteau, 1996; Croteau et al., 2000; Lidderdale et al., 2007). In addition, based on qualitative reports of LGB workers, we know that workplace discrimination itself is a complex construct, connecting with felt access to power and survival as well as experiences of social connection and self-determination.

An important aspect of the early workplace discrimination-related literature was reliance on the voices of LGB workers to describe and shape understanding of these experiences (see Croteau, 1996; Croteau et al., 2000). Reliance on workers' own descriptions was important to the development of this literature and illustrates the necessity of what POW calls "experience-near" research. Based on LGB workers' descriptions of their experiences, research on discrimination has included both formal and informal discrimination. This distinction, coined by Levine and Leonard (1984), highlights the impact of both "institutionalized procedures to restrict officially conferred work rewards" such as hiring, firing, promotion, and compensation decisions (formal discrimination) as well as "harassment and other unofficial actions taken by supervisors or co-workers" (informal discrimination) (p. 706).

Over time, the study of discrimination has become increasingly more rigorous, moving from a reliance on convenience samples to include both probability sampling and experimental designs (Badgett et al., 2007). The study of discrimination has also become increasingly more inclusive of understanding the impact of work context or climate (Croteau, Bieschke, et al., 2008). In fact, there has been an overall evolution toward a more overarching understanding of "workplace climate" that includes formal and informal discrimination as well as other aspects of the workplace that contribute to making it hospitable to LGB workers. In the sections that follow, we review recent progress in understanding experiences of workplace discrimination and the broader experience of workplace climate.

Continued, and More Rigorous, Evidence of Pervasive Discrimination

The prevalence of discrimination against LGB workers is documented in a recent review of formal aspects of workplace discrimination, including 15 studies of LGB workers' experiences published since the mid-1990s (Badgett et al., 2007). Drawing on literature from a broad range of social science disciplines, including economics, sociology, and psychology, Badgett et al. also document the frequency of discrimination complaints filed with government agencies, evidence of wage inequities, and differential treatment of LGB workers evidenced in controlled experiments. The literature reviewed by Badgett et al. emphasizes understanding of organizational perspectives and behaviors that result in unequal treatment of LGB workers/employees. In contrast, the LGB vocational psychology literature focuses more on the psychological experiences of individual employees. The psychology of working is an inclusive perspective, and the need to advance knowledge across disciplinary perspectives fits well in its scope. Clearly, examining the organizational and psychological literature together provides a more complete understanding of LGB workers' experiences.

Badgett et al.'s (2007) review of the more recent surveys of LGB workers documents the pervasive and continued nature of discrimination. Although much of this literature focuses on specific occupations, populations, or geographical locations, the results of three recent studies based on national probability (or random) samples are also reviewed. The 15 studies published between the mid-1990s and 2007 suggest that the experience of discrimination remains common, with 15% to 43% of LGB workers reporting such experiences. For example, LGB workers report discrimination in hiring and firing (8% to 17%); discrimination in promotion and evaluation (10% to 28%); unequal compensation, including unequal pay and benefits (10% to 19%); and experiences of vandalism, verbal or physical harassment, and abuse (7% to 41%).

Badgett et al.'s (2007) review adds to our understanding of formal discrimination by analyzing wage inequity studies drawn on multiple national databases, including the National Health and Social Life Survey, the General Social Survey, the U.S. Census, and the National Health and Nutrition Examination Survey. Research using these data sources indicates that gay men earn 10% to 32% less than heterosexual men with comparable jobs and personal characteristics. Although evidence of a wage differential is not as consistent when lesbian women are compared to heterosexual women, lesbians do consistently earn less than men.

Badgett et al. (2007) also report on six studies employing traditional experimental designs to isolate the effects of sexual orientation in employment selection. Five of these studies found evidence of discrimination against gay and lesbian job applicants. Differential treatment was evident in lesbian and gay workers receiving fewer interview invitations; lower ratings on application materials (though as with wages, this is more apparent for gay men than lesbian women); fewer hiring recommendations; and negative interpersonal interactions.

Overall, this recent review of the literature (Badgett et al., 2007) clearly documents the pervasiveness of discrimination across a variety of research methods, including three national random probability-based samples, six traditional experimental design studies, and sophisticated analysis of wage inequities. While there is likely some merit in continuing this trend in rigorous documentation of formal discrimination, we recommend increasing scholarship aimed at identifying means for developing more hospitable workplaces for LGB workers. The vocational psychology literature of the past decade has begun to shift in this direction, focusing on the broader rubric of workplace climate, a concept that includes notions of formal and informal discrimination as well as positive indicators of both formal (i.e., policy) and informal (i.e., relationships at work) support at work.

Expanding the Focus to Workplace Climate

An exemplar in the progression toward consideration of the broader concept of workplace climate is Liddle, Luzzo, Hauenstein, and Schuck's (2004) work on measuring workplace climate. A core rationale for developing this new climate measure was to include a broad range of climate-related experiences. Building on the work of Chojnacki and Gelberg (1994), Liddle et al. sought to assess workplace environments ranging from overtly or covertly discriminatory to tolerant and even LGBT-affirming environments. The potential to measure the full breadth of workplace climates is an important shift in thinking about LGBT workers' experiences—one that has the potential to create more positive work outcomes than focusing solely on negative workplace climates.

With respect to measurement development, the authors began by collecting LGBT (primarily lesbian and gay) workers' descriptions of "what it's like to be a gay, lesbian, or bisexual employee at your current workplace" (Liddle et al., 2004, p. 37). Qualitative analysis was used to develop initial items including both positive and negative experiences. Efforts were made to be exhaustive of the experiences reported by participants and to use their wordings in item construction. Since initial data seemed to come from those in more supportive climates, particular attention was given in later recruitment to obtain data from participants working in settings experienced as "not very good for LGBT employees" (p. 38). At each stage of the study, particular emphasis was placed on the inclusion of workers from a broad range of occupations. The resulting measure will be useful in research aimed at identifying what contributes to and follows from more or less supportive climates, as well as measuring changes in workplace climate. We also agree with Liddle et al.'s challenge to future researchers to be more specific and contextual in their assessment of climate; workplace climate may vary across departments or other workgroups within the larger workplace, resulting in complex relationships between workplace variables and LGB workers' behaviors and experiences.

In addition to broad conceptions, and subsequent measures, of climate as exemplified in Liddle et al.'s (2004) research, theoretical understandings about LGB workers and workplace climates are needed to explore effective change. Chung's (2001) use of existing vocational psychology theory and research to develop a framework for understanding LGB workers' experiences of and strategies for coping with discrimination and other workplace hostility toward LGB workers is a good example of theoretical development. Expanding upon the distinction between formal and informal discrimination noted previously, Chung developed a model for conceptualizing coping with what he called work discrimination. In relation to the notion of workplace climate, Chung used the term "discrimination" broadly, focusing on coping with a breadth of negative experiences at work. Although we use Chung's term "work discrimination," his conceptualization includes experiences that fall under the broader and more inclusive rubric of workplace climate (e.g., interpersonal negativity toward LGB people or issues).

Chung (2001) identifies three dimensions of work discrimination: formal versus informal; potential versus encountered; and perceived versus real. The formal-versus-informal distinction contrasts institutional policies and decisions (formal) with interpersonal dynamics and the atmosphere of the workplace (informal). Potential discrimination refers to discrimination that is possible if and when sexual orientation is revealed; encountered discrimination refers to discrimination that has been experienced by LGB workers. The contrast between perceived and real discrimination refers to LGB workers' assessment of the opportunity structure of the workplace, highlighting the influence of real limits as well as perceived limits of access to power and opportunity.

According to Chung's (2001) model, LGB workers can be conceptualized as coping with discrimination through vocational choice as well as work adjustment behaviors. Coping with discrimination through vocational choice refers to the decisions workers make about pursuing particular jobs or occupations based on their perceptions of discrimination they may encounter. These choices involve decisions regarding self-employment (retaining power for self), job tracking (working in tolerant or affirming professions or companies), and risk taking (working in more varied contexts, including those that may be known to be actively homophobic and discriminatory).

Coping with discrimination through work adjustment involves two broad on-the-job strategies. The first is discrimination management, which was initially conceptualized as including quitting without reference to the experience of discrimination, silence, seeking social support, and confronting the perpetrator or supervisor. The second is identity management, which refers to choices about revealing and/or concealing one's sexual orientation in the workplace. Strategies for identity management, including behaviors ranging from acting or passing as heterosexual to implicitly or explicitly revealing a minority sexual identity, are explored more fully in the identity management section of this chapter.

Initial validity evidence for Chung's (2001) conceptual framework comes from semistructured qualitative interviews with eight lesbian and nine gay workers (Chung, Williams, & Dispenza, 2009). In this study, participants' descriptions of workplace experiences with discrimination were coded using the discrimination and coping strategy definitions from the model. When participants reported workplace experiences and responses that did not fit the proposed dimensions/categories, new categories and definitions were developed.

As expected, participants' reported experiences of discrimination included examples of formal and informal as well as potential and encountered discrimination. Similarly, participants' descriptions of coping with discrimination were determined to support the proposed model, with participants using self-employment and job-tracking strategies when seeking future employment and using varied identity management strategies for coping with potential discrimination in the workplace. Although no participant reported using risk taking as a vocational choice strategy, and no participant reported either acting or passing as an identity management strategy, all reported vocational choice and identity management behaviors fit within the remaining categories in the proposed models (Chung et al., 2009).

In terms of discrimination management strategies, however, findings suggested important revisions in the originally proposed strategies of quitting, silence, social support, and confrontation (Chung et al., 2009). Quitting and silence were combined to make up a new category labeled "nonassertive" coping, while the broad strategies of social support and confrontation were retained. All three broad strategies (nonassertive coping, social support, and confrontation) were expanded to include multiple subcategories descriptive of the varied ways LGB workers manage discrimination in the workplace. Nonassertive coping encompasses varied behaviors such as quitting, silence, avoidance, and self-talk. Social support strategies were classified by sources of support, including partner, friends, family, coworkers, and professional help. Confrontation strategies were classified as interpersonal (e.g., confronting the offender or supervisor directly) or more systemic (e.g., confrontation via human resources, legal action, publicity, etc.)

Application of Chung's (2001; Chung et al., 2009) model of work discrimination to the development of future research as well as the integration of existing findings has the potential to support development of more hospitable workplace climates. Core concepts from traditional vocational development theories (vocational choice and work adjustment) are integrated with core concepts from LGB vocational psychology literature (formal and informal discrimination; identity management strategies) and connected with outcomes that are often a focus in the organizational literature (job tenure and system change). The resulting framework is offered from the perspective of LGB workers navigating the systems at work, making it a strong exemplar of the POW perspective and highlighting aspects of workers' experiences that are less often discussed in the literature. In particular, the focus on discrimination management as distinct from workplace sexual identity management and coping with discrimination through vocational choice provides another avenue for moving toward more positive workplace climates.

We concur with Chung et al. (2009) that we have limited knowledge about the kind of resilience being demonstrated by LGB workers using internal or nonassertive coping strategies, and note that this bias toward studying and supporting more external and assertive behaviors is also evident in the existing literature on workplace sexual identity management (Croteau, Anderson, & VanderWal, 2008). We recommend increased focus on these less visible aspects of discrimination management as well as continued exploration of social support and confrontation strategies. Connecting these latter, largely interpersonal, strategies with other recent literature concerning the interpersonal climate at work and the role of systems in promoting climate change (e.g., Embrick, Walther, & Wickens, 2007; Smith & Ingram, 2004; Hill, 2009; Willis, 2010) would likely facilitate thinking about how we might begin to develop hospitable and affirming climates for LGB workers.

Hill (2009) provides another exemplar of approaching the theoretical understanding of climate in ways that might have implications for change, but this time beginning from an organizational perspective that emphasizes policy implementation and systemic change. Although Hill takes a narrower focus than Chung by zeroing in on a neglected specific aspect of what may occur as workplace climates change, his exploration of backlash/blowback highlights the importance of working to facilitate both internal psychological and interpersonal behavioral changes.

Backlash or blowback is a form of resistance to change that occurs when implementation of new external policies or structures is experienced as threatening to individuals; when there is real organizational movement toward inclusion, employees may respond with active resistance and retaliatory behaviors directed at LGBTQ employees. Calling on human resource development (HRD) professionals to be leaders of organizational change, Hill (2009) offers an analysis of backlash and methods for promoting change that recognize the importance and difficulty of facilitating internal psychological changes for all employees.

Hill (2009) offers multiple reasons that some employees may respond with backlash and develops a framework for diversity training that can support the internal changes necessary to promote systemic change. Five specific reasons for blowback are discussed: threats to majority group entitlement; resentment for what is labeled "LGBTQ special rights"; fear and anxiety; negative stereotypes and heteronormativity; and government- and politician-sponsored antigay speech. All of these reasons are supported by dominant discourses of heterosexism, heteronormativity, and gender conformity. When dominant discourses go unchallenged, the lives and experiences of sexual minorities are invisible to members of the dominant heterosexual or gender identity traditional (cisgender) group, making inclusion unimportant and not compelling for them. In addition, when members of the dominant group operate from an unexamined sense of entitlement, their needs and perspectives take precedence over the needs of others, making efforts at inclusion appear unfair or unnecessary. Efforts at inclusion are experienced as uncomfortable and/or threatening because they disrupt dominant discourses and press for reexamination of internalized beliefs about sexuality and gender.

Hill (2009) recommends working from a perspective that embraces difference and frames diversity initiatives as relevant for all employees—a perspective of celebrating diversity rather than just tolerating those who are perceived as different. From this perspective a focus on diversity is inclusive of everyone: all people have a sexual orientation and a gender identity (and other aspects of self). Thus diversity groups and programs should be open to and focused on all people, rather than on perceived deficiencies within the organization. This perspective interrupts the tendency to just build "tolerance" of the other by the dominant group and opens the possibility of valuing people because of rather than in spite of their diverse characteristics and ways of being. Although the article falls short of describing how oppression of sexual minorities harms everyone, including those in the dominant group, the recommendations are consistent with this perspective on working toward systemic change.

Overall, Hill's (2009) discussion of anticipating and responding to blowback extends understanding of workplace climate by encouraging critical thinking about the hostility and discrimination that workers may experience in *apparently inclusive environments*—those where a nondiscrimination policy exists. At its core, blowback is understood as occurring as a result of heterosexual workers experiencing the increased inclusivity of LGB workers as threatening. The strategies that Hill suggests for anticipating and responding to blowback further broaden the previous focus in the literature on level of LGBT supportiveness in the workplace to explicitly call for celebration (not mere tolerance or islands of support) of diversity. In addition, Hill's recommendations for how to accomplish this mesh nicely with other perspectives on raising awareness of dominant group privileges and perspectives and developing anti-oppressive identities (Helms, 1995; Mohr, 2002; Todd & Abrams, 2011; Worthington, Savoy, Dillon, & Vernaglia, 2002). We encourage more explicit and extended application of these and similar ideas and models to further develop strategies for developing hospitable and positive workplace climates.

Focusing particularly on the interpersonal aspects of climate. Each of the exemplars of workplace climate-focused literature reviewed above incorporates or even emphasizes the role of interpersonal interactions in shaping the experience of workplace climate. This perspective is consistent with core POW tenets: work is a primary place for social connections and work is a primary place where oppressive systems of social categorization play out. Our review of recent literature on the workplace experiences of LGB workers uncovered a small body of literature on workplace relationships and interpersonal interactions. We point to four studies (Embrick et al., 2007; Huffman, Watrous-Rodriguez, & King, 2008; Smith & Ingram, 2004; Willis, 2010) we found to have potency for illustrating and pointing in constructive directions for understanding and intervening in interpersonal aspects of LGBT workplaces.

Huffman et al. (2008) is a good exemplar of theory-based research on the workplace experiences of LGB workers. Using Minority Stress Theory (Meyer, 1995) as a foundation for understanding the experiences that LGB workers are likely to

encounter in the workplace, the authors employed Social Exchange Theory (Blau, 1964) and discussion of existing research to develop a series of hypotheses concerning the influence of work-related social support on LGB workers' job and life satisfaction as well as their level of openness about their sexual orientation at work.

This study extends understanding of workplace climate by focusing on the differential effects of three specific kinds of support: supervisor support, coworker support, and organizational support. Supervisor support and coworker support are conceptualized as informal and interpersonal sources of support, whereas organizational support is conceptualized as a more overarching form of support inclusive of both formal (policies) and informal (LGB employees are treated with respect) aspects of workplace climate (assessed with Liddle et al.'s [2004] measure). In addition, organizational support may be viewed as being ongoing and systemically influencing all (LGB) workers in fairly global ways, while supervisor support and coworker support are more individualized and targeted at particular workplace experiences or stresses.

Based on the data from 99 mostly (84%) White, well-educated, and mostly lesbian and gay (4.3% bisexual) employees, supervisor support was associated with more positive job satisfaction, coworker support was associated with more positive life satisfaction, and organizational support was associated with more openness about one's sexual orientation at work. This pattern of findings fits the authors' hypotheses. Implications from this study include the value of promoting support through each of these three means and the importance of additional study of how to increase the interpersonal aspect of support in particular. In addition, it would likely be useful to gather more experience-near data about how workers experience these sources of support and why different sources are associated with different outcomes.

Smith and Ingram (2004) also employ Minority Stress Theory (Meyer, 1995) and Social Exchange Theory (Thibaut & Kelley, 1959) to develop hypotheses concerning the effects of social interactions on LGB workers. This study focuses in particular on the effects of unsupportive social interactions that follow LGB workers' discussion of experiences with workplace heterosexism. Unsupportive interactions, "defined as upsetting or hurtful responses from social network members in reaction to a specific stressor" (Smith & Ingram, 2004, p. 58), include minimizing the significance of the stressor, blaming the distressed person for his or her role in the stressor, distancing or disengaging from the interaction, and bumbling, awkward, or inappropriate attempts to fix the concern (Ingram, Betz, Mindes, Schmitt, & Smith, 2001).

Based on data from 97 mostly (82%) White, well-educated, lesbian and gay (10% bisexual) employees, unsupportive social interactions following LGB workers' discussion of experiences with workplace heterosexism (i.e., minimizing or blaming) were associated with higher levels of psychological distress. Minimizing interactions were directly related to psychological distress, whereas blaming interactions moderated the relationship between heterosexism and psychological distress. The nature of the relationship between blaming interactions, heterosexism, and psychological distress suggests that blaming exacerbates negative consequences at low levels of experienced heterosexism such that the psychological distress experienced is on par with high levels of experienced heterosexism. Both minimizing and blaming interactions appear to be potent stressors (Smith & Ingram, 2004).

In the Smith and Ingram (2004) study, LGB workers provided information about unsupportive interactions in their own social networks. It seems likely that these networks included people in the workplace and beyond. To further our recommended focus on the development of positive workplace climates, future research could examine the role of interactions in the workplace in particular, examining the role of both supportive and unsupportive interactions. More specifically, it seems worth exploring the climate-related and psychological distress-related outcomes of coworkers and supervisors who acknowledge or validate LGB workers' experiences of heterosexism and the systemic nature of heterosexist privilege.

Willis (2010) offers an additional new perspective for thinking about the role of interpersonal interactions and social support in the workplace. This qualitative study focuses on young (18 to 26) LGBQ workers' experiences working with other (older) LGBQ employees and managers. Acknowledging that work has the potential to be a primary source of interpersonal connection, a core purpose of this study was to critically examine the assumption that relationships among LGBQ-identifying workers necessarily function as sources of support and commonality in the workplace. Although sexual minority role models are often highlighted as important sources of support in career development (Croteau et al., 2000), Willis notes that sexual identity may

not be the defining feature of biographies of LGBQ young people, particularly those who may be navigating multiple oppressed social identities.

Using an interesting and creative mix of data collection approaches, including a Web-based survey, online interviews, and face-to-face interviews, Willis (2010) explored the workplace relationship experiences of 34 young LGBQ workers (18 men, 16 women) in Australia. Participants were drawn from a wide range of occupational groups and industries, and some were employed in "queer-majority" workplaces. Findings indicate that participants' relationships with other LGBQ workers included both relationships of connection and support and relationships of conflict and division. Supportive relationships were sources of extended work and social networking, and mentoring, as well as buffers against discrimination. In "queer-identified" workplaces in particular, young LGBQ workers expressed appreciation for not having to worry about whether to reveal their sexual identity, but instead being affirmed and valued and even assumed to be gay.

Relationships characterized by conflict or division ranged from an absence of connection due to having nothing in common beyond identifying as a sexual minority to experiences of discrimination and abuse. For those participants reporting the most difficult experiences with other queer-identified workers, clear power differentials existed between the participant and his or her coworker. Gender and age were also interactive aspects in workplace interactions, with multiple participants observing that youth and maleness are more rewarded or valued in workplaces (Willis, 2010).

Consistent with Hill (2009), Willis (2010) suggests that efforts to provide LGB-focused social support at work should not be limited to LGBQ employee groups and networks. Rather than assuming that all LGBQ workers will feel most drawn to and supported by other LGBQ workers, Willis recommends developing diversity-focused support across broader ranges of individual differences, perhaps grounded in a "common commitment to valuing diversity and addressing processes of workplace exclusion" (p. 240).

Embrick, Walther, and Wickens (2007) represent a unique perspective on the interpersonal workplace climate in regard to sexual orientation by focusing on the attitudes and behaviors of heterosexuals toward lesbians and gay men and doing so in a working-class context. This study serves as an exemplar of depth-oriented research focused on the nuances of climate in a single workplace (a baked goods company). Employing both the more customary in-depth interviews as well as 6 months of in vivo participant observations, the authors demonstrate how interpersonal attitudes and workplace policies and procedures combine to form an inhospitable climate for LGBT employees. Semistructured interviews with 20 workers, supervisors, and lower-level managers, all of whom were identified by the researchers through contextual information as "practicing heterosexuals," revealed strong negative attitudes about LGBT workers. Two women participants were seen as having neutral or positive general attitudes, while all the men held negative views that fell into three categories: "outright disgust, don't ask—don't tell, and ostracism and fear."

The researchers also considered the hiring process at the bakery operation, mapping a complex chain of policy/procedure and interpersonal attitudes that formed barriers to hiring and retention of LGBT workers. They demonstrated how negative general attitudes and stereotypes concerning LGBT workers, combined with an interpersonal networking-driven hiring/probation process, made it unlikely that lesbian or gay men would be hired and/or retained. Perhaps most interesting in these data is how bias plays out through concern about the image of the company in conjunction with held negative stereotypes (largely of gay men; e.g., effeminacy, not able to handle stress, etc.).

Lastly, the authors consider the influence of gender and present an analysis that takes into account both stronger negative reactions to gay men and the male-dominated nature of this workplace (90% male). They frame their understanding around heterosexual men's construction of appropriate masculinity and femininity and its relation to heteronormativity, all to the advantage for heterosexual men and to the disadvantage of gay men, heterosexual women, and lesbians. In this way the results extend understanding of the concept of White male solidarity to sexual orientation. Previously such solidarity has been defined as how White working-class men coalesce to exclude men and women of color and White women. In this study the solidarity group is clearly also organized around heterosexuality and the exclusionary group also includes gay men and lesbian women.

While theoretical frames and multimethod qualitative data are important exemplars of research directions consistent with POW, what is unique about this study is its setting in a male-dominated working-class institution. By focusing on understanding the complexities of how heterosexuals think and behave in the workplace, we gain a relatively rare glimpse of how social constructions of social class and gender combine to create a climate inhospitable to gay men and lesbian women.

Limited focus on complexities of identity for LGBT workers. While two of the interpersonal climate studies discussed in the previous section include some consideration of age and social class diversity, the considerations of LGBT workers from multiple social group perspectives is extremely limited. Despite growing recognition that understanding sexual orientation more fully requires increased focus on sexual orientation in the context of race, gender, class, and other social locations (e.g., Croteau, Bieschke, et al., 2008), we identified only two exemplars (Bowleg, Brooks, & Ritz, 2008; Nelson & Probst, 2004) that directly approach the idea of multiple oppressed social identities among sexual minority workers.

Bowleg et al. (2008) explicitly focus on the combined experience of race, gender, and sexual orientation for 19 Black, lesbian (including 3 who identified as gay, 1 as queer, and 2 as other), predominantly middle-class and highly educated workers. Although their study was not initially aimed at understanding the workplace experiences of these participants, 18 out of 19 reported experiences of discrimination and workplace stress, leading the authors to examine these experiences in more depth. The emergence of the workplace as a primary place where multiple-minority stress, resilience, and coping play out is consistent with POW tenets that work serves as a central place for self-determination as well as societal oppression.

Participants reported a range of workplace stressors in response to broad questions concerning what they like most and least about being a Black lesbian, and what day-to-day challenges they faced in terms of race, gender, or sexual orientation. Workplace stressors included experiences of heterosexism, racism, sexism, and the intersections among them. Understanding these places of intersection goes beyond much of the literature that looks at workplace climate with a focus on only one form of oppression. The following quotes begin to give voice to varied experiences of this understudied group:

> "... a lot of [masculine-appearing Black lesbians] work jobs that are on the margin. You know you're not going to see them in corporate offices, although White dykes can be looking like [a big football player] in a dress and they'll still hire her and promote her." (p. 76; 47-year-old attorney)

" ... it took at least 7 or 8 years before I really got [the] respect of the Black men in my work place, and the White men choose not to deal with me at all." (p. 76; 42-year-old physical therapist)

"My boss was Black, and he hired me [I later learned] because I was Black ... But he soon found out via someone else that I was gay, female-liking women, whatever, and he had an issue with it. There was tension. And I didn't want to let him down because I worked with him. (p. 77; 30-year-old medical clerk)

Although participants had a sense of not knowing whether the stressors they encountered were "because I'm Black or because I'm woman or queer" (Bowleg et al., p. 77; 47-year-old attorney), there was some consistency to how they coped. Their descriptions of coping with discrimination were grouped into three main strategies: being out and managing being out; covering sexual orientation; and confronting or educating coworkers. Using Chung's model as an organizational tool, these on-the-job strategies can be conceptualized as coping with discrimination through work adjustment, spanning both discrimination management and identity management behaviors.

In summary, in this experience-near study, Black lesbian women identified work as a central place where oppression is experienced, and articulated an intersection or additive experience of discrimination associated with multiple oppressed aspects of their identities/social selves. This study helps us begin to move beyond the otherwise apparent frame that Black (women) workers are heterosexual (and middle class), and that LGBT workers are White (and middle class). In addition, although most participants reported being strategic about when and how to disclose their sexual orientation in order to minimize potential negative interactions, their efforts to confront and educate coworkers highlight the importance they placed on working for organizational change.

Nelson and Probst (2004) offer an organizational-level strategy for examining climate, providing a strong complement to the experience-near focus of Bowleg et al. (2008). They begin by describing organizational diversity climate as a distinct way of understanding workplace experiences of discrimination, and build on existing discrimination and harassment literature to develop a broad diversity-focused measure of organizational climate. Here organizational diversity climate is defined as "shared employee perceptions regarding predicted consequences of various forms of workplace harassment

and discrimination .... a positive organizational diversity climate will be intolerant of workplace harassment and discrimination, whereas a negative diversity climate will convey to employees that harassment and discrimination are tolerated" (p. 196).

The Organizational Diversity Climate Scale assesses perceptions concerning five major types of workplace discrimination: harassment due to age, race, gender, disability, and sexual orientation. The tool presents two scenarios describing discriminatory incidents related to each of these areas; in one scenario a coworker perpetrates the harassment, while in the other the perpetrator is a supervisor. Scenarios are firmly grounded in the domain of interpersonal interactions, focusing on comments, jokes, and references to lower competence or morality of workers who hold a particular minority status. For each scenario, respondents indicate "how risky it would be for a harassed employee to file a complaint"; "how likely it would be that the complainant would be taken seriously"; and "the likely consequences for the alleged harasser."

Like Bowleg et al., Nelson and Probst (2004) are also particularly interested in the experiences of workers who hold multiple minority statuses. They extend our understanding through conceptual-based discussion of multiple minority status and utilize the concept of cultural distance from the dominant group (Triandis, Kuroski, & Gelfand, 1994) to explore how or why we might expect multiple minority statuses to compound difficulties for individual workers. Experienced distances are thought to contribute to barrier-sustaining outcomes such as lack of personal or intimate friendships with coworkers, lack of trust in the organization, and lack of organizational commitment. This kind of conceptualization also supports the development of a conceptual perspective on how identity salience might operate. When minority identities are salient, the cultural distance from the dominant group is more tangible; thus, individual workers may be both more perceptive of discrimination experiences they encounter, as well as more exposed to discrimination through their stronger expression of aspects of self that differ from the dominant group.

Nelson and Probst (2004) examined these conceptually based ideas using data from 719 people at a single university. The sample was mostly White (87.4%) and mostly heterosexual (95.8%) and the majority of participants were female (66%). When multiple minority status was examined, using sexual orientation, race, religious affiliation, ability status, veteran status, age, and sex as indicators (total = 7), the highest reported number of minority identity statuses was six; sufficient data were available to make comparisons among individuals reporting one, two, three, or four minority statuses.

As the authors expected, organizational diversity climate accounted for most variability in workplace harassment and discrimination and multiple minority status was positively related to experiences of harassment and discrimination. There was also a significant interaction between identity importance and minority status such that for individuals placing low importance on identity, multiple identities were less related to negative workplace experiences, whereas for individuals placing high importance on identity, multiple minority status was even more strongly related to experiences of discrimination and harassment. In addition, job-gender context mattered; gender-imbalanced (either high male or high female) contexts yielded more negative experiences for the less represented gender. This finding was strongest for men in traditionally female occupations, suggesting a potentially dominant role of sexism in policing interpersonal interactions. The finding also supports the idea that building a more diverse workforce may decrease individual minority workers' experiences of "otherness."

We concur with Nelson and Probst's (2004) suggestion to regularly assess organizational climate (perhaps in addition to interpersonal climate). The Organizational Diversity Climate Scale can be used to identify specific aspects of the climate that are problematic; more specifically, the tool allows for identification of the minority status being targeted in the harassment as well as who is doing the harassing (coworker vs. supervisor). Used in conjunction with suggestions for successful implementation of diversity policies (e.g., Hill, 2009) and examining various subcontexts (e.g., workgroups, department, etc.) within the organizational context (e.g., Liddle et al., 2004), this tool could contribute to the development of more affirming/hospitable workplace environments.

Moving Toward a POW Perspective on LGBT Workplace Climate

The quantity and rigor of evidence for discrimination on the basis of sexual orientation in workplaces has grown, and there can be little doubt as to its pervasiveness. The review of, and additions to, the research by Badgett et al. (2007) establishes this very well. While there is certainly room for continued research that rigorously establishes the presence of discrimination, we believe that there is a greater need for scholarly attention to follow the trend we have discussed toward understanding the broader notion of workplace climate, which includes but is not limited to formal discrimination. We encourage consideration of the broader notion of climate that includes informal discrimination and other negative aspects of climate that make workplaces hostile to LGBT workers, as well as positive indicators of both formal (i.e., policy) and informal (i.e., relationships at work) support at work. In fact, more focus on positive factors in climate is needed as well as the study of workplaces that are positive; several of the studies reviewed previously include some focus on these ideas.

Research and scholarship on the factors that constitute and are related to workplace climate will allow an intentional focus on improving LGBT workers' lives that is consistent with POW—that is, to have more direct implications for social change, in this case discovering specific factors related to climate that will suggest organizational and psychological interventions to make workplace climate more hospitable and inclusive toward LGBT workers. Exemplars of this movement include the measurement research of Liddle et al. (2007) that will allow the identification of factors related to this broader notion of climate that can be targeted for climate improvement. Chung's theoretical model has a similar effect, facilitating a more complete mapping of a fuller range of experiences of coping with discrimination that, in turn, allows insight into, and study of, psychological and organizational factors that could also be targeted for change. Hill's examination of backlash and how its prevention can be incorporated intentionally in organizational efforts provides a clear example of the trend we encourage involving examining specific aspects of climate that can be targeted for change. Aspects of climate that are interpersonal in nature seem especially potent areas for future work and are consistent with a central tenet of POW. The studies by Huffman et al. (2008) and Smith and Ingram (2004) are exemplars of this focus and point in directions for how interpersonal interactions in the workplace shape climate, and consequently, yield ideas of climate change that go beyond policy and procedures. However, this broader focus on LGBT workplace climate is just beginning; the extant literature primarily comprises isolated studies with limited connection among them, and there remains little in the way of systematic lines of research or scholarship on how to improve climate and create positive change in workplaces.

The studies by Willis (2010) and Embrick et al. (2007) also fall within this important emerging trend of focus on interpersonal aspects of climate. Both add important contexts for understanding the experiences of sexual minority workers: age and social class. Further, the study by Embrick et al. emphasizes the need to examine climate from the perspectives of the heterosexual worker and supervisor to fully understand the interpersonal and organizational factors that might influence climate. The studies by Bowleg et al. (2008) and Nelson and Probst (2004) recognize the notion becoming more frequent in the broader LGBT literature concerning multiple socially oppressed identities and their intersection. The experience-near reports of Black lesbians in Bowleg et al.'s research indicate that identities can be experienced more holistically and that separating "sources" of oppression can be problematic in understanding the experience of LGBT workers. Nelson and Probst approached this notion from the organizational angle in a broad way. They considered seven areas of oppression and developed a measure that is about overall organizational diversity climate across participants with varying numbers of socially oppressed identities. Despite some exemplars that are considering minority sexual orientation in the workplace in conjunction with other areas of oppression, this approach remains rare.

While our literature search for this chapter was selective and focused on bringing the POW perspective to LGBT workplace issues, we are confident that the studies reviewed here are among the very few contributions in the work-related area that consider sexual orientation along with other social oppression issues. There are many more manuscripts calling for such an approach than there are actual studies advancing that approach. Further, the scholarship that does exist, at its best, focuses on intersectionality among multiple oppressed social identities. There has been almost no work on intersectionality across oppressed and privileged identities (see Croteau, Talbot, Evans, and Lance, 2002, for an example of this outside the specific workplace focus). Further, even this notion of intersectional identities is limiting, emerging from a binary perspective of social identities that fails to consider the complexity of holding multiple social identities. The actual idea of intersecting social group identities may well be a "White European cultural perspective that tends to view the world in reductionist terms and sees the self as made up of separate parts," albeit overlapping separate parts (Croteau, 2008, p. 648). More holistic approaches

may be needed. The overall point we want to make most strongly, however, is that work is needed on the area of understanding sexual orientation, in conjunction with, instead of in isolation from, other issues of oppression. In fact, this expansion is key if LGBT workplace scholarship is to move to the more inclusive notions advocated by the POW perspective.

Workplace Sexual Identity Management

The other early and continued area of study within LGBT vocational psychology focuses on workers' disclosure or management of their minority sexual identity at work. Though variability in degree of openness about sexual orientation in the workplace was only one of five broad areas of research identified in Croteau's (1996) integrative review of the LGBT vocational psychology research literature, this theme was present in all nine empirical articles reviewed. From these nine studies, we learned that degree of openness varies widely across LGB workers and work contexts. In addition, though the literature on correlates of openness was extremely limited at that time, there was interest in exploring the relationship between degree of openness, fear of discrimination, experiences of discrimination, and job satisfaction.

Perhaps most important, though, was the recognition that three qualitative studies of gay and lesbian workers (Griffin, 1992; Hall, 1986; Woods & Harbeck, 1992) highlighted management of one's sexual identity in the workplace as a central and recurring activity. This perspective, supported by subsequent research, suggests that although workers may be able to be described as falling along a continuum ranging from concealment to openness about sexual orientation in the workplace, the experience of sexual identity management is a good deal more complex than how "out" one is at work (Croteau et al., 2000; Croteau, Anderson, et al., 2008; Lidderdale et al., 2007). Workplace sexual identity management is understood as an ongoing process, involving numerous daily choices about expressing sexual identity at work. Consistent with the POW perspective that work is a central place for self-determination as well as societal oppression, day-to-day behavioral choices as well as more enduring strategies for identity management have been associated with both anticipated or potential and experienced or encountered discrimination and hostility in the workplace (Anderson, Croteau, Chung, & DiStefano, 2001; Chung, 2001; Lidderdale et al., 2007).

Over the past decade, scholarship on workplace sexual identity management has begun to evolve from a sparse collection of individual studies to a more theoretically driven and methodologically rigorous body of scholarship. Important contributions to this newer literature have been the development of two multidimensional measures of identity management (Anderson et al., 2001; Button, 2004) and three models of identity management-related decision making (Clair, Beatty, & MacLean, 2005; Lidderdale et al., 2007; Ragins, 2004, 2008). In the sections that follow, we first summarize the definitional clarification afforded by these recent contributions. Then we discuss progress on understanding factors related to identity management, with particular attention to understanding more about choices to conceal sexual identity at work. Finally, we focus on the much-needed newer direction of connecting sexual identity management to broader understandings of identity that include other social and cultural group identities.

Continued Focus on Definition

Croteau, Anderson, et al. (2008), writing in an LGB-focused special issue of *Group and Organization Management*, provide a critical integrative analysis of the literature that defines workplace sexual identity management. They review the three conceptual models of identity management noted above, highlighting the complementary lenses of organizational and vocational psychology perspectives on sexual identity management and the need to develop multifaceted definitions of the construct. Two of the conceptual models of workplace sexual identity management, by Clair et al. (2005) and Ragins (2004, 2008), apply concepts from stigma theory (Goffman, 1963), while the third model, by Lidderdale et al. (2007), applies concepts from social-cognitive career theory (Bandura, 1986, 1997; Lent, 2005; Lent, Brown & Hackett, 2002). The stigma-based models emphasize an organizational perspective focused on understanding how the context and climate of work influence LGB workers' decisions about disclosing their sexual orientation. In contrast, the social-cognitive model emphasizes internal cognitive processes that contribute to the development of a breadth of sexual identity management preferences and behaviors while considering general work and personal contexts.

When these models and other similar literature are considered together, it becomes clearer that identity management has been defined in at least three distinct ways in the literature: "identity management as a summary of disclosure actions over time; identity management as a particular approach or strategy for presenting one's identity in the workplace; and identity management as a specific disclosure decision" (Croteau, Anderson, et al., 2008, p. 547). Consistent with the recommendations in the special issue of *Group and Organization Management* (Croteau, Anderson, et al., 2008), we recommend a continued focus on only two of these perspectives: *identity management strategies* and *disclosure decisions*. These two perspectives capture both the ongoing process (strategies) and the daily choices (disclosure decisions) about revealing or concealing sexual identity at work articulated by LGB workers. Continued focus on how both identity management strategies and disclosure decisions are formed and implemented, including increased understanding of the role of workplace climate and other contextual factors, is sorely needed. In particular, more attention is needed to understanding choices to conceal sexual identity at work, as well as expanding the focus to how other social and cultural identities influence the development of sexual identity and subsequent identity management strategies and disclosure decisions.

Expanding Understanding of Factors Related to Concealing and Revealing

Much of the existing literature on workplace sexual identity management frames disclosure of sexual identity as more ideal than concealing. Perhaps building on the early literature concerning lesbian and gay workers' experiences (e.g., Griffin, 1992; Woods & Harbeck, 1992), research and scholarship have been largely based on the (narrow) idea that need for integrity and fear of discrimination are the central motivating factors in identity management preferences and behaviors. Although additional motivations have been offered in subsequent literature (e.g., Creed, 2000, 2006; Lidderdale et al., 2007), the experiences of LGBT workers who choose to conceal their sexual identities in the workplace, somewhat ironically, have remained largely invisible. The two recent articles reviewed in this section are notable exceptions and extension of the literature (DeJordy, 2008; Ragins, Singh, & Cornwell, 2007).

DeJordy (2008) developed a conceptual model to explore potential unintended consequences of passing. In this model both intra- and interpersonal sequelae to passing are examined, with the ultimate goal of understanding individual work performance in an organizational setting. Grounded in broader social identity literature such as Stigma Theory (Goffman, 1963) and Self-Verification Theory (Swann, Stein-Seroussi, & Giesler, 1992), the model builds on the work focusing on workplace sexual identity disclosure by Clair et al. (2005) and Ragins (2008). DeJordy extends understanding of workplace sexual identity management in three ways: by distinguishing the construct of passing from other constructs, by proposing a set of researchable propositions, and by encouraging that future scholars seek an even more nuanced understanding of passing.

DeJordy initially defines passing using Goffman's (1963) words as "the management of undisclosed discrediting information" (p. 42). He goes on to highlight that this definition frames passing as conceptually distinct from the idea of simply not revealing one's identity, as well as from other conformity-focused behaviors such as compliance and impression management. Passing is described as distinct from not revealing because it involves the intentional ongoing portrayal of an expected or dominant social identity rather than one's actual (potentially discrediting) social identity. In this way, passing goes beyond displaying a socially or contextually expected set of behaviors or values to altering one's presentation of the self. In addition, though the negative consequences of revealing are only anticipated, the irreversibility of revealing makes for higher stakes associated with passing than with other conformity-focused behaviors, resulting in a high need for vigilance.

A core aspect of viewing passing from an organizational perspective rests on the notion that within organizations the ongoing nature of interactions among people demands a certain amount of self-disclosure, which passing inhibits. Interestingly, despite making a strong call for the need to look beyond existing bias in favor of revealing identity management strategies, DeJordy develops a model of passing in organizational contexts that highlights a number of potentially unintended negative consequences of passing. More specifically, he offers a series of research propositions suggesting that "passing results in disengagement from the organizational context, mediated by a lack of self-verification, ego depletion, and cognitive dissonance" (p. 506), ultimately resulting in less "workplace initiative, collaboration, and extra role behaviors" (p. 519).

Recognizing that his proposed model is limited by lack of attention to the potential benefits of passing, DeJordy further suggests that future research might focus intentionally on examining possible unintended positive consequences, perhaps through the use of qualitative or experience-near research methods. We concur with this suggestion as well as his discussion of recommendations to incorporate an understanding of how identity itself matters, and to increase understanding of the wide range of passing and other identity management behaviors that may be used. DeJordy hypothesizes that the unintended negative consequences of passing may be lessened for less salient identities, and that passing behaviors involving fabrication of an alternative identity will require more self-regulation and create more cognitive demand than those relying more on discretion. This latter distinction is consistent with the separation of passing and covering (Griffin, 1992) or counterfeiting and avoiding (Woods & Harbeck, 1992) strategies described in early models of sexual identity management.

Ragins et al. (2007) also extend understanding of the choices to conceal sexual identity at work, through focused exploration of the effects of fear of disclosure of sexual identity in the workplace. Noting inconsistent and inconclusive findings in the existing literature concerning the relationship between workplace disclosure of sexual orientation and a wide variety of work-related outcomes, including work attitudes, psychological strain, and experiences of formal and informal discrimination, Ragins et al. hypothesized that fear of disclosure may have a bigger impact on workplace experiences than disclosure itself. This possibility is consistent with Chung's discussion of potential discrimination, and DeJordy's suggestion that even anticipated negative consequences of disclosure may have significant effects on workplace behaviors. The study by Ragins et al. extends understanding of workplace sexual identity management in multiple ways. They developed a tool specifically aimed at measuring fear of disclosure; they undertook comparative analysis of both antecedents and consequences of disclosure versus fear of disclosure; and they recruited a national sample that is substantially more diverse than typical samples in the workplace sexual identity literature.

The Fear of Disclosure Scale was developed from a review of "related literature" (Ragins et al., 2007, p. 1110) and focuses on commonly raised possible outcomes of workplace disclosure of sexual orientation. Sample items include *I would lose my job*, *I would be excluded from informal networks*, and *Coworkers would feel uncomfortable around me*. Initial factor analysis of the measure yielded a single factor accounting for 64.9% of the variance, and internal consistency for the development sample was estimated at .95. Although these initial psychometric data are promising, additional reliability and validity data are needed. One specific needed clarification concerns whether the measure may tap something like expectations or anticipation of negative outcomes of disclosure rather than fear; the idea of fear is not included in either the scale directions or the items themselves.

Also based on their review of existing literature, Ragins et al. (2007) investigated five potential predictors of fear of disclosure: perceived sexual orientation of workplace supervisor, perceived sexual orientation of coworkers, perceived social support from supervisors, perceived social support from coworkers, and previously perceived experiences of discrimination due to sexual orientation. These same five predictors were also examined in relationship to degree of disclosure (measured with a single item asking participants about their own disclosure of sexual orientation in the workplace). As expected, fear of disclosure was lower and degree of disclosure was higher when supervisors and coworkers were perceived as gay and lesbian and when they were perceived as supportive. In addition, though past experiences with discrimination were associated with greater fear of disclosure, they were also associated with greater degree of disclosure. This latter finding is consistent with existing research and theory suggesting multiple motivations underlying individual differences in workplace disclosure and identity management (Croteau, Anderson, et al., 2008).

Ragins et al. (2007) also investigated the relationships between both fear of disclosure and degree of disclosure, and 15 work-related outcomes. The variety of work-related outcomes investigated was extensive, including six commonly assessed work and career attitudes (job satisfaction, organizational commitment, turnover intentions, satisfaction with opportunities for promotion, career commitment, and organization-based self-esteem); three work environment variables (role ambiguity, role conflict, and workplace participation); four indicators of psychological strain at work (somatic complaints, depression, anxiety, and irritation); and two career outcome variables (promotions and compensation).

Comparison of the results from these analyses was quite striking: 13 of the 15 (all except anxiety and compensation) outcome variables were associated with fear of disclosure, while only 1 (workplace participation) was partially associated with degree of disclosure. For workers who had not disclosed

or not fully disclosed their sexual orientation in the workplace, those who feared more negative consequences of disclosure reported less positive work attitudes; more role ambiguity and conflict; less workplace participation; more work-related somatic stress, depression, and irritation; and fewer promotions. When the entire sample was considered (both those who had fully disclosed and those who had not), greater degree of disclosure was associated with more participation in the workplace; looking only at those who had not disclosed or not fully disclosed their sexual orientation, this relationship was no longer statistically significant. This pattern of results supports existing calls for more complex perspectives on workplace sexual identity management: the absence of relationship between degree of disclosure and work-related outcome variables challenges the prevailing bias that disclosure alone leads to more positive work experiences.

A final important contribution of this study is the successful recruitment of a fairly diverse national sample. Participants were drawn from a large national random sample of three gay rights organizations in the United States. Although recruitment through gay-identified organizations suggests some homogeneity in how sexual identity is constructed, the obtained sample includes greater racial diversity (15.2% African American; 12.2% Latino/a), more bisexual participants (7.1%), and greater variation in degree of workplace disclosure (11.7% out to no one, 37% out to some, 24.6% out to most, 26.7% out to everyone) than is prototypical of LGBT work-related research. As described more fully in the following section, increased focus on sampling the full breadth of LGBT workers is a central need in the literature.

Focusing Particularly on Other Social and Cultural Identities

LGBT vocational psychology and POW perspectives both call for increased attention in the literature to the full breadth of workers. Systems of social categorization, marginalization, and oppression work to sustain the invisibility of particular groups of people, making it urgent that we expand our focus to include nonprofessional workers, workers from diverse racial backgrounds, and workers reflecting the full range of sexual and gender identities. Despite repeated calls for increased inclusion, a primary continuing limit of the sexual identity management literature is overreliance on White, well-educated, middle- and upper-class samples. We did, however, identify three notable exceptions in the recent literature that are reviewed here. More specifically, two recent qualitative studies provide initial information about the mediating effects of social class on the experience of lesbian or gay workers (McDermott, 2006; Rumens & Kerfoot, 2009), while the qualitative study of Black lesbian workers initially reviewed in the climate section also yields information about race and gender in relationship to sexual identity management (Bowleg et al., 2008).

McDermott (2006) conducted a qualitative study examining the combined influence of workplace sexual identity performances and social class on the psychological health of sexual minority women. Though not explicitly defined in the article, identity performance appears to refer to the full range of ways identities may be expressed, including the breadth of ongoing and day-to-day behaviors captured by the concept of identity management. This study is important for extending understanding of workplace sexual identity management because of the explicit focus on the interaction between social class and sexual identity performances in the workplace. In addition, the conceptual framework for the study emphasizes the notion of performance of both social class and sexual orientation. The emphasis on performance of identities serves to highlight the systemic and socially constructed nature of both heterosexism and classism, helping to focus thinking beyond the identity management decisions and strategies of individual workers to the broader context (of work) that reproduces heteronormativity and social class inequalities.

Participants in the study were 24 women aged 21 to 56 in the United Kingdom. They self-identified as lesbian, gay, or dyke; and as White (17), Black or mixed race (5), and Jewish (2). With respect to social class, three groups were examined: those identifying as working class (10), those identifying as middle class (7), and those university-educated women from a working-class background (7). Consistent with other research, these women reported that workplace homophobia was pervasive and persistent, contributing to experiences of stress and strain as they navigated the hetero-gendered nature of workplace interactions. Performing a lesbian identity at work was perceived as risky overall, and each individual worker's identity performances were shaped by complex and careful evaluations of the risk involved. As expected based on earlier research, participants' performance of sexuality in the workplace was quite varied, including embracing opportunities to reveal their identity to others they judged as likely

to be more accepting; contesting or disputing heterosexual norms; and masquerading as heterosexual (McDermott, 2006).

Although participants also described specific aspects of the workplace that influenced their level of perceived risk from sexual identity performance, the most striking finding from this study was the differences in experiences of women across social class. Middle-class and educated-from-working-class participants were mostly open about their sexuality at work. They tended to work in environments with less risk—including workplaces that were female-dominated, had other lesbian or gay workers, or had explicit endorsement of alternative/non-mainstream politics. In addition, these women were more likely to hold workplace roles that provided them more power and authority, which they experienced as providing more control of (less vulnerability to) potential negative outcomes of revealing their sexual identity (McDermott, 2006).

Working-class women and some of the educated-from-working-class women tended to view their workplaces as high-risk settings where heterosexuality was strongly policed. Often these workplaces were highly male-dominated, resulting in high levels of scrutiny for female workers. Another aspect of class that influenced the experiences of these women was the sense of access to work; middle-class women may have changed jobs in order to escape homophobic workplaces, while working-class women tended to remain in their jobs or face unemployment (McDermott, 2006).

These findings indicate that social class clearly interacts with sexual identity performances and that there is an important dynamic related to social power that contributes to this interaction. Both of these findings are consistent with POW core values and perspectives involving social class consciousness and how social power is an important aspect of the experience of working. Though not too distant from understanding motivation for identity management choices from a fear-versus-integrity perspective, a focus on social power adds an important system perspective for choices around how (not just whether) to perform minority sexual identity. In focusing on the notion of identity performance for both social class and sexual identity, McDermott (2006) makes a clear connection to the social construction of both sexual identity and social class, including the means by which the social system regulates heterosexuality and maintains gender- and class-related inequities.

Rumens and Kerfoot (2009) conducted a qualitative study of gay men that provides further evidence of the interweaving of the performance of sexuality and social class in the workplace. The unique perspective offered by this study is that it focuses on how workers construct a professional self, and the ways in which a gay identity is incorporated into this professional presentation. In addition, participants (10 gay men, aged 20 to 48) were employed in a range of roles at a single British public-sector gay-friendly workplace. This context is salient for extending understanding of workplace sexual identity management because of national legislation prohibiting workplace discrimination on the grounds of sexual orientation in the United Kingdom, a context that is shared only in certain locations in the United States.

Though at least some participants in this study reported experiencing more acceptance in this gay-friendly–identified workplace than they have in other work contexts, participants also reported a continued experience of "dominant professional norms and discourses on heteronormativity that position sexuality and professionalism as polar opposites" (Rumens & Kerfoot, 2009, p. 763). The gendered nature of professionalism itself is also acknowledged, and linked to the gendered nature of sexuality. Participants describe the performance of sexuality as heavily monitored by supervisors and coworkers, and report using performance of social class and gender to enhance professional credibility.

Some participants reported that the "gay-friendly" environment of their workplace allowed them to "behave as a normal professional, and be regarded as a professional by others … it's a place where gay men are just accepted that way" (Rumens & Kerfoot, 2009, p. 773). However, other participants highlight the boundaries around this acceptance: "I can be an openly gay professional … I am the new acceptable face of homosexuality … straight acting, a professional who drives an Audi with a partner at home, has holidays abroad, wears nice clothes, what's wrong with that? Just blending in … rather than being a thorn in the side of society" (p. 774). In this latter example, the authors note that economic independence and gender conventionality are used to create a "normal gay professional" identity; middle-class affluence and blending into the heterosexual milieu are highlighted as means for being viewed as professional in the workplace.

Other gay workers with less financial resources describe more struggles to claim a professional identity (Rumens & Kerfoot, 2009). Though knowledge and technical skills may lead such workers to self-identify as professional, they struggle to display behaviors associated with a professional lifestyle, a lifestyle that is perceived as very connected to class. Overall, being an openly gay professional even in gay-friendly workplaces is still perceived as requiring a good deal of self-regulation. Expression of sexuality is viewed as needing to be monitored, and sexuality that flagrantly transgresses gender norms is seen as problematic and unprofessional. The message seems to be that it's okay to be gay as long as you are masculine in your expression of professionalism.

At the same time, Rumens and Kerfoot (2009) note that gay-friendly workplaces provide a context where workers may construct a sense of self as professional. In a context where diversity of sexual orientation is relatively recognized and valued, workers may focus on the expression of professionalism more so than on the expression of sexuality, claiming a place as valued members in the organization. They suggest that in a gay-supportive context, more implicit expression of sexuality may not reflect "shame or self-loathing" but rather reflect a choice to emphasize other aspects of self. This perspective is consistent with the suggestion from Croteau, Anderson, et al. (2008) that sexual identity management may be more varied in gay-supportive workplaces because choices around expression of sexuality will be less constrained by a singular focus on fear of discrimination present in more oppressive contexts. At the same time, the qualitative data from this study of gay workers highlight that the dominant societal discourses on gender, sexuality, and work continued to limit self-determination.

The study of predominately middle-class, well-educated Black lesbians by Bowleg et al. (2008) explicitly addressed issues of identity management in ways conscious of racism and sexism in the workplace. Ten of the 19 participants were described as being out in the workplace, while 6 of the 18 discussed covering or concealing their sexual orientation at work.

Of particular interest for expanding understanding of workplace sexual identity management are the motivations participants reported for revealing sexual orientation in the workplace. Motivations for being out included managing stress and self-expression ("'I'm clear at work. I don't say friend; I say 'partner'. I say 'she'. I don't change the pronoun. People can get it or not get it, but I don't want to play circles with myself" [p. 77]) and challenging heterosexist assumptions ("I don't like for people to assume that I'm heterosexual, because that happens a lot: 'Oh how's your boyfriend? Or your husband?' … things like that. I don't like that. So it's very important [that] I'm out to everybody" [p. 77]).

In addition, while a majority of participants reported no negative experiences as a result of being out and those with LGBT supervisors or support groups reported positive experiences of being out in the workplace, most also reported being strategic about managing information about their sexual orientation, and being strategic about when and how to disclose, in order to minimize negative reactions. Some of these participants also discussed confronting and educating coworkers. These efforts included directly confronting oppressive coworker behavior, being involved with the LGBT-related work organization, and serving as an example for others.

For those participants who discussed covering or concealing their sexual orientation at work, two broad strategies were employed: monitoring speech and behavior revealing of sexual orientation, and sharing little or no information about personal lives. These workers tended to perceive that they really had no other options, and at least for some workers this was perceived as different from other colleagues who held other social privileges, such as being male. This sense of difference in experiences between those participants holding multiple oppressed social identities (race, gender, and sexual orientation) and those who may also hold a privileged social identity as well as the broad categories of coping employed by these participants echo findings reported by McDermott concerning intersections of sexual orientation and social class and point to the need for increased intentional focus on the complexities of identities and identity management overall.

Moving Toward a POW Perspective on LGBT Workplace Sexual Identity Management

In some ways the concept of identity management is at the crux of what it means to think from a POW perspective. The literature concerning the workplace experiences of LGBT workers consistently identifies identity management as a core component of navigating work—and that navigation spans organizational, interpersonal, and intrapersonal perspectives. The focus on how self-portrayal in the workplace is connected to workplace rewards, relationships, and sense of self clearly connects with POW notions of work as providing means for survival and access to power, social connection, and self-determination.

Although even the early literature on identity management emphasized the complex and ongoing nature of managing a minority sexual identity in the workplace, the growing edge and the continued growth edge in this topic area is on increasing complexity of thinking and understanding of the full range of identity management (e.g., Croteau, Anderson, et al., 2008). Recent measurement and theoretical developments have facilitated some important growth and can be used as jumping-off points and models for highlighting the most recent developments and encouraging more developments in this area.

The identity management measures developed by Anderson et al. (2001) and Button (2004) are multidimensional measures that capture the conceptualization of identity management strategies based on early qualitative research with mostly lesbian and gay workers. These tools are valuable because they allow measurement of the full range of identity management on a continuum from concealing to revealing that was highlighted in this early literature. Although scholarship on identity management is becoming more programmatic and rigorous, there has been very limited additional research on or with these tools since they were developed. An important limit of both tools is that the items are phrased so that they apply to workers who identify as lesbian or gay much better than to those who identify as bisexual or transgender—not focused on gender perceptions, focusing on same-sex partners, etc. An important alternative to the development of more inclusive measures might involve distinct measures for bisexual people and for transgender people. The experience of identity and its management for workers who identify as bisexual or transgender are probably distinct enough to warrant consideration of this alternative. Further, there needs to be a consideration of the extent to which White and/or middle- and upper-class bias exists in current constructs and measures of identity management.

We strongly encourage further development of these identity management measures (or ones like them) so that they work well with a broader range of workers identifying as sexual minorities. We again note that such efforts are a major part of moving the current scholarship toward the POW vision of worker inclusivity. We also strongly encourage use of these tools (or ones like them) to assess identity management in future LGBT workplace-focused research; this will facilitate increased rigor and allow more meaningful examination of the relationships between various aspects of the experience of work and identity management. This idea is particularly important in light of another core development in the literature—increased clarity in the definition of identity management.

Recent theoretical work has identified two distinct perspectives for thinking about management of a minority sexual identity in the workplace (Croteau, Anderson, et al., 2008). More specifically, broad ongoing strategies for managing one's sexual identity in the workplace can be understood as related to but distinct from specific daily decisions workers make about disclosure (or not) of sexual identity in the workplace. Further exploration of each of these constructs is needed to reach the goals of inclusion that are central to a POW perspective. In particular, increased focus on how both identity management strategies and disclosure decisions are formed and implemented is sorely needed. Though largely untested at this time, the conceptual models reviewed by Croteau, Anderson, et al. offer promising frameworks for integrating existing scholarship and developing future research. Effective application of these models will also likely require development of additional tools to measure core theoretical constructs such as identity management-related self-efficacy and outcome expectations, and organizational and professional norms concerning sexual identity disclosure, etc. Ragins et al.'s (2007) development of the Fear of Disclosure scale and subsequent investigation of workplace outcomes associated with both fear of disclosure and disclosure itself offers one of these important tools and provides data relevant to their stigma-based model (Ragins, 2004, 2008).

When advances in measurement and theory-based clarification of construct definition are considered in combination, two core limits to our understanding of sexual identity disclosure and management are highlighted. More information about the full range of ways LGBT workers portray their sexual identity in the workplace is needed, as well as more information about the full range of motivations that underlie specific disclosure decisions and broad identity management strategies. The bias in the literature is to value revealing strategies and disclosures; this bias likely occurs for many reasons, including the need for visibility for social change efforts and the over-reliance on White, middle- or upper-class, highly educated samples for which the bias might best apply. Information about the experiences of workers who do not reveal or who conceal their sexual identity in the workplace is extremely limited.

The basic conceptualization of identity management as ranging from concealing to revealing emphasizes the contrast between fear of disclosure and wish for integrity articulated by lesbian and gay workers in the 1980s. One of the models reviewed by Croteau, Anderson et al. (2008), the Workplace Sexual Identity Management Model (Lidderdale et al., 2007), provides a useful framework for beginning to think about additional motivations underlying identity management in combination with a broad range of contextual influences. Workplace climate is the most studied contextual influence in the existing literature. We recommend combining increased study of affirmative workplace environments with a broader range of other contextual and personal variables to improve understanding of the varied motivations that potentially underlie sexual identity management strategies and disclosure decisions. The Rumens and Kerfoot (2008) study of gay men's professional identities provides an example of how additional social and cultural identities may emerge as prevalent shapers of workplace behavior in gay-friendly contexts.

DeJordy's (2008) conceptual discussion of differences between passing and other forms of not revealing, as well as Ragins et al.'s (2008) separation of fear of disclosure and disclosure itself, should also help us move beyond the contrast between fear of disclosure and wish for integrity to consider additional motivations underlying identity management strategies and disclosure decisions. In particular, the finding that it is *anticipated discrimination rather than encountered discrimination* that contributes to most negative workplace outcomes suggests that nondisclosure that is not grounded in this fear may have very different outcomes. Bowleg et al.'s (2008) observation that there were mostly no negative consequences of being out—and yet workers were also mostly strategic about identity management—further supports the need to think more complexly about the motivations underlying these choices. Intentional exploration of the theoretical mechanisms for developing, changing, and implementing identity management strategies suggested in the workplace sexual identity management model proposed by Lidderdale et al. (2007) could guide identification of additional motivations to explore. The qualitative studies by McDermott (2006) and by Bowleg et al. (2008) yield some ideas of other motivations that may be operating—such as stress management and promoting social change. The social change motivation in particular connects to POW perspectives concerning the central role of work in allowing access to social power, and the importance of using scholarship on work to create positive changes in the conditions of work, particularly for historically marginalized workers. We encourage continued exploration of identity management strategies that may be motivated by a desire for and lead to changes in workplace climate, and note that Creed et al.'s exploration of identity deployment may provide additional fruitful conceptualization of these ideas (Creed, 2006; Creed & Scully, 2000)

Imbedded in the models that explore predictors of identity management strategies and disclosure decisions, as well as the call for understanding more about choices to conceal or not reveal, is a recognition that choices about revealing or expressing sexual identity in the workplace must be contextualized in a broader understanding of identity. Although we gave focused attention to identifying literature that would help us understand more about variation in workplace sexual identity management associated with additional aspects of diversity, we identified only a few exemplars to discuss. The three qualitative studies that we reviewed illustrate that lesbian and gay workers do report considering other social group identities as they make identity management-related choices (Bowleg et al., 2008; McDermott, 2006; Nelson & Probst, 2004). The hints we have here about moderating effects of social class and race are strongly connected to core POW concepts. A core continued limit of this literature, however, is the constrictive notion of traditional definitions of sexual identity itself. There is emerging recognition in the broader LGBT psychology literature that these conceptualizations of sexual identity are themselves limited by a dominant group perspective that centralizes the experience of White, often lesbian, middle- or upper-class, and well-educated individuals (Bieschke, Hardy, Fassinger, & Croteau 2008). In responding to the repeated calls for broadening understanding of sexual identity itself in the LGBT workplace experiences literature, scholars are encouraged to at least incorporate an assessment of identity development or identity salience and better yet to incorporate newer notions in LGBT psychology literature on fluid, contextual, and nonbinary understandings of gender and sexual identities (e.g. Fassinger & Arseneau, 2007).

Conclusion: Toward an Authentic LGBT Psychology of Working

Our focus in this chapter has been on moving LGBT vocational psychology toward an LGBT psychology of working. This is not a comprehensive review of LGBT vocational literature, but rather a selective review in order to highlight and illustrate the directions we think are particularly important for this movement. The most developed areas of scholarship within LGBT vocational psychology,

LGBT workplace climate and discrimination and LGBT workplace sexual identity management, are strong exemplars of the POW focus on broadening our understanding of the experience of work. Exploration of this literature using a POW lens, however, reveals multiple potentially fruitful expansions. We used the POW perspective to make recommendations for future research and scholarship throughout our discussion of LGBT workplace discrimination and climate and our discussion of LGBT workplace sexual identity management.

Integrating the POW perspective across these core areas in LGBT vocational psychology, we offer some final thoughts about potent and critical expansions required by an LGBT POW perspective. The first three of these final thoughts are recommendations for how to continue building incrementally on the strong foundations within LGBT vocational psychology; these three sets of ideas are summarized briefly. The fourth and final set of ideas connects the POW emphasis on intentional inclusion of the full range of work and workers with an emerging perspective within LGBT psychology. This emerging LGBT psychology perspective calls for a more integrated understanding of identity itself that challenges binary conceptions of sexual and gender orientation and identity, unidimensional considerations of sexuality apart from other aspects of identity including race, gender, and social class, and simplistic additive understandings of such intersections. Transformation of knowledge in this area requires a much bigger shift in current thought; thus we offer more extended discussion and suggestions for change in this area.

Building on Foundations Within LGBT Vocational Psychology

Recognizing that LGBT workplace discrimination continues to be a pervasive experience for LGBT workers, we have two core recommendations for advancing this literature and/or moving it toward a POW perspective. We recommend focusing more on the broad notion of climate, with particular emphasis on increasing understanding of the dynamic interplay among varied aspects of climate and including attention to LGBT workers' experiences of positive workplace climates. We also recommend intentional focus on changing workplace climates to be more hospitable and affirming of LGBT workers. Both of these recommendations will require more programmatic research as well as intentional focus on systemic forces (not just individual and organizational ones) that sustain oppressive workplace climates.

The pervasiveness of workplace discrimination and broader systemic heterosexism sustain the other core focus of this chapter: LGBT workers' sense of ongoing and daily need to manage expression of sexual identity in the workplace. The POW continuing press toward inclusion and uncovering obstacles toward inclusion can be seen as a point of interrogation of the bias toward uncritical valuing of more revealing workplace sexual identity management behaviors and strategies in much of the existing literature, a bias that likely developed in part out of a broader bias in the field toward primarily studying, theorizing, and representing experiences of predominantly White, well-educated, middle- and upper-class people. Our primary recommendation for this broad area of research and scholarship is to continue to move toward fuller understanding of day-to-day behaviors, ongoing strategies, and motivations underlying expression of sexual identity in the workplace among a wider range of workers. Further exploration of the connections and distinctions among discrimination management, identity management strategies, and disclosure decisions should prove fruitful. In addition, recent qualitative literature exploring the intersections of race, gender, social class, and sexual identity points to the potential value of integrating additional perspectives, such as the notion of identity performances and the importance of a broader conceptualization of worker well-being beyond the impact of experiences with discrimination.

Literature on LGBT workplace discrimination and climate and LGBT workplace sexual identity management has been growing more rigorous in the past decade. The discrimination and climate literature has expanded to include national probability samples and more traditional experimental designs. The identity management literature has benefitted from better measurement and more theory use. We encourage continued focus on rigor and note the particularly fruitful expansion of understanding of LGBT discrimination management and identity management that has been supported through development of LGBT-specific models, and application of Social Cognitive Career Theory, Stigma Theory, Social Exchange Theory, and Minority Stress theory, all of which have been previously discussed. The concept of microaggressions has recently expanded to nascent consideration of sexual orientation microaggressions and microaggressions in the workplace context (see Sue, 2010). We recommend using the perspective of workplace sexual orientation microaggressions to further extend our understanding of workplace climate.

Building Inclusivity

Psychology, vocational psychology, LGBT psychology, and here specifically LGBT vocational psychology have too long been bounded by economic and social privilege—thus yielding a LGBT vocational psychology of White, middle- and upper-class, lesbian women and gay men. The POW perspective is an insistent challenge that scholarly efforts go beyond boundaries of privilege. Bieschke et al. (2008) point to a new paradigm emerging in the broader LGBT psychology, a paradigm that "recognizes to fully understand sexual orientation, it must be explored in conjunction with gender, race, ethnicity, religion, class, disability, and other aspects of social or cultural location" (p. 177). An LGBT psychology of working would embody that recognition. Though we have pointed to several exemplars of this work in the material reviewed previously, such embodiment has barely begun.

In regard to advanced inclusivity along racialized lines, the recent work in a major contribution to *The Counseling Psychologist* is essential for shaping a racially conscious and inclusive LGBT psychology of working (see Moradi, DeBlaere, & Huang, 2010). Of particular note is the article on conducting research on LGBT people of color (DeBlaere, Brewster, Sarkees, & Moradi, 2010). DeBlaere et al. present a careful consideration of barriers to such research and offer suggestions for how to overcome them. They offer a comprehensive overview considering such issues as sampling and recruitment, measurement and instrumentation, methods, and analyses. They also encourage deeper critique and interrogation of existing literature, pointing out for example that existing LGBT constructs are limited by having been developed primarily from research on White sexual minorities. Their concluding 12 recommendations should be required reading for anyone doing research on sexual and gender minorities in any context, including that of working. The recommendations include specific method suggestions (e.g., how to assess sexual identification, settings for recruitment, etc.) as well as guidance on an overall approach that recognizes racist structural obstacles and intentionally prioritizes the establishment of networks, relationships, and leadership from communities of color out of which productive research can arise.

Inclusion of bisexual- and transgender-identified people, not just lesbian and gay people, is a major aspect of the "new paradigm" of LGBT psychology (e.g., Bieschke et al., 2008). Bisexual men and women have begun to be considered in much of the newer sexual minority work-related research, but often in small numbers that contribute little to understanding the experiences of bisexual workers that may be distinct from lesbian and gay workers. While there has been research on bisexual men and women specifically in the larger LGBT psychology research, such research is largely nonexistent in relation to work. Surprisingly, there has been work-specific attention to transgender people.

In their review of workplace discrimination literature, Badgett et al. (2007) identified a small body of studies focused particularly on discrimination on the basis of gender identity or transgender status; findings from six studies conducted between 1996 and 2006 indicated that transgender employees report similar or higher levels of employment discrimination as LGB employees. In addition, in our review of workplace experiences literature published since this time, we identified four additional articles aimed at supporting transgender individuals (Budge, Tebbe, & Howard, 2010; Kirk & Belovics, 2008; O'Neil, McWhirter, & Cerezo, 2008; Sangganjanavanich & Cavazos, 2010). These articles primarily emphasize development of effective career counseling practice for transgender persons through provision of basic information about gender identity and gender variance; legal issues and common experiences of discrimination, harassment, and aggression; and encouragement of social advocacy and increased scholarship. As a whole the literature on workplace experiences of transgender people is best described as mostly focused on raising awareness and educating career development professionals about the basics of transgender experiences; research and theory development is sorely lacking.

In reference to the larger LGBT psychology literature, Bieschke et al. (2008) note there is almost no research that examines the lives of LGBT people who are specifically in lower social or economic classes. Samples continue to be predominantly White, well-educated, middle and upper class, and little research targets social class in particular. Despite the obvious link between social and economic class and the experience of working, the only research we found on this link in the context of work has been reviewed here: Embrick et al. (2007) targeted a largely working-class environment as the setting for their study, and McDermott (2006) focused on social class as a factor that could make for distinct work-related experiences among a group of female workers.

We recommend much more research focused on working-class settings and encourage direct examination of the effects of social class on the working experiences of LGBT people. Finally, in regard to social class, we must note the almost total disregard of issues of poverty among LGBT people in LGBT vocational psychology literature. Badgett et al. (2007) expose income disparities but do not focus particularly on experiences of poverty. We think that among the factors related to poverty, anti-LGBT discrimination and hostility need consideration.

We also recommend expanding existing notions of inclusivity and suggest that even the work-related experiences of White, well-educated, upper- and middle-class LGBT people may be less than fully understood due to the lack of racial and social class consciousness within that research and scholarship. For example, the experience of stigma by a White middle-class gay man at work can only be fully understood, perhaps, in the context of an assumption of White male social class privilege that is disrupted by sexual orientation stigma. As we consider such privilege in relationship to race and class, we also want to promote the consideration of heterosexual workers, their own sexual orientation management, and their contributions to LGBT workplace climate. The experimental studies reviewed by Badgett et al. (2007) and the studies by Willis (2010) and Embrick et al. (2007) are examples of looking at heterosexual workers' and managers' exercise of bias in the workplace. Hill's (2009) conceptual work on heterosexual backlash to progress on LGBT workplace inclusion is another such example. This work needs to continue and expand in many ways. In particular, we suggest expansion of experience-near research that can capture positive effects of working in an LGBT-supportive workplace on heterosexual workers.

The only examination of LGBT issues in explicit relationship to the psychology of working prior to this one are a handful of pages in Blustein's (2006) original work on POW. We think the meta-perspective of the POW has much to offer in terms of pointing toward future directions that will extend understandings of the experience of working among LGBT people toward more depth and much greater inclusivity. Blustein notes that "working is the battleground for social justice" (2006; p. 26); in this light, an authentic POW can play a significant role in bringing more justice to wider range of LGBT lives.

References

Anderson, M. Z., Croteau, J. M., Chung, Y. B., & DiStefano, T. M. (2001). Developing an assessment of sexual identity management for lesbian and gay workers. *Journal of Career Assessment, 9*, 243–260.

Badgett, M. V. L., Lau, H., Sears, B., & Ho, D. (2007). *Bias in the workplace: Consistent evidence of sexual orientation and gender identity discrimination.* Los Angeles, CA: The Williams Institute.

Bandura, A. (1986). *Social foundations of thought and action.* Englewood Cliffs, NJ: Prentice Hall.

Bandura, A. (1997). *Self-efficacy: The exercise of control.* New York: Freeman.

Bieschke, K. J., Hardy, J. A., Fassinger, R. E., & Croteau, J.M. (2008). Intersecting identities of gender-transgressive sexual minorities: Toward a new paradigm of affirmative psychology. In B. Walsh (Ed.), *Biennial review of counseling psychology* (vol. 1, pp. 177–208). New York: Psychology Press.

Blau, P. M. (1964). *Exchange and power in social life.* New York: Wiley.

Blustein, D. L. (2006). *The psychology of working: A new perspective for career development, counseling, and public policy.* Mahwah, NJ: Erlbaum.

Blustein, D. L., Kenna, A. C., Gill, N., & DeVoy, J. E. (2008). The psychology of working: A new framework for counseling practice and public policy. *Career Development Quarterly, 56,* 294–308.

Bowleg, L., Brooks, K., & Ritz, S. (2008). Bringing home more than a paycheck: An exploratory analysis of black lesbians' experiences of stress and coping in the workplace. *Journal of Lesbian Studies, 12*(1), 69–84.

Budge, S., Tebbe, E., & Howard, K. (2010). The work experiences of transgender individuals: Negotiating the transition and career decision-making processes. *Journal of Counseling Psychology, 57*(4), 377–393.

Button, S. B. (2004). Identity management strategies utilized by lesbian and gay employees: A quantitative explanation. *Group & Organization Management, 29,* 470–494.

Chojnacki, J. T., & Gelberg, S. (1994). Toward a conceptualization of career counseling with gay/lesbian/bisexual persons. *Journal of Career Development, 21,* 3–10.

Chung, Y. B. (2001). Working discrimination and coping strategies: Conceptual frameworks for counseling lesbian, gay, and bisexual clients. *Career Development Quarterly, 50,* 33–44.

Chung, Y. B., Williams, W., & Dispenza, F. (2009). Validating work discrimination and coping strategy models for sexual minorities. *Career Development Quarterly, 58,* 162–170.

Clair, J. A., Beatty, J. E., & MacLean, T. L. (2005). Out of sight but not out of mind: Managing invisible social identities in the workplace. *Academy of Management Review, 30,* 78–95.

Creed, W. E. D. (2006). Seven conversations about the same thing: Homophobia and heterosexism in the workplace. In A. Konrad, P. Prasad, & J. Pringle (Eds.), *Handbook of Workplace Diversity,* (pp. 371–400. Thousand Oaks, CA: Sage.

Creed, W. E. D., & Scully, M. A. (2000) Songs of ourselves: Employees' deployment of social identity in workplace encounters. *Journal of Management Inquiry, 9,* 391–412.

Croteau, J. M. (1996). Research on the work experiences of lesbian, gay, and bisexual people: an integrative review of methodology and findings. *Journal of Vocational Behavior, 48,* 195–209.

Croteau, J. M. (2008). Reflections on understanding and ameliorating internalized heterosexism. *Counseling Psychologist, 36,* 645–653.

Croteau, J. M., Anderson, M. Z., DiStefano, T. M., & Kampa-Kokesch, S. (2000). Lesbian, gay, and bisexual vocational psychology: Reviewing foundations and planning construction. In R. M. Perez, K. A. DeBord, & K. J. Bieschke (Eds.), *Handbook of counseling and psychotherapy with lesbian, gay, and bisexual clients* (pp. 383–408). Washington, DC: American Psychology Association.

Croteau, J. M., Anderson, M. Z., & VanderWal, B. (2008). Models of workplace sexual identity disclosure and management: Reviewing and extending concepts. *Group Organization Management, 33,* 532–565.

Croteau, J. M., & Bieschke, K. J. (1996). Beyond pioneering: And introduction to the special issue on the vocational issues of lesbian women and gay men [Special issue]. *Journal of Vocational Behavior, 48,* 119–125.

Croteau, J. M., Bieschke, K. J., Fassinger, R. E., & Manning, J. L. (2008). Counseling psychology and sexual orientation: History, selective trends, and future directions. In S. D. Brown & R. W. Lent (Eds.), *Handbook of counseling psychology* (4th ed., pp. 194–211). Hoboken, NJ: Wiley.

DeBlaere, C., Brewster, M. E., Sarkees, A., & Moradi, B. (2010). Conducting research with LGB people of color: Methodological challenges and strategies. *Counseling Psychologist, 38,* 331–362.

DeJordy, R. (2008). Just passing through. *Group Organization Management, 33*(5), 504–531.

Embrick, D., Walther, C., & Wickens, C. (2007). Working class masculinity: Keeping gay men and lesbians out of the workplace. *Sex Roles, 56*(11-12), 757–766.

Fassinger, R. E. (1995). From invisibility to integration: Lesbian identity in the workplace. *Career Development Quarterly, 44,* 148–167.

Fassinger, R. E., & Arseneau, J. R. (2007). "I'd rather get wet than be under that umbrella": Differentiating the experiences and identities of lesbian, gay, bisexual, and transgender people. In K. Bieschke, R. Perez, & K. DeBord (Eds.), *Handbook of counseling and psychotherapy with lesbian, gay, and bisexual clients* (2nd ed., pp. 19–50). Washington, DC: American Psychological Association.

Goffman, E. (1963). *Stigma: Notes on the management of spoiled identity.* Englewood Cliffs, NJ: Prentice-Hall.

Griffin, P. (1992). From hiding out to coming out: Empowering lesbian and gay educators. In K. M. Harbeck (Ed.), *Coming out of the classroom closet* (pp. 167–196). Binghamton, NY: Harrington Park Press.

Hall, M. (1986). The lesbian corporate experience. *Journal of Homosexuality, 12,* 59–75.

Helms, J. E. (1995). An update of Helm's White and people of color racial identity models. In J. G. Ponterotto, J. M. Casa, L. A. Suzuki, & C. M. Alexander (Eds.), *Handbook of multicultural counseling* (pp. 181–198). Thousand Oaks, CA: Sage.

Hill, R. (2009). Incorporating queers: Blowback, backlash, and other forms of resistance to the workplace diversity initiatives that support sexual minorities. *Advances in Developing Human Resources, 11*(1), 37–53.

Huffman, A., Watrous-Rodriguez, K., & King, E. (2008). Supporting a diverse workforce: What type of support is most meaningful for lesbian and gay employees? *Human Resource Management, 47*(2), 237–253.

Ingram, K. M., Betz, N. E., Mindes, E. J., Schmitt, M. M., & Smith, N. G. (2001). Unsupportive responses from others concerning a stressful life event: Development of the unsupportive social interactions inventory. *Journal of Social and Clinical Psychology, 20*, 173–207.

Kirk, J., & Belovics, R. (2008). Understanding and counseling transgender clients. *Journal of Employment Counseling, 45*(1), 29–43.

Lent, R. W. (2005). A social cognitive view of career development and counseling. In S. D. Brown & R. W. Lent (Eds.), *Career development and counseling: Putting theory and research to work* (pp. 101–127). Hoboken, NJ: John Wiley.

Lent, R. W., Brown, S. D., & Hackett, G. (2002). Social cognitive career theory. In D. Brown & Associates (Eds.), *Career choice and development* (4th ed., pp. 255–311). San Francisco: Jossey-Bass.

Levine, M. P., & Leonard, R. (1984). Discrimination against lesbians in the work force. *Signs: Journal of Women in Culture and Society, 9*, 700–710.

Lidderdale, M. A., Croteau, J. M., Anderson, M. Z., Tovar-Murray, D., & Davis, J. M. (2007). Building LGB vocational psychology: A theoretical model of workplace sexual identity management. In K. J. Bieschke, R. M. Perez, & K. A. DeBord (Eds.), *Handbook of counseling and psychotherapy with lesbian, gay, bisexual, and transgender clients* (2nd ed., pp. 245–270). Washington, DC: American Psychological Association.

Liddle, B., Luzzo, D., Hauenstein, A., & Schuck, K. (2004). Construction and validation of the lesbian, gay, bisexual, and transgendered climate inventory. *Journal of Career Assessment, 12*(1), 33–50.

Maher, M., Landini, K., Emano, D., Knight, A., Lantz, G., Parrie, M., Pichler, S., & Sever, L. (2009). Hirschfeld to hooker to herek to high schools: A study of the history and development of GLBT empirical research, institutional policies, and the relationship between the two. *Journal of Homosexuality, 56*(7), 921–958.

McDermott, E. (2006). Surviving in dangerous places: Lesbian identity performances in the workplace, social class and psychological health. *Feminism Psychology, 16*(2), 193–211.

Meyer, I. (1995). Minority stress and mental health in gay men. *Journal of Health Sciences and Social Behavior, 36*, 38–56.

Moradi, B., DeBlaere, C., & Huang, Y, (2010). Centralizing the experiences of LGB people of color in counseling psychology. *The Counseling Psychologist, 38*, 322–330.

Milburn, L. (1993). Career issues of a gay man: Case of Allan. *Career Development Quarterly, 41*, 195–196.

Mohr, J. J. (2002). Heterosexual identity and the heterosexual therapist: An identity perspective on sexual orientation dynamics in psychotherapy. *Counseling Psychologist, 30*(4), 532–566.

Nelson, N. L., & Probst, T. M. (2004). Multiple minority individuals: multiplying the risk of workplace harassment and discrimination. In J. L. Chin (Ed.), *The psychology of prejudice and discrimination: Ethnicity and multiracial identity* (Vol. 2, pp. 193–217). Westport, CT: Praeger Publishers/Greenwood Publishing.

O'Neil, M., McWhirter, E., & Cerezo, A. (2008). Transgender identities and gender variance in vocational psychology. *Journal of Career Development, 34*(3), 286–308.

Pope, M. (1995). Career interventions for gay and lesbian clients: A synopsis of practice knowledge and research needs. *Career Development Quarterly, 44*, 191–203.

Ragins, B. R. (2004). Sexual orientation in the workplace: The unique work and career experiences of gay, lesbian and bisexual workers. *Research in Personnel and Human Resources Management, 23*, 35–120.

Ragins, B. R. (2008). Disclosure disconnects: Antecedents and consequences of disclosing invisible stigmas across life domains. *Academy of Management Review, 33*, 194–215.

Ragins, B. R., Singh, R., & Cornwell, J. M. (2007). Making the invisible visible: Fear and disclosure of sexual orientation at work. *Journal of Applied Psychology, 92*(4), 1103–1118.

Rumens, N., & Kerfoot, D. (2009). Gay men at work: (re)constructing the self as professional. *Human Relations, 62*(5), 763–786.

Sangganjanavanich, V., & Cavazos, J. (2010). Workplace aggression: Toward social justice and advocacy in counseling for transgender individuals. *Journal of LGBT Issues in Counseling, 4*(3), 187–201.

Smith, N. G., & Ingram, K. M. (2004). Workplace heterosexism and adjustment among lesbian, gay, and bisexual individuals: The role of unsupportive social interactions. *Journal of Counseling Psychology, 51*(1), 57–67.

Sue, D. W. (2010). *Microaggressions in everyday life: Race, gender and sexual orientation*. Hoboken, NJ: Wiley.

Swann, W. B., Jr., Stein-Seroussi, A., & Giesler, B. (1992). Why people self-verify. *Journal of Personality and Social Psychology, 62*, 392–401.

Thibaut, J. W., & Kelley, H. H. (1959). *The social psychology of groups*. New York: Wiley.

Todd, N. R., & Abrams, E. M. (2011). White dialectics: A new framework for theory, research and practice with White students. *Counseling Psychologist, 39*, 353–395.

Triandis, H. C., Kurowski, L. L., & Gelfand, M. J. 1994. Workplace diversity. In H. C. Triandis, M. P. Dunnette, & L. M. Hough (Eds.), *Handbook of industrial and organizational psychology* (2nd ed., vol. 4, pp. 769–827). Palo Alto, CA: Consulting Psychologists Press.

Willis, P. (2010). Connecting, supporting, colliding: The work-based interactions of young LGBQ-identifying workers and older queer colleagues. *Journal of LGBT Youth, 7*(3), 224–246.

Woods, S. E., & Harbeck, K. M. (1992). Living in two worlds: The identity management strategies used by lesbian physical educators. In K. M. Harbeck (Ed.), *Coming out of the classroom closet* (pp. 141–166). Binghamton, NY: Harrington Park Press.

Worthington, R. L., Savoy, H. B., Dillon, F. R., & Vernaglia, E. R. (2002). Heterosexual identity development: A multidimensional model of individual and social identity. *Counseling Psychologist, 30*, 496–531.

Poverty, Social Class, and Working

Saba Rasheed Ali

Abstract

The psychology-of-working perspective (Blustein, 2006) outlines an agenda that promotes social and economic justice. As part of this agenda, Blustein argues for an integrative approach to address the problems associated with work, social class, and poverty. The current chapter describes ways in which the psychology-of-working perspective can be used as the framework to address issues that influence access to resources that foster greater volition for work among individuals and families living in poverty. In this chapter, I also outline some of the different interventions that can address these issues and discuss how these interventions promote the tenets of economic justice and social justice espoused in the psychology-of-working perspective. The chapter includes (1) a discussion of the connection among working, wages, and poverty; (2) an overview of the historical and contemporary perspectives of the interface between vocational psychology/career counseling and poverty eradication efforts; and (3) implications that the psychology-of-work paradigm has for public policy efforts.

Key Words: poverty, working poor, psychology of working, social class

The U.S. Census Bureau estimates that approximately 15.1% of the U.S. population earned an income that was below state-determined poverty thresholds. Thus, roughly 46.2 million Americans live in poverty, with 31 of the 50 states seeing an increase in both the number and percentage of people living in poverty in the past decade (DeNavas-Walt, Proctor, & Smith, 2010). Economists, sociologists, and psychologists all have varied explanations for the increase in poverty rates in the past few years, and politicians and lawmakers have heated debates over the causes of poverty and how to alleviate the problem (Bane, 2009). Despite all the different theories and explanations about why poverty exists, most of the disciplines involved in the study or understanding of poverty agree on the centrality of the relationship between work or lack thereof and poverty. Considering this, it is important that vocational psychologists begin to more seriously consider interventions and resources that assist clients in overcoming poverty through gainful employment that provides livable wages.

The psychology-of-working perspective (Blustein, 2006) developed recently reflects a critique of existing assumptions in vocational psychology and recommendations for a revitalized and expanded mission for the field. One of the main objectives of the psychology-of-working initiative is to attend to the inextricable relationship between poverty and working and to offer a psychologically integrative approach to address the problems associated with work, social class, and poverty. This perspective also examines the psychological and financial implications that result from unemployment, underemployment, and lack of educational resources as the root causes of poverty. The purpose of the present chapter is to describe how issues related to working, social class, and poverty affect access to resources that foster greater volition for work and to discuss possible interventions within the context of the psychology-of-working perspective. The chapter will be organized in the following way. First, I discuss the connection among working, wages, and poverty. Next, I turn to the historical and contemporary perspectives of the relationship between vocational psychology/career counseling and poverty eradication efforts. Finally, I discuss the implications that the psychology-of-working paradigm has for public policy efforts that aim to assist people living poverty with employment issues.

Working, Wages, and Poverty

For the past 20 years, earnings mobility (moving out of poverty through gainful employment and work advancement) within the United States has been the predominant view on how to alleviate poverty. Politicians have touted individual participation in the paid workforce as the means to escape poverty (Theodos & Bednarzik, 2006) and have sought to reform assistance programs such as welfare to encourage labor market participation. Fundamental to this proposition is that once individuals enter the workforce, they will be able to garner sufficient financial resources to support themselves and their families and to advance to higher pay levels. Policy researchers highlight the important debate among scientists on this issue.

Theodos and Bednarzik (2006) discuss the debate between sociologists and economists on the reality of whether or not this type of upward mobility of workers can be applied equally across all workers, citing that earnings mobility is not a reality for low-wage workers. Further, Theodos and Bedenarzik (2006) point out that "low wage jobs are not evenly distributed throughout the economy, but are concentrated in certain industries ....Sectors most frequently containing low wage workers include agriculture, retail trade, private households, personal services, entertainment and recreation services, and social services" (pp. 35–37). These sectors are also where people of color (specifically African Americans, Latinos) and women are overrepresented. Thus, poverty is also a function of a far-from-equal work opportunity structure and for some no real opportunity for advancement, which is further complicated by racism, sexism, homophobia, classism, etc. (Blustein, 2006).

Statistics demonstrate the complicated interactions of race and poverty in the United States. For example, African, Latino, and Native Americans are more likely to live in poverty-stricken neighborhoods, and one out of nine immigrants to the United States lives in high-poverty neighborhoods.

This is in direct contrast to the figures for White Americans: only one in 25 non-Hispanic Whites lives in high-poverty areas (Pendall, Davies, Frieman, & Pitingolo, 2011). Sociologists have been studying the impact of employment issues in high-poverty, predominantly African American neighborhoods for decades. The results of these studies have indicated that among a myriad of other factors, a significant decline in urban manufacturing employment has contributed to the declining job availability in low-income Black neighborhoods. Wilson (1996) contends that the transition in the U.S. economy from a manufacturing base to service and technology bases has largely contributed to this lack of work and has served to disenfranchise urban communities.

Furthermore, Wilson (2011) argues that persistent racial discrimination in hiring practices has hindered young and less-experienced minority workers from achieving gainful employment. For example, most new jobs that are available that do not require advanced degrees are relegated to the service sector. Since these jobs require a great deal of public contact, Black men from the inner city are far less likely to be employed in these positions due to negative stereotypes (e.g., they are dangerous or threatening). These perceptions hinder the employment prospects for Black men and are deeply embedded in American culture. According to Wilson, Black Americans may have gained legal access to opportunity, but cultural forces of racism have shaped patterns of "inferior" and "superior" between White Americans and Black Americans from 100 years ago and now contribute to a new form of "laissez faire racism" (Wilson, 2011, p. 20). This type of racism, while not necessarily overtly segregationist, perpetuates a perception that Blacks have created their own economic problems and are unworthy of governmental assistance (Wilson, 2011). Examples of this attitude can be seen in the political sphere: the "welfare queen" championed by Ronald Reagan was resurrected in the 2012 election cycle, yet these political messages completely ignore the societal factors such as racism and wage discrepancies that are the roots of poverty in the United States.

Lott and Bullock (2007) argue that wage discrepancies in the United States are the foundational source of poverty, indicating that approximately 20% of the jobs in the United States pay less than poverty-level wage for a family of four. This information highlights that the majority of the poor in the United States are employed, dispelling the common myth that the majority of poor are on government assistance programs. Lott and Bullock use the phrase "working for wages not salaries" to describe wage discrepancies of low-income workers, which brings to light the sector of the workforce for whom earnings mobility is not a reality. Consistent with Wilson's contentions, statistics demonstrate that a higher representation of women, non-Whites, and those with poor health or disabilities are among the low-income groups (Theodos & Bedenarzik, 2006). Lott and Bullock contend that among the lowest-paid workers are immigrant migrant workers, who often look for work on a daily basis and who are typically hired for day work at minimum wage or less. The majority of these workers are women who are hired to work in factories and in domestic service in middle-class homes. Typically these jobs do not provide medical benefits, sick pay, or vacation days and certainly do not provide opportunities for earnings mobility.

Furthermore, in times of economic recession, it is more likely that those at the bottom of the earnings stratification experience the recession most strongly, which more seriously hinders earnings mobility. A recent report by the Center for Labor Market Studies highlights the impact of the recession for low-income workers compared to their affluent counterparts. Sum and Khatiwada (2010) write:

> A true labor market depression faced those in the bottom two deciles of the income distribution, a deep labor market recession prevailed among those in the middle of the distribution, and close to a full employment environment prevailed at the top. There was no labor market recession for America's affluent. (p. 13)

Consistent with the issue of lack of earnings mobility is the issue of education stratification and a "broken chain of achievement" (Shapiro, Meschede, & Sullivan, 2010, p. 2). The National Poverty Center at the University of Michigan issued a working paper series in 2011 that outlined the different aspects of poverty associated with the national recession. One of these reports summarized the evidence on how recessions affect the annual labor market earnings of vulnerable workers using longitudinal administrative earnings data (Shaefer, 2011). Shaefer reported that of all the measures of vulnerability. the key one affecting labor market earnings during recessions is education level. Shaefer's (2011) report details how highly educated workers have experienced actual growth in earnings during the recession and recovery years, while lower-educated workers experienced significant and pronounced declines in their annual incomes during these same years.

Further, Shapiro et al. (2010) describe the "broken chain of achievement" that contributes to higher poverty rates among African Americans. Through decades of social policy research, these authors concluded that the data demonstrate huge disparities in wealth between White Americans and their African American counterparts in the same income categories (i.e., comparing those in the same jobs). Essentially, it would be assumed that those in the same income bracket would be able to accumulate wealth at the same rate, but the data show that income equality does not lead to wealth equality and that job achievements cannot predict a family's wealth holdings. Largely, this is due to African American families' reliance on credit for emergency purposes as opposed to other financial resources available to Whites (e.g., inheritance, monetary gifts from parents). Because of decades of an unequal opportunity structure, African Americans cannot rely on past generations to assist them with financial needs. Shapiro et al. (2010) write: "African Americans who have worked hard at well paying jobs to achieve the American Dream are still not able to achieve wealth of their peers in the workforce, which translates into very different life chances" (Shapiro et al., 2010, p. 2). Clearly, the evidence supports the argument that the cycle of poverty is not easily corrected without attention to the issues of lack of earnings mobility, educational stratification, racism, and wealth disparity. Current federal programs that support only a "get back to work" mentality can be problematic when they do not attend to the problem of lack of opportunity. For example, programs like TANF (Temporary Assistance for Needy Families) replaced the ADFC (Aid to Families with Dependent Children), commonly known as welfare, in 1997 under the Personal Responsibility and Work Opportunity Act (PRWOA). The goal of both TANF and the PRWOA was to limit government financial assistance in order to encourage people to find and maintain employment. Lott and Bullock (2007) argue that while the implementation of the TANF program may have resulted in decreased state welfare caseloads, it has done little to alleviate poverty. Largely, this is because TANF does not provide money for education or training opportunities and does not pay for assistance while individuals are being retrained, forcing the majority of TANF recipients into low-skilled and low-wage jobs (Lott & Bullock, 2007) with little opportunity for earnings mobility or educational advancement. These issues also highlight the pernicious role of classism in the opportunity structure and how racism and classism are often intertwined. As mentioned previously, recent examples of this can be seen in the 2012 Republican nomination process, where candidates repeatedly used phrases like "welfare queen" and "food stamp president" to make distinctions between the "hardworking middle class" and the "freeloading poor."

Lott and Bullock (2007) argue that psychologists have a duty to better understand the needs of poor families and to examine public policy issues that have perpetuated the cycle of poverty, classism, and education stratification. The early history of the discipline of vocational psychology was heavily associated with social justice and public policy initiatives to help immigrant and low-income families and to create a less stratified economic system (Pope, 2000). Toward the middle of the 20th century, a focus on career counseling emerged that tended to emphasize career advancement and college-educated populations (Blustein, 2006). Within the past 20 years, vocational psychologists have returned to their roots and have become more proactive in seeking opportunities to inform policy practices through research initiatives on the needs of low-income youth and their families. Vocational psychologists have much to offer in this area and have begun to address this concern on a more macro level (e.g., Blustein, 2006; Fassinger, 2008; Fouad & Bynner, 2008). The psychology-of-working perspective was born out of this new renewal and offers a framework for vocational psychologists to frame research questions that answer broader questions about the employment and educational needs of families and individuals living in poverty. Studying working from this perspective offers a new alternative to models that offer only a more privileged "career" perspective and that are generally more applicable to individuals with more volition and choice in their work lives. Examining the history of vocational psychology provides us with a better understanding of the ways that vocational psychologists in the early 20th century were effective in simultaneously working with individuals and families and helping to shape educational and political reforms. Next, we turn to a discussion of the past, present, and future of the relationship between vocational psychology and poverty alleviation efforts.

Poverty and Vocational Psychology
Historical and Contemporary Perspectives

As mentioned previously, the discipline of vocational psychology (or vocational guidance) was initially associated with helping individuals to overcome poverty and unemployment. Frank Parsons, who is considered the founder of vocational guidance (Miller, 1961), developed interventions to assist immigrant youth in the early 20th century to make vocational decisions. However, Parsons' writings reflect a deeper desire to use vocational guidance to deal with social inefficiency and inequality. He and his colleagues were a part of the "Progressive Movement" that focused on "enhancing the efficiency of individual adjustment to the new industrial and social order" (Baker, 2009, p. 57).

Parsons, in particular, believed that part of this adjustment was to help immigrant youth find work that was "a function of the fit between a person's capacities and characteristics on one hand and the requirements of routines of the occupation on the other (Crites, 1969)" (Savickas & Baker, 2005; p. 25). Parsons was a frequent lecturer at a Boston settlement home that was established to assist neighborhood immigrant residents to develop English fluency, complete high school, and advocate for needed services (Baker, 2009). His favorite topic was the importance of matching one's abilities to a vocation. Largely, Parsons' work was built upon the premise of creating a more efficient society by assisting youth in becoming and *staying* employed in occupations that would provide them with life's necessities and ultimately transcend poverty. He was an ardent critic of the U.S. educational system, believing that it was not useful for preparing immigrants for the new industrial workforce (Baker, 2009). Within vocational psychology, Parsons is often revered as a pioneer in social justice—yet he is not without his critics, who argue that Parsons and colleagues were merely reinforcing the existing social order (i.e., that the industrial society could be built on the backs of immigrant labor at the expense of their obtainment of education) (Savickas & Baker, 2005). Regardless with which view one agrees, it is important to understand that the discipline of vocational psychology was predicated on the recognition of social status inequality; in this context, the disagreements between Parsons and his critics stemmed from how best to change the social status of immigrants (via education or labor).

While early in the 20th century the focus of vocational psychology (or vocational guidance) was on the educational and employment needs of immigrants and war veterans, there was a shift in the mid-20th century in which theoretical and research advancements centered on the needs and concerns of college students and college-educated populations, the majority of whom were men (Fitzgerald & Betz, 1994). Blustein (2006) discusses how the focus from a vocational perspective to a career was, to some extent, an inadvertent function of Donald Super's laudable attempt to take vocational psychology from a person–environment fit discourse and locate it within the realm of human development. This era of vocational psychology produced "career" theories that attended to linear career progression and upward mobility, ignoring those living in poverty and non–college-bound individuals (Fitzgerald & Betz, 1994). Within the past 20 years, there has been a paradigm shift that calls for a return to a social justice agenda in vocational psychology, evoking a revitalization and development of new perspectives of vocational psychology that are geared toward a broader understanding of the meaning and role of work in people's lives.

For example, Blustein, McWhirter, and Perry (2005) applied the work of Prilleltensky's (1997) emancipatory communitarian approach to vocational psychology, coupling it with Social Cognitive Career Theory (SCCT; Lent, Brown, & Hackett, 1994). Blustein et al. (2005) put forth this approach arguing that a framework for vocational psychology that attends to the needs of the people who experience little volition in their work lives is sorely needed. This work has spawned critical thought and research in the area of vocational psychology, with a specific emphasis on the importance of contextualizing the experiences of workers with little volition. Further, this paradigm promotes vocational psychologists' role in addressing individual and systemic barriers that individuals living in poverty face in relation to their work lives (e.g., low wages, lack of educational opportunities, etc.). Drawing upon this work, Blustein (2006) used the psychology-of-working perspective to put forth an agenda for how to shape vocational psychology for the 21st century. Within this agenda is a need to go beyond the academic silos that exist to understand how the work of other disciplines can be helpful in shaping interventions and public policy.

Contemporary Vocational Psychology and Poverty

Building on the work of Blustein et al. (2006), Diemer and Ali (2009) argued that social class and poverty issues need to be better addressed within the vocational psychology literature and offered an interdisciplinary review of literature to address how to integrate and conceptualize these issues within the field. Among the most important conceptualizations of social class discussed in this review were the sociological and structural perspectives, which entail a number of important implications for reconceptualizing the relationship between work and poverty. Diemer and Ali (2009) argue that these perspectives offer contextual evidence that counters individualistic ideologies of equal opportunity and meritocracy (Hotchkiss & Borow, 1996; Rossides, 1990) that are often consistent themes within the career development and occupational attainment literatures. An overemphasis on individual factors in ideologies of equal opportunity and meritocracy neglects the structural inequities and contextual factors such as the asymmetrical access to resources that disproportionately affect the occupational attainment of oppressed/marginalized groups (Blustein, 2006). These perspectives offer vocational psychologists broader systemic interpretations of the relationship between opportunity structures and poverty and can help to better inform interventions at the individual and broader systemic levels. Vocational psychologists are starting to bridge the gap between the sociological and structural perspectives that often focus on the macro-level understanding of poverty by investigating how macro-level constructs affect the occupational attainment of individuals with varying levels of access to resources.

Within the emerging social justice literature in vocational psychology, we see glimpses of contemporary research and writings that reflect a shift in trying to better understand issues of poverty while challenging the emphasis on linear career progression and upward mobility that is central to the career development literature. We will turn next to a discussion of some contemporary examples of research and conceptual literature that explores the vocational and educational development of those living in poverty and is consistent with the psychology-of-working paradigm.

Adolescents and poverty. One focus that is emerging within the vocational psychology literature is an emergent understanding of how lowered income and poverty are affecting adolescents' occupational development. Ali, McWhirter, and Chronister (2005) examined the role of SCCT (Lent, Brown, & Hackett, 1994) in the career development of students from lower socioeconomic backgrounds. Results of this study indicated that sibling and peer support accounted for a significant amount of variance in vocational/educational self-efficacy beliefs, and that vocational/educational self-efficacy beliefs predicted outcome expectations. Surprisingly, parental support did not contribute unique variance to either vocational/educational self-efficacy or outcome expectations with this group. This research suggests that further examination of how the career development process is different for adolescents living with fewer resources is desperately needed and that understanding of specific contextual factors (environmental factors such as support and barriers) affects the career development process. Lent, Brown, and Hackett (2000) articulated the role of social support for career plans and offered the conceptualization that support may be more powerful in the career development process than external and internal barriers. In other words, for individuals with fewer resources, it may be that social support and relationships are the factors that heavily influence individual differences in career success.

In an effort to understand the career development process for poor youth of color (PYOC), Diemer (2009) focused on the role of sociopolitical development in the occupational attainment of PYOC. He contends that while sociopolitical barriers constrain the occupational expectations and attainment of PYOC, sociopolitical development, which is defined as "the consciousness of and motivation to transform sociopolitical inequity," can serve as a buffer to these sociopolitical barriers (p. 6). Diemer analyzed longitudinal data from the National Educational Longitudinal Survey (NELS) of 1988 to examine the role of sociopolitical development in adult occupational attainment of PYOC 8 years after they had finished high school. Specifically, this study examined the longitudinal impact of sociopolitical development upon adult occupational attainment, while controlling for academic performance. Results indicated that sociopolitical development had a positive association with occupational expectations in 12th grade and had a longitudinal impact upon adult occupational attainment. While the model was a reasonably good fit for male and female participants in the study, the results suggested that the model was actually a better fit for female participants. Diemer suggested that the findings from this study can be used to enhance career interventions. For example, he argued that development of "critical consciousness" (or an understanding of the uneven playing field) may facilitate engagement and achievement because of the desire to transform the opportunity structure. This may have a more pronounced impact for women because of dealing with multiple barriers such as racism and sexism in the process of occupational attainment. For women living in poverty, this is especially poignant.

Women and poverty. Heppner and O'Brien (2006) offered a contextualized perspective of the lives of women living in poverty, underscoring that women and children bear "the heaviest brunt of the impact of poverty" (p. 75). Heppner and O'Brien elucidate factors such as disparity in the occupational pay structure, racism, divorce, responsibility for children and aging relatives, and violence against women as major contributor to women's poverty. Despite the explosion of literature that attends to the career development of women, there has been very little research dedicated to examining the factors that contribute to women being poor. Heppner and O'Brien contend that this lack of attention is largely a function of psychologists' reluctance to study lives that are different from our own. Lott (2002) suggested that psychologists, in general, are seemingly oblivious to the plight of the poor because the majority of psychologists are themselves White middle-class individuals who study and develop theories that are concerned with the lives of those who are most like them. She notes that when psychologists do write about or research those living in poverty, they often referred to individuals from a distanced perspective that helps to separate their experiences from the middle-class norm, resulting in a form of classism that excludes and discounts the experiences of those living in poverty. Heppner and O'Brien argue that vocational psychologists have also engaged in cognitive distancing and proposed that as vocational psychologists, we begin to examine "our own classism" so that we can avoid the ramifications of cognitive distancing such as stereotyping working lives of the poor. They argued that this examination may lead to a reconceptualizing of poverty from an internal "blame-the-victim" perspective to a more macro-level understanding of the systemic causes of poverty.

Heppner and O'Brien further explicate an ecological model of career development first proposed by Cook et al. (2002) to understand the systems and subsystems that influence women's career development and may be useful to design interventions for women living in poverty. This may help to put poor women's career development into a perspective that offers broader ways of intervening. One area that has been largely ignored in the career development literature in general and in particular in relation to women's career development is the examination of public policy initiatives that contribute to women living in poverty. As mentioned previously, Lott and Bullock have underscored the importance of "welfare reform" legislation such as TANF that has often forced women into low-wage jobs. One tenet that the psychology-of-working perspective and the ecological model of women's career development share is an emphasis on psychologists taking an active role in shaping legislation and public policy around workforce issues. For example, vocational psychologists have knowledge about the process of career development and occupational attainment that could inform policy to direct federal funding to go beyond job placement strategies and also offer services to help women obtain retraining or further education (Fouad & Bynner, 2006). These issues will be further explicated in subsequent sections of this chapter.

Unemployment and poverty. Within the psychology-of-working perspective, Blustein (2006) is among a handful of vocational psychologists who have underscored the importance of attending to the links between unemployment and poverty. While sociologists and economists have illuminated the macro-systemic factors that relate to unemployment, there is very little research and literature that explicates the actual individual experiences of unemployed persons and the poverty issues that arise. Blustein (2006) writes, "the perspective offered by the psychology of working has the potential to help place the *human dimensions* of unemployment and underemployment onto the agendas of policymakers and government officials" (p. 215).

One of the human dimensions that is often ignored is the shift in social class identity that results from job loss (Ali, Fall, & Hoffman, in press). Ali et al. (in press) contend that paying more attention to the psychological ramifications such as social class identity shift may help to better understand the types of services that unemployed individuals need to ultimately obtain work. Services to help families to garner income for needed resources are crucial; equally crucial is the need to attend to the psychological ramifications of social class shifting. Research that incorporates multiple disciplines would be useful to help inform what services may be needed. Often the psychological consequences of unemployment (depression, anxiety, shame) can lead a person to either choose to withdraw from social networks or to be ostracized from his or her own community. Sociological research has demonstrated that this social isolation can further exacerbate the unemployment situation, as research has long established the link between social networking and re-employment (Brand & Burgard, 2008).

Ali et al. (in press) propose that using a psychology-of-working perspective to frame research and interventions can help to shift vocational psychology from an emphasis on career counseling from a decision-making perspective to a more practical emphasis on helping clients to find and maintain gainful employment and access training. Next, we will turn to a discussion of the types of practices and interventions that are consistent with the psychology-of-working paradigm.

Practices and Interventions
Career Counseling Versus Vocational Counseling

From a psychology-of-working perspective, Blustein (2006) advocates for a shift away from the term "career counseling" to the term "vocational counseling." He argues that the term "career counseling" is associated with the elitist concept of career that focuses on a very small minority of individuals with access to power and resources. Vocational counseling, in contrast, refers to a broader concept that incorporates interventions designed to help clients explore the options available.

I would further argue that a focus on vocational counseling helps to reframe the ultimate goal of any type of career counseling from an ideal match between interests and work environments to assisting individuals to find and maintain gainful employment that provides a living wage. In this definition, we are able to expand the idea of career counseling from a focus on decision making to include prevention efforts, educational and guidance efforts, and unemployment counseling. Vocational counseling then would focus on various stages of the processes of preparing for, finding, and maintaining meaningful work and would encompass the full spectrum of developmental interventions, from pre-kindergarten math programs for the underserved to assisting individuals with unemployment and retirement issues. With this focus, we can expand our ideas of what is possible within vocational psychology to promote the psychology-of-working agenda of inclusion in our theories and research and improvement in access to services for marginalized groups. Through an expanded idea of vocational counseling, we can begin to reinvent or augment services that currently exist.

Liberatory Psychology and Vocational Counseling

Expanding the idea of vocational counseling, Blustein et al. (in press) advocate for a liberatory emancipatory approach to unemployment interventions. They critiqued the current literature and policies related to unemployment from a critical psychology perspective and suggested that one of the major flaws in the current discourse around unemployment is that current practices and policies often serve to further marginalize the unemployed.

Blustein et al. (in press) suggest that current unemployment intervention models do not address mental health issues that are related to unemployment, nor do they adopt an emphasis on retraining individuals for the 21st-century workforce. They suggest that applied psychologists and career counselors could provide input on how to redesign current unemployment systems so that vocational counseling, infused with an emphasis on mental health treatment, is integrated into interventions to help with re-employment. Blustein (2006) suggests a multidimensional approach to providing assistance to unemployed individuals that focuses on both the pressing needs and the psychological impact of job loss. These dimensions that are important include (1) focus on the individual's psychological construction of the job loss; (2) help clients develop their skills both in vocationally relevant areas and in conducting job searches; and (3) develop supportive and engaged social, economic, and educational systems that will furnish resources for unemployed individuals. However, many unemployed people are focused on day-to-day survival and may consider seeking any type of counseling a luxury. Smith (2005) argues that if we want to help those who need us the most, we might have to provide them with services in locations that are convenient to them. Therefore, it may be helpful for psychologists to move out of our offices to places where individuals are seeking services (Ali et al., 2013).

For example, workforce development agencies are charged with the duty of determining a person's eligibility for and dispensing unemployment compensation, assisting clients with re-employment, résumé writing, interviewing skills, and job searches and placement. With federal funding to these agencies dwindling, it may be crucial for psychologists and career counselors to take a more active outreach role in helping communities deal with the impact of unemployment by partnering with local workforce development centers. Services that vocational psychologists and career counselors could easily tackle, given our training and background, include conducting résumé, job search, and interviewing skills workshops and interest identification assessments and leading support groups (Dodge, 2009, personal communication). Because a major emphasis of career counseling and vocational psychology is the understanding of work as a major domain of life, and training in this area is provided by graduate training programs, counseling psychologists and professional counselors are uniquely positioned to do this type of *pro bono* work. Blustein (2006) argues that the psychology-of-working perspective can help to frame the new interventions or reformat old interventions to assist clients with re-employment opportunities. Further, getting to know the resources that clients depend upon for re-employment would help counselors and psychologist to become more familiar with government-provided assistance programs.

Another example of liberatory efforts within career interventions is the ACCESS program (Chronister & McWhirter, 2006). The ACCESS program provides career education services to women who have experienced domestic violence and was developed using SCCT (Lent, Brown, & Hackett, 1994) as the theoretical framework. To test the effectiveness of the program, Chronister and McWhirter randomly assigned 73 women to either an ACCESS group that did or did not incorporate critical consciousness as a component, or a wait-list control group. Both the ACCESS interventions included the five most effective career intervention components identified by Brown and Krane (2000), and one of the interventions also was designed to enhance critical consciousness (i.e., empowerment for self-protection and awareness of domestic violence impact). The results demonstrated that both groups of ACCESS participants had higher career-search self-efficacy than those in the control group and that the enhanced ACCESS program participants had higher critical consciousness at posttest. At follow-up, enhanced ACCESS participants had higher critical consciousness scores and made more progress toward goal achievement than those who participated in only the standard ACCESS program. Those individuals who participated in the enhanced ACCESS program were more likely to discuss and acknowledge the impact of oppression and lack of power in their relationships but were also more aware of the survival techniques they used and how these skills would be useful to make future changes. This research study is the first to apply and empirically test the role of critical consciousness in career education programming and provides strong evidence for the importance of incorporating liberatory, consciousness-raising efforts into vocational counseling and career education for those living in poverty.

Poverty Prevention and Career Education

"The best poverty prevention program is a job [and] education" wrote Marc H. Morial, President of the National Urban Leauge, in the *District Chronicles*. In this column, Morial (2008) discussed the importance of federal youth employment programs such as the Summer Youth Employment and Training Program (SYETP), which lost its federal funding in 2000. Morial described the importance of such training programs in helping urban youth of color to develop important work readiness skills. He argued that for over 30 years, the federal government was involved in providing summer jobs through SYETP. In 2000, funding for SYETP was eliminated and reallocated to programs within the Workforce Investment Act. However, because SYETP was effectively "buried" within the Workforce Investment Act, it no longer provides the types of work experiences and compensation that poor youth need in order to gain valuable skills, earn much-needed money to help support their families, and use it as an alternative to gang affiliation (Morial, 2008).

Morial (2008) underscores the importance of career education and employment programs in the prevention of life problems. We also know that adolescent work experiences (or lack thereof) can have implications for poverty. For example, Holloway and Mulherin (2004) investigated the long-term effects that living in a poverty-stricken neighborhood has on adult employment using the National Longitudinal Survey of Youth. They concluded that an adolescent raised in a poor neighborhood can have a marked labor market disadvantage caused, in part, by lack of early work experiences.

Kenny et al. (Kenny, 2008; Kenny et al., 2010) conducted research on the importance of school-to-work programs that foster the links between academic material and the world of work as one way to assist students in finding the motivation for school. One of the major components of these programs are work-based learning opportunities where students are placed in real-life work environments and given the opportunity to connect academic content with success in the workforce. Kenny et al. (2010) examined the relationships of work hope, autonomy, support, and achievement beliefs among a sample of urban minority students who were enrolled in a work-based learning program in a major metropolitan area. Findings indicated that work hope and teacher autonomy support were the most powerful predictors of achievement beliefs for this group of students. They concluded that interventions that provide youth with the opportunity to establish goals and develop plans can be especially helpful. Further, -workbased learning programs that provide the opportunity for students to internalize the immediate gains of accomplishing work-related, future oriented goals, and applying academic content of school to the context of a real job. increase motivation for the completition of education. It also would be important for students (especially students of color) to connect these goals to the needs of their community.

Another career education program that has shown some promise for helping students to connect world-of-work experiences with academics and community needs is Project HOPE (Healthcare Opportunities, Preparation, and Exploration). This interdisciplinary program at the University of Iowa involves collaboration among the University's College of Education and the health science colleges (medicine, public health, pharmacy, nursing, dentistry), the State Hygienic Laboratory, and several K–12 schools in rural Iowa districts. Project HOPE has been implemented with eighth-grade students in two middle schools with large immigrant populations (predominantly Latino). The project is conducted from a participatory action-oriented research perspective in which the participants are also active in the development of the program. The purpose of the program is preventive in nature from two perspectives. The first is to ensure that Latino immigrant students have the knowledge and skills to explore job opportunities in potentially lucrative fields and to help them plan how to attain in these fields. One of the major strategies behind the development of Project HOPE is to ensure that exploration of job opportunities was consistent with projected labor market demands in the areas where the students served by the program live. In Iowa (as in many states), the healthcare industry is the most rapidly growing job market, and many rural areas of Iowa are considered medically underserved. Therefore, there is great demand for healthcare professionals in Iowa. In concert with the first prevention goal, the second goal is to increase the diversity of the health science workforce in order to deal with health disparities issues for underserved population such as Latinos. Increasing the diversity of the workforce has been a strong recommendation of a number of entities, including the Sullivan Commission, the Pew Healthcare Commission, and the U.S. Congress to deal with health disparity issues. Project HOPE administrators seek to connect understanding between lucrative career opportunities and community healthcare needs.

There are two important components to Project HOPE. The curriculum component, developed from the perspective of SCCT (Lent et al., 1994), connects students to career-related information, resources, and planning related to a career in a health science profession and helps students make the link between high school academic subjects such as science and math and career opportunities in the health sciences. Further, students participate in simulated healthcare experiences that are coordinated by the health science colleges. Ali, Lee, Gibbons, Hoffman, Dean, and Williams (2011) used case study methodology to determine the effectiveness of the bridging program in increasing students' interests, confidence, knowledge, and planfulness for a career in the healthcare/science professions. Preliminary pretest and posttest survey information indicates an increase in math and science career interests and outcome expectations, but no change for math/science self-efficacy or vocational skills self-efficacy. Focus group data revealed that the school administrators believed the program to be helpful and integrative and also repeatedly mentioned parents commenting on the benefit of the program to school personnel. Data also revealed that students enjoyed the program and learned a great deal but acknowledged the need for better linkages to family life and more opportunities to learn about the specific skills needed for different healthcare job opportunities. Furthermore, focus group data revealed that students do believe that health careers would help them to attain the level of financial security they need to support their families and satisfy their interests; however, they also acknowledged the need for continuous mentoring, support, and an emphasis on skill development from Project HOPE staff, parents, teachers, and school administrators.

One major concern for programs like Project HOPE is the need for funding to support career education programming in K–12 schools. In Iowa, as in many other states, the majority of rural schools are underfunded and operating with limited personnel whose time and energy is often spent on meeting the immediate pressures of the school day. For example, teachers are often faced with teaching specific content that will be later tested, with results of these tests affecting the school's No Child Left Behind (NCLB) standing. School counselors are also overwhelmed by other responsibilities and cannot consistently provide career counseling or interventions for students. Current analysis of counselors' perceptions of their own role indicates

that they see themselves spending too much time in administrative functions, such as scheduling, disciplinary functions, and clerical duties, and not providing enough services to students (Zalaquett, 2005). Foster, Young, and Hermann (2005) surveyed school counselors and found that facilitating students' development of job/career search skills was rated as only somewhat important and a rarely performed work activity. In areas of extreme poverty, career guidance and education is crucial to assist students to identify and acquire skills to be competitive in the 21st-century workforce.

In the early 1990s, legislation known as the School-To-Work Opportunities Act (STWOA; 1994) focused national attention on the ways in which public schools could better prepare adolescents to make more successful post-high school occupational and educational transitions (Blustein, Juntunen, & Worthington, 2000). STWOA provided funding for K–12 students to obtain the experience, knowledge, and skills required to explore the world of work and to identify and pursue occupational goals (McWhirter, Rasheed, & Crothers, 2000). One of the specific goals of the STWOA "was to establish community-based partnerships that would empower students to overcome barriers related to demographics, geography, socio-economic level, or disability/health status" (Lapan, Tucker, Kim, & Kosciulek, 2003, p. 330). With the election of a next executive branch of government (George W. Bush), new federal legislation (NCLB) reshifted the focus of public schools from providing transition from school to the world of work to a heavy emphasis on academic achievement as measured by standardized testing. Thus, STWOA federal money was no longer available for programs that focus on career development or exploration of work-related issues.

During the Obama administration, educational policy has centered on reforming NCLB through initiatives such as Race to the Top, a program that allocates federal funding for charter schools, technological advancements, and evaluating teachers partly through increases in student performance on standardized tests. It is clear that these types of educational policies have important implications for education as well as for the workforce readiness of students. They also have implications for how well students see the connection between the academic content that is being tested and their own future career opportunities. Yet few of the current federal policies and programs are funding career or vocational education programming that seeks to help students make the links between academic content and the world of work.

From a psychology-of-working perspective, Blustein (2006) advocates for vocational psychologists and counselors to become more involved in public policy efforts that will help to steer legislation and funding allocations for workforce development and career guidance programs for K–12 students, as well as adults living in poverty. He argues that vocational and other psychologists can offer a complementary individual focus to the work of other social scientists and economists, who tend to view poverty, education, and work issues from a macro-level perspective. I turn now to a discussion of some of the current efforts on the part of vocational psychologists, career development researchers, and experts in the area of public policy.

Poverty/Employment Research and Public Policy

Blustein (2006) called for more interdisciplinary collaboration to deal with the complex social problems associated with poverty, education, and work. I would argue further that it would be almost impossible for psychologists and career counselors to influence public policy alone without working in tandem with those who have been doing social policy research for decades.

International Career Guidance Initiatives

We can learn a great deal from other countries, in particular European countries, which are putting career guidance initiatives at the forefront of poverty reduction programs. For example, Tony Watts, a sociologist by training, has conducted several comparative studies of guidance systems around the world. In a paper delivered at the National Career Development Association's annual conference in 2008, Watts presented the main findings from a series of national reviews of career guidance policies in over 30 countries around the world. One of the main findings from the reviews was concerned with the interface between career guidance and public policy. In the majority of the countries that were reviewed, career guidance services were publicly funded and free to the public, with a foundational premise that these services provide a public good as well as a private good. Policymakers in these countries expected career guidance services provided in their countries to align with three major public policy goals: (1) learning goals to improve efficiency in education and training, (2) labor market goals, including improving the match between supply and demand and managing adjustment to labor market changes, and (3) social equity goals, which include supporting an equal opportunity structure and inclusion (Watts, 2008). The national reviews also found that public policymakers in the majority of these countries increasingly recognize that career guidance services need to be accessible to all sectors of the public across the lifespan and life situations.

Watts (2008) noted that while the United States did not participate in any of the reviews and is not an international leader in policy in this area, scholars in the United States provide leadership in the area of career theory development and research. However, he also noted it was not always the case that the United States lacked federal initiatives to provide quality career guidance services to sectors of the public. During the 1970s and 1980s, several federal initiatives and laws were enacted to augment quality career guidance services, in particular in the K–12 system, in the United States. However, Watts (2008) argues that because of the shift toward state-controlled education, there have been few federal initiatives in this area. Watts (2008) recommended that a national review of a sample of states might be a good starting point to understand this diversity and to build a consensus on the types of services needed to individuals across the lifespan.

Watts' (2008) recognition of U.S. researchers as leaders in the development of theories and research studies is important because vocational psychologists and career development researchers have been prolific in developing theories that are used to understand career development behaviors and develop interventions around the world. However, very little of this research has produced evidence that directly links career guidance services with increased workforce readiness outcomes in the United States; in particular, there is a lack of evidence that links K–12 career guidance services with employability skills (Wills & Mack, 2009). In a policy brief written for the U.S. Department of Labor, Wills and Mack (2009) contend that there is a direct link between the lack of evidence and no clear national policy regarding the accountability metrics that schools and organizations should use to evaluate these services. Because education and workforce development programs to a large degree are governed by individual states, there is a huge diversity between states in terms of the implementation of career guidance programming, and there is no clear metric being used by these states to evaluate the quality of guidance services. Hence, federal dollars are often directed away from guidance services to other concerns and issues within public education, and it is often up to states to find adequate funding to develop and implement career guidance programming. This has serious implications for the amount and quality of career guidance services delivered in poor and underresourced schools and also has implications for preventive career education programming, as well as programs for adults in the workforce (i.e., TANF).

Recently, the Pennsylvania State University formed the Center for the Study of Career Development and Public Policy with several notable researchers in the area of career development. The purpose of the center is to serve as a "clearinghouse for legislation information, policy statements, and related documents; engaging in research related to the analysis of career development public policies; and partnering with other entities engaged in the study of career development and public policy" (Center for the Study of Career Development and Public Policy, n.d.).

One of the featured papers of the Center is Edwin Herr's (2008) invited keynote speech for the National Career Development Association, in which he outlined the importance of career development in this economically untenable period. In this address, Herr outlines how vocational psychologists and career counselors can further the provision of career services from the standpoint of public policymakers. For example, Herr suggests that policymakers and legislators largely view career interventions as sociopolitical processes that are developed to meet national priorities and goals, which are often steeped in the major sociopolitical and economic events occurring at a period in time. Currently, the economic recession and issues related to the globalization of the American economy are driving many of the national policies. Therefore, Herr (2008) strongly advocates for academics and practitioners who are testifying in front of Congress to study the vernacular that policymakers use. For example, currently language related to economic recovery and unemployment is immensely popular, so such terms as "frictional unemployment," "structural unemployment," "offsourcing," etc. are being used quite frequently (Herr, 2008). Further, it is important for researchers and practitioners to use terms such as "evidence-based" and "best practices" when promoting federal initiatives for career guidance services.

Herr and other experts in the area of public policy have made many important practical suggestions for researchers and career counseling practitioners

that can provide a specific framework for how to incorporate the agenda put forth by the psychology of working into policymaking venues. Specifically, the psychology-of-working perspective outlines a number of areas germane to public policy that are in need of attention, including (1) developing a body of research that focuses on documenting the specific vocational needs of individuals living in poverty, as well as evidence for the usefulness of interventions with these populations; (2) describing the evidence base that can lead to a systematic set of ideas that can form an accountability metric for which to evaluate different interventions; and (3) training for vocational psychologists and career counselors to be public policy advocates for the vocational needs of marginalized groups (i.e., figuring out how to translate the research to public policy). As Blustein (2006) suggests, public policy efforts can be the strategies that we use to ameliorate the external barriers that often impede our clients from achieving gainful employment. Through our active engagement in these issues, we begin to truly use the skills we have developed as counselors and psychologists to engage in social justice efforts that could make a structural impact on the issues of working for those living in poverty.

Training Initiatives

More recently, Fouad and Bynner (2008) discuss the need for psychologists to become more involved in facilitating the adjustment of individuals to various work transitions. In particular, they advocate that psychologists (I would extend this to career counselors as well) can assist in the development and advocacy of policies that promote training experiences for unemployed individuals or individuals entering the workforce for the first time (women, high school graduates). As previously mentioned, programs such as TANF or unemployment insurance programs do not provide funding for retraining or relocation so that individuals who are enrolled in these programs can acquire new skills. Often individuals living in poverty reside in areas where work has been tied to manufacturing jobs, which have been eroded within our economy. These individuals need retraining for different employment opportunities (e.g., computer training) that provide needed skills in today's post-technological environment. Influencing transitional career guidance public policy to include retraining or further training is one large-scale initiative where vocational psychologists and career counselors have the potential to make a lasting and far-reaching impact on the lives of those living in poverty. The psychology-of-working perspective advocates that we begin to train practitioners, students, and researchers to be better advocates of public policy initiatives to make larger-scale changes at a national level.

Conclusion

Blustein's (2006) psychology-of-working perspective is an ambitious agenda that pulls to the forefront issues of poverty, social class, and working. As outlined in this chapter, research that specifically serves to examine the needs of individuals living in poverty is desperately needed, especially research that takes a comprehensive perspective on how classism, racism, poverty, and lack of educational opportunity combine to keep many Americans from realizing gainful employment across the lifespan. Collaborative research partnerships with other disciplines such as sociology, geography, and economics and within divisions of psychology (counseling, vocational, community, social) have the potential to better inform our understanding of these issues. Further, public policy efforts that specifically tie together the need for career guidance services and national interests may help to shape a 21st-century focus on workforce issues from a poverty prevention perspective.

References

Ali, S. R., Fall, K., & Hoffman, T. D. (2013). Life without work: Understanding social class changes and unemployment through theoretical integration. *Journal of Career Assessment, 21,* 111–126. doi: 10.1177/1069072712454820

Ali, S. R., Lee, S., Gibbons, S. J., Hoffman, T., Dean, A., & Williams, J. (2011, August). Health science career education programming: A collaborative/preventive Approach. In E. H. McWhirter & S. Hage (Chairs), *Using career interventions as a prevention strategy: Implications for policy.* Paper presented at the 119th Annual Convention of the American Psychological Association, Washington, DC.

Ali, S. R., McWhirter, E. H., & Chronister, K. M. (2005). Self-efficacy and vocational outcome expectations for adolescents of lower socioeconomic status: A pilot study. *Journal of Career Assessment, 13,* 40–58.

Baker, D. B. (2009). Time, context, and change: Vocational guidance at 100. *Career Development Quarterly, 4,* 31–39.

Bane, M. J. (2009). Poverty politics and policy. *Focus,* Retrieved September 9, 2012 from http://www.irp.wisc.edu/publications/focus/pdfs/foc262m.pdf

Blustein, D. L. (2006). *The psychology of working.* Mahwah, NJ: Lawrence Erlbaum Associates.

Blustein, D. L., McWhirter, E. H., & Perry, J. (2005). An emancipatory communitarian approach to vocational development theory, research, and practice. *Counseling Psychologist, 33,* 141–179.

Blustein, D. L., Juntunen, C. L., & Worthington, R. L. (2000). The school-to-work transition: Adjustment challenges of the forgotten half. In S.D. Brown & R.W. Lent. *Handbook of counseling psychology* (3rd ed., pp. 435–470). New York: Wiley.

Brand, J. E., &. Burgard, S.A. (2008). Job displacement and social participation over the life course: Findings for a cohort of joiners. *Social Forces, 87,* 211–242. doi:10.1353/sof.0.0083

Center for the Study of Career Develoment and Public Policy (n.d.). Retrived on January 16, 2013 from http://www.ed.psu.edu/educ/cscdpp

Chronister, K. M., & McWhirter, E. H. (2006). An experimental examination of two career counseling programs for battered women. *Journal of Counseling Psychology, 53,* 151–164.

Cook, E. P., Heppner, M. J., O'Brien, K. M. (2005). An ecological model of women's career development. *Journal of Multicultural Counseling and Development, 33,* 165–179.

DeNavas-Walt, C., Proctor, B. D., & Smith, J. C. (2010). *Income, poverty, and health insurance coverage in the United States: 2010, current population reports, consumer income,* pp. 60–239. Retrieved September 19, 2010, from http://www.census.gov/prod/2011pubs/p60-239.pdf.

Diemer, M. A. (2009). Pathways to occupational attainment among poor youth of color: The role of sociopolitical development. *Counseling Psychologist, 37*(1), 61), Codoi:10.1177/0011000007309858

Diemer, M. A., & Ali, S. R. (2009). Integrating social class into vocational psychology. *Journal of Career Assessment, 17,* 247–265. doi:10.1177/1069072708330462.

Fassinger, R. E. (2008). Workplace diversity and public policy: Challenges and opportunities for psychology. *American Psychologist, 63,* 252–268.

Fouad, N. A., & Bynner, J. (2008). Work transitions. *American Psychologist, 63,* 241–251.

Fitzgerald, L. F., & Betz, N. E. (1994). Career development in cultural context: The role of gender, Race, class, and sexual orientation. In M. L. Savickas & R. W. Lents (Eds.), *Convergence in career development theories* (pp. 103–118). Palo Alto, CA: CPP Books.

Foster, L. H., Young, J. S., & Hermann, M. (2005). The work activities of professional school counselors: Are the national standards being addressed? *Professional School Counseling, 8,* 313–321.

Heppner, M. J., & O'Brien, K. M. (2006). Women and poverty: A holistic approach to vocational interventions. In W. B. Walsh & M. J. Heppner (Eds.), *Handbook of career counseling for women* (pp. 75–102). Mahwah, NJ: Lawrence Erlbaum.

Herr, E. L. (2008, July). *The importance of career development for an uncertain world: Public policy, legislation and professional advocacy.* Keynote presented at the annual National Career Development Global Conference, Washington, DC.

Holloway, S. R., & Mulherin, S. (2004). The effect of adolescent neighborhood poverty on adult employment. *Journal of Urban Affairs, 4,* 427–454.

Hotchkiss, L., & Borow, H. (1996). Sociological perspective on work and career development. In D. Brown & L. Brooks (Eds.), *Career choice and development* (3rd ed., pp. 281–336). San Francisco: Jossey-Bass.

Kenny, M. E., Walsh-Blair, L. Y., Blustein, D. L., Bempechat, J., & Seltzer, J. (2010). Achievement motivation among urban adolescents: Work hope, autonomy support, and achievement-related beliefs. *Journal of Vocational Behavior, 77,* 205–212.

Kenny, M. E. (2008, August). Advancing social justice through school-based career development. In Paul A. Gore (Chair),

Celebrating a century of vocational psychology practice. Symposium conducted at the 116th annual convention of the American Psychological Association, Boston, MA.Lapan, R. T., Tucker, B., Kim, S., & Kosciulek, J. F. (2003) Preparing rural adolescents for post-high school transitions. *Journal of Counseling and Development, 81*, 330–342.

Lent, R. W., Brown, S. D., & Hackett, G. (1994). Toward a unifying social cognitive theory of career, and academic interest, choice and performance. *Journal of Vocational Behavior, 45*, 79–122.

Lent, R. W., Brown, S. D., & Hackett, G. (2000). Contextual supports and barriers to career choice: A social cognitive analysis. *Journal of Counseling Psychology, 47*, 36–49.

Lott, B. E. (2002). Cognitive and behavioral distancing from the poor. *The American Psychologist, 57*, 100–110.

Lott, B., & Bullock, H. E. (2007). *Psychology and economic injustice.* Washington, DC: APA.

McWhirter, E. H., Rasheed, S., & Crothers, M. (2000). The effects of high school career education on social cognitive variables. *Journal of Counseling Psychology, 47*, 330–341.

Miller, C. H. (1961). *Foundations of guidance.* New York: Harper and Brothers.

Pendall, R., Davies, E., Freiman, L., & Piringolo, R. (2011). *Lost Decade: Neighborhood Poverty and the Urban Crisis of the 2000's.* Retrived May 14, 2011 from http://www.jointcenter.org/docs/Lost%20Decade%20Fact%20Sheet.pdf

Morial, M. H. (2008) The best poverty prevention program is a job [and] education. *District Chronicles.* Retrieved September 30, 2010 from http://www.districtchronicles.com/

Pope, M. (2000). A brief history of career counseling in the United States. *The Career Development Quarterly, 48*, 194–211.

Rossides, D. W. (1990). *Social stratification: The American class system in comparative perspective.* Englewood Cliffs, NJ: Prentice Hall.

Savickas, M. L., & Baker, D. B (2005). The history of vocational psychology: antecedents, origin, and early development. In M. L. Savickas & W. B. Walsh (Eds.), *Handbook of vocational psychology* (pp. 15–50). Mahwah, NJ: Lawrence Erlbaum.

School to Work Opportunities Act (1994), Pub. L. No. 103-239 (1994).

Shaefer, L. H. (2011, July). Recessions and the annual labor market earnings of vulnerable workers: New evidence using longitudinal administrative earnings data. *National Poverty Center Working Paper Series, #11-05.* Retrieved from http://www.npc.umich.edu/publications/working_papers/

Shapiro, T. M., Meschede, T., & Sullivan, L. (2010). *The racial wealth gap increases fourfold* (Research and Policy Brief). Retrieved from Institute on Assets and Social Policy website: http://iasp.brandeis.edu/.

Smith, L. (2005). Psychotherapy, classism, and the poor: Conspicuous by their absence. *American Psychologist, 60*, 687–696. doi: 10.1037/0003-066X.60.7.687

Sum, A., & Khatiwada, I. (2010, February). *Labor underutilization problems of U.S. workers across household income groups at the end of the great recession: A truly great depression among the nation's low income workers amidst full employment among the most affluent.* Northeastern University, Center for Labor Market Studies.

Theodos, B., & Bednarzik, R. (2006). Earnings mobility and low-wage workers in the United States. *Monthly Labor Review, 129*, 34–47.

Watts, T. (2008, July). Lessons learned from national reviews: Implications for the United States. In *Strategic Leadership for Career Development in Public Policy: Identifying challenges, creating solutions, implementing strategies.* Symposium at the annual National Career Development Association Global Conference, Washington, DC.

Wills, J., & Mack, D. (2009). *Comprehensive career planning and its role in the competitive global economy.* (Research brief prepared for the U.S. Department of Labor, Office of Disability Employment). Retrieved August 20, 2011, from http://www.freshmantransition.org/ccp.pdf.

Wilson, J. J. (1996). *When work disappears.* New York: Alfred A. Knopf.

Wilson, J. J. (2011). Being poor, black, and American: The impact of political, economic, and cultural forces. *American Educator, Spring*, 10–46.

Zalaquett, C. P. (2005). Principals' perceptions of elementary school counselors' role and functions. *Professional School Counseling, 8*, 451–457.

From Work and Family to a Dual Model of Working

Mary Sue Richardson *and* Charles Schaeffer

Abstract

This chapter is informed by the counseling for work and relationship perspective that posits two major contexts of work, market work and unpaid care work. Examination of the work and family literature through this lens, especially that having to do with work–family conflict and work–family expansion, reveals a general lack of attention to unpaid care work, which typically is folded into more general considerations of family. The need to pay more attention to the significance of unpaid care work is framed by a social policy context in the United States that is not supportive of unpaid care work, demographic changes, changes in the context of market work, and radical changes in the ways that adults form relationships and care for others. A dual model of working for men and women across the lifespan encompassing market work and unpaid care work is proposed for the psychology of working. This dual model of working is based on a single adult worker model for the market economy, an analysis of the linkages among market work, unpaid care work, and paid care work, and a broad definition of unpaid care work applicable to all. This chapter suggests that this dual model of working will contribute to the ability of people to co-construct lives worth living and to the amelioration of prevailing gender and social inequities.

Key Words: market work, care work, social justice, work–family

"Work and family" is the name of a multidisciplinary field of scholarship that extends across developmental, social, and industrial/organizational psychology, history, anthropology, sociology, occupational health, economics, and social work (Barnett, 1998; Pitt-Catsouphes, Kossek, & Sweet, 2006). It is a field that addresses the connections between work and family. In this chapter we approach this literature through the lens of the counseling for work and relationship perspective (Richardson, 2012b). Among other things, the counseling for work and relationship perspective recommends to the field of vocational psychology a discourse about market work and unpaid care work as central to the co-construction of lives rather than the more familiar discourse about career. Market work is defined as the work that people do for pay

as well as the work they do in educational institutions preparing for market work. Unpaid care work is defined as the work that people do in their private lives to care for people (themselves and others), relationships, institutions and communities, and the physical world that is unpaid.

This definition of care work deliberately expands the traditional definition of care work that usually refers to the care of dependent others. The rationale for this broad definition of care work is elaborated in the final section of this chapter. While the focus of this chapter is on unpaid care work, the relationship between unpaid and paid care work is central, especially in relation to issues of social equity.

In making this recommendation, the counseling for work and relationship perspective extends the critique of career discourse in the psychology of working (Blustein, 2006, 2008) by advocating for the use of two separate terms to refer to work for pay in the public sector of lives and to unpaid work in the private sector. A basic point of the counseling for work and relationship perspective is that the discourse of career, and of work and family contribute to the marginalization and "disappearance" of unpaid care work as work in the life experience of contemporary women and men. Without explicit attention to both market work and unpaid care work, even the discourse of the psychology of working risks marginalizing unpaid care work.

This emphasis on the role of discourse reflects a social constructionist understanding of how language constructs experience (Gergen, 1994; Harre, 1998; Harre & Gillett, 1994; Henriques, Holloway, Urwin, Venn, & Walkerdine, 1998; Richardson, 2012a, Shotter, 1993). Social constructionism posits that personal experience is a product or outcome of the interaction between selves and the social world. In other words, personal experience flows from social interaction and is shaped by that interaction. Discourse analysis focuses on how language itself, the words we use and how we use them, is critical in the co-construction of personal experience. In short, what we call something affects how we experience it. Thus, our decision to label and refer to two different kinds of work in the language we use is significant.

In this chapter, we look at the work and family literature with the explicit intention of bringing to light the extent to which and how unpaid care work is addressed. Inevitably, our lens also addresses issues of paid care work. Our goal is to challenge the prevailing discourse of work and family as well as career discourse with a new discourse about market work and unpaid care work and to "reappear" unpaid care work as work. Ultimately, issues of market work and care work can be framed more broadly as issues that have to do with economic production and social reproduction. Market work essentially involves economic production or the production of the goods and services needed by the economy; care work is about social reproduction or the reproduction of people, the communities in which they live, and the environment that sustains them. Both of these functions are critical for healthy and sustainable societies.

This lens is explicitly feminist in that it seeks to revalue care work, both paid and unpaid, that traditionally has been done mostly by women. Feminist standpoint theory (Haraway, 1988; Harding, 1991), one strand of social constructionist thought, has taught us that the world looks different depending upon where you are located in this world. Personal and social realities are not separate entities; experience differs for people who inhabit different social locations such as gender, race, and class. Dismantling, or at least proposing an alternative to, career, and work and family discourse is necessary to understand more fully the social experience of women who have specialized in, or, some might say, have been marginalized in the provision of care work. This new discourse goes some way toward helping to revalue this kind of work. This feminist lens also embraces men who increasingly have a stake in revaluing the care work in their lives (Calasanti & King, 2007; Coltrane & Galt, 2000).

We begin our exploration of the work and family literature with an historical review of the ways in which the normative picture of the appropriate roles of men and women in relation to market work and care work created the social context from which this literature emerged. We then examine some notable examples of how social scientists have addressed issues of work and family, linking this scholarship to underlying assumptions about normative gender roles, on the one hand, and to the ways in which unpaid care work is addressed in this literature, on the other hand. We then contextualize this scholarship in relation to social policy regarding work and family in the United States, a policy profile that differs markedly from that of other advanced economies. Throughout, we attend to whether and how poor people are represented in this literature.

In the next section of the chapter we address some contemporary social changes that are radically altering the landscape of lives and that underline the increasing significance of unpaid care work in the lives of individuals and in the sustainability of the society in which we live. These include demographic changes, changes in the context of market work, and changes in families.

Finally, we develop a rationale for a dual model of working for all encompassing market work and unpaid care based on a single adult worker model for the market economy, an analysis of the linkages among market work, unpaid care work, and paid care work, and the expanded definition of unpaid care work. In conclusion, we suggest the kinds of changes at both the individual and social level that we believe are needed to enable our social system to engage maximally in both economic production and social reproduction and with regard to ameliorating prevailing gender and social inequities. We believe that the lens of the psychology of working that has designated working as its primary focus of scholarship needs to embrace this larger picture of work and working.

Three Historical Models of Social Organization

The past two centuries have been witness to breathtaking and radical changes in the realms of economic production and social reproduction. In many ways, it is not at all surprising that social science has had a hard time keeping up with the rapid rate of change and the radical kind of change that is occurring in the organization of our lives. If, as Fouad (2007) so aptly noted, it is difficult to make a career choice when the world of market work is a moving target, so too, it is difficult to develop theory and to do research on social worlds that, in so many ways, are also moving targets. In this section, we examine three relatively recent historical models regarding normative expectations of gender roles and the corresponding organization of society that set the stage for the emergence of the social science literature on work and family in the United States (Boris & Lewis, 2006).

The Household Economy Model

The Household Economy Model characterized gender roles and social organization during the colonial and the Early Republican period of American history (Boris & Lewis, 2006). All people who constituted a household, including family groups such as parents and children, extended kin, and boarders, were expected to contribute to the economic productivity of the household. Although work was certainly organized along gender lines, with men taking more responsibility for work located outside the home, such as farming or working in the family store, and women taking more responsibility for work done within the home, such as canning, mending, food preparation, and childcare, both kinds of work were valued and were recognized as work. This was true across class and racial lines, though, of course, this picture was severely distorted for Black people who were enslaved (Jones, 1985; Mintz & Kellogg, 1988).

This household economy model persisted into the 19th and 20th century in farm communities, among the newly freed African American community in the South, and among the urban working class in cities, many of whom were immigrants. While in each of these cases the kind of work that was done as a family or household group might differ, the household was the center of economic

production and all members of a family or household group, including children, were expected to contribute to earning a living. For example, African Americans in the South might work in family groups as sharecroppers and urban immigrant families in the North might work in family groups in a business such as a store or restaurant.

At the same time as the household was the center of economic production, the household was also the center for accomplishing the care tasks that were needed. Economic production and social reproduction, though not designated as such, were thoroughly intertwined in this model. While a new model of social organization began to emerge among the urban, White, middle class in the early 19th century, the household economy model continued to characterize less affluent groups.

The Male Breadwinner/Female Caregiver

The male breadwinner/female caregiver model emerged in the early 19th century in response to the industrialization of the economy that enabled a single adult, typically a man, to earn a wage outside of the household economy and to support a wife and children who stayed at home (Boris & Lewis, 2006). Thus, the household economy model was split in two in a very radical way. First of all, it was split into a public sphere where market work and economic production were predominant and a private sphere comprising home and family. Each of these spheres was thoroughly genderized. Under the influence of what came to be known as the cult of domesticity, women's role in the home and family was valorized as emotional and expressive and the male role was shifted to that of provider, wage earner, and breadwinner (Boydston, 1990; Cott, 1977).

According to the cult of domesticity, a woman's role at home was to nurture her mate and family. Her labor in doing the care work that continued to need to be done, except in richer families who could pay others to do these tasks, was redefined as a labor of love and disappeared as work. Unpaid care work was designated as caring, and the doing of this work was designated as caregiving, or the giving of care. The ideal of a nuclear heterosexual family with a wage-earning husband and father doing market work and a wife and mother at home providing the care that the family needed was the beating heart of this model. Care work became thoroughly privatized in this model and relegated to the realm of personal responsibility.

This very powerful model and the ideal family type that it personified persisted into the mid-20th century and became institutionalized in social policy, despite the fact that it didn't fit the lives of the less affluent (Boris & Lewis, 2006). Many women needed to earn money through wages of some sort. For young women before marriage, their wage or market work outside of the home was thought of as only temporary, until they married, hopefully well, and could fully enact the male breadwinner/female caregiver model. Other married women who did wage or paid work to earn an income, such as taking in sewing or putting up boarders, did this "on the side." In these cases, their market work was "supplemental." Poor women who had no men to support them or whose partners were unable to support them, and who had to do market work outside of the home, were disparaged and provided little social support (Mink, 1994). Fathers who could not support their families according to the ideals dictated by the male breadwinner/female caregiver model were also disparaged (Wellrich, 2001). These deeply ingrained attitudes toward what were considered to be appropriate gender roles had particularly negative consequences on African American families whose men had limited access to better-paying jobs and whose women had to do market work (Feldstein, 2000; Levy, 1998).

Throughout the history of the male breadwinner/female caregiver model there was reluctance on the part of policymakers to provide any kind of support for the care of the children of mothers who had to do market work, since they shouldn't have been working outside of the home in the first place. The meager mother's pension provided to women with children who did market work morphed into the demeaning and inadequate subsidies entrenched in the Aid to Dependent Children legislation. The policy system that developed linked social benefits such as pensions, social security for the elderly, unemployment insurance, and health insurance to wage work that was gendered male. Far more limited benefits were linked to childbearing status for women who were mothers (Kessler-Harris, 2001).

The male breadwinner/female caregiver model began to fragment in the years following World War II as women of all social classes increasingly began to participate in market work. We now turn to the dual breadwinner/female caregiver model that emerged in this time period and that characterizes our most recent history (Boris & Lewis, 2006). The dual breadwinner/female caregiver model is the social context from which the work and family literature emerged.

Dual Breadwinner/Female Caregiver

The dual breadwinner/female caregiver model is the one with which we are most familiar and that extends into the 21st century. It encompasses the revolution in women's roles that has occurred in the United States and across the world in the past 50 or 60 years (Collins, 2009). Basically, and with the explicit encouragement of the women's movement in the United States, women have increasingly participated in unprecedented numbers throughout their lives in market work. While initially the labor market participation of women with very young children lagged behind other groups of women, statistics now indicate that most women participate in market work most of their lives, including mothers of young children (Wharton, 2006).

While popular literature tends to depict this revolution as a matter of women's choice, underlying economic factors tell another story. Essentially what happened is that a family wage sufficient to support a wife and family eroded (Casper & Bianchi, 2002; Warren & Tyagi, 2003; Wharton, 2006). To support a family and to maintain a middle-class life style, women's wages became necessary and could no longer be considered supplemental. In some ways, this third model is a recasting of the old household economy model in which both men and women worked and participated. Only this time, both men and women participate in waged market work rather than in the household economy. What is different is that now unpaid care work, redefined as the giving of care and a labor of love, is located outside of this web of economically productive work and continues to be gendered female.

In the late 20th century, as middle-class women moved into market work and the dual breadwinner/female caregiver model evolved, caregiving, especially the care of children, was recognized as problematic. It was no longer embedded in the household economy, nor did economic conditions enable the continued idealization of a stay-at-home mom and family caregiver. However, the weak social welfare support for families with children in which both fathers and mothers had jobs continued (Boris & Lewis, 2006; Michel, 1999). Women and families made private arrangements with neighbors, friends, and extended kin to care for their children while they worked at their jobs. Those who were more affluent were able to pay others to do their care work, and paid care work done by poor and otherwise marginalized women, such as immigrants, became increasingly important (Abel, 2000; Parrenas, 2001, 2005).

This rapid and revolutionary change in women's roles drew the attention of social scientists to problematic connections between work and family. Rosabeth Moss Kanter's (1977) groundbreaking work in which she challenged the myth that work and family are separate worlds, a myth enshrined in social theory by Parsons and his colleagues (Parsons, 1964; Parsons & Bales, 1955), is frequently cited as the major impetus for the development of this literature across disciplines (Barnett, 1998). Work-family conflict initially was the paradigmatic conceptual scheme for capturing and understanding what was happening to families as women moved into market work. We now turn to a selective consideration of several major lines of research on work–family conflict and, especially, to an examination of the ways in which unpaid care work is or is not addressed in this literature.

Research on Work and Family

Research considered in this section is drawn largely from industrial/organizational psychology, along with some attention to research in family studies and sociology. We begin with research that is dominated by a conflict perspective and then turn to several reconceptualizations of the field that provide a comprehensive framework for work and family research across disciplines and that make a case for work–family expansion as well as work–family conflict. We conclude this section with consideration of the research on the changing nature of work patterns in both market and family contexts from the mid-20th century until the early years of the 21st century.

Work–Family Conflict

Role theory, highly influential in the 20th century, dominated the discussion of what was happening to women's and men's lives as women moved into market work. Based on the earlier model of male breadwinner/female caregiver in which worlds of work and family were conceived as separate domains and separate roles, it was assumed that conflict between these roles would be the outcome when women participated in both work and family roles. Note here that the earlier model in which the social world was split into work and family continued to constrain and determine how roles were defined. Work meant only market work; care work was buried in the family, which, in turn, was considered to be a role. The notion of conflict was predicated on what is referred to as the scarcity hypotheses; that is, there is only so much time in a day and energy to spend. If a

person needs to meet the demands of two separate and competing roles, it is a zero–sum game and conflict between roles in a likely outcome (Burke, 1988; Edwards & Rothbard, 2000; Katz & Kahn, 1978; Sieber, 1974; Zedeck & Mosier, 1990).

Greenhaus and Beutell (1985), early and influential theorists in this area, defined work–family conflict as "a form of interrole conflict in which the role pressures from the work and family domains are mutually incompatible" (p. 77). They further elaborated three dimensions along which this role conflict might play out: pressures due to time, the strain due to the physical and mental rigors of the roles, and participation in behaviors adaptive in one role and maladaptive in the other role. Within this more general consideration of roles, the problem of caregiving or unpaid care work, especially with respect to the care of children at home and doing housework, appears but is not highlighted. Rather, it is folded into a more general consideration of the family role and is typically referred to as one of the structural aspects of the family role.

The conceptualization of work–family conflict continues to influence research in the work and family literature today, most notably in its elaboration into two separate constructs, work-to-family conflict and family-to-work conflict (Byron, 2005; Carlson & Kacmar, 2000; Frone, 2003; Frone, Russell, & Cooper, 1992; Frone, Yardley, & Markel, 1997; Netemeyer, Boles, & McMurrian, 1996). Research on these two separate and reciprocal constructs, each with its own antecedents, outcomes, and moderators, continues to reference unpaid care work only tangentially, most frequently as measured by the presence and age of children at home and responsibility for household chores. Childcare and household chores are only a part of a more general picture of conflicting work and family roles. Nowhere in this literature does the ability to hire others to do the care work needed in families appear as a central factor.

An especially interesting research program on work–family conflict by Jacobs and Gerson (2004) that is grounded in the notion of competing time demands and based on national surveys at two points in time, 1992 and 1997, concludes that work interferes or conflicts with family more than family interferes with work and that the culture of families has changed more than the culture of the workplace, or in the parlance of this chapter, the market workplace. However, as with most of this research, the focus of the research is on the perception and experience of conflict, and not on how people actually spend their time.

Work–Family Expansion

A critical expansion of this literature beyond the narrow confines of conflict was signaled by Barnett's (1998) radical reconceptualization of the field. Building on the work of others who challenged the scarcity hypotheses (Marks, 1977; Marks & MacDermid, 1996), Barnett directly challenged the myth and the metaphor of work and family as two separate worlds, the dominance of the scarcity hypothesis, and the related conceptualization of people as having separate selves linked to each of these major life roles. In its place, she proposed a more holistic and contextual model of people engaging in multiple life contexts in which they develop adaptive strategies for meeting the demands of their jobs and what she most broadly refers to as social system demands or life demands. This model is offered as a framework for organizing research across the many fields that contribute to the study of work and family. In this model, Barnett attempts to step outside the frame of family discourse to acknowledge the full set of social system demands or tasks outside of jobs that need to be performed. Her conceptualization of social system demands is quite similar to the definition of unpaid care work we are using in this paper in that it encompasses tasks that include care of people, relationships, and institutions and communities.

Rather than conflict, Barnett (1998) proposes the construct of fit as the outcome of a process in which people develop adaptive strategies for meeting the demands of their jobs and the social system. She also proposes a set of both distal and proximal factors on the job side and the social system side that influence the ability of people to develop adaptive strategies and to find a good fit. People who are able to fashion a good fit are more likely to find that participation in jobs and in the broader social system are mutually enhancing rather than conflicting. Conversely, conflict is more likely to be the result if adaptive strategies fail to find a good fit. This more process-oriented approach to understanding the interface of work and family resonates with the recommendation by vocational psychologist Donna Schultheiss (2006), who suggests that work–family "navigation" is a better metaphor than work–family "balance." Building on the work of MacDermid, Leslie, and Bissonnette (2001), Schultheiss notes that family and work contexts change over time and the challenge is to navigate through the challenges of competing work demands as they arise. "Staying the course" (Schultheiss, 2006, p. 328) through a process of navigation is a more useful goal than attempting to achieve an illusory and necessarily unstable sense of balance.

In her attention to distal factors such as prevailing economic conditions, workplace policies and practices, social policies and practices, and job conditions, Barnett (1998) shifts the focus away from the individual to the conditions that affect the ability of individuals to find adaptive strategies. Most importantly, she acknowledges the significance of economic circumstances on the ability to find adaptive strategies. Having more money enables people to pay for care work when needed. Having higher-level jobs is also likely to be associated with greater job flexibility that, in turn, facilitates the ability to forge adaptive strategies.

Patricia Voydanoff (2002, 2007) is responsible for a second model that reconceptualizes the work and family field and sets an ambitious agenda for research and policy. Her model, grounded in ecological theory, is similar to Barnett's in its consideration of ways in which work and family might or might not fit and, thus, moves beyond the conflict paradigm to one of work–family balance. She also considers economic deprivation to be an important factor influencing balance. This model also extends the parameters of work and family discourse by postulating that work and family, each of which are mesosystems in ecological theory, are embedded with a third mesosystem, that of community. This formulation is an elaboration of social system demands in that it trains a spotlight on the kinds of community resources that enable people to find or negotiate a better fit between work and family. This is especially important for policy-related research in that it draws attention to community factors such as those included in Bookman's (2004) family-friendly community index and Halpern's (2005) recommendations to schools and communities for working families. These are factors that are not typically associated with the policy context of work and family research and include issues such as housing affordability, public transportation services, public safety, and neighborhood stability (Voydanoff, 2005). Also, most importantly, Voydanoff's model includes elder care as a component of family demands. Elder care is becoming increasingly important, as we will discuss later in this chapter.

Barnett's (1998) pioneering reconceptualization of the field and the more recent model developed by Voydanoff (2002, 2007) have had interesting effects on the work and family field. Most notable is that the narrow focus on work–family conflict has given way to a much broader consideration of the ways that work and family might be related to one another as indicated by terms such as "work and family satisfaction" (Ford, Heinen, & LangKamer, 2007), "work and family enrichment" (Greenhaus & Powell, 2006), "work–family balance" (Grzywacz & Carlson, 2007; Grzywacz, Carlson, Kacmar, & Wayne, 2007), "work–family interaction" (Halpern & Murphy, 2005), and "work–family enhancement" (Wiese, Sieger, Schmid, & Freund, 2010), with a number of theorists and researchers proposing bidirectional models of work–family facilitation similar to the bidirectional models prevalent in the conflict literature (Frone, 2003; Frone, Russell, & Cooper, 1992; Frone, Yardley, & Markel, 1997; Grzywacz & Marks, 2005; Parasuraman, Purohit, Gotshalk, & Beutell, 1996; Voydanoff, 2005). As it has become normative for women to work most of their adult lives, it is clear that many men and women have developed adaptive strategies that enable them to participate in the multiple contexts of their lives in ways that are enhancing and facilitative. In other words, many have adapted with good fit to the changing economic circumstances of lives that increasingly require all able-bodied adults to engage in market work most of their adult lives.

The assumption of conflict between work and family has shifted to include both theory and research about the benefits of participation in work and family roles, especially to the extent that the family side of the equation conforms to the dual breadwinner/female caregiver model that assumes a married heterosexual couple in which both parties have jobs (Barnett & Rivers, 1996; Caspar, Eby, Bordeaux, Lockwood, & Lambert, 2007). What is not acknowledged in this rosier picture of participating in jobs and in families is the extent to which this picture is constrained by economic circumstances. Little research has attended to what happens to poor people who struggle to do the market and unpaid care work in their lives. While economic circumstances are acknowledged as important in these comprehensive models proposed by Barnett (1998) and Voydanoff (2002, 2007), we do not yet have a body of empirical research on conflict or enhancement between work and family among poor people.

Research on conflict and enhancement between work and family has also, for the most part, not carried through on Barnett's (1998) challenge to family discourse to attend to a broader array of social system demands or tasks that need to be accomplished outside of jobs. While research in this tradition has expanded its consideration of what family means, the kind of tasks that need to be accomplished in families, and the nature of the supports and resources available to families in accomplishing these tasks, the metaphor and discourse of work and family continues to dominate, and caregiving or unpaid care work continues to be embedded in a much broader conceptualization of the work and family interface (Barnett & Gareis, 2006). A central problem here is one of measurement. Voydanoff (2007) notes that using proxy measures of caregiving such as number and age of children and whether or not one is caring for elderly relatives is inadequate to assess the nature of the work involved in providing this kind of care.

It is also notable that the ability to pay others to do care work does not figure in either of these models except indirectly as a potential outcome of financial or economic resources. If unpaid care work is marginalized in this literature, paid care work is truly invisible.

Changing Work Patterns in Market and Family Contexts

In contrast to most of the work and family literature that tends to marginalize unpaid care work within a broader conceptualization of roles, another body of research has examined time use and unpaid care work in families (Budlender, 2010). One notable research program has tracked how parents with jobs actually spend their time in paid and unpaid work over a period spanning the 1960s to the early 21st century (Bianchi, Robinson, & Milkie, 2006). The activities measured by the time use diaries in this research project incorporate the breadth of Barnett's conceptualization of social demands and approximate the definition of unpaid care work in this chapter. For example, these activities include obtaining goods and services, attention to self-care, commitments to political, religious, and other community organizations, the use of information and computer technology, and visiting others, in addition to the set of activities having to do with childcare and housework. While the methodology of time diaries has evolved over these decades, including both extensive scrutiny of what people do on a specific day as well as assessment of what they do during a specific week, the use of a basically comparable method over many decades enables a fine-grained analysis of what parents actually do with their time and how these patterns have evolved as women's roles have been transformed.

What is particularly noteworthy from our point of view is the acknowledgment in this research that time given to both paid and unpaid work merits attention and that unpaid work includes activities that line up roughly equivalent to the definition of unpaid care work in this chapter. The one caveat is that the focus of this research is on the care of children in samples of married fathers, married mothers, and single mothers. Due to this focus on childcare, this research does not explicitly address elder care or the kind of kin work that involves caring for members of extended families that extends across household boundaries, a form of unpaid care work that is especially important in Black, Latino/a, and Asian American populations (Gerstel & Sarkisian, 2006). However, it is notable that the inclusion of single mothers as one of three specific research samples moves beyond the presumption of a normative family unit comprising father, mother, and child(ren) that dominates much of the work and family research literature.

In their recent volume, Bianchi et al. (2006) come to some startling and important conclusions. First of all, they conclude that married mothers are spending as much time with their children in the early years of the 21st century as they were 40 years ago, even though many more of them are engaged full time or part time in market work. While this seems to fly in the face of the logic of only 24 hours in the day, their analysis reveals that women are accomplishing this feat by making their children higher priorities in their lives, spending less time on personal activities and personal time with their spouses, more time in family activities with both spouses and children, and doing less housework. In short, they are multitasking and doing less housework.

Their second conclusion is that both married fathers and married mothers have equal workloads, considering both paid and unpaid work. However, men spend twice as much time as women engaged in market work activities while women spend twice as much time in childcare and household work. This pattern of market work also differs for married fathers and married mothers. For married fathers, rates of participation in market work do not change with number and age of children. For married mothers, participation rates do vary with number and age of children, especially when children are less than 6 years old.

A third conclusion is that fathers are now doing more of the unpaid work in families, including the basic care of children such as feeding and bathing. While married mothers still do more of this work, this imbalance has definitely moderated over the past 40 years. These conclusions support the research by Jacobs and Gerson (2004) that families have changed more than market workplaces in adapting to the revolutionary changes in women's roles.

With respect to single mothers, on almost all indices, the results of this research begin to document the effects of economic deprivation and poverty on single mothers. Although the research focuses on marital status as opposed to income level, the single mothers in this research are less educated, are younger, and have fewer financial resources than their married counterparts. These women are spending less time with their children than the married mother cohort, and their workload across market work and unpaid care work is significantly higher than both married men and married women. This group of mothers also scores higher than married mothers and married fathers on subjective reports about the sacrifices they are making for both their market work and their family time.

What is most important about this research is that its focus on how people actually spend their time enables the significance of market work and unpaid care work to come to the foreground. Rather than a more general consideration of roles that tends to mask the work that is associated with roles, this research puts work in both public and private domains front and center. Thus, it helps to set the stage for a new model of working that acknowledges that most people have two sets of work activities that, following Schultheiss (2006), they must negotiate. It is not just a question of accomplishing two sets of work tasks and demands; it is a question of continually negotiating within and between these two work contexts in order to find some kind of fit.

Further, this research demonstrates the extent to which the dual breadwinner/female caregiver model has moderated over the years but continues to produce gender inequities. Married women with children continue to suffer what is often referred to as the motherhood wage penalty, in which the earnings of women who are mothers are less than that of other women across the lifespan (Budig & England, 2001; Misra, Budig, & Boeckmann, 2011a, 2011b; Crittenden, 2001; Hersch & Stratton, 1997; Noonan, 2001).

This body of research also reveals the extent to which paid care work is ignored as a critical factor in the accomplishment of market and care work. In an article entitled "Is anyone doing the housework: Trends in the gender division of household labor," Bianchi, Milkie, Sayer, and Robinson (2000) conclude that the steady decline in the total hours devoted to housework by both men and women over the past two decades is likely due to factors such as lowering of standards and the availability of labor-saving technologies. What is not considered is whether and to what extent people are paying others to do their housework.

Finally, and most provocatively, the single mother data pose two challenges. First, it challenges in a fundamental way the viability of the dual bread-winner/female caregiver model. These data raise the question as to how families should be defined. Are single mothers an exception to the norm or are families with two parents the exception? Second, these data shift attention away from gender inequities *per se* to the question of how fundamental economic inequities, which affect women more than men, undermine the struggle of people with few economic resources to engage in both market work and unpaid care work.

Before turning to a consideration of some fundamental contemporary social changes that affect working in public and private domains of life, it is first necessary to address the policy context that so powerfully shapes the conditions that affect men and women in their struggles to engage in both market work and unpaid care work.

The Policy Context

Research on work–family conflict and work–family enhancement in the United States has taken place in a policy context in which there has continued to be little public policy designed to assist people who participate in the market work economy and might need help in managing their unpaid care work. The lack of public support for unpaid care work in the United States is striking in comparison to countries in the European Union (Kelly, 2006). Public policies such as paid leaves for caretaking responsibilities, childcare, and flexible work arrangements are woefully lacking in the United States compared to these countries. For example, one analysis of the care policies for children and the elderly identified roughly three groups of European countries, ranging from those who mostly consider care work a family matter, to those whose policies support families, to those that offer adults a wide range of options for the provision of care (Daly, 2001a). However, across the board, at least in the European Union, some level of paid leave is available for care work. In comparison, the United States provides public policy support only for unpaid caretaking leaves

(Kelly, 2006). Workers in the United States also have no protection from mandatory overtime, and there is no legal maximum to the number of hours of required work in a day (Appelbaum, Bailey, Berg, & Kalleberg, 2002).

Rather than public policy, the United States has a well-developed set of employer-based policies, typically referred to as family-friendly policies, that are designed to help individuals and families deal with the demands of jobs and unpaid care work. Naturally, these kinds of market-based policies are most common in companies and industries that rely on more educated workers and are least likely to benefit those who are likely to need them the most, such as the poor and uneducated. This policy situation help to explain why workers in the United States report more work–family conflict and stress than workers in other countries with more supportive policies and suggests that the benefits of work–family enhancement are likely to be limited to higher-income groups (Jacobs & Gerson, 2004; Kelly, 2006).

Contemporary Social Changes

The three sets of changes considered in this section set the stage for the final section of this chapter that more fully elaborates a dual model of working for the psychology of working. These changes are demographic changes, changes in market work, and changes in families.

Demographic Changes

Of these three changes, the demographic profile of the population is the most fundamental in shifting awareness of the patterning of market work and unpaid care work over the lifespan. While elder care is mentioned more frequently in recent literature in the work and family field, it is the demographic picture itself that is most startling. According to Riche's (2006) analysis of demographic trends, up until contemporary times, the demographic picture in most countries conformed to a population pyramid with many more people in younger generations at the base and broader levels of the pyramid and declining numbers of older people in the narrower, upper ends of the pyramid. At the present time and in relation to expectations for the future, the population picture most resembles a pillar, with approximately as many people in the older generations as in the younger ones. While there is a little blip in this picture having to do with the baby boomer generation, the changing distribution of age groups in the population extends beyond the baby boomer phenomenon. People are living longer overall and, even with the large immigration rates in the United States, younger people will no longer outnumber the aging.

This population picture has stark implications for issues having to do with unpaid care work, especially care of children and the elderly. Issues of childcare are becoming less salient as fewer people overall in the society are involved with raising children. The overall societal resources needed to care for children are becoming less burdensome from this perspective, but it is quite a different story regarding elder care. The care of the elderly is especially problematic given the weakening of family and generational ties and the expected number of older people who are likely to develop dementias and demand high levels of care (Alzheimer's Association, 2010; Arno, 2002). This is all taking place in an economic environment in which public economic resources for social welfare services of all types are most limited. From a demographic perspective, there is a looming crisis of care for the elderly.

On a more general level, the expected changes in the patterning of care needs reflect the ways in which care needs shift and change in response to not only demographic factors, but also to other kinds of radical societal changes that characterize modern societies. The point here is that a dual model of working needs to consider the broad picture of care work rather than single-mindedly focusing on one kind of care work (Folbre, 2008).

Changes in Market Work

While globalization and technology have radically altered the face of market work in many ways, in this section we address two changes that are most significant for affecting the dynamic relationship between market work and unpaid care work. The first has to do with changes in the nature and structure of market work; the second concerns the kinds of jobs most likely to be growth areas in the future. These issues together suggest that a very different situation regarding market work and unpaid care work confronts more educated and affluent workers versus those who have more limited economic resources, that the problems of the less affluent are affecting an ever-greater proportion of the population, and that issues of care work are deeply implicated in the growing economic inequities in the United States.

With respect to the first issue, changes in the nature and structure of market work, there is strong evidence that more educated and affluent workers are exposed to and espouse a new kind of work ethic in which the ideal worker is one who is highly committed to his or her job and is able to respond as needed to the demands of this job (Gambles, Lewis, & Rapoport, 2006). What is not said explicitly is that this new ideal worker is one who is unencumbered or who appears to be unencumbered by the demands of unpaid care work. Jacobs and Gerson (2004) note that an "ethic of 'professionalism', once reserved for a small slice of jobs, is becoming a solid and organizational standard" (p. 157) and that better jobs occur in workplaces that can be characterized as high commitment (Osterman, 1999).

This push for a unilateral commitment to the workplace may be due to factors such as increased productivity (Nyland, 1989), meaning that more work has to be done in a shorter period of time, and two decades of corporate downsizing that have concentrated more tasks in the hands of fewer workers (Cappelli, 2001). Regardless of what has caused this change in expectations for workers, most educated workers, both male and female and across race and ethnicity, have high expectations that their market work will be both personally satisfying and financially remunerative and, in many ways, endorse this new work ethic (Hochschild, 1989; Jacobs & Gerson, 2004). The ubiquitous invasion of technology that operates 24/7 across boundaries of public and private worlds only exacerbates the demands of this new work ethic. On the negative side, fear due to the specters of unemployment and underemployment may also drive workers to overcommit to their market work. While more educated and affluent workers are also far more likely to be employed in market work environments characterized by family-friendly policies, the new work ethic militates against the willingness of workers to take advantage of these policies.

While the lack of stability in market work certainly has affected workers at all levels of the economy, the newest permutation of career discourse, the boundaryless career, spins this instability in such a way as to support the new work ethic among the more educated and the more affluent. The high and single-minded commitment to market work is now placed in the service of one's own career progression—that is, in one's boundaryless career rather than in an organization that may be only a temporary home. The net result of this new work ethic, especially for people who are, in fact, encumbered by their unpaid care commitments, is to feel overburdened and overworked.

Changes in the nature and structure of market work take a totally different form among the less educated and less affluent. These are the prevalence of nonstandard hours and nonstandard contracts, especially among those who work in service jobs (Wharton, 2006). Nonstandard hours refer to work schedules that do not conform to a traditional 9-to-5, Monday through Friday work week. Nonstandard contracts refer to employment arrangements that are characterized as part-time, temporary, or with limited contracts, or, in other words, contingent employment (Kalleberg & Schmidt, 1996). Savickas (2011) describes this most evocatively as the disappearance of jobs. In contrast to the problems of the more educated and affluent, in which jobs consume too much time, the problem with contingent employment is that there is not enough work to be done. Not enough work translates into not enough money.

Research indicates that, among a high percentage of couples with children under 5, at least one parent works nonstandard hours (Presser, 2003). While these data provide some evidence that nonstandard hours may be helpful to some families, we know little about the emotional and physical costs of this kind of market work and childcare arrangement. Some research suggests that a range of physical and psychological problems can be traced to nonstandard hours (Fenwick & Tausig, 2001). Similarly, while some have suggested that nonstandard contracts or contingent market work may be especially useful to those struggling to combine market work and unpaid care work, research indicates that, compared to those who have standard contracts, contingent workers are more dissatisfied with their jobs (Mishel, Bernstein, & Boushey, 2003).

Essentially, scholars describe a bifurcated workplace in which the more educated and affluent have too much work to do to the detriment of their commitments to unpaid care work in the private domains of their lives, and the less educated and the less affluent do not have enough work to do, and when they do have work, they may be powerless to control the kinds of hours they can be expected to work, both of which may have a negative impact on their ability to accomplish unpaid care work (Jacobs & Gerson, 2004). For both groups of workers, market work is invasive, though in very different ways. This bifurcated workplace reflects and contributes to a bifurcated and increasingly unequal economy, especially in the United States, in which a small number of people have become much more affluent while the middle class stagnates or declines in

earning power (Judt, 2010; Mishel, Bernstein, & Shierholz, 2009). While both of these situations present problems for people trying to combine market work and unpaid care work, it is the problems of the poor that are most compelling. At least the affluent are more likely to have jobs in organizations characterized by family-friendly policies and, even if they are reluctant to take advantage of these policies, they have the resources to purchase the care work that needs to be done in their private lives.

Expectations for job growth only exacerbate these problems of inequality. Recent statistics compiled by the Bureau of Labor Statistics and reported by Hacker (2011) indicate that the occupations expected to show the greatest growth between 2008 and 2018 are mostly low-wage occupations. Most tellingly, among these low-wage occupations, jobs that can be characterized as paid care work are prominent. For example, positions for home health aides are expected to increase 50%, licensed practical nurses 20.7%, and nursing aides and orderlies 18.8%. These statistics do not include the underground economy of housekeepers, babysitters, and housecleaners who are paid under the table and do not even make it into these charts (Razavi, 2007). Thus, it appears that the ranks of the less affluent will only increase. While low-wage work is a complex and multifaceted problem, there is some evidence that low-wage work that can be characterized as paid care work is paid less well than other kinds of low-wage jobs that are comparable in skill level (England & Folbre, 1999). Thus, the problems with the devaluation of care work have serious economic consequences for those who do this work for pay. We will return to this issue in the final section of this chapter.

Changes in Families

The third major change has to do with the composition and the ultimate meaning of family. Marks (2006) documents the extent to which diversity in family type is increasingly the norm, making the traditional family, a nuclear heterosexual couple with children, "an ideological trope that hides rather than reflects empirical diversity" (p. 42). The two-parent family is in decline while single-parent families in single households are in ascendance. Blended families, people living alone, and families headed by LGBT persons are increasing. While people are having fewer children, the birth rate in the United States has not fallen below replacement levels as it has in many advanced economies. However, the more affluent and educated tend to delay having children, while the less affluent and less educated have children at earlier ages and outside marriage. In fact, marriage is becoming less common, in general, among the poor than among the more affluent. Marriage is also increasingly less stable, especially for the poor (Taylor, 2011).

Although Marks (2006) includes racial and ethnic diversity as a factor interpolated with the generally increasing diversity of family types, what is particularly relevant in the context of this chapter is the extent to which the extended families of Black, Latino/a, and Asian populations and the importance of unpaid care work having to do with kin requires a consideration of relational and caregiving ties that extend beyond the household (Gerstel & Sarkisian, 2006). With respect to issues of negotiating market work and unpaid care work, kin play a far greater role among these racial and ethnic groups and among the poor, two intersecting markers of privilege and hierarchy. Kin are both a resource for helping out with unpaid care work and a source of unpaid care work demands.

What emerges from this picture is the diversity and complexity of the ways that people are forming and dissolving intimate and relational networks with others, having and raising children, and caring for the elderly, the sick, or the disabled, with and without partners and kin, and engaging in unpaid care work that extends beyond the boundary of the household. What is more important than family type is the nature and extent of the unpaid care work and the caregiving relationships that are formed across all types of families and all types of living arrangements. These changes in what is represented by family suggest that what is most important is not the sexual relationship or sexual status of the adults in a household but the nature and extent of the web of unpaid care work commitments that characterize an individual in any kind of family or any kind of living arrangement.

The salience of unpaid care work is reflected in the language used by Gerson (2010) in her interview study of a group of young people, mostly in their early 20s, who are diverse across categories of race, ethnicity, socioeconomic status, sexual orientation, and experience, being raised in single-parent or two-parent households. Although across the board these young people expressed expectations for committed sexual relationships and for meaningful market work, Gerson describes their expectations for adult life in terms of caregiving and breadwinning. This is language that resonates with the dual model of working that informs this chapter. That

is, people have to earn a living and they have to take care of themselves and others, their relationships, the institutions in which they participate and the communities in which they live, and the physical world. These are the two kinds of working that make up the dual working model we recommend in this chapter and to which we now turn to in the next and final section of this chapter.

A Dual Working Model

The rationale for a dual working model in which all people can expect to engage in market work and unpaid care work, in different amounts and in different ways, across the lifespan rests on an analysis of the current market work economy that is moving to a single adult worker model from the dual worker/female caregiver model, an analysis of the dynamic and problematic relationship between market work, unpaid care work, and paid care work, and a discussion of the expanded definition of care work by Tronto, endorsed in this chapter, that challenges the hegemony of the value of economic productivity. We address each of these issues in the sections to follow.

The Single Adult Worker Model for the Market Economy

The model that seems to be in line to replace the dual breadwinner/female caregiver model is one that assumes that all adults will participate in market work for a significant percentage of their adult life and that the web of social policy that links a wide range of societal benefits for insurance and various forms of social security to market work will continue (Lewis, 2001). In many ways, the move to reform welfare in the United States through the 1996 Work Responsibility and Personal Opportunities Act presaged this shift in model. The social policy of economic support for single mothers with dependent children can be viewed as a throwback to an earlier time and an earlier model in which mothers were supposed to stay home with children. Only in this case, it was the state and not husbands who were supporting these families. Before welfare reform, not only were these single mothers poorly supported by the state, they also were cut off from the social benefits that accrue to those who participate in market work. Ending welfare put these mothers in somewhat of the same shoes as most women who had to earn a living. What was different is that they had to take a market work job with little social policy support for retraining to prepare for 21st-century market work and for the care of their children in a context of very limited economic resources. Thus, welfare reform undercut both the market work and the unpaid care work of poor single mothers (Boris & Lewis, 2006).

However, what is important here is to note that the move to a single adult worker model for all, including mothers of small children, is a model that is based on the value of economic productivity. Across the board, developed economies are moving in the direction of expecting all adults who are able to participate in market work for a significant portion of their adult life (Lewis, 2001). The more people in a society who participate in market work, the higher is the gross national product of that society. Given this model, the provision of necessary care work becomes a critical issue.

The Relationship Between Market Work, Unpaid Care Work, and Paid Care Work

The relationship between market work, unpaid care work, and paid care work is problematic and ignored in much of the work and family literature. Essentially, as women have moved into the market work economy, the ranks of those who do paid care work at both professional and nonprofessional levels have increased (England, 2005; England & Folbre, 2000a; Wharton, 2006). The problem is with the increase in the kinds of low-wage paid care work identified by Hacker (2011) and referenced earlier in this chapter. His statistics, moreover, seriously underestimate low-wage paid care work in that they do not include the legions of mostly women who work in an underground economy as housecleaners, housekeepers, babysitters, and nannies. These numbers include poor women in the United States, frequently women of color (Gerstel & Sarkisian, 2006; Helburn & Bergman, 2002), as well as the continued flow of immigrant labor, many of whom come to the United States looking for work in the domestic labor market (Ehrenreich & Hochschild, 2002; Hochschild, 2000, 2003; Parrenas, 2002, 2005).

Thus, much of the shift in care work from unpaid to paid care work sectors that has accompanied women's increased participation in market work has resulted in an increase in low-wage jobs. What this means is that more educated and affluent women who have market work jobs that pay adequate income can afford to pay others to help them with their unpaid care work. They can pay household cleaners, babysitters, nannies, and others to help at home. The people whom they pay, mostly women, receive comparatively low wages that do not enable them to pay for their unpaid care work at home.

This, in turn, leads to a situation of inequitable care. Tronto (2009) labels this "the vicious circles of inequality" (p. 6). The children or other dependents of more educated and affluent parents are recipients of both paid and unpaid care and are presumably well taken care of. The children or other dependents of poor and immigrant women are forced to rely on a more fragile, uncertain, and vulnerable network of care such as extended families and kin, or no care at all, and are presumably less well taken care of. With respect to immigrant women, Hochschild (2000, 2003) has described this as a care drain from developing countries to more developed ones. Thus, the children and dependents of poor and immigrant women who do paid care work suffer from both income and care inequality, a situation that doubly compromises their future opportunities in life.

The reasons for the poor wages paid for care work in the market economy are complex. One major reason is that care work is expensive to provide. As we will see in the next section when we talk about definitions of care work, care work implies a relationship between the taker of care and the receiver of care. It implies a "caring for" and a "caring about" (Abel & Nelson, 1990). It is not the kind of work that lends itself well to the maximization of profits and productivity increases that characterize the market work economy. While some would argue that the commodification of care work in the market economy necessarily degrades the quality of care work that is then available for pay, others argue that care work can be marketized rather than commodified in ways that preserve its quality and its essential relational and nurturing character (Folbre, 2006; Folbre & Nelson, 2000; Razavi, 2007). What this means, for example, is the development of systems of paid care work that provide high-quality, well-compensated or at least decently compensated care and that have found ways to resist the downgrading of care work by market-oriented demands for productivity.

The point here is not to point fingers at those who pay low wages for help with their unpaid care work, but rather to sketch out the outlines of an interlocking system of market work and care work that poses challenges to all who need to negotiate their market work and their unpaid care work and that is especially challenging to those who do care work for pay. This is an interlocking structure that is critical for the psychology of working that seeks to address the issues of all who work, including the poor and disadvantaged. Increasingly the poor and disadvantaged are doing paid care work. Our market work-oriented economy has responded to the radical change in women's rate of participation in the market work economy by producing an increase in low-wage paid care work. It is in the context of these "vicious circles of inequality" (Tronto, 2009, p. 6) that how we define care work becomes most significant. It is to this task we now turn.

A Definition of Care Work

The evolution of our capitalist economy in which market work is prioritized and the Gross National Product (GNP), a measure of economic productivity, is widely accepted as an indicator of the health of a nation has been accompanied by the privatization of care work, which has fallen off the map as a locus of work activity. After all, in a capitalist mindset, care work does not lead to economic productivity and, therefore, it cannot be work. While the initial impetus in our efforts to "reappear" care work as work was feminist in that our intent was to revalue the work that historically has been done mostly by women, in this section we broaden the lens to consider more fully the meaning of care work and its role in the life of a nation. It is only after women, who had been doing most of the societal care work for free, flooded into the market workplace and after Kanter (1977) addressed the myth of two separate worlds that scholars and policymakers began to be concerned about care work and who was going to do it.

The literature on care work reveals an emerging struggle to articulate the value of care and caring to society and to move it out of its wholly privatized status. Early efforts focused on unpaid work without differentiating between work that had to do with caring and other unpaid work that more easily fit into economic indicators (Razavi, 2007). Increasingly, however, issues of care and caring, the labor of love that constituted the cult of domesticity described earlier, became the focus of attention and were addressed in language that was seemingly more compatible with a capitalist economy in which economic concerns were the driving force. Thus, scholars began to address the ways in which care work and care activities produced human and social capital that were needed for economic success (Coleman, 1993; England, 2005; England & Folbre, 2000b; Folbre, 2001; Williams, 2010).

More recent efforts have sought to establish an ethic of care that counterbalances the ethic of productivity and that is relevant to all people in a society. Scholars such as Tronto (1993, 2006, 2009), Daly (2001b), and Standing (2001) articulate a basic human need and right to care and to be cared for. Just as people have a right to a job, they have a right to care and be cared for. These scholars posit that caring is essential to human development and to human society. "Caring is part of the fabric of society and is integral to social development" (Daly, 2001a, p. 33). To value caring we have to recognize that caring is work, but it is work that cannot be subsumed into the values of economic productivity. Standing (2001) posits that we have to move from a labor-based society to a work-based one, in which the work of caring needs to be "adequately recognized as part of a total person as a working being" (p. 32). Care work is work that has an essentially different aim from economic productivity. How we articulate that aim has profound implications, and it is here that the diversity in the definitions of care work become most significant.

Many definitions of care work focus on the care of dependent others such as children, the sick, the disabled, and the elderly (Abel & Nelson, 1990; Folbre, 2008) and include activities "encompassing both instrumental tasks and affective relations" (Abel & Nelson, 1990, p. 4). In this focus on the care of dependent others, there is recognition of the relationship between the caregiver and the care recipient and that the aim of the care work is not just to respond to needs but to foster the capabilities of individuals (England & Folbre, 2000b). Razavi (2007) notes that this kind of care work can extend from pragmatic acts that are not necessarily very emotionally engaging, such as various kinds of physical care, to acts that involve deeply emotional caring. She also includes in care work many tasks such as shopping and cleaning that are preconditions to care.

The care of dependent others captures our attention because it epitomizes the kinds of care that seemed most compromised when women left home for market work, most especially the care of children. It is a meaning of care work that responds to the crisis of care for the elderly discussed early in this chapter. Tronto (1993, 2006, 2009) is a prominent feminist theorist who offers a more expansive definition of care work that goes beyond the care of dependent others to address the ways that care work functions to enable the reproduction of the social order (i.e., the social reproduction that we referred to early in this paper). The term *social reproduction* clearly signals that the care work essential to social reproduction is essentially different from economic production in its aims.

Tronto's (1993, 2006, 2009) expanded definition of care work rests, in part, on a critique of the false dichotomy between autonomous selves and dependent others that enables those designated as autonomous to deny and to project their dependency onto those designated as dependent others. Her analysis presumes that dependency is a part of all lives, in different ways and to different degrees, across the lifespan. Rather than dichotomizing independent selves and dependent others, Tronto proposes that all people exist in a web of interdependent social connections that characterize human lives. Interestingly, this analysis resonates with the work of contemporary relational theorists in the field of psychology and psychotherapy who have radically revised the story of human development from one that moves from symbiosis to independence to one that one that moves through increasingly complex and mutually interdependent networks of relationships (Jordan, Kaplan, Miller, Stiver, & Surrey, 1991; Miller & Stiver, 1997 Mitchell, 2000; Wachtel, 2008). The social interdependence of humankind extends as well to an appreciation of the interdependence of all people on the natural environment. By acknowledging the need of all for care, care work becomes relevant to all people. We are all givers and receivers of care. Care is not a women's issue; care is a human issue.

This broadening of the meaning of care work also challenges the ethic of ever-increasing productivity and unlimited growth that characterizes our market economy with a contrasting ethic of a world with limits to growth in which sustainability competes with growth. Social reproduction through this lens has to do with reproducing and caring for people (selves and others), relationships, institutions and communities, and the physical world. It provides a potentially powerful counterbalancing force to the pressures for unlimited growth. As Tronto (2009) puts it, the construction of a world with "livable lives" (p. 3) must necessarily encompass both economic production and social reproduction. Without care work, the market collapses. Without market work, there is no money to support care.

An expanded definition of care work informed by this analysis is provided by Fisher and Tronto (1990): "A species activity that includes everything that we do to maintain, continue, and repair 'our world' so that we can live in it as well as possible. That world includes our bodies, our selves, and our environment, all of which we seek to interweave in a complex life-sustaining web" (p. 40). Thus, the definition of care extends beyond dependent others to include care of people (self and others), relationships, institutions and communities, and the physical world. It provides a basis for a full-scale dual model of working that applies to all. Tasks of care work and tasks of market work, in different ways and to different extents over the lifespan, characterize the working lives of all.

By making care work visible and applicable to all across the lifespan, it is hoped that a dual model of working will contribute to the construction of lives worth living. It is also in line with the recommendations of others regarding the need to revalue care work and mitigate the pressures of market-based work so that people may maximally engage in both contexts of their working lives (Appelbaum, Bailey, Berg, & Kalleberg, 2002; Gambles, Lewis, & Rapoport, 2006). This revaluing of care work and repositioning it as one of the two contexts of all working lives will, we hope, foster the continued dismantling of the genderization of public and private worlds that occurred with the rise of industrialization. Gender flexibility, in turn, with respect to both market and care work will contribute to the ability of both men and women to develop adaptive strategies for negotiating the ever-changing mix of market work and unpaid care work that characterizes lives (Gerson, 2010). A revaluing and degendering of care work will also contribute to efforts to find ways to productively marketize rather than commodify paid care work, thereby contributing to the lessening of the social inequities currently embedded in much of paid care work.

Conclusion

Counteracting the invasiveness of paid work into private lives and revaluing care work in both its unpaid and paid manifestations are daunting challenges. As elaborated by Gambles, Lewis, and Rapport (2006) in their investigation of work-life challenges in seven countries, including the United States, these kinds of changes require both a change in mindsets and changes in public policy. The current Caregiving Initiative of the American Psychological Association (Goodheart, 2010) epitomizes the attempt to change mindsets about care work. However, public policy is essential in order to provide conditions that will facilitate the ability of people across the socioeconomic spectrum to find strategies and negotiate a fit between their market and their unpaid care work. We suggest that the recognition of a dual model of working that characterizes all lives will go some way toward changing mindsets about market work and care work and bringing the need to support both kinds of work to the attention of policymakers.

References

Abel, E. (2000). *Hearts of wisdom: American women caring for kin, 1850–1940*. Cambridge, MA: Harvard University Press. doi:10.1086/343265

Abel, E. K., & Nelson, M. K. (Eds.) (1990). Circles of care: An introductory essay. In E. K. Abel & M. K. Nelson (Eds.), *Circles of care: Work and identity in women's lives* (pp. 4–34). Albany, NY: SUNY Press.

Alzheimer's Association (2010, May). Alzheimer's disease facts and figures. Accessible at www.alz.org.

Appelbaum, E., Bailey, T., Berg, P., & Kalleberg, A. L. (2002). *Shared work, valued care: New norms for organizing market work and unpaid care work*. Washington, DC: Economic Policy Institute. doi:10.1177/0143831X02231007

Arno, P. S. (2002, February). The economic value of informal caregiving, U. S. 2000. Paper and updated figures presented at the 15th Annual Meeting of the American Association for Geriatric Psychiatry, Orlando, Florida.

Barnett, R. C. (1998). Toward a review and reconceptualization of the work/family literature. *Genetic, Social, and General Psychology Monographs, 124*(2), 125–182.

Barnett, R. C., & Gareis, K. C. (2006). Role theory perspectives on work and family. In M. Pitt-Catsouphes, E. E. Kossek, & S. Sweet (Eds.), *The work and family handbook: Multidisciplinary perspectives, methods, and approaches* (pp. 209–222). Mahwah, NJ: Lawrence Erlbaum.

Barnett, R. C., & Rivers, C. (1996). *She works/he works: How two income families are happier, healthier, and better off*. San Francisco, CA: Harper.

Bianchi, S. M., Milkie, M. A., Sayer, L. C., & Robinson, J. P. (2000). Is anyone doing the housework? Trends in the gender division of household labor. *Social Forces, 79*(1), 191–228. doi:10.2307/2675569

Bianchi, S. M., Robinson, J. P., & Milkie, M. A. (2006). *Changing rhythms of American family life*. New York: Russell Sage Foundation.

Blustein, D. L. (2006). *The psychology of working*. Mahwah, NJ: Lawrence Erlbaum.

Blustein, D. L. (2008). The role of work in psychological health and well-being: A conceptual, historical, and public policy perspective. *American Psychologist, 63*, 228–240. doi:10.1037/0003-066X.63.4.228

Bookman, A. (2004). *Starting in our own backyards*. London: Routledge.

Boris, E., & Lewis, C. H. (2006). Caregiving and wage-earning: A historical perspective on work and family. In M. Pitt-Catsouphes, E. E. Kossek, & S. Sweet (Eds.), *The work and family handbook: Multidisciplinary perspectives, methods, and approaches* (pp. 73–98). Mahwah, NJ: Lawrence Erlbaum.

Boydston, J. (1990). *Home and work: Housework, wages, and the ideology of labor in the early republic*. New York: Oxford University Press.

Budig, M., & England, P. (2001). The wage penalty for motherhood. *American Sociological Review, 66*, 204–225. doi:10.2307/2657415

Budlender, D. (2010). *Time use studies and unpaid care work*. New York: Routledge.

Burke, R. J. (1988). Some antecedents and consequences of work–family role conflict. *Journal of Social Behavior and Personality, 3*, 287–302.

Byron, K. (2005). A meta-analytic review of work–family conflict and its antecedents. *Journal of Vocational Behavior, 67*, 169–198. doi:10.1016/j.jvb.2004.08.009

Calasanti, T., & King, N. (2007). Taking "women's work" like a man: Husbands' experiences of care work. *Gerontologist, 47*(4), 516–527. doi:10.1093/geront/47.4.516

Cappelli, P. (2001). Assessing the decline of internal labor markets. In I. Berg & A. Kalleberg (Eds.), *Sourcebook of labor markets: Evolving structures and processes* (pp. 207–245). New York: Kluwer Plenum. doi:10.1007/978-1-4615-1225-7

Carlson, D. S., & Kacmar, K. M. (2000). Construction and initial validation of a multidimensional measure of work–family conflict. *Journal of Vocational Behavior, 56*, 249–276. Doi:10.1006/jvbe.1999,1713.

Caspar, W. J., Eby, L. T., Bordeaux, L., Lockwood, A., & Lambert, D. (2007). A review of research methods in IO/OB work–family research. *Journal of Applied Psychology, 92*, 28–43. doi:10.1037/0021-9010.92.1.28

Casper, L. M., & Bianchi, S. M. (2002). *Continuity and change in the American family*. Thousand Oaks, CA: Sage.

Coleman, J. S. (1993). The rational reconstruction of society. *American Sociological Review, 58*, 1–15. doi:10.2307/2096213

Collins, G. (2009). *When everything changed: The amazing journey of American women from 1960 to the present*. New York: Little, Brown and Company.

Coltrane, S., & Galt, J. (2000). The history of men's caring: Evaluating precedents for fathers' family involvement. In M. H. Meyer (Eds.), *Care work: Gender, labor, and welfare states* (pp. 15–36). New York: Routledge.

Cott, N. (1977). *The bonds of womanhood: "Women's sphere" in New England, 1780–1835*. New Haven, CT: Yale University Press.

Crittenden, A. (2001). *The price of motherhood*. New York: Henry Holt.

Daly, M. (2001a). Care policies in western Europe. In M. Daly (Ed.), *Care work: the quest for security* (pp. 33–55). Geneva, Switzerland; International Labour Office.

Daly, M. (Ed.) (2001b). *Care work: The quest for security*. Geneva, Switzerland: International Labour Office.

Doucet, A. (2012). Gender roles and fathering. In N. J. Cabrera & C. S. Tamis-LeMonda (Eds.), *Handbook of father involvement: Multiciplinary perspectives* (2nd ed., pp. 297–319). New York: Routledge

Edwards, J. R., & Rothbard, N. P. (2000). Mechanisms linking work and family: Clarifying the relationship between work and family constructs. *Academy of Management Review, 25*, 178–199. doi:10.2307/259269

Ehrenreich, B., & Hochschild, A. R. (2002). *Global women: Nannies, maids and sex workers in the new economy*. New York: Hall.

England, P. (2005). Emerging theories of care work. *Annual Review of Sociology, 31*, 381–399. doi:10-1146/annurev. soc.31.041304.122317

England, P., & Folbre, N. (1999). The cost of caring. *Annals of the American Academy of Political and Social Science, 561*, 39–51. doi:10.1177/0002716299561001003

England, P., & Folbre, N. (2000a). Capitalism and the erosion of care. In J. Madrick (Ed.), *Unconventional wisdom: Alternative perspectives on the new economy* (pp. 29–48). New York: Century Foundation Press.

England, P., & Folbre, N. (2000b). Reconceptualizing human capital. In W. Raub & J. Weesie (Eds.), *The management of durable relations* (pp. 126–128). Amsterdam, the Netherlands: Thela Thesis.

Feldstein, R. (2000). *Motherhood in black and white: Race and sex in American liberalism, 1930–1965*. (editing not clear - should be a dash between 1930 and 1965) Ithaca, NY: Cornell University Press.

Fenwick, R., & Tausig, M. (2001). Scheduling stress: Family and health outcomes of shift work and schedule control. *American Behavioral Scientist*, *44*, 1179–1199. doi:10.1177/00027640121956719

Fisher, B., & Tronto, J. C. (1990). Toward a feminist theory of caring. In E. Abel & M. Nelson (Eds.), *Circles of care* (pp. 36–54). Albany, NY: SUNY Press.

Folbre, N. (2001). *The invisible heart: Economics and family values*. New York: New Press.

Folbre, N. (2006). Demanding quality: Worker/consumer coalitions and "high road" strategies in the care sector. *Politics & Society*, *34*(1), 11–31. doi:10.1177/0032329205284754

Folbre, H. (2008). Reforming care. *Politics & Society*, *36*(3), 373–387. doi:10.177/0032329208320567

Folbre, N., & Nelson, J. A. (2000). For love or money—or both? *Journal of Economic Perspectives*, *14*(4), 123–140. doi:10.1257/jep.14.4.123

Ford, M. T., Heinen, B. A., & LangKamer, K. L. (2007). Work and family satisfaction and conflict: A meta-analysis of cross-domain relations. *Journal of Applied Psychology*, *92*, 57–80. doi:10.1037/0021-9010.92.1.57

Fouad, N. A. (2007). Work and vocational psychology. *Annual Review of Psychology*, *58*, 1–22. doi:10.1146annurev.psych.58.110405.085713

Frone, M. R. (2003). Work–family balance. In J. C. Quick & L. E. Tetrick (Eds.), *Handbook of occupational health psychology* (pp. 143–162). Washington, DC: American Psychological Association. doi:10.1037/10474-000

Frone, M. R., Russell, M., & Cooper, M. L. (1992). Prevalence of work–family conflict: Are work and family boundaries asymmetrically permeable? *Journal of Organizational Behavior*, *13*, 723–729. doi:10.1002/job.4030130708

Frone, M. R., Yardley, J. K., & Markel, K. S. (1997). Developing and testing an integrative model of the work–family interface. *Journal of Vocational Behavior*, *50*, 145–167. doi:10.1006/jvbe.1996.1577

Gambles, R., Lewis, S., & Rapoport, R. (2006). *The myth of work-life balance: The challenge of our time for men, women, and societies*. New York: John Wiley & Sons. doi:10.1002/9780470713266

Gergen, K. J. (1994). *Realities and relationships: Soundings in social constructionism*. Cambridge, MA: Harvard University Press.

Gerson, K. (2010). *The unfinished revolution: How a new generation is reshaping family, work, and gender in America*. New York: Oxford University Press.

Gerstel, N., & Sarkisian, N. (2006). Sociological perspectives on family and work: The impact of gender, class, and race. In M. Pitt-Catsouphes, E. E. Kossek, & S. Sweet (Eds.), *The work and family handbook: Multidisciplinary perspectives, methods, and approaches* (pp. 237–266). Mahwah, NJ: Lawrence Erlbaum.

Goodheart, C. (2010). Caregiving: What's APA got to do with it? *Monitor on Psychology*, *41*(3), 5.

Greenhaus, J. H., & Beutell, N. J. (1985). Sources of conflict between work and family roles. *Academy of Management Review*, *10*, 76–88. doi:10.2307/258214

Greenhaus, J. H., & Powell, G. N. (2006). When work and family are allies: A theory of work–family enrichment. *Academy of Management Review*, *31*(1), 72–92. doi:10.5465/AMR.2006.19379625

Grzywacz, J. G., & Carlson, D. S. (2007). Conceptualizing work–family balance: Implications for practice and research. *Advances in Developing Human Resources*, *9*(4), 455–471.

Grzywacz, J. G., Carlson, D. S., Kacmar, K. M., & Wayne, J. H. (2007). A multi-level perspective on the synergies between work and family. *Journal of Occupational and Organizational Psychology*, *80*, 559–574. doi:10.1177/1523422307305487

Grzywacz, J. G., & Marks, N. F. (2005). Reconceptualizing the work–family interface: An ecological perspective on the correlates of positive and negative spillover between work and family. *Journal of Occupational Health Psychology*, *5*, 111–126. doi:10.1037//1076-8998.5.1.111

Hacker, A. (2011, February 24). Where will we find the jobs? *New York Review of Books*, pp. 39–42.

Halpern, D. F. (2005). Psychology at the intersection of work and family: Recommendations for employers, working families, and policymakers. *American Psychologist*, *60*, 397–409. doi:10.1037/0003-066X.60.5.397

Halpern, D. F., & Murphy, S. E. (2005). *From work–family balance to work–family interaction: Changing the metaphor*. Mahwah, NJ: Lawrence Erlbaum.

Haraway, D. J. (1988). Situated knowledges: The science question in feminism and the privilege of partial perspective. *Feminist Studies*, *14*(3), 575–599. doi:10.2307/3178066

Harding, S. (1991). *Whose science, whose knowledge?* Milton Keynes, UK: Open University Press.

Harre, R. (1998). *The singular self: An introduction to the psychology of personhood*. London: Sage.

Harre, R., & Gillet, G. (1994). *The discursive mind*. London: Sage.

Helburn, S. W., & Bergmann, B. R. (2002). *America's child care problem: The way out*. New York: Palgrave/St. Martin's Press.

Henriques, J., Hollway, W., Urwin, C., Venn, C., & Walkerdine, V. (1998). *Changing the subject: Psychology, social regulation, and subjectivity*. New York: Routledge. doi:10.1177/0959353502012004003

Hersh, J., & Stratton, L. S. (1997). Housework, fixed effects and wages of married workers. *The Journal of Human Resources*, *32*, 285–307. doi:10.2307/146216

Hochschild, A. R. (1989). *The second shift*. New York: Avon Books.

Hochschild, A. R. (2000). Global care chains and emotional surplus value. In W. Hutton & A. Giddens (Eds.). *On the edge: Living with global capitalism*. (pp. 130–146). London: Jonathan Cape.

Hochschild, A. R. (2003). *The commercialization of intimate life: Notes from home and work*. Berkeley, CA: University of California Press.

Jacobs, J. A., & Gerson, K. (2004). *The time divide: Work, family and gender inequality*. Cambridge, MA: Harvard University Press.

Jones, J. (1985). *Labor of love, labor of sorrow: Black women, work, and the family from slavery to the present*. New York: Basic Books.

Jordan, J. V., Kaplan, A. G., Miller, J. B., Stiver, I. P., & Surrey, J. L. (1991). *Women's growth in connection: Writings from the Stone Center*. New York: Guilford Press.

Judt, T. (2010). *Ill fares the land*. New York: Penguin Press.

Kalleberg, A. L., & Schmidt, K. (1996). Contingent employment in organizations. In A. L. Kalleberg, D. Knoke, P. V. Marsden, & J. L. Spaeth (Eds.), *Organizations in America* (pp. 253–275). Thousand Oaks, CA: Sage.

Kanter, R. M. (1977). *Work and family in the United States: A critical review and agenda for research and policy*. New York: Russell Sage Foundation.

Katz, D., & Kahn, R. (1978). *The social psychology of organizations*. New York: Wiley.

Kelly, E. L. (2006). Work–family policies: The United States in international perspective. In M. Pitt-Catsouphes, E. E. Kossek, & S. Sweet (Eds.), *The work and family handbook: Multidisciplinary perspectives, methods, and approaches* (pp. 99–124). Mahwah, NJ: Lawrence Erlbaum.

Kessler-Harris, A. (2001). *In pursuit of equity: Women, men, and the quest for economic citizenship in 20th-century America*. New York: Oxford University Press.

Levy, F. (1998). *The new dollars and dreams*. New York: Russell Sage Foundation.

Lewis, J. (2001). Legitimizing care work and the issue of gender equality. In M. Daly (Ed.), *Care work: The quest for security*. Geneva, Switzerland: International Labour Office.

MacDermid, S. M., Leslie, L. A., & Bissonnette, L. (2001). Walking the walk: Insights from research on helping clients navigate work and family. *Journal of Feminist Family Therapy, 13*, 21–40.

Marks, S. R. (1977). Multiple roles and role strain: Some notes on human energy, time and commitment. *American Sociological Review, 42*, 921–936. doi:10.2307/2094577

Marks, S. R. (2006). Understanding diversity of families in the 21st century and its impact on the work–family area of study. In M. Pitt-Catsouphes, E. E. Kossek, & S. Sweet (Eds.), *The work and family handbook: Multidisciplinary perspectives, methods, and approaches* (pp. 41–66). Mahwah, NJ: Lawrence Erlbaum.

Marks, S. R., & MacDermid, S. M. (1996). Multiple roles and the self: A theory of role balance. *Journal of Marriage and the Family, 58*, 417–432. doi:10.2307/353506

Michel, S. (1999). *Children's interests/mothers' rights: The shaping of America's child care policy*. New Haven: CT: Yale University Press.

Miller, J. B., & Stiver, I. P. (1997). *The healing connection: How women form relationships in therapy and in life*. Boston: Beacon Press.

Mink, G. (1994). *The wages of motherhood: Inequality in the welfare state, 1917–1942*. Ithaca, NY: Cornell University Press. doi:10.2307/2945573

Mintz, S., & Kellogg, S. (1988). *Domestic revolution: A social history of American family life*. New York: Free Press.

Mishel, L., Bernstein, J., & Boushey, H. (2003). *The state of working America, 2002–2003*. Ithaca, NY: ILR Press.

Mishel, L., Bernstein, J., & Shierholz, H. (2009). *The state of working America, 2008/2009*. Ithaca, NY: Cornell University Press.

Misra, J., Budig, M., & Boeckmann, I. (2011a). Cross-national patterns in individual and household employment and work hours by gender and parenthood. *Research in Sociology of Work, 22*, 169–207.

Misra, J., Budig, M., & Boeckmann, I. (2011b). Work–family policies and the effects of children on women's employment hours and wages. *Community, Work, and Family, 14*(2), 139–147.

Mitchell, S. A. (2000). *Relationality: From attachment to intersubjectivity*. Hillsdale, NJ: Analytic Press.

Netemeyer, R. G., Boles, J. S., & McMurrian, R. (1996). Development and validation of work–family conflict and family-work conflict scales. *Journal of Applied Psychology, 81*, 400–410. doi:10.1037//0021-9010.81.4.400

Noonan, M. C. (2001). The impact of domestic work on men's and women's wages. *Journal of Marriage and Family, 63*, 1134–1145. doi:10.1111/j.1741-3737.2001.01134

Nyland, C. (1989). *Reduced overtime and the management of production*. Cambridge: Cambridge University Press.

Osterman, P. (1999). *Securing prosperity: The American labor market: How it has changed and what to do about it*. Princeton, NJ: Princeton University Press.

Parasuraman, S., Purohit, Y. S., Gotshalk, V. M., & Beutell, N. J. (1996). Work and family variables, entrepreneurial career success, and psychological well-being. *Journal of Vocational Behavior, 48*, 275–300. doi:10.1006/jvbe.1996.0025

Parrenas, R. S. (2001). *Servants of globalization: Women, migration, and domestic work*. Stanford, CA: Stanford University Press.

Parrenas, R. S. (2005). *Children of global migration: Transnational families and gender woes*. Stanford, CA: Stanford University Press.

Pitt-Catsouphes, M., Kossek, E. E., & Sweet, S. (2006). Charting new territory: Advancing multi-disciplinary perspectives, methods, and approaches in the study of work and family. In M. Pitt-Catsouphes, E. E. Kossek, & S. Sweet (Eds.), *The work and family handbook* (pp. 1–16). Mahwah, NJ: Lawrence Erlbaum.

Parsons, T. (1964). *Essays in sociological theory*. New York: The Free Press.

Parsons, T., & Bales, R. T. (1955). *Family socialization and interaction process*. Glencoe, IL: Free Press.

Presser, H. B. (2003). *Working in a 24/7 economy: Challenges for American families*. New York: Russell Sage Foundation.

Razavi, S. (2007). *The political and social economy of care in a development context* (Gender and Development Programme Paper Number 3). Geneva, Switzerland: United Nations Research Institute for Social Development.

Richardson, M. S. (2012a). A critique of career discourse practices. In P. McIlveen & D. Schultheiss (Eds.), *Social constructionism in vocational psychology and career development* (pp. 87–104). Rotterdam: Sense Publishers.

Richardson, M. S. (2012b). Counseling for work and relationship. *The Counseling Psychologist, 40*(2), 190–242. doi:10.1177/0011000011406452

Riche, M. F. (2006). Demographic implications for work–family research. In M. Pitt-Catsouphes, E. E. Kossek, & S. Sweet (Eds.), *The work and family handbook: Multidisciplinary perspectives, methods, and approaches* (pp. 125–140). Mahwah, NJ: Lawrence Erlbaum.

Savickas, M. (2011, April). Career development: Retrospective and prospective. Keynote Presentation at the International Career Conference, Cairns, Queensland, Australia.

Schultheiss, D. E. P. (2006). The interface of work and family life. *Professional Psychology: Research and Practice, 37*, 334–341. doi:10.1037/0735-7028.37.4.334

Shotter, J. (1993). *Cultural politics of everyday life: Social constructionism, rhetoric and knowing of the third kind*. Buckingham, UK: Open University Press.

Sieber, S. D. (1974). Toward a theory of role accumulation. *American Sociological Review, 39*, 567–578. doi:10.2307/2094422

Standing, G. (2001). Care work: Overcoming insecurity and neglect. In M. Daly (Ed.), *The quest for security* (pp. 15–32). Geneva, Switzerland: International Labour Office.

Taylor, P. (2011). The decline of marriage and rise of new families. Pew Research Center's Demographic Trends Project. Retrieved from http://www.pewsocialtrends.org/files/2010/11/pew-social-trends-2010-families.pdf.

Tronto, J. C. (1993). *Moral boundaries: A political argument for an ethic of care*. New York: Routledge.

Tronto, J. C. (2006). Vicious circles of unequal care. In M. Hamington (Ed.), *Socializing care* (pp. 3–25). Lanham, MD: Rowman and Littlefield.

Tronto, J. C. (2009, March). Democratic care politics in a world of limits. Keynote address, The Political and Social Economy of Care. Conference of the United Nations Research Institute for Social Development, New York.

Voydanoff, P. (2002). Linkages between the work–family interface and work, family, and individual outcomes: An integrative model. *Journal of Family Issues, 23*(1), 138–164. doi:10.1177/0192513X02023001007

Voydanoff, P. (2005). The differential salience of family and community demands and resources for family-to-work conflict and facilitation. *Journal of Family and Economic Issues, 26*, 396–417. doi:10.1007/s10834-005-5904-7

Voydanoff, P. (2007). *Work, family, and community: Exploring interconnections*. Mahwah, NJ: Lawrence Erlbaum.

Wachtel, P. L. (2008). *Relational theory and the practice of psychotherapy*. New York: The Guilford Press.

Warren, E., & Tyagi, A. W. (2003). *The two-income trap*. New York: Basic Books.

Wellrich, M. (2001). Home slackers: Men, the state, and welfare in modern America. *Journal of American History, 87*, 460–489. doi:10.2307/2568760

Wharton, A. S. (2006). Understanding diversity of work in the 21st century and its impact on the work–family area of study. In M. Pitt-Catsouphes, E. E. Kossek, & S. Sweet (Eds.), *The work and family handbook: Multidisciplinary perspectives, methods, and approaches* (pp. 17–40). Mahwah, NJ: Lawrence Erlbaum.

Wiese, B. S., Seiger, C. P., Schmid, C. M., & Freund, A. M. (2010). Beyond conflict: Functional facets of the work–family interplay. *Journal of Vocational Behavior, 77*, 104–117. doi:10.1016/j.jvb.2010.02.011

Williams, F. (2010). *Claiming and framing in the making of care policies*. (Gender and Development Programme Paper Number 13). Geneva, Switzerland: United Nations Research Institute for Social Development.

Zedeck, S., & Mosier, K. L. (1990). Work in the family and employing organization. *American Psychologist: Special Issue: Organizational Psychology, 45*, 240–251. doi:10.1037//0003-066X.45.2.240

Approaches to Aging and Working

Harvey L. Sterns *and* Anthony A. Sterns

Abstract

The demarcation of work–nonwork that has been characterized by sharp retirement (e.g., ending a long-term job) is now more often characterized by individuals seeking either to continue working or opting for a dull or gradual retirement (move to a bridge job or part-time work). The growing percentage of older adults in the population is increasing the percentage of older workers; moreover, low-wage workers are older and more educated than in the recent past. The health status of the future workforce will include individuals with and without chronic disease, and predictions of improved health must be tempered by trends in the percentage of adults with obesity and obesity-related health changes. With the economic uncertainties since 2007, many older workers are finding they need to continue working longer than they had expected. These shifting financial, needs as well as an interest in continuing to contribute to society, are drawing many older workers into steady or episodic market work and volunteer work. This chapter will examine the relationship between aging and working from two psychology-of-working perspectives, the organizational perspective and the self-management perspective.

Key Words: older worker, age and performance, retirement, self-management, lifespan, training, Americans with Disabilities Act, Age Discrimination and Employment Act, job analysis

Perspectives on Continuing to Work

The issue of jobs and slowing economic growth is a continuing global concern. The unemployment rate continued above 9% in the United States from 2007 until 2011, when the rate finally declined below that threshold to 8.6%. By the end of 2011, there were between 100,000 and 150,000 jobs being created, but twice as many people were no longer actively looking for work and becoming categorized as discouraged workers. This level of slow employment growth is expected to remain, but, more importantly, it seems to have reset perceptions of the opportunities for continuous employment for both those new to and continuing in the workplace.

For those individuals planning on retirement at 65 as has been the norm, there may now be a belief in the need for continued employment to 70

and beyond. The impact is pervasive, affecting high school and college graduates entering the workforce and those eligible for retirement. Importantly, it differentially and potentially more negatively influences the poor and less educated (Taylor & Geldhauser, 2007). In this chapter, we examine how older adult workers are managed from the perspective of the organization, and how they navigate and self-manage this changing employment and post-retirement landscape.

Many of those just starting their careers have a unique burden of high debt from their education. Those finishing their career may be working longer as a result of less-than-expected stock market and savings returns. For those whose careers are interrupted, up to 25% of the U.S. workforce at the Great Recession's (first) peak, unemployment benefits may soon be expended, if they have not already been. This level of employment turmoil has not been seen since the 1980s, and in some respects since the Great Depression of the 1930s. Of those who are employed, there is the constant concern regarding layoffs, downsizing, or being let go from a present position. There is also a similar impact on the decision to retire both for those close to retirement today, but, perhaps more importantly, for those who will be retiring more than a decade from now.

Many adult and older adult workers are continuing to work and have stated as a group for some time that they plan to work longer (H. Sterns & A. Sterns, 1995). This desire to work longer has been tracked through a gradual evolution in the approaches to writings on aging, work, and retirement (in chronological order, Sterns & Patchet, 1984; Sterns, 1986; Sterns & Alexander, 1987; Sterns & Doverspike, 1989; Sterns & Huyck, 2001; Hedge, Borman, & Lammlein, 2006; Rothwell, Sterns, Spokus, & Reaser, 2008; Shultz & Adams, 2007; Czaja & Sharit, 2009; Cappelli & Novelli, 2010). From the organizational perspective, it is important for managers to have a clear understanding of what the aging workforce means in terms of planning, training, and knowledge management. It is critical that management and executives have a clear understanding of the legal obligations to workers as disabilities that co-vary with age become more common. They must not be driven by stereotypes, but, rather, have a clear understanding of the specific approaches that will retain the embedded knowledge of senior workers, retaining those best workers, and retraining workers to ensure they are fully competent and have the requisite skills to maximally perform.

Equally important is the perspective of the worker, who is now fully responsible for self-managing both career and retirement. Beginning in the 1970s, organizations moved away from paternalism and maternalism, with workers being increasingly responsible for themselves (Hall, 1971; Sterns & Kaplan, 2003). That means issues such as career updating, training to maintain expertise, and decisions to change careers are individual decisions alone. How self-relevant experiences (Carstensen, 2009), and work positive experiences in particular, (Warr, 2001) affect decisions to continue working are now being explored; both are important elements in understanding individual decisions about employment (Sterns & Chang, 2010; Sterns & Kaplan, 2003).

Barriers and Opportunities to Employment Across the Lifespan

RESILIENCE

Sterns and Dawson (2012) emphasize that improved health and longevity are allowing some older adults the option of remaining in the workforce longer and postponing retirement. For those with a choice of staying in the workforce, continuing work can bring forth fulfillment and improved self-esteem. For others, particularly those who must continue working to provide sufficient income, there are also many challenges that older adults uniquely face during their continued employment (Blustein, Kenna, Gill, & Devoy, 2008). The tools, resources, and networks available to assist the older worker to respond to the environmental demands, both at work and outside of work, determine the amount of resilience an individual will have and the likelihood of success (McLoughlin, Taylor, & Bohle, 2001).

There is a significant body of literature outlining age-related deficits that older workers have to overcome to successfully remain in the workforce (Rothwell, Sterns, Spokus, & Reaser, 2008). Some of these adverse stressors include changes in cognitive capacity, sensory decline, musculoskeletal decline, and motor deficits. Older workers must also contend with their changing roles in the workforce as well as potentially confounding roles at home, such as caregiver. Changes in the work environment may also increase levels of adversity for the older worker. Not only can the physical environment pose stressors, but also social stressors such as attitudes of supervisors and coworkers.

UNEMPLOYMENT

Making decisions about work and retirement is particularly challenging for those who are unemployed or underemployed. It has become extremely clear that many older workers who did not have a position a year ago have not been able to find new employment over the period of a year (Rix, 2011c). Workers and non workers alike are experiencing a new awareness of their financial challenges as they consider the endgame of their careers. It is apparent that they are forming new expectations and reforming the assumptions required to plan for the coming decades. With the considerations of healthcare, retirement savings, pension solvency, and general economic conditions, many people are reporting that they plan to remain in the workforce considerably longer than in the recent past.

LOW INCOME

Those older adults living at or near the poverty line have considerably less freedom in choosing to work. They may work because they require the income to cover basic needs for shelter, heat, food, and medicine (Blustein, Kenna, Gill, & Devoy, 2008). Poverty disproportionately affects older women and minorities (Taylor & Geldhauser, 2007). Historically, there have always been more women living in poverty than men. The median income for women 65 and older is just over $12,000 per year, just $3,000 over the U.S. Census Bureau standard for living in poverty (Beedon & Wu, 2005).

Low-income older adults rely more heavily on Social Security. Intended to be one support in addition to pension and savings, those living at the bottom of the economic ladder are much more reliant on Social Security payments. For example, over 75% of older Hispanics rely on Social Security for 50% or more of their total income. Without it, 33% of older Hispanics would fall into poverty (Taylor & Geldhauser, 2007).

Perhaps the greatest barrier for low-income older workers is that they are the least likely to have the education, information skills, and training to be a good match for many of today's job tasks (Sterns & Sterns, 1996; Taylor & Geldhauser, 2007). Those without a choice to continue working, due to social disadvantage or oppression (racism, sexism, ageism, etc.), are addressed by the psychology-of-working perspective. This perspective is intended to provide a framework to address these disadvantages, not by the traditional career guidance approaches but through practical support, connection with financial planning and skills training support, in the context of public programming and the policy to support and implement such programs. Several researchers have made specific policy recommendations that include education of social workers and career counselors (Blustein, Kenna, Gill, & Devoy, 2008) and the implementation of financial planning and skills training for older workers (Sterns, 1986; Sterns & Sterns, 1986; Taylor & Geldhauser, 2007).

RETIREMENT

Over the past three decades of industrial gerontological research, work expectations and our understanding of retirement has evolved (Rothwell et al., 2008). The possibility of large-scale corporate collapses, changes in the global economy, and shifts from manufacturing to service to information industries all are considered in the discussions.

Individual career issues that include organizational commitment and benefits, financial planning and investment returns, housing and community support choices, age discrimination, and the ability to maintain professional expertise or to retrain have also been topics that have evolved along with the economic and business issues. Still, the experts and older workers themselves were not prepared for the scope of the changes that began with the recession and banking crisis that began in 2005 and continues past the official end of the recession in 2009. Different economic levels and different cohorts are feeling the impact of these changes and it is differently affecting their attitudes about continuing to work and approaches to retirement. This chapter will consider the continuing impact of the economic and social challenges of the decade of the 2010s and attempt to fit these changes into an historical context.

In this chapter, we present each issue from two major perspectives on approaching older workers, the organizational perspective and the self-management perspective. We will present a definition of older workers and their characteristics. We will describe the makeup of the current workforce, focusing on middle-aged and older workers, and issues with older workers' job performance and self-management. Lastly, organizational characteristics related to supporting and attracting older workers are discussed. We will address how the current economic and social situation may have an impact on the aforementioned issues throughout the chapter.

Approaches to Defining the Older Worker

The phenomenon of the increasing numbers of older individuals in the United States has been forecast for decades. In particular, low-wage middle-aged workers (those making $10/hour or less) now represent 38.1% of those age 35 to 64, up from 30% in 1979 (Schmidt & Jones, 2012). Social policy planners have used this time to modest effect to modify the protections, entitlements, services, and benefits that this large and growing group receives. With the leading edge of the baby boom generation reaching age 65, the challenges of their impact on workforce participation, role in continued work and retirement, and representation in entitlement programs have become mainstream issues. This chapter will examine the impact of aging and its impact on the productivity and capacity of workers. This chapter also will consider a set of important categories of changes this group will experience, both within themselves and in the environment around them, and examine how these changes affect work. Mechanisms for coping with and adapting to these changes will then be considered.

How we talk about older workers has changed over time. There are five unique ways of defining who is an older worker: chronological, functional, psychosocial, organizational, and lifespan developmental (Sterns & Doverspike, 1989; H. Sterns & Miklos, 1995; A. Sterns, H. Sterns, & Hollis, 1996).

Chronological age is the earliest and most common approach of defining older workers. The Age Discrimination in Employment Act (ADEA) (1967) and its amendments (1978, 1986) define an older worker as any individual 40 and over who is still an active worker (Snyder & Barrett, 1988; Sterns, Sterns, & Hollis, 1996; H. Sterns, Doverspike, & Lax, 2005). Chronological age has been favored by courts in the assessment of individual performance capacity (over functional age, discussed below). Chronological age has consistently been supported as a *bona fide* occupational qualification (BFOQ) when reasonably related to job performance. Commercial airline pilots, for example, are still subject to mandatory retirement, now at 65 raised from 60, based on their chronological age (Avolio, Barrett, & Sterns, 1984; Culler & H. Sterns, 2010).

Functional age focuses on the individual's performance to define the person's age. Functional age is presented as a single index that combines assessments based on biological and psychological changes. These changes take into account the range of abilities as well as the changes in skill, wisdom, and experience (Birren & Stafford, 1986). These changes may either increase or decrease in the individual. The index is an indication of how the person performs compared to the average individual of a given age. So if a specific 50-year-old individual can run a mile as fast as the average 25-year-old, we would say that person has a functional age of 25. Two examples of functional age approaches are physical abilities analysis and functional capacity assessment, discussed later in the chapter.

Psychosocial definitions of older workers come from societal norms and the social perceptions of older workers. The age at which a worker is perceived as older, the attitudes others have toward older workers, and the impact and implications for personnel decisions of giving a worker the label of "older worker" are central issues within this view. Research has shown considerable change in organizations' views on how older workers are perceived.

Researchers have found both negative and positive perceptions. Research in the 1970s and 1980s has found that negative perceptions about older workers included being regarded as more difficult to train, less receptive to technological changes, more accident-prone, less promotable, and less motivated (e.g., Avolio & Barrett, 1987; Bird & Fisher, 1986; Schwab & Heneman, 1978; Stagner, 1985). On the positive side, older adults were perceived as more dependable, cooperative, conscientious, consistent, and knowledgeable (Schwab & Heneman, 1978). In the 1990s, perceptions changed such that a sizeable minority of older workers desired to continue working (H. Sterns & A. Sterns, 1995). Most recently, older workers are perceived as likely to continue working, due in equal parts to the desire to be active and financial necessity (Rix, 2011a). The stereotypes of older workers remain (Posthuma & Campion, 2009). Older workers today are still viewed as having less flexibility, energy, disinterest in training, and poorer health on the negative side. They are also positively stereotyped as more loyal and reliable employees.

According to Pitt-Catsouphes and Smyer (2007) from the Sloan Center on Aging & Work, one of the dimensions in which workers can be viewed is through the generational lens. Each cohort not only is similar in age but has also been exposed to significant historical events that may alter their views or values expressed in the workplace. Examples may include the technological savvy of the Millennials (born between 1981 and 1999), as they grew up with easy access to computers and the Internet, or the baby boomers (born between 1946 and 1964), who were exposed to significant loss and turmoil during the Vietnam War. Adversity may be encountered by (1) an individual misusing the generational lens and overgeneralizing certain characteristics of a "generation" to all members of the cohort instead of treating each employee as an individual or (2) different views, values, or work ethic causing conflict during work responsibilities requiring team interaction and collaboration. The relational pattern of resilience is easily applied here as the older worker must count on positive peer interactions and support to maintain a successful work environment.

The organizational approach is the aging perspective that focuses on understanding the roles of individuals in an organization and the impact of the mix of ages of personnel on the organization as a whole. This perspective emphasizes expertise, seniority, and tenure rather than age. An organization is considered old when the average age of its members is older. For example, employees at a startup software company may have an average age in the 30s, with tenures of employees less than 1 year, whereas employees at an established manufacturing company may have an average age of 45 and tenures of 15 years or more. As the average age of personnel increases, attitudinal and financial demands on the organization may change. This approach is most concerned with the nature and interactions of the organization. The mix of cognitive and physical requirements determined by the activities of the personnel as a whole is the important consideration when examining the impact of aging on workers in an organization. For the startup, software languages and programming are likely changing quickly, whereas in manufacturing environments the change is likely much more gradual, with rare discontinuous sudden changes.

The lifespan orientation combines each of the above approaches with an understanding that people are dynamic and that behavioral change occurs over the entire working life of individuals. The emphasis in this approach is the recognition of substantial individual differences as individuals age (Baltes, Reese, & Lipsitt, 1980; Bowen, Noack, & Staudinger, 2011; Sterns, 1986). Individuals are influenced by normative, age-graded biological and environmental influences (physical and cognitive changes as one ages), normative, history-graded factors (generational events), and nonnormative influences unique to every individual. These normative and nonnormative influences interact to influence and steer an individual's career path. Over time, they determine the strengths and limitations, the skills and experience that an individual brings to his or her organizational role. Each worker begins with different potentials and each person will improve and decline uniquely.

Finally, the psychology-of-working perspective (Blustein, Kenna, Gill, & DeVoy, 2008) goes beyond the traditional approaches of industrial/organizational and vocational psychology. It formally considers the impact of social barriers that prevent individuals from fully achieving their potentials. It focuses on the realities of individual working lives as they are experienced regardless, or perhaps specifically because they are not pursuing a hierarchical self-managed career. This perspective is particularly helpful for understanding those individuals who are challenged by a poor regional economy, disability or addictions, or work limitations due to care of children, spouse, or older loved ones.

These definitions of older workers temper how the impacts of future technological changes, employment opportunities, and incentives to remain in the work force are understood and interpreted. Also to be considered is whether individuals have a career track or experience a disconnected series of jobs over their lifetime of work. Individuals with more education tend to have better abilities to adapt and succeed financially over their working lifetimes. Regardless, interventions can be tailored to be effective when the combination of these issues is appropriately considered.

Each of the six approaches emphasizes a unique viewpoint and produces recommendations for interventions specific to that perspective. The chronological definition emphasizes legal issues. Functional age perspectives emphasize the capacity of the worker, both physically and cognitively, and measurement of that capacity. Psychosocial perspectives require methods for monitoring the attitudes of individuals and determining perceived norms in organizations and in industry. Organizational perspectives focus on the management of human resources and require measures of productivity and efficiency. The lifespan perspective and the psychology-of-working perspective remind us of the important role of individual differences and to be cautious of overgeneralizing. These six perspectives must each be considered in turn as assessments of productivity and functionality are weighed and policies and practices are determined regarding older workers.

To understand the role of aging on the productivity of a workforce, the advantages and the limitations of aging's impact on individual workers, the tasks involved in a job must be well defined and understood. Defining formally the requirements of the person doing the job is determined by a process known as job analysis.

Older Worker Norms and Statistics
Age Norms for Work and Retirement

The total labor force is projected to increase by 8.5% during the period 2006–2016 (see Figure 10.1) (BLS, 2010). The youngest group (age 16 to 24) will decrease and a slight increase in the 25-to-54 group is projected. In contrast, workers age 55 to 64 will increase by a predicted 36.5%. At 55, 75% of people are still working, at 60 the figure is 65%, but at 66 less than 33% are still working, and at 70 about 20% of people are working (Rix, 2011c). Workers 65 years of age and older are expected to nearly double, increasing by more than 80%, representing over 6% of the total labor force by 2016 (Toossi, 2007).

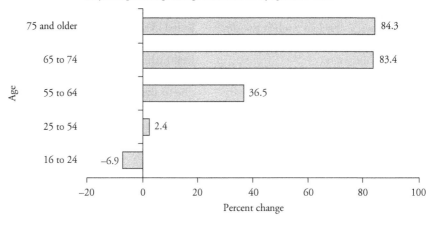

Projected percentage change in labor force by age, 2006–2016

Age	Percent change
75 and older	84.3
65 to 74	83.4
55 to 64	36.5
25 to 54	2.4
16 to 24	−6.9

Figure 10.1 Bureau of Labor Statistics Employment Projections.
Source: http://www.bls.gov/opub/ted/2008/jul/wk4/art04.htm

Work–life cycles are not uniform among demographic groups (Sterns & Chang, 2010). Labor force participation rates are increasing for women as well as for racial and ethnic groupings (Toossi, 2006, 2007). The number of employed women who are 65 years of age and older increased approximately 147% over the past three decades. For men, there was a smaller but significant 75% increase in labor force participation (Bureau of Labor Statistics, 2008). Throughout the developed world, older women between ages of 55 and 64 continue working today in most countries (Rix, 2005). In the era of the Great Recession, men are more adversely affected, possibly because the construction, manufacturing, and financial activities, where men are more prevalent, have been disproportionately affected. (Borbely, 2009; Kelter, 2009).

According to the projections by the Bureau of Labor Statistics (2007), by 2016, Caucasians will be the major racial group, occupying 79.6% of the U.S. labor force. African Americans (16.2%) and Asians (29.9%) will grow in their participation rates relatively faster than that of Whites (5.5%) through 2016. The Hispanic labor force will grow by 29.9%, which is nearly six times the projected non-Hispanic labor force increase of 5.1%. The already diverse workforce will be even more diverse in every aspect, including being older, into the indefinite future.

There has been an increase in the number of full-time older workers beginning in 1995. This trend is likely strengthening, given the current economic situation. In parallel, the number of persons employed part time increased drastically during 2008 because older workers (and workers in general) could not find full-time work even though full-time work was preferred (Borbely, 2009). Labor force participation is also driven by work attitudes, which we focus on in the next section.

Age and Work Attitudes

As reflected in recent surveys, many baby boomers have said for many years they are planning to work in retirement (Rix, 2011c). Of employed boomers at 65, 1 in 3 report having retired from an earlier career. As of 2010, nearly 74% of persons age 45 to 64, mostly baby boomers, are in the labor force, up from 62% in 1950 and 66% in 1985. By 2010, those age 55 to 64, leading-edge boomers, were more likely to be in the labor force than in any time in the past 60 years.

Women had a participation rate in the workforce of 27% in 1950. Women who are part of the baby boomer generation (1946–1964) joined the workforce in the 1960s and 1970s and increased female participation rates, which reached 60% in 2010. Participation rates of boomer men are well below that of men in the 1950s, 70% today versus 87% in 1950. Only 29% of new male Social Security beneficiaries 62 to 64 gave health problems as the reason for leaving their last job (Rix, 2011a). This is down from 54% in 1968 (Sherman, 1985). Participation rates for work are expected to become more equal as the workforce ages.

Age and Training

One in six (16.7%) of those classified as unemployed or classified as looking for work are over the age of 50 (Rix, 2011b). Nearly 13% were involuntarily unemployed but were working when surveyed. A sizeable 13.4% reported being out of the labor force but had been working during the past 3 years. Seven out of 10 (70%) were employed at the time of the survey; 57.2% had a job at the time of the survey and had not been involuntarily unemployed during the past 3 years.

Age and Work Withdrawal

It seems that most workers do not directly retire from career jobs; rather, they get to full retirement via some kind of transition employment or bridge job, which may be self-employment (Rothwell et al., 2008). These post-career transitions may involve a voluntary career change, follow a job loss, or represent an attempt to phase or ease into retirement that requires a job change (Rix, 2011b).

Declining disabilities with greater age and increased lifespan imply that health status and work ability for older adults are improving. Some potentially work-limiting conditions such as arthritis, hypertension, heart disease, and diabetes rise with age, as do hearing and vision impairments.

Mature Services held a series of 3-week job clubs for older adults looking for work (Ferrel & Nakai, 2012). The group members were assessed on seven dimensions. Four of the dimensions were components of the participants' attitudes toward their job search: optimism, perceived stress, confidence, and general feelings toward the job search tasks. The other three dimensions related to the perceptions about skills gained through the job club process: excitement, usefulness of the acquired information, and learning new techniques for looking for employment. The job club experience was found to be uniform among the groups. Female participants experienced greater stress compared to male participants. Non-Caucasian participants had higher levels of optimism, confidence, and positive feelings and lower stress compared to Caucasian participants. Participants who had retired felt less stress and considered the job club less useful than those participants who did not retire. Most importantly, participants developed more positive attitudes toward their job search and reported increases in information and techniques learned to find work. This report shows that there are benefits to training older adults who are looking for work in terms of both skills to find and apply for work as well as improving the motivation to look for work.

Munnell, Soto, and Golub-Sass (2008) estimated that life expectancy for 50-year-olds increased 4.3 years from 1970 to 2000; healthy life expectancy, measuring disability-free remaining years, increased by less than 3 years. This improvement was explained by increased educational attainment. In 2000, college-educated White men at age 50 were projected to have 22.8 healthy years, while those with a high school education had only 13.3 more years of healthy life. This trend seems to have plateaued.

Health is playing a smaller role in the workplace due to the aforementioned protections and accommodations. Many of those who need to work longer, low-wage workers dependent on Social Security, have onerous jobs that keep them under stress and have the least education to manage their health optimally (Blustein et al., 2008; Taylor & Geldhauser, 2007).

A Theory of Self-Management of Employment

Conceptualizations of work and retirement continue to evolve, and in the 1990s three very important publications appeared in the literature (Hall, 1996; Hall & Mirvis, 1995a, 1995b). *The Career is Dead—Long Live the Career* (Hall & Associates, 1996), perhaps the most illustrative of the three contributions, presents the strongest statement regarding the protean career. The emphasis is on self-management of career in a dramatically changing work environment.

Sterns et al. (Sterns & Gray, 1999; Sterns & Kaplan, 2003; Sterns & Subich, 2005) emphasized the challenge faced by midlife and older workers in terms of self-management. As organizations transition from pyramid to flatter, more streamlined configurations through downsizing and restructuring, employees may experience job loss, job plateauing, and skills obsolescence (Farr et al., 1998; Sterns & Miklos, 1995). Furthermore, depending on age of career entry, middle-aged and older workers may be more likely to occupy midlevel managerial positions and may need to take increased involvement and responsibility in terms of further career management. More recent discussions (Rix, 2011a) emphasize that one may want to continue in a present job since re-employment may not be possible in challenging economic periods.

Career self-management is carefully discussed by Hall and Mirvis (1996) in their discussion of the protean career. A protean career is directed by the individual rather than the employing organization. Greater responsibility for learning, skill mastery, and reskilling is also placed on the individual (Hall & Mirvis, 1995b). The individual is in charge, in control, and able to change the shape of his or her career at will—similar to a free agent in sports (Hall & Mirvis, 1996). This perspective and the goals of this type of career (e.g., psychological success, identity expansion, and learning) also recognize the artificiality of the distinction between work and nonwork life. Personal roles and career roles are highly interrelated and the boundaries between these roles tend to be fuzzy rather than clear cut (Hall & Mirvis, 1995b). One disadvantage of protean careers is that an individual's identity is not likely to be tied to any one organization.

Older workers, however, may also be at a disadvantage in terms of moving toward greater career self-management. Transitioning from a typical, organizational-driven career to a protean career may be a rather difficult task, particularly if an individual entered the workforce with a one career/one employer ideal. Additionally, stereotypical beliefs about older workers may lead to the underutilization of this group within new relationships between organizations and employees (Mirvis & Hall, 1996).

Sterns (1986), in his model of career development and training, sees the option of full- or part-time retirement as part of the decision to no longer be actively involved in career development and work activities. Decisions regarding career and updating are based on many dimensions. However, individuals can move in or out of the work role. A similar multidimensional model is proposed for self-management of retirement. A person's self-concept (Fig. 10.2), work environment (Fig. 10.3), significant relationships (Fig. 10.4), and community connections (Fig. 10.5) all influence and are factors in consideration of the decision to continue to work or to retire. Self-concept is influenced in the many ways illustrated by the model. What is critical is our ability to bridge from the individual level to the broader work and societal context.

Impact of Trends from the Organizational and Self-Management Perspectives

The conclusions from the statistics and research presented above are mixed. For organizations, it is clear that there will be a near doubling of older workers. They will be in the labor force for two very different reasons. One group is motivated to work because they want to be engaged and another group is motivated by financial realities that necessitate continuing to work. Although generally healthier than the past, workers with disabilities that co-occur more frequently with age must be accommodated, so organizations should be prepared to increase their expertise to support their older workers. For those industries challenged to meet diversity targets, it is likely that as all the protected classes increase their

representation, creating a diverse workforce will be one area where less attention will be required.

Assessing Adult and Older Workers
Job Analysis and Job Descriptions

Job analysis is the fundamental methodology for the development of a job description. The job description documents the knowledge, skills, and abilities required of a person to successfully perform the job described. A job analysis establishes the credentials, training, duties, responsibilities, and tools required of a job. Determining the knowledge, skills, and abilities of a job is important for two main reasons. First, the employer will want to consider only the applicants who possess the required qualifications for the position. The availability of qualified persons in the population can be determined based on the job description. This is important for a company to achieve diversity targets. The second reason is that job analysis defines the criteria for evaluating and comparing the qualified candidates when hiring. From these criteria, it can be determined which candidate is thus the most qualified. With current employees, the job analysis can be used to validate decisions related to training, selection, compensation, and performance appraisal (Cascio & Aguinis, 2005; Sterns, Sterns, & Hollis, 1996).

Once criteria for a job are established, testing or evaluation items tied to the job's critical abilities can be developed. Then cutoff scores should be validated with existing job incumbents to establish appropriate criterion performance levels. Repeated assessment of individuals can track their performance levels over time and detect when substantial drops have occurred. For example, a word processor who develops arthritis would keep the position until performance drops below the criterion levels. Arthritis would affect a customer service position less dramatically as typing is relatively less important, and it may never have a substantial impact on job performance, or play a role in retirement. This approach provides the means for a legally defensible method of performance appraisal that is job-related, sensitive to disabilities and limitations, and not directly related to age (Capelli & Novelli, 2010; Sterns, Sterns, & Hollis, 1996).

A number of methodologies are used to carry out a job analysis. The most common method requires a combination of observation, interviews with job incumbents and supervisors, and surveying to validate the qualitative results. Other methods may include review of job classification systems (e.g., www.onetcenter.org), expert panels, structured

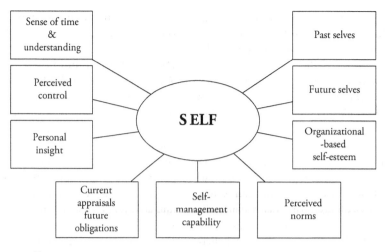

Figure 10.2 Influences on self.

questionnaires, task inventories, checklists, work logs or diaries, activity sampling, or using critical incidents techniques. The job analysis process results in a job description detailing the knowledge, skills, and abilities required of the position as well as essential and marginal functions performed on the job. This sets the stage for ensuring there is an equal opportunity for all qualified candidates to be evaluated on qualifications and job performance.

Needs Assessment

A needs assessment (Goldstein & Ford, 2002) is also essential to thoroughly understand the requirements of a job. A needs analysis is important because it is the methodology for connecting the organizational need to the personnel required to fill that need. A needs analysis consists of three separate analyses that examine the organization, the personnel, and the job tasks.

Organizational analysis is concerned with issues of manpower, organizational strategy, and organizational climate (Wexley & Latham, 2002). The person conducting the organizational analysis should be on the lookout for potential obstacles. Supervisor and peers and job objectives should reinforce the desired skills, and measures to evaluate those objectives should be in place. How the organization manages knowledge, promotes the organizational culture, and supports interorganizational communication are all issues that would be of interest during an organizational analysis.

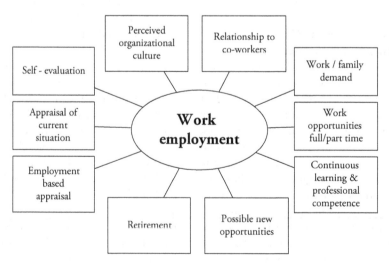

Figure 10.3 Work influences.

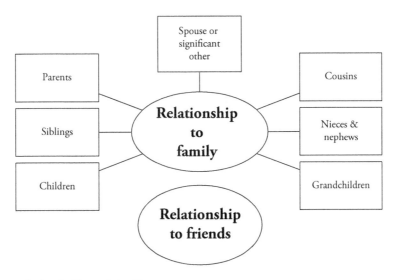

Figure 10.4 Marriage and other significant relationships.

Personnel analysis examines such issues as the need for performance appraisal, consideration of trainability of personnel, and the existing abilities, motivation, and perceptions of the work environment by job incumbents (Noe, 1986). Other personnel issues would include training priorities and readiness and motivation for training (Wexley & Latham, 2002).

Task analysis is closely tied to job analysis (Wexley & Latham, 2002). Task analysis will reveal testing and appraisal concerns and allow for consideration of potential obstacles. Modern testing such as Web-based tools for tailored testing, 360-degree feedback, and training should be considered as part of the needs analysis (Cascio & Aguinis, 2005).

Needs analysis supports and enhances the human resource functions present in most organizations, such as maintenance of job descriptions, planning, training, and career management. Products of needs analysis include identification of the knowledge, skills, and abilities (KSAs) required to perform jobs, ability to assess which training program would be best for a job, designing future training across jobs, and the creation of a database of pertinent KSAs throughout the organization. These activities will also be used for many other essential human resource functions such as determining benefits and compensation. They also spell out the requirements for workers so that older workers can be provided with the proper support and guidance to be fully engaged in the organization as long as both the organization and the person want to remain engaged.

Job and needs analysis techniques emphasize the tasks required to perform the job, but other analysis

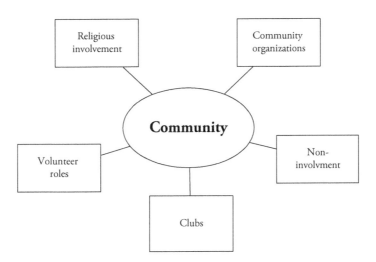

Figure 10.5 Community influences.

techniques focus on defining the capabilities and capacities of the person. These approaches originate from the functional age perspective. Two of these approaches are the physical abilities analysis and functional capacity assessment.

Neither approach concerns itself directly with aging or disabilities; rather, the physical demands of the job are defined and the applicants are evaluated to determine if they can achieve and maintain those demands (Sterns, Sterns, & Hollis, 1996). The physical abilities analysis attempts to measure job effort using the job incumbent's perceptions of effort, exertion experienced while performing work, or time studies of actual efforts over extended work periods.

Similarly, a functional capacity assessment evaluates an employee, applicant, or job incumbent in terms of his or her capacity to perform essential functions of a job. This approach is commonly used for jobs involving public safety or military service (Fraser, 1992; Sterns, Sterns, & Hollis, 1996).

Age-Related Physical and Cognitive Changes in Performance
Age-Related Physical Change and Functional Capacity

Aging research has indicated that age and job performance are generally unrelated (Sterns & McDaniel, 1994). The problem, therefore, is not the general skill performance of older workers as much as it is their ability to maintain skill competency in response to changes in technology. Certainly, learning capabilities do not significantly decline with age (Hedge, Borman, & Lammlein, 2003; Sterns & Doverspike, 1989). Therefore, it is important to review age-related decline factors for older workers (e.g., sensory decline) and propose appropriate ergonomic interventions that the organization may utilize to support work-life extension of older adults.

Changes in Strength

There is some indication that physical strength declines beyond the age of 40, but the extent of the decline is not clear, nor is the effect of the decline on work performance. Welford (1988) cites research that suggests moderately heavy muscular work is well tolerated by older adults, especially if it is intermittent. Other research has found, however, that older workers are more likely to leave jobs that are highly physical in nature. It has been argued that repetitive loading, twisting of the torso, and rapid lifting may result in special risk to older workers

who have decreased strength. Thus, it has been suggested that design/redesign efforts should be used to reduce some of the physical demands on older workers (Fisk, Rogers, Charness, Czaja, & Sharit, 2009; Immerian, 2009; Sterns, Sterns, & Hollis, 1996; Vercruyssen, 2009; Welford, 1988).

Changes in Health and Rehabilitation

A recurrent theme in work-life extension is the health of the older worker. There are implications that health is one of several variables affecting the functional capacity of older persons. Thus, the working capacity of older workers needs to be assessed.

It is important to identify aspects of health that are central to measuring disability and its impact on work life. Health may be defined in several ways, such as total well-being and absence of disease. Further distinctions between chronic and acute disease and subjective feelings of sickness must be made clear.

These distinctions highlight that disability or functional capacity is not directly tied to the presence of disease or impairment. Heart disease, cancer, stroke, and lung and liver disease are major conditions that increase with age. Other disabling conditions that affect people in all ages include arthritis, deformities or orthopedic impairments, hearing and speech impairments, and mental retardation. These disabilities may limit the kind of work an individual can do, but they do not prevent work altogether.

Disability is defined by its impact on one or more major life activities an individual is to perform. Disabilities affected more than 11% of Americans in 2002. This means that 51.2 million people have functional limitations that prevent them from working, attending school, or maintaining a household (Office of Disease Prevention and Health Promotion, 2009). There are 20.2 million Americans with a work disability, of whom 7.4 million (37%) are over the age of 55 (Waldrop & Stern, 2003).

Older persons over 65 have more health problems than middle-aged persons (45 to 64). However, there are no major differences between the age groups. Large numbers of middle-aged and older persons are able to work. Age 65 was not found to be a point where dramatic changes in health patterns take place. A sizable minority of the older population experiences functional impairment. A sizable percentage of older persons experience partial work disability. Health patterns differ by sex, with women frequently reporting more problems than men. The health states of older Hispanics and Blacks are poorer than that of older Whites. Older Blacks are especially disadvantaged in terms of health status.

Health problems increase gradually across groups as age increases. Only small differences are found between groups close in age. Young-olds (ages 65 to 74) are more like the middle-aged (ages 45 to 64) in their health level than old-olds (ages 75 and over).

The majority of the population 45 years and over report no functional limitations due to chronic conditions. Over two thirds of persons age 45 and above rate their health as good or excellent; thus, a large segment of the older population can be characterized as able-bodied. Thirty-two percent of individuals ages 45 and older report some level of impairment due to health limitations. Ten percent of this population report that they are unable to work or do housework because of chronic conditions.

While health problems are more frequently experienced by older compared to younger persons in their groups, differences between the groups were small. In terms of continuing work, a sizable percentage of older people report partial work disability (defined as limited in amount or kind of major activity they can perform).

It is of utmost importance that older adults are not treated as one homogeneous age group. The lifespan perspective emphasized the unique development of each individual, and this is especially true of health. There is greater variability in the older population compared to the younger population, so reporting older workers as a single group can distort the reality of health and aging.

Age-Related Sensory and Perceptual Changes and Limitations

Reviews by Fozard (1990), Kline and Schieber (1985), and Fozard and Gordon-Salant (2001) present information pertaining to sensory and perceptual capabilities in hearing and vision that exhibit different degrees of age-related decline across the lifespan. Keeping in mind there are always individual differences in the degree of decline with age, the following aspects of the aging process still need to be noted.

Before proceeding, the point needs to be mentioned that different aspects of age-related sensory decline may potentially be ameliorated to some degree with proper ergonomic interventions (Charness & Bosman, 1990; Fisk et al., 2009), but more empirical research in the workplace is needed before definitive conclusions regarding this issue can be made.

It is important to reiterate that the most significant decline probably does not begin until approximately age 70 or older, and there are always individual differences in decline such that some individuals in the workplace may not be affected by any of the following decline factors.

CHANGES IN VISION

Reactions to Illumination. Older adults are more likely to be adversely affected by changing levels of illumination. Reactions to light and dark adaptation may not be as quick or complete, although recent research suggests that dark adaptation may not be as problematic as had been previously thought. In addition to adaptation, older adults have been shown to be more affected by glare from light sources.

In response to these age-related changes, it has been suggested that conditions causing glare at work should be modified or eliminated if possible (Charness & Bosman, 1990; Welford, 1988). For example, installation of lighting that has soft white reader bulbs, allowing diffusion of light in the workspace and a reduction of glare, would be an effective intervention. Glare on computer screens is another relevant source to focus on for intervention purposes; installation of a glare-free computer screen on a computer terminal would help in reducing glare in the workplace. Design of work stations should include adjustable light sources in order to alter lighting in the workspace according to the perceptual needs of the employee over the course of the day. Placement of a computer or other equipment in relation to the windows in an office is another related workspace design issue. Covers should be placed on light bulbs and furniture should be arranged to face away from the source of glare. Lastly, sudden shifts in illumination should be avoided in the workplace; walking from one area of the workplace to the next area, an employee should not perceive a drastic shift in lighting of rooms.

Poorer Contrast. A second change in vision with age is that older adults have more difficulty detecting differences between visual stimuli. Older workers need greater contrast between the stimuli to be able to distinguish them (Fozard, 1990). This could create problems for an older worker with respect to navigating stairs at work or accurately utilizing visual information.

In response to this, it has been suggested that the work environment should be designed to avoid difficult contrasts for older workers (Fisk et. al, 2009). Difficult contrast, such as blue–green, should not be used for visual displays (computerized or written) that older workers will use. In fact, it has been suggested that black print on a white computer screen is the most effective for older adults (Charness & Bosman, 1990).

Useful Field of View. A third age-related change in vision concerns the useful field of vision (UFOV). Older adults have a smaller UFOV in which to process information from the environment. Stimuli outside the UFOV may not be processed as well by older adults (Fozard, 1990). Driving research by Owsley et al. has indicated that older adults' performance can be impaired due to a shrinking UFOV in their perceptual range (Owsley, Ball, Sloane, Roenker, & Bruni, 1991). The findings from driving research are applicable to the workplace context; older workers may be impaired in their information processing capabilities if their attention to environmental stimuli is outside the periphery of their reduced field of view.

A possible ergonomic response to this would be to create workspaces organized such that important information for task performance on the job is easily perceived within an older worker's UFOV perceptual span. It has been suggested the lighting should be focused on select areas in a workspace to enhance the perceptual and selective attention capabilities of workers across the lifespan.

Reduced Visual Acuity. Older adults, in general, are less able to make fine visual discriminations, although the extent of this difficulty is not clear from the existing research (Fozard, 1990; Kline & Schieber, 1985).

Researchers have suggested that employers should revise printed material to ensure an adequate size for legibility (Charness & Bosman, 1990; Garg, 1991). Such measures as the use of larger print on signs and adjustable font sizes for computerized displays and tablets aid older adults especially.

CHANGES IN HEARING

Some auditory changes that occur with age include difficulty hearing sounds at high frequencies, greater distractibility, and increasing difficulty with the speed of presentation (Fozard, 1990; Stine, Wingfield, & Poon, 1989). In addition to these auditory changes, older adults are sometimes able to hear a pure tone at a given loudness but cannot understand a spoken word at the same noise level. This is known as the phonemic regression effect. Older adults also may respond more dramatically to slight increase in volume (Stine et al., 1989). Other studies indicate, however, that consonants and consonant–vowel combinations may have different

intensity without causing the overall noise level to be too high for older adults. This could lead to potentially interesting interventions, in and out of the workplace (Fozard, 1990).

Suggestions have been given for improving the auditory characteristics of the work environment for older adults (Charness & Bosman, 1990). Noise levels in general should be decreased to reduce distracting noise. Noise from machinery, heating equipment, etc., should be muffled if possible (e.g., use of sound-absorbing materials such as curtains or sound-canceling headphones). Eliminate possible echoes in a room (e.g., position the speaker and audience to best utilize the room acoustics). Avoid high-frequency sounds (i.e., 4000 hertz and above) in the work or living space. To assist the older adult in selectively attending to important noises (e.g., a smoke alarm), increase the volume of such noises so there is a good auditory contrast effect. In a group discussion format, it is important to enhance visual cues of communication to compensate for older adults' decline in auditory functioning capabilities (e.g., a speaker should facilitate use of visual cues when speaking and listening; seat groups in a circle to improve visual cue attendance of older adults; limit the size of the group to help integration of auditory and visual communications).

CHANGES IN PERCEPTUAL SPEED

The generalized slowing hypothesis proposes that age-related deficits are spread throughout the cognitive processing system, and that performance declines are tied to the amount of processing rather than any specific component (Salthouse, 1985). Cerella (1990) attributes these declines to random breaks in the neural connections in the brain that build linearly over time but exponentially affect the pathways along which thoughts and motor responses travel. Cerella describes two slowing functions for older adults, finding they take 1.22 times longer to complete perceptual-motor functions and 1.82 times longer to complete cognitive functions. Using these functions, Cerella ignores higher-level cognitive processes, taking the position that generalized slowing can adequately account for age-related declines.

Another generalized approach has theorized that age-related changes can be attributed to changes in the quantity of mental resources. Resources that have been proposed are working memory and processing rate. Researchers, however, have found support for multiple aging mechanisms (i.e., several factors) that contribute to age-related declines (Salthouse,

Kausler, & Saults, 1988). Future research is still required to understand these cognitive declines.

Age-Related Cognitive Changes in Performance

There are real complexities in the relationships between cognitive change and work ability. There are also very different concerns from the perspective of the organization and from the perspective of the person self-managing his or her career. Generally, changes in intelligence, memory, and learning would be discussed (Schaie, 2011). With a thought for stimulating what trends may emerge in the future, we will instead present our thinking regarding effortful and automatic processing and the development and maintenance of expertise. In particular, we will examine how well-practiced skills can be affected by changes in cognitive ability. Dynamic approaches may not be as palatable or well understood to managers and business researchers; however, the efforts by the cognitive sciences over the past decades have produced mental models reflecting great diversity and individual change in adult and older adult workers. These models are beginning to help us understand how well-documented general declines in perceptual and motor speed affect the combined effects of increasing knowledge, skills, and practice that are experienced by workers. This naturally leads to suggestions on appropriate interventions and accommodations that can support work functioning and behaviors challenged by changing abilities, disabilities, and emerging chronic conditions.

CHANGES IN INTELLIGENCE

Over 40 years of gerontological research has provided important information regarding intellectual ability, learning, and memory. Major longitudinal studies (Schaie, 1985) have shown that most individuals maintain stable intellectual functioning well into their 70s and beyond. Unless there is a major health problem, most people remain at the same level of intellectual ability up to very late life.

There are age-related changes in the central nervous system, and as a result a person's information processing capacity also changes. Neuronal loss with age in the brain is highly individual and is particularly affected by behaviors such as reading and smoking and chronic conditions such as dementia. Recent evidence has demonstrated that plasticity and modifiability in brain function continue well into late adulthood (Papalia, Sterns, Feldman, & Camp, 2007). In cases where adults must divide attention and process complex information,

performance goes down with age. While speed and efficiency of processing may be affected by aging, most job situations do not involve maximal levels of performance. Thus, most adult and older adult workers can perform satisfactorily (Papalia et al., 2007). For many work-related cognitive abilities, there is no age variation across the working years (Warr, 1993).

This raises the methodological issue of proper measurement of changes across the lifespan, particularly as they are not often studied from an organizational perspective and in a work context. As a result, there are potential limitations of cognitive research in terms of the implications for working adults. Specifically, there are different results when examining age-related change if the research design of a study is cross-sectional, time lag, or longitudinal (Schaie, 1965, 2011). Studies involving cross-sectional design tend to show changes in cognitive ability (Schaie, 1974, 2011) when longitudinal designs do not show such significant changes, each with respective confounds of selective sampling, selective dropout, selective survival, practice effects (longitudinal), and generation effects (cross-sectional) (Schaie, 1965, 2011).

Kanfer (2009) discusses the role that intelligence may play in person–job fit. Person–job fit is the match of a person's knowledge, skills, and abilities to the task requirements of a specific job. Employees who perform jobs that have strong demands on fluid abilities or general problem-solving abilities may experience a change in levels of ability that may eventually affect maximal levels of job performance. This creates a gap in performance that the person may be aware of and can lead to changes in self-perceptions of a person's ability to do the job. This is in contrast to crystallized abilities or knowledge-based skills, which are not likely to be affected by changes in cognitive function. However, greater effort may be required to maintain a professional knowledge base as one ages, such as the latest rules and regulations in a field, and that effort may be tempered by a person's ability and motivation to continue learning. Kanfer concludes that individuals may require management support in terms of awareness of performance and that a person may need to be moved into a position that has a better person–job fit with his or her current abilities. From our perspective, we would support regular assessment through proper performance appraisal that would provide the necessary data for both the employee and employer to monitor person–job fit (A. Sterns & H. Sterns, 1995).

From a self-management perspective, taking a lifespan approach research shows changes in some capabilities (e.g., fluid intelligence in problem-solving capabilities) while there is stability in other areas of performance (e.g., areas of expertise, crystallized knowledge). This has direct implications for how organizations manage their workforce in terms of understanding ways to monitor change, provide training and skill maintenance (e.g., transfer), and reward job-related performance through the use of knowledge management and appraisal systems (i.e., proceduralized knowledge bases).

Bowen, Noack, and Staudinger (2011) talked of the importance of selective optimization with compensation in the maintenance of older adult performance. This idea of compensatory behaviors has direct relevancy for appropriately measuring performance, as in the classic transcription typing study by Salthouse (1984). The study found older expert typists were able to compensate for age-related slowing in reaction time (e.g., finger tapping) through the utilization of an expanded eye–hand span and parallel processing (overlapping) of underlying performance segments of input, parsing, translation, and execution (Salthouse, 1984). Similarly, experts' ability to more readily identify patterns of events and propose workable solutions may also compensate for general cognitive slowing. Job experience has certainly been a better predictor of job performance than the age of an employee in the workplace (r = .18) (Avolio, Waldman, & McDaniel, 1990; Giniger, Dispenzieri, & Eisenberg, 1983; McDaniel, Schmidt, & Hunter, 1988).

There is an ever-growing need with today's rapidly aging workforce to identify key, scientifically supported, age-related changes in performance and the limitations they impose in order to develop appropriate remedial and preventive interventions and reasonable accommodations for older workers (Kliegl & Baltes, 1987). Only then can appropriate organization-based policies be developed and interventions implemented.

Skill obsolescence is particularly relevant to both the organization and the person (A. Sterns, H. Sterns, & Hollis, 1996). Organization-based policies play a role in motivating employees to maintain expertise, and organizational-based factors may often work against older workers' being encouraged or reinforced to maintain their skill and knowledge base (Rosen & Jerdee, 1995; Stagner, 1985).

CHANGES IN COGNITIVE TASK PERFORMANCE

Laboratory performance by older adults presents an apparent paradox with real-world job performance. While clearly still capable of maintaining a good level of work-related performance in the workplace, older adults demonstrate age-related declines in performance on lab-related cognitive tasks. It is important to discuss the relevant meta-analytic research exploring the relationship between age and performance and how to approach the lab/job performance paradox.

Examining the findings of job performance data, two well-cited meta-analytic studies concluded that the relationship depends importantly on the type of job performance being measured and the type of job. Waldman and Avolio (1986) found that objective measures showed some increases with age, but subjective supervisory ratings showed slight declines. McEvoy and Cascio (1989) did not find any relationship between age and performance, which should be considered a positive finding in that no negative age effect was found. Because the age–performance link may vary with particular performance dimensions, individual differences that are rarely explored longitudinally, and contextual situations within an organization, it is not unexpected that the research would be inconsistent given the challenges (Sterns & Miklos, 1995; Warr, 1994).

There are a few examples of attempts to account for individual characteristics and organizational and contextual situations to address the age–performance question. Because of such studies' scarcity, we note several interesting model studies over the past three decades. First, a series of garment industry studies were conducted by Giniger, Dispenzieri, and Eisenberg (1983) to determine the extent of age differences in speed of sewing performance and inspection skill. The studies revealed that older workers' performance was superior to younger workers' performance, and this was attributed to older workers' increased experience on the job that ameliorated any age-related decline factors. Similarly, Perlmutter, Kaplan, and Nyquist (1990) found that though older food service workers showed age-related declines on measures of reaction time, they were still comparable in job knowledge and performance to younger workers on the job.

From a self-management perspective, the main issue for the individual worker is how to keep current and competitive (Sterns & Huyck, 2001). In terms of learning and memory, the general conclusion for learning is that older adults can learn as well as younger individuals, but it will take them more time. This means that people maintain intellectual and learning ability, should be able to continue to perform in familiar job roles, and can be trained for new ones. The best way is to take advantage of relevant training both within as well as outside the current employment situation (Sterns & Doverspike, 1989).

From the organizational perspective, it is important to realize that older adults are capable of learning and growing through educational experiences (Peterson, 1986), and this has direct implications for ensuring the availability of older adult education and training opportunities for older learners in the organization. Maintaining and updating discipline-specific knowledge and skills is particularly important for scientists and engineers. Sturman's (2003) study of 115 empirical studies examined job complexity in terms of age and performance. The meta-analysis found that performance increased with mean age of the sample in high-complexity jobs (like science and engineering) while declining in low-complexity jobs. Hedge, Borman, and Lammlain (2006) emphasize that older workers with a higher level of expertise or experience can be as effective as younger workers, particularly when both have equal access to skill-updating opportunities. With dramatic changes in Web-based and now mobile training opportunities, it can be expected that opportunities will become more equally available, and the role of motivation to learn will become the key factor. What is important to keep in mind is that both the organization and the individual have a part to play. Evidence is mounting that intrinsic rewards of work, job satisfaction, relationships with coworkers, and a sense of participating in meaningful work become more important as an individual ages. Most jobs allow older adults to continue to participate in these benefits until they feel that they have the financial resources and personal network outside of the workplace to retire (Bowen, Noack, & Staudinger, 2011).

Organizational-based barriers to training and retraining opportunities are serious in terms of limiting the true growth potential of individuals across the lifespan and present the issue of blatant ageism (Kimmel, 1988; Sterns, Sterns, & Hollis, 1996) and age discrimination in the context of availability of updating skill opportunities for older workers who may be in the position of losing their jobs and work skill competency in the workforce (Rothwell et al., 2008; Sterns & Alexander, 1987, 1988).

Willis and Dubin (1990) proposed that a preventive approach to skill obsolescence, the maintenance of professional competency, is an important issue for older workers. An organization that encourages workers to maintain and improve the skills required to excel at their job and provides challenging work and the opportunity to inject new ideas will not only be more likely to stay ahead of its competitors, but also will have reduced turnover and retain more productive employees.

Older adults bring experience and extensive skills to any job. They have had a lifetime of communicating, overcoming hardships, solving problems, and acquiring lessons learned. Older employees have had years to integrate their knowledge with practical experience to develop efficient methods of accomplishing their work. When new techniques arise, open-minded older workers are often the best source to determine how successful new ideas will be and how best to implement them.

EXPERTISE, PROBLEM SOLVING, AND DECISION MAKING

A majority of executives, senior politicians, and world leaders are older adults. They make most important and far-reaching decisions on a daily basis and successfully carry out their leadership responsibilities. Despite many decades of research attention to information processing, how cognitive changes over the lifespan affect performance are not well understood.

Even if performance does decline with age, this still leaves open the source of the decline. KSAs that affect job-specific performance may simply become obsolete (Fossum, Arvey, Paradise, & Robbins, 1986). The mainframe computer systems and machine language programming skills of the 1980s have been replaced with new languages controlling cloud-based server farms and cross-platform mobile programming environments. KSA obsolescence resulting in inadequate performance may be due to changes over time in job characteristics, motivation, individual orientations, organizational factors, and organizational structure (Howard & Bray, 1988; Kanfer, 2009). If obsolescence is the cause of decline, this is encouraging because with training this is correctable. But other evidence supports other causes of decline that may be more fundamental.

In one of the only studies of age and management team performance, Streufert, Pogash, Piasecki, and Post (1991) presented different age groups with a challenging day-long, decision-making simulation. Groups composed of older subjects (75 and older) demonstrated significantly different performances and strategies from those composed of middle-aged (45 to 55) and young (28 to 35) subjects. Strategy differences included asking for less additional information, having less breadth to their overview of the simulation (having a more restricted conceptualization of the task), using fewer avenues to effect changes, and planning that was less effective and less optimal. The older groups performed more poorly in the simulation, and their planning was of less complexity than that of the other groups. The older groups were similarly motivated and expressed satisfaction with their performance, unaware of their much longer decision making and less extensive information searches as compared to younger groups. Interestingly, no differences emerged in responding to emergencies between the different age groups, perhaps due to shorter information searches. Importantly, cognitive processes, rather than motivational differences, both of which were assessed, appeared to play a strong role in explaining the differences between the older and younger managers, though these differences may be cohort-specific rather than age-related.

Clearly, older workers are in positions of responsibility in every occupation and make important decisions affecting employees throughout their organizations. Is their decision making affected by the aging process? And if so, to what extent?

CHANGES IN CREATIVITY AND IDEA PRODUCTIVITY

Creativity is an important area of study in lifespan changes in cognitive abilities. Creativity may be indicative of originality and productivity. While some researchers have found that creativity may decline in the later years (see Kausler, 1992; Simonton, 1990; Sternberg & Lubart, 2001, for reviews), a recent meta-analysis by Ng and Feldman (2008) examined the relationship between age and job performance, focusing on ten performance dimensions, including core task performance and creativity. They found that age was not related to most of core task performance and creativity. Research focusing on creative productivity has led to conclusions of decline in later career production compared to that in the earlier stage of a career. Other researchers have considered the relationship between age and creative processes using more standardized measures and more controlled conditions.

If previous knowledge is linked to creativity in older adults, then it is important to understand how previously stored information can be optimally transferred from one problem to another. If this process is understood, interventions can be designed and applied to the training of older employees.

Research on transferring information from one problem to another has focused on the distinction between surface and deep structure problem features. Surface features are defined as the characteristics of a problem. Deep structure features are the underlying relationships between the problem characteristics. Deep structures can be thought of as the rules necessary for solving a problem.

Stein (1989) argues that both surface and deep structure features must be present to guarantee transfer of knowledge from one situation to the next. In contrast, Kotovsky and Fallside (1989) argue that transfer of knowledge from one problem to another is optimized when the task is designed to evoke established naturally organized memories.

Novick (1988) considered expert and novice differences in transferring information from one problem to another. When two problems share deep structure features, experts are more likely than novices to appropriately transfer information from the first problem to the second. When the two problems shared surface features but not deep structure features, novices were more likely than experts to inappropriately transfer information from the first problem to the second.

Thus, the findings from expertise research, such as the above studies, offer valuable information in the design of training programs and job design that utilize existing knowledge bases of older workers to optimize transfer and maintain professional competencies across the lifespan. When experts feel their skills are no longer a good fit, or their knowledge base provides insufficient experience with new situations and technology, and the desire to obtain the necessary training to return to an expert state wanes, then this may be the trigger that leads to retirement. But it is not only knowledge changes that may challenge experts' abilities to collect and process information; there may be other biological changes that contribute.

Impact of ADEA and ADA on the Workplace

The basis of the chronological perspective is the Age Discrimination in Employment Act (ADEA) of 1967. The ADEA protected workers with a chronological age greater than 40 years to an age of 65. In 1978, the ADEA was amended to extend its coverage to age 70. In addition, the amendment abolished mandatory retirement for federal employees. The most recent amendment, in 1986, removed the maximum age restriction with certain exceptions. In terms of the ADEA, an older worker is any individual 40 and over who is still an active worker (Snyder & Barrett, 1988). Being classified as an older worker affords certain protections against discrimination. Stereotypes about declining abilities and declining productivity may contribute to discrimination against older workers, which these laws were designed to defend against.

The Americans with Disabilities Act (ADA) of 1990 offers additional protection to older adults, as well as the disabled. Many of the ailments associated with older adults are now classified as disabilities (Papinchock, 2005). To fail to hire or promote an older worker because of some belief about older workers' abilities based on their age is illegal and leaves an organization open to potential litigation.

ADA defines disabled as any physiological disorder or condition, cosmetic disfigurement, or anatomical loss affecting one or more body systems (neurological, musculoskeletal, special sense organs, respiratory, cardiovascular are examples) and also includes infectious and contagious diseases. In contrast, if an individual does not take medication as prescribed or cannot read, the person is not considered disabled according to case law. A communicable disease, however, such as tuberculosis or HIV, is considered a disability (School Board of Nassau County v. Arline, 1987).

The ADA requires that an employer make reasonable accommodations in administering employment tests to eligible applicants or employees with disabling impairments in sensory, manual, or speaking skills. The test must be in formats that do not require the use of the impaired skill. Reasonable accommodation may be acceptable in one instance but not in another. Very specific position analysis must now be used to determine the essential skills and the experience and education level needed for a position and to test only those skills. The job analysis techniques described above, if done correctly and thoroughly, will provide the level of detail required.

It is important to understand that employers do not have to alter the qualification requirements for the position. In addition, a medical exam cannot be required prior to hiring the individual. These changes should aid older adults as well as the disabled. The ADA requires that individuals be allowed to demonstrate their qualifications. If an employer does not select the most qualified applicant, this is discrimination and the applicant has grounds to pursue litigation. Again, it must be emphasized that an employer does not have to alter standards and

does not have to initiate an affirmative action program. Any function that is critical to the job, such as attendance, can be an essential function. Critical tasks, such as a firefighter carrying a person out of a building, though seldom done, must be able to be performed in order to hold that job (Landy, 1992).

The ADA should provide additional protections for older adults, especially those returning from illnesses, such as heart attacks and strokes. The employee has demonstrated qualification by already holding the position prior to illness. The employee must be allowed to return to work, even with impairments, if he or she can perform the essential functions of the position with reasonable accommodation (Sterns & Barrett, 1992).

Though disabilities and limitations become more likely as people age, these changes do not affect most older adults. Further, disabilities are not a result of normal aging; they are a result of genetics, accidents, or disease. Laws now in place protect older workers with disabilities as well as young workers. When older adults are impaired by a disability, they should seek the support necessary to accommodate their disability and continue receiving the intrinsic and extrinsic rewards of working.

Despite the statutory text stating that the ADEA prohibits discrimination because of "age," in *Hazen Paper Co. v. Biggins*, 507 U.S. 604 (1993), the Supreme Court reasoned that the ADEA only prohibits actions based on inaccurate or stigmatizing stereotypes about age. In *Kentucky Retirement Systems v. EEOC*, 554 U.S. ___, 128 S.Ct. 2361 (2008), the Supreme Court held that the use of age as an explicit factor in determining eligibility for benefits is not on the issues face discriminatory. Despite seven decades of research on employment and age, research has not been the driving factor in decisions on age discrimination and employment cases.

The recent transformation of the Administration on Aging to the Administration on Community Living provides a new opportunity to further explore ways in which issues of aging and disability can be considered jointly with a new perspective. Community living embodies the idea of aging-in-place and remaining engaged in the community. Turning the emphasis to community living, the administration can set policy and research that addresses the combined needs of individuals who are experiencing age-related change and disability, with an emphasis on new solutions and new interventions that allow people of all cultures and economic backgrounds to age-in-place both in work and in retirement.

Prolonging Productivity of Workers Across the Lifespan

Designing a workplace that supports older workers in their efforts to remain updated and competent is one important application of motivation research. The design of training equipment that has age-sensitive considerations that take into account age-related factors (e.g., decline in visual acuity) has many advantages for an older adult learner and the employer.

First, the equipment, particularly mobile devices such as smartphones and tablets, will assist older workers in adopting compensatory behaviors to adapt to the work demands of the task (A. Sterns, 2005). Other modifications, such as cues giving more attention to monitoring oneself for safety reasons, can also have a substantial impact on older workers. Second, a deeper degree of learning the training material may be achieved if the training design allows the avoidance of distractions that may hinder the allocation of working memory in learning the task. It is hypothesized that there will be an increase in trainees' feelings of trainability and job performance competency, especially among older trainees, if age-related factors are accounted for when designing training programs.

From an organizational perspective, the potential loss of productivity that can occur if proper design/redesign of training and job equipment is not taken into account may be substantial. Organizations may have to use limited time, capital, and human resources to correct for this oversight by implementing corrective training programs, changes in selection process, and/or supervision techniques (Howell, 1992). It is pragmatic for organizations to evaluate and understand the underlying cognitive subsystem of the man–machine system to ensure that there is a proper match between employee and equipment characteristics in equipment design, especially for older adults.

The following section will address specific examples of workplace interventions that could be designed to enhance the work experience of older adults.

Suggestions for Organization-Based Interventions

The following will be a discussion of some specific workplace design considerations that have been addressed in the ergonomic literature and their implications for older workers. For example, workspace and computer design are two areas that can be examined with specific consideration for the needs

of older workers. In addition, the transfer of trained skills to the workplace is a special issue that should be considered when discussing how to design training programs suited for the learning needs of older workers (A. Sterns & H. Sterns, 2007).

General Workplace Design

According to Fisk et al. (2009), there should be an increase in the level of illumination (e.g., at the top and bottom landings of stairs, hallways, and elevators) for older adults. To compensate for decreasing dark adaptation capabilities of older adults, sudden and pronounced transitions in the level of illumination should be avoided. For example, lighting in a workplace should be designed with considerations of consistent lighting levels between different areas of an industrial manufacturing plant, especially avoiding a transition from high- to low-level lighting in a room that may contain disability-related dangers for older employees (e.g., steps descending to a lower level).

Since older adults have more difficulty with some color discriminations, avoid using materials that are within the blue–green range of colors, and avoid using colors of the same hue (e.g., do not have carpet colors of the same hues when there is a step or transition from one level to another level).

Using soft white bulbs and glare-free computer screens would help reduce glare in the workplace, and design of workstations should include adjustable light sources.

Because of the age-related decline in ability to read certain sizes of print, larger print sizes should be used in text material (i.e., font size should be at least size 8 millimeters) and on signs (i.e., print size should be at least 15 mm). Lastly, a way to compensate for age-related visual decline is to increase contrast (target luminance) in a room to enhance older adults' visual discrimination capabilities.

Workspace Design

The importance of a well-designed workstation cannot be stressed too much. It is usually the standard to design office equipment so it can be adjusted to the needs of most individuals, from the 5th to the 95th percentile of the relevant population characteristics (e.g., anthropometric consideration of arm reach and sitting height of workers in the workspace). The standards of equipment design tend to focus on the average worker's physical characteristics, but as will be discussed, there are physical dimension changes that occur with age (e.g., decrease in height of worker).

Although age-related physical changes of older workers may not require significant equipment design measures, it is a consideration for organizations as the percentage of individuals over age 65 is projected to represent approximately 17% of the total population (Sanders & McCormick, 1993). Future research may focus upon age-related changes in physical stature (e.g., height, weight). Horizontal work-surface design, seated work-surface heights, and standing work-surface heights in reference to older workers' anthropometric needs would be areas for further ergonomic research.

Proper seating design can promote computer operator comfort and bodily support by examining the relationship between the body structure of the employee and the physical demands of the workspace (e.g., the reaching distance according to the design of the desk/table, the keyboard, and the placement of the chair) (Sanders & McCormick, 1993).

To compensate for losses in strength, an older worker could use a mechanical lift to carry heavy objects overhead. If lifting is required of the older worker, the load should be kept close to the body, and lifting that requires bending, stooping, or twisting should be eliminated. This can be done by rearranging storage facilities and providing lifting aids for heavier objects. Also, workers should be given a rest between lifts and given good foot traction to reduce tripping hazards.

With regard to changes in mobility, one suggestion has been to use "buffer" stocks between assembly line positions (Welford, 1988). Buffer stocks are small surpluses of assembly items either feeding into or along assembly lines or process lanes used to minimize the impact of items requiring more labor time. The stock moves out of the buffer at the line pace, but the stock is replenished at a slower pace. The buffer may be replenished by working additional hours off-shift, or increasing the number of labors filling the buffer.

Computer Design

In addition to designing the workspace of computer users, the design of the computer itself is relevant (Charness & Bosman, 1990). While older adults can effectively use computers (Czaja, 2001; Elias, Elias, Robbins, & Gage, 1987; Gist, Rosen, & Schwoerer, 1988; Hartley, Hartley, & Johnson, 1984; Jay & Willis, 1992), they are still less likely to do so than younger cohorts—but they are catching up quickly. Smartphone adoption has accelerated to include over half of teen, adult, and older adult

consumers in the United States, with over 25% of adults over 55 having a smartphone in the second quarter of 2010, growing to 30% in the following quarter. Tablets are similarly being adopted in great numbers by older consumers.

There are not yet any formal studies on the adoption of mobile tablets, and there are only a handful of studies on training with smartphones (Mayhorn & Sterns, 2006; Sterns, 2005). Training older adults on the computer has been shown to improve their attitudes toward computers (Jay & Willis, 1992; McNeely, 1991). From an ergonomic standpoint, the design of the computer can influence its user friendliness. Because of the constantly changing form factors, determining which design is most effective for older adults is an ongoing challenge. As previously mentioned, installation of a glare-free computer screen would be a viable intervention in the workplace to ameliorate age-related increases in glare sensitivity. Another work-related issue for older adults is that they may be wearing eyeglasses with bifocals or trifocals, which cause difficulties in reading information off a stationary computer screen; older employees who wear these types of eyeglasses would benefit from a computer screen that is adjustable and thus permits easier readability of information on the screen. Charness and Bosman (1990) also reviewed research that a computer system with a mouse may help reduce speed differences between older and younger adults in operating computers. Fisk et al. (2009) point to modifiable adjustments to change the sensitivity of the mouse to match the capabilities of the older user. Another workspace design issue suggested by the research of Jaschinski-Kruza (1990) is that older computer users may be more comfortable with somewhat longer viewing distances from the computer screen; thus, an adjustable workstation that permits such adjustments would be a possible consideration.

Conclusions and Recommendations for Future Researchers and Practitioners

Organizations and individuals self-managing their careers are faced with coping with many changes in the occupational environment. One change that is not often discussed is the changes occurring as workers age. It is clear that many older adults experience declines in physical, sensory, and, to some extent, cognitive abilities, although individuals may not experience significant cognitive decline across the lifespan. What is not clear, however, is how these declines affect performance at work and how such effects can be ameliorated through effective ergonomic design. It is also not clear the extent to which organizations today, and organizations with nearly twice as many older workers in the near future, will focus on, monitor, and act on these issues.

It is important to reiterate the point that although there can be recommendations for ergonomic interventions to ameliorate age-related decline factors (e.g., sensory decline), there may be no significant age-related decline for some individuals across most of their adult life. Moreover, there has been a relative paucity of research that has tested whether these ergonomic interventions actually do have significant ameliorating effects for older employees. Thus, more research to understand the real impact of ergonomic interventions for older adults in the workplace is recommended as an important area for future research.

An additional work-related issue to be considered is stress in the workplace. Sources of stress at work may include task-related factors such as information overload, equipment underload, and deficiencies of equipment design; interpersonal factors such as overcrowding; environmental factors (e.g., noise, heat, lighting, dirt, and squalor); and personal threats to physical safety, economic security, or self-esteem.

In dealing with stress, individuals have mediating factors such as personality, attitude, and coping skills. These ameliorate the subjective or perceived effects of stressors. In addition, it is important to understand mediating factors concerning how the perceived stress will manifest itself physically. For older workers, some stressors, such as information overload or poor air quality, may be exaggerated. For example, older adults are more affected by carbon monoxide, a common indoor air pollutant, than younger workers. Combined with less physical reserve to mediate the effects of perceived stress, this puts older workers at greater risk of stress-related difficulties. Not only does stress have physical outcomes, but performance and job satisfaction may also be sacrificed. Controlling sources of stress such as task design and environment will bolster older workers' capability to withstand stress. Research on how to best arm older workers who may be more vulnerable to the effects of stress should be another focus for future research.

Workplace design characteristics have been linked to the incidence of disability, but the specific effects of design on the performance of older workers have not been investigated. Results of various studies provide indirect, albeit conflicting, evidence concerning this issue. Some research in the area of fatigue and shiftwork demands indicates than younger workers may be at an advantage, but performance levels remain the same (Fuller, 1981, 1984; Snook, 1971; Zedeck, Jackson, & Summers, 1983).

Some research suggests that older adults may be less able to work in physically demanding occupations. Older men are more likely to leave physically demanding occupations (Hayward & Grady, 1986), while women are more likely to leave mentally demanding jobs. Past research addressed by Welford (1958) discovered that older workers were less often found in positions characterized by high time pressures. Thus, the possibility exists that older workers can compensate for the negative, physical effects of work in some occupations but not in others. Research should be conducted to identify the characteristics of the work environment, physical, functional, and psychological (e.g., stress associated with task), that could influence an older worker's performance. This topic of research is especially relevant when older workers are faced with the likelihood of entering a second career (e.g., entrepreneurial role in smaller business) or a bridge job that is similar to the former primary career.

In addition to the effects of physical characteristics of the work environment, the research has also shown that psychological characteristics of work, such as possibilities for development, can alleviate the negative effects of poor physical design (Hayward & Grady, 1986). Therefore, the psychological characteristics of the job as well as the physical aspects must be considered. The workplace should be designed to promote health for older adults (e.g., implementation of a "wellness" program). The job should be designed to promote mental stimulation, autonomy, and room for development.

It is important to address the quality of the lives of individuals who have lived with a disability or who have been ignored or forgotten as a result of poverty, racism, sexism, ageism, or other forms of social oppression (Blustein et al., 2008). There continues to be a need to develop employment-based approaches and programs to assist these individuals in a more successful and fulfilling work experience. It should never be considered too late to provide marketable work-based skills to marginalized individuals at any time or any age. Such programs should support continued employment, provide new knowledge and skills, and provide the global self-management skills to support ongoing work and contributions through volunteerism and enable the execution of successful late-life leisure and retirement. Moreover, broader systemic interventions are needed to ensure that older workers do not fall into poverty as they live longer, often with diminishing financial resources and constricting relational resources.

In conclusion, a combination of changing demographics with an increasingly sophisticated workplace puts greater emphasis on ergonomic and technological interventions in workspace design to extend the work life of older adults who desire to participate in the workforce. More empirical research in this area is greatly needed to understand and meet the needs of this growing aging workforce.

References

Age Discrimination in Employment Act of 1967, 29 U.S.C. Sec. 621 et seq. (1976 & Supp V. 1981 & 1986).

Americans With Disabilities Act of 1990 (P.L. 101-336), 42, U.S.C. 12101.

Avolio, B. J., & Barrett, G. V. (1987). The effects of age stereotyping in a simulated interview. *Psychology & Aging, 2,* 56–63.

Avolio, B. J., Barrett, G. V., & Sterns, H. L. (1984). Alternative to age for assessing occupational performance capacity. *Experimental Aging Research, 10,* 101–105.

Avolio, B. J., Waldman, D. A., & McDaniel, M. A. (1990). Age and work performance in nonmanagerial jobs: The effects of experience and occupational type. *Academy of Management, 33*(2), 407–422.

Baltes, P. B., Reese, H. W., & Lipsitt, L. P. (1980). Life-span developmental psychology. *Annual Review of Psychology, 31,* 65–110.

Beedon, L., & Wu, K. (2005). Women age 65 and older: Their sources of income. AARP Public Poverty Institute, October 2005. http://www.aarp.org.

Bird, C. P., & Fisher, T. D. (1986). Thirty years later: Attitudes toward the employment of older workers. *Journal of Applied Psychology, 71,* 515–517.

Birren, J. E., & Stafford, J. I. (1986). Changes in the organization of behavior with age. In J. E. Birren, P. Robinson, & J Livingston (Eds). *Age, health, & employment,* (pp. 1-26). New Jersay; Prentice Hall.

Blustein, D. L., Kenna, A. C., Gill, N., & DeVoy, J. E. (2008). The psychology of working: A new framework for counseling practice and public policy. *Career Development Quarterly, 56,* 294–308.

Borbely, J. M. (2009). U.S. labor market in 2008: economy in recession. *Monthly Labor Review, 132,* 3–19.

Bowen, C. E., Noack, M. G., & Staudinger, U. M. (2011). Aging in the work context. In K. W. Schaie & S. L. Willis (Eds.), *Handbook of the Psychology of Aging* (7th ed., pp. 263–277). Boston: Academic Press.

BLS: U.S. Department of Labor. Bureau of Labor Statistics. (2007). Washington, DC: U.S. Government Printing Office.

BLS: U.S. Department of Labor. Bureau of Labor Statistics. (2008). Washington, DC: U.S. Government Printing Office.

BLS: U.S. Department of Labor. Bureau of Labor Statistics. (2010). Washington, DC: U.S. Government Printing Office.

Cappelli, P., & Novelli, W. (2010). *Managing the older worker: How to prepare for the new organizational order.* Boston: Harvard Business Press.

Carstensen, L. L. (2009). *A long bright future.* New York: Broadway Books.

Cascio, W. F., & Aguinis, H. (2005). *Applied psychology in human resource management.* New Jersey: Prentice Hall.

Cerella, J. (1990). Aging and information processing rate. In J. E. Birren & K. W. Schaie (Eds.), *Handbook of the psychology of aging* (3rd ed., pp. 201–221). New York: Academic Press.

Charness, N., & Bosman, E. A. (1990). Human factors and design for older adults. In J. E. Birren & K. W. Schaie (Eds.), *Handbook of the psychology of aging* (3rd ed., pp. 446–463). New York: Van Nostrand Reinhold.

Culler, K. L., & Sterns, H. L. (2010, November). *The impact of ADA and ADEA on employment after later life disability.* For Policy Series Symposium: Age Discrimination and Employment Issue of Older Workers in Good Times and Bad Times presented at the Gerontological Society of America Annual Conference, New Orleans, LA.

Czaja, S. J. (2001). Technological change and the older worker. In J. E. Birren & K. W. Schaie (Eds.), *Handbook of the psychology of aging* (5th ed., pp. 500–522). Boston: Academic Press.

Czaja, S. J., & Sharit, J. (2009). *Aging and work: Issues and implications in a changing landscape.* Baltimore, Md: Johns Hopkins University Press.

Elias, P. K., Elias, M. F., Robbins, M. A., & Gage, P. (1987). Acquisition of word-processing skills by younger, middle-age, and older adults. *Psychology and Aging, 2*(4), 340–348.

Farr, J. L., Tesluk, P. E., & Lein, S. R. (1998). Organizational structure of the workplace and the older worker. In K. W. Schaie & C. Schooler (Eds.), *Impact of work on older adults* (pp. 143–185). New York: Springer.

Ferrel, J., & Nakai, Y. (2012). *Job club experience.* Report for Mature Services Employment and Training Solutions, Akron, Ohio.

Fisk, A., Rogers, W., Charness, N., Czaja, S., & Sharit (2009). *Designing for older adults: Principles and creative human factors approaches* (2nd ed.). Boca Raton, FL: CRC Books.

Fossum, J. A., Arvey, R. D., Paradise, C. A., & Robbins, N. E. (1986). Modeling the skill obsolescence process: A psychological/economic integration. *Academy of Management Review, 11*(2), 363–374.

Fozard, J. L. (1990). Vision and hearing in aging. In J. E. Birren & K. W. Schaie (Eds.), *Handbook of the psychology of aging* (3rd ed., pp. 150–170). New York: Academic Press.

Fozard, J. L., & Gorsdon-Salant, S. (2001) Changes in vision and hearing with aging. In J. E. Birren & K. W. Schaie (Eds.), *Handbook of the psychology of aging* (5th ed., pp. 241–266). New York: Academic Press.Fraser, T. M. (1992). *Fitness for work.* London: Taylor and Francis.

Fuller, R. G. (1981). Determinants of time headway adopted by truck drivers. *Ergonomics, 24*(6), 463–474.

Fuller, R. G. (1984). Prolonged driving in convoy: The truck driver's experience. *Accident Analysis and Prevention, 16*(5/6), 371–382.

Garg, A. (1991). Ergonomics and the older worker: An overview. *Experimental Aging Research, 17*(3), 143–155.

Giniger, S., Dispenzieri, A., & Eisenberg, J. (1983). Age, experience, and performance on speed and skill jobs in an applied setting. *Journal of Applied Psychology, 68*(3), 469–475.

Gist, M., Rosen, B., & Schwoerer, C. (1988). The influence of training method and trainee age on the acquisition of computer skills. *Personnel Psychology, 41,* 255–265.

Goldstein, I. L., & Ford, J. K. (2002). *Training in organizations: Needs assessment, development, and evaluation*. Belmont, CA: Wadsworth.

Hall, D. T. (1971). Potential for career growth. *Personnel Administration, 34*, 18–30.

Hall, D. T. (1996). *The career is dead: Long live the career*. San Fransisco: Jossey-Bass.

Hall, D. T., & Mirvis, P. H. (1995a). The new career contract: Developing the whole person at midlife and beyond. *Journal of Vocational Behavior, 47*, 269–289.

Hall, D. T., &Mirvis, P. H. (1995b). Careers as lifelong learning. In A. Howard (Ed.), *The changing nature of work* (pp. 323–361). San Fransisco: Jossey-Bass.

Hall, D. T., &Mirvis, P. H. (1996). The new pretean career: Psychological success and the path with a heart. In D. T. Hall (Ed.), *1he career is dead: Long live the career*. San Fransisco: Jossey-Bass.

Hartley, A. A., Hartley, J. T., & Johnson, S. A. (1984). The older adult as computer user. In P. K. Robinson, J. Livingston, & J. E. Birren (Eds.), *Aging and technological advances* (pp. 347–348). New York: Plenum Press.

Hayward, M. D., & Grady, W. R. (1986). The occupational retention and recruitment of older men: The influence of structural characteristics of work. *Social Forces, 64*(3), 644–666.

Hazen Paper Co. v. Biggins, 507 U.S. 604 (1993).

Hedge, J., Borman, W., & Lammlain, S. (2006) *The aging workforce: realities, myths, and ipliocations for organizations*. Wasington D.C.: American Psychological Association.

Howard, A., & Bray, D. (1988). *Managerial lives in transition: Advancing age and changing times*. New York: Guilford Press.

Howell, W. C. (1992). Human factors in the workplace. In M. D. Dunnette & L. M. Hough (Eds.), *Handbook of industrial and organizational psychology* (Vol. 2, pp. 210–269). Palo Alto, CA: Consulting Psychologists Press, Inc.

Immerian, J. (2009). Aging and work: An international perspective. In S. Czaja & J. Sharit (Eds.), *Aging and work: Issues and implications in a changing landscape* (pp. 51–73). Baltimore: Johns Hopkins University Publishing.

Jaschinski-Kruza, W. (1990). On the preferred viewing distances to screen and document at VDU workplaces. *Ergonomics, 33*(8), 1055–1063.

Jay, G. M., & Willis, S. L. (1992). Influence of direct computer experience on older adults' attitudes toward computers. *Journal of Gerontology, 47*(4), 250–257.

Kanfer, R. (2009). Work and older adults: Motivation and performance. . In S. Czaja & J. Sharit (Eds.), *Aging and work: Issues and implications in a changing landscape* (pp. 209–231). Baltimore: Johns Hopkins University Publishing.

Kausler, D. H. (1992). *Experimental psychology, cognition, and human aging*. New York: Springer-Verlag.

Kelter, L. A. (2009, March). Substantial job losses in 2008: weakness broadens and deepens across industries. *Monthly Labor Review, 132*, 20–33.

Kentucky Retirement Systems v. EEOC, 554 U.S. ___, 128 S.Ct. 2361 (2008).

Kimmel, D. C. (1988). Ageism, psychology, and public policy. *American Psychologist, 43*, 175–178.

Kliegl, R., & Baltes, P. B. (1987). Theory-guided analysis of mechanisms of development and aging through testing-the-limits and research on expertise. In C. Schooler & K. W. Schaie (Eds.), *Cognitive functioning and social structure over the life course* (pp. 95–119). Norwood, NJ: Ablex.

Kline, D. W., & Schieber, F. (1985). Vision and aging. In J. E. Birren & K. W. Schaie (Eds.), *Handbook of the psychology of aging* (2nd ed., pp. 296–331). New York: Van Nostrand Reinhold.

Kotovsky, K., & Fallside, D. (1989). Representation and transfer in problem solving. In D. Klahr & K. Kotovsky (Eds.), *Complex information processing* (pp. 69–108). Hillsdale, NJ: Lawrence Erlbaum.

Landy, F. J. (1992). Alternatice to chronological age in determining standards of sutiability for public safety jobs. Tehcnical report. Pennsylvania State University.

Mayhorn, C., & Sterns, A. (2006). Perfecting the handheld computer for older adults: From cognitive theory to practical application. *Cognitive Technology, 12*(1), 15–21.

McDaniel, M. A., Schmidt, F. L., & Hunter, J. E. (1988). Job experience correlates of job performance. *Journal of Applied Psychology, 73*(2), 327–330.

McEvoy, G. M., & Cascio, W. F. (1989). Cumulative evidence of the relationship between employee age and job performance. *Journal of Applied Psychology, 74*(1), 11–17.

McLoughlin, C., Taylor, P., & Bohle, P. (2001) Promoting working resilience over the lifecourse. In B. Resnick, L. P. Gwythei, & K.A. Roberts (Eds.), *Reslience in agin: Concepts, research, & outcomes* (pp. 121–131). New York: Springer Publishing.

McNeely, E. (1991). Computer-assisted instruction and the older-adult learner. *Educational Gerontology, 17*, 229–237.

Munnel, A. H., Soto, M., & Golub-Sass, A. (2008). *Will people be healthy enough to work longer?* CRR WP 2008-11. Chestnut Hill, MA: Center for Retirement Research at Boston College.

Ng, T. W. H., & Feldman, D. C. (2008). The relationship of age to ten dimensions of job performance. *Journal of Applied Psychology, 93*, 392–423.

Noe, R. A. (1986). Trainees' attributes and attitudes: Neglected influences on training effectiveness. *Academy of Management Review, 11*, 736–749.

Novick, L. R. (1988). Analogical transfer, problem similarity, and expertise. *Journal of Experimental Psychology: Learning, Memory, and Cognition, 14*, 510–520.

Office of Disease Prevention and Health Promotion (2009). *Developing Healthy People 2020: The Road Ahead*. Washington, DC. US Department of Health and Human Services.

Owsley, C., Ball, K., Sloane, M. E., Roenker, D. L., & Bruni, L. (1991). Visual/cognitive correlates of vehicle accidents in older drivers. *Psychology and Aging, 6*(3), 403–415.

Papalia, D. E., Sterns, H. L., Feldman, R. D., & Camp, C. J (2007) *Desarrollo del adulto y vejez* (Spanish edition). Mexico: McGraw Hill.

Papinchock, J. M. (2005). Title I of the Americans with Disabilities Act; The short but active history of ADA enforcement and litigation. In F. J. Landy (Ed.), *Employment discrimination litigation: Behavioral, quantitative, and legal perspectives* (pp. 294–335). San Francisco, CA: Jossey-Bass.

Perlmutter, M., Kaplan, M., & Nyquist, L. (1990). Development of adaptive competence in adulthood. *Human Development, 33*, 185–197.

Peterson, D. A. (1986). *Facilitating education for older learners*. San Francisco, CA: Jossey-Bass Publishers.

Pitt-Catsouphes, M., & Smyer, M. (2005) *Older workers; What keeps them working? The Center on Aging and Work/Workplace Flexibilty*. Chesnuts Heill, MA: Boston College. Retrieved August 20, 2008, from: https://agingandwork.bc.edu/documents/Center_On_Aging_and_Work_Brief_One.pdf.

Posthuma, R. A., & Campion, M. A. (2009). Age stereotypes in the workplace: Common stereotypes, moderators, and future research directions. *Journal of Management, 35*, 158–188.

Rix, S. (2005). *Rethinking the role of older workers: Promoting older worker employment in Europe and Japan.* Washington, DC: AARP.

Rix, S. E. (2011a). *Recovering from the Great Recession: Long struggle ahead for older Americans.* Insight on the Issues. Washington, DC: AARP Public Policy Institute

Rix, S. E. (2011b). Employment and aging. In B. Binstock & L. George (Eds.), *Handbook of aging and social sciences* (7th ed., pp. 193–206). Burlington, MA: Academic Press.

Rix, S. E. (2011c). *Boomers sail into retirement or do they?* Public Policy and Aging Report, pp. 34–39. Washington, DC: National Academy on an Aging Society.

Rosen, B., & Jerdee, T. H. (1990). Middle and late career problems: Causes, consequences, and research needs. *Human Resource Planning, 13*(1), 59–70.

Rosen, B. & Jerdee, T. H. (1995). *The persistence of age and sex stereotypes in the 1990s: the influence of age and gender in management decision making.* Washington, DC: AARP Public Policy Press.

Rothwell, W. J., Sterns, H. L., Spokus, D., & Reaser, J. M. (2008). *Working longer: New strategies for managing, training, and retaining older workers.* New York: American Management Association.

Salthouse, T. A. (1984). Effects of age and skill in typing. *Journal of Gerontology, 113*, 345–371.

Salthouse, T. A. (1985). Speed of behavior and its implications for cognition. In J. E. Birren & K. W. Schaie (Eds.), *Handbook of the psychology of aging* (pp. 400–426). New York: Van Nostrand Reinhold.

Salthouse, T. A., Kausler, D. H., & Saults, J. S. (1988). Investigation of student status, background variables, and feasibility of standard tasks on cognitive aging research. *Psychology and Aging, 3*, 29–37.

Sanders, M. S., & McCormick, E. J. (1993). *Human factors in engineering and design.* New York: McGraw-Hill.

Schaie, K. W. (1965). A general model for the study of developmental problems. *Psychological Bulletin, 64*, 91–107.

Schaie, K. W. (1974). Translation in gerontology—from lab to life: Intellectual functioning. *American Psychologist, 29*, 802–807.

Schaie, K. W. (1985). Intellectual development in adulthood. In J. E. Birren & K. W. Schaie (Eds.), *Handbook of the psychology of aging* (pp. 291–310). New York: Van Nostrand Reinhold.

Schaie, K. W. (2011). Historical influences on aging and behavior. In K. W. Schaie & S. L. Willis (Eds.), *Handbook of the psychology of aging* (7th ed., pp. 263–277). Boston: Academic Press.

Schmidt, J., & Jones, J. (2012). *Low-wage workers are older and better educated than ever.* Washington, DC: Center for Economic and Policy Research. Retrieved from www.cepr. net on July 20, 2012.

School Board of Nassau County v. Arline (1987).

Schwab, D. P., & Heneman, H. G., III (1978). Age stereotyping in performance appraisal. *Journal of Applied Psychology, 63*, 573–578.

Sherman, S. R. (1985). Reported reasons retired workers left their last job: Findings from the New Beneficiary Survey. *Social Security Bulletin, 48*, 22–30.

Shultz, K. S., & Adams, G. A. (2007). *Aging and work in the 21st century.* Mahwah, NJ: Lawrence Erlbaum Associates.

Simonton, D. K. (1990). Creativity and wisdom in aging. In J. E. Birren & K. W. Schaie (Eds.), *Handbook of the psychology of aging* (3rd ed., pp. 320–329). New York: Academic Press.

Snook, S. N. (1971). The design of manual handling tasks. *Ergonomics, 21*, 963–985.

Snyder, C. J., & Barrett, G. V. (1988). The Age Discrimination in Employment Act: A review of court decisions. *Experimental Aging Research, 14*, 3–55.

Stagner, R. (1985). Aging in industry. In J. E. Birren & K. W. Schaie (Eds.), *Handbook of the psychology of aging* (pp. 789–815). New York: Van Nostrand Reinhold.

Stein, B. S. (1989). Memory and creativity. In J. A. Glover, R. R. Ronning, & C. R. Reynolds (Eds.), *Handbook of creativity* (pp. 163–176). New York: Plenum Press.

Sternberg, R. J., & Lubart, T. I. (2001). Wisdom and creativity. In J. E. Birren & K. W. Schaie (Eds.), *Handbook of the psychology of aging* (5th ed., pp. 500–522). Boston: Academic Press.

Sterns, A. A. (2005). Evaluation of a curriculum design and program to train older adults to use personal digital assistants. *Gerontologist, 45*, 828–834.

Sterns, A. A., & Sterns, H. L. (2007). Developing products for seniors. In D. L. Owens & D. R. Hausknecht, *Marketing in the 21st century, Vol. 4: Consumer behavior and integrated marketing communications* (pp. 82–106). New York: Praeger Perspectives.

Sterns, A. A., Sterns, H. L., & Hollis, L. A. (1996). The productivity and functional limitations of older adult workers. In W. H. Crown (Ed.), *Handbook on employment and the elderly,* (pp. 276–303). Westport, CT: Greenwood.

Sterns, H. L. (1986). Training and retraining adult and older worker. In J. E. Birren & J. Livingston (Eds.), *Age, health, and employment* (pp. 93–113). Englewood Cliffs, NJ: Prentice-Hall.

Sterns, H. L., & Alexander, R. A. (1987). Industrial gerontology: The aging individual and work. In K. W. Schaie (Ed.), *Annual review of gerontology and geriatrics* (pp. 93–113). New York: Springer.

Sterns, H. L., & Alexander, R. A., (1988). Performance appraisal of the older worker. In H. Dennis (Ed), *Fourteen steps in managing an aging workforce* (pp. 85–93). New York: Lexington.

Sterns, H. S., & Barrett, G. V. (1992). *Work (paid employment) and aging.* Paper presented at the National Institute of Aging Workshop entitled "Applied Gerontology Research: Setting A Future Agenda," August 12–13, 1992. Bethesda, MD: Department of Health and Human Services, National Institute on Aging.

Sterns, H. L., & Chang, B. (2010). Workforce issues and retirement. In J. Cavanaugh & C. Cavanaugh (Eds.), *Aging in America: Societal issues* (pp. 81–105). Sanata Barbara, CA: Praeger.

Sterns, H. L., & Dawson, N. (2012). Emerging perspectives on resilience in adulthood and later life: Work, retirement, and resilience. In B. Hayslip Jr. & G. Smith (Eds.), *Annual review of gerontology and geriatrics:. Emerging perspectives on resilience in adulthood and later life, 32,* (pp. 211–230). New York: Spring.

Sterns, H. L., & Doverspike, D. (1989). Aging and training and learning process. In R. A. Katzell (Ed.), *Training and development in organizations* (pp. 299–332). San Francisco, CA: Jossey-Bass Publishers.

Sterns, H. L., Doverspike, D., & Lax, G. A. (2005). The age discrimination in employment act. In F. S. Landy (Eds.),

Employment discrimination litigation: Behavioral quantitative and legal perspectives (pp. 256–293). San Francisco: Jossey-Bass.Sterns, H. L. & Gray, J. H. (1999). Work, leisure, and retirement. In J. Cavanaugh & S. Whitbourne (Eds.), *Gerontology* (pp. 355–390). NY: Oxford University Press.

Sterns, H. L., & Huyck, M. H. (2001). Midlife and work. In M. E. Lachman (Ed.), *Handbook of midlife development* (pp. 447–486). New York: John Wiley & Sons, Inc.

Sterns, H. L., & Kaplan, J. (2003). Self-management of career and retirement. In T. Beehr & G. Adams (Eds.), *Retirement: Current research and future directions* (pp.188–213). New York: Springer Publishing Co.

Sterns, H. L., & McDaniel, M. A. (1994). Job performance and the older worker. In S. E. Rix (Ed.), *Older workers: How do they measure up?* (pp. 27–51). Washington, DC: Public Policy Institute, American Association of Retired Persons.

Sterns, H. L., & Miklos, S. M. (1995). The aging worker in a changing environment: Organizational and individual issues. *Journal of Vocational Behavior, 47*, 248–268.

Sterns, H. L., & Patchett, M. (1984). Technology and the aging adult: Career development and training. In P. R. Robinson & J. E. Birren (Eds.), *Aging and technology* (pp. 261–277). New York: Plenum Press.

Sterns, H. L., & Sterns, A. A. (1995). Health and employment capability of older Americans. In S. Bass (Ed.), *Older and active* (pp. 10–34). New Haven, CT: Yale University Press.

Sterns, H. L., & Subich, L. M. (2005). Counseling for retirement. In S. D. Brown & R. W. Lent (Eds.), *Career development and counseling: Putting theory and research to work.* (pp. 506–521). Hoboken, New Jersey: Wiley.

Stine, E. L., Wingfield, A., & Poon, L. W. (1989). Speech comprehension and memory through adulthood: The roles of time and strategy. In L. W. Poon, D. C. Rubin, & B. A. Wilson (Eds.), *Everyday cognition in adulthood and later years* (pp. 195–221). Cambridge: Cambridge Press.

Streufert, S., Pogash, R., Piasecki, M., & Post, G. M. (1991). Age and management team performance. *Psychology and Aging, 5*, 551–559.

Taylor, M. A., & Geldhauser, H. A. (2007). Low-income older workers. In K. Shultz & G. Adams (Ed.), *Aging in the 21st century* (pp. 25–49). London: Lawrence Erlbaum Associates.

Toossi, M. (2006, November). A new look at long-term labor force projections to 2050. *Monthly Labor Review, 129*, 19–36.

Toossi, M. (2007, November). Employment outlook: 2006–16: Labor force projections to 2016: more workers in their golden years. *Monthly Labor Review, 130*, 33–52.

Vercruyssen, M. (2009). Movement control and speed of behavior. In A. D. Fisk & W. A. Rogers (Eds.), *Handbook of human factors and the older adult* (pp. 55–86). San Diego, CA: Academic Press.

U. S. Department of Labor (1965). *The dictionary of occupational titles* (3rd ed.). Washington, DC: U. S. Government Printing Office.

Waldrop, J., & Stern, S. M. (2003). *Disability status: 2000.* Washington: U.S. Department of Commerce, Census Bureau.

Waldman, D. A., & Avolio, B. J. (1986). A meta-analysis of age differences in job performance. *Journal of Applied Psychology, 71*(1), 33–38.

Warr, P. (1994). Age and employment. In M. Dunnette, L. Hough, & H. Triandis (Eds.), *Handbook of industrial and organizational psychology* (Vol. 4). Palo Alto: Consulting Psychologists Press.

Warr, P. B. (2001). Age and work behavior: Physical attributes cognitive abilities, knowledge, personality traits, and motives. *International Review of Industrial and Organizational Psychology, 16*, 1–36.

Welford, A. (1958). *Aging and human skills.* London: Oxford Press.

Welford, A. (1988). Preventing adverse changes of work with age. *International Journal of Aging and Human Development, 27*(4), 283–291.

Wexley, K. N., & Latham, G. P. (2002). *Developing and Training Human Resources in Organizations* (3rd ed.). Upper Saddle River, NJ: Prentice Hall.

Willis, S. L., & Dubin, S. S. (1990). Maintaining professional competence: Directions and possibilities. In S. L. Willis & S. S. Dubin (Eds.), *Maintaining professional competence* (pp. 306–314). San Francisco, CA: Jossey-Bass.

Zedeck, S., Jackson, S. E., & Summers, E. (1983). Shift work schedules and their relationship to health, adaptation, satisfaction, and turnover intention. *Academy of Management Journal, 26*(2), 297–310.

Work and Disability

Ellen Fabian

Abstract

In American society, a job confers significant benefits, both extrinsic (standard of living) and intrinsic (psychosocial). For the vast majority of people with disabilities, access to these benefits has been severely limited, and even, in some cases, denied. Similar to other groups who have experienced attitudinal and environmental barriers to work, people with disabilities have engaged in a decades-long struggle to mitigate them. While there has been significant attention in the rehabilitation literature on barriers to employment, there has been much less attention toward understanding why people work, or the psychology of working for people with disabilities. This chapter presents an overview of some of the historical issues regarding work and people with disabilities, including vocational rehabilitation, attitudes, and predictors of employment. It concludes with a description of a theoretical model based on the psychology of working.

Key Words: disability, work, impairments, rehabilitation, models of disability

Introduction

For hundreds of years, and across the globe, people with disabilities have been among the most disenfranchised, impoverished, and unemployed groups in society (Barnes, 2000). Although having a disability in a developing country is an almost certain predictor of poverty and unemployment, the status of people with disabilities in the developed world is not much better. For example, in the United States, recent data released by the Bureau of Labor Statistics (BLS) reported that the employment–population ratio in 2009 for persons with disabilities was 19.2%, compared to 64.5% for people without a disability (BLS, 2010). The *unemployment* rate among persons with disabilities was 14.5% in 2009; and, perhaps most important, about 8 in 10 individuals with disabilities were not in the labor force, meaning that they are neither working nor looking for a job. Although the incidence of disability increases with age (about 50% of the population of people with disabilities is 65 and older), across all

age groups people with disabilities were more likely than those without to be out of the labor force. In terms of wanting a job, periodic surveys conducted by the National Council on Disability report that more than 60% of respondents with disabilities indicate their willingness to work (Bertoni, 2010). This is not surprising, as work is a central element of identity in American society, promoting access to social and material benefits.

There has been a long and expansive discourse in disability and rehabilitation research regarding the factors that facilitate and impede employment, a discussion that has evolved into considering the complex interplay among the person, behavioral, environmental, political, and social forces that influence work. These individual and contextual factors will be briefly reviewed in this chapter. However, significantly less attention has been paid to the psychological meaningfulness of work in the lives of people with disabilities, perhaps because of the complex political and social philosophies of disability, which have influenced thinking about the meaning of disability but have not expanded to a theoretical discourse on work and well-being (Barnes, 2000; Shaw, Segal, Polatajko, & Harburn, 2002). The purpose of this chapter is to consider work in the lives of people with disabilities from theoretical perspectives on disability. The chapter will (1) review the origins of policies and programs related to work and people with disabilities; (2) discuss the social and environmental circumstances that affect work-related behavior; and (3) examine the meaning of work from a theoretical framework.

Programs and Policies Related to Employment of People with Disabilities

Work or employment has been central to the field of vocational rehabilitation (VR) since the beginning of the 20th century, and historically, legal definitions of disability have been in part predicated on the ability to work. The public VR service system in the United States, which dates to 1917 (Patterson, Bruyere, Szymanski, & Jenkins, 2005), grew out of national policy designed to assist people with acquired disabilities to return to work; indeed, work was the central goal and rationale for the existence of the public VR program. Similar to the vocational guidance movement that was emerging in the United States at about the same time, VR service providers adopted a pragmatic approach to achieving employment goals by matching individual capacities to job requirements and demands. The early emphasis in the public VR program was on adults with acquired disabilities rather than those who had been born with them. During this period and until the mid-1970s, many children with congenital or developmental disabilities were excluded from mainstream public education in America and remained marginalized, frequently institutionalized and segregated, until the 1975 Education of all Handicapped Children Act was passed (Loprest & Maag, 2007). This law, together with the Rehabilitation Act of 1973, which addressed nondiscrimination in employment, reflected the dramatic shift in social attitudes and public policy toward educational, vocational, and social inclusion of children and youth with disabilities. However, the relatively recent enactment of these laws, together with uneven implementation across states, has resulted in many youth with disabilities having poor-quality academic experiences, a factor that significantly curtails their entry into employment (Loprest & Maag, 2007).

The policy shift that marked educational inclusion for children with developmental disabilities also affected the provision of services for adults. While the early intent of the public VR system was focused on retraining adults who acquired disabilities to facilitate their reentry into employment, community-based vocational rehabilitation programs (CRPs) serving adults with congenital disabilities proliferated in the 1970s and later. Early on, vocational training programs tended to be located in segregated work settings, called "sheltered workshops" or "transitional employment programs." The goal of these CRPs was habilitation into competitive jobs, but the majority of adults within them never achieved this goal, as federal incentives and viable employment support models were lacking until the late 1980s (Cimera, 2008). Even with these expanded incentives and significantly increased funding, an individual's likelihood of leaving a CRP and entering and maintaining employment remains fairly unlikely (Revell, Kregel Wehman, & Bond, 2000). In other words, while employment among all people with disabilities is poor, competitive employment rates for individuals with significant developmental disabilities were reported recently as less than 25% (Winsor & Butterworth, 2007). The challenges encountered by individuals with acquired disabilities, or those who were born with them, will be discussed in this chapter as they relate to motivating and sustaining employment. However, it is first important to explore the definition of disability.

Defining Disability

Another contextual issue critical to understanding the psychology of working for people with disabilities is the definition of disability. Altman (2001) stated that there is "no neutral language with which to discuss disability, and yet the tainted language itself and the categories used influence the definition of the problem" (p. 97). As national estimates of the proportion of Americans who are disabled range from 25 million to over 50 million, one can see that there must be confusion as to the definition of disability, with the emerging definitional ontology being ascribed to the individual's subjective perspective on his or her own condition. "My disability is how others view my disability" (Frank, 1988) captures some of the paradoxical difficulties in attempting to define disability. Unlike gender or race, "disability" can be a status that requires people to prove or document that they "belong," yet doing so can evoke the stereotypes and attitudes that are such pervasive barriers to employment access and advancement for people with disabilities. Moreover, as Stone (1984) and others have observed (Albrecht

& Bury, 2001), the recent history of disability in America (and the Western world) can be viewed from the perspective of disability being a "privileged" status. Stone goes on to explain that the disability label confers certain economic and social benefits, such as access to healthcare, income transfer payments, housing vouchers, and so on. While this point is perhaps worth noting, there is no doubt that the economic, social, and psychosocial benefits that potentially accrue to those who work certainly outweigh the "privileged" status of being a beneficiary of federal or state disability compensation programs. However, it is also important to note that federal and state disability compensation programs continue to present considerable work disincentives, as recipients weigh the relative costs of risking their loss when they enter or return to work (Orszag, 2010), even though the income benefits offered by these programs are quite small, because the access to public health insurance benefits (either Medicaid or Medicare) is what really matters. The way that this plays out in an individual's life relates to the meaning derived from work and the social and financial costs incurred from engaging in it. Perhaps in no other arena is federal policy so important in individual meaning making or decision making.

To some extent, the way that disability has been legally defined in the United States reflects social attitudes toward it. For example, early federal definitions of disability included in rehabilitation laws enacted prior to the 1970s considered it solely as a biological limitation of the individual. This "medical model" view considered return-to-work services as either "training around the disability" (Altman, 2001) or matching the individual to a job on the basis of the impairment. For example, people who were deaf or hard of hearing were employed in the production departments of publishing companies, where the excessive noise of the printing presses was not a barrier to work, nor a liability. With the rise of the disability rights movement in the 1970s, the strict biological definition of disability was expanded to include the extent to which the environment offered supports to facilitate functioning. The intent in federal laws such as the 1973 Rehabilitation Act and subsequent amendments emphasized the interaction of the person in the environment as constituting an employment barrier, not simply the individual's impairment. This perspective gradually evolved in the Americans with Disabilities Act of 1990 (ADA), where "disabled persons" who merited the protections of the ADA were defined as those who (a) have a physical,

mental, or emotional impairment; (b) have a history of such an impairment; or (c) are regarded as having an impairment. The phrase "my disability is how others see my disability" was codified in the ADA, as the Congressional intent was to prevent employment discrimination based not only on actual limitations resulting from impairments, but also from limitations imposed by negative attitudes and stereotypes (Dart, 1993). Interestingly, subsequent Supreme Court decisions began to so severely limit the expansive Congressional intent in defining disability that Congress enacted the ADA amendments in 2009 to preclude them from doing so. This national policy is referred to as the "civil rights" model of disability (Altman, 2001). However, disability is still defined as work incapacity in Social Security laws (SSA, 2009) under which individuals with disabilities must document their "total incapacity" to engage in gainful employment in order to qualify for income transfer and healthcare benefits; thus, the "medical" or biological determinant model remains powerful. Unfortunately, and perhaps as a consequence of this definitional requirement, once an individual is a beneficiary of one of these programs, the likelihood of returning to work is less than 1% (Orszag, 2010).

One contemporary model for defining disability emerged from the World Health Organization in 2001 (WHO, 2002). The WHO developed the International Classification of Functioning (ICF) based on a dynamic biopsychosocial approach to defining and measuring disability (See Figure 11.1). The ICF is an interactive model of the "disability process" rather than simply a definition of disability, as it accounts for the way biological impairments may be experienced as barriers to functioning depending on environmental and individual resources. In this model, the "disablement process" is ascribed not simply to the type or severity of disability, but to reciprocal interactions among the body, the individual, and the environment. Thus, health conditions do not act directly to create barriers to functioning across generic environments, but are moderated by social attitudes and resources in specific functional domains, as well as individual contextual factors, such as race, gender, psychological disposition, and so on.

The ICF provides a comprehensive framework for exploring the dynamic interactions at play in an individual's decision to seek or retain employment. For example, an individual with arthritis who experiences mobility and range-of-motion impairments can be faced with different scenarios when

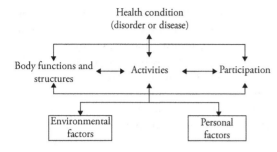

Figure 11.1 A model of disability, health, and functioning. World Health Organization (2002). Towards a common language for functioning, disability and health: ICF. World Health Organization, Geneva: Author. Retrieved July 31, 2011 from: http://www.who.int/classifications/icf/training/icfbeginnersguide.pdf. Reprinted with Permission.

considering a job as an account specialist for a large company. If the work environment incorporates universal design elements, such as elevators and alternative computer software technology (speech rather than typing), and the surrounding community provides adequate public transportation, then person-based factors become more salient regarding the decision to work. Some of the person factors include age, marital status, level of education, and psychological attributes such as coping behaviors and self-efficacy (Szymanski & Hershenson, 2005). Environmental factors include an individual's financial and social resources, as well as eligibility for certain disability benefits such as pensions and health benefits. In addition, other factors relevant to the decision, and not clearly specified in the ICF model but discussed further in this chapter, include the individual's assessment of the benefits to be derived from work, weighed against the risks of disability disclosure, among other issues. Finally, the broader sociopolitical and cultural context of disability may influence the decision—values such as economic self-sufficiency, independence, and so on.

It is clear that definitions have power, and that the way an individual defines his or her impairment, no matter how visible, can be influenced by prevailing social attitudes and national policies, as well as cultural and personal values. Disability is not a "thing" as is gender, but a perception (Davis, 2001). As Davis (p. 536) notes, "disability is a very postmodern identity because although one can somaticize disability, it is impossible to essentialize it the way one can with the categories of gender or ethnicity." Perhaps because of this, people with disabilities have been largely excluded from the discourse on diversity and multiculturalism and ignored in courses, curriculum, and textbooks. Davis also attributes

their marginalization in diversity studies as resulting from the "porous" nature of disability (anyone can become disabled and a person with a disability can be cured). Moreover, disability represents a vast and heterogeneous category—there are over 1,000 conditions included in the ADA, including HIV, Down syndrome, blindness, dyslexia, schizophrenia, and so on. These features or factors create a central difficulty—even a contradiction—in "essentializing" the meaning of disability in political, social, and personal arenas. Yet these basic issues are critical to understanding the context in which people with disabilities (the vast heterogeneous group) make meaning of their lives, and how in their lives they derive meaning from work. Is work understood differently by the individual with a significant intellectual disability who finally gets his first job as a courtesy clerk in a Wal-Mart as compared to the professor who returns to the classroom after a serious motor vehicle accident that leaves her using a wheelchair and computer-assisted devices to operate instructional technology? Both of these individuals chose to work, because both would qualify for federal benefits programs that would effectively "excuse" them from participation in the workforce. In the United States, conditions that compromise productivity (impairments, motherhood, old age), free one from the social and economic obligations of productivity (Stone, 1984). In the case of people with disabilities, as Stone says, the "deserving poor," what are the psychological, social, cultural, and environmental circumstances that motivate the courtesy clerk and the professor to return to work? Understanding some of these issues is the basis for understanding the meaning of work in the lives of people with disabilities.

Individual and Environmental Factors Related to Employment

It is clear that people with disabilities are significantly underrepresented in the labor market. The issue of why this is so has been rigorously studied for decades from the perspectives of both the supply side (labor supply) and the demand side (jobs) of the labor market (Gilbride & Stensrud, 1999). Supply-side studies have examined personal characteristics, sociodemographic issues, and disability/health conditions and how these generally function as facilitators or barriers to employment. These studies represent the majority of the research on factors related to labor market outcomes. The demand-side studies have focused on social attitudes and environmental barriers, and they represent a smaller volume of research. Fewer studies have examined factors or influences that contribute to decisions by people with disabilities to enter or return to work (Shaw et al., 2002). Interestingly, the predominant focus of studies in the broad area of the meaning and benefits of work has been people with psychiatric and cognitive disabilities, perhaps due to the common history of oppression these groups experienced (e.g., Grob, 1994; Wolfensberger, 1972) and the multidisciplinary nature of research studies in this area (i.e., from psychology, psychiatry, rehabilitation, education). This section examines social and political policies influencing work entry and reentry for people with disabilities, beginning with a discussion of workplace attitudes.

Attitudes of Employers

Attitudinal surveys of employers' willingness to hire individuals with disabilities have generally indicated an overall positive response (e.g., Hernandez, Keys, & Balcazar, 2000; Unger, 2002), although employer attitudes vary depending on the nature of the disability (Dalgrin & Bellini, 2008; Unger, 2002). These differential attitudes seem to be related to more highly stigmatized disabilities (or those that are less well understood), such as psychiatric and other invisible disorders (e.g., Beatty & Kirby, 2006; Corrigan, 2004; Mathews & Harrington, 2000). In these cases, employer attitudes reflect more stereotyped responses, such as fear of litigation, skepticism regarding the nature of the disability, or casual attribution of disability being the fault of the individual (Balser, 2007; Florey & Harrison, 2000).

Despite these relatively positive general attitudes toward the idea of hiring people with disabilities, there is a fairly large gap between attitudes and practices. For example, a recent report from the Department of Labor (Domzal, Houtenville, & Sharma, 2008), based on a nationally representative survey of more than 4 million businesses, indicated that only 19% of large companies (those with more than 250 employees) and 23% of small businesses reported having an employee with a disability in the organization. While hiring was down across all segments of the population during the recent job recession, only 9% of all employers had hired someone with a disability during the past 12 months. In the same study, employers' rationale for not hiring hinged on negative stereotypes, such as "increasing worker's compensation costs" and "fear of litigation." While the overall picture of how attitudes influence hiring practices remains somewhat murky, it is clear that individuals with disabilities, particularly those

with invisible ones, may encounter negative perceptions in the hiring and retention phases of employment that influence their decision to disclose their disability in order to invoke legislative protections.

National Policies

Federal and state policies that strongly influence return to work address the economic consequence of having a disability sufficiently severe to qualify for monetary benefits such as worker's compensation, federal disability pension plans, or personal insurance payouts. Although the research here is complicated (based on the type of disability and the amount of financial remuneration), the consensus is that it can exert a sufficient effect on the decision to work so as, coupled with personal factors such as coping behaviors, self-efficacy beliefs, and other environmental resources (access to jobs, barrier-free environments), to depress return-to-work rates (Dekkers-Sanchez, Wind, Sluiter, & Frings-Dresen, 2010; Kennedy, Olney, & Schiro-Geist, 2004). In support of this point, economists point to the "exploding" number of individuals with disabilities receiving federal social security disability pensions of various kinds as evidence of the powerful force it may exert on these decisions. However, studies of social security beneficiaries indicate that they manifest a general pattern of higher age, lower educational level, and more significant impairment—all of which are negative indicators of return to work (Davies, Rupp, & Wittenburg, 2009; Kennedy et al., 2007). Related to federal pensions, and perhaps more important given the healthcare crisis in America, is that these beneficiaries, such as those receiving Social Security Disability insurance or Supplemental Security Income, qualify for federal healthcare, either Medicare or Medicaid. Beneficiaries who choose to return to work may be risking a much more powerful resource—access to health insurance—rather than simply relinquishing the relatively small monetary benefit of some of these federal pension programs (Fabian & MacDonald-Wilson, 2005). As the process for regaining eligibility for federal disability programs once an individual returns to work can be excessively burdensome, this economic and political reality can substantially influence the behavior of even those who are the most motivated to work (Orszag, 2010).

Federal laws such as the ADA also influence decisions to return to work. Under the ADA, an individual who meets the three-pronged definition of disability described earlier is both protected from employment discrimination and eligible to seek "reasonable accommodations" that enable "qualified employees with disabilities" to perform the "essential functions of the job" (MacDonald-Wilson, Fabian, & Dong, 2008). Reasonable accommodations include modifications to physical structures, assistive technology, modified work schedules, and restructured jobs. To invoke the protections of the ADA, however, individuals with a disability must reveal their condition to their employer and often must provide medical evidence documenting their need for workplace accommodations. Thus, requesting workplace accommodations is called a "two-edged sword" in that doing so can invoke negative stereotypes and attitudes on the part of employers; a factor that has been shown to depress the likelihood of requesting them (MacDonald-Wilson et al., 2008), particularly for people with nonapparent disabilities.

Individual Factors Influencing Work-Related Behavior

Researchers in rehabilitation, psychology, and medicine have explored numerous biological and psychosocial factors influencing both the return to work for individuals with acquired disabilities and work entry for those with developmental or related types of disorders (e.g., Chan, Cheng, Chan, & Rosenthal, 2006; Tsang, Lam, Ng, & Leung, 2000; Wehman, Targett, West, & Kregel, 2005; Wewiorski & Fabian, 2004; Yasuda, Wehman, Targett, Cifu, & West, 2002). In general, demographic, psychosocial, and impairment-related factors have been studied. For example, self-efficacy has been found to predict work entry and work retention for individuals with a variety of disabilities in several studies (e.g., Dionne & Noven, 2011; Fabian & Leisener, 2005; Martoreu, Gutierrez-Recarchor, Preda, & Ayuso-Mateus, 2008), as have impairment-related factors such as the severity of the condition or injury (e.g., Lancourt & Kettelhut, 1992; Reisine, McQuillan, & Field, 1995; Xu & Martz, 2010). Among the most robust predictors of work for individuals with disabilities have been educational level, severity of impairment, and prior work experience (e.g., Lidal, Tuan, & Biering-Sorensen, 2007; Wewiorski & Fabian, 2004; Xu & Martz, 2010). In terms of organizational factors, the provision of workplace accommodations affects both work entry and work retention (e.g., MacDonald-Wilson et al., 2008), as does the provision of other organizational and systemic supports (e.g., Chadsey & Beyer, 2001; Mank, Cioffi, & Yovanoff, 1997; Schroer et al., 2005).

Individual impairments have also been studied in terms of their links to job and workplace demands, such as physical labor (Lancourt & Kettelhut, 1992), speed and endurance (Shaw et al., 2002), interpersonal issues in the workplace (Novak & Rogan, 2010), and workplace culture (Soklaridis, Ammendolia, & Cassidy, 2010). Generally, the physically demanding nature of the jobs has been the most important factor in determining return to work for people with acquired disabilities, although social and interpersonal characteristics of work environments have been strongly correlated to work retention for individuals with significant cognitive and psychological disabilities.

As can be seen, there have been decades of research examining individual and setting factors that predict work entry and work retention, as well as employer attitudes and other obstacles that facilitate or impede it. Given the political and economic context of work for people with disabilities, much of the research has been linked to efforts to improve VR programs in order to motivate work entry, as well as systemic changes to decrease work disincentives such as current Social Security Administration policies regarding receipt of benefits (SSA, 2009).

I think one of the major obstacles to achieving work participation among people with disabilities remains the prevailing medical model assumption in disability policy and service; in other words, the emphasis is still on the problem within the individual, rather than focusing efforts on remediating policy, cultural, or systemic issues that depress employment entry for people with disabilities. One small example of the prevailing medical model assumption is evident, I think, in the concept of "reasonable accommodations" required by the ADA to enable qualified individuals with disabilities to participate fully in employment and the community. Of course, nothing is legally wrong with this right, but politically it rests on the assumption that society is compensating for the impairment of the individual, rather than for the obstacles in the environment. The latter approach is consistent with the philosophy of "universal design," exemplified by simple curb cuts, which were originally designed for wheelchair users but are widely preferred by people pushing baby strollers, bicyclists, the elderly, and so on. A solution designed to compensate for individual impairments became a universal solution to an environmental barrier—the curb cut. It obviously takes some imagination to envision the world of work as universally accessible, but recent efforts in incorporating elements of universal design into academic environments have shown that they benefit all students, not just those with disabilities (Scott, Mcguire, & Shaw, 2003). New technological developments—such as the "cloud"—have already provided more universal access to assistive technology (screen reader software for people with visual impairments, for example) that can be accessed anywhere and anytime. These types of innovations (curb cuts, clouds) will eventually foster a social and cultural environment that acknowledges human variation as just one more aspect of diversity, with, one hopes, positive implications for changing attitudes and mitigating workplace barriers. When that occurs, more attention can be focused on some of the issues raised in the next section regarding the psychology of working.

Psychology of Working and Disability

> The vast literature of psychiatry and clinical psychology includes little concerning the human problems of working. (Neff, 1977, p. 3)

More than for any other group in society, the decision to enter or return to work among people with disabilities is influenced by political, social, and environmental forces. Although people with disabilities largely shaped the broader political and social context of work, especially in terms of advocating for nondiscrimination and socially inclusive laws and policies, recent employment data suggest that they are not benefitting. Not only does participation in the labor market remain troublesome, but data also show that even when people with disabilities do work, they fare far worse than their nondisabled peers in terms of pay, full-time employment, and re-employment after layoff (Burkhauser, Daly, & Houtenville, 2001; Houtenville & Burkhauser, 2004).

As this chapter has indicated, much of the research in rehabilitation counseling and psychology has been devoted to exploring the complicated reasons contributing to this dismal employment picture, with fewer studies examining the positive forces—that is, what are the motivators and benefits of a "working life" for people with disabilities? Moreover, getting and keeping a job can be challenging, in terms of dealing with social attitudes, having to disclose or reveal private information in order to obtain necessary accommodations, and coping with a chronic illness or disabling condition (Baron & Salzer, 2002). Nonetheless, a small but growing body of research in rehabilitation suggests that work is an important aspect of recovery from illness (Dunn, Wewiorski, & Rogers, 2008) and that it fosters self-determination (e.g., Algozzine, Browder, Karvonen, Test, & Wood, 2001; Wehmeyer & Bolding, 2008) and contributes to overall quality of life (Beyer, Brown, Akandi, & Rapley, 2010). To understand the benefits and meaning that people might derive from work, this section reviews some of the literature on the meaning of work for people with disabilities.

The Meaning of Work

Neff (1977) and some of the other pioneers in the VR field (e.g., Hershenson, 1981; Lofquist & Dawis, 1969) stimulated significant interest in the study of the meaning of work in the lives of people with disabilities. Philosophically, the VR field has moved from the assumption that disability is a determinant of work capacity to the prevailing notion that "any individual who desires to work, and has sufficient supports, can do so" (Luecking, 2009; Wehman, Brooke, & Revell, 2007). The shift in attitude parallels changes in public policy and law discussed earlier in this chapter and reflects the move from a strict "medical model" of impairment to a more social and contextual model of disability. Unlike the early discourse giving rise to the psychology of working (e.g., Richardson, 1993), where the criticism was directed toward an exclusive focus on choosing a vocation rather than simply getting a job, the history of VR is almost the opposite—the exclusive focus has always been (and remains) getting a job, with little attention to choosing one (Pumpian, Fisher, Certo, & Smally, 1997; Szymanski, Enright, Hershenson, & Ettinger, 2009). This inadequate attention gave rise to the charge that people with disabilities generally worked in secondary labor market, "dead-end" jobs (Baron & Salzer, 2002; Fabian, 1999; Hagner, 2000) and that people with the most significant disabilities worked in jobs described as the three "Fs"—food, flowers, and filth (fast food, nurseries, and janitorial). These types of jobs led some of us to wonder (e.g., Fabian, 1992; Petrovsky & Gleeson, 1997) whether competitive employment did significantly improve an individual's quality of life. While later research has identified benefits accruing from even entry-level jobs described earlier in the chapter, the idea of choosing a vocation remains troublesome in disability studies (Cinamon & Gifsh, 2004).

Work, as it is socially constructed in the United States, is predicated on two underlying assumptions: willingness and capacity. Although results of national surveys of people with disabilities who are not working indicate their desire and willingness to do so (National Organization on Disability, 2010), willingness implies choice and opportunity. As we have seen in this chapter, job choice for people with disabilities has historically been limited by negative employer attitudes and theirs pernicious effects on job opportunities and, subsequently, choice (Domzal et al., 2008; Hernandez et al., 2000). Choice (and opportunities) is also constrained by the poor educational experiences of youth exiting special education programs (National Longitudinal Transition Study, 2005), the continuing reluctance by employers to provide workplace accommodations (Basas, 2008), and other obstacles discussed earlier in the chapter.

Work capacity presents implicit and explicit challenges for people with significant disabilities. As indicated earlier, people with disabilities who want to return to work, but who rely on the health and income benefits of Social Security Administration programs (such as Social Security Disability Income), must document work incapacity while simultaneously seeking work opportunities. Another challenge is the requirement under the ADA that employees with disabilities must provide evidence of their impairments in order to request a reasonable accommodation that would enable them to perform the essential functions of the job. This circumstance (revealing a "hidden" health condition in order to invoke legal rights) focuses attention on incapacity and helps explain why many employees with disabilities are reluctant to request accommodations that would enhance their work performance (Gioia & Brekke, 2003; Granger, 2000). From their perspective, work requires "normative behaviors" and capacity, yet the need for job accommodations suggests "non-normative" needs. These paradoxes relate to what Neff (1977) called the necessary and sufficient conditions for work, with the necessary conditions being performance requirements and the sufficient ones being whether one can meet the psychological, cultural, and social demands of the work environment.

Beyond necessary and sufficient conditions, though, is the subjective meaning of work. More contemporary rehabilitation research has convincingly established that work (when it is the result of choice) positively affects quality of life for people with disabilities (Schonherr, Groothoff, Mulder, & Eisman, 2005; Vestling, Tufvesson, & Iwarsson, 2003). In fact, it is interesting that some of the earliest research on the psychology of work (in terms of its benefits and opportunities) is derived from

rehabilitation psychology (Blustein, Kenna, Gill, & DeVoy, 2008), particularly research on people with psychiatric conditions, where paid employment has been strongly correlated with recovery from illness (Dunn et al., 2008; Provencher, Gregg, Crawford, & Mueser, 2002). However, there is also a growing acknowledgement that jobs can demand substantial psychological, social, and physical resources (back to Neff's condition of sufficiency) that can exhaust personal resources (Baron & Salzer, 2002). In a way, these demands create similar situations to those encountered by women raising young children who find that the demands of competing requirements (childcare and work) challenge them either to develop strategies to endure (if there is no choice) or, if there is choice, to temporarily leave the labor force, depending on the meaning and value they derive from paid employment. For individuals with disabilities, addressing these challenges can heighten the risk of exacerbating symptoms, which in turn can result in job loss.

People with disabilities desire employment, an assertion supported by periodic polls of the population conducted by the National Organization on Disability. Despite the barriers discussed earlier in this section, it seems to me that it is important to understand some of the motivating factors and incentives associated with a working life. The next section discusses an approach to understanding work motivation and incentives within a theoretical framework of disability.

Theoretical Model of Disability and Work

There has been surprisingly little research to explain why some people with disabilities enter or return to work (such as our courtesy clerk or injured professor) based on the perceived cultural, social, material, and personal benefits of it, and there are few theoretical models of disability to assist in explaining it. As Shaw et al. (2002) suggest, given the diverse models of disability (as reviewed earlier in this chapter), it might be most helpful to explore the facilitators and barriers to employment, and the benefits derived from it, from a theoretical perspective.

One theoretical framework developed by Priestley (1998) generated a fourfold typology based on the various models of disability described earlier in the chapter. This approach, which has been used in subsequent studies on the meaning of disability and work (e.g., Shaw et al., 2002), used two explanatory dimensions to form a 2×2 matrix: an individual and social continuum and a materialistic and idealist one (Table 11.1). The individual/social continuum refers to the extent to which the disability is experienced as an individual or social phenomena—or, as Priestley suggests, "whether disability has some real collective existence in the social world beyond the existence or experience of the individual" (p. 83). The materialist/idealist continuum embodies the distinction between structural/material conditions (including biological and social structures) and idealist conditions (such as cultural symbols or social mores). For example, the medical model described earlier in this chapter would be consistent with the first position in the 2×2 matrix (individual/materialist) in that the explanation of disability relies on strict biological factors, distinct from individual or social interpretations of their meaning. The positions in the conceptual framework illustrated in Table 11.1 are not, as Priestley indicated, mutually exclusive, but they can help "explain some of the underlying differences between contemporary disability theorists and serve as a starting place for understanding why people work and the meanings and benefits they derive from it" (Shaw et al., 2002, p. 185). Although people choose to work based on

individualistic needs, beliefs, assumptions, values, and goals, these values and motivators are influenced by social and environmental factors, as well as prevailing political and social policies, particularly for people with disabilities.

Position 1: Individual/Materialist

This position incorporates the medical model of disability where the work-related barrier is attributed to the individual's functional impairment, which in turn creates the disability. In this approach, disability (impairment) is often viewed as a "personal tragedy," and those who overcome biological "deficits" (such as President Franklin Roosevelt) are admired, as FDR was, for "what the human spirit can ultimately accomplish" (Goodwin, 1994, p. 532). In work-related research, studies here focus on the effect of the impairment itself on vocational functioning, such as its nature, severity, or manifestation, as reviewed earlier in the chapter. To an extent, studies that have shown how work can improve self-efficacy (e.g., Strauser, O'Sullivan, & Wong, 2010) would be relevant here as well because the rewards of work can be both extrinsic (enhancing quality of life by

Table 11.1. Theoretical Positions Related to Disability and Work

Perspective	Materialist	Idealist
Individual	Philosophical point of view: Disability is a biological determinant of function and the focus is on the individual's impairment and resulting functional limitations. Work-related research emphasizes minimizing the impairment through training, compensatory strategies, or devices. Working "despite the disability" is a symbolic achievement, whereas disability itself remains a personal tragedy.	Philosophical point of view: The meaning of disability resides in the individual's subjective experience. The focus is on phenomenology. Work-related research emphasizes adjustment to disability in terms of negotiating new identities, shifting personal values and beliefs. Work provides an opportunity to reformulate a new identity. Work is part of recovery as it represents a way to reframe an identity within a more positive narrative.
Social	Philosophical point of view: Disability is the result of socioeconomic barriers (including attitudes); often called the "civil rights model of disability." The focus is on collectivist action for political change in order to eliminate barriers to economic and civil participation. The "socially oppressive" disability service system is the charitable embodiment of powerlessness. Studies emphasize the deleterious consequences of not working, particularly the costs to society in terms of exploding disability benefits programs, and the marginalized impoverished lives of people with disabilities who lack economic opportunity. Work is a way to exercise and increase political and economic power and to improve overall quality of life.	Philosophical point of view: Disability is a social constructivist concept that is dependent on cultural values, mores, norms, and beliefs; an "ableist" culture devalues and diminishes people who are different. The focus is on a group identity model. Studies are qualitative and emphasize common shifts in individual values and social roles in order to construct a "working life." Work can be viewed as a means of affirming a new cultural identity and social empowerment (negating oppressive cultural values). Deaf culture as a source of identity and pride is an example of this perspective.

improving socioeconomic status, for example), and intrinsic (self-efficacy). The individualistic and objectified nature of this perspective suggests that individuals with disabilities who "manage" to work do so at great personal cost—and deserve considerable approval for their efforts. Probably the most iconic symbol of this position would be Christopher Reeve, the actor who survived a fall from a horse and sustained a severe cervical spinal injury that left him paralyzed from the neck down. The media stories admired his personal courage, stamina, and stubbornness both to regain functioning and to continue his acting career. Or, as one participant in a qualitative study of return to work for a sample of individuals with diverse disabilities put it, "I take pride in my job and I don't look for handouts" (Shaw et al., 2002; p. 192).

Position 2: Individual/Idealist

Position 2 also focuses on the individual's experience of disability, but the point of view emphasizes not the objective impairment but the cognitive and affective meaning of it to the person. In rehabilitation psychology, much of the research on adjustment to disability is consistent with this position, where, for example, individuals acquire new perspectives (or value shifts) on the meaning of disability in their lives (e.g., Wright, 1983). In this regard, the individual is not compensating for or "overcoming" an impairment by returning to work, but changing the meaning of the impairment and thus creating a new identity that incorporates it. Wright refers to this as "enlarging the scope of values" and "containing disability effects." In mental health or psychiatric disabilities, work has an important role in the recovery process (e.g., Dunn et al., 2008), as it empowers the person to create a new identity and expands possibilities beyond Parson's (1972) classic reference to "succumbing to the sick role." There have been several studies on the positive relationship between work and quality of life (e.g., Beyer et al., 2010;; Fabian, 1992; Priebe, Warner, Hubschmid, & Eckle, 1998), which are also relevant to understanding position 2.

Disability itself can be subjectively defined, and people with similar disabilities might report different types of limitations regarding the capacity to work (e.g., Yates, 2010). These perceptions are shaped not only by individual psychological factors (such as self-efficacy or coping skills) but also availability and accessibility of structural and social resources. Of course, the nature and extent of the impairment also plays a role, although even here two people with ostensibly similar conditions, such as blindness, may still have vastly different views of their resulting limitations interfering with the capacity to work. Self-determination theory (Algozzine, 2001) is also relevant, as people may perceive work as a means of empowerment or personal agency fostering a new identity that incorporates disability.

Within position 2, individuals with disabilities, particularly those with nonapparent ones, might struggle with the issue of revealing their condition or impairment to others in the workplace, depending on the subjective view of disability and the perception of the risk of disclosure to their identity as a worker (Beatty & Kirby, 2006). For example, one participant in a qualitative study examining patterns of return to work among a sample of people with nonapparent back injuries said, "I somehow kept on going to work normally. So that it was not visible on the outside and I was treated as … a healthy person'" (Svajger & Winding, 2009, p. 447). Or, as a wheelchair user in another study put it, "the salaried work enables me to feel like everyone else" (Ville & Winance, 2006, p. 427).

Position 3: Social/Materialist

The social/materialistic position incorporates the view of disability as a structural or institutional barrier that exists outside the person—that is, in the broader physical, social, and economic environment, or "the philosophical basis for that strand of disability theory which has been central to the mobilization of the disabled people's movement" particularly because "the form of poverty principally associated with physical impairment is caused by our exclusion from the ability to earn a living on par with our able bodied peers," the mission statement of the Union of the Physically Impaired Against Segregation (Barnes, 2000, p. 442). Or, as one noted scholar put it, "Dependency is created amongst disabled people not because of the effects of functional limitations of their capacities for self-care, but because their lives are shaped by a variety of economic, political and social forces which produce it" (Oliver, 1990, p. 94). Within this perspective, the assumption is that the socioeconomic climate has largely impeded access to the workplace for people with disabilities, a factor supported by recent evidence that employers resist employing people with disabilities based on the faulty assumption that there aren't "any jobs in the company that people with disabilities can do" (Domzal et al., 2008). Because position 3 assumes a commonality among all people with disabilities, well-known disability activists such as Judith Heumann (1980) or Ed Roberts (see Fleisher & Zames, 2001) find significant meaning in their "power struggle" against a perceived "oppressive system" that denies access to employment while relegating people with disabilities to marginalized economic and social lives (Albrecht & Bury, 2001). The political advocacy of the disability community against "collective oppression" is often compared to the civil rights or women's movements (e.g., Fleisher & Zames, 2001).

From the civil rights perspective, individuals might seek meaning from their fight to gain access to jobs through their advocacy efforts. One well-known case is that of Judith Heumann, a wheelchair user as a result of childhood polio who was denied a teaching certificate from the New York City Board of Education because, they said, she would be unable to lead elementary school children safely out of the building in case of fire (Heumann, 1980). Heumann made the personal political, publicizing her case in the *New York Times* and being one of the founders of Disabled in Action. Later, she served as Assistant Secretary in the Department of Education under President Carter. A similar career story unfolded in the life of Ed Roberts, also severely disabled as a result of polio. Roberts, who was denied VR services by the state of California because he was assessed as "too disabled to work," later was appointed the director of that agency in the 1970s (Fleisher & Zames, 2001). These well-known examples from the disability rights movement (although not nearly as well known as, for example, leaders of the women's movement for equality) found meaning in work by struggling against social and political stereotypes that impeded their lives. Although their stories are dramatic, the issue of working despite attitudinal or environmental barriers is reflected in the career stories of more ordinary citizens. For example, one participant in a qualitative study of the career trajectories of high-achieving women with disabilities said she worked in order to "engage and peel away [people's] biases, their fears, their issues, and to teach people about disability in a nonthreatening way. But I know that no matter where I go, in whatever arena, I have to do that and that's always a challenge, to deal with the same questions and the same attitudes" (Noonan et al., 2004, p. 72). The sense of injustice implied in this response, as well as the personal commitment to continue to struggle against it in the work arena, captures the essence of position 3.

Position 4: Social/Idealist

Similar to position 3, in position 4, social phenomena have "objective reality beyond the individual, but this social reality exists more in ideas than in material relations of power" (Priestley, 1998, p. 68). In the literature, this position would be described as the "social constructivist" perspective on disability, where cultural and social mores and values shape public attitudes and treatment toward disability, as well as influence how disability is understood and defined (Gill, 2001). Within position 4, the lack of work for people with disabilities is consistent with the history of social marginalization and exclusion. Wolfensberger (1972), among the first to address the issue of "normalization" of the lives of individuals with intellectual disabilities, used the phrase "social role valorization" to capture the sense that work confers a legitimate social and cultural role for people with disabilities.

Social stereotypes of disability, derived from cultural symbols and values (i.e., independence, health, and beauty), are among the most entrenched barriers to workplace access (e.g., Ware, 1999). As a business participant in a focus group I conducted said, "We don't have any jobs for people who are blind." Davis (1961) coined the phrase "deviance disavowal" to define the way that individuals with disabilities need to "manage social impressions" in order to reduce the threat and ambiguity that can result from stereotypes. From position 4, sometimes it is just the reality of being a visibly disabled person who has a job that can challenge stereotypes. For example, one young woman participating in a focus group said that having a job gives people the "impression that you exist, and that you're not just some poor little disabled woman who can't do anything on her own" (Ville & Winance, 2006, p. 434). From this position, people with disabilities who work acquire a legitimate social identity, resist social exclusion, and, indirectly at least, challenge fairly well-entrenched social stereotypes. Murphy (1990), an anthropologist, referred to wheelchairs as "portable isolation huts," suggesting how people with disabilities occupy a marginalized culture unless they take assertive action to take on valued social roles, such as work, in order to "reclaim their lives" (Linton, 2010).

People with disabilities have been largely excluded from American workplace as a result of structural and attitudinal barriers. Although several laws, most notably ADA, sought to "level the playing field" by mandating accessibility, the disappointing labor market figures cited earlier in the chapter suggest that the ideals of the ADA have not been realized for a number of complex reasons, including individual beliefs about the nature and limitations of disability, persisting structural and political barriers that impede opportunity, and negative stereotypes. While the issues relating to work and disability are complex, the majority of interventions designed to achieve better outcomes do not have roots in theoretical discourses on disability. This exploration of how the difference in a person's perceptions of the "disabled role" may influence the meaning and benefits derived from work offers a start for this exploration. It also leads to the discussion of implications and recommendations for work-based interventions.

Implications for Interventions

The previous section discussed four positions or perspectives on disability and how they might be operationalized in terms of individual beliefs regarding the psychology of working; that said, it is also important to consider how strong social stereotypes and long-held beliefs continue to impede access to employment opportunities—and vocational well-being—for people with disabilities. For example, children with disabilities, even with the advent of educational inclusion, continue to experience social exclusion and even segregation compared to their nondisabled peers, which negatively affects career aspirations and vocational identity (Loprest & Maag, 2007). Many of these children, as they "age out" of the educational system, are placed in segregated vocational facilities, such as day habilitation programs and sheltered employment, even though recent interventions such as supported employment have been shown to be efficacious in enabling competitive employment (e.g., Cook et al., 2005; Revell et al., 2000).

On the other hand, adults who acquire disabilities have already established a vocational identity and a career history, but tend to face other barriers mentioned earlier. These include issues such as recreating an identity around the disability, managing workplace stigma, and dealing with the complex issues around work disincentives embedded in the country's social security laws.

This brief discussion might suggest that the different positions on disability described in Table 11.1 have implications for different types of interventions, depending on a complexity of factors, including the timing of the disability, accessibility to career and vocational resources, and personality characteristics and traits, among others. For example, a young adult with intellectual disabilities who recently "aged out" of the educational system will benefit from participating in self-advocacy and self-determination vocational interventions (positions 1 and 2), designed to improve self-efficacy beliefs and manage workplace stereotypes by redefining the personal meaning of disability.

From the perspective of position 3, young women might seek others as role models or mentors in order to share common experiences and acquire new skills to address social stereotypes that impede workplace access. For example, one participant in a qualitative study of high-achieving career women with disabilities said that, "hands down, you know, knowing other women with disabilities … going to conferences, hanging out more, you know, doing the old thing" empowers the individual through belonging to a community (Noonan et al., 2004, p. 72).

Position 4, characterized as a social constructivist view of disability, offers the possibility of redefining disability based on more positive social attitudes and cultural symbols. This perspective is closely related to disability identity politics, or what Linton (2010) calls "claiming disability." The assumption of a commonality of experience, based on positive perspectives (such as those associated with Deaf culture), is a key issue in this position. As cultural mores and social stereotypes influence individual meaning, Schriner (2001) and others have encouraged people to look "upstream" to identify the roots of beliefs that contribute to personal values regarding the role of work. For example, how do cultural stereotypes evoked by disability benefits programs ("the deserving poor") affect an individual's identity as a worker? Regarding children with congenital disabilities, how do current educational policies affect the development of a vocational identity? Although many special education curricula incorporate self-determination and self-advocacy skills training, recent studies on the career trajectories of children and youth in special education indicate considerable disparities in their dropout rates, enrollment in postsecondary education, and work (Loprest & Maag, 2007) compared to their nondisabled peers. Their early education experiences strongly influence the value and meaning they attribute to work. Working "upstream" by transforming social beliefs is a slow process, although heightened awareness of some of these issues is proceeding. For example, Congress recently passed "Rosa's Law" to replace the term "mentally retarded" with "intellectual disability" in all subsequent federal legislation dealing with disability issues.

Summary

In American society, a job confers significant benefits, both extrinsic (standard of living) and intrinsic (psychosocial). For the vast majority of people with disabilities, access to these benefits has been severely limited, and even, in some cases, denied. Similar to other groups who have experienced attitudinal and environmental barriers to work, people with disabilities have engaged in a decades-long struggle to mitigate them. Moreover, for many people with disabilities, this condition may be only one of the multiple characteristics subject to overt or implicit employment discrimination, such as race or gender. On the other hand, as Williams (2001, p. 139) noted, we need to "acknowledge the near universality of disability," meaning that this "minority group can include any of us today, tomorrow, or the day after." While laws have been enacted and intensive public relations campaigns targeted at changing attitudes have been launched over the past few decades, the employment rate of individuals with disabilities illustrates the distance yet to go, particularly when compared to public opinion polls of individuals with disabilities asserting their willingness and desire to work (National Council on Disability, 2010). However, as this chapter has shown, the issue of work is more complicated than simply matching people's employment skills with available jobs, the predominant perspective in VR service systems.

Work and disability is further complicated by its surprising absence in the disability studies scholarship on the one hand, and the career psychology literature on the other. For example, the most recent edition of the *Disability Studies Reader* (2010), one of the major sources of scholarship in the field, did not include a chapter on work in its 48, and the well-known *Handbook of Disability Studies* (published in 2001) had only one. And disability, as many scholars have pointed out (e.g., Hershenson, 2005; Szymanski & Hershenson, 2005), is largely missing from texts on career and vocational theory and development. While the source of much of what we know about work and disability emerges from rehabilitation psychology and counseling scholarship (Blustein, 2008), the major focus in this literature tends to be on remedying the impairment (the medical model) or addressing barriers (the civil rights model). This research has certainly informed our practices and policies in terms of designing rehabilitation programs and interventions, but it hasn't contributed significantly to answering the question of why people work, particularly from various theoretical positions on understanding the meaning of disability to the individual and in a broader social context. Research that starts with the premise of understanding the costs and benefits of work to the individual from a broader theoretical perspective will promote a "shift in which the prevailing medical/biological perspectives are supplemented with personal perspectives" (Shaw et al., 2002, p. 195), to which I would add social and cultural perspectives. These types of studies may finally help to address the dismal employment outcomes for people with disabilities, and develop perspectives related to youth identity and employment that may have some long-term promise.

References

Albrecht, G., & Bury, M. (2001). The political economy of the disability marketplace. In G. L. Albrecht, K. D. Seelman, & M. Bury (Eds.), *Handbook of disability studies* (pp. 585–609). Thousand Oaks, CA: Sage Publications.

Algozzine, B., Browder, D., Karvonen, M., Test, D., & Wood, W. (2001). Effects of intervention to promote self-determination for individuals with disabilities. *Review of Educational Research*, *71*, 219–277.

Altman, B. (2001). Disability definitions, models, classification schemes and applications. In G. L. Albrecht, K. D. Seelman, & M. Bury (Eds.), *Handbook of disability studies* (pp. 97–122). Thousand Oaks, CA: Sage Publications.

Balser, D. B. (2007) Predictors of workplace accommodations for employees with mobility-related impairments. *Administration & Society*, *39*, 656–669

Barnes, C. (2000). A working social model? Disability, work and disability politics in the 21st century. *Critical Social Policy*, *65*, 441–457.

Baron, R. C., & Salzer, M. S. (2002). Accounting for unemployment among people with mental illness. *Behavioral Science and the Law*, *20*, 585–599.

Basas, C. G. (2008). Back rooms, boardrooms: Reasonable accommodations and resistance under the ADA. *Berkeley Journal of Employment & Labor Law*, *29*(1), 59–62.

Beatty, J. E., & Kirby, S. L. (2006). Beyond the legal environment: How stigma influences invisible identity groups in the workplace. *Employee Responsibilities and Rights Journal*, *18*, 29–44.

Bertoni, D. (2010). *Actions that could increase work participation for adults with disabilities. Highlights of a forum.* Washington, DC: US Government Accountability Office: Eric Document # ED511105

Beyer, S., Brown, T., Akandi, R., & Ripley, M. (2010). A comparison of quality of life outcomes for people with intellectual disabilities in supported employment and day habilitation programs. *Journal of Applied Research in Intellectual Disabilities*, *23*, 290–295.

Blustein, D. L. (2008). The role of work in psychological health and well being: A conceptual, historical and public policy perspective. *American Psychologist*, *63*, 228–240.

Blustein, D. L., Kenna, A. C., Gill, N., & DeVoy, J. E. (2008). The psychology of working: A new framework for counseling practice and public policy. *Career Development Quarterly*, *56*, 294–308.

Bureau of Labor Statistics (August, 2010). *Persons with a disability: Labor force characteristics—2009.* Washington, DC: Department of Labor, Bureau of Labor Statistics.

Burkhauser, R., Daly, M., & Houtenville, A. (2001). How working-age people with disabilities fared over the 1990's business cycle. In P. Burdett, R. Burkhauser, J. Gregory, & H. Hunt (Eds.), *Ensuring health and income security for an aging workforce* (pp. 291–353). Kalamazoo, MI: Upjohn Institute for Employment Research.

Chadsey, J. G., & Beyer, S. (2001). Social relationships in the workplace. *Mental Retardation and Developmental Disabilities Research Reviews, 7*, 128–133.

Chan, F., Cheng, G., Chan, J. Y., & Rosenthal, D. A. (2006). Predicting employment outcomes of rehabilitation clients with orthopedic disabilities: A CHAID analysis. *Disability and Rehabilitation, 28*(5), 257–270.

Cimera, R. E. (2008). The cost trends of supported employment versus sheltered employment. *Journal of Vocational Rehabilitation, 28*(1), 15–20.

Cinamon, R. G., & Gifsh, L. (2004). Conceptions of work among adolescents and young adults with mental retardation. *Career Development Quarterly, 52*, 212–224.

Cook, J. A., Lehman, A. F., Drake, R., McFarlane, W. R., Gold, P. B., Leff, S., Blyler, C., et al (2005). Integration of psychiatric and vocational services: A multisite randomized controlled trial of supported employment. *American Journal of Psychiatry, 162*, 1948–1956.

Corrigan, P. (2004). How stigma interferes with mental health care. *American Psychologist, 59*, 614–625.

Dalgrin, R. S., & Bellini, J. (2008). Invisible disclosure in an employment interview: Impact on employers hiring decisions and views of employability. *Rehabilitation Counseling Bulletin, 52*, 6–15.

Dart, J. (1993). Introduction—the ADA: A promise to be kept. In L. O. Gostin & H. A. Beyer (Eds.), *Implementing the Americans with Disabilities Act* (pp. xxii). Baltimore, MD: Paul H. Brookes Publishing.

Davies, P., Rupp, K., & Wittenburg, D. (2009). A lifecycle perspective on the transition to adulthood among children receiving Supplemental Security Income. *Journal of Vocational Rehabilitation, 30*, 133–151.

Davis, F. (1961). Deviance disavowal: The management of strained interactions by the visibly handicapped. *Social Problems, 9*(2), 120–132.

Davis, L. J. (2001). Identity politics, disability and culture. In G. Albrecht, K. Seelman, & M. Bury (Eds.), *Handbook of disability studies* (pp. 535–545). Thousand Oaks, CA: Sage Publications.

Dekkers-Sanchez, P. M., Wind, H., Sluiter, J. K., & Frings-Dresen, M. (2010). A qualitative study of perpetuating factors for long-term sick leave and promoting factors for return to work: Chronic work disabled patients in their own words. *Journal of Rehabilitation Medicine, 42*, 544–552.

Dionne, R. S., & Noven, A. (2011). Self-efficacy and health care locus of control: Relationship of occupational disability and workers with low back pain. *Journal of Occupational Rehabilitation, 21*, 421–430.

Domzal, C., Houtenville, A., & Sharma, R. (2008). *Survey of employer perspectives on the employment of people with disabilities: Technical report.* (Prepared under contract to the Office of Disability and Employment Policy, U.S. Department of Labor). McLean, VA: CESSI.

Dunn, E. C., Wewiorski, N. J., & Rogers, E. S. (2008). The meaning and importance of employment to people in recovery from serious mental illness: Results of a qualitative study. *Psychiatric Rehabilitation Journal, 32*, 59–62.

Fabian, E. S. (1992). Supported employment and the quality of life: Does a job make a difference? *Rehabilitation Counseling Bulletin, 36*, 84–97.

Fabian, E. S. (1999). Re-thinking work: The example of consumers with significant mental health disorders. *Rehabilitation Counseling Bulletin, 42*, 302–316.

Fabian, E., & Liesener, J. (2005). Promoting the career potential of youth and young adults with disabilities. In S. D. Brown & R. W. Lent (Eds.), *Career development and counseling: Putting theory and research to work* (pp. 551–573). Hoboken, NJ: John Wiley & Sons, Inc.

Fabian, E., & MacDonald-Wilson, K. (2005). Professional practice in rehabilitation service delivery systems and related system resources. In R. M. Parker, E. M. Szymanski, & J. B. Patterson (Eds.), *Rehabilitation counseling: Basics and beyond* (4th ed., pp. 56–87). Austin, TX: Pro-Ed.

Fleisher, D. Z., & Zames, F. (2001). *The disability rights movement: From charity to confrontation.* Philadelphia: Temple University Press.

Florey, A. T., & Harrison, D. A. (2000). Response to informal accommodation requests from employees with disabilities: Multi-study evidence on willingness to comply. *Academy of Management Review, 43*, 224–233.

Frank, G. (1988). Beyond stigma; visibility and self-empowerment of persons with congenital limb deficiencies. *Journal of Social Issues, 44*, 95–115.

Gilbride, D., & Stensrud, R. (1999). Demand-side job development and systems change. *Rehabilitation Counseling Bulletin, 42*, 329–342.

Gill, C. J. (2001). Divided understandings: The social experience of disability. In G. L. Albrecht, K. D. Seelman, & M. Bury (Eds.), *Handbook of disability studies* (pp. 351–372). Thousand Oaks, CA: Sage.

Gioia, D., & Brekke, J. S. (2003). Knowledge and use of workplace accommodations and protections by young adults with schizophrenia: A mixed method study. *Psychiatric Rehabilitation Journal, 27*(1), 59–68.

Goodwin, D. K. (1994). *No ordinary times.* New York: Simon & Schuster

Granger, B. (2000). The role of psychiatric rehabilitation practitioners in assisting people in understanding how to best assert their ADA rights and arrange job accommodations. *Psychiatric Rehabilitation Journal, 23*(3), 215.

Grob, G. (1994). *The mad among us: A history of the care of America's mentally ill.* Cambridge, MA: Harvard University Press.

Hagner, D. (2000). Primary and secondary labor markets: Implications for vocational rehabilitation. *Rehabilitation Counseling Bulletin, 44*, 22–29.

Hernandez, B., Keys, C., & Balcazar, F. (2000). Employer attitudes toward workers with disabilities and their ADA employment rights: A literature review. *Journal of Rehabilitation, 66*, 4–16.

Hershenson, D. B. (1981). Work adjustment, disability and the three r's of vocational rehabilitation: A conceptual model. *Rehabilitation Counseling Bulletin, 25*, 91–97.

Hershenson, D. B. (2005). INCOME: A culturally inclusive disability-sensitive framework for organizing career development concepts and interventions. *Career Development Quarterly, 54*, 150–161.

Heumann, J. E. (1980). *Civil rights issues of handicapped Americans: Public policy implications.* Washington, DC: A Consultation sponsored by the U.S. Commission on Civil Rights, May 13–14, 1980, pp. 234–235.

Houtenville, A. J., & Burkhauser, R. V. (2004). *Did the employment of people with disabilities decline in the 1990s and was the ADA responsible?* Ithaca, NY: Employment and Disability Institute, School of Industrial & Labor Relations, Cornell University.

Kennedy, J., Olney, M., & Schiro-Geist, C. (2004). A national profile of SSDI recipients and applicants: Implications for early intervention. *Journal of Disability Policy Studies, 15*, 178–185.

Lancourt, J., & & Kettelhut M (1992). Predicting return to work for lower back pain patients receiving worker's compensation. *Spine, 17*, 629–640.

Lidal, I. B., Tuan, K. H., & Biering-Sorensen, F. (2007). Return to work following spinal cord injury: A review. *Disability & Rehabilitation, 29*, 1341–1375.

Linton, S. (2010). Reassigning meaning. In L. J. Davis (Ed.), *The disability studies reader* (pp. 223–236). New York: Routledge.

Lofquist, L. H., & Dawis, R. V. (1969). *Adjustment to work: A psychological view of man's problems in a work-oriented society.* New York: Appleton-Century-Crofts.

Loprest, P., & Maag, E. (2007). The relationship between early disability onset and education and employment. *Journal of Vocational Rehabilitation, 26*(1), 49–62.

Luecking, R., (2009). *The way to work: How to facilitate work experiences for youth in transition.* Baltimore, MD: Paul H. Brookes.

MacDonald-Wilson, K. M., Fabian, E., & Dong, S. (2008). Reasonable accommodation factors that predict employment or return to work—Practices based on the literature. *Rehabilitation Professional, 16*(4), 221–232.

Mank, D., Cioffi, A., & Yovanoff, P. (1997). Analysis of the typicalness of supported employment jobs, natural supports, and wage and integration outcomes. *Mental Retardation, 35*, 185–197

Martoreu, A., Gutierrez-Recachor, P., Pereda, A., & Ayuso-Mateus, I. C. (2008). Identification of personal factors that determine work outcomes for adults with intellectual disabilities. *Journal of Intellectual Disabilities Research, 52*, 1091–1101.

Mathews, C. K., & Harrington, N. G. (2000). Invisible disability. In D. O. Braithwaite & T. L. Thompson (Eds.), *Handbook of communication and people with disabilities* (pp. 405–421). Mahwah, NJ: Erlbaum.

Murphy, R. F. (1990). *The body silent.* New York: W. H. Norton & Co.

National Longitudinal Transition Study-2 (November 2005). *High school completion by youth with disabilities.* Menlo Park, CA: SRI International. Retrieved July 30, 2011, from: www.nlts2.org/fact_sheets/nlts2_fact_sheet_2005_11.pdf

National Organization on Disability (2010). *Survey of Americans with Disabilities, July 26, 2010.* Retrieved March 11, 2011 from: http://www.2010DisabilitySurveys.org/indexold.html

Neff, W. S. (1977). *Work and human behavior.* Chicago: Adeline Publishing Co.

Noonan, B. M., Gallor, S. M., Hensler-McGinnis, N., Fassinger, R. E., Wang, E., et al. (2004). Challenge and success: A qualitative study of the career development of highly achieving women with physical and sensory disabilities. *Journal of Counseling Psychology, 51*, 68–80.

Novak, J. A., & Rogan, P. M. (2010). Social integration in employment settings: Application of intergroup contact theory. *Intellectual and Developmental Disabilities, 48*(1), 31–51.

Oliver, M. (1990). *The politics of disablement.* London, UK: Macmillan.

Orszag, P. (December 9, 2010). Making disability work. Op-ed, *The New York Times.*

Parsons, T. (1972). Definitions of health and illness in the light of American values and social structure? In E. Jaco (Ed.), *Patients, physicians and illness* (2nd ed., pp. 107–127). New York: Free Press.

Patterson, J., Bruyere, S., Szymanski, E. M., & Jenkins, W. (2005). Philosophical, historical and legislative aspects of the rehabilitation counseling profession. In R. M. Parker, E. M. Szymanski, & J. B. Patterson (Eds.), *Rehabilitation counseling: Basics & beyond* (pp. 27–54). Austin, TX: Pro-ed.

Petrovsky, P., & Gleeson, G. (1997). The relationship between job satisfaction and psychological health in people with intellectual disability in competitive employment. *Journal of Intellectual & Developmental Disabilities, 22*, 199–211.

Priebe, S., Warner, R., Hubschmid, T., & Eckle, I. (1998). Employment, attitudes toward work, and quality of life among people with schizophrenia in three countries. *Schizophrenia Bulletin, 24*, 1701–1745.

Priestley, M. (1998). Constructions and creations: idealism, materialism and disability theory. *Disability and Society, 31*, 75–94.

Provencher, H. L., Gregg, R., Crawford, S. M., & Mueser, K. T. (2002). The role of work in the recovery of persons with psychiatric disabilities. *Psychiatric Rehabilitation Journal, 26*(2), 132–145.

Pumpian, I., Fisher, D., Certo, N. J., & Smally, K. A. (1997). Changing jobs: An essential part of career development. *Mental Retardation, 35*, 39–48.

Reisine, S., McQuillan, J., & Field, J. (1995). Predictors of work disability in rheumatoid arthritis patients. *Arthritis & Rheumatism 38*, 1630–1637.

Revell, G., Kregel, J., Wehman, P., & Bond, G. (2000). Cost effectiveness of supported employment programs: What we need to do to improve outcomes. *Journal of Vocational Rehabilitation, 14*, 173–178.

Richardson, M. S. (1993). Work in people's lives: A location for counseling psychologists. *Journal of Counseling Psychology, 40*, 425–433.

Schonherr, M. C., Groothoff, J. W., Mulder, C. A., & Eisman, W. H. (2005). Participation and satisfaction after spinal cord injury: Results of a vocational and leisure outcome study. *Spinal Cord, 43*, 241–248.

Schriner, K. (2001). A disability studies perspective on employment issues and policies for disabled people: An international view. In G. L. Albrecht, K. D. Seelman, & M. Bury (Eds.), *Handbook of disability studies* (pp. 642–662). Thousand Oaks, CA: Sage.

Schroer, C. A., Janssen, M., Van Amelsvoort, L. G., Bosma, H., Swaen, G. M., Nijhuis, R. W., & van Eijk, J. (2005). Organizational characteristics as predictors of RTW disability: A prospective study. *Journal of Occupational Rehabilitation, 15*, 434–445.

Scott, S., McGuire, J., & Shaw, S. (2003). Universal design for instruction: A new paradigm for instruction in post-secondary education. *Remedial and Special Education, 24*, 369–379.

Shaw, L., Segal, R., Polatajko, H., & Harburn, K. (2002). Understanding return to work behaviors: promoting the importance of individual perceptions in the study of return to work. *Disability and Rehabilitation, 24*, 185–195.

Social Security Administration (2009). *The Red Book—A Guide to Work Incentives*. SSA Publication No. 64-030. Retreived February 20, 2000, from: http://www.socialsecurity.gov/redbook.

Soklaridus, S., Ammendolia, C., & Cassidy, D. (2010). Looking upstream to understand low back pain and return to work: Psychosocial factors as the product of system issues. *Social Science & Medicine, 17*, 1557–1566.

Stone, D. (1984). *The disabled state*. Philadelphia: Temple University Press.

Strauser, D. R., O'Sullivan, D., & Wong, A. L. (2010). The relationship between contextual work behaviour self-efficacy and work personality: An exploratory study. *Disability & Rehabilitation, 32*, 1999–2008.

Svajger, A., & Winding, K. (2009). Perceptions of possibilities of returning to work with chronic musculoskeletal disorders. *Work, 32*, 443–454.

Szymanski, E. M., Enright, M. S., Hershenson, D. B., & Ettinger, J. M. (2009). Career development theories and constructs: Implications for people with disabilities. In E. M. Szymanski & R. M. Parker (Eds.), *Work and disability: Contexts, issues and strategies for enhancing employment outcomes for people with disabilities* (pp. 91–154). Austin, TX: Pro-Ed.

Szymanski, E. M., & Hershenson, D. B. (2005). An ecological approach to vocational behavior and career development of people with disabilities. In R. M. Parker, E. M. Szymanski, & J. B. Patterson (Eds.), *Rehabilitation counseling: Basics & beyond* (pp. 225–280). Austin, TX: Pro-Ed.

Tsang, H., Lam, P., Ng, B., & Lueng, O. (2000). Predictors of employment outcomes for people with psychiatric disabilities: A review of literature since the mid-80s. *Journal of Rehabilitation, 66*, 19–38.

Unger, D. (2002). Employers' attitudes toward persons with disabilities in the workplace: Myth or reality? *Focus on Autism and other Developmental Disabilities, 17*, 2–10.

Vestling, M., Tufvesson, S., & Iwarsson, S. (2003). Indicators for return to work after stroke and the importance of work and subjective well-being. *Journal of Rehabilitation Medicine, 35*, 127–131.

Ville, I., & Winance, M. (2006). To work or not to work? The occupational trajectories of wheelchair users. *Disability and Rehabilitation, 28*, 423–436.

Ware, N.C. (1999). Toward a model of social course in chronic illness: The example of chronic fatigue syndrome. *Culture, Medicine and Psychiatry, 23*, 303–331

Wehman, P., Brooke, V. A., & Revell, W. G. (2007. Inclusive employment: Rolling back segregation of people with disabilities. In P. Wehman, K. Inge, W. G. Revel, & B. A. Brooke (Eds.), *Real work for real pay* (pp. 3–18). Baltimore, MD: Paul H. Brookes.

Wehman, P., Targett, P., West, M., & Kregel, J., (2005). Productive work and employment for persons with traumatic brain injury: What have we learned after 20 years? *Journal of Head Trauma Rehabilitation, 20*(2), 115–127.

Wehmeyer, M. L., & Bolding, N. (2008). Enhanced self-determination of adults with intellectual disability as an outcome of moving to community-based work and living environments. *Journal of Intellectual Disabilities Research, 45*, 371–383.

Wewiorski, N. J., & Fabian, E. S. (2004). Association between demographic and diagnostic factors and employment outcomes for people with psychiatric disabilities: A synthesis of recent research. *Mental Health Services Research, 6*(1), 9–21.

Williams, G. (2001). Theorizing disability. In G. Albrecht, K. Seelman, & M. Bury (Eds.), *Handbook of disability studies* (pp. 123–144). Thousand Oaks, CA: Sage Publications.

Winsor, J., & Butterworth, J, (2007). National day and employment service trends in MR/DD agencies. Data Note 11B. Retrieved January 11, 2011 from: http://www.community-inclusion.org/article.php?article_id=210&type=topic&id=5

Wolfensberger, W. (1972). *The principle of normalization in human services*. Toronto: National Institute on Mental Retardation.

World Health Organization (2002). *Towards a common language for functioning, disability and health: ICF.* World Health Organization, Geneva: Author. Retrieved July 31, 2011 from: http://www.who.int/classifications/icf/training/icfbeginnersguide.pdf.

Wright, B. (1983). *Physical disability: A psychosocial approach*. New York: Harper & Row.

Xu, Y. J., & Martz, E. (2010). Predictors of employment of individuals with disabilities: A Bayesian analysis of the Longitudinal Study of the VR Services Program. *Journal of Vocational Rehabilitation, 32*, 35–45.

Yasuda, S., Wehman, P., Targett, P., Cifu, D. X., & West, M. (2002). Return to work after spinal cord injury: A review of recent research. *NeuroRehabilitation, 17*(3), 177–186.

Yates, B. (2010). *Enabled voices: An interpretive study of the "lived experiences" of young adults with disabilities transitioning to work*. Dissertation Abstracts International, Vol. 17(7A). Order Number: AA1336697.

PART 3

Organizational Implications

Redefining Work, Work Identity, and Career Success

Douglas T. Hall *and* Philip H. Mirvis

Abstract

This chapter explores changing definitions of careers in terms of work, work identity, and career success. It enlarges the concept of career *space* by considering how nonwork activities—in one's home and personal life, in social networks, and in the community—can all contribute to self-development and self-image and ultimately to a sense of psychological success in one's career. It also expands the concept of career *time* by opening the relationship between chronological age and career stage to show how people today move in and out of the paid workforce, and across work roles, occupations, and organizations, to put together a boundaryless career. This poses psychological and economic challenges but opens new possibilities for development of self and identity. The chapter examines the personal and environmental resources needed for people to successfully navigate this new career space/time landscape.

Key Words: careers, protean career, psychological success, work identity

In their volume *The Career is Dead, Long Live the Career*, Hall and Associates (1996) make the case that the psychological contract between organizations and employees, based in welfare capitalism and offering lifelong job security, was shattered in the United States in the 1980s and to some extent throughout Europe a decade later. Today, continuous restructuring, outsourcing, and offshoring are common in the private and increasingly public sectors, and the attendant downsizing and preferences for hiring part-time or contingent workers have made employment unstable for many people. As a result, increasing numbers follow a boundaryless career that sees them regularly change jobs and organizations over their life course, experience career "breaks" (voluntary and not) to retool themselves, and along the way, engage in self-study or go back to school, attend to childcare or elder-care responsibilities, transition from old to new friendships and support systems, and rethink and change their career directions.

The self-directed career has several features that differentiate it from the traditional career path, including peaks and valleys of advancement and achievement and movement in and out of the full-time paid workforce. This rollercoaster ride can provide people with new opportunities for self-development and self-expression, but it can also exact material and psychic costs. For instance, larger numbers of working people in the United States and other industrialized countries today go through periods of under- or unemployment, face uncertainty about their future employability, and, in some instances, harbor self-doubts about themselves as providers and career achievers.

Hall and Associates framed this new career in a relational perspective. This framing acknowledges the central role of the individual in setting personal and career goals, making occupational and employment choices, and carving out a career path, but it also nests individual agency in a social/relational context that can include more (and less) supportive employers, family systems, social networks, and communities, as well as cultural influences and public policies regarding work, employment, and success. To successfully navigate the new career, the individual has to be able to make sense of and draw effectively upon the resources of this contextual environment. In addition, the actors, interests, and resources in this environment have to be accessible and responsive.

In his update to the "psychology of working," Blustein (2006) observes similar contours in the occupational terrain and adopts a relational perspective on the architecture and meaning of work. In his frame, work is undertaken by people in both market and nonmarket roles that can enable their material provision and power, social connection, and self-determination. Blustein treats the social/relational context of work as a potential barrier to and facilitator of achieving these three ends.

In this chapter, we join these two distinct but overlapping lines of theory and research to examine how people ask and answer fundamental questions about their work and themselves as they maneuver through the new career:

- Redefining My Work—What is my work?
- Redefining My Identity—What is my work identity?
- Redefining My Career—What is career success?

As we shall see, answers to these questions hinge not only on what individuals are doing, how they define themselves, and how they mark their progress, but also and especially how they configure their experiences into an integrated self-picture of work, themselves, and their career.

The Contemporary Career

As a starting point, consider the new contours of the contemporary career. Three features have been noted as changes over the past two or three decades (Hall, 2002).

From an Organizational to a Protean Career

Over the past decades, there has been a shift in conceptions of career development as more people move from an "organizational" to a "protean" career where they assume greater responsibility for their own career definition and development. Named after Proteus, the Greek god who shifted shape to adapt to new situations, Hall (1976) describes this career as follows:

The protean career is a process which the person, not the organization, is managing. It consists of all of the person's varied experiences in education, training, work in several organizations, changes in occupational field, etc.... the protean career is shaped more by the individual than by the organization and may be redirected from time to time to meet the needs of the person. (Hall, 1976, p. 201)

This decouples the concept of career from a connection to any one organization (or to an organization, period) and from its exclusive association with lifelong paid employment. If the "old career contract" was with the organization, the contract in the protean career is with one's self and is defined by the boundaries a person draws around work or "what I do" (Mirvis & Hall, 1994).

From a Single Life-Long Career to Multiple Mini-Learning Cycles

Much of the theory and research on careers from 1950 to 2000 has focused on the ways people work their way up an organization, emphasizing career stages, life cycles, and ladders (Hall & Associates, 1986). This notion of a career was forged in the post–World War II era and appealed to people who grew up during or heard first-hand stories of the Great Depression and the Great War. Many entered the workforce in the 1950s with the idea of a lifetime career with one employer. Those who began their careers in the next 30 years recognized, to some extent, the necessity of more frequent job changes, but most were still imbued with expectations of upward mobility and looked forward to mastering a job and then savoring the satisfactions of seniority.

However, Hall and Mirvis (1994) have argued that, because of the increased complexity and turbulence in the contemporary work environment, the traditional notion of a single life-long career cycle, with a series of stages, has been replaced with a series of shorter learning cycles. Each career learning cycle looks like an abbreviated version of the Super (1957) career stages: exploration, trial, establishment, and mastery. In the new model, there are short mini-cycles of goal setting, effort, and achievement as the person gains experience and achieves a high level of performance and mastery. Then, near the end of each learning cycle, the person starts exploring again, necessitated by changes in technology, products, markets, or economic factors, or in personal values, needs, or life situation.

From an Objective to a Subjective Definition of Career Success

In this formulation, career development is more cyclical—involving periodic cycles of retrenchment and reskilling. In addition, it will be marked by more lateral, rather than upward, movement and could culminate in a phased retirement. The problem is that this model of career progress is not yet accepted as the norm, and it seems the antithesis of the onward-and-upward ideal that fires the traditional success ethic. What is more, it raises questions as to the timeworn notion that through hard work and diligence one can "make it" in a chosen field of endeavor.

However, the protean career is *not* what happens to the person in any one organization or occupation. The protean person's own personal career choices and search for self-fulfillment are the unifying and integrative elements in his or her life. The criterion of success are not objective, but subjective, and not externally but rather internally defined. The term used to describe this subjective view of assessing success outcomes is *psychological success* (Hall, 1976).

Redefining My Work

Blustein (2006) proposes three sets of basic human needs that can be fulfilled by working—material (survival and power), social connection, and self-determination. To these, we add a fourth dimension: psychological success, which embodies aspects of these three basic needs but also considers how work contributes to people's self-expression and sense of purpose.

Psychological Functions of Work

Consider, first, how the rewards of work relate to these fundamental needs. A key distinction in the psychology of working is made between the extrinsic versus intrinsic rewards of working (Amabile, 1993; Herzberg, 1966). Extrinsic rewards include pay, benefits, job amenities, and chances for advancement, which link directly to people's material needs. Working also provides access to financial (i.e., money) and social (i.e., status, prestige, and privilege) resources that can empower people and aid in their self-determination.

Working is also a way to develop interpersonal relationships outside of the family and neighborhood, and to develop new group affiliations. Studies find that interpersonal relationships enable people to experience their work as more important and meaningful (c.f., Kahn, 1990, Wrzesniewski, 2003,

Wrzesniewski, Dutton, & Debebe, 2003). Research on broader social networks also finds that these can enhance employees' motivations, opportunities, and resources at work (Ibarra, 1993; Leana & Rousseau, 2000; Rangan, 2000).

Finally, psychologists have focused considerable attention on the intrinsic rewards of jobs and identified how task variety, autonomy, and completeness yield more challenge and meaning in a job (Hackman & Lawler, 1971). Studies find that when employees have intrinsically motivating work and can participate in job-related decisions, they feel more engaged in their work roles and feel better about themselves as a person. These are key ingredients in experiencing psychological success.

Need Satisfaction Versus Psychological Success

Studies of work motivation are often premised on the notion, à la Abraham Maslow (1943), that people operate through a hierarchy of needs that motivate them—stretching from basic needs for survival and security, to social needs, to "higher-order" needs associated with self-esteem and self-actualization. Thus there has been a tendency to equate higher-order need satisfaction with psychological success.

Certainly employers have embraced Maslow's hierarchy of needs. For instance, in the 1970s and 1980s, when baby boomers entered the workforce, organizations responded with job enrichment and employee involvement programs. These prescriptions seemed to fit the needs of better-educated and comparatively well-off "new breed" workers, as they were called, for more interesting work and a voice in job-related decisions (Yankelovich, 1981). More recently, under similar logic, organizations are using personal growth and corporate social responsibility programs to "engage" their employees: these seem to fit the needs and aspirations of today's more self-expressive and socially conscious millennial generation (Mirvis, 2012).

A key problem with the "need-based" approach is that studies have shown that Maslow's theory, insightful as it is, doesn't apply mechanically to people in their everyday work lives and circumstances. Research demonstrates, for example, that nearly everyone has some motivations concerning their material provision, social relations, and self-expression and growth—no matter what their current socioeconomic status is (Alderfer, 1972). Thus so-called higher-order needs don't "go away" even when financial concerns predominate.

Furthermore, interests in personal growth and in helping others are found among people of all ages, classes, and colors (Batson, 1990).

The broader point is that psychological success is not realized simply by meeting needs arrayed hierarchically. On the contrary, it is a deeply subjective judgment that hinges on how people set their life and work goals, frame and experience rewards, and perceive themselves in a societal and organizational context (Shepard, 1984; Weiss et al., 2004). This situates psychological success in a more elastic, contextualized, and socially constructed view of the self whereby people interpret their experiences to make sense and meaning of their lives (Baumeister, 1991). In his relational theory of working, Blustein (2011) argues that we need an "expanded vision of working along with an integrative understanding of the complex, reciprocal relationships between work and other life domains" (p. 2). This helps in redefining "work" and self-definitions of "what is my work" to encompass both "market jobs" and what has traditionally been described as "nonwork" or "life settings."

Work in "Nonwork" Settings

Consider a sampling of research about the work that people do in four "nonwork" contexts:

• **Home and family**. As the literature on work and family makes clear, there are many work tasks in the "family" arena (Harrington & Hall, 2007). The care of and responsibility for children and in some instances parents, maintenance and management of the home, not to mention organizing one's own leisure and personal development activities all involve intentional, goal-directed activity, and they all represent work. On the rewards of work, Hochschild (1997) has argued that today's workplaces offer more satisfaction to people than their home environments. However, longitudinal data say otherwise: more people find fulfillment in their home lives than they do in the workplace (Kiecolt, 2003).

• **Friends and social networks.** Planning and organizing a social life with friends, developing new relationships, living in a community and meeting one's responsibilities there, and investing the requisite time and energy to maintain these connections in a mutually rewarding way is also a major area of task activity for most people. In general, the research finds only a modest relationship between friendship and people's overall life satisfaction. However, the relationship increases significantly in cases where friends provide a social support system (Rojas, 2006).

• **Education/learning experiences and personal growth**. When thinking of nonwork settings and activities, it is easy to overlook one's *self* and *self-identity* in the form of one's physical, emotional, and spiritual health and development. Vast numbers of people care for themselves through exercise, hobbies, and myriad types of "soul work." Ironically, the literature of work–life relationships cites these as ingredients for "balance" but scarcely mentions their relevance for self-development and growth. It should: self-awareness and self-development are requisite components in life planning and integral to the experience of psychological success over the life course.

• **Community, church, and civic life**. People live not only in their homes and with their families but also in communities with neighbors, churches, schools, politics, local organizations, cultural activities, and problems or issues requiring collective responses. Engagement in community can involve significant and satisfying task activities.

Enlarging Definitions of What Is My Work

There is considerable research on the question of whether or not the rewards derived from these nonwork settings can "substitute" or in a sense "compensate" for those not realized via an employer (Staines, 1980). While the evidence is mixed, what seems clear is that bad experiences on the job can "spill over" into one's mood and work performance in other life spheres, and vice versa. This means that the rewards derived from family, friendships, community, and personal life cannot compensate for dissatisfaction in a paid job. That said, under the rubric of psychological success, there is potential to bundle together rewards from work and nonwork roles into a larger package that can prove fulfilling and meaningful to people (see Fig. 12.1).

Figure 12.1 depicts an array of "life spheres" involving work and rewards. The past decades have witnessed unprecedented efforts to make work in these settings more explicit and rewarding. There are, for example, countless guidebooks, workshops, support groups, and resources on childrearing, elder care, getting along with your spouse, taking better care of yourself, and so on. The "self-help" movement in the United States alone represents a $10–12 Billion industry. Social media technologies, such as Facebook, LinkedIn, and the like make friendship networks a stronger resource. Educational

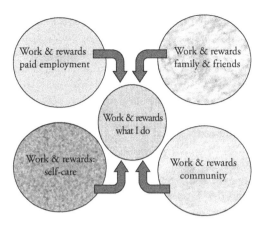

Figure 12.1 Redefining My Work: "What I Do".

resources are more accessible, too, whether through community colleges, the local Y, or online. And community support groups, churches, etc. are all doing their part to help people access material provisions, make social connections, and direct their lives and futures. The sum total of these resources and experiences often outweighs those provided by a work organization. How does this "work" add to the human experience?

A body of research on life satisfaction contends that it is an "additive" function of satisfactions in each of life spheres (Argyle, 2001). Closer examination, however, reveals considerable individual differences in how people calibrate, weigh, and combine their experiences across the life domains. This, in our view, makes life and career planning especially important in the contemporary work world and an essential part of a worker's lifelong learning, best started at an early age.

Progressive employers recognize and respect the challenges and rewards of work in all of these settings. Increasing numbers, for example, have work–family and work–life programs to help their employees to integrate their engagement across these life spheres. They also enable their employees to get involved in community support and service programs. And many insist that their employees prepare personal development programs that encompass their development in work and in other life spheres.

Work for an employer on a paid job and in nonmarket jobs in the home, with family and friends, in the community, and on tasks associated with self-development and helping others all serve important psychological functions. What does it mean for people to achieve psychological success? Hall (1986) has emphasized the importance of adaptability, which he calls a meta-competency,

as it enables people to accommodate themselves to new tasks and relationships in work and nonwork settings and to incorporate new roles and responsibilities into their personal repertoires. There is no denying that working across these multiple spheres can generate role conflicts and overload. What is open to exploration is the extent to which people can mix their relative success experiences in work and nonwork roles together into a recipe for psychological success. Increased "mindfulness" in daily tasks is one inner resource. So, too, employers, communities, and societies overall can facilitate and legitimize work in nonwork settings.

Redefining what I do to encompass the varied mix of joys and frustrations of work in employment and nonwork settings increases the scope and variety of rewards available to people from their work. Still, there can be a tendency to categorize and rate these rewards in each setting. To synergize them, working people also have to redefine "who am I" when working.

My Work Identity: Who I Am

To shift from an occupational to relational model of work invites a shift in how people define their work identity. To say someone needs something emphasizes his or her individualistic and atomistic nature. A relational perspective, by comparison, stresses his or her social and connected self. Adding this perspective to developmental psychology, Miller (1976) argues that the self cannot be separated from its relation to others and that an "interacting sense of self" is present for all infants and informs development of the self over the life course. In a sociological frame, Mead (1934) likewise contended that one's sense of self is formed in relation to multiple expectations and demands from society. In this construction, the self is a "whole" that encompasses and integrates people's identities in various roles—as, say, employee, coworker, parent, community member, and the like.

The relevance of this idea for employee engagement took shape decades ago when it was posited that people think of themselves and embody identity in the workplace in the form of gender, race, ethnicity, sexual preference, and age, and in their life roles as, for instance, caregivers and providers. These forms of identity have been the subject of debate, consciousness raising, and policymaking throughout societies and within companies as well. In top firms today, for example, employee diversity is valued not only as a human resource management driver but as a source of fresh ideas, as a means of mirroring and better serving the multicultural marketplace, and as a source of learning and effectiveness, as Thomas and Ely (1996) point out in their analysis of the changing contours of diversity management in corporations. A parallel argument has been made by Parker and Hall (1993) for the benefits of flexible work arrangements and other work–family programs.

Building on this logic, Googins, Mirvis, and Rochlin (2007) see a broader move in identity engagement whereby employers engage their employees as "citizens." This naturally means recognizing and respecting employees in their many dimensions of self-identity—race, gender, age, and so on—and in their multiple work and work–life roles as workers to be sure, but also as working parents and members of a community. It also means recognizing and validating them in relation to their roles as citizens of a society and inhabitants of the planet (see Fig. 12.2). The argument is that this further enables the engagement of the "whole self" and can yield benefits for an individual, an organization, and society.

How Organizations Engage Identity

Organizations are today engaging the employee's identity with respect to age, gender, race, sexual orientation, and the like—facets of personal identity that are socially situated in people's upbringing, families, and identity groups on and off the job. Leading organizations go further by hosting diversity and work–family forums to steer corporate conduct, as well as associations of minorities, women, and LGBTs where employees can share common interests and advocate for their concerns. These affinity groups not only provide input to and

feedback on company matters, they also influence the public policy positions taken by their organization—witness, by way of example, the increasing number of organizations in the United States taking an affirmative stand on gay/lesbian rights or supporting professional associations of women and minorities that span multiple companies and industries.

Pitt-Catsouphes and Googins (2005) contend that work–family support is an employer's social responsibility because the way organizations respond to the needs of working parents has implications not only for the children and elders they might care for but also for the broader society. Thus socially responsible employers are devising community-based strategies to work–family issues that have them engaged in local transportation forums, before- and after-school childcare programs, education reform programs, and the like. Several organizations have joined forces with others in a coalition of businesses, Corporate Voices for Working Families, to promote work–family balance nationally and globally.

How about engaging people's self-in-the-world? Many corporate social responsibility programs honor and extend people's aspirations to redress social problems such as the rich–poor gap and digital divide or to care for the planet. In this sphere encompassing people's societal roles, engagement often takes the form of volunteerism, increasingly of a type where employees' talents and the firm's resources are marshaled to address significant and relevant social challenges. Beyond this, innovative employers are educating their people about social and environmental matters, gaining their hands-on participation in eco-friendly, cause-related, or fair-trade marketing, and involving them in triple-bottom-line audits.

Best Buy and Identity Engagement

The electronics retailer Best Buy exemplifies the relational aspects of employee engagement. Individual employees, for example, are engaged through the company's "strength-based" human resources model that encourages job involvement and development around their personal strengths and passions. On the work–life boundary, many employees are part of a results-only work environment (ROWE) that allows them to flexibly manage their work and personal time, so long as results are achieved. The company also hosts a women's leadership forum (WOLF) that engages female managers, employees, and customers in "Wolf Packs"

Figure 12.2 Redefining Who I Am: Engaging the "Whole Person".

that provide leadership counsel and social support. Going further on identity engagement, Best Buy also supports affinity groups revolving around race (Black Employees Network, Asian Employees Network, Latin Employees Network), age (Teenage Employees and SaGE—The wisdom of experience), sexual orientation (PRIDE), faith, military service, and personal abilities/disabilities (INCLUDE).

Best Buy is expanding its engagement program to focus employee energy and entrepreneurism on society through a "venture citizenship" program. For example, store employees, rather than professional staff, run the company's community grant program and decide which nonprofits to support. In turn, they work with students in the @15 program to teach them how to run their own volunteer programs. And the company's Geek Squad donates its time and talents to supporting community-based groups. On the job, employees take part in the company's program to recycle used electronics, whether purchased at Best Buy or not, and share ideas on "greening" their operations through Blue Shirt Nation, employees' social media conversation.

Why would a company concern itself with and seek to activate people's identities as citizens of a corporation, community, society, and planet? One reason is that when employees find that their company welcomes the full range of their interests and aspirations, including for instance a personal desire to serve society and/or protect the planet, they feel welcome to bring their "whole self" into the workplace. In a relational context, corporate social responsibility initiates a conversation between individual and corporate identity that shapes a company's culture and also its employees' career orientation (c.f., Schein, 1984). Employees whose aspirations to live and work responsibly are fulfilled through their companies thereby serve as effective brand ambassadors for their firms through their word-of-mouth commentary. They also produce social capital—a web of positive relevant relationships—that connects their companies to other stakeholders and the public at large.

Enriching My Work Identity

Blustein (2006) defines work as "effort, activity, and human energy in given tasks that contribute to the overall social and economic welfare of a given culture" (p. 3). Ironically, it was Maslow (1968) who laid the foundation for this deeper level of psychological engagement by working people in his depiction of people's "Being Values," which include, among other themes, fundamental human preferences for truth, goodness, beauty, wholeness, and justice. Early on, Maslow, like many of his contemporaries, expressed concern that the existing "social order" thwarted people's personal growth and countered inclinations toward altruism and generativity. However, in *Eupsychian Management* (Maslow, 1965), he confessed that his earlier depictions of human motivation were too "individualistic" and failed to acknowledge the positive potential of groups, organizations, and communities to promote human development. This marked his embrace of humanistic psychology with its emphasis on human potential and the importance of people discovering their fundamental purpose in life.

The idea that work organizations could serve a liberating and generative purpose for employees was variously expressed in the 1960s and 1970s by Douglas McGregor (1960) in depictions of Theory X and Y management models, in the practices of group and organization development during that era, and in employee engagement efforts that drew from the theories of Erich Fromm to show how companies might promote an "ethic of being" as opposed to an "ethic of having" among their employees (Mills, 1975).

Needless to say, the human potential movement was downplayed in practices of employee engagement in the 1980s and 1990s that stressed the material aspects of organizational involvement (Kanter & Mirvis, 1989). However, interest in human potential is being resurrected today in many complementary ways. Csikszentmihalyi (1993), as one example, depicts humans as having an "evolving self" whose growth hinges on attaining fuller consciousness of their inner nature and of the world that surrounds them. In developmental terms, this posits that human potential expands as people gain a deeper sense of their individual uniqueness and connect it to the processes at work in the world. In so doing, Csikszentmihalyi (1993, p. 281) contends, "One needs to step out of the cocoon of personal goals and confront larger issues in the public arena."

What would it take for people to enrich the work identity to include a full range of life spheres? Hall (1986) calls personal identity development another meta-competency needed to experience psychological success over the course of a career. Identity integration is a major part of adult development (Kegan, 1982). As people move through various levels of growth, the self becomes more differentiated. That is, people's lives become richer, with more varied activities in more varied roles. Their emotional world becomes bigger and more complex. And the self must grow and create new components that serve to connect people to this richer set of engagements with the world.

However, as the self becomes more differentiated and complex, it is necessary to integrate these facets into a cohering self-picture, so that the individual feels whole. The psychologically healthy person is able to hold all of these different parts of the self, or "sub-identities," in one larger, unifying identity. This attainment of an integrated identity is a highly demanding activity, as one is literally growing a new self as one moves through levels of development.

What seems necessary is for a person to establish some distance between his or her core self and engagement in multiple life spheres. In this holistic view of identity, the tasks associated with work, family, friends, community, and such can be separated and distinct, but the person performing these tasks integrates them in a larger identity that embodies roles as a worker, parent, friend, and citizen. The challenge posed by the protean career is for people to integrate many more stimuli and experiences into their sense of self. This means finding fresh answers to ambiguous questions: "What is my work? What is my work identity? What is career success?"

Redefining My Career: What Is Success?

There are several advantages that accrue from the protean career concept. First, it opens up new ways to think about career activity over *time*. The traditional model of one life/one career development has individuals explore occupations and employers early on, increase their talents and productivity from early to middle stages of their employment, and then either "plateau" or "drop off" in terms of their own career aspirations and what they have to offer an organization. The protean concept, however, introduces a more elastic and socially constructed *time span*. It encompasses early career development marked by high achievement in, for example, a startup or fast-moving technical field as well as the challenge of recent college graduates "living at home" and cobbling together internships and part-time jobs while searching for something more sustainable. It includes mid-career retrenchment, to attend to family or reskill for new pursuits, as well as forays into self-employment as, say, a consultant. And it covers late blooming, whereby one finds one's passions to pursue or at least stays active in a post-retirement job.

Second, it enlarges the career *space*. There is a tendency to associate a career with paid work and to draw sharp distinctions between people's work and nonwork lives. A more elastic concept, however, acknowledges that work and nonwork roles overlap and shape jointly a person's identity and sense of self. In practical terms, an enlarged definition of career space enables people to consider seriously taking time off to spend with growing children or to care for aging parents under the rubric of attaining psychological success. There are, in addition, many examples of people "downshifting" in their careers to pursue hobbies or regain peace of mind, combining a part-time job with volunteer work to give back to the community, and pursuing the option of self-employment and freelancing.

As partial evidence of the popular interest in the protean career, there is now a protean career group on LinkedIn (http://www.linkedin.com/groups/Protean-Careers-3533493?trk=myg_ugrp_ovr). Many of the active members on this site seem to be career coaches, consultants, and teachers, who share their views on modern careers, as well as how to respond to some of the major issues and dilemmas facing people in their careers today.

Toward Psychological Success: Career as Calling

Research by Derr (1986) suggested that people have different orientations to career success. (In recent years, career success has been one of the most widely studied concepts in the careers literature; see Arthur, Khapova, & Wilderom (2005); Briscoe, Hall, & Mayrhofer, 2012.) For those concerned with getting *ahead*, for instance, a prime objective is upward mobility. Others seek to be *secure* or strive to *be free* and autonomous. The goals are challenge and stimulation for those who want to get *high*. Finally, there are those who want to get *balanced* and combine personal and family life with career achievement. Although these career orientations seem to represent individual differences in temperament and aspiration, Derr's research suggests that they can change in response to life experiences. More flexible definitions of a career will give people the freedom to change their career orientations over the life course.

To illustrate: if we take seriously the notion that people will age over several career cycles, then an early-career man, needing more education to move up the career ladder, may choose instead to emphasize his parental role, take more time off to be with young children, and "switch gears" to a balanced identity, thereby putting off an MBA until his mid-30s or later or not at all. In the same way, a mid-career woman, whose career has peaked with a small employer or on a functional career track, may "rev up" by moving to a nonprofit service organization or simply increasing her volunteer time.

Blustein et al. (2008) make the case that "work is also a means to contribute to the larger economic structure of society, thereby offering individuals a sense of connection to their broader social world" (p. 299). Thus it is relevant to ask whether or not people feel that they are doing something *useful* on their jobs. On this count, Grant (2007) reviews evidence that makes a strong case for "relational job design" that enables people to express their prosocial motives by making a "positive difference" in other people's life. Some of this is encompassed through the idea of "task significance" in the job design literature. It is also captured more fully in service learning. Grant's field studies connect this specifically to corporate social responsibility by documenting how engaging employees in community service gave them an opportunity to support others, which in turn strengthened their organizational commitment. In a felicitous turn of the phrase, he makes the point that linking corporate social responsibility to employee engagement is about employees "giving" rather than "receiving." (Grant, Dutton, & Rosso, 2008).

Finally, one of the deepest forms of psychological success can occur when the person experiences work as more than a job or career—when it is a calling, work that a person perceives as his or her purpose in life. The early notion of a calling was described as a divine inspiration to do morally responsible work (Weber, 1958). Later work moved beyond a strictly religious connotation of calling and toward a broader secular view. Bellah et al. (2007) described a work orientation that they referred to as a "calling," which is an orientation that describes those who work for the fulfillment of doing so and, in addition, believe that their work affects society in some way.

More recent work has viewed a calling as a strong sense of inner direction—work that would contribute to a better world (c.f., Dobrow, 2006; Hall & Chandler, 2005; Lips-Wiersma, 2002; Wrzesniewski, 2003). In this secular view, the calling comes from an internal motivation that is not driven by instrumental goal seeking. Rather, it reflects a generalized form of psychological engagement with the meaning of one's career work (c.f., Kahn, 1990; Wrzesniewski et al., 1997). For example, Hansen (1997) describes how a person's career self-assessment and development often involves a self-reflective quest for personal and professional purpose, as part of the development of the "whole person."

Lips-Wiersma and Morris (2011) have identified two major dimensions of a calling orientation: a focus on others versus on self, and a focus on doing versus being. Although all of these concerns can have positive effects, a person who moves too far in one direction does so at the expense of the related dimension. For example, if the person who is spending great amounts of time in service to others may not have enough time to care for himself or herself. And if the person spends great amounts of time in "doing" mode (such as doing community service, perhaps in far-flung parts of the developing world), he or she will not have much time for "being" (e.g., personal growth, developing self-awareness). Moving too far in any direction away from the center creates a loss of equilibrium. On the other hand, when one has a balance of all four of these meaningful activities, one is in equilibrium—a state that Lips-Wiersma calls "spiritual coherence" (Lips-Wiersma, 2002).

To illustrate these elements of a sense of calling and how they can provide strong intrinsic motivation, Hall and Chandler (2005) describe the experience of Laura, who has pursued a career in the public and nonprofit sectors:

> In high school, she was the associated student body president and almost single-handedly reformed the associated student government election system in her senior year. In college, she was one of three keynote speakers at a major political conference in Washington, DC. As Laura described the effect of this experience, "The … experience bolstered my self-confidence."
>
> After college, she was granted a fellowship to go to Israel for a year. Early during her stay in Israel, she was asked to be the American student representative at a conference sponsored by the Israeli President on Israel–Diaspora relations. At lunch, the Israeli President invited her to sit at his table and they discussed how much students would benefit from a conference specifically structured around their needs. She volunteered to organize it and the President promptly accepted and offered his residence as the conference location. Ultimately, 120 students from all over the world participated the next year." (Hall & Chandler, 2005, pp. 167–168)

After finishing her education, Laura worked in state government and became Chief of Staff for an agency deputy commissioner at the age of 30 after being there for 4 years. When we last heard, she reported that she was exploring a change: "I think I've just reached my learning plateau and I'm getting a bit bored" (Hall & Chandler, 2005, p. 168).

Career Development in a Stratified Workforce

While the protean career model is increasingly visible in today's economy, it can have different contours in the increasingly stratified workforce. To recruit and retain well-educated, technically skilled, in-demand workers, for instance, employers have launched a "war for talent" that has them pitch starting bonuses, flexible hours, challenging projects, the latest technology, and amenities ranging from a concierge service to health club memberships. These higher-end workers and professionals are very mobile and seek employment offering both meaning and money throughout their careers. Some operate as "free agents" and regularly transfer their skills to whichever employer is the "highest bidder."

While this mobile career path can be a recipe for psychological success, some who have followed it are taking a fresh look at work purpose and lifestyle. Growing numbers of young people, eschewing the fast track, are refashioning themselves as social entrepreneurs, starting social enterprises, or moving into established nonprofits to address community and social problems. A growing number of businesses, in turn, are offering their employees a chance to "do good" through service learning assignments (Mirvis, Thompson, & Gohring, 2012). IBM, for example, has sent over 1,000 employees on 100 teams to 24 countries on one-month service assignments through its Corporate Service Corps. Modeled on the U.S. Peace Corps, the program engages teams of volunteers in three months of pre-work, one month in country, and two months in post-service, where they harvest insights for themselves and their business.

At the other end of the employment spectrum are less-educated, less-skilled workers who have high rates of joblessness today and whose future prospects for full-time employment are chancy. The recent recession has ravaged the employment prospects of millions in the United States, but the hardest-hit have been low-income and disadvantaged populations. The poverty rate in the United States has risen sharply (reaching a 15-year high in 2012); rates of unemployment among racial minorities and 18- to 29-year-olds have skyrocketed; and community resources, ranging from food banks to shelters to medical care, have lagged behind needs.

For this segment, unemployment assistance and training are essentials to gaining any foothold in the labor market. International training and temporary work organizations like Manpower provide extensive life and personal counseling to unemployed youth and sponsor programs to boost their self-confidence and self-definition. Focus: HOPE, a nonprofit based in Detroit, Michigan, is an example of local responsiveness. It has trained (or retrained) over 12,000 men and women (primarily African Americans) to become machinists, CAD/CAM operators, IT specialists, and systems engineers in partnership with auto companies, high-technology firms, and area universities (which provide college degrees for trainees). Focus: HOPE also runs a daycare center, operates a food bank, and runs community development programs—all in support of promoting economic development and eliminating racism in the Detroit area.

Employers also have a role in supporting low-income employees and communities. A 2009 survey (BCCCC, 2009) found that one in four U.S. employers have programs to purchase goods and services from women- and minority-owned suppliers, and as many provide training and development opportunities for their lower-wage employees. Fewer (18%) take special steps to hire employees from poor communities. This study found that large employers do considerably more than smaller ones to support low-income workers and communities, but their support declined in the recession. Obviously more is needed from the private sector to assist low-income and disadvantaged populations to get on (and stay on) a career track.

In the vast middle of the workforce are growing numbers who are dissatisfied with their jobs but who cannot move to new ones because of the lack of opportunity, outdated skills, or limited personal mobility. To stay in the labor market, many in the middle ranks have to update their training and, as Hall and Mirvis (1996) put it, "learn a living." The most youthful and most mature of this work population will also have to accept part-time job opportunities and cobble together, respectively, a beginning or ending career stage.

While a career path of lifelong learning may sound appealing to self-starters and self-developers, it has its downsides. The resulting sense of overload and regular movement across work/nonwork boundaries poses practical problems and can fragment people's work identities and family systems. Furthermore, people who more or less start over in a new occupation can have lower overall lifetime earnings than those in the traditional single-career path. Taking into account the costs of retraining and redeployment, plus the value of lost earnings, the protean career may well prove less remunerative than the stable career paths of the past.

Resources for Career Redefinition

Nevertheless, there are resources to draw on to successfully navigate the boundaryless career. What kinds of occupational and psychological supports can contribute to integrated identity development as people live and work through the self-construction required by a protean career? Consider a few of them.

• **Lifelong learning.** Hall and Mirvis (1994) contend that to be successful in a protean career requires more than periodic retraining; instead, people need to embark on a course of continuous lifelong learning. This can involve formal schooling and online learning, of course, but it also means intentionally seeking jobs that call for skill development and taking stock of personal learning experiences. Expanding this point, Gratton (2011) contends that working people should also associate themselves with a "big-ideas crowd" to stay abreast of the latest thinking and developments that could pertain to their occupation and industry.

• **Smart jobs.** Hall and Las Heras (2010) also speak to the importance of "smart jobs." Here the combination of demanding task characteristics, varied interpersonal relations, and rich developmental opportunities can contribute to self-development and expression. In a sense, the work in paid employment and nonwork settings can be conceived of as providing "modules" of smart tasks. Making connections between work on the job and at home, between service to customers and community, and so on enables people to "practice" adaptability and to see their work identity in a more integrated way.

• **Collaborative workspaces**. It is also notable how new social forms are emerging to help people enact a protean career. There are, for example, growing numbers of "collaborative workspaces" arising in big cities where individuals have access not only to an office and telecommunications but also to a diverse set of independent peers. Hub operators have begun to offer professional development programs for their clientele. In addition, there are growing numbers of online marketplaces like oDesk and freelancer.com, which secure fringe benefits for individual contributors, and like Mom Corps, which offer a portfolio of paid and bartered services for professional women.

Making Space for Self-Development and Career Development

To grow, the person thus needs to evolve to a higher level of consciousness. This requires that the person receive support in an unconditional way, despite any mistakes he or she might make. This means the creation of a "safe space" containing *psychological safety* for experimentation and personal growth. This is what Kegan calls a "holding environment." What, specifically, would a holding environment look like in a paid employment setting? Let us propose a few possibilities:

• *A period of time in which the person's primary task (or a major task, if not the primary task) would be to grow in some way.* Examples might be time off the job at a one-week retreat or training program, a one-year period when the person is engaged in a formal educational program (e.g., an executive MBA program), or an expatriate job assignment in which the person is expected to spend significant time in learning about the local culture and business practices. And some organizations, of course, do have formal sabbaticals, where employees, following a certain number of years of service, are granted a number of months of paid leave to pursue their personal interests.

• *A formal educational component is helpful but not required.* It helps legitimize the time spent in a learning role if the person is enrolled in a formally defined learning program. Many of the other steps listed below are easier to "sell" to the person's role senders if he or she is in the role of student.

• *Explicit recognition from one's major role senders of this liminal period and a reduction in their work role expectations.* This change in the expectations of role senders means that the person's job has been redesigned to a certain extent, to allow for the new time devoted to learning. This, in turn, would mean a renegotiation of the work role with these role senders. This gets us to the next point ...

• *The supervisor, representing the employing organization, must lead and provide ongoing support for the reduced work role expectations.* This means that the boss must "run interference" and help maintain the boundary between the person's regular work responsibilities and the time required for development. This may require additional staffing or a reallocation of responsibilities within the work group.

• *For the organization, this can be a time for staff and role revitalization.* Often this can be a good opportunity to revisit and revise the design of a job, eliminating outdated activities. It can also be a good opportunity to delegate important tasks to more junior employees or to bring interns into the organization on temporary assignments, and thus provide trial work for potential new staff members.

• *Relational resources for development must be provided.* Since much adult learning comes from relational sources, it is important to provide explicit "guides" to the learner. These could be professional coaches, peer coaches (i.e., other people going through a similar development process), or teachers who help impart specific skills and knowledge. A person who has recently gone through a similar kind of development process can be a particularly powerful source of relational learning.

• *Opportunities for personal reflection are critical to help the learner extract the lessons of the holding environment.* This may sound obvious, but it rarely happens. One of the great ironies of most adult learning experiences is that they entail the investment of considerable resources (time, effort, and money), and much learning does in fact occur—but it is often not retained because the learner does not do the final work of getting "up on the balcony" and reflecting on the experience and formally culling out the wisdom and lessons that he or she has gained. With the online technology now available, it is possible to automate periodic (e.g., weekly) "time outs," when the person is reminded of his or her learning goals and prompted to recall opportunities that came up that week to work toward those goals, and is then asked to assess progress made. (For one example, see Fort Hill Company's "Results Engine" http://www.forthillcompany.com/solutions/retransfertool/).

Redefining Career Time

To make sense of all these, work identity learning requires *reconceptualizing career time*—the traditional relationship between chronological age and career stage. Recognizing increasing longevity and better health in the aging population, for example, popular culture has adopted the mantra that "70 is the new 50." This, along with material requirements to do so, makes it quite acceptable to speak of a "third stage" or "encore" career (Kim, 2010) where erstwhile retirees instead continue working for their employers, but for fewer hours and less income, connect to another organization or perhaps a nonprofit, or start their own enterprise.

Another requirement is to rethink "aging." Pitt-Catsouphes, Matz-Costa, and Brown (2010), for instance, have developed the "prism of age" that compares how people see themselves in terms of their chronological age, life stage, and career stage. The permutations yield patterns whereby older workers often see themselves at midlife (60 is the new 40) and at a midcareer stage (places to go, things to do). There are psychological markers of this new prism in the outlooks of aging adults. Bateson (2010), for example, posits an Adulthood II stage in late-adult development marked by a developmental crisis between "engagement versus withdrawal." This stage fits in between the Eriksonian stages of mature adulthood (generativity) and old age (integrity). In seeking and exercising "active wisdom" in this Adulthood II stage, older adults have to cycle back through challenges associated with identity formation, intimacy, and generativity as they embark on a new life and career stage.

Furthermore, there is a need for language, labels, and concepts that enable people to understand where they are and where they are going in career time. In lieu of traditional career anchors (Schein, 1974) that define and give meaning to traditional career development stages and mark a path toward upward mobility, the protean career requires signposts that tell people how to travel "on" and "off" ramps to new jobs and employers (Hewlett & Luce, 2005).

Note that this attention to career time is not limited to aging adults. Another societal mantra is that "30 is the new 15." This has young adult children living in their parents' homes, not fully employed, and lacking any picture of career progress. Psychological and sociocultural forces figure into their conceptions of career time. Arnett (2000), for instance, has assigned a stage of development to 20-somethings that he calls "emerging adulthood" that continues identity exploration and involves instability, self-focus, feeling in-between, and "a sense of possibilities." In turn, Gerson (2009) focuses on how these young people grew up during the gender revolution of the workplace and the rise of two-career couples as well as divorce. These have fundamentally shaped career and work–life balance aspirations of 20-somethings.

The net effect of these changes at the early and later career stages will be to prolong the working and learning stages of a person's work career. In contrast to the earlier career stage model identified by Super (1957) in the mid-20th century, with perhaps a 35- or 40-year period of productive employment

(25 to 60 or 65), we are now seeing some combinations of working and learning taking place in the teens and continuing into the 70s and 80s, a potential career span of roughly 70 years. This means that for a person in high school or college today, his or her career may be almost twice as long as that of his or her parents or grandparents. However, not only is such an extended span possible in terms of health and physical capability, it will also be necessary for the person's physical and fiscal—not to mention emotional and spiritual—health.

Conclusion

In sum, it appears that our traditional concepts of work are simply not working. The locus of work, which was at one time external, rooted in an objective role or position in organizational space, is now more relational and subjective. The nature of the work that a person does and the social or relational space in which that work is carried out has much more permeable boundaries than earlier, more traditional conceptions of work that formed the basis of what was a job and what was a career. Now the paid employment role is just one part of what a person does, along with key relationships with family and friends, personal development (i.e., one's relationship with oneself), and one's embeddedness in and contributions to a larger community in the world.

And in a related way, one's work identity is also the property of a more fluid set of influences. One's work identity is a negotiated construct that is the result of a social exchange process involving the focal individual and the members of her or his relevant reference groups (Grote & Hall, 2012; Ibarra, 1993). A person's work identity is influenced not only by work roles, but also by personal affinities and social identities (groups in which he or she feels membership), personal and family connections, and one's connection to personally meaningful purposes and activities in the world. These more diffuse and diverse influences upon one's sense of work identity make the process of choice and personal integration much more difficult than it was in earlier eras (Kegan, 1994).

The key currencies in all of this complexity and ambiguity are the individual's awareness of self as he or she navigates various role and self-expectations, as well as his or her adaptability, or facility in shaping and responding to these changing expectations. The ability to be comfortable with change, to anticipate and move smoothly through ongoing transitions, and to be a continuous, lifelong learner is critical to success, both subjective and objective.

Achieving this comfort with ambiguity and change will become the new norm for personal and career development.

References

Alderfer, C. P. (1972). *Existence, relatedness, and growth: Human needs in organizational settings.* New York: Free Press.

Amabile, T. (1993). Motivational synergy: Toward new conceptions of intrinsic and extrinsic motivations in the workplace. *Human Resource Management Review, 3*(3), 185–201.

Argyle, M. (2001), *The psychology of happiness.* London: Routledge.

Arnett, J. J. (2000). Emerging adulthood: A theory of development from the late teens through the twenties. *American Psychologist, 55*(5), 469–480.

Arthur, M. B., Khapova, S. N., & Wilderom, C. P. M. (2005). Career success in a boundaryless career world. *Journal of Organizational Behavior, 26*(2), 177–202.

Bateson, M. C. (2010). *Composing a further life: The age of active wisdom.* New York: Knopf.

Batson, C. D. (1990). How social an animal? The human capacity for caring. *American Psychologist, 45,* 336–346.

Baumeister, R. F. (1991). *Meanings of life.* New York: The Guilford Press.

BCCCC (2009). *The state of corporate citizenship in the U. S. 2009.* Boston: Center for Corporate Citizenship, 2009.

Bellah, R., Madsen, R., Sullivan, W., Swidler A., & Tipton, S. (2007). *Habits of the heart* (3rd ed.). Berkeley: University of California Press.

Blustein, D. L. (2006). *The psychology of working: A new perspective for career development, counseling, and public policy.* Mahwah, NJ: Erlbaum.

Blustein, D. L. (2011). A relational theory of working. *Journal of Vocational Behavior, 79,* 1–17.

Blustein, D. L., Kenna, A. C., Gill, N., & DeVoy, J. E. (2008). The psychology of working: A new framework for counseling practice and public policy. *Career Development Quarterly, 56*(4), 294–308.

Briscoe, J. P., Hall, D. T., & Mayrhofer, W. (Eds.) (2012). *Careers and cultures—A global perspective: The collaboration for the cross-cultural study of contemporary careers.* New York: Routledge.

Csikszentmihalyi, M. (1993). *The evolving self: A psychology for the third millennium.* New York: Harper/Collins.

Derr, C. B. (1986). *Managing the new careerists.* San Francisco: Jossey Bass.

Dobrow, S. R. (2006). *Having a calling: A longitudinal study of young musicians.* Doctoral dissertation, Harvard University.

Gerson, K. (2009). *The unfinished revolution: How a new generation is reshaping family, work, and gender in America.* New York: Oxford University Press.

Googins, B., Mirvis, P. H., & Rochlin, S. (2007). *Beyond good company: Next generation corporate citizenship.* New York: Palgrave MacMillan.

Grant, A. M. (2007). Relational job design and the motivation to make a prosocial difference. *Academy of Management Review, 32*(2), 393–417.

Grant, A. M., Dutton, J. E., & Rosso, B. (2008). Giving commitment: Employee support programs and the prosocial sensemaking process. *Academy of Management Journal, 51,* 898–918.

Gratton, L. (2011). *The shift: The future of work is already here.* London: Collins.

Grote, G., & Hall, D. T. (2012). Reference groups: A missing link in career studies. Unpublished technical report, ETH, Zurich.

Hackman, J. R., & Lawler, E. E. (1971). Employee reaction to job characteristics. *Journal of Applied Psychology, 55,* 259–286.

Hall, D. T. (1976). *Careers in organizations.* Santa Monica, CA: Goodyear Publishing Company.

Hall, D. T. (2002). *Careers in and out of organizations.* Thousand Oaks, CA: Sage.

Hall, D. T., and Associates. (1986). *Career development in organizations.* San Francisco, CA: Jossey-Bass.

Hall, D. T., and Associates. (1996). *The career is dead—long live the career.* San Francisco, CA: Jossey-Bass.

Hall, D. T., & Chandler, D. E. (2005). Psychological success: When the career is a *calling. Journal of Organizational Behavior, 26,* 155–176.

Hall, D. T., & Las Heras, M. (2010). Reintegrating job design and career theory: Creating not just good jobs but smart jobs. *Journal of Organizational Behavior, 31(2-3),* 448–462.

Hall, D. T., & Mirvis, P. (1996). The new protean career: Psychological success and the path with a heart. In D. T. Hall and Associates, *The career is dead—long live the career* (pp. 15–46). San Francisco, CA: Jossey-Bass.

Hall, D. T., & Mirvis, P. H. (1994). Careers as lifelong learning. In A. Howard (Ed.), *The changing nature of work* (pp. 323–361). San Francisco, CA: Jossey-Bass.

Hansen, L. S. (1997). *Integrative life planning: Critical tasks for career development and changing life patterns.* San Francisco, CA: Jossey-Bass.

Harrington, B., & Hall, D. T. (2007). *Career management and work life integration: Using self-assessment to navigate contemporary careers.* Thousand Oaks, CA. Sage.

Herzberg, F. (1966). *Work and the nature of man.* Cleveland, OH: World.

Hewlett, S. A., & Luce, C. B. (2005). Off-ramps and on-ramps: keeping talented women on the road to success. *Harvard Business Review,* March, *83*(3), 43–54.

Hochschild, A. (1997). *The time bind: When work becomes home and home becomes work.* New York: Metropolitan Books, 1997.

Ibarra, H. (1993) Personal networks of women and minorities in management: A conceptual framework. *Academy of Management Review, 18,* 56–87.

Kahn, W. A. (1990). The psychological conditions of personal engagement and disengagement at work. *Academy of Management Journal, 33,* 692–724.

Kanter, D. L., & Mirvis, P. H. (1989). *The cynical Americans: Living and working in an age of discontent and disillusion.* San Francisco, CA: Jossey-Bass.

Kegan, R. (Ed.). (1982). *The evolving self: Problem and process in human development.* Cambridge, MA: Harvard University Press.

Kegan, R. (1994). *In over our heads: The mental demands of modern life.* Cambridge, MA: Harvard University Press.

Kiecolt, K. J. (2003). Satisfaction with work and family life: no evidence of a cultural reversal. *Journal of Marriage and Family, 65,* 23–35.

Kim, N. (2010). *Who am I, what I do, and where I belong Revisited: Older workers' identity change and their work in post-retirement years.* Academy of Management Conference, Montreal.

Leana, C., & Rousseau, D. M. (2000). *Relational wealth: Advantages of stability in a changing economy.* New York: Oxford.

Lips-Wiersma, M. (2002). The influence of spiritual "meaning-making" on career behavior. *Journal of Management Development, 7,* 497–520.

Lips-Wiersma, M., & Morris, L. (2011). *The map of meaning: How to sustain our humanity in the world of work.* London: Greenleaf Publishing.

Maslow, A. A. (1943). Theory of human motivation. *Psychological Review, 50(4),* 370–396.

Maslow, A. H. (1965). *Eupsychian management.* Homewood, IL: Irwin/Dorsey.

Maslow, A. H. (1968). *Toward a psychology of being.* New York: D. Van Nostrand Company.

McGregor, D. (1960). *The human side of enterprise.* New York: Wiley.

Mead, G. H. (1934). *Mind, self and society.* Chicago, IL: University of Chicago Press.

Miller, J. B. (1976). *Toward a new psychology of women.* Boston: Beacon Press.

Mills, T. (1975). Human resources—Why the new concern? *Harvard Business Review,* March-April, 120–134.

Mirvis, P. H. (2012). Employee engagement and CSR: Transactional, relational, and developmental approaches. *California Management Review, 54(4),* 93–117.

Mirvis, P. H., & Hall, D. T. (1994).. Psychological success and the boundaryless career. *Journal of Organizational Behavior, 15,* 365–380.

Mirvis, P. H., Thompson, K., & Gohring, J. (2012). Toward next generation leadership: Global service. *Leader to Leader, 24,* Spring, 20–26

Parker, V., & Hall, D. T. (1993). Workplace flexibility: Faddish or fundamental? In P. H. Mirvis (Ed.), *Building the competitive workforce: Investing in human capital for corporate success* (pp. 122–155). New York: Wiley.

Pitt-Catsouphes, M., & Googins, B. (2005). Recasting the work–family agenda as a corporate responsibility. In E. E. Kossek & S. J. Lambert (Eds.), *Managing work-life integration in organizations: Future directions for research and practice* (pp. 469–490). Boston: Erlbaum.

Pitt-Catsouphes, M., Matz-Costa, C., & Brown, M. (2010). The prism of age: Managing age diversity at the 21st century workplace. In S. Tyson & E. Parry (Eds.), *Managing an Age Diverse Workforce* (pp. 80-94). London: Palgrave Macmillan.

Rangan, S. (2000). The problem of search and deliberation in economic action: when social networks really matter. *Academy of Management Review, 25(4),* 813–828.

Rojas, M. (2006). Life satisfaction and satisfaction in domains of life: is it a simple relationship? *Journal of Happiness Studies, 7(4),* 467–497.

Schein, E. H. (1974). *Career anchors and career paths: a panel study of management school graduates.* Working papers 707–74, Massachusetts Institute of Technology (MIT), Sloan School of Management.

Schein, E. H. (1984). Culture as an environmental context for careers. *Journal of Occupational Behavior, 5,* 71.

Shepard, H. A. (1984). On the realization of human potential: A path with a heart. In M. B. Arthur, L. Bailyn, D. J. Levinson, & H. A. Shepherd (Eds.), *Working with careers* (pp. 25–46). New York: Center for Research on Careers, Graduate School of Business, Columbia University.

Staines, G. L. (1980). Spillover versus compensation: A review of the literature on the relationship between work and non-work. *Human Relations, 33*(2), 111–129.

Super, D. E. (1957). *The psychology of careers.* New York: Harper & Row.

Thomas, D. A., & Ely, R. J. (1996). Making differences matter: A new paradigm for managing diversity. *Harvard Business Review,* September–October, pp. 80–90.

Weber, M. (1958). *The protestant ethic and the spirit of capitalism.* New York: Scribner.

Weiss, J. W., Skelley, M. F., Haughey, J. C., & Hall, D. T., (2004). Calling, new careers and spirituality: A reflective perspective for organizational leaders and professionals. In *Spiritual intelligence at work: Meaning, metaphor, and morals* (Research in Ethical Issues in Organizations, vol. 5, pp. 175–201). Amsterdam: Elsevier Ltd.

Wrzesniewski, A. (2003). Finding positive meaning in work. In K. S. Cameron, J. E. Dutton, & R. E. Quinn (Eds.), *Positive organizational scholarship: Foundations of a new discipline* (pp. 327–347). San Francisco, Berrett–Koehler.

Wrzesniewski, A., Dutton, J. E., & Debebe, G. (2003). Interpersonal sensemaking and the meaning of work. *Research in Organizational Behavior, 25,* 93–135.

Wrzesniewski, A., McCauley, C., Rozin, P., & Schwartz, B. (1997). Jobs, careers, and callings: People's relations to their work. *Journal of Research in Personality, 31,* 21–33.

Yankelovich, D. (1981). *New rules: Searching for self-fulfillment in a world turned upside down.* New York: Random House.

A More Inclusive
Industrial-Organizational Psychology

Michael J. Zickar

Abstract

This chapter discusses the need for industrial-organizational (IO) psychology to be more inclusive. Historically, IO psychologists have focused on research topics that are of prime interest to management and have neglected topics that are of interest largely to workers. Topics such as personnel selection and productivity have received much more attention than topics such as unionization and making working lives more meaningful. In addition, IO psychologists have generally preferred quantitative methods instead of qualitative methods; this preference has made it more difficult for IO psychologists to understand phenomena from workers' perspectives. This article discusses the history of these biases and provides a series of suggestions for scholars to incorporate into their professional lives so that they can be more inclusive in their choice of topics, perspectives, and methodologies.

Key Words: history of IO psychology, methodological bias, qualitative methodology, graduate training, labor–management relations

The mission statement for the Society of Industrial-Organizational Psychology (SIOP) includes the goal "to enhance human well-being and performance in organizational and work settings" (SIOP Mission Statement, n.d.). This is a general statement that most industrial-organizational (IO) psychologists would likely embrace, though I will argue in this chapter that this goal has rarely been met throughout the history of the field. In this chapter, I will advocate that the science and the practice of IO psychology would benefit from a more inclusive approach that better embraces the ideals espoused in SIOP's mission statement. This more inclusive approach is consistent with the psychology of working that Blustein has been advocating and outlining (see Blustein, 2006). For IO psychology to better reflect the psychology of working, or to reflect the diverse everyday experiences of those who work, I will advocate that IO psychology must change and adapt. In its current state, the field

reflects a relatively narrow range of stakeholders' interests and a relatively restrictive range of topics, both which have been partially determined by historical, cultural, and economic forces. Throughout this chapter, I argue for a culture of more inclusiveness in a wide variety of domains, not just how our research is used (i.e., whether to improve efficiency or improve well-being) but inclusiveness in several other aspects. I will outline the need for more tolerance for diversity of value systems, methodologies, research questions, publication outlets, and career paths. I will argue that the field of IO psychology can make itself more viable and important by broadening its scope, rather than focusing on its existing strengths. I will use a variety of methods including historical analysis as well as analysis of existing practices to convince the reader that IO psychology can do better to reach a broader audience. Finally, I end with a list of suggestions that can be used to make sure that IO psychology becomes more relevant to a broader range of constituents, and that it becomes more interesting and helpful in improving the lot of a wider range of workers.

Before proceeding into the history of the field, I want to warn the reader that this chapter uses the word "I" much more than any other piece that I have written. Throughout this chapter, I provide my own idiosyncratic view of the field and share anecdotes and experiences that have led to my current state of thinking. Although the use of the first person is often discouraged in academic writing, I have taken the liberties to purposely share these stories, biases, and assumptions with the hope that this will help the reader to better understand my perspective, and to encourage other researchers to be more explicit in their own intellectual biases and affections.

A Brief History of IO Psychology

In this section, I provide a selective review of the history of IO psychology, focusing on two themes: psychology's relationship with management and our obsession with quantification. The history of IO psychology has been reviewed much more broadly and in more depth by others, notably Koppes (2007), and the reader is encouraged to consult that contribution and other sources if so motivated. I have written elsewhere on a summary of IO psychology's history within the United States (Zickar & Gibby, 2007). I acknowledge that the following is an idiosyncratic view of the history of IO psychology, but it is one, I would argue, that fits the historical data quite well.

Psychology's Relationship with Management

IO psychology (originally called simply applied psychology and then later industrial psychology) was founded in the decade of the 1910s with the publication of Hugo Munsterburg's textbook *Psychology of Industrial Efficiency* (1913) (note the title for future reference) and the creation of the first program in industrial psychology, at Carnegie Tech (later Carnegie Mellon), around the same time. The early days of industrial psychology were shaped by World War I, with the most noted applied psychologists working on early problems of selection, training, performance appraisal, and placement. The needs for these services were enormous given the need for rapid deployment of hundreds of thousands of troops into a military force that prior to 1917 had been quite small. In short, a massive organization had to be created overnight with little guidance from past practices. Psychologists such as

Walter Van Dyke Bingham, Walter Dill Scott, and Robert Yerkes developed tests to identify which recruits had the intelligence to perform complex tasks, to identify which candidates had the requisite trade knowledge in important crafts such as electricity, and to evaluate the performance of officers.

After the war, these psychologists disseminated the scientific knowledge they had learned and marketed their advances to industry. Robert Woodworth, who developed the Woodworth Personality Inventory to identify soldiers likely to experience "shell shock" while under combat fire, marketed his inventory to organizations who were interested in screening out psychologically vulnerable employees (i.e., people who had adjustment problems and were likely to cause emotional problems at work). Similar marketing efforts were made by developers of the ability tests used to screen entry-level recruits; these tests were adapted and marketed to different occupations for help in hiring new workers. The acceptance of these personnel devices helped organizations that were becoming bigger and more bureaucratic and needed a systematic way to staff their new positions (see Jacoby, 2004). Selection tests were developed to identify successful employees in a variety of positions, including sales agents, managers, steelworkers, cable car operators, and clerical staff.

The process of validating tests was just being developed during this period. Some psychologists validated tests by correlating test scores with subjective rankings and ratings, a process still popular among IO psychologists. Others related test scores to objective criteria to determine a link between scores and "hard" criteria deemed important by the organization. Vinchur (2007) identified 45 studies that used objective criteria to validate selection exams from 1906 to 1930. It is illustrative to get a sense of what organizations valued by examining their choice of criteria. Forty-two percent of those studies chose production numbers and 31.1% used sales figures. Nearly 16% of the studies used job level or salary, whereas 11.1% used accidents as a criterion. In summary, 73.3% of the studies used criteria clearly of value primarily to the organization; in effect, tests were judged to be good or not based on their ability to help organizations increase productivity. There were very few considerations on whether these tests would result in employees being safer or whether they would increase job satisfaction.

It is possible to argue that this use of tests to increase productivity indirectly benefited employees by ensuring that people were chosen for jobs in which they were likely to succeed, and that by increasing organizational productivity, employees would be more likely to have long-term job security. In the 1930s, however, some employers used employment tests to directly undermine employee interests. As mentioned previously, personality tests were adapted from military use, where they were used to predict who would experience "shell shock" while experiencing enemy fire for the first time, to employment use. In the 1920s and 1930s, there was a belief that the primary reason for poor performance in the workplace was maladjustment or neuroses. Management experts led by Elton Mayo argued that troublemakers would spoil the morale of other employees, sabotage the workplace, and agitate for militant labor unions.

The latter was a significant concern for management, who was facing aggressive attempts to organize the workplace. In the 1920s and early 1930s, there was a significant rise in militant efforts to unionize the workforce, with more aggressive strikes often leading to violence (perpetrated by both management and labor). Management fought these unionization efforts, often abetted by management-friendly laws that allowed hiring managers to force workers to sign "Yellow Dog" contracts that forbade workers from joining unions; they could be fired if they engaged in unionization efforts. As part of his ambitious New Deal efforts to stabilize the economy during the Great Depression, President Franklin Delano Roosevelt signed into law the National Labor Relations Act of 1935, which made it illegal for managers to terminate employees because of unionization activities, and forbade managers from even asking potential employees about their views related to unionization.

Hiring managers turned to personality tests to identify potential troublemakers who could be excluded from hiring without ever explicitly asking applicants about their union proclivities. Psychologists like Doncaster Humm marketed their personality inventories directly to companies by offering to "root out troublemakers" and reporting reductions in labor problems in companies that used the Humm-Wadsworth Inventory (see Zickar, 2001). Although there was never any validity evidence that demonstrated that these instruments were useful in weeding out likely union members, companies desperate to eliminate likely union members used these inventories frequently.

In 1960, historian Lorenz Baritz published his doctoral dissertation, *Servants of Power*, in a paperback book that was cited widely in the social sciences

and even got some attention from some nonprofessional readers. The thesis of the book was that social scientists, both industrial psychologists and sociologists, had been co-opted by management to exploit workers. He cited much of the personality/unionization work by Humm and others and also presented numerous other examples where social scientists were used to brainwash employees and to mislead consumers into making decisions that were against their own interests.

As a beginning academic, I was fascinated by Baritz's book as it was a corrective to much of the Pollyanna-ish description of the field I had learned in graduate school (University of Illinois at Urbana-Champaign). In graduate school, we read article after article praising the importance of the contributions of IO psychology to the improvement of the workplace and the economy. (I must note that Chuck Hulin gave a more balanced view of the field of IO psychology than most of the articles we were assigned.) Reading *Servants of Power* for the first time was similar to the experience that I hear many undergraduates get when reading Howard Zinn's left-wing tour of American history, *A Peoples' History of the United States* (Zinn, 2003). Both books provide an interesting critique of knowledge that is often treated as undebatable and force readers to consider alternative explanations for what had always been assumed to be true.

As a scholar interested in historical analysis, however, I decided to investigate some of the historical claims asserted by Baritz, leading to my analysis of the use of personality tests to root out labor agitators (Zickar, 2001). In that case, Baritz was partially correct in that there were some nefarious companies and psychologists who worked to circumvent the laws of the land and to weaken labor unions. After reading and delving more into Baritz's work and sources, I later concluded that the work is more of an ideological polemic against the use of social science in industry, and not that accurate of a historical analysis. The book made me appreciate the damage that our field can do and the narrow interests that we have typically served, but in later years I grew to reject Baritz's strident view of IO psychology as beholden to management interests only.

Some of that change was inspired by another historical investigation (Zickar, 2003), this time into the work and career of Arthur Kornhauser. Kornhauser was a second-generation applied psychologist trained by Walter Van Dyke Bingham and was very widely cited in the early period of our field, although the few historical sources in the

1990s mentioned him infrequently. He was an IO psychologist who fiercely advocated for a field that served workers' interests as well as management's interests, and he was prescient in complaining that the field was likely to ignore the former in an effort to be relevant to management. Kornhauser was not antagonistic to management and conducted some of the first research on validating tests that managers could use to better select appropriate workers. His heart, however, was blatantly on the side of workers, and he let his heart guide most of his research career. His work focused on understanding the sources of job satisfaction, wanting to know what aspects of work made individuals happy or distressed. He conducted one of the first large-scale investigations of how factory work could result in negative mental health issues, studying auto workers in the Detroit area. He worked with labor unions so that they could benefit from some of the knowledge that was typically only given to management. He conducted training sessions for United Auto Workers' leaders to help them become better union stewards.

Kornhauser had a successful career: he was elected president of the precursor organization to SIOP and was widely heralded and cited by peers throughout his career. But despite his success, Kornhauser never traded his reputation for lucrative corporate work. He wrote frequently about the importance of academics asking questions that psychologists employed by management would not be able to ask. At that time, as is the case now, psychologists generally had the view that management and workers had convergent interests (e.g., management and workers have an interest in having an organization succeed) and that conflict in the workplace was the result of poor communication, inept management, or workers with psychopathology. Kornhauser certainly agreed that management and workers often had convergent interests, but he also recognized that there can be an aspect of the relationship that is inherently contentious and full of conflict. Issues such as workplace rights and compensation issues were inherently full of conflict. Kornhauser embraced this conflict and argued that everybody would benefit from an honest appraisal of the structural dynamics of the employment relationship. Two recent authors who examined these issues with a similar level of lucidity are Kaufman and Lefkowitz (see especially Kaufman, 1993, and Leftkowitz, 2003).

Kornhauser's fierce advocacy for the rights of employees to participate in labor unions was in stark contrast to the field's relationship to organized labor

at the time I was in graduate school and beyond (1990s to today). In today's field, labor unions are rarely studied, especially within the United States. Some of that is due to the decline in the power of labor unions and the diminished proportion of workers they represent within the economy, but much of that was due to an anti-union bias that I discovered among my fellow psychologists. Most of these psychologists subscribed to the view that everybody in the workplace could just get along with an enlightened management. And when labor unions were brought up, they were usually mentioned in the context of unions' unrealistic criticisms of psychologists who came to do work in their unionized organizations. Unions were mentioned as just another hurdle to jump through when implementing selection systems and another level of unpredictable bureaucracy that had the power to quell the best-intentioned projects. Upon further investigation, I learned that the field of employee attitude surveying had taken on a new level of exploitation that validated the worst of Baritz's nightmares. Just enter the phrase "union avoidance" into an Internet search engine and you will find firms that openly push their services to helping employers identify problem areas where unions are likely to strike as well as offering their services to run the anti-union campaign once the unionization process begins. I found out that one of my former graduate students who was working in an attitude survey firm was sent to a "union avoidance" conference and that another graduate worked in a healthcare firm that administered attitude surveys only in order to determine where management needed to mobilize the anti-union "SWAT forces." Clearly, Kornhauser's vision of an IO psychology that was balanced in the battle between labor and management had failed to materialize. Baritz's worst nightmares were starting to come true.

This one-sided approach to labor unions surprised me because my cursory readings of other fields that study working life showed that those fields had a much more vibrant investigation into organized labor. Economics and industrial sociology still have a vibrant set of researchers who investigate both the positive and negative aspects of labor unions. Given the difference in the fields, I conducted a historical analysis on why psychology ended up clearly on the side of management whereas economics and sociology were more balanced (though it could be easily argued that sociology actually lines up generally on the side of organized labor). Although it is impossible to answer such a question definitively, I considered a wide range of hypotheses, some which had been speculated on by others (see Zickar, 2004).

Some of these hypotheses were easy to prove false. One hypothesis was that perhaps early applied psychologists had been anti-labor, which influenced later generations of psychologists who perpetuated this bias of their founders. This was false, though, because most early psychologists were explicitly neutral with respect to the role of labor. In fact, Walter Dill Scott refused to work with a company who wanted to take a more antagonistic role in defeating a labor union within its ranks. Bingham corresponded with American Federation of Labor founder Samuel Gompers and made sure to include labor representatives in an organization that was designed to promote psychology within businesses. Although the field became more indifferent to labor throughout its history, it did not start out that way.

The one hypothesis that I believe most readily explained this bias was that psychology had learned to market its services to management and many applied psychologists made lucrative incomes from selling their services to corporations. Sociologists and labor economists never learned or did not wish to profit from private industry and consequently were largely employed only in the academy or government, giving them freedom to pursue a wider range of questions and perspectives. The success of IO psychologists with management provided the field with a substantial cadre of psychologists (at least 50% of our graduates are now employed in private industry in one guise or the other) who are restricted to pursuing questions deemed important by management. As Kornhauser wrote, "I know of no instance in which a study undertaken to improve employee morale has discovered that the company needs a stronger, more vigorous labor union to represent its employees" (Kornhauser, 1957, p. 199).

Another case study is important to consider about the role of management interests in shaping our field. Personnel selection is an important topic that has been with the field from its inception. Psychologists are good at measuring individual characteristics and abilities, and so it is a legitimate activity that we help companies pick employees who will best succeed in their organizations. The other side of workplace selection is equally meaningful: it is important from a societal perspective to help individuals make the best decisions about what type of career would be best to pursue given their unique set of abilities, characteristics, and interests. This side of workplace selection was an important part of early applied psychology, with psychologists

such as E. E. Strong and Donald Paterson conducting research on both sides of the workplace selection perspective. Paterson worked with companies to choose tests that would best predict who would be successful, and he administered tests to individuals to help them with their vocational choices (see Erdheim, Zickar, & Yankelevich, 2007).

The latter is still an important and vibrant field, vocational counseling, but IO psychologists have largely ceded this type of selection to other fields, such as educational and counseling psychology. Rarely is there an article in IO-related journals on such a topic, even though it would clearly fit within the purview of IO psychology as defined by SIOP's mission statement. I argue that IO psychology has a tendency to shed topics to other fields based not on whether that topic has relevance to the psychological functioning within the workplace, but whether the topic fits the management perspective that dominates our field.

It is instructive to examine the construct of job satisfaction. Clearly, whether workers are satisfied on their job or not should be a matter of supreme importance to IO psychologists regardless of the consequences of satisfaction or dissatisfaction. It is a good thing for society when people are happy; we are concerned whether people are happy in their marriages and relationships, and there is a new concern for using happiness as a meaningful variable to evaluate and compare well-being across countries. But for many years, researchers grappled with whether job satisfaction was related to performance or not, with the assumption that if job satisfaction was unrelated to work performance (i.e., if happier workers were not more productive), then job satisfaction should not be that much of a concern. Walter Nord (1977), one of the few IO psychologists unafraid to critique the underlying assumptions of the field, wrote an *American Psychologist* article basically asserting that he did not care whether job satisfaction was related to performance or not (at the time it looked like there was a marginal relationship), but that this was an important dependent variable in its own right.

To be fair, the field has broadened its range of topics in recent years to include research questions that are more focused on worker quality-of-life issues rather than productivity or efficiency. The field of occupational health psychology (OHP), of which IO psychology is an important contributor, investigates worker stress and health issues that certainly have an impact on the bottom line of organizations, though the questions have even more relevance to the experiences of daily lives of workers. Other researchers are investigating retirement, examining questions such as what makes one worker have a miserable experience in retirement whereas another has increased bliss. These areas are important questions to ask that relate to the working life of people, but I worry that these topics will soon be ceded to other academic disciplines, just like what happened to vocational counseling research. I see this already happening with IO psychologist colleagues who attend OHP conferences and are less likely to attend general IO psychology conferences. This specialization is natural in a field, especially ones that are inherently interdisciplinary (e.g., OHP and retirement research), but it is telling that other disciplines are more likely to co-opt these topics whereas IO psychology's core always comprises the bread-and-butter issues most relevant to management.

In the mid-1990s, President Clinton signed into law a sweeping overhaul of the welfare laws proposed by the Republican Congress, entitled Welfare-to-Work. The bill placed strict limits on most welfare payments but ostensibly provided job training for welfare recipients so that they could be more easily integrated into the workplace. Helping the hardcore unemployed develop workplace skills was a topic that seemed well suited for IO psychologists and certainly within the purview of the field. But I can remember only a single session at an SIOP conference on how IO psychologists might get involved in the government programs that were sure to come about. IO psychologists never got involved and missed an important opportunity to provide input on one of the most important work-related initiatives put forward by the government in recent years. Again, this was a topic that did not fit nicely within the management focus of the field.

A few years ago, I put together a symposium at the SIOP conference, inviting researchers to discuss neglected populations in the field. There was a presentation by Virginia Schein on the challenges of poor women in the workplace and how single mothers had significant challenges unique to that population. Schein asserted that there had not been a publication related to poor women at work in the *Journal of Applied Psychology* since the early 1970s. Other presentations focused on young African American entrepreneurs, disabled workers, and the challenges of people working largely at night. Again, these are topics that are of supreme importance to a subset of the working population, though the questions being asked might be limited to a small subset of employers.

King and Cortina recently published an article advocating more research on gay/lesbian/bisexual/transgendered (GLBT) employees in the workplace (King & Cortina, 2010). They argued persuasively that issues of discrimination faced by GLBT workers are important for us to investigate and that our research might be used to better the lives of these employees. In addition, they argued that studying issues related to GLBT employees might be beneficial to employers because having GLBT-friendly workplaces might result in increased retention of a subset of employees, and that would help organizational profitability. In a commentary piece on the target article, I commended them on their urging the field to choose a broader range of topics and to be focused on the humanitarian concerns of workers (Zickar, 2010). Also, I argued that it was a prudent strategy to try to link these humanitarian concerns to management concerns (i.e., efficiency and productivity)—but that even if those linkages cannot be made, this topic would be a legitimate topic on its own right (Zickar, 2010). IO psychologists, especially those with tenure, should feel the right to pursue any research topic as long as it is within the purview of psychology and work.

There is a recent movement within the field to branch out and apply IO psychology topics to nonprofit organizations and nongovernmental organizations (NGOs) that work with Third World nations. This is an important movement in the field; if it can gain momentum, it has the potential to transform the field. Again, I am skeptical, given the history of the field, but it is important to encourage these efforts. In an inclusive IO psychology, the potential topics for IO researchers and practitioners become much broader. For example, if we address the needs of different stakeholders, not just management, possibilities widen. In terms of personnel selection, companies are always interested in identifying the brightest and hardest-working talent. What is often left out of the equation is what happens with people who, for whatever reason, score lowest on the tests we deem to have the best predictability. Low-cognitive-ability or "g" employees are going to be viewed as undesirable by nearly every selection process created by an IO psychologist. No company will want these people, but our society has an interest in finding meaningful work for these people so that they can feel a sense of meaning in their lives and earn at least a portion of the income necessary to provide for basic living. The same could be said for people with serious mental illnesses. There is some research on the employability of people with serious mental illnesses, though none of it (as far as I can tell) has been conducted by IO psychologists, and it is rarely ever cited by us (e.g., Campbell, Bond, & Drake, 2011).

Issues related to management exploiting workers should also be a topic ripe for study by IO psychologists. Although I have heard many people talk about how important labor unions were in the 1920s, when management "really did exploit" workers, this view that exploitation of workers is part of our distant past is simply not true. There are occasional high-profile workplace disasters (e.g., the Massey mine disaster, sweatshop labor conditions in developing nations) that remind us of the terrible working conditions that a subset of workers face. These working conditions that lead to high-profile workplace disasters should be studied, but in addition we should study issues related to the economic exploitation that exists in many different economies around the world. For example, I have a relative who is continually trying to sell me some kind of home-marketing product. One year it is "all-natural vitamins, much better than you can get in any store," and another year it is cleaning supplies that work "more effectively than anything you can buy in the store, and much more environmentally friendly." Currently, about twice a year, I buy a 24-pack case of "all-natural" energy drinks because I am indebted to this particular family member for many other reasons. I buy the case (overpriced, disgusting taste) and put the pack out for our doctoral students, who grab this stuff because they will drink anything purported to give them needed energy. There are millions of people in this country trying to make a quick buck by selling these products out of their home via multilevel marketing techniques. You see them when you are driving down the highway with signs on their cars that say things like "Need Zanga, Call My Cell …" or "I lost 30 pounds in 30 days and can help you do the same." Most of these people will never make any money through these products; often they actually lose money because they are required to purchase expensive starter kits. The people who make money are those who are successful in recruiting willing salespeople underneath them, who then give them a small portion of every sale. Sure, some people actually do make serious amounts of money in these businesses, but for the most part, these companies exploit the dreams and aspirations of everyday workers who think someday they will be able to quit their regular jobs (in my relative's case, a bartender) and live the high life. There have always been get-rich-quick schemes: in my youth,

I always dreamed of responding to the ads in the back of comic books with offers to make thousands of dollars a month stuffing envelopes from home. So our field could and should study issues related to economic exploitation. We should be studying why people fall victim to these pyramid schemes and the characteristics of the few who actually succeed. We should be studying the stresses of migrant farm workers, often immigrant labor, who work in the farms in Northwest Ohio and other regions, and then migrate south or north depending on the season. We should be documenting the psychological effects on workers of not having health insurance and how that affects their daily lives. We should be studying the effects that working multiple jobs to make ends meet has on a particular worker, who has more than one boss and more than one set of daily stressors. Academic IO psychologists should be asking these and many more questions that, frankly, private industry does not care to ask. We should be asking our government to provide funding for some of this research. And we should be promoting and giving tenure to researchers who do this research well, regardless of any success with external funding. In my view, the field is big enough to support a group of researchers who pursue these topics. We have enough journal space to publish high-quality articles on these topics.

I am not advocating that the field give up on the management-focused research that has defined the field since its inception. Nor am I arguing that such research has no greater value. Clearly, it is important for our society and our economy to have organizations that are productive and efficient, and it is important that IO psychologists contribute toward these goals. I wish, however, that our field had a niche of researchers who did not feel compelled to study topics related to management issues. Others have issued similar calls. Katzell and Austin, after a review of the history of IO psychology, concluded: "I-O psychology is still oriented overwhelmingly to the needs of management, and despite occasional exceptions, shows proportionately little concern for the outcomes of work (or nonwork) on workers, their families and their communities, nor is it very much interested in their unions" (1992, p. 823). For this to develop, as Arthur Kornhauser argued in the 1950s, it is incumbent on IO psychologists employed in academia to be the leaders. Unfortunately, the corporatization of our universities provides a disincentive for many IO psychologists to pursue research topics that corporations do not care about.

History of Quantification

Another obsession that makes it difficult for our field to be more inclusive and limits our understanding of everyday workers' concerns is our obsession with quantitative methods and the scientific assumption of logical positivism. The field of IO psychology has been preoccupied with statistical tools from its inception, and as these tools have progressed, our obsession has advanced. This focus on quantification has led to some excellent techniques and tools that have truly helped managers make better personnel decisions. Yet, as I will argue after a brief review of the history, by focusing nearly exclusively on quantitative methods, we have lost a depth of insight that might help us better understand the concerns and needs of workers and make IO psychology a richer discipline.

Nearly all historians of psychology identify Wilhelm Wundt as the founder of modern-day scientific psychology. Wundt was instrumental in applying scientific methods to questions of perception and thinking that had previously been relegated to philosophers. Wundt's students, such as Hugo Munsterburg, E. B. Titchner, and G. Stanley Hall, were instrumental in bringing back Wundt's scientific approach to psychology to U.S. universities, where such methods would later thrive. Although Wundt's work on applying scientific methods was well known, he also published a series of books under the title *Völkerpsychologie* (often translated as social psychology, but perhaps better translated as folk psychology), in which he advocated that there were some questions and issues related to psychology that were best understood not by the scientific method but by other techniques that were less scientific and more idiographic and qualitative in nature. Unfortunately, this work was not brought over to the United States, and very little of the original work was even translated into English (see Danzinger, 1994). Right from the start of the history of psychology within the United States, quantitative and scientific approaches dominated.

Early applied psychologists quickly co-opted the statistical techniques that were being developed in various scientific endeavors. Psychologists used correlation and regression techniques as well as analysis of variance techniques. Psychologists such as L. L. Thurstone, who were crucial in the development of statistical techniques, were also associated with applied psychology groups, often developing personnel selection inventories. Psychometric theory was developed largely in the realm of educational testing, but it was quickly adapted by IO psychologists and used to provide a scientific evaluation of tests. As statistical techniques were developed, they were quickly adapted by IO psychologists, who learned how to use factor analysis, structural equations modeling, meta-analysis, and item response theory; IO psychologists also increasingly contributed to the basic advances of these important statistical tools. These techniques were used to develop inductive theory and to refine existing theory as well as to validate psychological tests.

There was also an early tradition that encouraged qualitative techniques within social science investigations of the workplace (see Zickar & Carter, 2010, for a summary of workplace ethnography tradition). A steel executive, Whiting Williams, decided that to better understand his workforce, he should go incognito and work alongside the steelworkers of Pennsylvania and then later throughout the world. He published his books under titles such as *What's On the Workers' Mind* (1920) and *Horny Hands and Hampered Elbows* (Williams, 1922) in editions that were widely read by businesspeople, the general public, and some of the early applied psychologists. Sociologist Elton Mayo, and a large team of other researchers, observed workers in the Hawthorne electrical plants and made important observations about worker motivation and group cohesion. Psychologist Rexford Hersey observed and interviewed railway workers to determine their emotional lives and how work influenced those emotional rhythms (Hersey, 1932). These were important studies that helped more quantitative-minded researchers better understand the phenomena that they were trying to measure and provided rich anecdotes that managers could use to better understand their workers and policymakers could use to generate more useful policy.

The field of IO psychology moved away from more qualitative methods as quantitative methods became more developed, even though other fields continued to embrace workplace ethnography. Sociologists and other management scholars continued to use ethnographic methods and published high-profile ethnographies that received much attention from workplace scholars. For example, Henry Mintzberg, in an effort to figure out what high-level managers actually did in the workplace, followed managers around and recorded their daily behavior, finding that much of what they spent their time on were mundane tasks just like other workers (see Mintzberg, 1973). Journalist Studs Terkel studied a variety of jobs and occupations, publishing conversations about jobs with a range of workers (from jazz musician to farmer to baseball player) in a popular book, *Working*, that was even turned into a play (Terkel, 1974). The concept of *Working* was updated in 2001 by Bowe, Bowe, and Streeter in *Gig*, a book that is a particular favorite of mine; the range of occupations was updated, but the basic concept was the same, with three- to five-page interviews with job holders (Bowe, Bowe, & Streeter, 2001).

These workplace ethnographies offer a wealth of information about the workers, in language chosen by the interviewees themselves. Sure, often the bias of the researcher comes out in these interviews, and it is difficult to determine how much editing took place with the reported interview data, but there is a richness of the responses that is simply not possible when administrating fixed-response surveys to workers. In most of the survey work that is done within organizations, questions are determined without much input from those being surveyed (often with off-the-shelf scales that were developed many years ago), and little context is provided to interpret participants' responses. I know that such survey research is important, especially to understand relations between various constructs, but we are often left still unaware of how particular constructs manifest themselves in the day-to-day lives of our workers.

In graduate school, I had the unforgettable experience of administering a job satisfaction inventory (along with other scales) to a series of workers in a food processing plant in rural eastern Washington. For most respondents, we administered our survey in group settings, getting responses of 1 to 3 on items such as "Is your work demanding?" and "Do you find your job fulfilling?" The data collection was efficient but a bit unsatisfying, as workers filled the survey out at the end of their shifts and rarely had any questions or comments (in person or written on their survey). There were a few illiterate workers, to whom we had to read the survey item by item and capture their responses. Given that the company was committed to having all employees participate, they made especial efforts to survey these workers, and I commend the organization for doing that. I remember vividly a particular respondent who was unable to read (due to some mild developmental disability); he drove a forklift truck throughout the warehouse, moving packages of potatoes throughout the plant. As he explained his job to me, before administering the survey, I thought, "This guy must hate his boring job." When I asked him items like "Do you find

your work challenging?" and "Do you find your work keeps you on your toes?" I was surprised when he answered affirmatively with a sparkle in his eyes. I thought maybe he did not understand the items, and so I asked him to clarify, and I remember him saying, with all sincerity, "I never know what to expect day to day. Some days we are moving boxes and pallets from the east side of the warehouse to the west side, other times it is the reverse." He went on to explain other similar challenges of his job with a same level of fascination. That one-hour survey administration changed my life as a researcher. I still realize the importance of nomothetic research using psychometrically developed scales (in fact, my main line of research is in psychometrics) that are analyzed using complex statistical techniques. That one-hour interview demonstrated to me, though, that if we fail to dig deeper than our correlations and our mean scores, we fail to understand the meaning of work as experienced by our respondents.

If we are to develop a true psychology of working that captures work as it exists within the minds and representations of those who work, we must do a better job of connecting with those who work. The value of the scientific research that has dominated our field has taken us very far, but I think we could improve our relevance and our impact by doing a better job of connecting with those we are studying. Although there has been a call for more qualitative research within IO psychology (e.g., Locke & Golden-Biddle, 2002), it remains a miniscule aspect of our published research. And more telling is that it is very rare for someone who has conducted quantitative research to engage in a qualitative study. The few qualitative researchers who work in the field seem to be respected but have little influence on the majority of researchers.

Idiosyncratic Steps for a Better IO Psychology

This final section of the chapter is a list of suggestions or steps that IO psychologists can take to make the field of IO psychology more consistent with the broader vision that I propose. It would be unrealistic for any IO psychologist to engage in all of these suggested practices, but I aver that if more of us engaged in at least some of these suggestions, the field would be much improved. Some of these suggestions I elaborate on in a lot of detail and others I casually mention. In each case, the reader should reflect on what practices would improve his or her career.

1. *Perform the jobs you are studying.* The television show *Undercover Boss* is currently popular, and I enjoy watching the show with my wife, who is an IO psychologist who consults for private industry. In the show, CEOs or other high-ranking corporate officials of large companies venture out into the field incognito (e.g., usually by changing their hairstyle or facial hair) and perform a range of low-level jobs within the organization. Inevitably, the CEO fails at one or more of these menial tasks, failing to meet the performance standards that corporate imposed. Also, during a lunch break, the CEO will typically listen to the personal challenges that a particular coworker-of-the-day faces (often related to the interplay of work and family), and the CEO will realize that some policy set by corporate is unnecessarily burdening the lives of the employees. At the end of the show, all is revealed (usually causing a mixture of anxiety and humor among the CEO's temporary coworkers, all to comic effect for the viewer) and the CEO makes small or major changes that benefit the everyday lives of the workers. Usually the CEO also promises to continue to maintain close contact with the "grunt workers" and nearly always asserts that this has been a life-changing event. Given it is only in its second season, it is difficult to determine the long-term effects of this incognito investigation, but in the short term, everybody feels good (except for the few employees who get terminated for egregiously bad behavior).

Contrast that with the typical IO psychologist, who rarely interacts with the workers he or she is studying. Data collection devices such as StudyResponse.com and Google's Mechanical Turk even allow researchers to get reasonably large samples without ever talking with a single person within any organization. I wish there was a rule that anybody conducting a study on a particular job would be required to perform that job for at least two days before formulating his or her hypotheses. There are precedents for such a suggestion. Best legal practices for job analyses suggest that IO psychologists observe the job before administering job analysis surveys to workers. In fact, one of the most common reasons for a judge rejecting a job analysis is that there had been no observation. In addition, retired Illinois professor Chuck Hulin told stories of working as a temp during the summer before conducting a study on the temporary workforce. As a full professor, one of his temp jobs was helping unload the belongings of a new faculty member on campus!

The problem of not knowing the job you are studying is exacerbated by the reality that most of our graduate students enter our programs with zero work experience (excepting the temporary summer jobs that most undergraduate students have). This provides little grounding in the world of work for our future theorists and encourages the boring circles, squares, and ovals that characterize most of our theories. My idol, Arthur Kornhauser, recognizing the importance of having significant work experience, delayed his migration from a master's program at Carnegie Tech to a doctoral program at University of Chicago, telling his advisor, Walter Van Dyke Bingham, that he wanted to bum around the East Coast to learn what it was really like to work.

Our research and practice would be much more enriched if we knew the people we were studying at more than a superficial level. I assert that our theories might be more complex and rich and less boring if we really tried to get into the job as experienced by its incumbents. I suspect our research would have more relevance to these workers as well. This idea of getting to know personally the experiences of the people you are studying is one of the central tenets of participatory action research (e.g., Whyte, 1991).

2. *Encourage diversity.* Most IO psychologists believe in the value of diversity in the workplace at least at some level. I would like to translate that respect for diversity in the workplace to respect for diversity within the profession. The field has been dominated by the idealistic scientist–practitioner model that was developed in clinical psychology (the Boulder model) and argues that the best IO psychologists are those who are excellent at both research and practice. The argument is that research should inform practice and that practice makes research more realistic. On the one hand it is hard to argue with such an ideal, and it is great to see individuals who truly excel at both of these demanding roles. My belief, however, is that science and practice are opposite ends of a continuum and that the field would be benefit from a wide range of individuals located throughout the continuum. There would be respect for pure researchers who are investigating topics that have no direct relevance to the bottom line of today's organizations, and there would be respect for practitioners who do their job well but do not contribute to the future knowledge base. In addition, there would be those in the middle who are reasonably adept at both of these tasks. My vision of a continuum allows individuals to flourish within their own skill set and their own aspirations. And if people throughout the continuum communicated

with each other, there would be no need for each person to encapsulate the ideals of science and practice. Let the scientists do science really well; let the practitioners apply that knowledge to organizations. And if both sides communicated with each other on a meaningful basis, they could each benefit from the others' contributions. In reality, the field already exists on such a continuum (despite the pervasiveness of the idealistic but unrealistic scientist–practitioner model), but the communication between the different camps is not particularly effective. Neither side takes the time to understand the others' challenges and perspectives (except in my household, where we talk about research and practice over the dinner table!).

Diversity need not be limited to various locations on the science–practitioner continuum. I would like to see increased diversity in terms of focus on the management–worker continuum and increased diversity in terms of philosophical perspectives on methodological assumptions as well as political biases. The field can tolerate some pro-worker researchers who focus on issues from a worker perspective as a counter to the typical perspective that views things through the management lens. The field is big enough now that it can tolerate researchers who reject the importance of the logical positivism model and focus on more of a social constructionist approach or any other approach (see Crotty, 1998). Finally, the field could benefit from researchers who approach questions from an explicit leftist view of the workplace and those who view the workplace from the right. Too often, researchers check their personal biases and beliefs at the door to the office where they do their writing; none of their personal beliefs make it into their own writing, even though those biases and beliefs may inspire the research questions that they choose to pursue.

Occasionally there are examples where researchers let their guards down. There was a provocative Marxist critique of the Hawthorne studies published by two social psychologists in *American Psychologist* (Bramel & Friend, 1981). It was fascinating to read the back-and-forth dialogue through the comments in subsequent issues between Bramel and Friend and unabashedly libertarian, right-wing-thinking Ed Locke, who often cites Ayn Rand as an authoritative source. This openness in terms of political biases is refreshing in a field where "showing your cards" is often anathema to getting published. The field is big enough and established enough now that we can tolerate a wider range of opinions, methodologies, and perspectives. I am heartened by the development of an SIOP publication outlet, *Industrial-Organizational Psychology: Research and Practice*, that provides regular publication of back-and-forth commentary between authors who have divergent opinions. Given our size, it is unrealistic and unhealthy to reach consensus on many important issues related to the workplace.

3. *Celebrate work.* I sense a cultural shift, at least in the United States, where work is viewed now as a means to obtaining an important income and status, with people who are stuck in low-level jobs either frowned upon or, perhaps worse, overlooked and ignored. If you study work, whether you are a counseling psychologist, a sociologist, an economist, or an IO psychologist, you should celebrate the phenomena you are studying. If nothing else, it has provided you likely with a decent income and a topic for much intellectual stimulation. Find ways to nurture some joy and excitement in the topic you are studying. I enjoy watching movies related to work—two of my favorite are documentaries: *The Salesman*, about a door-to-door Bible salesman, and *Harlan County USA*, about the famous 1973 coal miners' strike in Kentucky. I love collecting songs related to work, with some favorites being Johnny Cash's *One Piece at a Time*, which tells the story of a disgruntled autoworker who steals from his employer in a comic fashion, to Merle Haggard's wistful look back at migrant labor, *They're Tearing the Labor Camps Down*, to half of Bruce Springsteen's oeuvre (*Highway Patrolman* or *Youngstown*, for just a couple of examples). Cultivate a love for the topic you study by collecting art or artifacts related to it. If you treat your topic in a cold, intellectual manner, your work will probably seem the same.

4. *Read outside your field.* There are a host of disciplines who study the same thing you do, just from different lenses and perspectives. This edited volume is a good example of how people with different training and experiences can participate in a volume with at least a modicum of common purpose. As our fields become more specialized, it is easier to spend your time reading within your own discipline. Within IO psychology, a literature develops—say, of personality within the workplace—and the members of that discipline, after its initial flourish, start citing each other and rarely branching outside of a small cadre of scholars. This is particularly depressing in the field of work where there are so many exciting books being published in a variety of fields. I try to keep an active reading life outside of my immediate professional demands and try to occasionally read a book on working life published by a labor historian,

an industrial sociologist, or a muckraking journalist who has decided to write about something related to working life. Search out work-related Internet websites. One of my favorites is www.FireMe.com, where respondents share their horror stories about why they should be fired or why they want to quit their jobs. Such wide-ranging reading keeps me fascinated with the working world and often rewards itself with an anecdote to share in class or even occasionally a citation for a journal article.

5. Don't be afraid to make the workplace better. I often like to reflect on how many applicants to our graduate program cite humanistic impulses in their personal statements. I would venture to guess that at least 50% want to make the workplace less stressful and help corporations become much more humane. Very few applicants admit wanting to become IO psychologists because they want to help corporations make more money. Someday I should content-code these personal statements to document these numbers. Despite these noble beginnings, when you examine the career choices of our graduates, rarely do they seem to be guided by the same humanistic impulses that led them into the field. It is as if we have stripped them of any of those do-gooder impulses after 4 or 5 years of personnel selection, statistics, and preliminary examinations! Even if you are employed in a private industry job where you are helping corporations make more money, do not be afraid to use your techniques and skill sets to help volunteer organizations to which you belong: churches, political organizations, and clubs. And if you have the good fortune to become rich and retire early, you could use your experience and your free time to help those truly less fortunate.

Conclusions

Understanding the psychology of working is a daunting and perhaps impossible task. In this chapter, I have used historical analyses and personal anecdotes to build the case that IO psychology has often failed to reach a broad audience and make itself relevant across a wide range of topics and constituencies. It has done an excellent job of aligning itself with management interests and has made many important advances in this line. Such advances have helped corporations become more productive and efficient, thus helping workers in many ways. As I argued in this chapter, however, a true psychology of working has yet to be achieved. Looking into the past, there are bright spots (e.g., the careers of Arthur Kornhauser and Donald Paterson) that give me hope, but without a concerted effort, I fear that

our field will continue along its same path. At best, I hope this chapter has given you a few ideas and convinced you of the gains that a more inclusive IO psychology can bring about.

References

Baritz, L. (1960). *Servants of power: A history of social science in American industry*. Westport, CA: Greenwood.

Blustein, D. L. (2006). *The psychology of working: A new perspective for career development, counseling, and public policy*. Mahwah, NJ: Erlbaum.

Bowe, J., Bowe, M., & Streeter, S. (2001). *Gig: Americans talk about their jobs*. New York: Broadway.

Bramel, D., & Friend, R. (1981). Hawthorne, the myth of the docile worker, and class bias in psychology. *American Psychologist, 36*, 867–878.

Campbell, K., Bond, G. R., & Drake, R. E. (2011). Who benefits from supported employment: A meta-analytic study. *Schizophrenia Bulletin, 37*, 370–380.

Crotty, M. (1998). *The foundations of social research: Meaning and perspective in the research process*. Thousand Oaks, CA: Sage.

Danzinger, K. (1994). *Constructing the subject: Historical origins of psychological research*. Cambridge: Cambridge University Press.

Erdheim, J., Zickar, M. J., & Yankelevich, M. (2007). Remembering Donald G. Paterson: Before the separation of industrial-organizational and vocational psychology. *Journal of Vocational Behavior, 70*, 205–221.

Hersey, R. (1932). *Workers' emotions in shop and home*. Philadelphia: University of Pennsylvania Press.

Jacoby, S. (2004). *Employing bureaucracy: Managers, unions, and the transformation of work in the 20th century* (rev. ed.). Mahwah, NJ: Erlbaum.

Katzell, R. A., & Austin, J. T. (1992). From then to now: The development of industrial-organizational psychology in the United States. *Journal of Applied Psychology, 77*, 803–835.

Kaufman, B. E. (1993). *The origins and evolution of the field of industrial relations*. Ithaca, NY: Cornell.

King, E. B., & Cortina, J. M. (2010). The social and economic imperative of lesbian, gay, bisexual, and transgendered supportive organizational policies. *Industrial and Organizational Psychology: Perspectives on Science and Practice, 3*, 69–78.

Koppes, L. (2007). *Historical perspectives in industrial and organizational psychology*. Mahwah, NJ: Lawrence Erlbaum Associates Publishers.

Kornhauser, A. (1957). Democratic values and problems of power in American society. In A. Kornhauser (Ed.), *Problems of power in American democracy* (pp. 184–217). Detroit, MI: Wayne State University Press.

Leftkowitz, J. (2003). *Ethics and values in industrial-organizational psychology*. Mahwah, NJ: Erlbaum.

Locke, K., & Golden-Biddle, K. (2002). An introduction to qualitative research: Its potential for industrial and organizational psychology. In S. Rogelberg (Ed.) *Handbook of research methods in industrial and organizational psychology* (pp. 99–118). Malden, MA: Blackwell Publishing.

Mintzberg, H. (1973). *The nature of managerial work*. New York: HarperCollins.

Munsterberg, H. (1913). *Psychology and industrial efficiency*. Boston: Houghton-Mifflin.

Nord, W. R. (1977). Job satisfaction reconsidered. *American Psychologist, 32*, 1026–1035.

SIOP Mission Statement (n.d.). Retrieved from http://www.siop.org/mission.aspx.

Terkel, S. (1974). *Working: People talk about what they do all day and how they feel about what they do.* New York: Pantheon.

Vinchur, A. J. (2007). A history of psychology applied to employee selection. In L. Koppes (Ed.), *Historical perspectives in industrial and organizational psychology* (pp. 193–218). Mahwah, NJ: Lawrence Erlbaum Associates Publishers.

Whyte, W. F. (1991). *Participatory action research.* Thousand Oaks, CA: Sage.

Williams, W. (1920). *What's on the workers' mind.* New York: Charles Scribner.

Williams, W. (1922). *Horny hands and hampered elbows.* New York: Charles Scribner.

Zickar, M. J. (2001). Using personality inventories to identify thugs and agitators: Applied psychology's contribution to the war against labor. *Journal of Vocational Behavior, 59,* 149–164.

Zickar, M. J. (2003). Remembering Arthur Kornhauser: Industrial psychology's advocate for worker well-being. *Journal of Applied Psychology, 88,* 363–369.

Zickar, M. J. (2004). An analysis of industrial-organizational psychology's indifference to labor unions in the United States. *Human Relations, 57,* 145–167.

Zickar, M. J. (2010). Recognizing the need for a humanistic movement within industrial–organizational psychology. *Industrial and Organizational Psychology: Perspectives on Science and Practice, 3,* 97–99.

Zickar, M. J., & Carter, N. T. (2010). Reconnecting with the spirit of workplace ethnography: A historical review. *Organizational Research Methods, 13,* 304–319.

Zickar, M. J., & Gibby, R. E. (2007). Four persistent themes throughout the history of I-O psychology in the United States. In L. Koppes (Ed.), *Historical perspectives in industrial and organizational psychology* (pp. 61–80). Mahwah, NJ: Lawrence Erlbaum Associates Publishers.

Zinn, H. (2003). *A peoples' history of the United States: 1492 to present.* New York: HarperCollins.

PART 4

Counseling and Psychotherapy

Counseling Clients with Work-Based Challenges

Sherri L. Turner, Julia L. Conkel Ziebell, *and* Robin A. Alcala Saner

Abstract

The field of vocational psychology is moving toward examining ways to counsel clients with work-based challenges and insufficient resources to meet these challenges. This chapter will review the current realities of disenfranchised groups with work-based challenges, including real and perceived barriers to obtaining and maintaining work. In addition, it will discuss the meaning of work for those with few career choices. The discussion will include factors found to be related to attaining and maintaining employment, such as cultural and community values, and racial identity development. Finally, the chapter will review counseling strategies, models, and interventions that counselors can use to assist clients with insufficient resources.

Key Words: Native Americans, African Americans, Hispanic/Latino(a)s, disabilities, sexual minority clients, poverty, homeless, working poor, nonworking poor

Work has many meanings and serves many functions. In modern career theory, work is an expression of one's personality, interests, and goals (Holland, 1997). Yet, there are large swaths of people who do not necessarily seek employment in order to satisfy intrinsic interests. Indeed, although some people with insufficient resources find work satisfying and rewarding, others find that they have no opportunities to work, or find that work is excruciatingly painful and arduous because of racism, discrimination, harassment, incivility, demanding physical tasks, cultural disrespect, or simply low pay and little opportunity (e.g., Blustein, 2006).

Nevertheless, work has meaning over and above the accomplishment of mundane tasks. This meaning is derived, at least in part, from cultural values and the cultural contexts that shape one's experiences (Blustein, 2006). It is also derived from the socioeconomic circumstances in which one finds oneself. For many people with some degree of career choice privilege, work is often a means of expressing individualism, gaining status and power, and augmenting wealth. For persons from groups who frequently have fewer social, cultural, and financial resources, work can mean survival, supporting an often-fragmented social and cultural community, evidence of equitable treatment after generations of disenfranchisement, and final acceptance into the fabric of American life with a promise of precious opportunities to come. Counseling clients with work-based challenges requires a shift in perspective away from traditional career counseling. When considering how to best provide counseling services for persons without sufficient resources, the task must be to understand individuals within their cultures, worldviews, and all of those elements that make people who they are within their frame of reference.

In this chapter, we will explore the barriers, supports, and meaning of work among groups without sufficient resources, as well as offer ideas about how to counsel effectively with clients from these groups. The groups we will focus on are ethnic minority clients (Native Americans, African Americans, Hispanic/Latino(a)s), sexual minority clients, clients with disabilities, and the unemployed, homeless, and working and nonworking poor. Barriers include low inclusion into the world of work, low educational attainment, poverty, lack of access to those structures that make working possible or career advancement likely, and psychological distress. Although we do not cover social change in this chapter, we acknowledge that social change and providing equal opportunities for all people are also necessary in meeting the work challenges of persons with insufficient resources.

Racial/Ethnic Minority Clients

In the following sections, we will identify and briefly describe populations that are overly affected by work-based challenges. We will describe how lack of access to work opportunities affects these populations, including descriptions of how many live in poverty daily, their employment/unemployment rates, and where people in these groups work, when work is available to them. We will then identify for each group barriers to employment, supports to obtaining and maintaining employment, and the meaning of work, including both financial meanings and the more intangible meanings of work, such as supporting the community or expressing one's identity and values. Finally, we will examine the models or strategies that have been suggested in the literature as being effective with people from each group.

Native Americans

As of 2008, the total racial minority population in the United States was estimated at 34%. Native Americans, including those of more than one race with a significant Native American heritage, made up 1.6% of the population, or approximately 4.9 million people (U.S. Census Bureau, 2009a). Lack of access to work opportunities among Native Americans is evidenced by a number of indicators. These include poverty, with the median household income for Native Americans in 2008 at $37,815 compared to $52,029 for all ethnic groups in the United States combined (U.S. Census Bureau, 2009b). Indicators also include joblessness. For example, only 51.5% of Native Americans of

working age in 2010 were employed, with a 15.2% to 21.6% unemployment rate among those people still actively looking for work (Ghosh, 2010).

For Native Americans living on reservations, unemployment rates are very high, ranging from 85% to 90% on some western reservations (e.g., Robbins, 2008). This lack of employment is associated with a lack of property rights, a lack of industry, a lack of affordable transportation, and a crumbling infrastructure. Those who are employed often work in low-paying retail, social, health, and human services occupations (National Drug Intelligence Center, 2008). Off-reservation Native Americans also have challenges related to unemployment, underemployment, and poverty. Many Native Americans are part of the rural poor, with 52% of Native Americans who live outside of metropolitan areas living in poverty. Additionally, among Native Americans who live in urban areas, the poverty rate is 1.6 times higher than among other urban residents, the unemployment rate is 1.7 times higher, and the rate of homelessness is 3 times higher (National Urban Indian Family Coalition, 2008).

BARRIERS, SUPPORTS, AND THE MEANING OF WORK

Work is meaningful to Native Americans. A qualitative study of adult American Indians from the northern plains revealed that career is typically seen as a lifelong endeavor that one enjoys or in which one specializes (Juntunen et al., 2001). Career success is seen as a collective experience that tends to minimize the importance of money and material gain. Career for some Native Americans means promoting traditional ways and tribal well-being (Juntunen et al., 2001).

However, researchers have identified numerous real and perceived barriers to Native Americans' access to work. For example, among Native American youth, only 50% receive a high school diploma, and only 3% of all Native Americans receive college degrees (Alliance for Excellent Education, 2009; Burton, 2010). Researchers have suggested that for Native American students, this low educational attainment is related to academic difficulties in math, science, and English, a belief that success is not related to effort, and ambivalence and uncertainty about how to achieve goals (Hoffman, Jackson, & Smith, 2005; Turner & Conkel, 2011). This lack of educational preparation among Native American youth can put them at a substantial disadvantage for competing in the world of work.

Additionally, among Native American adolescents, there is mixed evidence of a restricted range of career interests. Compared to Caucasian American adolescents, Native American adolescents have greater Realistic and Conventional interests, but similar levels of Investigative, Artistic, Social, and Enterprising interests. Native American adolescents have greater interests in careers requiring high school or two-year college educations, but similar levels of interests in careers requiring four-year college educations (e.g., Turner & Lapan, 2003). Restrictions in interests could lead to a narrower range of occupations that Native American young people will consider (Gottfredson, 1981).

Among adult Native Americans, researchers have identified a lack of support from others, single-parent homes, a lack of childcare resources, domestic violence, alienation, oppression, and discrimination as barriers to work and career success (Juntunen et al., 2001). Additionally, pressures to live biculturally, with adherence to the sometimes-competing sets of values derived from both the dominant culture and the indigenous culture, can also function as a psychological barrier that affects the career development of Native American clients (Juntunen & Cline, 2010). Although living biculturally is successfully accomplished by some Native Americans, for others this demand creates anxiety and uncertainty about the correct way to proceed. The barriers that have been identified in these and other research studies affect to varying degrees Native Americans' abilities to attain or maintain satisfying employment.

HELPING CLIENTS CHANGE

Researchers have suggested that effective counseling with Native American clients is dependent on cultural competency (e.g., Garrett, Garrett, Torres-Rivera, Wilbur, & Roberts-Wilbur, 2005). Culturally competent counseling for Native Americans includes knowledge of Native American customs, lifeways, and spiritual ceremonies (e.g., the use of sweat lodges). It also includes knowledge of and openness to discussing the impacts of historical relationships between Native Americans and other Americans (e.g., population loss and loss of customs and languages; Turner & Pope, 2009), knowledge of communication styles among Native Americans (e.g., using indirect communication and humor in counseling; Garrett et al., 2005), and building relationships with other Native American service providers (e.g., tribal elders or medical personnel). Using empowerment models, narrative counseling, and nondirective counseling mirrors the values

and communication styles often found in Native American communities. Working to interpret the results of vocational appraisal activities within the complexities evidenced in Native American lives can assist counselors in more effectively addressing the work and career needs of their clients (Turner, Trotter, et al., 2006). For example, counselors can help clients understand how working in various occupations identified through interest inventories can help them meet their spiritual goals and how the tasks required to work in those occupations can be congruent with their own values, such as providing service to the community.

Additionally, Native Americans are a widely dispersed population group, living in urban areas, reservations, tribal towns or other small towns, and rural areas. Moreover, there are over 560 tribes in the United States, indicating that counselors should understand the customs and values of the local Native Americans that make up their client base. Counselors also must understand the level of acculturation of their Native American clients (Juntunen & Cline, 2010), as this knowledge can influence their treatment decisions and counseling goals.

There are a number of areas that vocational counselors can address that can help their Native American clients meet their vocational goals and that can result in client change. These include helping them explore how working, not working, or the type of work they choose will affect their families and communities. Next, counselors can help clients explore what collective success means to them. Clients should be able to articulate the parameters of their collective identity (i.e., that metaphysical relationship to one's family, tribe, or community that de-emphasizes individual identity in deference to the common good) and how this collective identity influences their work and career choices. In this way, counselors can help clients make the implicit explicit, so that clearer and more informed choices can be made. These choices, for example, could include moving away to get a better job, or attending a local or tribal college in order to maintain geographical closeness to families and friends.

Regarding helping Native American clients experience vocational success, counselors should not impose their own values on Native American clients concerning the meaning of success. Instead, clients should be helped to explore and articulate what success means to them. Clients should be helped to explore the meanings of money, material wealth, how money can be obtained through working, and how work, family, and tribal life can be balanced. Clients should be helped to explore their work and career aspirations and should be challenged to understand potential connections between their level of aspiration and perceived barriers to education and training, such as not having money for tuition for college. Counselors should help their Native American clients explore barriers to seeking, obtaining, and maintaining work (e.g., alienation and oppression). Counselors should help clients plan how they can overcome each of these barriers in ways that are effective and consistent with client values. Finally, counselors may be helpful to their Native American clients by exploring their feelings and behaviors around living biculturally and helping them make choices that are consistent with their own values, as well as choices that can help them meet their employment and earning needs when they are working in cross-cultural situations.

Additionally, counselors should become familiar with the strides in employing Native Americans that are being taken by the tribes themselves. Native American tribes have found ways to create their own labor markets. From training Native Americans in entrepreneurship in colleges serving primarily Native American students (Silvey & Turner, in preparation), to tribally owned tobacco shops, convenience stores, gas stations, and casinos, Native American tribes have found ways to support education, medical care, and retirement for tribal members, as well as providing employment opportunities to some Native Americans that were previously unavailable. Assisting Native American clients to explore, prepare for, and pursue these opportunities optimally will allow them to find work that not only supports individual workers and their families, but also allows Native American people to give back to their communities.

For the many Native Americans who do not live in areas where work opportunities provided by tribes are available, or who do not have interests that match these opportunities, other strategies to help clients obtain satisfying work can be offered in culturally sensitive and clinically effective ways. For example, along with identifying interests, abilities, and work skills, counselors can help Native American clients learn coping skills (Grandbois, 2009), identify sources of instrumental support that can assist them in working (e.g., affordable childcare, transportation), and assist them in identifying people who can serve as mentors and role models and who can provide psychological support in job search and employment situations.

African Americans

African Americans represent 13.4% of the U.S. population (U.S. Census Bureau, 2009a). Nationally, the unemployment rate for African Americans is approximately three times greater than it is for Caucasian Americans (U.S. Department of Labor, 2011a). Concomitantly, the poverty rate among African Americans is almost three times as great as among Caucasian Americans (U.S. Census Bureau, 2010). African Americans are underrepresented in high-paying, high-status occupations, and overrepresented in low-paying, low-status occupations (Christie, 2010). In the second quarter of 2010 and the second quarter of 2011, African Americans nationally earned 80% of what Caucasian Americans earned (U.S. Department of Labor, 2011b). Only 51% of African American students graduate from high school (Alliance for Excellent Education, 2009).

BARRIERS, SUPPORTS, AND THE MEANING OF WORK

Regarding what work means to African Americans, researchers have found that African American college students believe that making money is important, and they aspire to having a good lifestyle, a secure work environment, job security, and good supervisory relationships (Duffy & Sedlacek, 2007; Hammond, Betz, Multon, & Irvin, 2010). Researchers also have shown that African Americans are interested in high-status occupations and have higher career aspirations than Caucasian Americans (e.g., Booth & Myers, 2011). However, many African American adolescents live in low-income neighborhoods where they are exposed to few working role models; therefore, they may not believe that their occupational aspirations are possible for them to achieve. Additionally, African Americans experience discrimination both when seeking employment (Riach & Rich, 2002) and at the workplace. This discrimination is related to psychological distress, low self-esteem, less efficacy (e.g., less perceived mastery), and an external locus of control (Williams, Neighbors, & Jackson, 2003). The most telling effect of racism and discrimination is the internalization of racial biases, so that, for example, African American elementary school children believe that occupations with higher concentrations of African Americans are lower in status than occupations with lower concentrations of African Americans (Bigler, Averhart, & Liben, 2003).

Cultural knowledge can be key to providing effective counseling interventions for African American clients (Atkinson & Lowe, 1995). Counselors need to have a thorough understanding of the effects of racism and discrimination, as well as an understanding of the broader African American culture and the culture specific to local communities. This knowledge can help counselors assist clients to counter the effects and internalization of racial biases as these biases affect clients' work and lives. This knowledge can also help counselors provide counseling that acknowledges the strength of the African American community and the importance of the African American culture to the individual client and to the environment in which he or she may work.

In addition to gaining cultural knowledge, when counselors provide vocational interventions for African American clients, they should incorporate a discussion of their ethnic identity (i.e., self-identification as an ethnic group member) and how this identity can affect work and career planning and decision-making. Ethnic identity has been associated with a positive self-concept, self-efficacy, and self-esteem (Fouad & Arbona, 1994). Ethnic identity encourages African American clients to consider the meaning of personal achievement as it relates to the larger context of one's own cultural group and can buffer African Americans against the discrimination and barriers that persist in the 21st-century world of work (Byars-Winston, 2010).

Regarding empirically validated interventions that career counselors can use to assist African American clients, an interesting line of research has recently emerged. The modality is constructivist career counseling, in which clients learn the skills of critical reflection, identification of personal strengths, problem solving, and reliance upon self to make meaning out of events (Grier-Reed & Skaar, 2010). Constructivist career counseling is designed to enhance personal power and freedom. Results of pre–post studies evaluating constructivist career counseling among African American college students have shown that this type of intervention leads to greater self-efficacy to make career decisions and overcome barriers, greater positive outcome expectations, and a more internalized locus of control (Grier-Reed & Ganuza, 2011; Grier-Reed, Skaar, & Conkel-Ziebell, 2009; Grier-Reed, Skaar, & Parson, 2009).

When planning counseling for African American adolescents, counselors also should consider ways to draw upon recent research on social cognitive models. In one study, for example, researchers found that within a milieu of perceived racism, poor academic performance in math was related negatively to math interests (Alliman-Brissett & Turner, 2010). Thus, when providing counseling focused on assisting African American young people to consider math careers, counselors should address ways for them to increase their math performance in order to prepare for the math careers in which they are interested and to explore the meaning of racism and the strategies available to manage the impacts of racism upon them. In another study, the researcher found expected associations between career decision-making self-efficacy, outcome expectations, and viable career-choice goals (i.e., goals to which one is committed, for which one is actively preparing, and that are measurable and specific; Lapan, 2004) among high school students (including a large sample of African American students). Efficacy was negatively related to perceptions of barriers to career attainment and positively related to career maturity, to engaging in more career exploration, and to being proactive in considering one's career options (Conkel-Ziebell, 2010). Results of this study suggest ways that counselors can focus on increasing decision-making self-efficacy in service of increasing goal-setting skills among African American young people.

Researchers have also found that the support of their family, peers, and community can help African American adolescents obtain additional sources of vocational knowledge. Moreover, helping African American young people identify individuals with compatible career interests and then encouraging them to job shadow these individuals could serve to promote greater career self-efficacy through appropriate role modeling (Bandura, 2002). Assisting African American clients to locate such role models can often be the first step to exploring a variety of previously foreclosed vocational pathways.

Hispanic/Latino(a)s

Hispanic/Latino(a)s are the largest and fastest-growing minority group in the United States, as well as the fastest-growing ethnic population in the labor force (U.S. Census Bureau, 2009a). Approximately 16.3% of the U.S. population is Hispanic/Latino(a), or about 1 in every 6 people. Hispanic/Latino(a)s make up approximately 14.2% of the U.S. civilian workforce (Kochhar, 2008).

The average income of Hispanic/Latino(a) Americans is significantly lower than the national average, which leads to large portions of the population being classified as part of the working poor. In 2009, the median household income among Hispanic/Latino(a)s was approximately $38,039, in comparison to Caucasian Americans, which was $51,861 (U.S. Census Bureau, 2009b). Research has indicated that this is due, at least in part, to low educational attainment, limited English proficiency, residency in concentrated poverty neighborhoods, and occupational segregation (e.g., National Center for Education Statistics, 2011; Toussaint-Comeau, Smith, & Comeau, 2005). Hispanic/Latino(a)s are overrepresented in low-skilled, low-paying service, manual labor, and agricultural jobs that are strongly identified by the general public as "Latino" (Catanzarite & Aguilera, 2002). High school graduation rates for Hispanic/Latino(a) students are 55% (Alliance for Excellent Education, 2009).

BARRIERS, SUPPORTS, AND THE MEANING OF WORK

A number of cultural values have been identified by researchers that differentiate the Latino(a) population from other populations and that influence "recruitment, retention, advancement, work climate, career and leadership development" for Latino(a)s in the workplace (Holvino, 2008, p. 6). Holvino identified seven of these cultural values (or scripts): (1) loyalty and strong obligation to the family, (2) gender differences in social roles in which males dominate and females nurture, (3) courtesy and respect required to develop meaningful, trusting relationships, (4) avoiding conflict and maintaining harmony, (5) group focus rather than individual focus, (6) present time orientation, and (7) respect for those in authority. While some of these values are consistent with work expectations (e.g., respecting those in authority), some values are inconsistent with a workplace culture that requires an overarching focus on work, quick and independent decision-making balanced with collaboration with coworkers and supervisors, egalitarianism and gender equity, and an orientation toward pursuing and obtaining future goals. Although adhering to traditional cultural values in the workplace may assist Hispanic/Latino(a)s in maintaining solidarity with their cultural community and in maintaining their own psychological integrity, it also could lead to stress due to conflicts with value systems of employers.

Among Hispanic/Latino(a)s, there can also be a disconnect between educational aspirations and attainment. For example, 50% of Mexican American junior high students aspire to attend graduate school, yet 57% of these students do not finish high school, and only 11% graduate from college (Ojeda & Flores, 2008; St. Hilaire, 2002; Stoops, 2004). Some researchers believe that school failure in this population is a result of a mismatch between the cultural context at school and the Hispanic/Latino(a) culture. For example, Valenzuela (1999) stated that the Hispanic/Latino(a) culture is devalued at school, which in turn separates students from social and cultural resources and leaves them susceptible to academic failure. Authors have also argued that Hispanic/Latino(a) students have limited access to academic preparation, career information, and guidance (Lee & Ekstrom, 1987).

Nevertheless, work itself is highly valued by Hispanic/Latino(a) persons. Hispanic/Latino(a)s "take pride in working hard and doing things well" (Benitiz, 2007, p. 46). Hispanic/Latino(a) persons have stated that they work from a sense of dignity, determination, and pride because they have opportunities in the United States, as well as working to provide for their families (Benitiz, 2007); and, although they are occupationally segregated in the United States and are at risk for low educational attainment, Hispanic/Latino(a) people report having a broad range of interests across the vocational world (Kantamneni & Fouad, 2011). Their career goals are influenced by interests and efficacy, as is true across many populations (Flores, Robitschek, Celebi, Andersen, & Hoang, 2010).

HELPING CLIENTS CHANGE

Recognizing clients' cultural values can help establish a solid working alliance and facilitate client change. For example, activating the value of courtesy and respect in the counseling session can be essential to establishing a strong working alliance (Flores, Ramos, & Kanagui, 2010). Understanding clients' vocational personalities as well as their strong loyalties and obligations to their families can guide counselors in helping them make work choices that are congruent and culturally appropriate. These are only a few examples of providing counseling that is informed by the cultural values of Hispanic/Latino(a) clients. Counselors who work with Hispanic/Latino(a) clients should become very aware of their guiding values and should become facile at entering into clients' worlds to facilitate change.

Counseling models that are founded on Hispanic/Latino(a) culture have been developed. For example, in a career counseling model based on the DSM-IV-TR Cultural Formulation Outline, authors (Flores, Ramos et al., 2010, p. 412) suggested that five dimensions be used to address their career concerns: "(a) self and cultural identity" (i.e., the way that individuals are defined and shaped by their culture), "(b) self and cultural conception of career problems, (c) self in cultural context, (d) cultural dynamics in the therapeutic relationship, and (e) overall cultural assessment for career counseling interventions" (including a thorough appraisal of clients' backgrounds, traditions, immigration histories, and acculturation).

In another example, researchers integrated cultural values into a career support group designed for baccalaureate-level Latino(a) college students (Berrios-Allison, 2011). Using this model, counselors addressed career planning, financial aid, academic training, mentoring, college climate, and exploration of ethnic identity issues. Results showed that across the four years of the baccalaureate programs in which students were enrolled, retention rates for those attending the groups ranged from 16% to 22% more than rates for those students not attending the groups. The use of this intervention highlights the success that counselors can have when focusing upon the career development needs of Hispanic/Latino(a) individuals while at the same time being sensitive to their cultural values and cultural identity.

Clients with Disabilities

The National Council on Disability (2008) estimates that 20.4% of the U.S. population has a disability. These disabilities include both low-incidence disabilities (e.g., autism, blindness, deafness, severe cognitive disabilities) and high-incidence disabilities (e.g., learning, communication, or emotional/behavioral disorders, mild cognitive impairments, other health impairments). Unemployment rates are high among people with disabilities, with only 22.6% of adults with disabilities employed (U.S. Department of Labor, 2009b), while in the general population, 71.9% of people without disabilities are employed. There is an inextricable link between disabilities and poverty. Almost two-thirds of working-age adults who experience consistent income poverty (more than 36 months of poverty in a 48-month period) have at least one disability. "People with disabilities are much more likely to experience various forms of material hardship—including food insecurity, not getting needed medical or dental care, and not being able to pay rent, mortgage, and utility bills—than people without disabilities" (Fremstad, 2009, p. 3).

Barriers, Supports, and the Meaning of Work

Persons with disabilities find great meaning in work. For example, researchers have found that working allows persons with disabilities to increase their activity levels and gain self-esteem (Freedman, 1996). Among persons with intellectual disabilities, work allows them to attain social recognition and connection with others and provides a means for integrating into the community, enjoyment in being part of a work group, camaraderie and fun, a sense of pride, satisfaction in performing work tasks, social comfort, and psychological empowerment (Kober & Eggleton, 2005; Lysaght, Ouellette-Kuntz, & Morrison, 2009). Among women with physical, visual, and hearing disabilities, work is associated with emotional welfare, self-esteem, social status, and a sense of independence and personal competence (Gonzalez, 2009). Among patients recovering from mental illness, work is associated with pride, self-esteem, and coping strategies, and work allows them to become consumers and providers for their families (Dunn, Wewiorski, & Rogers, 2008).

Nevertheless, there are structural challenges in regard to attaining and maintaining work among persons with disabilities, including lack of adequate educational preparation (high school dropout rates of persons with disabilities are more than double those of persons without disabilities, or slightly more than 50%; National Council on Disability, 2004), lack of job availability, lack of transportation, lack of job information, inadequate training, fear of losing health insurance or Medicaid, family responsibilities, and being discouraged from working by family or friends (Loprest & Maag, 2001). Other reasons include lack of required training for specific jobs, a lack of skills or experience regarding specific occupations, lack of supervisors' knowledge about accommodations, attitudes and stereotypes of coworkers and supervisors, restricted social networks, poverty, the presence of symptoms, lack of interpersonal skills, and the lack of rehabilitation programs (Baron & Salzer, 2002; Dauwalder & Hoffmann, 1992; Loprest & Maag, 2001).

There are also psychological barriers that can impede satisfactory employment. For example, among persons in recovery from workplace injuries, pain catastrophizing (i.e., characterizing pain as awful and unbearable; Gracely et al., 2004), pain-related anxiety, depression, and activity avoidance have been found to be barriers to successful re-employment (e.g., Carleton, Abrams, Kachur, & Asmundson, 2009). Other psychological barriers include finding work boring and frustrating in sheltered work settings (Szivos, 1990), feeling lonely and excluded because of the perceived stigma of having a disability (Petrovski & Gleeson, 1997), and feeling anxious about not having the competence to meet employers' expectations or the work-related skills appropriate to job demands (Jahoda et al., 2009).

Regarding career decision-making, there are a number of challenges involved in this process among persons with disabilities. Persons with disabilities may have less confidence to make effective career decisions than persons without disabilities have, and may be more dependent on others to make decisions for them (Luzzo, Hitchings, Retish, & Shoemaker, 1999). They are less likely to have engaged in career exploration, are less likely to have taken career education courses in high school, and are less likely to have had opportunities to practice connecting knowledge of self and the world of work (Luzzo, 2000; Ochs & Roessler, 2004; Trainor, 2007). In high school, this could be due, at least in part, to the demands of taking transitions or life-skills classes so that career exploration activities that could lead to more informed career decision-making are not pursued. However, it could also be that because of the public's expectations regarding the employment of persons with disabilities, these opportunities are not as readily available for either adolescents or adults.

An example of these challenges in career decision-making is the high rate of mismatch between career interests, self-estimated abilities, and procured employment among persons with disabilities (Turner, Unkefer, Cichy, Peper, & Juang, 2011). Although researchers have shown that both high school students and adults who are matched with jobs according to their Holland Theme interests have higher performance ratings, lower rates of absenteeism, fewer conduct problems, and greater job satisfaction than those who are not matched (Jagger, Neukrug, & McAuliffe, 1992; Wilkes, 2002), among a sample of young adults with disabilities, researchers found that only 31% were employed in jobs that matched their interests, and only 33% were employed in jobs that matched their self-estimated work abilities. Moreover, across the United States, persons with disabilities are overemployed in Realistic (R) jobs, with 70% of persons with disabilities who work employed in R jobs, even though only 35% of the available jobs in the United States are R-type occupations (Turner et al., 2011; U.S. Department of Labor, 2006).

Helping Clients Change

Establishing a working alliance with persons with disabilities can depend upon the type and level of the disability. However, approaches have been identified for working with persons with disabilities independent of the type or level of their disability. For example, researchers suggest that "(1) treating all clients as adults regardless of the severity of the disability condition, (2) using age-appropriate language and techniques, (3) placing emphasis on client strengths, and (4) respecting client values and beliefs" (Kosciulek & Wheaton, 2003) can serve as a beneficial foundation for forming a strong working alliance. It is important for psychologists to "strive to recognize that there is a wide range of individual response to disability, and collaborate with their clients who have disabilities, and when appropriate, with their clients' families to plan, develop, and implement interventions" (American Psychological Association, 2011).

A strong working alliance also can be promoted by providing appropriate accommodations during counseling. These accommodations can include the use of interpreters, the use of computers for communicating questions and answers, the availability of wheelchairs or elevators, or assistance in parking and moving from a car to the office and back. Counselors should consider carefully the needs of their clients with disabilities, and should ask them to state specifically what types of accommodations they desire rather than assuming that each client will want the same accommodations. For example, researchers have found that among the deaf and hard of hearing, 50% of sign language users preferred to have an interpreter with them, and 43% preferred to work with a counselor who also signs (Middleton et al., 2010).

In regard to counseling strategies, a very important tactic for assisting clients with disabilities to change is helping them develop the skill of self-advocacy. Self-advocacy means that clients can express, in ways understandable and acceptable to their audiences, their interests, desires, rights, and needs, can make informed decisions, and can take responsibility for their decisions (VanReusen, Bos, Schumaker, & Deschler, 1994). Helping persons with disabilities learn to engage in self-advocacy and become self-determined can also help them become the primary causal agents in their own lives and work environments. Self-advocacy can help clients ask for more career development assistance. Self-advocacy can also help clients negotiate structural challenges, such as family responsibilities, transportation arrangements, adequate training, or insurance payments. Self-advocacy can help clients inform supervisors about their accommodation needs and can help clients challenge the inaccurate beliefs and attitudes of employers and coworkers. Self-advocacy can help clients negotiate inclusion into a network of coworkers and ask for social support. Among persons with disabilities, self-advocacy has been positively associated with self-efficacy, perceived ability to work, and satisfaction with work (Bedell, 2007; Tschopp, Frain, & Bishop, 2009).

Clients with disabilities also can benefit from learning career development skills. Strategies to help clients understand themselves and the world of work (Turner et al., 2011) and participate in career planning, career decision-making, and work assistance planning are critically important to help them gain and maintain full and satisfying employment. An example of a model that can guide counselors in providing this type of assistance is the Individualized Career Planning Model (Condon & Callahan, 2008), in which a step-by-step method of career planning and job development is specified. In this model, clients with disabilities participate in the assessment of their interests, preferences, learning strategies, skills and abilities, environmental supports, and the job-relevant tasks that they are able to perform. Counselors then write thorough vocational profiles and meet with clients to develop customized job plans. Narrative portfolios are then created to represent clients' potential contributions to employment situations and those ideal conditions that can help them work successfully. Portfolios can then be used by job developers to represent the clients to employers, or by clients to design their own businesses. Finally, Social Security Work Incentives are utilized to fund needed services, such as job coaching, job development, transportation, equipment, and training. Using this model can promote self-determination and informed choice-making of clients with disabilities.

Additionally, clients with disabilities can benefit from learning work readiness skills. Helping clients develop work readiness skills can help them learn to thrive in the work environment. For example, in an 18-month intervention designed to support persons recovering from mental illness in returning to meaningful work, training in soft skills (e.g., social and interpersonal skills) and coping skills was given. Services specific to each participant's mental health and career development needs were also offered. These services included day treatment, crisis stabilization, vocational rehabilitation, career development instruction, work adjustment and support services, job development/job seeking/job placement services, educational support services, assistance in applying for entitlements, and supported work opportunities. Results of a one-sample, pre–post study of this intervention showed that there were significantly more employed participants at the end of the intervention than at the beginning. There was a significant increase in the number of hours worked per week, and participants had significantly greater earnings. Moreover, there were significant increases in independent living and overall self-esteem (Hutchinson, Anthony, Massaro, & Rogers, 2007). These are only a few examples of recent studies that counselors can draw from regarding assisting persons with disabilities in their work and career development.

Finally, clients with disabilities can benefit from rehabilitation services. Assisting persons with disabilities to relearn lost skills (National Institutes of Health, 2011), or to learn to use job-related accommodations in order to perform work functions, can greatly enhance their employability and work satisfaction. Examples of these accommodations include writing notes, keeping daily calendars, writing to-do lists, keeping items that need attention in visible places, learning to use technologies such as personal digital assistants (PDAs) with verbal prompting, and learning to use Web-based instruction to enhance digital literacy (Assistive Technology Solutions, 2011; Center for Gerontology, 2006; Starcic & Niskala, 2010). While vocational counselors and psychologists should work with clients to advocate for appropriate and accessible accommodations, a wide referral network of professionals specializing in this type of education can help clients find accommodation resources and become proficient in using accommodations.

Sexual Minority Clients

The current estimate of gay, lesbian, bisexual, and transgendered (GLBT) individuals in the United States is 3.8%. This equates to approximately 9 million GLBT adults (Gates, 2011). There is a high unemployment rate among transgender and gender-nonconforming persons, with unemployment rates two to four times higher than in the general population. The rates of unemployment among gay, lesbian, and bisexual persons are not as definitively known. Similarly qualified gay/bisexual men earn 15% to 30% less than straight men (Carpenter, 2007). There is less clarity in the literature that such a wage gap exists between lesbian and non-lesbian women.

There is national discussion about the discrimination that GLBT clients experience in employment, with 15% to 43% of gays reporting that they have experienced some form of job discrimination, including being fired indiscriminately from jobs and being denied employment opportunities and employment rights (Burns & Krehely, 2011). Outcomes of work discrimination result in very negative consequences for GLBT people. For example, transgender people experience a disproportionate rate of homelessness and poverty, with four times as many as in the general population living in households with incomes less than $10,000 a year, which is classified as extreme poverty (Grant et al., 2011). Moreover, few companies have domestic partner rights for GLBT employees, such as family medical leave if one's domestic partner becomes ill, or the availability of company-provided health insurance for one's domestic partner (Ash & Badgett, 2006).

Barriers, Supports, and the Meaning of Work

Work and career can have multiple meanings for GLBT persons. Work can provide a focus for one's life (Hook & Bowman, 2008). Work also can enhance the quality of life and can be a source of prestige, security, financial gain, and social relationships among GLBT individuals.

Nevertheless, GLBT persons have reported great work-related distress related to unfair treatment, heterosexist discrimination, job loss or inability to be promoted due to one's sexual orientation or transgender status, and harassment in the workplace (Bowleg, Brooks, & Ritz, 2008; Budge, Tebbe, & Howard, 2010; Lombardi, Wilchins, Priesing, & Malouf, 2001; Smith & Ingram, 2004; Trau & Härtel, 2004). Some gay men suffer from isolation, ridicule, and a lack of peer support in the workplace, and some who are closeted feel disingenuous and are worried that their sexual orientation will be discovered (Trau & Härtel, 2004). Some transgender individuals report that they experience rejection by coworkers or are fired, physically threatened, or physically or emotionally abused (e.g., Budge et al., 2010; Lombardi et al., 2001). Because of this they are anxious, and some have suicidal thoughts.

Some gay, lesbian, and bisexual individuals report being the victim of slurs or feeling that they have to act straight at work (Smith & Ingram, 2004). These heterosexist events are associated with depression and distress (Smith & Ingram, 2004). Some lesbians report workplace distress related to feelings of marginalization, the heterosexist assumptions underlying workplace conversations, and the need to monitor behaviors and interactions with others in order to ward off presumptions of sexual attraction to coworkers (Bowleg et al., 2008).

Because of these types of discriminatory behaviors, the consideration of one's own sexual orientation and reactions from others to that orientation can be factors considered when GLBT clients choose careers. GLBT clients may welcome opportunities to express their sexual orientation at work or through work (Chung, 1995). However, theorists have suggested that adult lesbians may consider such factors as being in more tolerant work environments, being in geographical locations where they can receive support for values and life choices, and having financial security (e.g., Fassinger, 1995, 1996) when choosing careers. Similarly, researchers have found that among transgender persons who made gender transitions while holding a job, real and perceived occupational barriers (e.g., anticipated job loss due to transgender identity) as well as occupational aspirations, opportunities to learn new skills, and workplace benefits (Budge et al., 2010) are considered.

There is also evidence that GLB persons receive less support from others regarding their career decision making (Nauta, Saucier, & Woodard, 2001), although support has been shown to be an important factor in this process for GLBT individuals. For example, GLB college students reported that a career role model's sexual orientation and the support of persons with their same sexual orientation were important to the decisions they made concerning their careers (Nauta et al., 2001).

Helping Clients Change

When planning vocational interventions for GLBT persons, researchers have found that a stronger working alliance is facilitated by counselors who have a universal diverse orientation (i.e., appreciation of and openness to others' similarities and differences; Fuertes, Sedlacek, Roger, & Mohr, 2000). Additionally, clients value counselors who have LGB-specific knowledge and general therapeutic skills (Burckell & Goldfried, 2006; Stracuzzi, Mohr, & Fuertes, 2011). Moreover, research among counselors has shown that from counselors' perspectives, there are important dimensions of counselor self-efficacy that can help establish a working alliance with LGB clients (Burkard, Pruitt, Medler, & Stark-Booth, 2009). These include efficacy to overcome negative feelings when working with LGB clients, efficacy to express feelings of compassion about LGB clients' disadvantages in society and the struggles they experience in coming out, efficacy to feel positive emotions toward clients and to support, show respect to, and care for them, efficacy to discuss religious and sexual concerns and to normalize clients' experiences, and efficacy to provide appropriate counseling and referrals. Further research should be conducted on how these dimensions relate to clients' ratings of the working alliance and both clients' and counselors' ratings of counselor competency; however, this study provides initial insight on ways that counselors can establish a working alliance with their LGB clients.

In regard to counseling strategies, there are few outcome studies of career counseling for GLBT individuals. Nevertheless, empirical studies have provided guidance concerning factors to consider in helping GLBT clients make career decisions, models have been developed that counselors can use to help meet GLBT clients' work and career development needs, and a pre–post study has been conducted on an intervention designed to help lesbians become comfortable with sharing their sexual orientation in the workplace (e.g., Chung, 2001; Chung & Harmon, 1994).

Regarding factors to consider in career decision-making, research has shown that GLBT persons may have more gender-nontraditional career interests than non-GLBT individuals. For example, in a study comparing gay and heterosexual men who were matched on age, socioeconomic status, ethnic background, student status, and education level, researchers found that gay men had less interests in Realistic and Investigative occupations and greater interests in Artistic and Social occupations than heterosexual men (Chung & Harmon, 1994). There were no differences in the prestige level of the careers to which they aspired. Similarly, in a qualitative study conducted 10 years later with Latino gay and lesbian youth (18 to 20 years old), respondents described career interests that they believed were less gender-role stereotyped. In this sample of eight young people, all of the males ($n = 5$) had artistic interests and all of the females ($n = 3$) had interests in science, medicine, engineering, and astronautics (Adams, Cahill, & Ackerlind, 2005). Although stereotyping GLBT clients' interest/prestige profiles would be ineffective in providing services for these clients, counselors should remain open to exploring clients' interests broadly and use this knowledge to help them find work and careers that satisfy their intrinsic interests.

Additionally, models to help clients make more informed career decisions (the Vocational Choice Model), manage the disclosure of sexual identities (the Identity Management Model), and respond to discrimination (the Discrimination Management Model) (Chung, 2001; Chung, Williams, & Dispenza, 2009) have been developed. Using the Vocational Choice Model to help clients make career decisions, counselors can help clients select occupations based on their level of comfort or efficacy in managing discrimination. Three strategies were identified in this model: self-employment, identifying whether an occupation or job is LGB welcoming, and taking a risk with the knowledge that work-based discrimination could occur. The strategies used in the Identity Management Model include passing or coming out (either through behaviors or explicit statements). In the Discrimination Management Model, strategies identified were quitting the job, silence, social support, and confrontation. Chung et al. emphasized that using any of the strategies identified in these models is a matter of individual choice, and that counselors should not push clients to choose one specific strategy over another. However, research has shown that coming out at work, being true to one's self, and taking pride in one's identity is associated with positive mental health benefits. GLBT persons who are open about their sexual orientation at work are more confident and more comfortable in their work situations, have more commitment to their work organizations, and have less conflict between work and home (Day & Schoenrade, 1997; Trau & Härtell, 2004).

For example, the results of a pre–post study (Morrow, 1996) designed to help lesbians become comfortable with sharing their sexual orientation at work by training them to be assertive and to deal with homophobia and heterosexism showed that experimental group participants had significantly greater ego development, lesbian identity development, empowerment, and the ability to disclose than control group participants at post-test. The ability to communicate, be assertive, and live openly can have a significant positive impact on lesbian women's ability to be comfortable in sharing their sexual orientation in the workplace. Considering the results of these studies can help counselors design useful work and career counseling interventions for their GLBT clients.

The Unemployed, the Homeless, and the Working and Nonworking Poor

In 2009, the U.S. Census Bureau reported that 14.3% of Americans, or 43.6 million people, have incomes that are under the federally established poverty level. Poverty rates are highest for families headed by single women, particularly if they are African American or Hispanic. Children under 18 (25% of the U.S. population) represent 35% of those who live in poverty. As shown in the previous sections of this chapter, poverty is a large part of the lived experience of groups who are also otherwise disenfranchised by racial, ethnic, sexual, or disability minority status (Smith, 2005); but there is no population group in the United States that is immune from poverty or from the devastating effects that poverty can have on people's lives.

Poverty in some cases leads to homelessness. Approximately 0.2% of the US population (about 650,000 people) is homeless on any given night. Approximately 1% of the US population is homeless at some time during one calendar year (U.S. Department of Housing and Urban Development, 2010). Of the homeless, men, African Americans, single adults, and persons with disabilities are overrepresented in the population at the rates of 1.3:1, 3:1, 5:1, and 2.4:1, respectively. Moreover, not all who are homeless are unemployed. Indeed, researchers have shown that 44% of people who are homeless have jobs (Long, Rio, & Rosen, 2007).

Barriers, Supports, and the Meaning of Work

The most obvious signs of poverty are found in inner cities, where crumbling neighborhoods and poorly maintained infrastructures are seen, and in rural areas, where there are dilapidated houses and a lack of visible employment opportunities. The host of problems associated with poverty are well known and numerous. These include inadequate nutrition, housing, medical care, and transportation, unsafe neighborhoods, underfunded schools, and low educational attainment. Extreme poverty and/or lack of access to resources such as mental health treatment can ultimately lead to homelessness, a chronic deficiency of basic necessities, and a potentially grim existence (Torey, 2008).

Just a few of the psychological barriers associated with unemployment and poverty are anxiety, depression, hopelessness, and aggression (Belle & Doucet, 2003; DeCarlo Santiago, Wadsworth, & Stump, 2011). Among clients in poverty, barriers to gaining or maintaining satisfactory employment include a lack of educational credentials, a lack of transitional skills (Nixon, 2006), and/or a lack of access to structures that make working possible (e.g., transportation, phones, addresses, or appropriate accommodations for disabled persons). While work

for some in poverty is simply a matter of survival, for others it is still a means of self-expression, social acceptance, self-identity, enjoyment, satisfaction, and self-respect.

Helping Clients Change

Research on the establishment of a working alliance between vocational counselors and clients in poverty is in the initial stages of development. However, one study did indicate that a strong working alliance between counselors and youth living in poverty should be founded on client attractiveness (e.g., whether the counselor can address his or her potential biases against a client in poverty) (Hutchison, 2010). Nevertheless, there has been a wealth of literature regarding the development of psychotherapeutic relationships between therapists and persons living in poverty that could be instructive for professionals who work in the vocational counseling realm. In sum, many of the preconceived notions about working with clients in poverty are incorrect. Clients in poverty do benefit from counseling. More clients who live in poverty drop out of counseling prematurely than clients who live in more comfortable circumstances do, but this could be because they are faced with the unacknowledged privilege and classism that can characterize psychologists' offices. The barriers that counselors have in working with clients in poverty could very well be due to their own internalized resistance to identifying with the poor, to their fear of poverty and what it means to their own presumptions of meritocracy, and to their feelings of non-efficaciousness, given that their clients will likely return to a life that is still bereft of what they consider to be basic necessities. Supervision, education, flexibility, and the willingness to try innovative treatment strategies can be first steps in learning to establish a change relationship with clients in poverty (Smith, 2005).

In regard to planning vocational interventions for clients in poverty, counselors should consider assisting them to attain educationally, acquire career development skills, and participate in rehabilitation services. Assisting young people to attain educationally is essential to helping them avoid poverty later in life. Young people who do not earn a high school diploma are less likely to gain and maintain employment. For example, in July 2009, the unemployment rate for high school dropouts was 15.4%, but for high school graduates, it was 9.4% (U.S. Department of Labor, 2009a). Yet, helping young people to persevere to graduation has continued to remain a problem: over 25% of all students in the

United States and approximately 50% of students from various minority groups drop out of high school (Snyder & Dillow, 2011).

A large body of research exists concerning helping young people develop skills to complete high school (e.g., Flum & Blustein, 2000). In these studies, researchers have identified educational skills, vocational planning skills, and various types of educational, vocational, and personal supports as important in assisting students in their educational efforts. For example, a recent 7-year longitudinal study was conducted that evaluated programs that were designed to increase high school graduation rates among multiethnic, primarily low-socioeconomic-status students. In this study, skills among student participants were identified that differentiated schools with increasing graduation rates from schools in which graduation rates did not increase. Skills related to students graduating included math and reading, exploring interests and abilities, reviewing academic progress, learning to use time wisely, learning to use information concerning college entrance, scholarships, and careers, learning about post-high school choices, and engaging in career planning (Mason-Chagil et al., 2011).

Research also shows that educational attainment beyond high school is related to superior employment outcomes (Stoll, 2010). However, students in poverty are at risk for not being able to afford higher education, or not being prepared academically for college-level work (Lapan, Turner, & Pierce, in press). To help remedy this, colleges often provide remedial courses that can increase students' academic skills preparation in order to promote greater academic success (Mina, Fulmer, & Smith, 2010). Researchers have shown that students who complete remedial coursework in math are less likely to drop out of college than students who do not complete this coursework (Bettinger & Long, 2005).

One useful way for counselors to help ameliorate poverty among adult workers is to help clients acquire career development skills. In a comprehensive model of career development, the Integrative Contextual Model of Career Development (ICM), Lapan (2004) identified six skill sets that lead to a variety of positive motivations and positive educational and vocational outcomes. The first set is career exploration skills, which includes skills to gain adequate labor market information. In particular, for semiskilled jobs, unskilled jobs, or part-time jobs, opportunities may not be publicized and jobs may be filled through informal networking (Holzer, 1996). The other skill sets identified in the ICM

model are person–environment fit skills, goal-setting skills, social, prosocial, and work readiness skills, self-regulated learning skills, and the consistent utilization of social support. Career development skills such as these can assist both young people and adults to make the transition from school to work, from job to job, or from occupation to occupation.

Regarding offering services to persons who are homeless or live in absolute poverty, rehabilitation services for disabled persons and both publically and privately funded community counseling agencies are available that offer assistance in gaining career planning skills as well as providing a host of mental health and case management services. For the chronically homeless, many programs have been developed across the United States, and some have been tested empirically. For example, in a program designed to serve homeless persons with severe mental illness, 97% of experimental group participants (compared to 67% of the comparison group participants) received vocational services, including vocational assessment and the development of jobs based on career preferences, vocational skills training, job placement in jobs that paid at least minimum wage in competitive employment situations in integrated community settings (not reserved for persons with disabilities), and employment supports upon finding a job. Results indicated that experimental group participants were more likely to secure competitive employment, work more hours, and have higher earnings than control group participants for most of the 24 months of the study (Cook et al., 2005). This model indicates that combining multiple strategies rather than career counseling or rehabilitation services alone can lead to successful work outcomes among persons in poverty.

Conclusion

In this chapter, a number of themes have become apparent concerning clients with work-based challenges and insufficient resources that if addressed could assist them to both attain and maintain productive, satisfying employment. The first is low educational attainment. Few jobs are available that do not require high school diplomas, and those few jobs typically do not pay more than minimum wage. Counselors should develop a strong focus in helping the approximately 50% of students in many minority communities who drop out of high school persist toward earning their high school diplomas. However, when working with students who are unable to complete their educations or when working with adults who have not completed high school, there are alternatives to returning to high school, including taking online courses, obtaining apprenticeships, completing GEDs, or participating in internships or work-based learning opportunities. In this way, counselors can promote skill building for adults who are struggling in their working lives. Working within a network of community–career partnerships can help counselors refer clients to these options in order to assist them with their educational development (Turner & Lapan, 2003).

The second theme is work-related discrimination. As has been discussed in this chapter, persons with work-based challenges face many different types of discrimination. However, most of this discrimination is based on nonconformity to the dominant way of being or behaving, or based on race, gender, or disability status. It is crucial that counselors address discrimination in the counseling session and help clients manage the effects of racism and discrimination on both their employment and on their mental health. Counselors should use empowerment models and models designed to help clients understand discrimination and make informed choices about how to counter its effects when working with clients who are experiencing discrimination.

Another theme is that work has great meaning to clients, and counselors should assist clients in tapping into that meaning. This could help buffer the distress that many face regarding work. It is not only structural issues with which persons with work-based challenges must contend; it is also their psychological responses to stresses caused by their environments. Counselors providing vocational counseling for these clients must truly integrate personal counseling into their work in order to provide effective and salient services to their clients. For example, counselors can help clients examine the emotional components of career problems, such as the fear and anxiety that drives career indecision and procrastination (Krumboltz, 1993).

Finally, in our review we saw that there is a dearth of research aimed at evaluating models and methods to provide vocational counseling to clients with work-based challenges and insufficient resources. Some progress is being made in examining career-based outcomes when using specific models or methods to counsel certain groups (e.g., constructivist counseling with African Americans), but less research is being conducted that examines outcomes among other groups (e.g., Native Americans). There is also little research on training counselors to provide services to clients with work-based challenges and insufficient resources. Research in both of these areas will be needed in the future in order to ascertain best practices for working with these groups of clients.

Reflections

One of the most complex challenges facing counselors who work with clients with less volition in their work lives is helping them develop careers when their initial need is to find a job. In considering this problem, counselors need to explore with clients their motivations to pursue employment. Work "works" for clients who actually benefit from working. It is challenging for clients who are the few who are working in a community of the many who do not have jobs. This is because much of what one can earn monetarily may be used to support as much as possible one's friends, family, and community. Clients need to grapple with not only the economic benefit of working, but also the tremendous psychological and social benefits that can inure to them as they participate in work. Cost–benefit analyses of what is at risk versus what can be gained by finding a job can be useful in helping clients make work and subsequent career choices.

Next, counselors may need to rethink their concepts of career. The traditional notion of career as the path to economic upward mobility may not have that same type of meaning to clients who are on the margins of the dominant European American society. Indeed, for some clients, family and community, or personal or cultural values may outweigh the urge to pursue careers that increase personal wealth. For those clients who desire an upwardly mobile career path and also for those clients who choose different types of career paths, counselors should help them develop the types of skills that they would help any person develop who is pursuing employment. These skills include developing a solid understanding of local as well as nonlocal opportunities and how their skills and interests can fit. Clients with work-based challenges should be accorded the same dignity as clients with greater resources in that their personal preferences should be considered. Even for less prestigious jobs, blue-collar jobs or entry-level jobs with lower pay, there are typically choices about which job to first pursue. If there are not, counselors can help clients learn how to market themselves in order to procure employment at an available job while helping them to plan and prepare for their next opportunity. Counselors should also assist clients with work-based challenges with what might be considered as less intense problems among middle-class persons, such as how to maintain reliable transportation, where to buy suitable clothing for work when one has little money, or how to arrange for quality childcare. This type of counseling could require helping clients not only set goals, but explore and commit to strategies and tasks to reach these goals. It could also require giving clients detailed information about possibilities and places to obtain assistance (e.g., babysitting co-ops).

Next, while pursuing employment, counselors should help clients with work-based challenges develop career development skills, positive outcome expectations, a stable internal locus of control, and hope. Soft skills and interpersonal skills, as well as job skills, should be developed. Clients should be helped to explore the resistances they might face when looking for a desired job, and to plan how to manage these resistances. Moreover, clients should be helped to explore their own dysfunctional thoughts in regards to work (e.g., no one will ever hire me, or what happened to me today will determine everything that happens to me for the rest of my life). Clients should also be helped to look for those hidden and unexpected sources of networking and support. These may not be job-related sources of support. They could be community sources, family sources, or mentors from professional associations.

Clients should also be helped to develop positive self-esteem (e.g., a positive opinion of themselves and their value as persons). They should be helped to understand who they are and what their personal worth is, no matter what their circumstances are or how others view them. The understanding of their core selves, which is based on their realistic appraisals of their own gifts and talents, along with hope and a belief that what they are doing will eventually lead them to their goals, can help keep clients from becoming discouraged by seemingly uncontrollable events and can keep them focused on obtaining their objectives.

Finally, counselors should be strong advocates for developing economic and work opportunities for those who have been disenfranchised. Counselors can participate in such activities as helping employers learn to communicate with their workers from diverse cultures, sharing with employers information about how to access state-supported employment services for persons with disabilities, and networking with employers to establish entry-level and part-time jobs for persons who are in the initial stages of work skill development. Along with this, counselors should remain engaged in activities that promote broader social change so that equal opportunities are available for all people, including people with work-based challenges.

Future Directions

Traditional vocational counseling rests upon presumptions of equality, opportunity, and resources. As has been discussed in this chapter, there are many, many people in the United States for whom these presumptions are inaccurate. Any type of career counseling needs to be rooted in an understanding of the strengths provided through specific communities and within individual clients, as well as the barriers experienced by persons from diverse social and cultural groups. It will require a shift in perspective in order to counsel clients with work-based challenges and insufficient resources effectively. Following are questions for the consideration of future directions in this endeavor:

1. How do counselors learn the cultural values of their clients well enough to provide needed services for them within their cultural context?

2. What types of pre–post studies can we develop in order to inform our practice on how to work most effectively with clients with work-based challenges and insufficient resources?

3. How can we best use standard vocational assessment methods with clients with work-based challenges?

4. At what point do we encourage clients to embrace the work culture rather than continuing to operate from their own cultural value systems?

5. How can we best utilize what we know about multicultural theory, research, and models to best serve clients with work-based challenges?

References

Adams, E. M., Cahill, B. J., & Ackerlind, S. J. (2005). A qualitative study of Latino lesbian and gay youths' experiences with discrimination and the career development process. *Journal of Vocational Behavior, 66*, 199–218.

Alliance for Excellent Education. (2009). *Understanding high school graduation rates in the United States*. Retrieved from http://www.all4ed.org/files/National_wc.pdf

Alliman-Brissett, A., & Turner, S. (2010). Racism and math-based career interests, efficacy, and outcome expectations among African American adolescents. *Journal of Black Psychology, 36*, 197–225.

American Psychological Association. (2011). *Guidelines for assessment of and intervention with persons with disabilities*. Retrieved from http://www.apa.org/pi/disability/resources/assessment-disabilities.aspx

Ash, M. A., & Badgett, M. V. L. (2006). Separate and unequal: The effect of unequal access to employment-based health insurance on same-sex and unmarried different-sex couples. *Contemporary Economic Policy, 24*, 582–599.

Assistive Technology Solutions. (2011). *Cognitive impairments.* Retrieved from http://www.atsolutions.biz/cognitive.htm#content

Atkinson, D. R., & Lowe, S. M. (1995). The role of ethnicity, cultural knowledge, and conventional techniques in counseling and psychotherapy. In J. G. Ponterotto, J. M. Casas, L. A. Suzuki, & C. M. Alexander (Eds.), *Handbook of multicultural counseling* (pp. 3–16). Thousand Oaks, CA: Sage.

Bandura, A. (2002). Social cognitive theory in cultural context. *Applied Psychology: An International Review, 51*, 269–290.

Baron, R. C., & Salzer, M. S. (2002). Accounting for unemployment among people with mental illness. *Behavioral Sciences & the Law, 20*, 585–599.

Bedell, G. (2007). Balancing health, work, and daily life: Design and evaluation of a pilot intervention for persons with HIV/AIDS. *Work: Journal of Prevention, Assessment & Rehabilitation, 31*, 131–144.

Belle, D., & Doucet, J. (2003). Poverty, inequality and discrimination as sources of depression among US women. *Psychology of Women Quarterly, 27*, 101–113.

Benitiz, C. (2007). *Latinization: How Latino culture is transforming the U.S.* Ithaca, NY: Paramount Market Publishing, Inc.

Berrios-Allison, A, C. (2011). Career support group for Latino/a college students. *Journal of College Counseling, 14*, 80–95.

Bettinger, E., & Long, B. T. (2005). Remediation at the community college: Student participation and outcomes. *New Directions for Community Colleges, 129*, 17–26.

Bigler, R. S., Averhart, C. J., & Liben, L. S. (2003). Race and the workforce: Occupational status, aspirations, and stereotyping among African American children. *Developmental Psychology, 39*, 572–580.

Blustein, D. L. (2006). *The psychology of working: A new perspective for counseling, career development, and public policy.* Mahwah, NJ: Lawrence Erlbaum Associates.

Booth, C. S., & Myers, J. E. (2011). Differences in career and life planning between African American and Caucasian undergraduate women. *Journal of Multicultural Counseling and Development, 39*, 14–23.

Bowleg, L., Brooks, K., & Ritz, S.F. (2008). "Bringing home more than a paycheck:" An exploratory analysis of Black lesbians' experiences of stress and coping in the workplace. *Journal of Lesbian Studies, 12*, 69–84.

Budge, S. L., Tebbe, E. N., & Howard, K. A. S. (2010). The work experiences of transgender individuals: Negotiating the transition and career decision-making processes. *Journal of Counseling Psychology, 57*, 377–393.

Burckell, L. A., & Goldfried, M. R. (2006). Therapist qualities preferred by sexual-minority individuals. *Psychotherapy: Theory, Research, Practice, Training, 43*, 32–49.

Burkard, A. W., Pruitt, N. T., Medler, B. R., & Stark-Booth, A. M. (2009). Validity and reliability of the lesbian, gay, bisexual working alliance self-efficacy scales. *Training and Education in Professional Psychology, 3*, 37–46.

Burns, C., & Krehely, J. (2011). *Gay and transgender people face high rates of workplace discrimination and harassment: Data demonstrate need for federal law.* Center for American Progress. Retrieved from http://www.americanprogress.org/issues/2011/06/workplace_discrimination.html

Burton, W. (December 19, 2010). Programs in place to boost Native American graduation rates. *Muskogee Phoenix.* Retrieved from http://muskogeephoenix.com/local/x1707770120/Programs-in-place-to-boost-Native-American-graduation-rates

Byars-Winston, A. (2010). The vocational significance of black identity: Cultural formulation approach to career assessment and career counseling. *Journal of Career Development, 37*, 441–464.

Carleton, R. N., Abrams, M. P., Kachur, S. S., & Asmundson, G. J. (2009). Waddell's symptoms as correlates of vulnerabilities associated with fear–anxiety–avoidance models of pain: Pain-related anxiety, catastrophic thinking, perceived disability, and treatment outcome. *Journal of Occupational Rehabilitation, 19*, 364–374.

Carpenter, C. (2007). Revisiting the income penalty for behaviorally gay men: Evidence from NHANES III. *Labor Economics, 14*, 25–34.

Catanzarite, L., & Aguilera, M. B. (2002). Working with co-ethnics: Earnings penalties for Latino immigrants at Latino jobsites. *Social Problems, 49*, 101–127.

Center for Gerontology. (2006). *Mild Cognitive Impairment (MCI): What do we do now?* Retrieved from http://www.gerontology.vt.edu/docs/Gerontology_MCI_final.pdf

Christie, L. (July 30, 2010). Pay gap persists for African-Americans. *CNNMoney.* Retrieved from http://money.cnn.com/2010/07/30/news/economy/black_pay_gap_persists/index.htm

Chung, Y. B. (1995). Career decision making of lesbian, gay, and bisexual individuals. *Career Development Quarterly, 44*, 178–190.

Chung, Y. B. (2001). Work discrimination and coping strategies: Conceptual frameworks for counseling lesbian, gay, and bisexual clients. *Career Development Quarterly, 50*, 33–44.

Chung, Y. B., & Harmon, L. W. (1994). The career interests and aspirations of gay men: How sex-role orientation is related. *Journal of Vocational Behavior, 45*, 223–239.

Chung, Y. B., Williams, W., & Dispenza, F. (2009). Validating work discrimination and coping strategy models for sexual minorities. *Career Development Quarterly, 58*, 162–170.

Condon, E., & Callahan, M. (2008). Individualized career planning for students with significant support needs utilizing the Discovery and Vocational Profile process, cross-agency collaborative funding and Social Security Work Incentives. *Journal of Vocational Rehabilitation, 28*, 85–96.

Conkel-Ziebell, J. L. (2010). Promoting viable career choice goals through career decision-making self-efficacy and career maturity in inner-city high school students: A test of social cognitive career theory. *Dissertation Abstracts International Section A: Humanities and Social Sciences, 71*, pp. 3527.

Cook, J. A., Leff, H. S., Blyler, C. R., Gold, P. B., Goldberg, R. W., Mueser, K. T.,…Burke-Miller, J. (2005). Results of a multisite randomized trial of supported employment interventions for individuals with severe mental illness. *Archives of General Psychiatry, 62*, 505–512.

Dauwalder, J. P., & Hoffman, H. (1992). Chronic psychoses and rehabilitation: an ecological perspective. *Psychopathology, 25*, 73–86.

Day, N. E., & Schoenrade, P. (1997). Staying in the closet versus coming out: relationships between communication about sexual orientation and work attitudes. *Personnel Psychology, 50*, 147–163.

DeCarlo Santiago, C., Wadsworth, M. E., & Stump, J. (2011). Socioeconomic status, neighborhood disadvantage, and poverty-related stress: Prospective effects on psychological syndromes among diverse low-income families. *Journal of Economic Psychology*, 32, 218–230.

Duffy, R. D., & Sedlacek, W. E. (2007). What is most important to students' long-term career choices: Analyzing 10-year trends and group differences. *Journal of Career Development*, 34, 149–163.

Dunn, E. C., Wewiorski, N. J., & Rogers, E. S. (2008). The meaning and importance of employment to people in recovery from serious mental illness: Results of a qualitative study. *Psychiatric Rehabilitation Journal*, 32, 59–62.

Fassinger, R. E. (1995). From invisibility to integration: Lesbian identity in the workplace. *Career Development Quarterly*, 44, 148–167.

Fassinger, R. E. (1996). Notes from the margins: Integrating lesbian experience into the vocational psychology of women. *Journal of Vocational Behavior*, 48, 160–175.

Flores, L. Y., Ramos, K., & Kanagui, M. (2010). Applying the cultural formulation approach to career counseling with Latinas/os. *Journal of Career Development*, 37, 411–422.

Flores, L. Y., Robitschek, C., Celebi, E., Andersen, C., & Hoang, U. (2010). Social cognitive influences on Mexican Americans' career choices across Holland's themes. *Journal of Vocational Behavior*, 76, 198–210.

Flum, H., & Blustein, D. L. (2000). Reinvigorating the study of vocational exploration: A framework for research. *Journal of Vocational Behavior*, 56, 380–404.

Fouad, N. A., & Arbona, C. (1994). Careers in a cultural context. *Career Development Quarterly*, 43, 96–104.

Freedman, R. I. (1996). The meaning of work in the lives of people with significant disabilities: Consumer and family perspectives. *Journal of Rehabilitation*, 62, 49–55.

Fremstad, S. (2009). *Half in ten: Why taking disability into account is essential to reducing income poverty and expanding economic inclusion*. Washington, DC: Center for Economic and Policy Research. Retrieved from, http://www.cepr.net/documents/publications/poverty-disability-2009–09.pdf

Fuertes, J. N., Sedlacek, W. E., Roger, P. R., & Mohr, J. J. (2000). Correlates of universal-diverse orientation among first-year university students. *Journal of the First-Year Experience & Students in Transition*, 12, 45–59.

Garrett, M. T., Garrett, J. T., Torres-Rivera, E., Wilbur, M., & Roberts-Wilbur, J. (2005). Laughing it up: Native American humor as spiritual tradition. *Journal of Multicultural Counseling and Development*, 33, 194–204.

Gates, W. (2011). *How many people are lesbian, gay, bisexual, and transgender?* Los Angeles, CA: The Williams Institute, UCLA School of Law. Retrieved from http://www3.law.ucla.edu/williamsinstitute/pdf/How-many-people-are-LGBT-Final.pdf

Ghosh, P. R. (November 19, 2010). Joblesssness among American Indians doubled during recession. *International Business News*. Retrieved from http://www.ibtimes.com/articles/83945/20101119/american-indians-unemployment-recession.htm

Gonzalez, M. L. (2009). Getting to know reality and breaking stereotypes: The experience of two generations of working disabled women. *Disability & Society*, 24, 447–459.

Gottfredson, L. S. (1981). Circumscription and compromise: A developmental theory of occupational aspirations. *Journal of Counseling Psychology*, 28, 545–579.

Gracely, R. H., Geisser, M. E., Giesecke, T., Grant, M. A. B., Petzke, F., Williams, D. A., & Clauw, D. J. (2004). Pain catastrophizing and neural responses to pain among persons with fibromyalgia. *Brain*, 127, 835–843.

Grandbois, D. M. (2009). An exploratory study of resilience in the lived experience of Native American elders. *Dissertation Abstracts International, Section A: Humanities and Social Sciences.* 69, 3273.

Grant, J. M., Mottet, L. A., Tanis, J., Harrison, J., Herman, J. L., & Keisling, M. (2011). *Injustice at every turn: A report of the National Transgender Discrimination Survey*. Washington, DC: National Center for Transgender Equality and National Gay and Lesbian Task Force.

Grier-Reed, T., & Ganuza, Z. M. (2011). Constructivism and career decision self-efficacy for Asian Americans and African Americans. *Journal of Counseling & Development*, 89, 200–205.

Grier-Reed, T. L., & Skaar, N. R. (2010). An outcome study of career decision self-efficacy and indecision in an undergraduate constructivist career course. *Career Development Quarterly*, 59, 42–53.

Grier-Reed, T. L., Skaar, N. R., & Conkel-Ziebell, J. L. (2009). Constructivist career development as a paradigm of empowerment for at-risk culturally diverse college students. *Journal of Career Development*, 35, 290–305.

Grier-Reed, T. L., Skaar, N. R., & Parson, L. B. (2009). A study of constructivist career development, empowerment, indecision, and certainty. *Career and Technical Education Research*, 34, 3–20.

Hammond, M. S., Betz, N. E., Multon, K. D., & Irvin, T. (2010). Super's Work Values Inventory-Revised Scale validation for African Americans. *Journal of Career Assessment*, 18, 266–275.

Hoffmann, L. L., Jackson, A. P., & Smith, S. A. (2005). Career barriers among Native American students living on reservations. *Journal of Career Development*, 32, 31–45.

Holland, J. L. (1997). *Making vocational choices: A theory of vocational personalities and work environments* (3rd ed.). Odessa, FL: Psychological Assessment Resources.

Holvino, E. (2008). Latinos y Latinas in the workplace: How much progress have we made? *Diversity Facto*, 16, 11–19.

Holzer, H. J. (1996). *What employers want: Job prospects for less-educated workers*. New York: Russell Sage Foundation.

Hook, M. K., & Bowman, S. (2008). Working for a living. *Journal of Lesbian Studies*, 12, 85–95.

Hutchison, B. (2010). The influence of perceived student poverty on school counselor ratings of client disturbance and attractiveness. *Dissertation Abstracts International Section A: Humanities and Social Sciences*, 70(11-A), pp. 4177.

Hutchinson, D., Anthony, W., Massaro, J., & Rogers, E. S. (2007). Evaluation of a combined supported computer education and employment training program for persons with psychiatric disabilities. *Psychiatric Rehabilitation Journal*, 30, 189–197.

Jagger, L., Neukrug, E., & McAuliffe, G. (1992). Congruence between personality traits and chosen occupation as a predictor of job satisfaction for people with disabilities. *Rehabilitation Counseling Bulletin*, 36, 53–60.

Jahoda, A., Banks, P., Dagnan, D., Kemp, J., Kerr, W., & Williams, V. (2009). Starting a new job: The social and emotional experience of people with intellectual disabilities. *Journal of Applied Research in Intellectual Disabilities*, 22, 421–425.

Juntunen, C. L., Barraclough, D. J., Broneck, C. L., Seibel, G. A., Winrow, S. A., & Morin, P. M. (2001). American Indian perspectives on the career journey. *Journal of Counseling Psychology*, 48, 274–285.

Juntunen, C. L., & Cline, K. (2010). Culture and self in career development: Working with American Indians. *Journal of Career Development*, 37, 391–410.

Kantamneni, N., & Fouad, N. (2011). Structure of vocational interests for diverse groups on the 2005 Strong Interest Inventory. *Journal of Vocational Behavior, 78,* 193–201.

Kober, R., & Eggleton, I. R. C. (2005). The effect of different types of employment on quality of life. *Journal of Intellectual Disability Research, 49,* 756–760.

Kochhar, R. (2008). *Latino labor report, 2008: Construction reverses job growth for Latinos.* Retrieved from http://pewhispanic.org/reports/report.php?ReportID=88

Kosciulek, J. F., & Wheaton, J. E. (2003). Rehabilitation counseling with individuals with disabilities: An empowerment framework. *Rehabilitation Education, 17,* 207–214.

Krumboltz, J. D. (1993). Integrating career and personal counseling. *Career Development Quarterly, 42,* 143–148.

Lapan, R. T. (2004). *Career development across the K-16 years: Bridging the present to satisfying and successful futures.* Alexandria, VA: American Counseling Association.

Lapan, R. T., Turner, S. L., & Pierce, M. E. (2012). College and career readiness: Policy and research to support effective counseling in schools. In N. A. Fouad, J. A. Carter, & L. M. Subich (Eds.), *APA handbook of counseling psychology* (pp. 57–73). Washington, DC: American Psychological Association.

Lee, V. E., & Ekstrom, R. B. (1987). Student access to guidance counseling in high school. American. *Educational Research Journal, 24,* 287–310.

Lombardi, E. L., Wilchins, R. A., Priesing, D., & Malouf, D. (2001). Gender violence: Transgender experiences with violence and discrimination. *Journal of Homosexuality, 42,* 89–101.

Long, D., Rio, J., & Rosen, J. (2007). *Employment and income supports for homeless people.* National Symposium on Homelessness Research. Retrieved from http://aspe.hhs.gov/hsp/homelessness/symposium07/long/.

Loprest, P., & Maag, E. (2001). *Barriers and supports for work among adults with disabilities: Results from the NHIS-D.* Washington, DC: The Urban Institute.

Luzzo, D. A. (2000). Career development of returning-adult and graduate students. In D. A. Luzzo (Ed.), *Career counseling of college students: An empirical guide to strategies that work* (pp. 191–200). Washington, DC: American Psychological Association.

Luzzo, D. A., Hitchings, W. E., Retish, P., & Shoemaker, A. (1999). Evaluating differences in college students' career decision making on the basis of disability status. *Career Development Quarterly, 48,* 142–153.

Lysaght, R., Ouellette-Kuntz, H., & Morrison, C. (2009). Meaning and value of productivity to adults with intellectual disabilities. *Intellectual and Developmental Disabilities, 47,* 413–424.

Mason-Chagil, G., Turner, S. L., Pabon, M., Conkel, J. L., Joeng, J., Landgraf, R., Kim, H., & Dade, S. (2011). *Bush high school completion program.* Bush Foundation.

Middleton, A., Turner, G. H., Bitner-Glindzicz, M., Lewis, P., Richards, M., Clarke, A., & Stephens, D. (2010). Preferences for communication in clinic from deaf people: A cross-sectional study. *Journal of Evaluation in Clinical Practice, 16,* 811–817.

Mina, L., Fulmer, D. D., & Smith, R. O. (2010). The role of the community college in redirecting careers of low-literate, low-income, and low-skilled citizens. In M. V. Alfred (Ed.), *Learning for economic self-sufficiency: Constructing pedagogies of hope among low-income, low-literate adults* (pp. 15–28). Charlotte, NC: Information Age Publishing.

Morrow, D. F. (1996). Coming-out issues for adult lesbians: A group intervention. *Social Work, 41,* 647–656.

National Center for Education Statistics. (2011). *The condition of education 2011* (NCES 2011–033). Retrieved from http://nces.ed.gov/fastfacts/display.asp?id=16

National Council on Disability. (2004). *Improving educational outcomes for students with disabilities.* Retrieved from http://www.educationalpolicy.org/pdf/NCD.pdf

National Council on Disability. (2008). *Keeping track: National disability status and program performance indicators.* Retrieved from http://www.ncd.gov/rawmedia_repository/3cf968b2_341c_4dfb_ad70_bcd01ed7472a?document.pdf

National Drug Intelligence Center. (2008). *Indian Country drug threat assessment 2008.* Retrieved from http://www.justice.gov/ndic/pubs28/29239/overview.htm

National Institutes of Health, National Institute of Neurological Disorders and Stroke. (2011). *Post-stroke rehabilitation fact sheet.* Retrieved from http://www.ninds.nih.gov/disorders/stroke/poststrokerehab.htm

National Urban Indian Family Coalition. (2008). *Urban Indian America: A discussion paper addressing the status of American Indian and Alaska Native children and families today.* Baltimore, MD: Annie E. Casey Foundation. Retrieved from http://www.aecf.org/~/media/Pubs/Topics/Special%20Interest%20Areas/SW%20border%20and%20American%20Indian%20Families/UrbanIndianAmericaTheStatusofAmericanIndianan/Urban%2020Indian%2020America.pdf

Nauta, M. M., Saucier, A. M., & Woodard, L. E. (2001). Interpersonal influences on students' academic and career decisions: The impact of sexual orientation. *Career Development Quarterly, 49,* 352–362.

Nixon, D. (2006). "I just like working with my hands": Employment aspirations and the meaning of work for low-skilled unemployed men in Britain's service economy. *Journal of Education and Work, 19,* 201–217.

Ochs, L. A., & Roessler, R. T. (2004). Predictors of career exploration intentions: A social cognitive career theory perspective. *Rehabilitation Counseling Bulletin, 47,* 224–233.

Ojeda, L., & Flores, L. Y. (2008). The influence of gender, generation level, parent's education level, and perceived barriers on the educational aspirations of Mexican American high school students. *Career Development Quarterly, 57,* 84–95.

Petrovski, P., & Gleeson, G. (1997). The relationship between job satisfaction and psychological health in people with an intellectual disability in competitive employment. *Journal of Intellectual and Developmental Disability, 22,* 199–211.

Riach, P. A., & Rich, J. (2002). Field experiments of discrimination in the market place. *Economic Journal, 112,* 480–518.

Robbins, R. H. (2008). *Cultural anthropology: A problem-based approach* (5th ed.). Belmont, CA: Wadsworth, Cengage Learning.

Silvey, R. E., & Turner, S. L. (in preparation). *An undergraduate curriculum designed to train Native American students in entrepreneurship: A case study.*

Smith, L. (2005). Psychotherapy, classism, and the poor: Conspicuous by their absence. *American Psychologist, 60,* 687–696.

Smith, N. G., & Ingram, K. M. (2004). Workplace heterosexism and adjustment among lesbian, gay, and bisexual individuals: The role of unsupportive social interactions. *Journal of Counseling Psychology, 51,* 57–67.

Snyder, T. D., & Dillow, S. A. (2011). *Digest of education statistics 2010* (NCES 2011–015). Washington, DC: National Center for Education Statistics.

St. Hilaire, A. (2002). The social adaptation of children of Mexican immigrants: Educational aspirations beyond junior high school. *Social Science Quarterly, 83*, 1026–1043.

Starcic, A. I., & Niskala, M. (2010). Vocational students with severe learning difficulties learning on the internet. *British Journal of Educational Technology, 41*, E155–E159.

Stoll, M. A. (2010). Labor market advancement for young men: How it differs by educational attainment and race/ethnicity during the initial transition to work. *Journal of Education for Students Placed at Risk, 15*, 66–92.

Stracuzzi, T. I., Mohr, J. J., & Fuertes, J. N. (2011). Gay and bisexual male clients' perceptions of counseling: The role of perceived sexual orientation similarity and counselor universal-diverse orientation. *Journal of Counseling Psychology.* Advance online publication. Retrieved from http://psycnet.apa.org.ezp1.lib.umn.edu/psycarticles/2011–10203–001.pdf

Stoops, N. (2004). *Educational attainment in the United States: 2003* (Current Population Reports, P20–550). Retrieved from http://www.census.gov/prod/2004pubs/p20–550.pdf

Szivos, S. E. (1990). Attitudes to work and their relationship to self-esteem and aspirations among young adults with a mild mental handicap. *British Journal of Mental Subnormality, 36*, 108–117.

Torey, E. F. (2008). *The insanity offense: How America's failure to treat the seriously mentally ill endangers its citizens.* New York: W. W. Norton & Company.

Toussaint-Comeau, M., Smith, T., & Comeau, Jr., L. (2005). *Occupational attainment and mobility of Hispanics in a changing economy.* Pew Hispanic Center. Retrieved from http://pewhispanic.org/files/reports/59.1.pdf

Trainor, A. A. (2007). Perceptions of adolescent girls with LD regarding self-determination and postsecondary transition planning. *Learning Disability Quarterly, 30*, 31–46.

Trau, R. N. C., & Härtel, C. E. J. (2004). One career, two identities: An assessment of gay men's career trajectory. *Career Development International, 9*, 627–637.

Tschopp, M. K., Frain, M. P., & Bishop, M. (2009). Empowerment variables for rehabilitation clients on perceived beliefs concerning work quality of life domains. *Work: Journal of Prevention, Assessment & Rehabilitation, 33*, 59–65.

Turner, S. L., & Conkel, J. L. (2011). The career beliefs of inner-city adolescents. *Professional School Counseling, 15*, 1–14.

Turner, S. L., & Lapan, R. T. (2003). Native American adolescent career development. *Journal of Career Development, 30*, 159–172.

Turner, S. L., & Pope, M. (2009). North America's native peoples: A social justice and trauma counseling approach. *Journal of Multicultural Counseling and Development, 37*, 194–205.

Turner, S. L., Trotter, M. J., Lapin, R. T., Czajka, K. A., Yang, P., & Brissett, A. E. A. (2006). Vocational skills and outcomes among Native American adolescents: A test of the Integrative Contextual Model of Career Development. *Career Development Quarterly, 54*, 216–226.

Turner, S. L., Unkefer, L. C., Cichy, B. E., Peper, C., & Juang, J. (2011). Career interests and self-estimated abilities of young adults with disabilities. *Journal of Career Assessment, 19*, 183–196.

U.S. Census Bureau. (2009a). *Census Bureau estimates nearly half of children under age 5 are minorities.* Retrieved from http://www.census.gov/newsroom/releases/archives/population/cb09–75.html

U.S. Census Bureau. (2009b). *Median household income for states: 2007 and 2008 American community surveys.* Retrieved from http://www.census.gov/prod/2009pubs/acsbr08–2.pdf

U.S. Census Bureau. (2010). Poverty. Retrieved from http://www.census.gov/hhes/www/poverty/data/incpovhlth/2010/highlights.html

U.S. Department of Housing and Urban Development: Office of Community Planning and Development. (2010). *The 2010 annual homeless assessment: Report to Congress.* Retrieved from http://www.hudhre.info/documents/2010HomelessAssessmentReport.pdf

U.S. Department of Labor, Bureau of Labor Statistics. (2006). *Employment projections.* Retrieved from http://www.bls.gov/emp/emptabapp.htm

U.S. Department of Labor, Bureau of Labor Statistics. (2009a). *Employment status of the civilian population 25 years and over by educational attainment.* Retrieved from http://www.bls.gov/news.release/empsit.t04.htm.

U.S. Department of Labor, Bureau of Labor Statistics. (2009b). *Labor force statistics from the current population survey.* Retrieved from http://www.bls.gov/cps/cpsdisability.htm

U.S. Department of Labor, Bureau of Labor Statistics. (2011a). *Economic news release.* Retrieved from http://www.bls.gov/news.release/empsit.t02.htm

U.S. Department of Labor, Bureau of Labor Statistics. (2011b). *News Release: Usual weekly earning of wage and salary workers; second quarter 2011.* Retrieved from http://www.bls.gov/news.release/pdf/wkyeng.pdf

Valenzuela, A. (1999). *Subtractive schooling.* Albany: State University of New York Press.

VanReusen, A. K., Bos, C. S., Schumaker, J. B., & Deschler, D. D. (1994). *Self-advocacy strategy for education and transition planning.* Lawrence, KS: Edge Enterprises.

Wilkes, L. S. (2002). A study of job performance of young adults with disabilities comparing those matched and not matched using the Holland self-directed search. *Dissertation Abstracts International (B), 63*(2-B), pp. 1078. Dissertation Abstract: 2002–95016–362.

Williams, D. R., Neighbors, H. W., & Jackson, J. S. (2003). Racial/ethnic discrimination and health: Findings from community studies. *American Journal of Public Health, 93*, 200–208.

Psychotherapy and the Integration of the Psychology of Working into Therapeutic Practices

Anderson J. Franklin *and* Mary Beth Medvide

Abstract

Psychotherapy and career counseling have traditionally been treated as two distinct forms of client care with mutually exclusive sets of presenting problems. The prevailing dogma of psychodynamic theories has created a therapeutic encounter in which the individual's inner world and early experiences provide the fertile ground for exploration at the expense of the larger social context. Lost within that social context is the experience of working as its own unique contributor to optimal functioning. Traditional career theories defined optimal functioning for the autonomous individual as having significant volition while largely neglecting the lives of people with varying degrees of privilege. Emergent relational approaches redefined individuals as interdependent entities and developed an expanded and more inclusive focus on work activity rather than career attainment. This new career paradigm nests work within an array of relationships, which has become a cornerstone in the argument in favor of integrating psychotherapy and career counseling. At present, a growing body of literature has proposed how to infuse vocational techniques into traditional psychotherapy, but a theoretical integration remains unexamined. This chapter will provide this examination and use a case study to exemplify the benefits of an integrated counseling perspective.

Key Words: counseling, career development, psychotherapy, work (attitudes toward)

Introduction

This chapter will consider how our theories of psychotherapy and ensuing practices constrain us from understanding more fully as practitioners and scholars how the meaning of work, the significance of work contexts, and work experiences shape the lives of people, which in turn mitigate our greater integration of vocational issues into conventional practices of counseling and psychotherapy. Moreover, from this chapter there should be further appreciation of how gender, race, culture, and socioeconomic levels amplify the complexity of understanding work experiences and contexts, as do many other different sectors of people's lives (e.g., relationships). The goal of this chapter is also to promote ways that psychotherapists and counselors

can become more effective and competent through greater awareness, expanded knowledge, and an augmented repertoire of skills by integrating patients' work issues into therapeutic conceptualizations and practices.

Relevance of Integrating Work-Related Issues into Counseling and Psychotherapy Practice

It is reasonable to assume that psychotherapy practices insufficiently encompass the meaning, significance, and contextual diversity of work in counseling interventions when it is an element ignored, or at best marginalized, in psychotherapy theory building. Accordingly, advocates of the psychology-of-working perspective (Blustein,

2006) promote that work issues and working in the lives of people should be integral to our conceptual approaches, assessment, and interventions in the practice of counseling and psychotherapy because work-related issues and the utility of work is a global experience basic to daily functioning of all individuals in their efforts to live and to survive (Blustein, 2006; Richardson, 1993, 2012). Fundamentally, persons' psychological well-being and overall mental health are directly or indirectly connected to work because it is nested within relationships to others and to society (Richardson, 2012). By this statement, we are promoting an understanding of work as not only what a person engages in but also as an encompassing psychosocial environment co-constructed by significant others in our family and community. Their working experiences affect us too. Therefore, working is as much a generic as it is a multidimensional and particularistic construct hinged to subjectivity of experience and objectivity of reality. It is also a social construction imbued with what we make of it, out of it, and our fulfillment from it. Our experience of working is a product of the multiple roles we assume over the lifespan (Blustein, 2006). A multitude of contexts (e.g., social, economic and political, public policy) structure it. Working and career development evolve over the lifespan (Savickas, 2005; Super, 1957), but there are many determinants. To fully grasp the scope of implications and to be fair in representation as scholars and practitioners, we must recognize that diverse groups (such as the poor and racial, ethnic, and gender groups other than white middle-class populations) have been left out of theory building, research samples, and developed practices in career and vocational counseling.

Although the evolution of a personal psycho-history of working is enmeshed in each person's lifespan, there is insufficient recognition of its value in actual therapeutic practices of counselors and psychotherapists (Blustein, 2011). Too often counselors and psychotherapists delegitimize the significance of working to clients because it is not congruent with their theoretical orientation and concomitant practices of case conceptualization. This is in part because the focus of many theories, as explanatory paradigms, is upon other formative elements (i.e., building blocks) of the person that are often considered more important. For example, the significance and role of working to the person is rarely considered a primary structuring agent of manifested or latent behaviors in theorizing about the importance of parent–child interactions so integral to many of our psychotherapy and developmental theories. It is important for us therefore to be mindful of just how much of our formulations or interpretations of people's behaviors in psychotherapy are guided by the particular theoretical dogma that underlies our practice perspective. Consequently, as we advocate for a greater inclusion of social justice, critical consciousness, empowerment, relational focus, and other emergent tenets of a psychology-of-working perspective, let us be mindful of the realities of practices in the profession that continue to prevail and will mitigate against appropriate change (Blustein, 2006; Richardson, 2012; Schultheiss, 2003). In other words, prevailing dogma remains focused upon the individual as context without providing an adjustable lens for the sociocultural milieu, thus making it a formidable task to infuse inferences from that source. It also guides us to overlook as well related social justice principles that could inform conceptualizations and treatment endeavors. The psychology-of-working meta-perspective does, however, provide the conceptual tools needed to achieve such integration as a viable framework for understanding human behavior while also respecting the intent of psychodynamic practice, as well as other theoretical paradigms. Let us first, though, explore some of the barriers to integrating the psychology of working into psychotherapy and counseling practices

Barrier to Inclusion: The Conceptual Box Created by Theoretical Dogma

The practice of counseling and psychotherapy is captive to our theory and what it tries to explain through conceptualization of people's lives. Although we promote awareness, knowledge, and skills in working with people, if our orientation is limited to conventional theoretical thinking, so too will be the applications that flow from it. Contemporary career and vocational theorists have advocated that our theory and practices be more inclusive and that service providers' thinking and practices change to be responsive to diverse peoples, experiences, motives, and contexts (Blustein, 2006; Richardson, 2012; Schultheiss, 2003). It is explicit recognition that people bring to us, as counselors and psychotherapists, an array of human experiences that should not be overlooked or disregarded.

Past career counseling theory and psychotherapy theorizing generally utilize biological perspectives in development, or organismic perspectives as conceptual etiology (Richardson, 2012). Many traditional psychotherapy theories and developmental theorists, for example Freud and Piaget, formulated stage-based developmental paradigms that were fundamentally organismic in their conceptualization. The ideal place for development meant passing from a primitive (infantile) stage to a more mature (adult) stage. Nonetheless, each theory, whether it is about stage development, personality structure and functioning, or understanding work in the context of people's lives, has principles evolved from experiences of the theorists' work with particular populations (Fall, Holden, & Marquis, 2010).

The capacity of our theories to explain phenomena is constrained by the limitations of experiences with our clinical sample. Moreover, the complexity and vastness of the behavioral and intrapsychic phenomena most of us study often forces us as theorists into parsimonious explanations. Given this reality, and our limitations in grappling with this complexity, our understanding lacks representativeness and leads to well-intentioned but ultimately inadequate explanations of the things we aim to comprehend. Consequently, theory building, and therefore theory itself, is contextual, which means so are applications that emanate from the theories. We, therefore, as counselors and psychotherapists, when faced with these complexities of the human experience in the counseling room, latch onto parsimonious explanations and practices provided by theoretical protocol out of convenience, a professional comfort zone from which to operate. This comfort zone creates a box, wallpapered by theoretical dogma and furnished with the creature comforts of conventional professionalism and practices. It is in this conceptual box that we invite our clients and patients to receive our practice of counseling and psychotherapy. But before we unduly blame counselors or psychotherapists for such circumstance, let us briefly reflect on the career pathway of the counselor and psychotherapist to see how we got into this position. Understanding the circumstances of training places us, as advocates of inclusive psychology of working, in a better position to gauge potential acceptance of a different perspective, resistance to it, and the likelihood of transforming thinking—if not the profession.

Realities of Training About Work Life for Counselors and Psychotherapists

An important question before us therefore is: How well does our training in psychotherapy theory prepare us to understand a person's development (from birth to death) by the relationships and experiences that groom us for working in the world? Not much, when we examine our training curriculum or practical experiences. Much more emphasis is placed upon our understanding of persons' development within family and other relational contexts. If we look at what is truly required of us in the practice of psychotherapy, there are a number of obvious explanations why work-related issues are not as central to our psychological thinking in practice. One apparent reason rests within our training, supervision, and work environments as counselors, psychotherapists, and human service providers. Our training, both predoctoral and postdoctoral, including continuing education, often is encapsulated by a theoretical orientation and related intervention skills. Competence in counseling and psychotherapy is most typically attained by experience with patients and supervision, relying upon specific theoretical perspectives informing practice. The student in training (as a function of beliefs conveyed in training) is encouraged to learn how to understand and use (i.e., inevitably fit the patient into) a theoretical model in the development of competence. This is emphasized much more than teaching students how to engage in theory-building skills that use the patient's life narrative for insights and interventions in a process consistent with the theorists they are studying and in the furtherance of theory building. True sophistication as psychotherapists requires maturing skills over many years through postgraduate training, although ultimately it is from simply (and frequently unsupervised) extensive patient contact experience. It is often how professional independence is attained. Nevertheless, our orientation, acquired from training, often persists deep into our years of professional practice, perhaps modified by other emergent professional interests and experiences during our career, but often we remain rooted in what we have learned from the start. Therefore, infusing the psychology-of-working perspective into conventional practice guided by predominant theories of psychotherapy is constrained and challenged by our adherence to the enduring models of human development that we internalize and embrace as we progress through our careers. Though we should seek to understand these models, we should not mistake understanding or competence for habituation, as the latter undergirds reluctance to explore new theoretical possibilities or to broaden ways of thinking.

The training in psychology of working is also at the mercy of the numerous goals and objectives of training programs educating in the multiple domains required for professional accreditation and licensure. Unless the training program has a mission in career counseling or vocational rehabilitation, a counselor's exposure to any orientation about the influences of work issues in the lifespan is minimal (e.g., one course). Given the manner in which the training curriculum is prioritized, it is no wonder that the conceptualization of work as a significant developmental shaper of behavior across the lifespan is not a sufficient part of counselors' approach to theory or practice (much less research) in their evolving professional skills (Robitschek & DeBell, 2002). Therefore, the concerns and arguments of proponents for greater inclusion or reintegration of the psychology of work in the profession have considerable merit if not a daunting uphill battle in fighting for greater inclusion (Blustein, Medvide, & Kozan, 2012). It will require taking on training in a strategy of inclusion. To do that we must be aware that training is the handmaiden of professionalization and training about theory is essential in the service of achieving competency and professional identity. Let's consider some examples of how our training professionalizes.

Professionalization by Traditional Psychotherapy Theories and Practices

Conventional psychotherapy theories, as noted, do not make working life essential in their explanatory models of intrapsychic behavior. Conceptualization of the individual's development in psychotherapy theories focuses upon early childhood interactions for evolving the inner world, particularly with the mother. Parenthetically, this highlights another theoretical limitation by the underrepresentation of fathers' influences in child development and intrapsychic structuring in psychotherapy theory building. Nevertheless, many conventional theories guide adherents or therapists to consider maladaptive behaviors or pathology as manifestations of early acquired dysfunctional behaviors. They have their own clear boundaries and guidelines for following proper psychotherapy processes and trajectory to uncover sources of dysfunctional behaviors. This becomes a hurdle for inclusive psychological practice that incorporates working in the theoretical frame or intervention strategy because training in any of the traditional psychotherapy theoretical orientations creates blinders to any other perspective if adherence to sacred tenets is a virtual necessity. A brief review of conventional psychotherapy theory and orientations further elucidates this dilemma for advocates of an inclusive psychological practice.

Psychodynamic Orientation

Traditional psychoanalysis epistemology, for example, is rooted in the conceptualization of the child's biological primitive instincts as primary formative agents. It is the experience of fulfilling these (i.e., by "pleasure principle") or gaining control of these biological drives, libido, early within the parent–child (greater emphasis upon mother) relationship that is shaping and solidifying the psyche. The topography of the psyche established and evolved during this early stage determines intrapsychic structure and function (i.e., the id, ego, and superego; conscious, preconscious, unconscious;) with concomitant defense mechanisms (e.g., repression, fantasy, displacement, projection, sublimation) of the individual that become enduring in a manner that governs the way a person processes, interprets, and internalizes interactions within the self and with others in the world (Fall et al., 2010).

Other conceptualizations, like Kohutian self psychologists, seek to understand the person's sense of himself or herself or evolved self within infantile and early childhood experiences in relationship with others, or "self-objects" (i.e., most often people), germinating the individual's subjective experiences that serve his or her intrapsychic functions. It is by means of these interactions with self-objects and integration of experiences facilitated by emphatic attunement and mirroring, idealization, twinship, and empathic failures that the self develops. Subsequent interpretations from this self psychology perspective, as well as many other psychodynamic perspectives, ultimately rely upon early parent–child relationships as the source of the contextual dynamics that molds psychological functioning (Fall et al., 2010).

A classic analyst by training interacts little with the patient or the analysand and occasionally employs strategic interpretations as the defining clinical process during analysis. The intent is to allow the insights of the patient to guide the therapeutic process, unimpeded by unwarranted interpretations by the analyst. Sandor Ferenczi and Otto Rank (1988) provide one critical retrospective of the development of psychoanalysis and a view of the process during its formative years:

> The analyst must always take into account that almost every expression of his patient springs from several periods, but he must give his chief attention to the present reaction. Only from this point of view can he succeed in the attempts of the patient to repeat into remembering. In this process he

need pay little attention to the future. One may quietly leave this care to the person himself who has been sufficiently enlightened about his past and present mental strivings. The historic, cultural and phylogenetic analogies also need, for the most part, not be discussed in the analysis. The patient needs hardly ever, and the analyst extremely seldom, occupy himself with this early period. (p. 31)

Therefore, from the viewpoint of Ferenczi and Rank (1988), inclusion of the psychology-of-working perspective is challenged by the tenets of conventional psychoanalytic theory, where conceptualization of the intrapsyche as much as the process of analysis would not permit the type of focus upon working in a person's life. Axelrod (1999), in contrast, saw the value of analysts interpreting work behaviors as a function of personality and a critical determinant of the adult self. He conceptualized unsatisfactory work experiences as primarily associated with underlying psychopathology that can be resolved in much the same way that an analyst might address the analysand's interpersonal difficulties. Axelrod believed that work is an important developmental task for adults, but his conceptualizations, which were true to psychoanalytic dogma, remained focused on the individual at the expense of the larger context. Blustein (2006) noted that although Axelrod's (1999) contributions are beneficial in reframing the importance of work, the significance of those ideas was hindered by the exclusivity of the focus on career attainment.

Fundamentally, psychodynamic theory and relational psychotherapy theories place considerable conceptualization of individuals' inner world and their relational interactions with others in the contextual foreground (Blustein, 2006). An array of other legitimate influential contexts and circumstances (e.g., the global economy and public policy as primary formative contexts) are relegated to the background as determinants within conventional theories and related therapeutic practices. Critical consciousness and social justice imperatives for counselor and client, therefore, are even less integral to conventional psychotherapy theories because they have not been emphasized and promoted as relevant.

Evidence-Based Psychological Practices and Inclusive Practices

Evidence-based psychological practices (EBPPs) and empirically supported therapies (ESTs) represent attempts within the psychology community to establish guidelines for ethical and valid treatments. The movement towards ESTs started in 1995 through an American Psychological Association (APA) initiative, which was based upon a biomedical paradigm, to identify standardized treatments derived from sound empirical research. study. The APA (2006) later moved away from a strictly biological model by proposing EBPP, which gave greater attention to social and cultural processes (LaRoche & Christopher, 2009). Unfortunately, neither approach is undergirded by values, beliefs, or assumptions about the interconnectedness of work and personal domains to make them conducive to the integrative approach central to the psychology of working. This is a function of at least several factors: (1) EST has its own struggles with the foundational theory that guides its perspective, except those practices linked to theories (and empirical studies) of learning, reinforcement, and acquisition of behaviors. In its areas of theoretical foundations, EBPP, much less EST, an understsanding of the psychology of working is not the focus (2) EST is guided by targeting the psychological treatment of mental disorders often represented within diagnostic categories in the *Diagnostic and Statistical Manual, Fourth Edition* (DSM-IV; American Psychiatric Association, 1994). The focus often is upon symptom relief and restructuring of manifest cognitions and behaviors of the individual as related to a particular disorder. Unless dysfunctional behaviors are linked to the working context for specific treatment intervention, the broader conceptualization of the psychology of working is not as relevant to these practices. (3) Because EST practices are often more manualized, with very prescribed and circumscribed psychological treatment protocols tailored to remedying behaviors associated with disorders (APA, 2006; Barlow, 2004), they move further away from inclusive psychology-of-working goals. Consequently, the encompassing perspective of the psychology of working with such broad concerns about critical consciousness or social justice is not that germane to the current focus of EBPPs.

EBPPs advocate for reliance upon general research evidence and empirically supported approaches and interventions for counseling practices, with specific evidence-based treatments subsumed under it. The growing standard of EBPPs presents a new challenge to conventional training of counselors. Whereas proponents of EBPPs give some acknowledgement to the utility of conventional psychotherapy practice in such areas of counseling for personal adjustment, self-discovery, and career decision making (Barlow,

2004) and are willing to debate psychotherapists who challenge their EBPPs as the new gold standard (Westen, Novotny, & Thompson-Brenner, 2004), they have not made the inclusion of psychology of working as a critical psychological domain in this difficult dialogue.

SUMMARY

There clearly will be adherents to any one of these conventional theories briefly discussed who would argue against rigid and simplistic views of their particular orientations. There is no desire to misrepresent or refute that there are exceptions of thinking and practice within schools of conventional theories that may come closer to the level of inclusion desired by a psychology-of-working perspective. The many different ideological camps that have come out of conventional psychotherapy theoretical schools attest to diversity in beliefs as well as practices (Fall et al., 2010). Some may rightfully argue there is more receptiveness within their school than others to the inclusion of work-related issues into their theoretical thinking and practices of psychotherapy. As previously stated, Axelrod (1999) is a notable exception as a psychoanalytic theorist who argued that a productive, satisfactory work life is fundamental to optimal functioning. Nevertheless, the argument here is that the possibility of including the psychology of working in the practices of an average trained counselor and psychotherapist is constrained by the conventions of professional training. For the vast majority of trainees, traditional psychotherapy theory and concomitant practices are emphasized and valued, with little to no attention devoted to the working context. As noted, even the advance of evidence-based treatment and practices still does not give sufficient credibility to the depth and breadth of work-related issues in the life of the patient (perhaps an exception is in treating work-related anxiety or phobia). Even so, this challenge does not preclude efforts to expand thinking and adoption in the profession of inclusive psychological practices embracing the psychology-of-working perspective. Nor does it diminish advocacy for the more lofty elements of critical consciousness and empowerment of self and others in the fight against inequities and any other social injustices acting as barriers to work life that engenders positive quality-of-life outcomes.

Blustein (2008) identifies three elements of human needs essential to work in people's lives: needs for survival, relatedness, and self-determination. They represent the global human experience and vast variation of experiences that make up the multitude of life contexts that exist from people's efforts to fulfill them. Like traditional psychotherapy theories, those theories within career and vocational counseling have suffered their own limitations to adequately represent the scope of work-related issues influencing people's lives, given both national and global population diversity.

Inclusion Challenges for Career Development Theory

In a little more than 100 years, career development has progressed from the study of vocational decisions to careers across the lifespan and most recently the place of work in people's lives, marking a trajectory that reflects the dynamic change in scholarship and the society it represents (Blustein, 2011; Richardson, 2012). These changes in scholarly perspectives range from expansion and revision of existing theory to paradigm shifts that fundamentally rethink the basic concepts that drive the field. When paradigm shifts have emerged, they have propelled thinking away from positivist assumptions about individuals and the counseling process toward a social constructionist framework and new theoretical perspectives built upon the tenets of subjectivity and multiple truths (Blustein, 2011). As a result, an emerging program of scholarship has become more inclusive through its focus on people's work decisions within a relational context and more politically minded through its attention to socially constructed barriers to fulfilling and meaningful work lives.

Traditional Career Development Paradigms

Much like psychotherapy theories of the early and middle 20th century, career development theories were built upon the pillars of logical positivism and post-positivism, which emphasize objectivity, neutrality, and empiricism (Richardson, 1993). Career development theories of the 20th century also became increasingly focused on groups in society with significant privilege and began to mirror the cultural values of the White upper and middle classes and their support of the rugged individualism ethos (Richardson, 1993; 2012). Much like psychotherapy theories, career development theory and assessment developed in response to contextual circumstances, such as the world wars, which served as a catalyst for the growth of theory, research, and practice. Thus, for both psychotherapy and career development theories, theoretical advances can be marked by context and cohort effects that defined society at large and the characteristics of optimal functioning within the individual.

The beginnings of career development can be traced back to Frank Parsons and the establishment of the Vocational Guidance Bureau in Boston at the turn of the 20th century. Parsons' agency provided training and education to recent European immigrants (Hartung & Blustein, 2002). This focus on the most vulnerable and disenfranchised members of the workforce diminished as society and its need for vocational interventions and assessments evolved starting after World War I and continued through the end of World War II and into the "space race" of the 1960s (Blustein, 2006). Early vocational psychologists who followed Parsons responded to the demands placed upon them in the years following World War I. These theorists devised the trait-factor approach (later renamed the person–environment fit model) in response to the growing need to match the personality traits of the individual with the characteristics of the workplace. The goal of this approach was the enhanced likelihood of adaptive career choices and a satisfying, productive work life through the optimal fit between the individual and the work environment (Hartung & Blustein, 2002). These theories, which continued to gain momentum through World War II, generally conceptualized work as an isolated activity characterized by the decision making of a rational, autonomous individual and gave considerably less weight to contextual factors that influence choice (Blustein, 2006).

In the mid-20th century, Donald Super (1957) developed the life-span, life-space theory of career development, which marked a radical departure from the limited scope of the person–environment fit model through the conceptualization of career choice in concert with ongoing life experiences and developmental stages beginning in childhood and extending into old age (Blustein, 2006). Super's (1980) later work also introduced the concept of multiple life roles, suggesting that career represents one domain of functioning and one area for self-actualization that can enhance or diminish functioning in other areas of life. This became a critical precursor to theory building on career in a relational context because Super recognized work within a matrix of influences on the individual. One of the unintended effects of Super's (1957) theory was an even farther departure from Parsons' focus on marginalized groups, which was already apparent through the contributions of the person–environment fit theorists (Richardson,

1993). Although Super (1980) later revised his theory to be more inclusive of women and racial and ethnic minority groups, his contributions continued to reflect the rugged individualism valued by the White middle and upper classes and neglected to consider the extent to which these groups may value interdependence over independence. Consequently, Super's (1980) work neglected the relational processes that support career decision making and optimal functioning more broadly, which can include different value orientations.

Despite the importance of Super's (1957, 1980) work, many scholars felt that his theoretical contributions lacked a unifying framework that could maintain its vitality with changing economic times (Lent, Brown, & Hackett, 1994). Lent et al. (1994) drew on social cognitive theory to develop social cognitive career theory (SCCT) to study how self-efficacy and expectations for the future affect career decision-making and goal-setting behaviors. In a critical development, Lent et al. (1994) also focused on how perceptions of barriers and relational supports influence career decision making by enhancing self-efficacy and fostering positive expectations. The attention to barriers was a critical theoretical advancement and facilitated dialogue on contextual impediments to career progress. Like previous theories, SCCT maintained allegiance to a positivist framework and shared a circumscribed focus on the White middle and upper classes and their cultural mindsets.

Much like SCCT (Lent et al., 1994), Savickas (2005) responded to the limitations of Super's (1957, 1980) work, although his theory diverged significantly from the central tenets of SCCT by rejecting positivist assumptions. Savickas (2005) appreciated the value of Super's (1957, 1980) work on vocational self-concept but also recognized that the linear career trajectory was no longer a reality for many individuals. Realizing that people are not likely to stay with one organization for the entirety of their careers, Savickas (2005) devised a theory to represent the evolving vocational landscape and changing market dynamics. By drawing on social constructionism (Gergen, 1999), Savickas (2005) moved away from the values of autonomy and rationality to explore how individuals make meaning of their work experiences and form an identity. Despite the significance of a departure from a post-positivist paradigm, this theory reflected the work lives of individuals with choice and volition and neglected to theorize on the lives of marginalized groups whose work experiences may be characterized by social injustices (Richardson, 1993). Therefore, Savickas (2005) succeeded in applying Super's (1957, 1980) contributions to a protean career, but his work did not extend past the White, middle-class worldview. The lives of people who must work to survive continued to be disregarded as a focus of the career development literature. The task of building upon the strengths of Super's (1957, 1980) work and making it resonate with the work experiences of diverse groups with varying degrees of privilege became the undertaking of scholars such as Blustein (2006, 2011) and Richardson (2012). Looking at these emergent new paradigms out of career development provides counselors and psychotherapists with broader and more inclusive ways of conceptualizing work within their practice.

The New Career Paradigm for the 21st Century

Richardson (1993) was among the first to call for a paradigm shift toward a more inclusive definition of work rather than a continued restriction to careers. This proposal is also central to Blustein's (2006, 2012) psychology-of-working perspective, and both see a relational lens as the means to achieve a more representative and socially just understanding of how people find meaning in their work. Richardson (1993, 2012) has focused much of her attention on the work lives of those experiencing economic disadvantage, whereas Blustein (2006) has applied this argument to other marginalized groups. Both scholars have argued that work is nested within relationships of personal and professional importance. Richardson (1993, 2012) further distinguished between work that contributes to social production, most notably caregiving, and work that contributes to economic production. She argued that people make meaning of their experiences and construct a meaningful work life within a matrix of relationships in public and private domains. Such a distinction has been largely missing from more conventional theories that privilege work that is undertaken for material gain. Thus, the position that Blustein (2006) and Richardson (1993, 2012) have taken promotes a view of work that makes it inseparable from other life domains. This assertion, which forms the core of their work, exemplifies how a relational perspective understands the value of social connection and the relationship between self and society.

Although these contributions by Blustein (2006, 2011) and Richardson (1993, 2012) are gaining momentum, a relational approach to career development has yet to dethrone the prevailing theories despite their applicability to a wide range of individuals and the contexts in which they work. Although there are a multitude of viewpoints under the auspice of the relational umbrella (e.g., Blustein, 2006; Richardson, 2012; Schultheiss, 2003), all of these writings converge on the belief that the lifespan experiences of the average working person are inadequately represented in our theorizing about career choices or the many vicissitudes of working. This becomes more complex to grasp when considering population diversity, the influence of systemic and structural barriers, and the changing labor market. A similar paradigm shift must emerge in the theory and practice of psychotherapy. The justifiable psychodynamic focus upon the inner world and attention to manifest behaviors of many psychotherapy theories along with EBPP and EST must be concomitantly transformed to incorporate how diverse populations internalize and enact affect and cognitions from their unique experiences of working and survival throughout their life.

Examining New Career Paradigms for Lives at the Margins

It was not until Smith's (1983) seminal work that the careers of racial and ethnic minorities were given significant attention. The late 1970s and early 1980s also marked increased attention to the career decision making of women, who had previously been ignored in mainstream career development theories or relegated to a position as caregiver while men were idealized for their contributions to economic production (Betz, 2005). The career experiences of members of other marginalized groups, such as the working poor and gays and lesbians, gained attention in the literature in the following two decades (Blustein, 2006). Below we will provide a brief review of research from traditional and contemporary theoretical perspectives on the careers and work lives of African Americans. This focus, although not entirely generalizable to the work lives of other marginalized groups in society, is nonetheless beneficial for considering the case study presented later in the chapter.

Among the influential theories of the 20th century, SCCT (Lent et al., 1994) is often used as a framework for understanding contextual factors that influence career decision making and attainment of African Americans (Constantine, Wallace, & Kindaichi, 2005). The unique aspect of SCCT is its attention to perception of barriers and supports situated proximally or distally to the individual.

Constantine et al. (2005) argued for studying the impact of prejudice and discrimination on career interests, choice, outcome expectations, and self-efficacy beliefs. Proximal support from family and mentors may have a buffering effect, given that these relationships are positively associated with career certainty and choice for African American college students (Constantine & Flores, 2006). Studies on the experiences of adults in the workforce have been consistent with findings from adolescent and college populations and suggest that experiences with prejudice and discrimination continue to act as barriers to success, whereas formal and informal support networks can facilitate career progress (Fouad & Kantamneni, 2008). Collectively, the body of research using an SCCT framework has generally been beneficial for understanding career interests and decision making across the lifespan, but SCCT is not without its detractors.

Through its theoretical conceptualization of the social context, whether that is defined proximally or distally, SCCT allows for a discussion of factors such as prejudice and discrimination that can quell the formation of career interests and foreclose career opportunities. However, SCCT was not explicitly developed to focus on social justice issues, and these are often framed as supplements to the core theory. This can potentially undermine its applicability in understanding the work lives of African Americans and other disenfranchised groups (Blustein, 2006; Richardson, 1993). Despite this potential limitation, researchers such as Alliman-Brissett and Turner (2010) have infused racial identity theory (Helms, 1990) into a SCCT framework to study self-efficacy beliefs and academic performance of African American youth. This has yielded valuable insight into how students perceive their prospects for success, but it could not fully overcome a cultural mindset endorsed by SCCT that is not fully reflective of the values and beliefs of racial and ethnic minority groups (Helms & Cook, 1999).

A relational approach to career development through its use of social constructionist ideas is more amenable to multiple cultural viewpoints and is more explicit in its treatment of social justice. Blustein (2006), for example, argued that traditional career development theories have relegated discussion of privilege and oppression to the background without ever critically evaluating what it means to have career choice. Through an appreciation of work within the broader social context, this question is at the forefront of relational perspectives that move beyond conventional skill-building exercises

to help clients to develop intentionality in their actions, both proximally within relationships and more distally as they confront socially constructed barriers (Richardson, 2012). This intentionality is accompanied by consciousness raising and empowerment that emerges in the counseling relationship and is carried into the work environment. Therefore, compared to traditional career theories, the relational perspectives of Blustein (2006, 2011) and Richardson (2012) may be particularly helpful for clients whose work environments are not conducive to well-being. The skill building valued within this framework helps clients to confront oppressive practices while relinquishing self-blame and maximizing social connectedness.

Despite the aforementioned limitations, research grounded in traditional career theories has contributed to understanding the career development of marginalized groups. Contemporary scholarship has begun to address some shortcomings by shifting the focal point from career to work (Richardson, 2012). However, whether focusing on career attainment or work activity, a potential pitfall is the treatment of vocational processes and outcomes as independent of psychological well-being, as in work-related decision making in a discriminatory work environment. The next section will review the literature on inclusive psychological practice and the work of scholars who have advocated for the marriage of career counseling and psychotherapy to provide a more holistic understanding of clients.

Inclusive Psychological Practice and the New Career Paradigm

Scholars in favor of a paradigm shift have also advocated for more inclusive psychological practice that integrates vocational and personal domains into treatment to provide a more comprehensive understanding of clients' lives (Blustein, 2006, 2011; Richardson, 2012). This stands in contrast to standard practice that makes career counseling and psychotherapy mutually exclusive (Richardson, 2012). This proposal is not limited to the new paradigm and actually precedes Richardson's (1993) first call for a paradigm shift (Betz & Corning, 1993). However, the cause has been championed by scholars such as Richardson (2012), who have worked from a politically minded, relational perspective and view work experiences as nested in multiple contexts, including a society characterized by differential access to opportunity.

Advocates of an integrated approach have long recognized underlying commonalities of psychotherapy and career counseling, such as the importance of the working alliance as the basis for interventions (Betz & Corning, 1993; Blustein, 2006). Richardson's (1996) stance on an integrative approach complemented previous work by Betz and Corning (1993) but shed light onto issues of privilege and oppression by arguing that therapists' disregard of the inequalities affecting the lives of marginalized groups is an implicit acceptance of oppression, or disempowerment by the status quo, without an intent to help clients to overcome its damaging effects, much less address the systemic factors. This argument was influential as the concepts of the new paradigm gained momentum in career development discourse (Blustein, 2006).

Much of the discourse on inclusive psychological practice has focused on the working alliance or on technical eclecticism that can bridge the two fields (Blustein, 2006). Blustein (2006) identified elements of inclusive psychological practice based on the work of Gergen (1999), Wachtel (1993), and Richardson (1996) and emphasized the role of empathy, interpretation, and challenging of discrepant beliefs. Juntunen (2006) later wrote about the psychology-of-working perspective in the clinical context and outlined a framework for addressing work issues alongside traditional psychotherapy presenting problems using assessments and counseling techniques. However, neither Blustein (2006) nor Juntunen (2006) achieved a systematic integration between career and psychotherapy theories.

Advocacy and Defiance in Psychotherapy Change

In sum, the psychology-of-working perspective (Blustein, 2006) has contributed a number of important concepts and factors for consideration by practicing psychotherapists. First is the importance of work in its various dimensions as primary to the lives of individuals, as well as its essential role in their psychological well-being and mental health. It is an acknowledgment that work therefore is central to the lives of people. Second, social constructionism (Gergen, 1999) is an important lens in considering the role of work in people's lives. There are many ways in which people view and internalize working, and they pertain not only to the meaning of work in people's daily lives but also to their personality structure, identity, self-concept, and self-esteem (Blustein, 2006). Another example would be how self-efficacy is a powerful determinant of job and life satisfaction (Perdue, Reardon, & Peterson, 2007; Wright & Perrone, 2010). Third,

critical consciousness can contribute to an understanding of how the work of the person fits within the larger social, political, and economic context (Blustein, 2006; Richardson, 2012). Blustein (2006) also stressed the historical contexts that affect our understanding of the determinants of market transitions from agrarian societies to industrial ones to our post-industrial, technologically based society. Ideally, critical consciousness in the tradition of liberation philosophies and emancipatory pedagogy helps persons to understand the role of societal infrastructure in the service of the most privileged. Comprehending how a particular social order can create inequities and social injustices can empower the most oppressed groups to harness their agency to overcome these injustices (Blustein, 2006). Fourth, it is from critical consciousness that we, as counselors and psychotherapists, become more sensitive to social injustices, marginalized populations, and discriminated groups such as ethnic minorities, the disabled populations, the working poor and unemployed, and powerless undesired immigrants victimized by xenophobia. Schultheiss' (2003, 2009) work, as another example influenced by a feminist relational perspective, has clearly drawn our attention to the struggle of women in the workforce and gender orientation to working. Equally important is the focus upon caregivers, of which a disproportionate number are women, as another distinct category of workers that is also quite diverse and at the margin of conventional thinking of counselors and psychotherapists (Richardson, 1993).

Lastly, drilling down into the types of working roles that marginalized populations assume to maintain a living at the subsistence level can yield numerous circumstances and conditions of survival linked to working. Given the distribution of family wealth in most countries, these circumstances are common, suggesting that the reach and relevance of an inclusive theory and practice extends beyond the United States but at the same time remains relevant domestically within a context of comprehending work for immigrant families (Blustein, 2006).

Fundamentally, the psychology-of-working perspective argues that counselors, psychologists, and the array of human service providers seek to include the diversity in working experiences and meaning of working to people's lives in our professional practice, assessments, interventions, research, and public policy (Blustein, 2006). Or as perhaps Leona Tyler, a historic contributor to counseling psychology, might affirm that it should be part of the "work of the counselor." Blustein (2006) notes that we should be "domain-sensitive" and "open to the full range of human experiences" (p. 254). In other words, we should be knowledgeable of and receptive to engaging the various areas or domains of a person's working experiences as well as other domains of a person's life. Life domains may be related to or independent of working experiences, but certainly both should be systematically integrated into the therapeutic process when the practitioner thinks of explanations and interventions. To realize this goal of the counseling process, Blustein (2006) encourages counselors to reinvigorate the value of empathy in understanding the interface of persons' working and personal circumstances when counseling. Moreover, counselors must attain particular competencies to connect with and to understand the circumstances of populations not ordinarily seen in conventional counseling settings (APA, 2003). We also particularly make this distinction out of awareness that too often marginalized populations are viewed through a narrow lens, "ghetto-izing" them into special group categories such as ethnic minorities, LGBT persons, at-risk youth (often a euphemism for minority youth), immigrants, and so forth when in fact there are many other different types and kinds of populations with intersecting identities (e.g., poor, minimum wage-earning, single young White adult mothers from Appalachia).

In the transition to an increasingly global high-tech economy, this contemporary transformation of working is creating major challenges for people wanting to work. For example, jobs in some sectors of the market remain unfilled because those who are laid off may not have the right skills for the available jobs (Bartsch, 2009). This discrepancy between job skill needs and worker skills highlights a contextual dilemma; it also highlights how contextual circumstances can socially construct outcomes. This state of affairs therefore creates another challenged population for career and vocational counselors that deserves inclusion in thinking about practices, given that this may well be an enduring circumstance for at least a generation.

Blustein (2006) advocated for a "domain-sensitive" approach from a psychology-of-working perspective that warns us about steering our process too much by conventional psychotherapy thinking:

> The domain-sensitive approach seeks to find balance in the conceptualizations and in the treatment strategies. A key element of the domain-sensitive approach is that work-related issues do not systematically become transformed into a psychotherapeutic or family systems framework that fit with existing theories or models. Although such conceptualizations might be indicated in given contexts, their utility would need to be weighed against other, more parsimonious conceptualizations. (p. 257)

Some major goals of inclusive psychological practice are empowerment and fostering critical consciousness. They are to be facilitated by the counselors' practice skills relying upon working alliance, interpretation, exploring discrepant beliefs and behaviors, and helping clients to change (Blustein, 2006, pp. 282–285). These are not that far out of the realm of skills considered for conventional psychotherapy, but rather an advocacy for elevating our awareness of the importance of sensitivity as therapists to integrate working issues meaningfully into the therapeutic context. As mentioned before, this is a challenge because theories were often not originally developed with issues of working and work life particularly pertinent to their conceptualization of the theory's paradigm.

Including Psychology of Working into Conventional Psychotherapy Theories

Up to this point, we have presented the challenges for integrating a psychology-of-working perspective into conventional counseling and psychotherapy theory and practices. In summary, they are (1) demonstrating the relevance of integrating work-related issues, (2) overcoming prevailing theoretical dogma, (3) incorporating a psychology-of-working perspective into standard professional training, (4) transforming career development theory and practices, and (5) advocating for new paradigms that include the variations of working across the expanse of people and life contexts globally. Changing the practices of counselors and psychotherapists to be more inclusive of a psychology-of-working perspective requires considering how to influence theoretical and case formulations as they inform interventions. As a next step in this chapter, we want to focus upon what that might entail as a hypothetical process toward restructuring conventional practices.

If we reconsider some of our conventional psychotherapy theories through an adjustable lens that includes the wider diversity of working persons, especially those workers whose lives are characterized by overcoming inequities or working to survive, there needs to be some revisionist's additions or at least conceptual reformulations to those theories. The challenge for psychology-of-working revisionists is the way that constructs and interventions are reconceptualized to view the client. Our thinking about key elements in theory, along with the particulars of William's life, will become part of our approach to the case presented in the subsequent section and illustrate how a psychology-of-working perspective can be integrated into case conceptualization.

For discussion purposes, let us use the sacred parent–child relationship as an example. It is considered a theoretical linchpin, certainly in the psychodynamic orientations mentioned previously, in which early stages of development establish the foundation of intrapsychic structure and processes. It helps explain childhood and many other subsequent adult behaviors. If we can hypothesize parents' experiences and satisfaction with working life as significant determinants of their interactions with their children, then a new interpretation, as well as etiology about psychological outcomes from parent–child relationships, might be more forthcoming. This observation certainly merits more scholarly study. In other words, how much do parents' working experiences (or parent at home working as caregiver) account for what we attribute as important outcomes in the equation of parent–child interactions? There are certainly many examples in the public domain (e.g., media) or our community narratives of critical after-work behavior, such as the proverbial "kicking the dog" to vent frustrations after a difficult day at work. Our demeanor and responsiveness coming into the home after a long day at work create varied and powerful post-working home atmospheres that are transformative and dynamic psychological contexts. Research trends have supported anecdotal evidence and indicated that difficulty at work negatively spills over into family dynamics, leading to marital discord and decreased attention to family responsibilities (Amstad, Meier, Fasel, Elfering, & Semmer, 2011; Ford, Heinen, & Langkamer, 2007).

Most psychotherapists have interpreted that parents reflecting upon and processing their workday events may be linked to a multitude of relational and family interactions. For example, satisfaction by family members about their quality of life and/ or socioeconomic status as outcome of their working circumstances can greatly affect parents' belief in their efficacy as workers, providers, and people. It can involve the intersection of numerous other roles and identities. Work satisfaction is a staple question included in domestic and international surveys, underscoring its significance in research. Parents' drinking behavior (for some, substance abuse) after a long day at work can be related to their attitude (or sense of obligation) about working. It is a common theme in couples and marital therapy. After-work behavior consistently is a powerful contextual variable in counseling and psychotherapy. Therefore, we cannot minimize the influences of parents' work life (and the meaning thereof) upon family dynamics and child development, much less upon our psychotherapy theories. How can we theorize about the importance of early stages of child development without marking the impact of parents' work lives on this formative stage of development and subsequent growth and behavior in adulthood? If you take the traditional nuclear two-parent family, with the father working and the mother as homemaker and caretaker (which is declining in contemporary times in industrialized countries), we can hypothesize, with some reasonable credence, that the satisfaction and fulfillment from working by both parents must influence how they viewed their children's dependency and attachment, which act as antecedents to their interactions with them. The multitude of circumstances intrinsic to the working person is a rich researchable area that would further our insights into family and person development.

Practitioners need to be better prepared with theories and empirical data that include the important influences of working upon individual development. In fact, in psychotherapy we should routinely consider how any person's fulfillment and sense of efficacy from his or her working life is linked to the intersection of other roles in his or her life, like the provider role, parenting, and marital partnership. Work life satisfaction and efficacy have to account for some of the variation in the parenting and family dynamics equation. How much is the question, and the fact of its contribution is not yet clear. Contemporary variations in family structure (e.g., divorce and the vast number of single-parent families) only complicate the development of appropriate theoretical and practice models.

If we elevate the determinant role that working plays in a person's life, there may be many ways to reconceptualize somewhat differently conventional theoretical perspectives informing psychotherapy processes and outcomes. The working context and working life have stimulus valence in shaping cognitions, affects, and interactions in normal and dysfunctional behavior. A composite of clients' circumstances in a fictional case will be used next to illustrate.

Transforming Case Conceptualization by Integrating a Psychology-of-Working Perspective: The Case of William

A colleague who does some consulting with the Metropolitan Transportation Company (MTA) of New York City referred William to me (first author). He has been a city bus driver for 8 years and requested in confidence if he could speak to someone who could help him sort out some personal issues. He preferred an African American male counselor, characteristics that the first author fulfilled.

BACKGROUND

William was a 35-year-old African American man, married for 10 years, with a 10-year-old son and an 8-year-old daughter. His wife, Rose, also 35, was one of his high school sweethearts; they married while he was in his first year of a local community college. He did not complete college because he "wanted to work and make some money." William admitted he had no interest in college despite achieving average to above-average grades while attending, which was consistent with his high school performance.

William arranged sessions for late afternoon after he got up and before he had to leave for his night shift. His presenting concerns were a need to reduce marital tension and sort out his thoughts and feelings about pressure from his wife and others in the extended family to return to college and get a better job than, as his wife puts it, "simply being an old bus driver." He has been feeling depressed after periodic, sometimes heated discussions with his wife about their future and related marital issues. These discussions trigger a life history overcoming self-doubts and ambiguous aspirations. He noted that his thoughts about the necessities of working keep him awake some nights, which is not good when rest is essential, especially given the demands of his job. These discussions with his wife bring up his own frequent musing about his choices of life path, job, and marriage. His wife, after high school and having their son, worked odd sales jobs, and the past few years has had regular employment as a part-time sales clerk in a major department store. She doesn't want to work full time because of the children, although as a good employee she is being courted for a full-time position. Both she and William have juggled work and childcare demands for years, having some coverage support from both grandmothers living nearby.

William routinely tries to get home from his nightly shift to help with breakfast and get the kids out to school. He and his wife spend time together before he has to go to bed. He spends a little time with the children when they come home from school and while having his early dinner before leaving for work. The grandmothers each alternate coverage in the afternoons or evenings, which allows Rose to work some school-day afternoons and nights, leaving William on his days off to cover those hours she works. This arrangement has been choreographed for years and adjusted according to William's changing work shifts, which is in part the source of Rose's frustration with William's job. She sees it as not going anywhere; he views his municipal job as stable with good "city union benefits." Moreover, this job is necessary for him to provide for the family; herein lies part of the couple's tension. William was quick to reassure me about their love and partnership as a couple and that this tension stems from concerns about the quality of life created by his job and Rose's personal frustrations with juggling work and taking care of the children. She expected a better life, which she believes is related to William getting a college education and a better job.

DISCUSSION

The initial task in this case was to assess William's mental status, ruling out major depression or any other serious pathology. In taking his family and work history during initial sessions, William indicated that he was the oldest of three children and was raised by a single mother. He had average to above-average grades in school, demonstrated no behavior problems, and was very sociable, with a wide network of friends. His high school and community college days were uneventful, except for considerable hanging out and socializing. After dropping out of college, he drifted into service jobs that paid slightly above minimum wage; they seemed to be acquired more for the paycheck than with a specific career focus in mind. It was at the urging of an uncle, a city bus driver with whom William had some attachment, that he applied and eventually was hired to train for a bus driver position. After getting married and having a son, William knew he had to get a good job. Circumstances made the bus driver position more important.

My assessing his view of and satisfaction with the job was an important part of the initial sessions. I asked what he liked about the job and what he disliked. It was consistent with what Blustein (2006) notes as an important element for the inclusion of work in psychotherapy by assessing strengths and challenges in the workplace (p. 277). This was also consistent with further determining his affective and cognitive state given his report of feeling depressed, not sleeping well, low self-esteem, suppressed anger, and discontents with his quality of life. Since acquiring this bus driver job, William has been reasonably happy. He doesn't particularly like the hours but believes with the advent of seniority he will get better shifts. In fact, this has been his "first real job." He notes that pulling the night shift is not that bad since he used to be out partying half the night when younger and he likes interacting with passengers who are out at night. Having a solid job and being able to provide for his family made William feel good. It was undergirded by a deeper satisfaction of defying the public's stereotype of Black men as absent providers, a theme in our sessions. Consequently, having a job and being able to provide for his family were relevant to William's racial and gender identity. For William, it was important to him that the therapist understood and had empathy for this Black male dilemma. He wanted to be seen as the exception rather than the rule in the public mind's eye. Franklin (2010) notes how Black fathers who are present and integral to family life are often invisible to the public mind's eye and how often they struggle with credibility from being overshadowed by stereotypes of Black men as irresponsible.

William was also personally committed to achieving upwardly mobile goals such as bettering the family's quality of life. He was not quite sure how he was going to do it, particularly since he saw discrimination as a major obstacle to his dreams. Although his wife's dreams were more associated with purchasing a house, William was more flexible and a bit less concrete in what fulfilled this goal, as manifested in his observation that "I just want us to have better times together and be happy." A dilemma for William was uncertainty (often triggered by Rose's priorities) that "my good bus driver" job will allow him to achieve the quality of life both he and Rose desired. He was also concerned about its influence upon their marital satisfaction. It is why he was always contemplating the possibility of pursuing other jobs, even though he viewed the security and acquisition of seniority in this strongly unionized occupation as offering more certainty than venturing forth on career proposals his wife suggested.

Traditional career counseling and vocational counseling theory places importance upon volition in choosing work pathways. Although William believed there were opportunities in the workplace, he was not convinced of their possibility, given what he believes are structural barriers for Black men in the workforce due to discrimination and racism. William also thinks more in terms of stable wage-earning jobs, because money is uppermost in his mind, in comparison to opportunities that are consistent with his interests and values. For William, pursuing a career that would offer more intrinsic satisfaction would require more preparation, time, and sacrifice than he feels able to give. Plus, he is not confident of the outcomes, given the risks of going back to school and financing it, when he is uncertain of attaining a career. William's thinking is a "bird in the hand is worth two in the bush"—in other words, he has a good job; why risk it?

Psychotherapy with Black men like William should include understanding their essential life issues, the concept of working for them, and their assessment of viable contexts to achieve work satisfaction. In many communities of color, persistently high unemployment rates, underemployment, and recognition of the cohort who has given up finding jobs make the significance and meaning of work hostage to the reality of structural inequalities. Given the social injustices and inequities in the labor history of generations of Black men and its impact upon the net worth of their families and communities, it is paramount for psychotherapists to understand the psychohistorical context of working for Black men and how it structures their views about their capacity to actualize job and career opportunities. Psychologists also need to be aware of the circumstances represented by a Pew Research Center Report (2011, p. 1) on the wealth gap, which indicates that by 2009 the median White family's net worth (i.e., assets minus debts) was 20 times greater ($113,149) than that of Black families ($5,677) and 18 times greater than that of Hispanic families ($6,325). In 2005 the median White family's net worth was $134,992, for Hispanics $18,359, and for Blacks $12,124.

It is these kind of drill-down statistics that provide another perspective on the labor market for privileged and marginalized populations both nationally and globally. It should also provide another perspective on theorizing about personal development and family interactions. Clearly, these data suggest that when someone like William, a member of a socially and economically marginalized population, comes into psychotherapy, it is not only his intrapsychic structure and functioning that is relevant therapy content (or even having a set of circumscribed behaviors susceptible to manualized interventions), but also the external structural inequities within society's infrastructure. These realities encapsulate his and his family's working life by determining conditions, opportunities, incentives, and rewards for him. It is why understanding the intersection of gender and racial identity for William (Franklin, 1999, 2004; Helms & Cook, 1999) is exemplary of what needs to be included within vocational and career counseling theory building, research, and practices. The counselor and the client should be guided by assessment of opportunity, capital, capacity, and efficacy in achieving desired quality of work. As counselors, we need to assess how people achieve family work goals given their social contextual factors (e.g., privileged vs. discriminatory). William exhibited a level of critical consciousness consistent with tenets of a psychology-of-working perspective by his insights being in harmony with the Black community's narrative about inequities in the marketplace. It was reflected in his views upon how the privileged had an advantage in contrast to marginalized populations. They had the "inside track" to navigate the workforce to achieve their quality of life. For William, social inequities remain an important contemporary reality that he must be vigilant about to succeed; in effect, the diverse sources of injustice have engendered a pronounced feeling of resignation and risk aversion in work life that he has internalized and that extends to many other domains of his life. Given the many levels of complexity represented in a case like William's life, not unlike that of many clients, it is easy for us as counselors to seek parsimonious explanations of our clients' problems. It is much easier to fit them into our theoretical comfort zones instead of reaching into other salient life domains to become more inclusive in our thinking and practices as counselors and psychotherapists. Nevertheless, recognizing the importance of and vast implications of working in clients' lives requires us to challenge convention and stretch our conceptual boundaries and make adjustments to our practices. The following sections offer some further possible ways of going about doing that.

Pathways for Integration of Working in Psychotherapy Practices
THINKING ABOUT DEVELOPMENT OF ATTACHMENTS

In considering this case of William in more inclusive ways in theory and practice, let's begin with an example of the domain of development viewed from a psychodynamic perspective. Earlier we noted, when discussing the conceptual box created by our adherence to theory, the importance of the parent–child relationship to essential psychodynamic theoretical thinking and how it guides practitioners with this particular orientation. An important area developed within psychodynamic thinking is attachment theory. Since Bowlby's (1973) articulation of the "internal working model" that influences an enduring manner of attachment and outcomes in the mother–child relationship (also evident in adult attachment), there have been numerous research studies illustrating these consequences (Grossman, Grossman, & Waters, 2005). For our purpose, the counselor and psychotherapist subscribing to this theoretical orientation may rightfully consider the nature of secure or insecure attachment of William to his mother, thus in part determining his relationship to his wife, Rose, and therefore the source of his relationship difficulties. It is a reasonable conceptualization consistent with following this line of thought. However, the many other factors formative to those attachment responses by the mother, such as the working context, are not adequately represented in our research knowledge, much less how determinant they are, thus limiting the adherent in his or her case conceptualization.

Wachtel (1993, 2008, 2011) cautions in his cyclical psychodynamics theory about the trap of limiting conceptualizations to just the formative past greatly emphasized by psychodynamic thinking. Instead he urges us to understand the mutuality of influences upon psychological structures of functioning by the interaction of details of the present with the past, as well as the past with the present, both of which can have restructuring properties and continuities within psychological functioning that sustain as well as change our behaviors. Such a perspective allows psychodynamic adherents (as well as others) to utilize external factors such as present-day experiences of social inequities to inform case conceptualization.

William's critical consciousness about structural inequities was a window into his attachments to adults and formative development as well as the continuities in his life. A belief that spanned generations throughout his extended family and influenced personal interactions was the perceived power differential from structural inequities. It created particular views and beliefs about work opportunities, the marketplace, and expectations about working. Therefore there was congruence between William's orientation toward working as an adult and what prevailed within his family and community narratives as he grew up. He observed that success in navigating these realities of structural inequities also influenced interpersonal dynamics and attachments. It was an element of how personal efficacy was evaluated by family and members of the community. William could portray how his mother and father's preoccupation with money and working while he was growing up structured his family environment. He was also aware of how it contributed to the formation of attachments within the family. Working was infused in their everyday discourse. Being attached to his father, he felt protective of his father's efforts at providing money for the family and angry at his mother's refusal to accept racism as a legitimate factor in his father's level of accomplishments, much less capacity to fulfill her marital satisfaction. William consequently considers these barriers created by work discrimination as a major risk to identity and well-being intrinsic to his personal efficacy.

Our theories about the development and attachments of a person do not adequately consider how these life circumstances shape them. For example, William's family life and his particular experiences with his parents, as he tells it, were greatly determined by the importance and consequences attributed to working every day. He constructs his father's leaving the family as a result of unresolved conflicts between his mother and father about working. His attachment to his father, plus his father and mother's legacy around working issues, helped form his sense of personal security. It has infused his current marital and family circumstances with insecurities. It orients his approach to parenting, where having a "good, stable job" reduces anxiety about risks to family destabilization more than any elusive, allegedly promising career possibilities can assure. Moreover, job stability keeps intact and protects William's sense of racial and gender identity and combats threats from stereotypes (Steele, 1997). These are all elements of his capacity to be resilient. His personality, however, can be viewed exclusively through the lens of his secure or insecure attachment to his mother with little inclusive formulation drawn upon a working experiences paradigm. A possible working experiences paradigm could hypothesize, in this case, that William's mother's capacity to nurture secure attachments was a product of her own development within a parental working environment that could also provide secure attachments. Counselors

or psychotherapists utilizing an attachment theoretical orientation could broaden and enrich their thinking in this manner if working experiences are integrated into their case conceptualization and treatment process.

THINKING ABOUT CAREER AND VOCATION

It is also easy to approach William's circumstances in counseling by elevating the importance of his career fit based upon his conflictual presentation, perhaps interpreted from his questioning of job adequacy, manifest depressive symptoms, and confusion and ambiguity in aspirations. He represents a history of low goal-directed motivation, low mood affect, and settling. We could view his representation of job satisfaction as accommodation to convenience from a job handed to him by his uncle. Although William's discontents are connected to marital strain, the status of working seems primary to this circumstance. Moreover, there is enough confusion and uncertainty within William that referring him for vocational and career interest assessment has merit as an intervention. The risk at this juncture of case conceptualization is to focus too much upon vocational and career domains, guided by our theoretical proclivities, at the expense of considering the influence upon William's development from socialization about gender and racial inequities. This is no less a clinical practice risk than a counselor or psychotherapist with a proclivity to focus upon theory informing intrapsychic structuring of William by his mothering.

THINKING ABOUT THE
COGNITIVE-BEHAVIORAL APPROACH

Another way a counselor or psychotherapist could approach William's circumstances is to focus upon his cognitions, the manner in which they have immobilized him and trigger his anxiety and depressive symptoms. The counselor could better sort out his dilemma about working as a bus driver and related marital strain by helping him gain control over his flooding thoughts (cognitions) and his response to them. By recognizing those chains of behaviors connected to his obsessive thinking, he can be taught techniques that disrupt this pattern, preventing the anxiety that typically governs the outcome of his process. Reducing debilitating thought processes will allow him to function better—and better functioning will help William to confront, in a greater state of well-being, his working and aspirational dilemma as well as marital strain. A more emotionally balanced and stable condition will also improve his engaging professional assessment and guidance about his vocational and career interests.

THINKING ABOUT THE MARITAL AND FAMILY SYSTEM

The prominence of marital strain and involvement of extended family in William's circumstances could easily lead a family counselor or psychotherapist into focusing upon formative relational issues within the family structure. Clearly the tense as well as loving relationship between William and his wife is interpersonally structuring not only for them but also for their children observing their dynamics. Exploring relational contexts and circumstances for William would provide insights into his orientation to working and the accompanying challenges he has in sorting out conflicts about work satisfaction and stated unfulfilled aspirations. A counselor or psychotherapist could approach William's circumstances from a family systems perspective. Bowen's (1978) emphasis upon transmission of intergenerational legacy is an appropriate frame for thinking about William's circumstances. It can accommodate understanding the origin of William's marital strain as seeded by his own observations and interactions with his parents as they struggled with issues of working on their relationship and that of the family. Moreover, William greatly represented the importance of working to the extended family's reputation. His uncle, who introduced him to the prospect of becoming a bus driver, had been a role model. The family a generation ago saw him, the uncle, as a good provider given his job stability.

Therefore, from a family therapy orientation, our clients are products of family as well as community intergenerational legacies of working. The interaction of a family's orientation to work with the continuities of intergenerational narratives from the community about working often determines how the family members enter the job market. One way in which family systems play a role in work-related contexts is that family members may follow work and career paths related to other family members. Relationships within family and community systems have an impact on the meaning that individual clients and families (and their family members also) attribute to the essentialism of working in their life (Richardson, in press). We often enter related occupations of family members or mentors because of this relational dynamic, and their access can privilege our access to those job areas. Breaking the work patterns of a family or community is more difficult than it would appear because the hold upon us from intergenerational legacies of values, beliefs, and practices of a family and community is so deeply embedded in our lives in an often unrecognized powerful fashion (Bowen, 1978; McGoldrick, Carter, & Garcia-Preto, 2010; Walsh, 2006).

Conclusion: Thinking in an Integrative and Inclusive Frame

Once again, almost any of our theoretical perspectives, if we choose flexibility in thinking, can lead us in unique ways into understanding the deep structural and systemic complexities that influence the meaning of working for individuals. The purpose of briefly presenting these different theoretical frames for conceptualizing William's circumstances is to highlight how quickly our orientation can guide us as well as constrain us. Our theoretical and practice orientations make it comfortable and easy to view circumstances of clients through a particular lens by virtue of the conceptual viewfinder and intervention guidebook we are provided. This is no secret, nor are these necessarily erroneous expectations given the reinforcement of credibility imparted to our respective orientations by supportive adherents. As we remain entrenched in our particular theoretical and practice camps, openness to new ways of thinking and practicing is not readily forthcoming, primarily due to the pervasiveness of conceptual boxes in our work. Nevertheless, we must continue to challenge our profession to become more inclusive and, ultimately, more effective.

Psychology-of-working advocates are doing just that (Blustein, 2006). Another way of approaching William's circumstances is from a more integrative and inclusive frame. For example, the different approaches briefly presented could be integrated into a treatment plan for William in which working is given more legitimacy and stature to formative processes of the person. The counselor or psychotherapist needs to have a level of sophistication to do this, thus making psychotherapy integration a foremost training goal. The challenges to curriculum development notwithstanding, another purpose of this chapter is to propose the feasibility of an integrated psychotherapy orientation that utilizes different theoretical and practice interventions when a client's circumstances make one more appropriate than the other at particular points in the treatment process. By taking this professional stance, we begin to loosen the shackles of absolute theoretical allegiance that can act as blinders at the expense of providing the best treatment practices for our clients' interest. It is theoretical and practice inflexibility that makes conceptualizing the multiple domains of our clients' life difficult more than its intrinsic complexity. This includes vocational and career counseling theory and practice, which also struggles to evolve out of its specialization box as much as other schools of thought.

For most therapists to include a psychology-of-working viewpoint in practice, as well as to engage marginalized populations and other nontraditional recipients of career or vocational counseling, a paradigmatic shift will be needed (Franklin, 2010). The paradigmatic shift will be even greater as we continue to advocate that not only theories and practices of psychotherapy but also psychology-of-working scholarship evolve from a more emic versus etic perspective in theory, research, and practice.

References

Alliman-Brissett, A. E., & Turner, S. L. (2010). Racism, parent support, and math-based career interests, self-efficacy, and outcome expectations among African American adolescents. *Journal of Black Psychology, 37*, 197–225. doi: 10.1177/0095798409351830

American Psychiatric Association. (1994). *Diagnostic and statistical manual of mental disorders* (4th ed.). Washington, DC: Author.

American Psychological Association (2003). Guidelines on multicultural education, training, research, practice, and organizational change for psychologists. *American Psychologist, 58*, 377–402. doi: 10.1037/0003-066X.58.5.377

American Psychological Association. (2006) Evidence-based practice in psychology. *American Psychologist, 61*, 271–285. doi: 10.1037/0003-066X.61.4.271

Amstad, F. T., Meier, L. L., Fasel, U., Elfering, A., & Semmer, N. K. (2011). A meta-analysis of work–family conflict and various outcomes with a special emphasis on cross-domain versus matching-domain relations. *Journal of Occupational Health Psychology, 16*(2), 151–169. doi:10.1037/a0022170

Axelrod, S. D. (1999). *Work and the evolving self: Theoretical and clinical considerations.* Hillsdale, NJ: The Analytic Press.

Barlow, D. H. (2004). Psychological treatments. *American Psychologist, 59*, 869–878. doi: 10.1037/0003-066x.59.9.869

Bartsch, K. J. (2009). The employment projections for 2008–18. *Monthly Labor Review, 132*(11), 3–11. retrieved from http://www.bls.gov/opub/mlr/2009/11/mlr200911.pdf

Betz, N. E. (2005). Women's career development. In S. D. Brown & R. W. Lent (Eds.), *Career development and counseling: Putting theory and research to work* (pp. 253–277). Hoboken, NJ: Wiley.

Betz, N. E., & Corning, A. F. (1993). The inseparability of career and personal counseling. *Career Development Quarterly, 42*, 137–142.

Blustein, D. L. (2006). *The psychology of working: A new perspective for career development, counseling, and public policy.* Mahwah, NJ: Erlbaum.

Blustein, D. L. (2008). The role of work in psychological health and well-being: A conceptual, historical, and public policy perspective. *American Psychologist, 63*, 228–240. doi: 10.1037/0003-066x.63.4.228

Blustein, D. L. (2011). A relational theory of working. *Journal of Vocational Behavior, 79*, 1–17. doi:10.1016/j.jvb.2010.10.004

Blustein, D. L., Medvide, M. B., & Kozan, S. (2012). A tour of a new paradigm: Relationships and work. *Counseling Psychologist, 40*, 243–254. doi: 10.1177/0011000011429032

Bowen, M. (1978). *Family therapy in clinical practice.* New York: Aronson.

Bowlby, J. (1973). *Attachment and loss: Vol. 2. Separation.* New York: Basic Books.

Constantine, M., & Flores, L. (2006). Psychological distress, perceived family conflict, and career development issues in college students of color. *Journal of Career Assessment, 14*, 354–369. doi: 2006-08839-00410.1177 /1069072706286491

Constantine, M., Wallace, C., & Kindaichi, M. (2005). Examining contextual factors in the career decision status of African American adolescents. *Journal of Career Assessment, 13*, 307–319. doi: 2005-07379-00410.1177/1069072705274960

Fall, K. A., Holden, J. M. & Marquis, A. (2010). *Theoretical models of counseling and psychotherapy* (2nd ed.). New York: Routledge.

Ferenczi, S., & Rank, O. (1988). The development of psychoanalysis: A historical critical retrospect. In B. Wolstein (Ed.), *Essential papers on countertransference* (pp. 25–35). New York: New York University Press.

Ford, M. T., Heinen, B. A., & Langkamer, K. L. (2007). Work and family satisfaction and conflict: A meta-analysis of cross-domain relations. *Journal of Applied Psychology, 92*, 57–80. doi: 10.1037/0021-9010.92.1.57

Fouad, N. A., & Kantamneni, N. (2008). Contextual factors in vocational psychology: Intersections of individual, group, and societal dimensions. In S. D. Brown & R. W. Lent (Eds.), *Handbook of counseling psychology* (4th ed., pp. 408–425). New York: Wiley.

Franklin, A. J. (1999). Invisibility syndrome and racial identity development in psychotherapy and counseling African American men. *Counseling Psychologist, 27*, 761–793. doi: 1999-01329-001.

Franklin, A. J. (2004). *From brotherhood to manhood: How Black men rescue their relationships and dreams from the invisibility syndrome.* New York: John Wiley & Son.

Franklin, A. J. (2010). Case illustration: Exploring an African American case with the AA-SISM. In M. E. Gallardo, J. E. Yeh, J. E. Trimble, & T. A. Parham, (Eds.), *Culturally adaptive counseling skills: Demonstrations of evidence-based practices* (pp. 65–74). Los Angeles: Sage.

Gergen, K. (1999). Agency: Social construction and relational action. *Theory & Psychology, 9*, 113–115. doi: 10.1177/0959354399091007

Grossman, K. E., Grossman, K., & Waters, E. (Eds.). (2005). *Attachment from infancy to adulthood: The major longitudinal studies.* New York: Guilford Press.

Hartung, P. J., & Blustein, D. L. (2002). Reason, intuition, and social justice: Elaborating Parsons' career decision making model. *Journal of Counseling and Development, 80*, 41–47. doi: 2002–10733–005

Helms, J. E. (Ed.). (1990). *Black and white racial identity: Theory, research, and practice.* New York: Greenwood.

Helms, J. E., & Cook, D. A. (1999). *Using race and culture in counseling and psychotherapy: Theory and process.* Boston, MA: Allyn & Bacon.

Juntunen, C. L. (2006). The psychology of working: The clinical context. *Professional Psychology: Research and Practice, 37*, 342–350. doi: 2006-09259-00310.1037/0735-7028.37.4.342

La Roche, M., & Christopher, M. (2009). Changing paradigms from empirically supported treatments to evidence-based practice: A cultural perspective. *Professional Psychology: Research and Practice, 40*, 396–402.2009-11890-01310.1037/a0015240

Lent, R. W., Brown, S. D., & Hackett, G. (1994). Toward a unifying social cognitive theory of career and academic interest, choice, and performance. *Journal of Vocational Behavior, 45*, 79–122. doi: 1994-47157-00110.1006/jvbe.1994.102

McGoldrick, M., Carter, B., & Garcia-Preto, N. (2010). *The extended family life cycle: Individual, family, and social perspectives.* Upper Saddle River, NJ: Prentice Hall.

Perdue, S. V., Reardon, R. C., & Peterson, G. W. (2007). Person-environment congruence, self-efficacy, and environmental identity in relation to job satisfaction: A career decision theory perspective. *Journal of Employment Counseling, 44*, 29–39. doi: 2007-04030-004

Richardson, M. S. (1993). Work in people's lives: A location for counseling psychologists. *Journal of Counseling Psychology, 40*, 425–433. doi: 1994-07341-00110.1037/0022-0167.40.4.425

Richardson, M. S. (1996). From career counseling to counseling/psychotherapy and work, jobs, and career. In M. L. Savickas & W. B. Walsh (Eds.), *Handbook of career counseling theory and practice* (pp. 347–360). Palo Alto, CA: Davies-Black Publishing.

Richardson, M. S. (2012). Counseling for work and relationship. *Counseling Psychologist, 40*, 190–242. doi: 10.1177/0011000011406452

Savickas, M. (2005). The theory and practice of career construction. In S. Brown & R. Lent (Eds.), *Career development and counseling: Putting theory and research to work* (pp. 42–70). New York: Wiley.

Schultheiss, D. E. P. (2003). A relational approach to career counseling: Theoretical integration and practical application. *Journal of Counseling and Development, 81*, 301–310.

Schultheiss, D. E. P. (2009). To mother or matter: Can women do both? *Journal of Career Development, 36*, 25–47. doi: 10.1177/08948453093407952009-12455-003

Robitschek, C., & DeBell, C. (2002). The reintegration of vocational psychology and counseling psychology: Training issues for a paradigm shift. *Counseling Psychologist, 30*, 801–814. doi: 2002–06392–002

Smith, E. J. (1983). Issues in racial minorities' career behavior. In W. B. Walsh & S. H. Osipow (Eds.), *Handbook of vocational psychology: Vol. 1, Foundations* (pp. 161–222). Hillsdale, NJ: Lawrence Erlbaum Associates.

Steele, C. M. (1997). A threat in the air: How stereotypes shape intellectual identity and performance. *American Psychologist, 52*, 613–629. doi: 1997-04591-00110.1037//0003-066X.52.6.613

Super, D. E. (1957). *The psychology of careers.* New York: Harper & Row.

Super, D. E. (1980). A life-span, life-space approach to career development. *Journal of Vocational Behavior, 13*, 282–298.

Wachtel, P. L. (1993). *Therapeutic communication: Knowing what to say when.* New York: Guilford Press.

Wachtel, P. L. (2008). *Relational theory and practice of psychotherapy.* New York: Guilford Press.

Wachtel, P. L. (2011). *Therapeutic communication: Knowing what to say when* (2nd ed). New York: Guilford Press.

Walsh, F. (2006). *Strengthening family resilience.* New York: Guilford Press.

Westen, D., Novotny, C., & Thompson-Brenner, H. (2004). The empirical status of empirically supported psychotherapies: Assumptions, findings, and reporting in controlled clinical trials. *Psychological Bulletin, 130*, 631–663. doi: 2004-15935-00510.1037/0033-2909.130.4.631

Wright, S. L., & Perrone, K. M. (2010). An examination of the role of attachment and efficacy in life satisfaction. *Counseling Psychologist, 38*, 796–823. doi: 10.1177/0011000009359204

Community-Based Interventions and Public Policy

The Promise of Work as a Component of Educational Reform

Maureen E. Kenny

Abstract

Education has long been understood as a vehicle for realizing the American dream, with the importance of education for entry and advancement in the world of work increasing in recent years. Although public officials and policymakers maintain that high schools must now prepare all students for college and career, many young people either graduate with inadequate skills or drop out prior to graduation. Education reform efforts have sought to bolster academic achievement, with particular concern for remedying achievement gaps among ethnic and racial groups. Overall results of these efforts have been inadequate, and policy formulations have overlooked relevant theory and research related to academic motivation and the context of students' lives. Theory and research related to career development and work-based learning can inform educational practice that strives to prepare all students for college and career.

Key Words: social justice, workplace skills, education reform, school engagement, academic motivation

Introduction

The role of work and education in society has changed radically in recent years. Completion of higher levels of education has become increasingly important for access to employment that offers a living wage and opportunities for advancement (Haskins & Kemple, 2009). This reality has had particularly negative consequences during the recent period of economic downturn, especially for those who are marginalized as a result of low levels of education and few marketable skills. The unemployment rate, for example, for Americans with less than a high school diploma was 14.6% in 2009, with that rate improving to 9.7% for high school graduates, 6.8% for those with an associate's degree, and 4.6% for holders of a bachelor's degree or higher (Bureau of Labor Statistics, 2010). As described in this chapter, recent data also reveal that racial discrepancies in high school and college graduation rates have not narrowed despite federal and state efforts to address this.

This chapter critically reviews extant research and policy that will serve to inform understanding and, I hope, promote action to correct these social injustices. I begin by considering the importance of education and work for youth, changes in the world of work, and skills demanded by the 21st-century workplace. In recognition of the importance of education, U.S. business and policy officials are adamant that all U.S. students should graduate from high school fully prepared for college and career (Haskins & Kemple, 2009). A variety of educational reform efforts have been attempted over the past several decades, with often disappointing results. I review these efforts and argue that reform strategies are bound to fail when they neglect the contexts that dominate the lives of youth and ignore theory and research related to academic motivation and career development. Theory and research addressing school engagement and academic motivation, particularly among students of color, are reviewed to gain insight regarding the limitations and successes of varied efforts. Finally, I argue that effective education must embrace both relevance and rigor and that career education and work-based learning are promising strategies that can be designed to meet both of these criteria.

Education and the American Dream

The importance of academic attainment to life quality is widely documented. The notion of the American dream is rooted in the premise that access to education is the vehicle for social mobility in the United States. Consistent with this premise, a higher level of educational attainment is correlated with greater job success, higher income, and lower levels of unemployment and poverty, as well as better health and higher levels of civic participation (Baum & Ma, 2007; Jerald, 2009). Although the correlation between education and income holds across gender and for all ethnic and racial groups, significant group differences in academic achievement, high school completion, and college enrollment and completion exist (Baum & Ma, 2007). While levels of academic achievement as assessed by standardized test scores have increased for all groups in the United States since 1990, Blacks, Latinos, and recent immigrant students obtain lower scores than White and Asian students (National Center for Education Statistics, 2009). Latinos and American Indian/Alaskan natives are also more likely than other groups to leave high school prior to completion, with the dropout rates being reported as 21.4% for Latinos and 19.3% for American Indian/Alaskan natives (National Center for Education Statistics, 2007). For those who complete high school, post-secondary enrollment and college completion rates differ by race, ethnicity, and income levels. Men and students from rural areas have relatively low rates of participation in higher education. Blacks, Hispanics, and low-income students are also more likely than other students to leave college without a degree (Baum & Ma, 2007).

Racial and ethnic differences in educational and occupational attainment persist as a function of racism and structural barriers in the United States. More than 50 years after *Brown vs. Board of Education*, public high schools differ enormously in the composition of their student bodies and the funding level of their schools, resulting in both separate and unequal high school experiences

(Balfanz, 2009). Public schools in large urban areas are increasingly segregated by race and social class (Weis & Dimitriadis, 2008). Minority youth disproportionately attend schools that are embedded in high-poverty neighborhoods, are attended by other minority students, are underfunded, and have low graduation rates. Students from the poorest families and the poorest communities attend large schools with high percentages of students performing below grade level, with high teacher–student ratios, and with low per-pupil expenditures (Balfanz, 2009).

The gaps that exist in educational attainment across race, ethnicity, and social class in the United States contribute to ever-widening gaps in income across the lifespan. High school dropouts are most vulnerable to long-term unemployment and poverty. On a national level in 2005, the median earning for a full-time worker with less than a high school education was $18,800, compared to $24,900 for a high school graduate, $39,000 for the holder of a bachelor's degree, and $74,500 for those with professional degrees (Baum & Ma, 2007). Moreover, those with less education have experienced declining economic opportunities over the past three decades (Haskins & Kemple, 2009). The financial benefits of a college education increased by 25% across the same time period, with the rate of return for each year of college completed being 13% to 24% (Jerald, 2009).

Earning a college degree remains a mechanism for social mobility: children whose parents are in the bottom-fifth income bracket quadruple their chance (from 5% to 19%) of moving to the top-fifth income bracket by earning a college degree. Unfortunately, only one third of youth from this income level actually enter college, and only 11% complete a degree (Haskins & Kemple, 2009). Parental educational level affects access to power and resources across generations, as the children of the more educated display a higher level of school readiness at an early age and are more likely to attend college as young adults (Baum & Ma, 2007). At a time when the number of children of immigrants in our schools is increasing, access to the American dream is diminishing.

Education and Social Justice

Within the United States and across the globe, educational attainment is key for access to employment opportunities. To the extent that work is a means for survival, power, social connection, and self-determination (D. Blustein, Kenna, Gill, & DeVoy, 2008), job instability and joblessness are social justice issues. Inequities persist in the U.S.

educational system and in academic and occupational attainment across social class, race, ethnicity, and disability status. I agree with authors (e.g., Fine, Burns, Payne, & Torre, 2004; Prilleltensky, 2001) who attribute these inequities to systemic and structural biases and sources of oppression at a societal level.

While broad structural and systemic changes at the political and economic levels are needed for the full realization of social justice, advanced academic and critical thinking skills are also critical to equip youth with the prerequisite competencies for success in the workplace and engagement in the political process (Cochran-Smith, Gleeson, & Mitchell, 2010). As noted by Prilleltensky and colleagues (Prilleltensky, 2001; Prilleltensky & Nelson, 1997), skills and competencies at the individual and group levels are essential for full and equal participation in society and for volition and self-determination in one's life. While it is vital to remove structural barriers that restrict access to opportunities, personal skills necessary for full societal participation also need to be developed (Prilleltensky, Dokecki, Frieden, & Wang, 2007). While injustices related to education and work are broad social issues requiring substantive social change (Prilleltensky & Nelson, 1997), creating educational and work policies that increase access to meaningful school and work opportunities and prepare youth to thrive in these settings are integral for advancing social justice. I maintain that education can and should be organized to promote social justice and prepare youth to resist oppression rather than to sustain the economic and social status quo.

This chapter critically examines relevant history, theory, and research with the goal of informing educational policy and efforts to structure school and work programs that will promote social justice and offer the next generation access to a better life. I begin by briefly discussing changes in the workplace, the interrelationship of school and work in U.S. education, and the nature of U.S. public education reform. I then review relevant educational and psychological research in efforts to realize more effective and just policies and practices that increase the capacity of all youth to participate fully in work and society.

The Changing World of Work

Increasingly, the workforce of the 21st century demands individuals who possess high levels of academic and technical skills. The U.S. economy has shifted drastically since 1997, when economic output was dominated by the manufacturing of material goods (e.g., automobiles and industrial equipment) and the delivery of materials (construction, transportation), to an economy now dominated by services, especially information services and technology (Partnership for 21st Century Skills, 2008). Globalization and automation are serving to eliminate routine jobs and those that can be programmed by a computer or completed by a robot. Assembly line and other routine work can be outsourced to persons thousands of miles away who will work for less money than U.S. workers (Jerald, 2009). According to the U.S. Department of Labor (Bureau of Labor Statistics, 2008), jobs that require a bachelor's degree or higher are expected to increase between 2006 and 2016 at a rate of two-to-one in comparison with those requiring high school graduation or less. Two thirds of new jobs are expected to require at least a high school diploma (Bureau of Labor Statistics, 2008). Individuals who lack higher-level education and possess only rudimentary literacy and technical skills are expected to struggle increasingly to find employment that offers a living wage (Baum & Ma, 2007).

Historically, the United States has prided itself as a world leader in education, with top institutions of higher education and K–12 schools. Indeed, the educational attainment of the U.S. workforce is recognized as a key factor in maintaining the strength of the U.S. economy since World War II (Jerald, 2009). International evaluations suggest that the status of the United States in comparison with other nations has diminished, however. According to the 2009 Program for International Student Assessment (PISA) study (Fleischman, Hopstock, Pelczar, & Shelley, 2010), U.S. teenagers (15 years old) scored average or lower level among 33 developed countries, ranking 18th in mathematics and 13th in science literacy.

In recognition of the changing workplace and concerns that the United States retain a competitive edge in the global economy, labor and business have sought to identify important workplace skills to be developed through the educational system. The Partnership for 21st Century Skills (www.p21.org), a leader in advocacy efforts for strengthening education to prepare students for success in the changing workplace, developed a collective vision for 21st-century learning and student outcomes with input from a national forum of employers, citizens, and K–12 and postsecondary educators. This vision is broad and reflects a range of complex skills, including critical thinking and problem solving, communication, collaboration and team building, and creativity and innovation, considered essential for current and future employees in applying academic knowledge to real-world problems. Economists maintain that Americans will need to offer more creativity and innovation in comparison with other workers if they are to maintain high wage levels (National Center on Education and the Economy, 2007). Despite the proclaimed importance of these skills, corporate senior executive and human resource managers view new employees as woefully unprepared in these areas. More than half of new workers at the high school graduate level are described as inadequately prepared, and only 25% of college graduates are reported as displaying excellent skill levels (www.p21.org).

While most experts agree that education for the 21st century must provide all students with advanced academic skills, along with a broad set of competencies to apply academic learning to real-world problems (Jerald, 2009), there is less consensus concerning the educational strategies for building these competencies. Some educators and policymakers argue that the academic skills required for college represent the best preparation for the workforce (ACT, 2010), while others argue that an exclusive focus on academic skills and college readiness neglects other valuable skills, involving interpersonal competence and experience in applying academic knowledge to real-life problems, that are important to work and life success (Grubb & Oakes, 2007; Stern, 2009). The Common Core State Standards (ACT, 2010), which are being adopted by states across the nation to increase the college and career readiness of high school graduates, focus exclusively on academic skills. This ambivalence about the role of the school in workforce preparation is evident in the history of U.S. education and in the range of educational reform initiatives that have been attempted.

The Fate of Work Preparation in Educational Reform

The American high school has been heralded historically as a conduit for upward mobility, workforce preparation, economic growth, and the development of citizenship (Balfanz, 2009). As the following historical review reveals, however, success in realizing these goals and the centrality of each over time has varied.

In the early 20th century, only a small and privileged percentage of the population attended high school as a means for college preparation. Many youth learned their trades through informal observation of family or community members or through formal apprenticeships. By the 1960s, however, high school attendance until the age of 16 was mandatory and the mission of schools had expanded to include socialization and life adjustment, as well as workforce preparation and academic skill development (Kliebard, 1999). Throughout the 20th century, academic education and vocational education, now referred to as career and technical education (CTE), were largely separate in U.S. high schools, requiring students to choose one pathway or the other. By the 1980s, vocational and technical education came under attack, however, for "tracking" students and limiting access to college preparation courses and college entry, especially for students from lower socioeconomic groups (Oakes & Saunders, 2008). Enrollment in vocational and technical education has declined since that time, with less than 3% of U.S. high school students attending vocational and technical schools in recent years (Stern, 2009). Among high school graduates in 2003–04, only 15% completed at least three high school credits in an occupational preparation course such as business, healthcare, and marketing (Stern, 2009).

A variety of educational reforms have been initiated over the past half-century out of concern for preparing a competitive workforce and for redressing racial and social class disparities in educational achievement. In 1981, the White House commissioned a study of U.S. education, stemming from evidence that the United States was beginning to fall behind other nations. The resulting report, entitled *A Nation At Risk* (National Commission on Excellence in Education, 1983), blamed U.S. educators for declines in student achievement, criticized schools for isolating students from the workplace, and cited inadequate educational and work preparation of U.S. students as a cause for economic instability (Hargreaves & Shirley, 2009). An influential report by the William T. Grant Foundation (1988) had also called attention to high levels of joblessness, job instability, and extended floundering in dead-end jobs experienced by that group of U.S. youth who were not college bound. The report spurred concern among educators and policymakers that many U.S. youth lacked both the academic and work readiness competencies to make a successful transition into the workplace.

The school-to-work (STW) movement, or school-to-career movement, that began in the United States in the 1990s (Olson, 1997) and the School-to-Work Opportunities Act (STWOA) of 1994 were outgrowths of concerns regarding diminishing opportunities for work-bound youth and declining quality in the U.S. workforce. The elaborate systems of student internships and collaborations between high schools and employers that had been developed in other nations, such as Germany, Austria, Switzerland, and Japan, to assist students in making successful transitions from school to the workplace were an impetus for reform in the United States (Mortimer, 2003). STW programs became an alternative to career-technical education and offered a new model for developing both academic and work readiness skills. In comparison with vocational or technical education that was separate from academic education, STW programs sought to integrate academic and work preparation in a new way. Connecting activities were conceptualized as an important mechanism for helping young people to understand the relationship between school and work and to link learning at school with activities in the workplace (D. L. Blustein, Juntunen, & Worthington, 2000). STWOA provided more than $1.5 billion to support career preparation activities, which included work-based learning or educational experiences embedded in a work environment (e.g., job shadowing, cooperative education, internships and youth apprenticeship programs that place students in paid workplace learning experiences and link students with workplace mentors), school-based learning focusing on careers (e.g., Tech Prep programs that emphasize technology-related instruction and occupations), and connecting activities (Mortimer, 2003). The availability of federal funding supported the development of many innovative programs, which were to rely on local support after the federal legislation expired in 2001.

Although the legislation expired before long-term outcomes were evaluated, short-term results of STW were promising. Evidence drawn from a variety of studies, including several using a randomized experimental design, revealed overall that students in STW programs had better attendance rates, higher grades, and broader career options and were less likely to drop out of high school than students in schools that did not offer STW programs (Hughes, Bailey, & Mechur, 2001). Positive effects on standardized test scores were not established (Hughes et al., 2001), although research demonstrated that graduates of one STW program enrolled in and completed postsecondary education at higher rates and had higher earnings than a matched non-STW sample (MacAllum & Bozick, 2001).

The 2001 reauthorization of the Elementary and Secondary Education Act (ESEA), better known as No Child Left Behind (NCLB), brought in sweeping changes in national educational policy. The emphasis of NCLB on academic achievement and the mounting financial and public pressures experienced by schools to improve student test scores contributed over time to an overall downsizing of STW and other initiatives that connected academics to out-of-school learning (Mortimer, 2003). As the title of the legislation suggests, the intent of the act was to ameliorate the achievement gap and to raise the achievement levels of all students, including children of color, new English language learners (ELLs), children with disabilities, and those living in poverty. While this overall goal was widely embraced, the methods for doing this, the support provided by the federal government to achieve that goal, and the effects of the reform have generated controversy.

A fundamental premise of NCLB and current educational policy is that rigorous assessment and accountability will enhance student, administrator, and teacher motivation and thereby improve academic achievement. Although school poverty is the strongest single predictor of whether a school will be labeled as "needing improvement" for failing to document student progress, NCLB holds administrators, teachers, and students accountable, rather than addressing underlying social and economic conditions. Available evidence suggests that firing school administrators is not an effective reform strategy (Good & McCaslin, 2008). With one out of four U.S. public high school students dropping out before graduation (Balfanz, Bridgeland, Moore, & Fox, 2010), the success of education reform to date is insufficient. The prevailing approach to reform adopts a business model of economic incentives, which ties teacher salaries with student test scores, and creates competition between charter and public schools for students and public funds.

Inadequate academic progress and increased dropout rates among low-performing students since the inception of NCLB suggest that high-stakes testing is inadequate and likely harmful as a method of educational reform (Good & McCaslin, 2008). Evidence suggests that some students, especially the growing number of immigrant students who are ELLs, racial and ethnic minorities, and special education students, expect that they will not pass the high-stakes tests required for high school graduation, become discouraged, and drop out of school (Fine, Jaffe-Walter, Pedraza, Futch, & Stoudt,

2007). Rather than motivating students, the rigorous accountability standards and assessments of NCLB seem like an insurmountable challenge for many ELLs. Critics also claim that pressures to demonstrate adequate yearly progress (AYP) inevitably contribute to a test-focused curriculum and neglect factors known to promote student engagement in learning, such as personalized and collaborative learning environments and an intellectually stimulating curriculum with assessment tied to real-world problems (Darling-Hammond, 2006; Fine et al., 2007). Preparations to pass standardized tests often overlook the development of critical thinking and application of knowledge needed for higher-paying jobs and civic participation (Cochran-Smith et al., 2010). In classrooms affected by NCLB reform policy, Good and McCaslin (2008) observed a focus on basic skills and factual material, with little or no discussion of the interrelationship of ideas or how they might be used in the future. Although relationships with teachers were pleasant, opportunities for student choice or initiative were absent. Amidst national concern for the international standing of U.S. students and workers, what is best for children and their overall well-being should not be forgotten (Shaker, 2010). Too many schools are failing to prepare students for success in post-high school education and work (Fleischman & Heppen, 2009).

Theory and Research Relevant to Educational Reform

Critics (e.g., Orfield, 2004) point out that NCLB transformed education policy in the United States without considering input from specialists in psychology, education, and educational measurement. Theory and research are integral for informing best practices in psychology and education (Hage et al., 2007). Recent educational policy initiatives (e.g., Investing in Innovation Funds) encourage partnerships between school districts and research entities to design and rigorously evaluate educational practices, identify those that work, and bring them to scale in new settings. In the hope of identifying knowledge that can serve to improve policy practice in education and vocational psychology, I now examine theory and research that pertains to the academic motivation and school engagement of high school youth and the role of systemic factors as constraints to school engagement and career progress. The work of counseling psychologists has been prominent in this domain. I also review the effects of programs that seek to integrate school and work and argue that efforts to separate academic

learning, work preparation, and out-of-school learning are misguided, neglect motivational factors that engage students in school and learning, and ignore the nurturance of creativity, critical thinking, and collaboration that are so important for the 21st-century workforce. The attention given here to student engagement and motivation is not intended to suggest that students are failing to make progress because they lack motivation, but that educational reform is being constructed without adequate understanding of student motivation and the factors that help students to cope with social and economic inequities.

School Engagement

School engagement, which refers to the students' levels of behavioral, affective, and cognitive investment in learning and mastering academic skills (Fredricks, Blumenfeld, & Paris, 2004), has received attention in the educational and psychological literature in recent years as a factor related to academic achievement. Dropping out of high school is understood as the endpoint of a long process of disengagement from school (Tyler & Lofstrom, 2009). Interest in the construct of school engagement is derived from the understanding that interest, motivation, and effort are needed for students to achieve commensurate with their abilities. Engagement is one "within-group" variable that may help to explain why some low-income and ethnic minority students are more or less successful academically than others (Sirin & Rogers-Sirin, 2005). Furthermore, engagement is identified as a modifiable construct that is seemingly more amenable to change in the short term in comparison with broad and deep-seated systemic factors (Fredricks et al., 2004; Perry, 2008). Research has consistently documented positive relationships between student engagement, academic performance and persistence, and negative relationships with school dropout, academic cheating, and substance abuse (Voelkl & Frone, 2000).

Given the potential value of the construct, research has also sought to identify factors that contribute to positive school engagement and those that lead to disengagement. Of concern is the large body of research indicating that student engagement is strong at the elementary school level but diminishes, sometimes drastically, across the middle school and high school years (Balfanz, Herzog, & MacIver, 2007). The decline in school engagement that occurs across the middle school grades has been linked to the spike in school dropout that occurs at grade 9, particularly in low-performing urban schools (Balfanz et al., 2007). A pervasive and disturbing level of disengagement is revealed by the 2006 national High School Survey of Student Engagement (Yazzie-Mintz, 2007). Based on that survey, the majority of students attend school because it is the law, rather than because they value what is taught in class. Two thirds of high school students report being bored in class at least some of the time. Students attributed their boredom most often to class material that is not interesting (75%), not relevant (39%), and not challenging (32%) and offers no interaction with teachers (31%) (Yazzie-Mintz, 2007).

Factors related to school engagement have been identified at varied ecological levels. At the individual level, for example, boys have been found to be more disengaged than girls across the middle and high school years, especially in urban schools (Balfanz et al., 2007; Sirin & Rogers-Sirin, 2005). Not only do girls report less disengagement than boys, but they are less likely to display the early warning signs of school dropout at grade 6 and are much less likely than boys to actually drop out prior to high school completion (Balfanz et al., 2007). This may be related to susceptibility among boys, prevalent across a range of ethnic minority and White cultures, to internalize peer norms that devalue school success and to associate doing well in school with being a "nerd" (Tyson, Darity, & Castellino, 2005).

At the micro-system level, support from parents, peers, and teachers is critical to student engagement (Close & Solberg, 2008; Kenny, Blustein, Chaves, Grossman, & Gallagher, 2003; Murray, 2009; Perry, Liu, & Pabian, 2010; Simons-Morton & Chen, 2009). Among Latin American immigrant youth, fluctuations in student school engagement from year to year have been associated with fluctuations in perceived support from teachers and other adults in the school (Green, Rhodes, Hirsch, Suarez-Orozco, & Camic, 2008). With regard to peers, when high school students perceive their peers as valuing school, they are more likely to be engaged in school as well (Kenny & Bledsoe, 2005). Qualities of peer relationships as early as third grade, including friendship quality, friend support, and level of peer aggression, correlate with school engagement in fifth grade (Perdue, Manzeske, & Estell, 2009). Experiences of racial discrimination at school are inversely related to school engagement (Dotterer, McHale, & Crouter, 2009). Neighborhood safety and moderate school size (less than 400 students per class) have also been positively related to student

engagement (Daly, Shin, Thakral, Selders, & Vera, 2009; Weiss, Carolan, & Baker-Smith, 2010).

At a broader level, societal inequities have been associated with school disaffection and disengagement. Fine, Burns, Payne, and Torre (2004) conducted focus groups with students attending poorly resourced schools across the elementary through high school grades. Fine et al. (2004) found that students were keenly aware of the social and economic inequities between the schools that they attended and those attended by more affluent youth. This awareness contributed, for many students, to feelings of anger, mistrust, shame, social cynicism, and alienation from school and civic matters.

As a whole, the body of research on school engagement, although correlational, highlights the need for educational reform to consider a range of ecological factors, including family, peers, social inequities, and students' understandings of those inequities, that affect students' engagement with learning. Although social justice demands effort to correct these inequities, consideration also needs to be given to ways to help students resist the negative effects of social and economic injustice.

Perception of Barriers

Concern for the role of social and economic inequality on school achievement and career development has spurred research examining the level and importance of perceived barriers to school success. Research on perceived barriers should be understood as assessing how individuals or groups internalize, understand, and are affected by the numerous real challenges to career development present in their environments (Constantine, Erikson, Banks, & Timberlake, 1998) rather than considering these perceptions as cognitive myths or distortions (Kenny et al., 2003). In comparison with European American students, McWhirter, Torres, Salgado and Valdez (2007) found that Mexican American high school students expected to encounter more barriers to pursuing postsecondary education and expected those barriers to be difficult to overcome. Furthermore, perceived educational barriers have been found to be inversely related to educational aspirations among Mexican American high school students, beyond the effects of gender, generational level, or parental level of education (Ojeda & Flores, 2008). Among ethnically and racially diverse urban high school students from low-income neighborhoods, a relationship of perceived family, financial, and societal barriers to school and job success with school engagement has also been demonstrated (Kenny et al., 2003; Kenny & Bledsoe, 2005). Systematic exposure to societal biases and inequities may contribute to school disinterest and a belief that one's efforts do not matter and will not be rewarded. Research examining the relationship between adolescents' perception of barriers and educational career progress has not been universally consistent, however (Lent, Brown, & Hackett, 2000; McWhirter et al., 2007). Among a sample of Mexican American girls, for example, McWhirter, Hackett, and Bandalos (1998) found that perceived educational and career barriers were not a predictor of postsecondary plans. Ali, McWhirter, and Chronister (2005) also failed to find a relationship between perceived barriers and postsecondary plans among European American high school students from lower socioeconomic backgrounds.

Racial Identity and Sociopolitical Development

The inconsistencies in studies focusing on barriers have led some researchers to postulate factors that might support youth in resisting or overcoming the potentially negative impact of barriers (Kenny et al., 2003). A positive ethnic or racial identity represents one individual factor that may help students to resist societally imposed negative stereotypes that can undermine academic interest and motivation (Nicolas, Helms, Jernigan, Sass, Skrzypek, & DeSilva, 2008; Spencer, 2005). Shin, Daly, and Vera (2007), for example, found among seventh- and eighth-grade students attending an urban public school that positive ethnic identity was associated with high levels of school engagement and resistance to negative peer norms. Chavous et al. (2003) followed over 600 African American youth for 2 years beginning in their senior year of high school and found that those students who regarded their race as positive and important were more likely than students with other racial identity patterns to have entered and remained in college.

These findings also converge with research documenting the protective value of sociopolitical development among students of color (Diemer, 2009; Diemer & Blustein, 2006; Watts & Flanagan, 2007). Sociopolitical development, coupled with personal agency and a means for collective action, may foster student achievement (Diemer & Blustein, 2006; Watts, Williams, & Jagers, 2003). According to Freire (1972), a process of *conscientization*, or analysis of the sources of oppression, is integral to reducing the psychological oppression that results when those who have been marginalized by society internalize a sense of inferiority and self-deprecation. Consistent with Freire's premise, research among students of color from low socioeconomic backgrounds reveals that critical consciousness of the reasons for structural inequalities and motivation to reduce this inequality are positively associated with vocational expectations and the view that work is important to one's future (Diemer & Hsieh, 2008; Diemer, Wang, Moore, Gregory, Hatcher, & Voigt, 2010).

Career Progress and School Engagement

With particular relevance to the topic of this chapter, research with urban high school youth reveals that career planfulness and positive career expectations contribute to an increase in school engagement over the course of the ninth grade (Kenny, Blustein, Haase, Jackson, & Perry, 2006). School engagement has also been positively associated among urban youth with career planfulness and racial identity (Perry, 2008). Career planfulness and work hope, including the presence of goals, thoughts about pathways or ways to achieve those goals, and the desire, confidence, or agency in one's capacity to achieve these goals, have also been associated among urban high school youth with adaptive achievement-related beliefs, including the enjoyment of learning, the belief that school is relevant to one's future, and feelings of confidence about one's capability to succeed at school (Kenny, Walsh-Blair, Blustein, Bempechat, & Seltzer, 2010). Perry et al. (2010) also found among a diverse sample of urban youth that career preparation, as assessed by career planning and career decision-making self-efficacy, mediated the effects of teacher support and parental career support on school engagement. In other words, support from parents and teachers contributed to career preparation, which in turn contributed to school engagement and academic achievement.

Not surprisingly, perhaps, many of the factors that contribute to school engagement also influence youth career progress. According to the Perry et al. (2010), study, for example, parental and teacher support contribute to career preparation. In other research (Kenny & Bledsoe, 2005; Metheny, McWhirter, & O'Neil, 2008), teacher support was positively related to career decision-making self-efficacy, vocational outcome expectations, and career planning and negatively associated with perceived educational barriers. Perceived parental support was positively related with career certainty and negatively associated with career indecision, with perceived occupational barriers having a negative relationship with career certainty and a positive relationship with indecision (Constantine, Wallace, & Kindaichi, 2005). The presence of supportive adults and the availability of work-based learning experiences have been identified as factors that prepare work-bound youth for the transition from school to work (Phillips, Blustein, Jobin-Davis, & White, 2002).

The interrelationships among teacher and family support, career planning, school engagement, and positive racial identity and critical consciousness, as evidenced in the above research, suggest that these factors should be considered in programmatic efforts to enhance the educational development and career preparation of American youth. The implications of motivational theory and research are considered next.

Academic Motivation

Efforts to understand the reasons for student disengagement and to increase engagement have been informed by theory and research focused on academic motivation. Although numerous motivational theories exist, I will consider several that have been given most attention in the literature pertaining to education and work in adolescents.

Self-determination theory (SDT; Ryan & Deci, 2000) focuses on social-contextual conditions that foster or suppress motivation. This theory is consistent with the psychology-of-working perspective (D. Blustein et al., 2008) in recognizing the salience of human needs for social connection and self-determination. Educational and work environments that provide opportunities for individuals to meet their basic psychological needs for relatedness and autonomy, as well as competence, are viewed as optimal for fostering motivation and self-regulation (Ryan & Deci, 2000). While satisfaction of these needs is important across the lifespan, these needs are particularly salient for adolescents, who are striving to increase autonomy and establish identity (Eccles & Midgley, 1989). Environments that provide both support and autonomy offer rules and structure but also provide some level of choice in selecting goals and strategies for achieving them (Newell & Van Ryzin, 2007). With regard to the need for competence in the school setting, the likelihood that students who are far behind academically and expect to fail will become unmotivated and disengaged is understandable. Research findings (e.g., Kenny & Bledsoe, 2005) that teacher, family, and peer support are positively related with school engagement

and career progress are also consistent with this theory. Critiques of the U.S. comprehensive high school as impersonal, rule-bound, and inattentive of student voice (Neild, 2009) add further evidence that the climate and structure of high schools may not be conducive to fostering school engagement and motivation among low-performing teens.

Expectancy-value theory (Wigfield & Eccles, 2000) postulates that achievement beliefs (e.g., self-perceptions of competence) and behaviors (e.g., persistence) are determined jointly by students' expectations for success and the perceived value of the task, including interest, importance, and perceived utility. Similar to SDT, expectancy-value theory offers a theoretical explanation as to why youth who experience consistent academic failure over time become disengaged. By recognizing the importance of success and utility to motivation, this theory also explains how students who view their academic learning as unimportant and unrelated to their future work life become bored, disinterested, and disengaged. Expectancy-value theory thus focuses on how competence and relevance affect motivation, but it neglects the roles of relatedness and autonomy highlighted by SDT.

Recent work derived from the perspective of positive psychology (Juntunen & Wettersten, 2006; Snyder, 2000) suggests that hope has a central role in fostering motivation and influencing human behavior. Snyder (2000) conceptualized hope as including the presence of goals, knowledge about pathways or ways to achieve those goals, and the desire, confidence, or agency in one's capacity to achieve these goals. This perspective is consistent with SDT and expectancy-value theory in recognizing the importance of perceived competence or efficacy and adds to those theories by highlighting the importance of goals and planning. Juntunen and Wettersten (2006) describe the relevance of hope in the vocational domain and suggest that identifying attainable career goals and the means for achieving them may foster motivation, while a lack of goals and unclear future possibilities may undermine motivation.

The above theoretical perspectives are consistent with a growing body of evidence linking academic development and career education. A number of studies, for example, support the application of SDT for understanding motivational processes for youth in school and work contexts. Kenny et al. (2010) found that students' perceptions of their teachers as providing both support and fostering autonomy were related to adaptive achievement-related beliefs, including feelings of academic competence and the desire to do well in school, both for its own sake and as a means to obtain a good job. In a study of middle school students attending urban public schools, Brogan (2010) found that students' levels of career progress were significantly associated with their expectations for school success and perceptions of school as valuable for the future, which were, in turn, related to their levels of school engagement. It thus appears that career progress may benefit middle school students by sustaining engagement in school through the mechanism of positive academic motivational beliefs. Also among middle school students attending high-poverty urban schools, Balfanz et al. (2007) found that students' perceptions of the utility of what they were learning at school, along with intrinsic interest, parental involvement, and teacher support, were related to attendance, behavior, and effort. The extent to which students' needs for autonomy, belonging, and competence are satisfied across multiple life contexts (e.g., school, home, peers, and work) has been related to their levels of psychological well-being and school adjustment (Milyavskaya et al., 2009).

Existing research has also documented positive relationships between student hope and achievement (Covington, 2000). High-hope students, for example, have been found to set challenging school-related goals and are likely to attain those goals even when they do not experience immediate success (Snyder, Shorey, Cheavens, Pulver, Adams, & Wiklund, 2002). Kenny et al. (2010) found, furthermore, that students' hope regarding their vocational futures was positively related to an understanding to the relevance of school, enjoyment of school, and confidence that they can do well in school. The construct of work hope may have heuristic value in explaining the relationship between career experience and achievement motivation. Work-based learning and career experiences may foster a sense of hope by helping youth to identify work goals, expand their understanding of how to reach those goals, and foster confidence in the likelihood of achieving those goals.

The Integrative Contextual Model of Career Development articulated by Lapan (2004) includes explicit attention to motivational factors. Lapan (2004) describes the importance of building hope and motivation for the future as part of efforts to empower young people across all social classes and ethnic/racial groups in realizing their desired futures. Consistent with SDT (Ryan & Deci, 2000), Lapan (2004) discusses the importance of experiences that explore and develop vocational interests as ways to enhance intrinsic motivation and to foster a sense of choice, purpose, and control among youth who may otherwise lack direction and interest in school. Experiences such as a career education, work-based learning, and comprehensive career development and counseling programs are expected to help youth develop career interests and goals, build self-mastery and hope, and increase attention and engagement in academic work that otherwise may seem boring and irrelevant. The integrative model focuses attention on six primary constructs emerging from career development research and practice that are intended to counteract internal and external barriers that prematurely limit vocational aspirations and expectations: (1) positive expectations for the future, (2) identity and goal development, (3) understanding of self and fit in the world of work, (4) the pursuit of intrinsic interests, (5) the ability to achieve academically and regulate one's attention and behavior in a learning environment, and (6) the development of work-readiness behaviors and the ability to make use of social support. Lapan's (2004) model was developed to provide a guide for practitioners that would integrate career development and motivational research and inform the development of theoretically based programs that integrate academic and career preparation at the K–12 level.

While educational reform and public policy are often formulated with insufficient attention to extant theory and research, the above reviews highlight scholarly evidence that should be considered in formulating new policy and practice. Fortunately, some promising educational models are emerging, which will be reviewed next.

Promising Whole-School Reform Models

One of the positive outcomes of educational reform as driven by NCLB has been the proliferation of new educational models at the high school level. Amidst these numerous efforts, a mounting body of evaluation evidence offers a "glimmer of hope" regarding some strategies for improving the academic development and work readiness of American youth (Fleischman & Heppen, 2009). A review of effective school reform approaches has identified some common elements believed to contribute to their success (Fleischman & Heppen, 2009). Programs with these elements show promise in engaging all students through high school and equipping them with skills for further learning, career, and involved citizenship. These elements include the presence of a personal, supportive, and orderly learning environment that attends to the social and emotional development of students, as well as their academic success. Effective schools have also been observed as offering instruction to help students who are behind to catch up, providing sound instructional practice and rigorous content for all students, and focusing on student preparation for either careers or postsecondary education or both. These elements are consistent with the educational and career theory and research reviewed in this chapter, and many integrate education and work preparation in innovative ways. Overall, these attributes affirm the notion that successful programs must consider contextual aspects of students' lives and must be designed with an understanding of the factors that support student motivation and engagement in their education.

The most comprehensive reform approaches seek to restructure whole schools to provide students with rigorous preparation for both college and the workplace. Whole-school reform initiatives began in the 1980s, increased in importance in the 1990s with support from Congress, and continue to be of interest, although they are not a focus of NCLB (Fleischman & Heppen, 2009). Several important models focus on the integration of academic and career preparation. Career academies, for example, originated in the 1970s as an alternative education strategy to prevent high school dropout (Grubb, 1995). In response to the 1980s critique of CTE for student tracking and inadequate academic preparation, career academies were expanded to provide college preparation and career awareness for students across the general high school population (Hooker & Brand, 2009). High Schools That Work (HSTW) was initiated in the 1990s by the Southern Regional Education Board (SREB) in efforts to improve CTE. Key components of the HSTW framework include upgrading the rigor of the academic core, providing academic and career guidance, and offering opportunities for CTE and academic teachers to collaborate in curriculum development (Wonacott, 2002). HSTW merged requirements for completing a college preparatory curriculum with completion of a planned sequence of career courses.

A number of contemporary approaches focus on the success of these earlier initiatives. For example, more than 2,500 career academies now exist in high schools across the country and continue to be an important element of many school reform initiatives. Although the specific themes and structures of career academies vary significantly, core components include academic and vocational curricula that focus on a broad career theme (e.g., Allied Health), partnerships with local employers who provide work-based learning opportunities, and a school-within-a school structure through which students and teachers participating in the same career theme or academy take several classes together each day (Hooker & Brand, 2009).

A solid body of evidence exists to support the impact of career academies on student outcomes. For example, an 11-year longitudinal experimental study of nine high schools across the country, conducted by MDRC (Kemple, 2008), showed especially positive results for students considered most at risk for high school dropout. Students attending career academies exhibited higher levels of school engagement and completion of the core high school academic curriculum and higher levels of post-high school earnings and employment than students attending non-academy schools. Although no impact was found for postsecondary enrollment or attainment, an unexpected positive outcome was that career academy students are more likely to be independent from their parents, to marry, and to be custodial parents at ages 22 to 26.

Several of the school models identified as most promising (Fleischman & Heppen, 2009) incorporate career academy components. Talent Development High Schools, for example, offer a freshman seminar and catch-up courses for ninth-grade students who enter the school behind grade level and career academies at the upper high school grades. Multiple Pathways in California (recently renamed as Linked Learning) also seeks to deliberately integrate college and career preparation. The model is described as following three research-based principles (Saunders & Chrisman, 2008): (1) learning is enhanced when academic and technical knowledge are integrated and practiced in real-life situations; (2) student interest and engagement are increased when academics are connected to real-work experiences; and (3) student college and career options are enhanced when students experience strong academic and career education. All students complete a college-preparatory academic core that includes project-based learning and emphasizes the relevance and application of academics to CTE. All students also complete a professional or technical knowledge core and demanding work-based learning, and are offered appropriate support services, such as supplemental instruction, counseling, and transportation. The work-based learning component is designed to support the academic and technical curriculum of the school and to develop increasingly sophisticated and complex skills across grade levels. By promoting both rigorous academic learning and career education, the Multiple Pathways model seeks to overcome the racial, ethnic and social class tracking that has been associated historically with vocational education (Oakes & Saunders, 2008). By providing opportunities to learn through multiple and contextually based methods (e.g., hands-on and project learning, cooperative learning), the Multiple Pathways model also strives to attend to the needs of ELLs and special education students. To effectively deliver this type of curriculum, teachers require special training for integrating academic and career knowledge (Saunders & Chrisman, 2008). While the principles that inform the Multiple Pathways model are evidence-based, schools developed from the model are now being studied, with promising evidence accruing (James Irvine Foundation, 2009). The Institute for Democracy, Education, and Access (IDEA) at the University of California Los Angeles (UCLA) (http://www.idea.gseis.ucla.edu) is conducting case studies of ten schools that have either successfully implemented the model or are moving toward full implementation. This research will seek to identify the conditions that contribute to successful Multiple Pathways schools and provide insights on effective implementation practices and challenges.

Many small learning communities, which have been designed to increase student support and personalization by breaking down larger schools into smaller theme-based schools or by creating new small schools, include freshman and career academies, as well as specialty academies. Specialty academies may offer a particular academic or curriculum focus, such as science, technology, or engineering. These specialties may be related to potential careers and emphasize both rigor and relevance but do not necessarily include work-based learning. Research on the overall effectiveness of these small learning communities has been mixed, suggesting that a small and personal learning environment is a necessary but insufficient condition for student learning (Fleischman & Heppen, 2009). This conclusion is not surprising given the research reviewed earlier in this chapter that revealed the importance of both teacher support and career school connection for student engagement in school. Small learning communities appear to reduce student alienation, decrease absenteeism and suspension, and increase student autonomy and engagement, but may not enhance student achievement if the curriculum is not strong.

Dual enrollment programs, which allow high school students to take college courses and earn credits toward a college degree while still in high school, have also grown in recent years. Although these programs were first created for high-achieving students, they are now becoming more common as a means of adding rigor to the high school curriculum for a broad range of students. Most dual enrollment programs are also designed to create a personal learning experience and incorporate "advisories" or other types of mentoring experiences to provide support and guidance for students. These programs have not been subject to the rigorous evaluation of career academies, but correlational studies suggest promising trends (Fleischman & Heppen, 2009). The opportunity for a critical mass of high school students to take college courses while still in high school is believed to build a college-going culture at the school and reinforce student beliefs that they can fit in and succeed at college.

Although career development interventions may be neglected in schools where college preparation is prioritized, the Inquiry School in New York City was designed to serve academically at-risk students, ELLs, and others students who may not typically expect to attend college by combining early college experience with a Career Institute that strives to foster career development competencies (Rivera & Schaefer, 2009). The decision to integrate academic and career development programming was derived from the research demonstrating links between career development intervention and personal, social, and academic success and the importance of understanding the importance of school for career success (Kenny et al., 2006; Lapan, Aoyagi, & Kayson, 2007). The Career Institute curriculum is developed collaboratively by the school counselor, teachers, and college faculty and is delivered by teachers in advisory groups. The advisory group meets daily and is intended to remain with the same teacher over the 7 years of school. At the middle school level, the curriculum focuses on student self-awareness and understanding the relationship between school and work. The high school level focuses more heavily on the acquisition of career information, college and career planning and college decision making. This program thus strives to incorporate a number of the effective elements of educational reform noted by Fleischman and Heppen (2009), including personalization, a strong curriculum, and preparation for higher education and career, although the effectiveness of this specific program has not been rigorously assessed over time.

Career Development Intervention

In addition to comprehensive school reform and redesign efforts, efforts to integrate education and work in American high schools also occur through a variety of career development interventions, which vary based on focus, duration, location, and scope. Such interventions may constitute advising, with a focus on academic planning, career counseling, and the promotion of personal and career awareness and planfulness. They may also include intermittent or sustained interactions with community worksites (e.g., internships, job shadowing, job coaching, mentorship) or may be delivered through a school-based curriculum designed to complement a work-based intervention (e.g., career information or career skills infused into curriculum, Tech Prep curriculum) (Dykeman, Ingram, Wood, Charles, Chen, & Herr, 2001).

Although a comprehensive developmental model of guidance is considered optimal (Gysbers, 2004), a number of focused guidance interventions have been developed to address some of the specific issues identified in the research literature as undermining the academic and career motivation of youth of color, particularly in low-income neighborhoods. Some of these interventions constitute the type of connecting activities recommended for helping students to understand the relationship between school and their vocational futures (D. L. Blustein et al., 2000). Although most of these specific programs have not been subject to the rigorous longitudinal evaluation of whole school reform approaches, such as career academies, modest data suggest some success, which should be assessed through further study. The literature assessing the effects of career education and career development programming across varied programs suggest positive impacts on career planning indices (Hughes & Karp, 2004) and high school graduation and college attendance (Visher, Bhandari, & Medrich, 2004), with costs and efforts much less than whole-school reform. Thus, I encourage further research on career intervention both as a component of whole-school reform models and as a separate entity.

With regard to specific programs, Achieving Success Identity Pathways (ASIP) (Howard & Solberg, 2006; Solberg, Howard, Blustein, & Close, 2002) was developed as a culturally relevant intervention to enhance youth motivation. The curriculum seeks to empower youth to challenge oppressive societal messages about the self and the world and to create identities of success. As part of the curriculum, students share their stories, identify challenges they face in school, set short- and long-term academic and work goals, learn about the world of work, and develop skills in interpersonal and conflict resolution. The expectation is that as students come to better understand how their social context shapes their behavior, they can gain more power and control over their choices. Evaluation results for the eight-session intervention are encouraging, with findings revealing that exposure to the program is related among low-income, ninth- and tenth-grade students with higher grades, higher attendance, fewer suspensions, and more classes passed and credits earned (Howard & Solberg, 2006). More extensive long-term follow-up with a comparison group is needed to further assess the impact of this intervention.

The Choices Program (Vera, Caldwell, Clarke, Gonzales, Morgan, & West, 2007) was also designed as a culturally relevant and responsive intervention with the intention of promoting positive identity development, social and academic efficacy and efficacy in responding effectively to peer pressure, and enhanced academic and career aspirations. Students are assisted in examining social barriers, developing organizational and study skills, and increasing knowledge of community-based academic resources. The eight-session program delivered to seventh- and eighth-grade urban public school students was developed after consulting existing research literature and conducting focus groups with students, parents, and teachers. A three-session parent program and a two-session teacher consultation complement the student program. Formative evaluation has informed ongoing modification and improvement of the program over the 9 academic years it has been offered, with summative evaluation documenting increases in student social efficacy. Although feedback from participants suggests that the program is beneficial, the program developers have not been able to arrange for a comparison group or to collect long-term academic outcomes.

Tools-for-Tomorrow (Kenny, Sparks, & Jackson, 2007; Solberg et al., 2002) was also designed specifically for low-income students of color with the goal of enhancing academic motivation by helping youth to internalize the connection between their current and future academic studies and their vocational futures. The weekly year-long curriculum includes three interrelated units focusing on self-exploration and identity, career exploration, and identification of resources and barriers. Although program evaluation data are limited, evidence suggests that program participants understand the connections between school and their vocational futures and gain more sophisticated articulation of their goals (D. L. Blustein et al., 2010; Perry, DeWine, Duffy, & Vance, 2007). Programmatic research also reveals that student career planning and career expectations contribute to increases in school engagement over the course of the curriculum (Kenny et al., 2006).

With awareness of the potential negative impact of perceived school and work barriers for the academic motivation of low-income inner-city youth and the adaptive impact of perceived resources (Kenny et al., 2003), Jackson, Kacanski, Rust, and Beck (2006) developed two 2-hour workshops for low-income, inner-city, mostly Black and Latino/Latina youth in grades 8 and 9. The workshops focused on learning about occupations, examining beliefs about the value of education for career rewards, and increasing awareness of personal and contextual supports for reaching their educational and career goals. Evaluation results reveal that students who perceived more school and work barriers had lower educational and career aspirations. Students' awareness of external resources (e.g., family, friends, teachers, coaches, counselors, program staff) to assist them in overcoming these barriers was increased through the brief intervention, although the impact of this change on future behavior or achievement was not examined.

McWhirter, Rasheed, and Crothers (2000) developed a 9-week career education course that was delivered to urban high school youth, largely European American, in a Midwestern U.S. city. After the course, students demonstrated increased outcome expectations and self-efficacy beliefs for career decision-making and vocational skills in comparison with a control sample. Although the researchers had expected that the experiential nature of the class would increase students' confidence in overcoming barriers to their career progress, this was not evidenced. The intervention did not give explicit attention to analyzing societal barriers, however. Given their European American status, most of the students in this sample were not contending with barriers associated with racial discrimination. Contrary to other research with more ethnically and racially diverse students (e.g., Kenny et al., 2003), perceived barriers were unrelated to career outcome expectations. The integration of contextual barriers in career education warrants further research attention.

Conclusion

The success of the U.S. education system is critical to the future economic vitality of our nation and to the well-being and prosperity of its citizens. Structural and systemic inequities underlie the lagging achievement of our nation's poorest youth, many who are recent immigrants and members of oppressed minority groups. I argue, however, that an effective and successful education can provide all youth with skills to fully participate in civic and work spheres of society. While education reform has occupied national attention over the past several decades, recent efforts have been disappointing, with high school graduation rates for African American, Hispanic, and Native American students being reported at just over 60% (Balfanz et al., 2010). I have argued that much recent educational reform has been misguided by not attending sufficiently to the contexts of children's lives and to psychological research on school engagement and motivation, including research on the impacts of racism and poverty and adaptive coping mechanisms.

Given the tremendous challenges that confront U.S. education and the U.S. labor market, it would be naïve to believe that any one educational model could address all of these challenges (Fleischman & Heppen, 2009). Yet attention to psychological research and evaluation evidence can guide the further development and adaptation of existing models, building on "glimmers of hope" (Fleischman & Heppen, 2009). An emphasis on testing and accountability has not been generally successful and has contributed to a loss of educational programs that promote the full development of students. Based upon a review of promising programs, I have argued that work-based learning and career education may be one component of education that can serve to enhance student engagement, motivation, and ultimately achievement. I state this with recognition that a broad range of educational activities, including art, music, and physical education, that are integral to student interest and engagement in school have been sacrificed in many school districts to focus on test preparation. These components of the curriculum are ultimately important not only for student engagement, but also for developing the type of creative and flexible thinking needed in the 21st-century workplace. Work-based learning and career education are not simple or complete solutions to the educational challenges faced by this nation. Indeed, if it is to have a broad and lasting impact, education reform must be accompanied by policies and programs that create fair labor laws and access to adequate healthcare and housing and counter residential segregation and poverty (Saunders & Chrisman, 2008).

Education reform at the secondary level must also consider the type of college or postsecondary experience that we advocate for all young people. Post-high school certificate programs of at least 1 year can offer academic and technical rigor, build a variety of job skills, and offer incomes equivalent to those with associate degrees (Gonzalez, 2010). While some post-high school education is needed to achieve 21st-century work-based skills and middle-class incomes, a bachelor's degree is not essential. One out of five persons with a vocational associate of arts degree earns more than workers with a bachelor's degree, and 14% earn more than those with graduate degrees. Career and technical education at the high school level may also benefit some students. Students who take CTE courses in high school are actually more likely to attend college than similar students who do not take CTE. Among those who do not go on to college, students who completed some CTE had higher earnings than students without CTE (Stern, 2009). In our zeal to prepare all students for college and career, it is wise to consider the value of technical training that is not offered in 4-year college settings. The interests of students and the needs of the labor market suggest that multiple pathways should be offered at the secondary and postsecondary levels.

Future Directions

Advancing efforts to promote the integration of career education and academic development, especially at the secondary level, will require considerable work. Besides the research on career academies, more rigorous research is needed to provide a compelling case for incorporating career education and work-based learning in the educational reform agenda. Although the research on career development and school engagement is informative, it is largely correlational and does not identify proven interventions for effecting change. Research that follows the gold standard of random assignment, follow-up with objective measures over the long term, and comparisons of alternative models is clearly needed to provide convincing evidence for public officials and policymakers. Research is also needed that demonstrates how to extend programs that have been shown to be effective in one setting to another setting. Consistent with current public policy initiatives, we need to examine the best strategies for expanding programs and identify the sites, conditions, and populations for whom they work best (Granger, 2010). Education is influenced by a complex array of factors, which need to be examined and considered both generally and in depth. Qualitative research can complement large-scale studies in elucidating the processes that influence program outcomes. Although the search for fast solutions can lead policymakers to embrace untried solutions and reject prior efforts, I believe that the "glimmers of hope" identified in prior evaluation need to be pursued to identify when they work and with whom and how they might be modified to extend their benefit. For psychologists interested in education and career development, the challenge is compelling and great.

In addition to program evaluation, vocational psychologists can bring their skills and experience to the development and enhancement of career intervention programs, especially for those low-income students and students of color who are still being left behind. A social justice concern for improving the lives of these youth should also propel psychologists to engage in public advocacy. We need to make sure that knowledge in psychology pertaining to education, career development, race, and culture is made known to the public and policy leaders so that educational policy and reform are formulated with this wisdom.

References

ACT (2010). *A first look at the Common Core and college and career readiness*. Retrieved from: http://www.act.org/news/data/

Ali, S. R., McWhirter, E. H., & Chronister, K. M. (2005). Self-efficacy and vocational outcome expectations for adolescents of lower socioeconomic status: A pilot study. *Journal of Career Assessment, 13*, 40–58. doi: 10.1177/1069072704270273

Balfanz, R. (2009). Can the American high school become an avenue of advancement for all? *Future of Children, 19*, 17–36. doi: 10.1353/foc.0.0025

Balfanz, R., Bridgeland, J. M., Moore, L. A., & Fox, J. H. (2010). Building a grad nation: Progress and challenge in ending the high school dropout epidemic. Retrieved from: http://civicenterprises.net/pdfs/gradnation.pdf

Balfanz, R., Herzog, L., & Mac Iver, D. (2007). Preventing student disengagement and keeping student on the graduation path in urban middle-grades schools: Early identification and effective interventions. *Educational Psychologist, 42*, 223–235.

Baum, S., & Ma, J. (2007). *Education pays: The benefits of higher education for individuals and society*. Washington, DC: The College Board.

Blustein, D. L., Juntunen, C. L., & Worthington, R. L. (2000). The school-to-work transition: Adjustment challenges of the forgotten half. In S. D. Brown & R. W. Lent (Eds.), *Handbook of counseling psychology* (3rd ed., pp. 435–470). Hoboken, NJ: John Wiley & Sons Inc.

Blustein, D., Kenna, A., Gil, N., & DeVoy, J. (2008). The psychology of working: A new framework for counseling practice and public policy. *Career Development Quarterly, 56*, 294–308.

Blustein, D. L., Murphy, K. A., Kenny, M. E., Jernigan, M., Pérez-Gualdrón, L., Castañeda, T., Koepke, M., et al. (2010). Exploring urban students' constructions about school, work, race, and ethnicity. *Journal of Counseling Psychology, 57,* 248–254. doi: 10.1037/a0018939

Brogan, D. T. (2010). *Stuck in the middle: Career progress, motivation, and engagement among urban middle school students.* Unpublished doctoral dissertation, Boston College, MA. Publication No. AAT 3397764. Retrieved from Boston College Library Digital Collections.

Bureau of Labor Statistics. (2008). *Occupational projections and training data* (2008–9 ed., p. 4, Table 1–3). Washington, DC: U.S. Department of Labor.

Bureau of Labor Statistics. (2010). *Labor force characteristics by race and ethnicity, 2009.*Washington, DC: U.S. Department of Labor. Retrieved from http://www.bls.gov/cps/cpsrace2009.pdf.

Chavous, T. M., Bernat, D. H., Schmeelk-Cone, K., Caldwell, C., Kohn-Wood, L. P., & Zimmerman, M. A. (2003). Racial identity and academic attainment among African American adolescents. *Child Development, 74,* 1076–1090. doi: 10.1111/1467-8624.00593

Close, W., & Solberg, S. (2008). Predicting achievement, distress, and retention among lower-income Latino youth. *Journal of Vocational Behavior, 72,* 31–42. doi: 10.1016/j.jvb.2007.08.007

Cochran-Smith, M., Gleeson, A. M., & Mitchell, K. (2010). Teacher education for social justice: What's pupil learning got to do with it? *Berkeley Review of Education,1*(1), 35–61. Retrieved from http://escholarship.org/uc/ucbgse_bre

Constantine, M. G., Erikson, C. D., Banks, R. W., & Timberlake, T. L. (1998). Challenges to the career development of urban racial and ethnic minority youth: Implications for vocational intervention. *Journal of Multicultural Counseling and Development, 26,* 83–95.

Constantine, M. G., Wallace, B. C., & Kindaichi, M. M. (2005). Examining contextual factors in the career decision status of African American Adolescents. *Journal of Career Assessment, 13*(3), 307–319. doi: 10.1177/1069072705274960

Covington, M. V. (2000). Goal theory, motivation, and school achievement: An integrative review. *Annual Review of Psychology, 51,* 171–200. doi: 10.1146/annurev.psych.51.1.171

Daly, B. P., Shin, R. Q., Thakral, C., Selders, M., & Vera, E. (2009). School engagement among urban adolescents of color: Does perception of social support and neighborhood safety really matter? *Journal of Youth and Adolescence. 38,* 63–74. doi: 10.1007/s10964-008-9294-7

Darling-Hammond, L. (2006). No Child Left Behind and high school reform. *Harvard Educational Review, 76,* 642–667.

Diemer, M. A. (2009). Pathways to occupational attainment among poor youth of color: The role of sociopolitical development. *Counseling Psychologist. 37,* 6–35. doi: 10.1177/0011000007309858

Diemer, M. A., & Blustein, D. L. (2006). Critical consciousness and career development among urban youth. *Journal of Vocational Behavior, 68,* 220–232. doi:10.1016/j.jvb.2005.07.001

Diemer, M. A., & Hsieh, C. (2008). Sociopolitical development and vocational expectations among lower socioeconomic status adolescents of color. *Career Development Quarterly, 56,* 257–267.

Diemer, M. A., Wang, Q., Moore, T., Gregory, S. R., Hatcher, K. M., & Voigt, A. M. (2010). Sociopolitical development,

work salience, and vocational expectations among low socioeconomic status African American, Latin American, and Asian American youth. *Developmental Psychology, 46,* 619–635. doi: 10.1037/a0017049

Dotterer, A., McHale, S.M., & Crouter, A. C. (2009). Sociocultural factors and school engagement among African American youth: The roles of racial discrimination, racial socialization, and ethnic identity. *Applied Developmental Science, 13,* 61–73. doi: 10.1080/10888690902801442

Dykeman, C., Ingram, M., Wood, C., Charles, S., Chen, M. Y., & Herr, E. (2001). *The taxonomy of career development interventions that occur in America's secondary schools.* University of North Carolina at Greensboro, NC: ERIC Clearinghouse on Counseling and Student Services. (ERIC Document Reproduction Service No. ED 475259.)

Eccles, J. S., & Midgley, C. (1989). Stage-environment fit: Developmentally appropriate classrooms for young adolescents. In C. Ames & R. Ames (Eds.), *Research on motivation in education* (pp. 139–186). New York: Academic Press.

Freire, P. (1972). *Pedagogy of the oppressed.* New York: Penguin Books.

Fine, M., Burns, A., Payne, Y., & Torre, M. (2004). Civic lessons: The color of class betrayal. *Teachers College Record, 106,* 2193–2223. doi: 10.1111/j.1467-9620.2004.00433.x

Fine, M., Jaffe-Walter, R., Pedraza, P., Futch, V., & Stoudt, B. (2007). Swimming on oxygen, resistance, and possibility for immigrant youth under siege. *Anthropology and Education Quarterly. 38,* 79–96.

Fleischman, H. L., Hopstock, P. J., Pelczar, M. P., & Shelley, B. E. (2010). *Highlights from PISA 2009: Performance of U.S. 15-year-old students in reading, mathematics, and science literacy in an international context (NCES 20111–004).* U.S. Department of Education, National Center for Education Statistics. Washington, DC: U.S. Government Printing Office.

Fleischman, S., & Heppen, J. (2009). Improving low-performing high schools: Searching for evidence of promise. *Future of Children, 19,* 105–133. doi: 10.1353/foc.0.0021

Fredricks, J. A., Blumenfeld, P. C., & Paris, A. H. (2004). School engagement: Potential of the concept, state of the evidence. *Review of Educational Research, 74,* 59–109. doi: 10.3102/00346543074001059

Granger, R. C. (2010). Learning from scale-up initiatives. *Education Week, 30,* 26–27.

Green, G., Rhodes, J., Heitler Hirsch, A., Suárez-Orozco, C., & Camic, P. M. (2008). Supportive adult relationships and the academic engagement of Latin American immigrant youth. *Journal of School Psychology, 46,* 393–412. doi: 10.1016/j.jsp.2007.07.001

Grubb, W. N. (1995). *Education through occupations in American high school: Approaches to integrating academic and vocational education.* New York: Teachers College Press.

Gonzalez, J. (2010). Certificate programs could play a key role in meeting the nation's educational goals. *Chronicle of Higher Education.* Retrieved from http://chronicle.com/article/Certificate-Programs-Could/125633/.

Good, T. L., & McCaslin, M. (2008). What we learned about research on school reform: Considerations for practice and policy. *Teachers College Record, 110,* 2475–2495. Retrieved from http://www.tcrecord.org

Grubb, W. N., & Oakes, J. (2007). *Restoring value to the high school diploma: Rhetoric and practice of higher standards.* Boulder, CO, and Tempe, AZ: Education and the

Public Interest Center & Education Policy Research Unit. Retrieved from http://www.epicpolicy.org/files/EPSL-0710–242-EPRU2.pdf.

Gysbers, N. C. (2004). The evolution of the Missouri Comprehensive Guidance Program. *Counseling Interviewer*, *36*, 9–12.

Hage, S., Romano, J., Conyne, R., Kenny, M., Matthews, C., Schwartz, J., & Waldo, M. (2007). Best Practice guidelines on prevention in practice, research, training, and social advocacy for psychologists. *Counseling Psychologist*, *35*, 493–566. doi: 10.1177 /0011000006291411

Hargreaves, A., & Shirley, D. (2009). *The fourth way: The inspiring future for educational change*. Thousand Oaks, CA: Corwin.

Haskins, R., & Kemple, J. (2009). A new goal for America's high schools: College preparation for all. *Future of Children Policy Brief*, *19*, 1–8.

Hooker, S., & Brand, B. (2009). *Success at every step: How 23 programs support youth on the path to college and beyond*. Retrieved from http://www.aypf.org/publications/SuccessAtEveryStep.htm

Howard, K. A., & Solberg, V. S. (2006). School-based social justice: The achieving success identity pathways program. *Professional School Counseling*, *9*(4), 278–287.

Hughes, K. L., Bailey, T. R., & Mechur, M. J. (2001). *School-to-Work: Making a Difference in Education. A Research Report to America*. New York: Institute on Education and the Economy. Retrieved from http://www.tc.columbia.edu/iee/PAPERS/Stw.pdf.

Hughes, K. L., & Karp, M. M. (2004). *School-based career development: A synthesis of the literature*. New York: Institute on Education and the Economy. Retrieved from http://www.tc.columbia.edu/iee/PAPERS/CareerDevelopment02_04.pdf.

Jackson, M. A., Kacanski, J. M., Rust, J. P., & Beck, S. E. (2006). Constructively challenging diverse inner-city youth's beliefs about educational and career barriers and supports. *Journal of Career Development*, *32*, 203–218. doi: 10.1177/0894845305279161

James Irvine Foundation (2009). *Making progress through California Multiple Pathways*. Los Angeles, CA: Author.

Jerald, C. (2009). *Defining a 21st-century education*. Alexandria, VA: Center for Public Education. Retrieved from: http://www.centerforpubliceducation.org/atf/cf/%7B00a4f2e8-f5da-4421-aa25-3919c06b542b%7D/21ST%20CENTURY[1].JERALD.PDF

Juntunen, C. L., & Wettersten, K. B. (2006). Work hope: Development and initial validation of a measure. *Journal of Counseling Psychology*, *53*, 94–106. doi: 10.1037/0022-0167.53.1.94

Kemple, J. J. (2008). *Career academies: Long-term impacts on labor market outcomes, educational attainment, and transitions to adulthood*. New York: Manpower Demonstration Research Corporation.

Kenny, M., & Bledsoe, M. (2005). Contributions of the relational context to career adaptability among urban adolescents. *Journal of Vocational Behavior 66*, 257–272. doi:10.1016/j.jvb.2004.10.002

Kenny, M. E., Blustein, D. L., Chaves, A., Grossman, J., & Gallagher, L. (2003). The role of perceived barriers and relational support in educational and vocational lives of urban high school students. *Journal of Counseling Psychology*, *50*, 142–155. doi: 10.1037/0022-0167.50.2.142

Kenny, M. E., Blustein, D. L., Haase, R. F., Jackson, J., & Perry, J. C. (2006). Setting the stage: Career development and the student engagement process. *Journal of Counseling Psychology*, *53*, 272–279. doi:10.1037/0022-0167.53.2.272

Kenny, M. E., Sparks, E., & Jackson, J. (2007). Striving for social justice through interprofessional university school collaboration. In E. Aldarondo (Ed.), *Advancing social justice through clinical practice* (pp. 313–335). Mahwah, NJ: Erlbaum.

Kenny, M. E., Walsh-Blair, L., Blustein, D. L., Bempechat, J., & Seltzer, J. (2010). Achievement motivation among urban adolescents: Work hope, autonomy support, and achievement related beliefs. *Journal of Vocational Behavior*, *77*, 205–212 doi:10.1016/j.jvb.2010.02.005

Kliebard, H.M. (1999). *Schooled to work. Vocationalism and the American curriculum, 1876–1946*. Reflective Histories Series. New York: Teachers College Press.

Lapan, R. T. (2004). *Career development across the K-16 years: Bridging the present to satisfying and successful futures*. Alexandria, VA: American Counseling Association.

Lapan, R. T., Aoyagi, M., & Kayson, M. (2007). Helping rural adolescents make successful postsecondary transitions: A longitudinal study. *Professional School Counseling*, *10*, 266–272.

Lent, R. W., Hackett, G., & Brown, S. D. (2000). Contextual supports and barriers to career choice: a social cognitive analysis. *Journal of Counseling Psychology*, *47*, 36–49. doi: 10.1037/0022-0167.47.1.36

MacAllum, K., & Bozick, R. (2001). *What happens after they graduate? Results from a longitudinal study of STC graduates*. Paper presented at the Association for Career and Technical Educational Annual Conference, New Orleans, LA. Retrieved from http://www.eric.ed.gov.proxy.bc.edu/PDFS/ED462598.pdf.

McWhirter, E. H., Hackett, G., & Bandalos, D. L. (1998). A causal model of the educational plans and career expectations of Mexican American high school girls. *Journal of Counseling Psychology*, *45*, 166–181. doi: 10.1037/0022-0167.45.2.166

McWhirter, E. H., Rasheed, S., & Crothers, M. (2000). The effects of high school career education on social-cognitive variables. *Journal of Counseling Psychology*, *47*, 330–341. doi: 10.1037/0022-0167.47.3.330

McWhirter, E. H., Torres, D. M., Salgado, S., & Valdez, M. (2007). Perceived barriers and postsecondary plans in Mexican American and White adolescents. *Journal of Career Assessment*, *15*, 119–138. doi: 10.1177/1069072706294537

Metheny, J., McWhirter, E. H., & O'Neil, M. E. (2008). Measuring perceived teacher support and its influence on adolescent career development. *Journal of Career Assessment*, *16*, 218–237. doi: 10.1177/1069072707313198

Milyavskaya, M., Gingras, I., Mageau, G. A., Koestner, R., Gagnon, H., Fang, J., & Boiché, J. (2009). Balance across contexts: Importance of balanced need satisfaction across various life domains. *Personality and Social Psychology Bulletin*, *35*, 1031–1045. doi:10.1177/0146167209337036

Mortimer, J. T. (2003). *Working and growing up in America*. Cambridge, MA: Harvard University Press.

Murray, C. (2009). Parent and teacher relationships as predictors of school engagement and functioning among low-income urban youth. *Journal of Early Adolescence*, *29*, 376–404. doi: 10.1177/0272431608322940

National Center for Education Statistics (2009). *The Nation's Report Card: Mathematics 2009* (NCES 2010–451). Washington, DC: Author.

National Center on Education and the Economy. (2007). *Tough choices or tough times: The report of the new commission on the skills of the American work force.* Washington, DC: Author.

National Commission on Excellence in Education. (1983). A nation at risk: The imperative for school reform. *Elementary School Journal, 84,* 112–130.

Neild, R. C. (2009). Falling off track during the transition to high school: what we know and what can be done. *Future of Children, 19,* 53–76. doi: 10.1353/foc.0.0020

Newell, R. J., & Van Ryzin, M. J. (2007). Growing hope as a determinant of school effectiveness. *Phi Delta Kappan, 88,* 465.

Nicolas, G., Helms, J. E., Jernigan, M. M., Sass, T., Skrzypek, A., & DeSilva, A. M. (2008). A conceptual framework for understanding the strengths of black youths. *Journal of Black Psychology, 34,* 261–280. doi: 10.1177/0095798408316794

Oakes, J., & Saunders, M. (2008). *Beyond tracking: Multiple pathways to college, career, and civic participation.* Cambridge, MA: Harvard Education Press.

Ojeda, L., & Flores, L.Y. (2008). The influence of gender, generation level, parents' education level and perceived barriers on the educational aspirations of Mexican American high school students. *Career Development Quarterly, 57,* 84–95.

Olson, L. (1997). *The school-to-work revolution.* Reading, MA: Perseus Books.

Orfield, G. (2004). Losing our future: Minority children left out. In G. Orfield (Ed.), *Dropouts in America: Confronting the graduating rate crisis* (pp. 1–11). Cambridge, MA: Harvard Education Press.

Partnership for 21st Century Skills. (2008). *21st century skills, education & competitiveness.* Tucson, AZ: Author.

Perdue, N. H., Manzeske, D. P., & Estell, D. B. (2009). Early predictors of school engagement: Exploring the role of peer relationships. *Psychology in the Schools, 46,* 1084–1097. doi: 10.1002/pits.20446

Perry, J. C. (2008). School engagement among urban youth of color: Criterion pattern effects of vocational exploration and racial identity. *Journal of Career Development, 34,* 397–422. doi: 10.1177/0894845308316293

Perry, J. C., DeWine, D. B., Duffy, R. D., & Vance, K. S. (2007). The academic self-efficacy of urban youth: A mixed-methods study of a school-to-work program. *Journal of Career Development, 34,* 103–126. doi: 10.1177/0894845307307470

Perry, J. C., Liu, X., & Pabian, Y. (2010). School engagement as a mediator of academic performance among urban youth: The role of career preparation, parent career support, and teacher support. *Counseling Psychologist, 38,* 269–295. doi: 10.1177/0011000009349272

Phillips, S. D., Blustein, D. L., Jobin-Davis, K., & White, S. F. (2002). Preparation for the school-to-work transition: The views of high school students. *Journal of Vocational Behavior, 61,* 202–216. doi:10.1006/jvbe.2001.1853

Prilleltensky, I. (2001). Value-based praxis in community psychology: Moving toward social justice and social action. *American Journal of Community Psychology, 29,* 747–778. doi: 10.1023/A:1010417201918

Prilleltensky, I., Dokecki, P., Frieden, G., & Wang, V. O. (2007). Counseling for wellness and justice: Foundations and ethical dilemmas. In E. Aldarondo (Ed.), *Advancing social justice through clinical practice* (pp. 19–42). Mahwah, NJ: Lawrence Erlbaum.

Prilleltensky, I., & Nelson, G. (1997). Community psychology: Reclaiming social justice. In D. Fox & I. Prilleltensky (Eds.), *Critical psychology: An introduction* (pp. 166–184) London: Sage.

Rivera, L. M., & Schaefer, M. B. (2009). The Career Institute. A collaborative career development program for traditionally underserved secondary (6–12) school students. *Journal of Career Development, 35,* 406–426. doi: 10.1177/0894845308327737

Ryan, R. M., & Deci, E. L. (2000). Self-determination theory and the facilitation of intrinsic motivation, social development, and well-being. *American Psychologist, 55,* 68–78. doi: 10.1037/0003-066X.55.1.68

Saunders, M., & Chrisman, C. A. (2008). *Multiple pathways: 21st century high schools that prepare all students for college, career and civic participation.* Boulder, CO, and Tempe, AZ: Education and the Public Interest Center & Education Policy Research Unit. Retrieved from http://epicpolicy.org/files/MP%20legislation%20Final.pdf.

Shaker, P. (2010). Fighting the education wars, metaphorically. *Teachers College Record.* Retrieved from http:// www.tcrecord.org ID Number 16232.

Shin, R., Daly, B., & Vera, E. (2007). The relationships of peer norms, ethnic identity, and peer support to school engagement in urban youth. *Professional School Counseling, 10,* 379–388.

Simons-Morton, B., & Chen, R. (2009). Peer and parent influences on school engagement among early adolescents. *Youth and Society, 41,* 3–25. doi: 10.1177/0044118X09334861

Sirin, S. R., & Rogers-Sirin, L. (2005). Components of school engagement among African American adolescents. *Applied Development Science, 9,* 5–13. doi: 10.1207/s1532480xads0901_2

Snyder, C. R. (2000). The past and possible futures of hope. *Journal of Social & Clinical Psychology Special Issue: Classical Sources of Human Strength: A Psychological Analysis, 19,* 11–28.

Snyder, C. R., Shorey, H. S., Cheavens, J., Pulvers, K. M., Adams, V. H., III, & Wiklund, C. (2002). Hope and academic success in college. *Journal of Educational Psychology, 94*(4), 820–826. doi: 10.1037/0022-0663.94.4.820

Solberg, V. S., Howard, K. A., Blustein, D. L., & Close, W. (2002). Career development in the schools: Connecting school-to-work-to life. *Counseling Psychologist, 30,* 705–725. doi: 10.1177/0011000002305003

Spencer, M. B. (2005). Crafting identities and accessing opportunities post-*Brown. American Psychologist, 60,* 821–830. doi: 10.1037/0003-066X.60.8.821

Stern, D. (2009). Expanding policy options for educating teenagers. *Future of Children, 19,* 211–239. doi: 10.1353/foc.0.0027

Tyler, J. H., & Lofstrom, M. (2009). Finishing high school: Alternative pathways and dropout recovery. *Future of Children, 19,* 77–103. doi: 10.1353/foc.0.0019

Tyson, K., Darity, W., & Castellino, D. (2005). It's not a "black thing": Understanding the burden of acting white and other dilemmas of high achievement. *American Sociological Review, 70,* 582–605. doi: 10.1177/000312240507000403

Vera, E. M., Caldwell, J., Clarke, M., Gonzales, R., Morgan, M., & West, M. (2007). The Choices program: Multisystemic interventions for enhancing the personal and academic effectiveness of urban adolescents of color. *Counseling Psychologist, 35,* 779–796. doi: 10.1177/0011000007304590

Visher, M. G., Bhandari, R., & Medrich, E. (2004). High school career exploration programs: Do they work? *Phi Delta Kappan, 86,* 135–138.

Voelkl, K. E., & Frone, M. R. (2000). Predictors of substance use at school among high school students. *Journal of Educational Psychology*, *92*(3), 583–592. doi: 10.1037/0022-0663.92.3.583

Watts, R. J., & Flanagan, C. (2007). Pushing the envelope on youth civic engagement: A developmental and liberation psychology perspective. *Journal of Community Psychology*, *35*, 779–792. doi: 10.1002/jcop.20178

Watts, R. J., Williams, N. C., & Jagers, R. J. (2003). Sociopolitical development. *American Journal of Community Psychology*, *31*, 185–194. doi: 10.1023/A:1023091024140

Weis, L., & Dimitriadis, G. (2008). Dueling banjos: Shifting economic and cultural contexts in the lives of youth. *Teachers College Record*, *110*, 2290–2316. Retrieved from http://www.tcrecord.org

Weiss, C. C., Carolan, B. V., & Baker-Smith, E. C. (2010). Big school, small school: (Re)testing assumptions about high school size, school engagement, and mathematics achievement. *Journal of Youth and Adolescence*. *39*, 163–176. doi: 10.1007/s10964-009-9402-3

William T. Grant Foundation. (January 1988). *The forgotten half: Non-college youth in America. An interim report on the school-to-work transition*. Washington, DC: Commission on Work, Family and Citizenship, WTGF. (ERIC Document Reproduction Service No. ED 290 822.)

Wigfield, A., & Eccles, J. S. (2000). Expectancy-value theory of achievement motivation. *Contemporary Educational Psychology Special Issue: Motivation and the Educational Process*, *25*, 68–81. doi: 10.1006/ceps.1999.1015

Wonacott, M. E. (2002). *High schools that work: Best Practices for CTE*. Practice Application Brief No. 19. Retrieved from: http://www.eric.ed.gov/PDFS/ED463445.pdf

Yazzie-Mintz, E. (2007). *Engaging the voices of students: A report on the 2007 and 2008 high school survey of student engagement*. Bloomington, IN: Center for Evaluation & Education Policy.

Training and Employment Services for Adult Workers

Cindy L. Juntunen *and* Tamba-Kuii M. Bailey

Abstract

The psychology-of-working perspective is a useful lens to focus on the unique needs of adult workers seeking employment and training services. This chapter presents common adult work transitions and a variety of employment services that an adult worker might see, both of which are analyzed from a psychology-of-working perspective. Alternatives and improvements are suggested, illustrated by a case example and by a set of specific recommendations for modifying extant employment and training services. The chapter concludes with a set of questions designed to further research and intervention development from the psychology-of-working perspective.

Key Words: adult vocational development, work transitions, employment and training services

Vocational psychology has paid limited attention to the needs of adult workers, particularly those who are in a state of transition that is not of their own volition. The majority of evidence-based vocational interventions have been developed with and applied to youth and young adults making the transition from education to work or, to a lesser extent, older adults preparing for retirement (Brown & Lent, 2005). In fact, Herr (2002) noted that the term "adult career development" was fairly new even at the turn of the 21st century. This lack of attention has translated into relatively few training or counseling services available to adults, and even fewer that have been influenced by the theories or research of vocational psychology. Yet the needs of adult workers are significant, and increasingly so in times of economic downturn, as is currently the case.

The impact of the U.S. economy is substantial for workers around the world, highlighting the reality that global labor markets are becoming increasingly interdependent. According to the International Labour Office (ILO, 2010), the 2008

crash of an investment bank in the United States contributed significantly, among other factors, to a global job crisis that has resulted in unemployment for millions of people around the world. Specifically, the number of unemployed people in the world jumped from approximately 178 million in 2007 to 212 million in 2009 (ILO, 2010). Beyond unemployment, there have been sharp global increases in discouraged workers (those no longer seeking work because they believe work is not available), vulnerable workers, and the proportion of employed people who are living in poverty (ILO, 2010). In fact, critics (Jensen & Slack, 2003) have pointed out that unemployment is not as hearty an indicator of the health of the labor force as underemployment, which includes a broader array of vulnerable and underutilized workers.

As of July 2011, the unemployment rate in the United States was 9.2% (representing approximately 14 million people); of these, 44% (approximately 6.3 million people) were identified as long-term unemployed, having been seeking employment for

27 weeks or more (U.S. Department of Labor, July 8, 2011). An additional 8.6 million people were identified as involuntary part-time workers, those who could not find full-time work or whose hours had been cut. An additional 2.7 million Americans were "marginally attached" to the labor force, in that they both wanted to work and were able to work, and had looked for work in the past 12 months, but had not sought work in the past 4 weeks. Of these 2.7 million people, 982,000 were discouraged workers (U.S. Department of Labor, 2011), more than twice as many people who were identified as discouraged workers in the first quarter of 2008 (U.S. Department of Labor, 2009). Further, the New Economic Paradigm Associates have identified a new group of "very discouraged workers" (Byrne & Derbin, 2011), which includes the significantly greater number of applicants for permanent disability and early retirement in the current U.S. economy.

Even before the economic downturn beginning in 2008, career counselors considering the changed environment of adult career development noted that "Adults are forced to acknowledge that although they have a job today, they may be unemployed tomorrow—regardless of how competent they are or how hard they work" (Niles, Herr, & Hartung, 2002, p.4). Based on current employment and underemployment statistics, this was a prophetic statement for an increasingly large number of adults around the world. Yet vocational psychology has done little to address the needs of this growing population. For example, the only reference to discouraged workers in a vocational psychology or career counseling publication in PsycINFO (as of July 2011) was from a 1988 textbook (Herr & Cramer, 1988).

The psychology-of-working perspective (Blustein, 2006) presents vocational psychology with a timely opportunity to focus more intently on the needs of working adults, whether or not they are part of the paid labor force. By attending to the meaning of work as a source of survival and power, social connection, and self-determination (Blustein, 2006), the psychology-of-working perspective creates several unique points of intervention for adult workers and help to improve upon the training and employment services currently available.

In this chapter, we briefly discuss the various ways in which adult workers might encounter voluntary and involuntary transitions that would benefit from vocational services, as well as the contextual factors that influence work transitions. This is followed by a description of the most common existing adult employment services. The psychology-of-working lens will be applied to identify the potential needs of working adults, and to offer a critical analysis of the extant models of adult employment services. We will then offer ideas for expanding and modifying existing services from a psychology-of-working perspective, as well as suggestions for radical change to the current support structure for adult workers. It is important to recognize that valuable work, including caregiving and childrearing, is occurring outside of the realm of paid employment. However, given the focus of this chapter on training and employment services, the bulk of our attention will be on transitions related to employment or paid work. Throughout, we will focus on the meaning of work in the multifaceted context of adult lives.

Work Transitions for Adults

Contemporary working adults are far more likely to encounter multiple and sometimes unpredictable work transitions than adults in previous generations, who were more likely to remain in a long-term relationship with a single employer (Fouad & Bynner, 2008; Niles et al., 2002). In fact, adaptability is an increasingly valued characteristic of the adult worker (Ebberwein, Krieshok, Ulven & Prosser, 2004; Fouad & Bynner, 2008; Savickas, 1997; Zikic & Hall, 2009). Unfortunately, there is also evidence that individuals' ability to successfully adapt to changes may be significantly influenced by their access to educational opportunities and resources (Schoon, 2007), and that educational opportunities are becoming increasingly important for younger generations (Schoon, Martin, & Ross, 2007).

While a significant number of adults will make the transition from school to work during adulthood, this chapter will focus on the transitions that occur into the workforce from a nonemployed situation, from one work situation to another, and from work to nonemployment. The role of relationships and family considerations is integrated throughout, in recognition of the relational aspect of work and the importance of considering the impact that work transitions have on relationships both at work and at home (Bauer & McAdams, 2004). Special attention will be paid to the impact of volition on these transitions, given that involuntary or forced changes in work are likely to have different impact on the worker and his or her family than are those that are voluntary (Fouad & Bynner, 2008).

Entry and Reentry Transitions

Adults who are seeking or beginning work for the first time, or who are seeking to find work after an extended period away from the labor market, are said to be making entry or reentry transitions. Making an initial entrance or reentrance to the workforce can precipitate significant stress related to changes in relationships, environments, and perceptions of one's self (Juntunen, Wegner, & Matthews, 2002). A voluntary decision to enter or return to work may be accompanied by positive feelings of excitement and satisfaction, among others, but uncertainty and caution are equally likely. Even when it is actively sought, a new work environment might challenge an individual's skill set, foster feelings of ambivalence about what has been given up to pursue work, or change the individual's social and family relationships (Juntunen et al., 2002).

The precipitating factors that contribute to an involuntary entry or reentry into work can add important complexity and stress to the entrance transition. Frequently, involuntary transitions involve significant financial distress. There may be a great deal of pressure on the individual to find work that provides a livable wage. For people reentering the work force after an extended time away, this might be coupled with the realization that the work environment and skills of a given job have changed significantly during their time away from work (Griffin & Hesketh, 2005; Juntunen et al., 2002). They may also occur subsequent to the loss of a wage-earning partner to death, divorce, or other means (Bobek & Robbins, 2005). In contrast to voluntary transitions, involuntary transitions to the workforce frequently allow insufficient time for planning, leading to additional challenges in balancing work and family roles (Fouad & Bynner, 2008). Involuntary transitions into the workforce may be primarily in response to the need for survival, with limited opportunity for attending to self-determination or social connection. Establishing access to the resources, via employment or other sources of social support, that will support survival of the individual and his or her dependents may be the necessary focus of psychology-of-working interventions.

In a qualitative study that assessed the work reentry needs of nonviolent offenders leaving incarceration, several psychology-of-working tenets were identified spontaneously by the participants (Shivy, Wu, Moon, Mann, Holland, & Eacho, 2007). Specifically, they identified the importance of social networks, empowerment through education, and the intersection of psychological, social, and emotional factors with vocational concerns. Although the authors did not set out to test a psychology-of-working perspective, this study provides a great example of the need for an inclusive approach to the reentry transition and the unique barriers encountered by ex-offenders, consistent with the major psychology-of-working tenets.

Work to Other Work Transitions

Given the dynamic state of the workforce addressed previously, work-to-work transitions are an increasingly normative experience for adults. For some workers, such transitions result in work opportunities. These transitions are exemplified in the ideas of the "boundaryless" (Arthur & Rousseau, 1996) and "protean" (Hall, 2004) careers, in which individuals, rather than their employers, are identified as being in charge of and responsible for their own career trajectories (Clarke, 2007). These frameworks assume a level of agency and volition that is likely to be available to only a percentage of working adults, and do not fully address the challenges accompanying limited personal, financial, and educational resources. Recently, Forrier, Sels, and Stynen (2009) proposed a conceptual model of career mobility that explores the interaction of the agency-driven protean career and the structural issues of the labor market. It is an intriguing model that addresses several complex issues, but also relies significantly on individual volition and perceptions of multiple options.

In contrast, many adult workers face involuntary work-to-work transitions, which can leave individuals feeling like they have very few options. Such transitions may come about if a worker is asked by an employer to change shifts, relocate, seek additional training to maintain his or her current position, or take a new position to accommodate downsizing or budget cuts. Such changes may affect the individual's identity as a worker (Juntunen et al., 2002) and may also result in changes to income and/or benefits. In addition, there may be significant pressure to make a change that disrupts family and social relationships, such as changing from a day to evening shift, to maintain financial security. Similar constraints may be in place when a worker changes from one employer to another, and the transition is compounded by the need to learn a new set of workplace norms and practices. When the work-to-work transition includes a shift to involuntary part-time work, the impact can include increased levels of depression (Dooley, Prause, & Ham-Rowbottom, 2000). Further, working in a poor-quality job, where security is low and pressure is high, can contribute to poor health indicators (Broom et al., 2006). When considering involuntary work-to-work transitions from the psychology-of-working perspective, it is important to attend to the impact this transition will have on access to further opportunities, access to social power, the nature of social connections, and the ability of the individual to identify ways in which he or she is able to experience a sense of autonomy or volition through one or more aspects of the work change.

Work to Nonemployment Transitions

The transition from work to nonemployment is arguably one of the more difficult transitions an adult might encounter, particularly when that transition is involuntary or unexpected (Fouad & Bynner, 2008). Even when voluntary, the transition to retirement or the intentional decision to leave work for some other reason requires significant adjustment to daily routines, social and collegial relationships, and family systems. Beyond those adjustments, people leaving the workforce may feel they are then making less of a contribution to society, something that is considered by many to be an important part of adult life.

Moving from work to unemployment, through layoffs or being fired, has a significant impact on several indicators of well-being, including increased levels of depression and anxiety and decreased self-esteem (Paul & Moser, 2009). The loss of income and benefits, and the security they provide, has important effects on family life as well, as unemployment is associated with increased child abuse and neglect (Sedlak et al., 2010) and marital and family conflict (Lobo & Watkins, 1995; Patton & Donohue, 2001). The importance of providing appropriate services to adults who are involuntarily unemployed or underemployed cannot be overstated. Training and employment services have the potential to influence the individual, his or her family, the surrounding community, and his or her future employers. The addition of a psychology-of-working perspective to the transition to unemployment may include attending to the importance of nonemployed work, as well as addressing the needs related to survival and social power that are precipitated by the loss of income.

Cultural Context in Career Transition

Fouad and Byars-Winston (2005) described work as a cultural construct and noted that many of the values and expectations associated with work are based on a cultural context. They asserted that individuals' cultural context makes a difference in the way decisions and choices are made about work. Fouad and Bynner (2008) stated that "people negotiating each new transition in their lives do not start on a level playing field" (p. 246). Thus, it is important to examine the influence of a cultural context (gender, race, age, and level of ability) when discussing adult workforce participation and career transition.

Gender. Gender can play an important role in career selection and transition. While the overall unemployment rate is lower for women than men (Bureau of Labor Statistics, 2009), there are many factors that may limit women's career mobility and career choices (Cabrera, 2007; Forret, Sullivan, & Mainiero, 2010). These factors include wanting to balance family and work, career restrictions related to societal norms and stereotypes (Forret et al., 2010), and experiences of sexual harassment and other forms of gender oppression on the job (Gelfand, Fitzgerald, & Drasgow, 1995; Gutek & Koss, 1993). Men's work transitions can be limited if they feel pressured to conform to more traditional work roles and career paths (Forret et al., 2010), particularly given the few role models of men taking on nontraditional career paths.

Gender differences are also relevant for involuntary transitions caused by job loss. While evidence indicates that men and women have similar responses to job loss, women appear to rebound better to this involuntary career transition and may experience more career growth (Eby & Buch, 1995). This may be due to the belief that men draw much of their identity from work, so the experience of job loss can create a sense of failure, whereas many women, drawing their identity from multiple, non–career-related roles, may view a job loss as an opportunity (Forret et al., 2010).

Race/Ethnicity. Employment statistics continue to demonstrate disparities by racial and ethnic identity. In 2009, unemployment rates for African Americans (14.8%) and Latinos (12.1%) were higher than for Whites (8.5%), while the rate of unemployment for Asian Americans (7.3%) was the lowest of all groups (Bureau of Labor Statistics, 2010). Rates of unemployment for African Americans and Latinos have been consistently higher than for Whites during the past three decades. Additionally, the Pew Research Center reported that the median wealth for white households is 20 times greater than Black households and 18 times greater than that of Latino households (Kochhar, Fry, & Taylor, 2011).

Many factors may contribute to the higher levels of unemployment, lower median wealth, and involuntary career transition for African Americans and Latinos. The U.S. Department of Labor hypothesized that high employment in jobs with high level of job loss, lower levels of education, high concentration in areas with limited job opportunity, and experiences of racism and discrimination are contributing factors (Bureau of Labor Statistics, 2010).

In terms of career aspirations and perceptions, which are connected to career participation, Fouad and Byars-Winston (2005), in their meta-analysis of racial and ethnic differences in career choice, found that race and ethnicity did not play a factor in career aspirations or decision making. However, they did find a difference among racial/ethnic groups in relation to perceptions of career opportunities and barriers. Thus, perceptions of career opportunities and barriers have the potential to affect career participation and transition.

Older Workers. Since 1995, there has been a dramatic rise in the number of workers over the age of 55, with the number of full-time workers almost doubling compared to the pre-1995 numbers (U.S. Bureau of Labor Statistics, 2008). It is projected that by 2016, the labor force participation will increase by over 36% for workers over the age of 55 and by 80% for workers over the age of 65 (U.S. Bureau of Labor Statistics, 2008). This increased participation in the labor force by older workers may be attributed to longer, healthier lifespans (Owen & Flynn, 2004), changes in retirement patterns and views about retirement (Quinn & Kozy, 1996), and the need for additional workers in some areas of the labor market. However, an alternate explanation for this surge in the labor force by older workers may be the global recession and the economic downturn that began in 2007. Older workers, even those with job seniority, found that they were not immune to the effects of the economy and were forced to adjust their career outlook and retirement plans (Brooke, 2009). With regard to career transitions for older workers, factors such as financial security, health, cultural characteristics, age discrimination, limited job security, and job mobility were identified as playing a major role (Brewington & Nassar-McMillan, 2000; Brooke, 2009; Miller, 2002; Quinn & Kozy, 1996).

There are limited programs where older adult workers can actively address career transitions and remain competitive in the labor market (Brewington & Nassar-McMillan, 2000). However, one option for dealing with career transitions is through the Senior Community Service Employment Program (SCSEP), a job training and education program for older workers (U.S. Department of Labor, 2011). This program, authorized by the Older Americans Act, provides subsidized, service-based training for low-income, unemployed individuals who are aged 55 or older and have poor employment prospects. Individuals in this program can utilize services through SCSEP and one-stop career centers (U.S. Department of Labor, 2011). This program provides older job seekers with the opportunity to update their job skills and gain more information on labor market needs and trends.

Level of Ability. The unemployment rate for individuals with disabilities is higher than that for individuals without disabilities (Schmidt & Smith, 2007). Adult job seekers represent all levels of ability. Enright (1996) noted that multiple environmental restrictions and personal beliefs, along with a disability, might alter the way that individuals with a disability perceive and follow various career options.

Some job seekers with disabilities may experience challenges in finding and gaining access to job training and services to meet their career transition needs. One way the federal government addressed this need was through the Workforce Investment Act (WIA) (Timmons, Boeltzig, Fesko, Cohen, & Hamner, 2007). The WIA requires that one-stop career centers be universally accessible so that any job seeker can utilize core services without asking for an accommodation. Other suggested interventions that have been proven to assist job seekers with disabilities are (1) access to broad assessment and individualized career planning, (2) psychoeducational programs with emphasis on work identity and interpersonal relationships, and (3) work experience (Szymanski & Hanley-Maxwell, 1996).

Extant Models of Adult Training and Employment Services

There are various adult employment service programs that provide unemployed and underemployed individuals with job skills training and education to obtain a job or start a new career (Goodman & McClurg, 2002). Categories of community-based and government-sponsored services include career coaching, faith-based programs, welfare-to-work (WTW) programs, and the one-stop delivery system. Community colleges also play an important role in adult vocational training, so we also address the relative strengths and weaknesses of community colleges in meeting adult employment needs.

With the exception of career coaching, most forms of adult employment training and services are in some way funded through the WIA and provided to job seekers at no cost (U.S. Department of Labor, 2011). In this section we will outline the basic components of the aforementioned programs as well as discuss some of their strengths and weaknesses.

Career Coaching

Career coaching, which grew out of the consultant movement of the 1990s (Chung & Gfroerer, 2003), primarily focuses on an infusion of career counseling, employment development, and organizational consulting concepts (Chung & Gfroerer, 2003; Stern, 2004). Inherent in the title, career coaching is most applicable for individuals with the resources, volition, and ability to see themselves creating a career. Coaches work individually with clients to identify work-related skills and to help them make better career choices in the future. Most career coaches have at least a bachelor's degree in business or a related area. And while the field of career coaching may consist of very similar components to that of career counseling, career coaching is very solution-focused, with emphasis placed on improving individuals' marketability and capacity to advance in their career (Amundson, 2006; Stern, 2004). Also, unlike career counseling, career coaching is not regulated by guidelines that delineate behaviors, methods of interaction, payment scale, or scope of practice. Although career coaching is not regulated, it has its own professional group (International Coach Federation) that offers training and credentials to those individuals interested in serving as career coaches (Stern, 2004).

The strengths of working with a career coach seem to be the individual attention and support that job seekers can receive during the coaching. Career coaches have relatively broad boundaries, which offer them the ability to interact with their clients in multiple settings and very different ways (Chung & Gfroerer, 2003). Coaching has been conceptually linked to positive psychology, as an intervention designed to improve the performance of individuals who may already be relatively successful (Kilburg, 2004).

Major criticisms of career coaching are the lack of guidelines and regulations of the field and the high cost associated with receiving services (Chung & Gfroerer, 2003). There is also a noted lack of empirical research on the methodology and outcomes of career coaching. Extant research focuses primarily on one type of career coaching—executive coaching, which is designed to develop performance among organizational leaders and managers (Kilburg, 2004). An increasing amount of research on executive coaching has emerged in the past decade (Greif, 2007), including findings that coaching interventions are positively related to increased self-efficacy (Baron & Morin, 2010; Evers, Brouwers, & Tomic, 2006), leadership skills (Thach, 2002), and productivity (Olivero, Bane, & Kopelman, 1997) among business managers. The small number of studies, heavy reliance on case studies, and limited empirical examination of the impact of coaching led Lowman (2005) to assert that "in the case of coaching, practice is considerably ahead of research" (p. 93).

Proponents of coaching argue that it is a new field whose growth is parallel to that of the evaluation of psychotherapy research (Kilburg, 2004) and that it holds potential as an evidence-based intervention for working adults. From a psychology-of-working perspective, career coaches may be well placed to emphasize the social connectedness and self-determination aspects of work. In fact, given the emphasis on assisting individuals to make decisions that maximize their career choices, there is a clear assumption that career coaching clients have volition. This suggests that the needs for survival and power would be overlooked in a traditional career coaching approach, as their presence is likely to be assumed.

Faith-Based Programs

Different from secular adult employment service programs, faith-based programs have a unique structure in that elements of religion are connected to the services provided by the faith-based organization. Uruh (as cited in Ebaugh, Pipes, Chafetz, & Daniels, 2003) identified two major components of faith-based programs that distinguish them from secular social service programs: (1) an affiliation with a religious denomination or church and (2) an active religious element that communicates religious messages or involves the individuals seeking services in a specific religious experience as a part of the program. Additionally, while many secular social service programs focus solely on the services offered by the program, faith-based programs tend to emphasize the need for more holistic relationships and interactions that go beyond the program (Lockhart, 2005).

In terms of funding, under the Personal Responsibility and Work Opportunity Reconciliation Act of 1996 (PRWORA), faith-based programs are allowed to apply and compete for federal grants without having to forfeit their religious character (Ebaugh et al., 2003; Lockhart, 2005). However, most faith-based programs receive little to no federal funding (Pipes & Ebaugh, 2002). Faith-based programs can also work with one-stop career centers and other secular organization when providing adult employment education and training (U.S. Department Labor, 2009).

A major strength of faith-based programs is the accessibility to job training and information by members of the denominations or churches (Ebaugh et al., 2003). Receiving services from faith-based programs may be a sought-after experience for those individuals who want to incorporate aspects of religion into their job training and job assistance. Empirical examination of religion and spirituality in work and career is limited (Duffy, 2006), but there have been a small number of studies that highlight ways in which faith-based employment services may be particularly relevant. The experience of work as a calling or vocation (Dik & Duffy, 2009) has been identified as relevant across multiple kinds of work (nursing, teaching, law) In a qualitative study with a small sample of practicing Roman Catholic participants (Hernandez, Foley, & Beitin, 2011). In an examination of working mothers, the sense of being called to a career was identified as a "sense or early recognition of God-given gifts and longings that manifested themselves later in life" (Sellers, Thomas, Batts & Ostman, 2005, p. 201). Religious beliefs and activity have also been linked a sense of calling for work and an orientation toward social justice in a large multidenominational sample (Davidson & Caddell, 1994). These studies suggest that there is ample room for research that examines the effectiveness of faith-based employment programs, at least for some populations. However, for job seekers who are not interested in combining religion with employment training and assistance, faith-based adult employment service programs may not be a good fit.

Faith-based programs may have more flexibility to consider the needs of the "whole person" than some government-funded services, and so in this way may be able to address several needs identified by the psychology-of-working perspective. Certainly the idea of making meaning from work may resonate for many individual who would seek faith-based support. Similarly, the social connectedness of faith practices is consistent with the emphasis of work as a source of social connection. Finally, assuming that the faith-based sponsor does not discriminate based on financial resources, the need to consider survival and power is consistent with many religious tenets that support meeting the needs of those without resources. Further inquiry and research is necessary to determine whether faith-based employment services are guided by any vocational theory in their use of interventions or supported by empirical evidence.

Welfare-to-Work Programs

PRWORA limited the amount of time that any one individual could receive welfare benefits to 60 months. As a result of the passage of this act, greater attention was placed on WTW programs. Hugh A. Bailey, an associate director with the Department of Employment Services in the District of Columbia who oversees all one-stop operations in Washington, DC, described WTW programs as government-sponsored programs that provide individuals who receive Temporary Assistance for Needy Families (TANF) with job training and job placement goals that move them from receiving assistance to being employed and self-sufficient (H. A. Bailey, personal communication, July 10, 2011; Pavoni & Violante, 2007).

Benefits of the WTW programs are access to job training and education for individuals receiving TANF (Hasenfeld & Weaver, 1996). There is no cost for individuals who participate in WTW programs, and programs are designed to provide a path toward self-sufficiency (H. A. Bailey, personal communication, July 10, 2011). Criticisms of WTW programs are that all TANF recipients, with some exceptions, must participate in the WTW programs with little control or autonomy (Pavoni & Violante, 2007); that these programs are time-limited (Hollenbeck & Kimmel, 2002) regardless of individual need; and that they are not accessible to non-TANF individuals. This means that working adults who are not responsible for the care of a dependent are not eligible for WTW services.

Research on the effectiveness of WTW programs has been complicated by the various ways in which the outcomes of PRWORA can be measured. Within a few years of the passage of welfare reform, the number of cases in the welfare system had dropped significantly (U.S. Department of Health and Human Services, 2006). This was viewed as a sign of success for the programs and policies instituted by PRWORA, but subsequent analyses have indicated that successful outcomes for recipients of WTW programs were not as clear. High dropout rates, low employment rates, and low incomes among participants who obtained employment have been identified in multiple studies across several states (Beimers & Fischer, 2007; Haennicke, Konieczny, & Raphael, 2000; Livermore, Davis, Powers, & Lim, 2011).

Because of their time-limited nature and emphasis on self-sufficiency, WTW programs are likely to focus on the needs of the worker related to survival and power, at least power as it is related to financial resources and security. Most WTW programs will not fully attend to social connectedness or self-determination. Interestingly, in one of the few WTW projects anchored in vocational psychology theory (Juntunen et al., 2006), participants demonstrated decreased levels of depression following a group vocational intervention focused on increasing self-efficacy. Further, participants indicated that the most valuable aspects of the intervention included exploring values, setting goals, bonding with group members, learning to manage stress, and developing self-confidence. Many of these aspects of change would be related to work as a means of social connectedness and work as a means of self-determination, suggesting the potential for the psychology-of-working perspective to add significant value to current WTW interventions.

One-Stop Career Centers

Starting in the earlier part of the 20th century, with the passage of the Wagner-Peyser Act of 1935, the Manpower Development and Training Act (MDTA) in 1961, the Comprehensive Employment and Training Act (CETA) in 1973, and the Job Training Partnership Act (JTPA) in 1983, the United States began providing job training and vocational education for individuals (Guttman, 1983). These acts created programs that provided individuals with vocational training and job search assistance as a means of creating a ready labor force; while also addressing poverty, reducing juvenile delinquency, and converting welfare recipients into wage earners. The Workforce Investment Act of 1998, the most recent job training legislation, was created "to consolidate, coordinate, and improve employment, training, literacy, and vocational rehabilitation programs in the United States" (U.S. Congress, 1998, para. 1).

While the programs associated with these job-training acts were viewed as essential to labor force development and readiness, there has been a constant redirection of these programs (Guttman, 1983). These revisions and shifts in the acts were, in part, based on varying congressional perceptions of the goals and objectives of the programs in relationship to the labor market needs. Another factor contributing to these shifts was the fact that all levels of government were involved in the development of programs from these acts, but the primary planning and implementation of these programs was carried out by the local governments.

The primary component of the WIA is the one-stop delivery system. It was first developed under the JTPA, and fully developed and strengthened as a centerpiece program in the job training legislation until the WIA (H. A. Bailey, personal communication, July 10, 2011). Direct oversight of the one-stop centers is provided by local boards that consist of individuals from local businesses (private and public sectors) and higher education (H. A. Bailey, personal communication, July 10, 2011). The one-stop delivery system comprises centers that offer a wide range of job training and job-related services primarily for unemployed and underemployed individuals (U.S. Department of Labor, 1998). One-stop career centers consist of two main types of services: core services and intensive services (U.S. Department of Labor, 2011). Core services include basic job search assistance such as labor market information for job seekers, résumé building, job interview training, basic computer skills training, and access to computers (H. A. Bailey, personal communication, July 10, 2011; U.S. Department of Labor, 2011). For those individuals who experience greater employment barriers, one-stop career centers offer intensive services that consist of a comprehensive assessment and development of an individualized employment plan (U.S. Department of Labor, 2011).

Some of the strengths of one-stop career centers are that they combine a number of employment resources and job training in one location (Jacobson, 2009). Also, they amass and distribute information about available jobs and training programs to which many unemployed individuals do not have access. A weakness of the one-stop career system is the limited preparedness of staff members when providing assistance and guidance to job seekers with disabilities (Timmons et al., 2007). Another weakness is the lack of national branding or a common name for all of the centers across the country (H. A. Bailey, personal communication, July 10, 2011). This lack of national branding makes it difficult for job seekers to locate local branches. Finally, there are no outlined competencies for staff related to case management skills. The absence of staff competencies decreases the one-stop career system's ability to provide a standard level of care and services in all of the centers. This challenge is highlighted in federal evaluation research, which focuses on program-level effectiveness and looks at the functioning of one-stop centers in individual communities (U.S. General Accounting Office, 2003). Such evaluation programs have also not fully considered the effectiveness of one-stop centers on consumers, and vocational psychology has paid only limited attention to the impact of such services. This is a rich area of future research for vocational psychologists interested in the experience of adults seeking work.

The one-stop career system was designed to unify access to career and vocational services in a single location (U.S. General Accounting Office, 2003). Prior to the one-stop career centers, adult job seekers expended large amounts of time and energy while attempting to access the multiple vocational resources and services from numerous locations in an area (H. A. Bailey, personal communication, August 1, 2011). This separation in vocational services has led many individuals to underutilize some vital sources of career assistance, as well as limiting their access to certain resources. Consistent with a psychology-of-working focus, the development and implementation of one-stop career centers has increased the equity and accessibility to vocational training and education for adult job-seeking individuals.

Community Colleges and Vocational Training

Many community colleges offer short-term training programs that allow individuals to obtain vocation-specific work training in a short period of time for entry into the workforce (Flannery, Yovanoff, Benz, & McGrath-Kato, 2008; Grubb, 2001; Lindstrom, Flannery, Benz, Olszewski, & Slovic, 2009). A significant factor contributing to this role of community colleges has been a need for local workforce development that takes advantage of community colleges' strengths such as organizational flexibility, the proximity to private-sector businesses, low tuition cost, technical expertise, and experience in teaching adult learners (Jacobs & Dougherty, 2006). Jacobs and Dougherty further argue that many states and communities have designed their work training and expansion programs around community colleges. The following assessment of community colleges will examine their strengths and weaknesses, particularly as they relate to the impact of community colleges on vocational training and career transitions for adult workers.

Community colleges have long played an important role in adult education because the training, course formats, and scheduling of community colleges are often geared toward educating adults and an older population (Jacobs, 2001). Some high-paying careers require more education than a high school diploma but less than a 4-year degree (Jacobs, 2001), which makes the training offered at community colleges ideal in meeting these needs. Many community colleges are able to alter and/or add new training programs to meet the changing vocational needs of the workforce.

The federal government also has contributed to building up and strengthening the presence of community colleges as it relates to vocational training. In 2003, the U.S. Department of Education, through its office of Vocational and Adult Education, established the College and Career Transition Initiative (CCTI), the goals of which were to strengthen the role of community and technical colleges in student transitions between secondary and postsecondary education and to improve academic performance in both secondary and postsecondary schools (League for Innovation in the Community College, 2008). Included in the CCTI, the U.S. Department of Education supported vocational training at the community-college level in five areas: education and training; health sciences; information technology; law, public safety, and security; and science, technology, engineering, and mathematics. This CCTI provided a transition outline for students from high school to college by setting a clear path to success through programs of study linked to high-demand, high-wage career fields (Kempner & Warford, 2009). These training areas were initially implemented at 15 sites and have since grown to include a network of 175 community colleges (Kempner & Warford, 2009). This initiative, as well as other funding and legislative acts, has contributed to community colleges serving as viable options for vocational education and training (Ankeny & Lehmann, 2010).

Accessibility and training for individuals with disabilities has also been identified as a strength of community colleges (Lindstrom et al., 2009). Lindstrom et al. note that many individuals with disabilities are less likely than those without disabilities to participate in postsecondary education. However, for those individuals who do receive some postsecondary education, the majority will attend a community colleges or some type of training program that is less than 2 years long (Ankeny & Lehmann, 2010). Ankeny and Lehmann identified the following as some of the factors that contribute to individuals with disabilities finding success in obtaining training from community colleges: open admission policies, location, reasonable costs, access to college counseling services, greater faculty focus on teaching as opposed to research, and transitional programs that help individuals prepare for postsecondary education. Lindstrom et al. (2009), in their study examining an occupational skills training partnership between Oregon's Office of Vocational Rehabilitation Services and several community colleges, found that many of the local rehabilitation counselors were more aware of training programs at the community colleges and were more likely to suggest these schools to individuals with disabilities. The aforementioned factors have contributed and will continue to contribute to a high number of individuals with disabilities receiving vocational training from community colleges.

In terms of weaknesses, community colleges have long been viewed as lowering the educational attainment of individuals by steering them away from attending 4-year institutions (Roksa, 2006). It is believed that the growth of workforce education in community colleges has contributed to the undercutting of the transfer function of those schools (Jacobs & Dougherty, 2006). This is highlighted by the fact that students who enter community or 2-year colleges are less likely to earn any kind of degree than those individuals who enter 4-year institutions.

Another weakness associated with community colleges is the non-credit workforce courses themselves. There is a growing concern that these courses may detract from the institutional mission of community colleges and potentially change the values of the colleges (Jacobs & Dougherty, 2006). Jacobs and Dougherty noted that many of these non-credit workforce courses do not have to meet the same standards as credit courses, which leads to concerns that these courses may be viewed as less rigorous than credit courses. Even with these identified weaknesses, community colleges are still leading the charge in terms of vocational preparation and development of the nation's workforce.

Assessing Adult Worker Needs via the Psychology-of-Working Perspective

It is clear from the preceding sections that adult workers have a high likelihood of requiring the assistance of employment and training services. Yet few of these services are adequately addressing the full spectrum of needs presented by adult workers, despite the existence of models such as the Integrated Life Planning approach (Hansen, 2002), which has been proposed for adults making work transitions in a changing global market. An assessment of adult workers' needs through the psychology-of-working perspective can provide important guidelines to improve existing resources.

The psychology-of-working perspective emphasizes the need to understand inner motivations and the way in which people make meaning from work, across the wide array of working sectors, both paid and nonpaid (Blustein, 2006). To address meaningfulness, inner motivation, and the broad array of needs presented by adult workers, Blustein (2006) and his colleagues (Blustein, Kenna, Gill, & DeVoy, 2008) have proposed an inclusive psychological practice perspective that includes both work and family life domains. Within that framework, the practitioner addresses work as a means of survival and power, work as a means of social connectedness, and work as a means of self-determination. As these constructs are addressed more fully elsewhere in this volume, we will demonstrate the use of these tenets to understand and assess the needs of adult workers in the following fictional case example.

Illustrative Case: Martha

Martha is a 56-year-old woman of Mexican American descent. She was born and has lived all of her life in California. She moved just a few blocks from her home of origin when she married at the age of 22, and she moved to a neighboring town at the age of 50, when she and her husband, Sam, retired. Sam, who was 10 years Martha's senior, died unexpectedly last year, after sustaining serious injuries in a car accident. Martha currently lives with her 7-year-old grandson, Cody. Martha and Sam took custody of Cody when he was 4 years old, after his parents were convicted of manufacturing and selling illegal drugs in their home. Cody's mother, Carolyn (who is Martha's daughter), is scheduled to be released when Cody is 9, but Martha expects that Cody will remain in her custody for several years after that, until his mother is able to "get things in her life back together."

Martha is seeking assistance in returning to the workforce, as she is increasingly worried about providing a financially stable upbringing for Cody. She worked for more than 30 years as the manager of the restaurant that she and Sam owned together. Martha really enjoyed that work and expressed some sadness about leaving the business. However, she was also looking forward to a long retirement and the opportunity to travel and enjoy free time with

Sam. They sold the restaurant when they retired, but the profits from the sale have been significantly reduced by the purchase of their retirement home, Sam's medical and funeral costs, and the expense of Carolyn's legal defense. Martha's assets at this point consist of her house, her household possessions, and her car. For income, she has a small monthly Social Security spousal benefit, child support from the state to meet Cody's basic needs, and whatever profit she can clear from bringing produce from her garden to the local farmer's market on Saturdays. Martha is determined to keep living in her home as it is "the only home Cody remembers." Martha also noted that it feels like the "only thing I can count on right now."

Martha has applied for close to 30 jobs in the past 2 months but has received only rejection letters. She has been looking for management-level work, similar to what she did in her family restaurant. Some of the letters she has received indicated she wasn't eligible for their openings because she does not have a college degree. She is also worried that people will think she is too old to get a new job.

Work as a Means of Survival and Power. At first glance, Martha appears to have adequate resources to ensure survival for herself and Cody. However, a closer assessment is required by the psychology-of-working perspective, and that reveals a more unpredictable circumstance. The bulk of Martha's income comes from government programs. In a time of economic downturn, even state and federal government programs are subject to disruption and even termination. If the programs she relied on are terminated or reduced, for example, Martha's income would be significantly reduced and extremely unpredictable. Martha's current assets include a safe home for herself and Cody. However, she may encounter significant barriers to liquidating that asset if the need arose. The ability to sell the house would need to be understood in the context of the local housing market. It would be critical for the counselor working with Martha to assess her perceptions of security and confidence in her ability to meet the survival needs of herself and Cody. The necessity and attending costs of childcare, if Martha is unable to find work that corresponds with Cody's hours in school, must also be considered as a basic safety need. Recognizing that the definitions of survival challenges can vary, practitioners need to look at their own assumptions regarding privilege and class (Blustein, 2006; Liu, 2010) to fully understand the client's survival needs.

In terms of power, it is important to assess the extent to which Martha feels she has volition or choices available to her in her current situation. It will also be important to explore the meaning that Martha attaches to work now, and the meaning that she ascribed to work during her 30-year paid work history. She has the experience of a long tenure in a position that did give her access to economic and social power, and she now is in a situation where she may feel relatively powerless. The potential impact of ageism and the possibility of racial discrimination must be explored and clearly attributed to social factors so that a "blaming the victim" mentality is not introduced into the counseling relationship. Part of the reality of Martha's situation is that employers are not fully prepared to understand the needs of older working adults (Miller, 2002). Working with Martha will include empowerment and consciousness-raising activities (Blustein et al., 2008), such as identifying skills and attitudes that are relevant to a new work setting and challenging the internalization of ageist or racist social norms. It is also important to recognize the value of nonpaid experiences to support empowerment. For example, one source of power that can be reinforced with Martha is the impact of her role as Cody's guardian and the strength she demonstrates in fulfilling that role despite numerous losses.

Work as a Means of Social Connectedness. Like many midlife and older adults seeking reentry to the work force, Martha is responding to a significant life change that likely has a direct impact on her need for social connectedness. The unexpected death of her husband is almost certain to be a factor here, and it will be important to assess the extent to which widowhood has affected Martha's social support network. Having guardianship of Cody may also be having an impact on her social connectedness outside of work, as it is possible that few of her peers have primary care of a child, and the parents of Cody's peers may be significantly younger than Martha. Drawing from a feminist relational perspective may be very useful in helping Martha identify ways in which her relationships with others can both support and deter her pursuit of work (Motulsky, 2010), and can lead to a more comprehensive understanding of Martha's current social connectedness.

It will also be important to assess the extent to which Martha's past work experience was related to social connectedness, both including and beyond connectedness with her husband. If Martha has previously had rewarding social connections at work, this may serve as a motivator to see work as a source of meaningful connections and contribute to the rewards present in work that might otherwise not seem worth pursuing. If Martha has not previously viewed work as a source of social support, it may be worthwhile to explore ways in which she can augment her current social connections through assessing the social climate in potential work settings. The extent to which a potential work setting will also allow her to attend to the needs of Cody will be an important consideration here as well, given that Martha may experience the need to prioritize one relationship over the other.

Work as a Means of Self-Determination. Attending to the tenet of internalization (Blustein, 2006; Deci & Ryan, 2000), it is important to assess Martha's current level of external and internal motivation to reenter the workforce. Internalization refers to the process by which external demands become increasingly internalized as values, beliefs, and self-regulating processes (Deci & Ryan, 2000). Initially, Martha's action may have been spurred purely by the external circumstances of Sam's death (external regulation), which may contribute to the perception of work (or job seeking) as a necessary but unrewarding task. If Martha is feeling guilty about not working in order to ensure a good future for Cody, she is beginning to internalize some of that external pressure (introjected regulation). Seeing work as a source of security for both herself and for Cody suggests that Martha is moving toward a more self-determined perspective on job seeking (identified regulation). Finally, if Martha identifies aspects of working or job seeking that are rewarding for her, above and beyond the external pressure of responding to need and caring for Cody, she may feel more autonomous and may ultimately see work as an expression of values that are important to her (integrated regulation). Martha might enter counseling with any one of these perspectives; depending on the extent to which she is externally motivated, an important part of counseling may be to help her identify internalized rewards such as competence, autonomy, and access to the opportunity structure (Blustein, 2006). In Martha's situation, it may not be possible to immediately find a job that is consistent with her past position; however, having access to the employment structure may be internalized as rewarding by offering the first step toward the job satisfaction she had previously.

Concluding Comments

In working with Martha, the psychology-of-working perspective would inform an inclusive psychological practice that would allow space to address the interaction of work and personal concerns (Blustein, 2006; Blustein et al., 2008). The interventions utilized by the counselor would include fostering empowerment, fostering critical consciousness, promoting skill building that meets current workforce demands, and providing scaffolding to support Martha's increased sense of volition and self-advocacy (Blustein, 2008). If Martha were to seek assistance from a counselor or psychologist versed in vocational issues, such a sequence of interventions would be accessible and personalized to fit Martha's needs.

However, many adult workers in need of vocational assistance will not seek that help from counselors or psychologists. Instead, they will approach or be referred to one of several employment and training agencies that exist in the private and public sector. Such services are engaging in a significant amount of vocational guidance, but their interventions are not necessarily anchored in the psychology of working, or even in vocational psychology generally. Identifying ways to integrate psychology-of-working principles into existing adult employment and training systems may allow more adult workers access to the space necessary to address their complex work and personal needs.

Modifications that Will Help Meet the Needs of the Contemporary Adult Worker

In this chapter, we discussed services available to adult job seekers as a means of dealing with career transitions. While assessing the many strengths and weaknesses of the programs, we explored how those programs aligned with the psychology-of-working conceptualization. And while some components of the programs were in line with the psychology-of-working perspective, we want to offer additional guidance for improving adult vocational services as a means of addressing career transition.

Increase Accessibility and Acceptability

As noted throughout this volume, vocational interventions are more readily available to individuals with choice and resources. One significant contribution that psychology of working can make to adult employment and training services is to normalize the need to access vocational services across the lifespan. Frequently, people with the greatest need for vocational interventions have not only the least access to these services but also the least awareness that they even exist (Zizic & Hall, 2009). Adopting an inclusive and integrative taxonomy of working (Blustein, 2006), which acknowledges that work serves multiple purposes for individuals across the lifespan, can make adult employment and training services more central to the well-being of individuals and the communities in which they live. For example, if an inclusive definition of work were part of career exploration activities beginning in early childhood, children and adolescents would be more likely to expect work transition and employment services as they become adults. Such expectations can over time influence policies and practices so that relevant services are more available and appropriate to meet the needs of working adults.

Finding a Job May Be Necessary but Is Not Sufficient

The primary functions of most vocational service programs are to provide individuals with job search assistance and vocational training. While these services are vital to individuals in obtaining employment and can increase their self-sufficiency, there are still gaps in extant models of adult vocational training as it relates to the delivery of comprehensive and effective services. Specifically, programs place minimal attention on empowerment, autonomy, a greater sense of identity, and connecting vocational theory to practice. However, a greater focus on these areas has the capacity to improve the utilization of services, thereby infusing the psychology-of-working perspective into practice.

Many programs will highlight the notions of empowerment and autonomy through employment, viewing these ideas as keys to success and foundational pillars to adult vocational programming. On the surface, it would appear that these components of adult vocational programs align very well with psychology-of-working perspectives in that they clearly emphasize survival needs. Although we agree that successful outcomes of adult vocational programs can lead to some empowerment and autonomy, the ways in which these ideas have been implemented also create boundaries and limitations for job seekers. The primary objective of adult vocational services is to assist adult job seekers in obtaining some level of employment. In having this focus, most programs do not address the needs of power, social connectedness, or self-determination. For example, very few programs support vocational education leading to an associate's or bachelor's degree (H. A. Bailey, personal communication, July 10,

2011). Bailey also indicated that adult vocational programs offer certifications only in certain fields designated as part of a high-growth industry. This is particularly unfortunate, as research suggests that programs that integrate employment and education, rather than just focusing on one or the other, are more likely to result in longer-term success for welfare recipients moving to work, for example (Deskins & Bruce, 2004). Limited opportunities for advanced training function to support and replicate the status quo, in which working adults continue to serve as a part of the major labor force with little power or influence. In not receiving any management training or being supported to obtain an associate's or bachelor's degree, adult job seekers have little chance for advancing into management-level career options or having a greater range of transferable skills as labor market needs shift. For an overview of one-stop programs and the components that have been identified as particularly successful, the interested reader is referred to the Research and Evaluation Portal of the U.S. Department of Labor Employment and Training Administration (http://www.doleta.gov/research/).

A psychology-of-working approach, integrated into existing programs, would support the adoption of wider training and educational models, which would support greater means of power and self-determination. Further, improved education opportunities allow for greater flexibility and career advancement and will increase the likelihood that recipients would remain in the labor force and not return to unemployment.

Support Holistic and Integrated Interventions

The current models of vocational training used in adult career programs place emphasis on the present (Chung & Gfroerer, 2003) and focus on the acquisition of skills for one specific job (Guttman, 1983). As we discussed earlier with faith-based programs, taking a more holistic approach that incorporates the needs of the "whole person" can lead to a greater meaning of work and possibly expand job seekers' view of their vocational identity and abilities. This expansion of career identity can benefit job seekers as they manage career transitions and the unpredictability of the labor market. Also, the development of a more complex career identity that incorporates a holistic perspective can encourage greater meaning associated with skill upgrades and can contribute to lasting change in job seekers' sense of identity. Finally, given the evidence that unemployment is linked to mental health concerns (Paul & Moser, 2009), comprehensive services may also include referral to and collaboration with counselors and counseling psychologists. These professionals are well prepared to integrate vocational and personal concerns and comprehensively address the needs of the individual.

The psychology-of-working perspective addresses this by explicitly acknowledging the interface between employment, nonemployed work, family and relationships, and socioemotional concerns (Blustein, 2006). Utilizing interventions that support empowerment and critical consciousness would significantly increase the ability of employment and training services to meet the needs of the whole client. Such interventions might include developing basic and transferable skills and abilities to further generalized empowerment, and helping clients recognize ways in which social and political barriers affect their work opportunities to increase critical consciousness (Blustein et al., 2008). Interventions that focus on skill building and adaptability to the changing workforce, as well as using the concept of scaffolding to help clients access multiple sources of help (Blustein et al., 2008), will also contribute to the ability of employment and training agencies to move beyond the present-oriented "get a job" emphasis.

There are limited examples of such efforts already in existence (Bhat, 2010; Juntunen et al., 2006). These two group programs highlighted the integration of personal and work empowerment, and both indicated some positive outcomes. Juntunen et al. developed a curriculum that focused on increasing self-efficacy and addressing common barriers (including transportation, childcare, and lack of familiarity with professional presentation and interviews) for welfare recipients. Participants who completed the program reported lower levels of depression and higher levels of self-efficacy, but there was a significant attrition rate related to the unstable living conditions of many recipients of social services. Bhat (2010) presented an intensive (15-day) group intervention that focused on empowerment and advocacy. She integrated a behavioral intervention for addressing unemployment with self-efficacy and self-awareness activities. In addition, the final week of the group includes advocacy efforts with local employers to increase their investment in hiring group members. Further research is needed to validate the impact of such group interventions. In addition, both were time-consuming activities for the consumer, which could serve as a barrier to participation for many work-seeking adults. In a related example, Clemens and Milsom (2008) describe the use of cognitive information process (CIP) in assisting military members manage the transition to civilian work. CIP is integrated into traditional military transition services to help service members address both immediate work concerns and learn skills that will support their future work transitions (Clemens & Milsom, 2008). From a psychology-of-working perspective, such interventions would be good examples of both empowerment and scaffolding.

Infuse Vocational Theory into Adult Employment and Training Services

Finally, there is a disconnect between the development and implementation of adult vocational programs and career theory. Vocational theory and research do not appear to have an influence on the development of adult employment training programs, based on the lack of inclusion of vocational psychology principles in the local, state, and federal laws that have mandated and shaped the design of most such programs. In another example of this disconnect, organizational management research indicates that the results of outplacement counseling, which helps executives manage transitions following job loss, will vary by personality factors, including agreeableness, conscientiousness, and openness (Martin & Lekan, 2008). The authors encourage outplacement counselors to attend to personality, but they fail to even mention the relationship between personality and vocational theory.

The omission of vocational theory and vocational psychologists from adult employment and training programs can limit program effectiveness, as well as keep program leaders uninformed of the many effective interventions that have been developed within the field of vocational psychology. To address this concern, we suggest the forging of a new partnership between vocational psychology and adult vocational programs. This partnership will offer adult vocational services with a theoretical foundation and reliable assessment measures as means of developing and assessing the effectiveness of these programs. For vocational psychology, a partnership such as this would offer psychologists access to these programs, where they can serve as consultants and obtain fresh data on the usefulness of vocational theories. This cyclical relationship may also lead psychologists to improve or develop new vocational theories and models that lead to more effective interventions that are appropriate across the wide range of working adult needs.

The psychology-of-working perspective is particularly useful in forging this improved relationship between employment and training agencies and vocational psychology, as it has been designed to augment and work in conjunction with other vocational theories (Blustein et al., 2008). By offering an inclusive perspective on the needs of adults traditionally underserved by vocational theory, yet still using vocational theory to understand work behavior, the psychology-of-working perspective can function as a bridge between the sometimes disparate worlds of employment services and vocational theory and research.

Future Directions

This review of adult employment training services has identified numerous areas of research and practice that can be more fully pursued by vocational psychology. The following questions outline some of the directions that psychology-of-working scholars might pursue to enhance employment services to adults.

1. How do we form more effective and productive partnerships with existing training and employment agencies? How do we demonstrate that vocational theory, especially the psychology of working, is relevant to the services they provide? This is a critical advocacy need, as policy changes at the federal and state levels will be necessary to support such partnerships.

2. What research needs to be conducted to demonstrate that relatively short-term interventions, which fit more readily into existing services, can be effective and add measurable value to what is currently offered? Given the needs of adult workers, and the difficulties inherent in attending extended workshops, for example, we need to develop more time-limited interventions to address critical consciousness, empowerment, and self-determination.

3. How can the contribution of social connectedness be more adequately assessed in the context of the adult worker's acquisition of skills and development as a member of the labor force? To support the integration of social connectedness as a key component of training and employment services, we need to demonstrate that it is related to job tenure and satisfaction, and therefore contributes to the overarching goal of adult employment agencies.

4. What steps are necessary to engage employers in the development of opportunities for working adults? Beyond that, how is this engagement sustained so that employers remain involved across changes in the larger economic and political context? Many existing approaches to vocational development focus on the individual and thereby reinforce the assumption that everyone has equal access to the opportunity structure. The psychology-of-working perspective can make a valuable contribution by clearly articulating that employers, as representatives of the opportunity structure, have a role to play in ensuring that working adults have meaningful and dignified work.

5. What can we do differently to bring vocational services to the adult workers who need them, rather than expecting them to come to agencies and offices? If a parent of three has to choose between paying the electric bill and paying for transportation to a local job services agency, we have removed the accessibility of vocational services. The psychology-of-working perspective might be expanded to consider ways in which we can "give away" vocational interventions by bringing them to communities in need. There are communities in the United States where a long-term unemployment rate of 25% or greater is the norm. How do we bring vocational psychologists, well prepared to provide meaningful interventions, to the adults who are historically disenfranchised and overlooked?

Conclusion

The needs of working adults with limited volition and few choices have long been underrepresented in the vocational psychologist literature. The psychology-of-working perspective can be used to identify the myriad ways in which adult work transitions can affect individuals, families, and communities. Interventions consistent with psychology of working can improve the services currently available to adult workers and work seekers by emphasizing the holistic needs of the adult, recognizing that work serves many purposes in a person's life, and providing an empowerment-based model of skills development that better prepare adults to respond to inevitable work transitions. Further, the psychology-of-working perspective provides a critical lens to consider the current contribution made by vocational psychology to adult employment and training programs, and suggests new questions and issues that can be pursued to make meaningful work more accessible to all adults.

References

Amundson, N. (2006). Challenges for career interventions in changing contexts. *International Journal for Educational and Vocational Guidance, 6*, 3–14. doi: 10.1007/s10775-0060002-4

Ankeny, E. M., & Lehmann, J. P. (2010). The transition lynchpin: the voices of individuals with disabilities who attend a community college transition program. *Community College Journal of Research and Practice, 34*, 477–496. doi: 10.1080/10668920701382773

Arthur, M. B., & Rousseau, D. M. (1996). *The boudaryless career.* New York: Oxford University Press.

Baron, L., & Morin, L. (2010). The impact of executive coaching on self-efficacy related to management soft-skills. *Leadership & Organization Development Journal, 31*, 18–38. doi:10.1108/01437731011010362

Bauer, J. J., & McAdams, D. P. (2004). Personal growth in adults' stories of life transitions. *Journal of Personality, 72*, 573–602. doi:10.1111/j.0022-3506.2004.00273.x

Beimers, D., & Fischer, R. L. (2007). Pathways to employment: The experiences of TANF recipients with employment services. *Families in Society, 88*, 391–400.

Bhat, C. S. (2010). Assisting unemployed adults find suitable work: A group intervention embedded in community and grounded in social action. *Journal for Specialists in Group Work, 35*, 246–254. doi:10.1080/01933922.2010.492898

Blustein, D., Kenna, A., Gill, N., & DeVoy, J. (2008). The psychology of working: A new framework for counseling practice and public policy. *The Career Development Quarterly, 56*(4), 294–308.

Blustein, D. L. (2006). *The psychology of working: A new perspective for career development, counseling, and public policy.* Mahwah, NJ: Lawrence Erlbaum Associates Publishers.

Bobek, B. L., & Robbins, S. B. (2005). Counseling for career transition: Career pathing, job loss, and reentry. In S. D. Brown, R. W. Lent, S. D. Brown, & R. W. Lent (Eds.), *Career development and counseling: Putting theory and research to work* (pp. 625–650). Hoboken, NJ: John Wiley & Sons Inc.

Brewington, J. O., & Nassar-McMillan, S. (2000). Older adults: Work-related issues and implications for counseling. *Career Development Quarterly, 49*, 2–15. Retrieved from http://proquest.umi.com.ezproxy.gsu.edu/pqdweb?vinst=PROD&fmt=6&startpage=-1&vname=PQD&RQT=309&did=59982911&scaling=FULL&vtype=PQD&rqt=309&TS=1312208930&clientId=19356

Brooke, L. (2009). Prolonging the careers of older information technology workers: Continuity, exit or retirement transitions?. *Ageing & Society, 29*, 237–256. doi:10.1017/S0144686X0800768X

Broom, D. H., D'Souza, R. M., Strazdins, L., Butterworth, P., Parslow, R., & Rodgers, B. (2006). The lesser evil: Bad jobs or unemployment? A survey of mid-aged Australians. *Social Science & Medicine, 63*, 575–586. doi:10.1016/j.socscimed.2006.02.003

Brown, S. D., & Lent, R. W. (Eds.).(2005). *Career development and counseling: Putting theory and research to work.* Hoboken, NJ: John Wiley & Sons.

Bureau of Labor Statistics (2010). Labor force characteristics by race and ethnicity, 2009. Retrieved from http://www.bls.gov/

Byrne, D. R., & Derbin, E. D. (Eds.). (June 11, 2011). Digging deeper into the details of the daunting jungle of unemployment statistics. *Economic Newsletter for the New Millennium, 2011* (5), 1–26. Retrieved from http://www.econnewsletter.com/media//DIR_66501/c78a99bf22391277ffff839b7f000101.pdf

Cabrera, E. F. (2007). Opting out and opting in: Understanding the complexities of women's career transitions. *Career Development International, 12*, 218–237. doi:10.1108/13620430710745872

Chung, Y. B., & Gfroerer, M. C. A. (2003). Career coaching, practice, training, professional, and ethical issues. *Career Development Quarterly, 52*, 141–152.

Clarke, M. (2007). Where to from here? Evaluating employability during career transition. *Journal of Management & Organization, 13*, 196–211. Retrieved from http://ezproxy.library.und.edu/login?url=http://search.ebscohost.com/login.aspx?direct=true&db=psyh&AN=2007-14328-001&site=ehost-live&scope=site

Clemens, E. V., & Milsom, A. S. (2008). Enlisted service members' transition into the civilian world of work: A cognitive information approach. *Career Development Quarterly, 56*, 246–256. Retrieved from http://ezproxy.library.und.edu/login?url=http://search.ebscohost.com/login.aspx?direct=true&db=psyh&AN=2008-02902-007&site=ehost-live&scope=site

Davidson, J. C., & Caddell, D. P. (1994). Religion and the meaning of work. *Journal for the Scientific Study of Religion, 33*, 315–147. doi: 10.2307/13866001994-44859-001.

Deci, E. L., & Ryan, R. M. (2000). The "what" and "why" of goal pursuits: Human needs and the self-determination of behavior. *Psychological Inquiry, 11*, 227–268.

Deskins, J., & Bruce, D. (2004, June). *Work requirements and welfare: Work or education first?* A Report to the Tennessee Department of Health and Human Services. Retrieved from http://cber.utk.edu/TDHS/ffjun0403.pdf

Dik, B. J., & Duffy, R. D. (2009). Calling and vocation at work: Definitions and prospect for research and practice. *Counseling Psychologist, 37*, 424–450. doi:10.1177/0011000008316430

Dooley, D., Prause, J., & Ham-Rowbottom, K. A. (2000). Underemployment and depression: Longitudinal relationships. *Journal of Health and Social Behavior, 41*, 421–436. Retrieved from http://www.jstor.org/stable/10.2307/2676295

Duffy, R. D. (2006). Spirituality, religion, and career development: Current status and future directions. *Career Development Quarterly, 55*, 52–63. Retrieved from http://web.ebscohost.com.ezproxy.gsu.edu/ehost/pdfviewer/pdfviewer?vid=3&hid=112&sid=279d51f1-fc66-412e-80b4-9f965546203a%40sessionmgr114

Ebaugh, E. R., Pipes, P. F., Chafetz, J. S., & Daniels, M. (2003). Where's the religion? Distinguishing faith-based from secular social service agencies. *Journal for the Scientific Study of Religion, 42*, 411–426. doi: 10.1111/1468-5906.00191

Ebberwein, C. A., Krieshok, T. S., Ulven, J. C., & Prosser, E. C. (2004). Voices in transition: Lessons on career adaptability. *Career Development Quarterly, 52*, 292–308.

Eby, L. T., & Buch, K. (1995). Job loss as career growth: Responses to involuntary career transitions. *Career Development Quarterly, 44*, 26–38. Retrieved from http://search.proquest.com.ezproxy.gsu.edu/docview/219436765/fulltext/130E0A9EC9222990031/1?accountid=11226

Enright, M. S. (1996). The relationship between disability status, career beliefs, and career indecision. *Rehabilitation Counseling Bulletin, 40*, 134–153. Retrieved from http://web.ebscohost.com.ezproxy.gsu.edu/ehost/detail?sid=84677591-fa75-46dc864ecaeef3102905%40sessionmgr113&vid=1&hid=108&bdata=JnNpdGU9ZWhvc3QtbGl2ZQ%3d%3d#db=a9h&AN=9709153563

Evers, W. J. G., Brouwers, A., & Tomic, W. (2006). A quasi-experimental study on management coaching effectiveness. *Consulting Psychology Journal: Practice and Research, 58*, 174–182. doi: 10.1037/1065-9293.58.3.174

Fitzgerald, L. F., Galfand, M. J., & Drasgow, F. (1995). Measuring sexual harassment: Theoretical and psychometric advances. *Basic and Aplied Socail Psychology, 17*, 425–445.

Flannery, K. B., Yovanoff, P., Benz, M. R., & McGrath-Kato, M. (2008). Improving employment outcomes of individuals with disabilities through short-term training. *Career Development for Exceptional Individuals, 31*, 26–36. doi:10.1177/0885728807313779

Forret, M. L., Sullivan, S. E., & Mainiero, L. A. (2010). Gender role differences in reactions to unemployment: Exploring psychological mobility and boundaryless careers. *Journal of Organizational Behavior, 31*, 647–666. doi:10.1002/job.703

Forrier, A., Sels, L., & Stynen, D. (2009). Career mobility at the intersection between agent and structure: A conceptual model. *Journal of Occupational and Organizational Psychology, 82*, 739–759. doi:10.1348/096317909X470933

Fouad, N. A., & Byars-Winston, A. M. (2005). Cultural context of career choice: Meta-analysis of race/ethnicity differences. *The Career Development Quarterly, 53*, 223–233. doi:10.1002/j.2161-0045.2005.tb00992.x

Fouad, N. A., & Bynner, J. (2008). Work transitions. *American Psychologist, 63*, 241–251. doi:10.1037/0003-066X.63.4.241

Gelfand, M. J., Fitzgerald, L. F., & Drasgow, F. (1995). The structure of sexual harassment: A confirmatory analysis across cultures and settings. *Journal of Vocational Behavior, 47*, 164–177. Retrieved from http://www.sciencedirect.com.ezproxy.gsu.edu/science?_ob=PublicationURL&_tockey

Goodman, J., & McClurg, S. (2002). Community-based adult career counseling. In S. G. Niles & S. G. Niles (Eds.), *Adult career development: Concepts, issues and practices* (3rd ed., pp. 307–320). Columbus, OH: National Career Development Association.

Greif, S. (2007). Advances in research on coaching outcomes. *International Coaching Psychology Review, 2*(3), 222–249.

Griffin, B., & Hesketh, B. (2005). Counseling for work adjustment. In S. D. Brown, R. W. Lent (Eds.), *Career development and counseling: Putting theory and research to work* (pp. 483–505). Hoboken, NJ: John Wiley & Sons Inc.

Grubb, W. N. (2001). From isolation to integration: Postsecondary vocational education and emerging systems of workforce development. *New Directions for Community Colleges, 115*, 27–37. doi: 10.1002/cc.28

Gutek, B. A., & Koss, M. P. (1993). Changed women and changed organizations: Consequences of and coping with sexual harassment. *Journal of Vocational Behavior, 42*, 28–48. Retrieved from http://www.sciencedirect.com.ezproxy.gsu.edu/science?_ob=PublicationURL&_tockey

Guttman, R. (1983). Job Training Partnership Act: New help for the unemployed. *Monthly Labor Review, 106*(3), 3–10. Retrieved from http://www.sciencedirect.com.ezproxy.gsu.edu/science?_ob=PublicationURL&_tockey

Haennicke, S. B., Konieczny, M. E., & Raphael, J. (2000, March). *Elements of success in welfare-to-work programs: Programmatic and policy recommendations.* Chicago: Center for Impact Research. Retrieved from http://www.impactresearch.org/documents/fryelementssuccess.pdf

Hall, D. T. (2004). The protean career: A quarter-century journey. *Journal of Vocational Behavior, 65*, 1–13. doi:10.1016/j.jvb.2003.10.006

Hansen, L. S. (2002). Integrative life planning (ILP): A holistic theory for career counseling with adults. In S. G. Niles & S. G. Niles (Eds.), *Adult career development: Concepts, issues and practices* (3rd ed., pp. 57–75). Columbus, OH: National Career Development Association.

Hasenfeld, Y., & Weaver, D. (1996). Enforcement, compliance, and dispute in welfare-to work programs. *Social Services Review, 70*, 235–256. Retrieved from http://www.jstor.org/stable/30012888

Hernandez, E. F., Foley, P. F., & Beitin, B. K. (2011). Hearing the call: A phenomenological study of religion in career choice. *Journal of Career Development, 38*, 62–88. doi:10.1177/0894845309358889

Herr, E. L. (2002). Adult career development: Some perspectives on the future. In S. G. Niles & S. G. Niles (Eds.), *Adult career development: Concepts, issues and practices* (3rd ed., pp. 385–393). Columbus, OH: National Career Development Association.

Herr, E. L., & Cramer, S. H. (1988). *Career guidance and counseling through the life span: Systematic approaches* (3rd ed.). Glenview, IL: Scott, Foresman & Co.

Hollenbeck, K., & Kimmel, J. (2002). The role of postsecondary education in welfare reform: Ohio's jobs student retention program. *Evaluation Review, 26*, 618–644. doi: 10.1177/0193841X0202600603

International Labour Office (2010, January). *Global employment trends.* Geneva, Switzerland: Author. Retrieved from http://www.ilo.org/public/libdoc/ilo/P/09332/09332%282010-January%29.pdf

Jacobs, J. (2001). Community colleges and the Workforce Investment Act: Promises and problems of the new vocationalism. *New Directions for Community Colleges, 115*, 93–99. Retrieved from http://web.ebscohost.com.ezproxy.gsu.edu/ehost/pdfviewer/pdfviewer?vid=3&hid=112&si =033ebb9a-999f-448a-ac32-94ceb04dee4c%40sessionmgr110

Jacobs, J., & Dougherty, K. J. (2006). The uncertain future of the community college workforce development mission. *New Directions for Community Colleges, 136*, 53–62. doi:10.1002/cc.259

Jacobson, L. (2009). *Strengthening one-stop career centers: Helping more unemployed workers find jobs and build skills.* Washington, DC: Brookings Institute.

Jensen, L., & Slack, T. (2003). Underemployment in America: Measurement and evidence. *American Journal of Community Psychology, 32*, 21–31. Retrieved from http://link.springer.com/article/10.1023%2FA%3A1025686621578?LI=true#page-1

Juntunen, C. L., Cavett, A. M., Clow, R. B., Rempel, V., Darrow, R. E., & Guilmino, A. (2006). Social justice through self-sufficiency: Vocational psychology and the transition from welfare to work. In R. L. Toporek, L. H. Gerstein, N. A. Fouad, G. Roysircar, & T. Israel (Eds.), *Handbook for social justice in counseling psychology* (pp. 294–309). Thousand Oaks, CA: SAGE Publications.

Juntunen, C. L., Wegner, K. E., & Matthews, L. G. (2002). Promoting positive career changes in midlife. In C. L. Juntunen, D. R. Atkinson (Eds.), *Counseling across the lifespan: Prevention and treatment* (pp. 329–247). Thousand Oaks, CA: Sage Publications.

Kempner, K., & Warford, L. (2009). The promise of the college and career transitions initiative. *Techniques: Connecting Education & Careers, 84*(7), 40–43. Retrieved from http://web.ebscohost.com.ezproxy.gsu.edu/ehost/pdfviewer/pdfviewer?vid=5&hid=112&sid=78e93549-c2e2-494a-8767-961195cbb3de%40sessionmgr110

Kilburg, R. R. (2004). Trudging toward Dodoville: Conceptual approaches and case studies in executive coaching. *Consulting Psychology Journal: Practice And Research, 56*, 203–213. doi:10.1037/1065-9293.56.4.203

Kochhar, R., Fry, R., & Taylor, P. (2011). *Wealth gaps rise to record highs between Whites, Blacks, Hispanics.* Washington, DC: Pew Research Center. Retrieved from http://www.pewsocialtrends.org/2011/07/26/wealth-gaps-rise-to-record-highs-between-whites-blacks-hispanics/

League for Innovation in the Community College (2008). *College and career transitions initiative.* Retrieved from http://www.league.org/league/projects/ccti/network/index.htm

Lindstrom, L. E., Flannery, K. B., Benz, M. R., Olszewski, B., & Slovic, R. (2009). Building employment training partnerships between vocational rehabilitation and community colleges. *Rehabilitation Counseling Bulletin, 52*, 189–201. doi:10.1177/0034355208323946

Liu, W. M. (2010). *Social class and classism in the helping professions: Research, theory and practice.* Thousand Oaks, CA: SAGE Publications.

Livermore, M., Davis, B., Powers, R., & Lim, Y. (2011). Failing to make ends meet: Dubious financial success among employed former welfare to work program participants. *Journal of Family and Economic Issues, 32*, 73–83.

Lobo, F., & Watkins, G. (1995). Late career unemployment in the 1990s: Its impact on the family. *Journal of Family Studies, 1*, 103–113.

Lockhart, W. H. (2005). Building bridges and bonds: Generating social capital in secular and faith-based poverty-to-work programs. *Sociology of Religion, 66*, 45–60. doi:10.2307/4153115.

Lowman, R. (2005). Executive coaching: The road to Dodoville needs paving with more than good assumptions. *Consulting Psychology Journal: Practice and Research, 57*, 90–96. doi:10.1037/1065-9293.57.1.90.

Martin, H. J., & Lekan, D. F. (2008). Individual differences in outplacement success. *Career Development International, 13*, 425–439. doi:10.1108/13620430810891455

Miller, J. V. (2002). Career counseling for mature workers. In S. G. Niles & S. G. Niles (Eds.), *Adult career development: Concepts, issues and practices* (3rd ed., pp. 267–283). Columbus, OH: National Career Development Association. Retrieved from http://ezproxy.library.und.edu/login?url=http://search.ebscohost.com/login.aspx?direct=true&db=psyh&AN=2003-02552-015&site=ehost-live&scope=site

Motulsky, S. L. (2010). Relational processes in career transition: Extending theory, research, and practice. *Counseling Psychologist, 38*, 1078–1114. doi:10.1177/0011000010376415

Niles, S. G., Herr, E. L., & Hartung, P. J. (2002). Adult career concerns in contemporary society. In S. G. Niles & S. G. Niles (Eds.), *Adult career development: Concepts, issues and*

practices (3rd ed., pp. 2–18). Columbus, OH: National Career Development Association.

Olivero, G., Bane, K. D., & Kopelman, R. E. (1997). Executive coaching as a transfer of training tool: Effects on aproductivity in a public agency. *Public Personnel Management, 26*, 461–469. Retrieved from http://www.vivirdelcoaching.com/docs/estudios_y_Estadisticas/Execcoachingtransfer.html.pdf

Owen, L., & Flynn, M. (2004). Changing work: Mid-to-late life transitions in employment. *Ageing International, 29*, 333–350. Retrieved from http://web.ebscohost.com.ezproxy.gsu.edu/ehost/pdfviewer/pdfviewer?vid=3&sid=18e0b3a4-3c1f-46c9-a3a8-eb8c703832f5%40sessionmgr113&hid=110

Patton, W., & Donohue, R. (2001). Effects on the family of a family member being long-term unemployed. *Journal of Applied Health Behaviour, 3*(1), 31–39.

Paul, K. I., & Moser, K. (2009). Unemployment impairs mental health: Meta-analyses. *Journal of Vocational Behavior, 74*, 264–282. doi:10.1016/j.jvb.2009.01.001

Pavoni, N., & Violante, G. L. (2007). Optimal welfare-to-work programs. *Review of Economic Studies, 74*, 283–318. doi:10.1111

Pipes, P. F., & Ebaugh, H. R. (2002). Faith-based coalitions, social services, and government funding. *Sociology of Religion, 63*, 49–68. doi: 10.2307/3712539

Quinn, J. F., & Kozy, M. (1996). The role of bridge jobs in the retirement transition: Gender, race, and ethnicity. *The Gerontologist, 36*, 363–373.

Roksa, J. (2006). Does the vocational focus of community colleges hinder students' educational attainment? *Review of Higher Education, 29*, 499–526. Retrieved from http://search.proquest.com.ezproxy.gsu.edu/docview/220851031/1346CEF8BE218F0026A 6?accountid=11226

Savickas, M. L. (1997). Career adaptability: An integrative construct for life-span, life-space theory. *Career Development Quarterly, 45*(3), 247–259.

Schmidt, M. A., & Smith, D. L. (2007). Individuals with disabilities perceptions on preparedness for the workforce and factors that limit employment. *Work: A Journal of Prevent, Assessment and Rehabilitation, 28*, 13–21. Retrieved from http://iospress.metapress.com/content/1fbxma1dr944v5el/

Schoon, I. (2007). Adaptations to changing times: Agency in context. *International Journal of Psychology, 42*(2), 94–101. doi:10.1080/00207590600991252

Schoon, I., Martin, P., & Ross, A. (2007). Career transitions in times of social change. His and her story. *Journal of Vocational Behavior, 70*(1), 78–96. doi:10.1016/j.jvb.2006.04.009

Sedlak, A., Mettenburg, J., Basena, M., Petta, J., McPherson K., Greene, A., et al. (2010). *Fourth national incidence study of child abuse and neglect. Report to Congress, Executive Summary.* Retrieved from http://www.acf.hhs.gov/sites/default/files/opre/nis4_report_exec_summ_pdf_jan2010.pdf http://www.acf.hhs.gov/programs/opre/abuse_neglect/natl_incid/nis4_report_congress_full_pdf_jan2010.pdf.

Sellers, T. S., Thomas, K., Batts, J., & Ostman, C. (2005). Women called: A qualitative study of Christian women dually called to motherhood and career. *Journal of Psychology and Theology, 33*, 198–209.

Shivy, V. A., Wu, J. J., Moon, A. E., Mann, S. C., Holland, J. G., & Eacho, C. (2007). Ex-offenders reentering the workforce. *Journal of Counseling Psychology, 54*, 466–473. doi:10.1037/0022-0167.54.4.466

Stern, L. (2004). Executive coaching: A working definition. *Consulting Psychology Journal: Practice and Research, 56*, 154–162. doi: 10.1037/1065-9293.56.3.0

Szymanski, E. M., & Hanley-Maxwell, C. (1996). Career development of people with developmental disabilities: An Ecological Model. *Journal of Rehabilitation, 62*, 48–55. Retrieved from http://homer.gsu.edu/search/metasearch/results/000191/003331

Thach, E. C. (2002). The impact of executive coaching and 360 feedback on leadership effectiveness. *Leadership & Organization Development Journal, 23*, 205–214. doi: 10.1108/01437730210429070

Timmons, J. C., Boeltzig, H., Fesko, S. L., Cohen, A., & Hamner, D. (2007). Broadening opportunities for job seekers with disabilities: Strategies to effectively provide assistive technology in One-Stop centers. *Work: A Journal of Prevent, Assessment and Rehabilitation, 28*, 85–93. Retrieved from http://iospress.metapress.com/content/1fbxma1dr944v5el/

U.S. Congress (1998). *Workforce Investment Act of 1998.* Public Law 105–220. Retrieved from http://www.doleta.gov/usworkforce/wia/wialaw.txt

U.S. Department of Health and Human Services. (2006). *Seventh annual report to Congress.* Administration for Children and Families, U.S. Department of Health and Human Services.

U.S. Department of Labor (1998). Workforce Investment Act of 1998. Retrieved from http://www.doleta.gov/usworkforce/wia/wialaw.pdf

U.S. Department of Labor, Bureau of Labor Statistics (July, 2008). *Spotlight on statistics: Older workers.* Retrieved from http://www.bls.gov/spotlight/2008/older_workers/

U.S. Department of Labor, Bureau of Labor Statistics (July 8, 2011). *Economic news release: Employment situation summary.* Report USDL-11-1011. Retrieved from http://www.bls.gov/news.release/empsit.nr0.htm

U.S. Department of Labor, Bureau of Labor Statistics (2009). *Ranks of discouraged workers and others marginally attached to the labor force rise during recession.* Retrieved from http://www.bls.gov/opub/ils/pdf/opbils74.pdf

U.S. General Accounting Office (2003, June). *Workforce Investment Act: One-stop centers implemented strategies to strengthen services and partnership, but more research and information sharing is needed.* GAO-03-725. Retrieved from http://www.doleta.gov/performance/guidance/gaoreports/d03725.pdf

Zikic, J., & Hall, D. T. (2009). Toward a more complex view of career exploration. *Career Development Quarterly, 58*(2), 181–192. Retrieved from http://ezproxy.library.und.edu/login?url=http://search.ebscohost.com/login.aspx?direct=true&db=psyh&AN=2010-12635-007&site=ehost-live&scope=site

Public Policy and the Psychology of Working

Spencer G. Niles *and* Edwin L. Herr

Abstract

This chapter provides an overview of the link between public policy and the psychology of working. Specifically, it emphasizes reasons for engaging in public policy, the changing organization of work and the shifting skills requirements for employment, conflicts between work and family, the psychology of work, public policy in historical context, and related themes. The chapter highlights the fact that these themes give expression to public policy and career development. Furthermore, it provides specific policy and legislative examples to illustrate the connection between context, policy, and career services. Finally, it discusses how these themes change as the larger societies change and constantly create new practices, new policies, and new research and scholarship in career development services.

Key Words: career development, emerging work contexts, public policy, legislation

Significant changes in work, occupational structures, and the psychology of working require reexamining the public policies supporting career development and career services. In this chapter, the authors highlight the emerging and expanding context of the worker; stress the important role for public policy in the work of career theorists, career practitioners, and other stakeholders; examine the relationship among public policy, the work context, and the psychology of working; highlight public policy and career development in a historical context; identify public policy and career development realities; and describe opportunities for public policy engagement as it relates to career development.

Career Development Professionals and the Emerging Context of the Worker

Career concerns evolve as the nature of work changes. Harsh evidence exists to indicate that the nature of work is changing substantially. To call attention to these changes, authors use such dramatic phrases as "the career has died" and "work has

ended" (Bridges, 1994; Rifkin, 1995). Although such declarations are not to be taken literally, they are to be taken seriously. The "career is dead" authors alert us to the fact that we must understand the changes occurring in the nature of work so that we can respond effectively to the career concerns confronting workers in contemporary society.

Indicators revealing ways in which work is changing include statistics about high levels of global unemployment, large numbers of jobs being transferred from one nation to another, rapidly changing occupational structures, corporate downsizing, offshoring, and a jobless economic recovery. Reports of these events appear daily in various news media. Technological advances change how business is conducted as small companies compete globally via cyberspace and computers perform tasks once assigned to workers, thereby creating nearly worker-less factories. Contingent employees perform project work; when the project is completed, so is their employment. Underlying these changes is the clear message that the social contract between employers and employees is being redefined (Niles, Herr, & Hartung, 2002; Rifkin, 1995). New challenges and career tasks emerge from these substantial changes in the nature of work.

Contemporary workers struggle to balance their various life-role commitments as predictions concerning ways in which technology would create a leisure society long ago gave way to reality. Rather than creating more leisure time, advances in technology have made it easier (and often necessary) to work more hours. Unfortunately, technology can change work, but it cannot change the fact that days still occur in 24-hour cycles and more of those hours are being filled by work activity (Blustein, 1997; Niles & Harris-Bowlsbey, 2009).

Other evidence that the nature of work is changing is found in media reports describing increases in the number of (a) companies offering daycare and parental leave, (b) families with dual earners, and (c) people working from home. Work concerns do not occur in isolation from life concerns. These reports highlight the increased intertwining of work and family roles and have important implications for the career concerns confronting workers (Niles, Herr, & Hartung, 2002).

Families and the Workplace

Changes in the workplace and the various types of pressure workers experience are reflected in the home and within families. In families in which both parents work, parents frequently come to their childrearing and/or marital roles in a state of fatigue. The strain of their work carries into the home. In selected occupations, where parents are subjected to pressure to work significant amounts of overtime or because of skill shortages in their workplace, time for balancing nonwork and other life roles becomes limited and problematic. In other circumstances, where one or both parents are under continuous pressure to keep their competencies current, they may find much of their discretionary time devoted to taking courses and learning new skills so they can compete for work opportunities. The pressures for people in dual-career or dual-income families to work harder, and maintain a high level of skill competence, are also often indirectly changing the nature of childrearing in the United States. Just as corporations outsource tasks that they previously did within the corporation to organizations outside the corporation that have specific specialties in security, food services, custodial work, advertising, marketing, accounting, transportation, or many other possibilities, many families are doing the same with

regard to maintaining their home and children. They are outsourcing daycare and birthday parties, eating out or ordering food to be delivered, and ordering groceries online rather than going to the store and selecting them; they are using cleaning services, lawn and snow removal services, and other mechanisms to try to balance work and nonwork roles. The term "virtual parenting" has come into the language to describe parents whose job requires them to work late or travel frequently. Their solution is to try to use e-mail, texting, Skype, digital recordings, family conference calls, and/or voicemail to stay in touch with their children (Herr, 2002).

Niles, Herr, and Hartung (2002) contend that many of the sorts of strains on families (and the responses cited) really affect the affluent members of society, not people of low economic wealth, the middle class, or single parents. Single parents who work two jobs or more to maintain financial viability may also have to use daycare, but, where possible, they are likely to use a relative or a friend to perform childcare tasks rather than an expensive preschool or daycare. Frequently, the financially impoverished of the nation, whose employment is uncertain, who are frequently laid off or terminated, whose unskilled jobs are replaced by outsourcing or other mechanisms, may spend much of their discretionary time seeking work and/or engaging in several part-time jobs. Many of these people are on the edge of financial insolvency all the time, trying to engage in multiple ways to obtain funds while taking on all of the tasks required by their children, their homes, and their employers. They are people for whom "life structure issues" (i.e., the struggle to engage in each of their salient life roles meaningfully) triangulate around financial strain and creating some sense of hope for a better future. Such divides between the affluent and those of low economic wealth continue to fragment society. The economically poor are not just rich people without money: their culture, worldviews, expectations, and realities about the roles they do and can play are quite at odds with other segments of the population. In a stunning statistic that affirms such disparities in how different the people's roles are, Robert Reich (1991) noted, "Bill Gates' net worth alone is equal to the total net worth of the bottom 50% of American families." Thus, to be useful in today's context, career development professionals must be responsive to the myriad contextual factors driving intra-individual and extra-individual factors that foster (or limit) career development. The growing socioeconomic divide cannot be ignored. Theories and practices must be applicable, and career services available, to people from all socioeconomic strata. Most importantly, career development professionals must engage in public policy initiatives to ensure that such services are available.

The Public Policy and Career Development Problem

Public policies provide the fiscal and conceptual support for the provision of career services (e.g., offering career planning assistance, job search coaching, career transition assistance) to people seeking to manage their career development, often under very challenging circumstances (e.g., long-term unemployment, sudden involuntary unemployment). Unfortunately, there is an historic disconnect, particularly in the United States, for many career theorists and career practitioners when it comes to public policy awareness and involvement. Many theorists and practitioners simply do not understand that there is a connection at all. Some question how public policy efforts relate to the work that they do and/or view career development public policy as being the work of others (e.g., lobbyists, state and federal officials, policy "wonks").

Perhaps this situation is a natural consequence of the fact that scant attention is paid to the policy/theory/practice connection in counselor training programs. For example, Niles and Nassar-McMillan (2009) reviewed 79 syllabi from career development courses in counselor training programs and found that no syllabi contained any reference to public policy. This is perplexing given the importance of social justice, multiculturalism, and advocacy within counselor training programs. A key action, especially when there is inequality relative to accessing the opportunity structure (whether it is occupational or educational), is advocating for more socially-just public policies and legislation.

Counselors-in-training, who subsequently are often the primary career development specialists in their work settings, are apparently not informed about the importance of public policy and/or legislation. Indeed, for the past 100 years, public policies in the United States have supported and funded counselors vis-à-vis the provision of career services, for whom the services would be provided, by whom the services would be delivered, and for what purposes the services would be offered. Thus, the career development-related activities of school counselors, employment counselors, college counselors, career counselors, and others have been supported in various legislative acts (e.g., the Workforce Investment

Act of 1998, the National Defense Education Act of 1958 [NDEA], the Carl D. Perkins Vocational Education and Applied Technology Act as amended in 1998). More specifically, governmental policies and legislative acts have been the impetus for helping students develop educational plans and to cope with the transition from school to work and from secondary school to postsecondary school. Likewise, legislative acts have sought to provide the support for increasing worker employability and reducing periods of unemployment as adults strive to cope with their career transitions. Thus, when there is a disconnect for career practitioners between their work and public policies supporting career services, the very future of the career development profession is at peril. Underneath it all is the reality that public policies create the service delivery pipeline for career practitioners, and the continued existence of these policies requires practitioner involvement.

The disconnect between public policy and career development becomes especially problematic during challenging budgetary periods. When policymakers must make difficult decisions about cutting funding, data are needed to inform the decision-making process. Unfortunately, career development researchers tend not to wonder about the cost effectiveness of the interventions they devise (Sampson, Jr., Dozier, & Colvin, 2011). Career practitioners focus on the costs to the individual as they relate to self-esteem and/or lost wages, but policymakers look at the costs to society as they pertain to phenomena such as unemployment (Herr, 1996). Herr notes: "The policies and legislation in any nation are typically intended to mirror national goals for strengthening the nation's well-being, for identifying and providing remedial assistance to individuals whose behavior or lack of skills are troublesome to them or to the larger society, for providing a safety net for those who cannot care for themselves, and for stimulating workforce preparation, development, and training that increases the quality of persons entering or in the labor market" (p. 12). Moreover, career practitioners typically do not systematically collect outcome data regarding their interventions. If practitioners cannot demonstrate the efficacy of their interventions, then they lack the evidence required to convince stakeholders that the funds allocated to support their salaries are, in fact, worthy expenditures. The vacuum created by this inattention to the relationship between the effectiveness of career development interventions and public policy also places the profession in peril as legislators consider extreme cuts in federal and state funding.

In the United States, these concerns relative to the continuation of public policies and legislation supporting career services are immediate. Currently, the United States Congress is considering multiple resolutions that could result in the largest spending cuts in U.S. history. Such reductions place in serious jeopardy legislation that contains funding for practitioners who provide career assistance to young people and adults. It is ironic that this is occurring despite the fact that opportunities to access quality educational experiences and job opportunities are significantly low for many people and the overall unemployment rate in the United States hovers between 9% and 10%, compared to 7.5% in Canada, 7.7% in the United Kingdom, and 6.4% in Germany (Bureau of Labor Statistics, 2012).

The unemployment rate in the United States reflects people experiencing several forms of unemployment. The form of unemployment a person experiences is important because it provides direction to policymakers regarding which sort of response is needed to ameliorate significant unemployment rates. For example, many people who are unemployed are said to be structurally unemployed. Structural unemployment reflects shifting skill set priorities within work settings. For instance, many skill sets related to assembly line employment 20 years ago have given way to technological skill set requirements because computers perform much of the work that once was performed by assembly line workers. Shifts such as these leave many workers behind if they don't have access to training programs intended to provide skills in areas of greater demand. Federal programs such as the Job Training Partnership Act and, before that, the Comprehensive Employment and Training Act have provided structurally unemployed workers with opportunities to acquire new skills so they can become more employable (Herr, Cramer, & Niles, 2004).

Workers can also be unemployed due to experiencing frictional unemployment. Frictional unemployment relates to the time between jobs or the time between school and jobs. These workers have the requisite skills but may need assistance in job search skills. One-stop career centers in the United States funded via the Workforce Investment Act provide job search assistance and job search skills training (e.g., résumé workshops, training in interview skills, networking). Such interventions are aimed at reducing the amount of time workers experience frictional unemployment.

Some workers are also unemployed due to cyclical unemployment. Cyclical unemployment occurs when changes in the business cycle lead to job lay-offs in particular industries. For example, because of increases in interest rates for home mortgages, fewer people can afford to buy a house and fewer houses are being built. Less home construction leads to workers in that industry being laid off. Workers in these circumstances may need assistance in identifying ways in which their skills sets are transferable to other jobs. In cyclical unemployment situations, once the business cycle becomes more favorable, the jobs also return and the workers' skills are once again in demand. Thus, retraining for workers experiencing cyclical unemployment is not necessarily required (although workers may opt for training in occupations that are less susceptible to economic fluctuations).

The primary point here is that different forms of unemployment require different responses and have implications for both career practitioners and policymakers. However, even when the need exists for career services, if data-based advocacy for public policies that support the provision of career services does not occur, those policies (and their related services) are not likely to be funded. Thus, career theorists and practitioners need to develop awareness of and become involved in public policy activities to support the provision of career services across the lifespan. Developing even a rudimentary understanding of these relationships and fostering a commitment to public policy involvement will have a major impact on the structure and processes of career development and, in turn, on the lives of many people in society who need competent career services.

Public Policy, the Work Context, and the Psychology of Working

Clarity regarding the current context for work and workers provides a foundation for public policy engagement. As the chapters of this book have demonstrated, the psychology of working is complex; it is a powerful medium that carries diverse meanings for individuals as they make career decisions or engage in work activity. Beyond the economic results of having a job, earning a livelihood, and being able to meet one's expenses and purchase goods and services, all work, paid and unpaid, has the additional potential to meet broad social and psychological needs, including power, effective interaction with others (affiliation), personal dignity (self-esteem, well-being), a sense of competency (mastery), identification with some purpose of mission larger than oneself (charity, philanthropy, spirituality), and human relations (positive communications, sharing, interaction) (Arthur, 2008). For many people, achievement of any of these needs, or others that could be cited, leads to a passionate attachment to the work they do.

However, if work is not valued, the specific work culture is substantially unsatisfying, the relationship to a supervisor is negative, and/or work tasks are not valued, etc., then it is likely that the needs of workers in such situations are not being met. In many instances, a variety of deleterious behaviors can arise in such situations. For example, substance abuse may become part of the worker's solution for coping with a challenging job situation (Frone, 2000), thereby exacerbating the situation. Negative workplace challenges can also result in a "spillover" effect in which participating in one role (e.g., work) affects participation in other life roles (e.g., family). Using nationally representative samples, Grzycaz, Almeida, and McDonald (2002) found that older workers (older than age 54) experience less negative work–family spillover than younger workers (ages 25 to 54). These results suggest the need for workplace policies that address negative spillover between work and family throughout most of the working years. Such policies would need to be attentive to the developmental differences in the nature of work–family spillover experiences. Specifically, younger workers with young children need different services and workplace policies (e.g., childcare) than workers in their 50s, who may have issues related to caring for parents. The primary point is that work does not occur in a vacuum. Essentially, every workplace is a human community with all the potential and all of the threat that is implied. Indeed, according to Landy (1989), "Work is something that happens to an individual. It is a treatment of sorts. People go to a work setting and are exposed to various elements. These elements include things such as heat and light and noise. In addition, there are such elements as pay and supervisory style and co-workers. Even the duties and responsibilities that make up the 'job' are treatments. Workers are exposed to a work place, a certain demand for productivity and accountability" (p. 600). These individual and collective person–environment interactions influence the individual's work satisfaction as well as the meaning he or she attaches to work.

The meaning of work, its language, its content, its processes, its information, its associated stresses, and its educational or skill requirements change across time and across generations. Indeed, the choice of, and adjustment to, work is intertwined with how one sees oneself, one's confidence that one can perform or master work tasks and that the work available will meet one's needs and values. Indeed, being successful in the workplace is, at the least, a blending of technical skills and psychological attitudes, self-efficacy, and values.

Various observers suggest that, compared to the past, individual career development in the future will become less linear, less predictable, more values-oriented, and more spontaneous and will consist of more frequent job changes and transitions, greatly affected by interruptions and fragmentation (Herr, Cramer, & Niles, 2004). Thus, in addition to the technical and technological skills required by occupations and workplaces, given the widening diversity of career patterns and worker experiences, emerging conceptions of new careers emphasize the importance of people acquiring the skills that underlie personal flexibility and the ability to adapt to change. Clearly, in the future, more workers will be expected to engage in multitasking, being able to perform multiple processes, rather than narrow specialties or skills. The term "job" will likely fade away as a reflection of older ways of thinking about work tasks, how they are packaged, and their boundaries. Facilitating such adaptations to changes in the workplace by workers will be a significant challenge for career practitioners, and it will increasingly be seen as the object of public policy and/or legislation (Herr, Cramer, & Niles, 2004).

Equity and access issues will also continue to be a focus of public policy and related legislation. The societal and economic costs associated with a lack of work readiness within the labor force, as that term pertains both to getting hired and to maintaining a job once one is hired, are clear, and a greater awareness of both achievement and opportunity gaps provides the impetus for policy and legislative action to address such issues. Such is the historical and evolving context of work that serves as the backdrop for the emergence of public policies and legislation to address career development challenges in contemporary society.

Public Policy Defined

There are several ways to think about the definitions of public policy and legislation. "Public policy" can be defined as any type of actual or proposed government action at the federal, state, or local level to address social problems. In this context, public policy contains the set of policies (laws, plans, actions) that direct the functioning of a government. Another way to think about public policy is that it can be considered a definite course or method of action selected to guide and determine present and future directions (Herr & Pinson, 1982). A more contemporary perspective would suggest that policy development could be conceived as the creation of a set of hypotheses that reflect the best guesses by which to change the circumstance giving rise to the policy. In such a view, policy is seen as based on a set of assumptions about the situation needing change as well as about the actions that will change them (Herr, 2008).

In the United States, public policy can emerge from many different power centers: governmental agencies, "think tanks," trade associations, learned societies, or other special interests, including grassroots activism. In this context, public policy can be defined as a system of laws, regulatory measures, courses of action, and funding priorities directed at a given topic.

Public policy can be viewed from two other somewhat different perspectives. In a macro sense, public policy can be seen as a large umbrella under which is included every element related to a particular area of concern: legislation, public statements, public policies, and government commitments to costs or methods of achieving the goals of the public policy. At a micro level, one can argue that a public policy is not as powerful as the legislation that it spawns. Thus, in many situations, legislation is likely to be adopted as an enactment of law. Therefore, a specific piece of legislation debated and approved by the U.S. Congress, for instance, becomes "the law of the land" as related to a particular topical area and includes the rules that define the implementation of the particular legislative authority.

Policy formulation is typically not a closed system. In fact, some observers would say that it is a porous system that can be entered at any time by statespersons, advocates, special interests, or lobbyists. Other observers would say the crafting of public policy assumes the art of compromise and also assumes that political activism by special interest groups ordinarily makes a difference in who is affected by the policy and how. The latter is most effective when it embraces "touch points" (i.e., emotionally charged social issues that many citizens react to in a similar way, such as poor treatment of service veterans) that inspire the average citizen to engage in advocacy activities related to public policy. Issues such as returning veterans who cannot find employment, workplace violence, increased substance abuse in dislocated worker populations, and minority groups experiencing a lack of access to

quality schools are recent examples of issues inspiring collective action to influence public policy.

As any potential form of public policy or legislative action is examined and debated, it is clear that public policies create realities. Over the past century, policy and legislation have had major input into the shape and substance of career development interventions, who provides them, where it is done, for what reasons it is done, the credentials and training one needs to practice career interventions on behalf of particular client groups, who receives the career interventions, and their likely outcomes. As such, public policy and legislation have been important influences on the acceptance and support that government and public agencies give to providing career services as reflected in the language used in legislation, the criteria by which it grants money, the outcomes to be achieved, and the accountability processes put in place.

Legislation can be limiting or freeing, facilitative or inhibiting. Legislation provides conditions that free and facilitate so that people employed, underemployed, and unemployed can receive job training and education, assessment, occupational information, financial support, career counseling, and other processes. Career professionals can be helpful in working with policymakers to ensure that public policies are timely and clear and include contributions that professionals in career development can make toward the goals of specific public policies, the need for funding resources to support career development services, and the conditions by which such career interventions will be funded and held accountable.

Public Policy and Career Development in a Historical Context

Legislation in support of career interventions in the United States occurred as early as the first decade of the 1900s and has typically been very active in defining and shaping the substance and the structure of career development in every decade since that time (Herr, 1974, 1993). Examples of such areas in which career services and career interventions have played prominent roles include social reform, child labor laws, and the growing awareness of individual differences in the early 1900s; concern for people with disabilities in the 1920s; the economic exigencies and the need to match people with available, but very limited, employment opportunities during the Great Depression of the 1930s and national defense in the 1940s and 1950s; assistance to veterans to return to the civilian workforce or take advantage of the GI Bill to complete their education in the 1940s and 1950s and again today; the democratization of job and educational opportunities in the 1960s; economic austerity in the 1970s; the transformation from an industrial to an information-based economy and the rise of the global economy in the 1980s and 1990s; and the global economic crisis and recession of the early 21st century and the wars in Afghanistan and Iraq.

At present, public policy, legislation, and career development are extremely timely and important. National attention to public policy in career development is seen by many observers in the United States and abroad as critical at this point in our history because of the comprehensive changes in the organization of work, how it is done, and its availability. In this context, many of these observers talk about the challenges, if not the worldwide crises, that job seekers are facing. These crises fall on youth and adults, on rich and poor, on employers and employees, and they are comprehensive in scope. Among such issues are the millions of people, unemployed but often well trained and educated, making up a global labor surplus that moves around the world seeking employment. In addition, altered career pathways are rapidly emerging as outsourcing and offshoring change the jobs available in different nations. Of particular importance is the meaning of "career" in an environment that is in constant and rapid change, in which many workers are anxious and on edge because of the uncertainty of their jobs and the need to be their own career manager. Furthermore, given the rapidly growing ratio of part-time, contingent, and guest workers to the less rapidly growing proportion of full-time workers, many workers are now working two or three jobs to support their families.

The definitions of career, career development, career interventions, and other terms have been changing decade by decade for the past 100 years. Since these terms are used throughout this book, we will limit our discussion to a few perspectives on the term "career" as it can be found in public policy or legislation. A "career defines how one sees oneself in the context of one's social environment, one's past accomplishments or failures, and one's present competencies and attributes" (Raynor & Entin, 1982, p. 262). Careers can be unique to each person and created by what one chooses or does not choose. They are dynamic and unfold throughout life. They include not only occupations but also prevocational and post-vocational concerns as well as the integration of work with other life roles (e.g., family,

community, and leisure roles) (Herr, Cramer, & Niles, 2004). Finally, many career professionals have viewed career as a staging phenomenon that occurs within the context of an age-related and linear process (Super, 1990). Given the changes in work and its availability, linear conceptualizations of career are less accepted currently because of today's more fragmented careers, more people working for small and medium-sized employers, more contingent workers, more workers experiencing periods of unemployment, and more people being self-employed. The economic crises and its associated uncertainty requires workers to make career choices more often as they struggle to manage what is often a nonlinear career trajectory or a "protean" career experience (Hall & Mirvis, 1996).

Currently, in the United States, the policies concerning career interventions are something of an uncoordinated mosaic; although there are pieces of legislation of major importance to career development (for example, the Workforce Investment Act of 1998; the Carl D. Perkins Career and Technical Education Improvement Act of 2006), many other important pieces of legislation dealing with career issues have been allowed to terminate. Sometimes important elements of their contents are integrated into more recent legislation; in other cases those ideas simply expire (Hoyt, 2005). In the United States there is no single policy direction in career development that spans the federal or state governments or, indeed, other entities. Although there is a wide range of legislative initiatives available, in some cases they are created independent of other legislation in place or in process. In general, legislation is focused on special problems, specific agencies, or targeted populations rather than as manifestations of a coherent, life-cycle policy designed to ensure that everyone with career concerns or problems at any point across the lifespan can obtain assistance with their career development, whatever state, institution, or geographic location they occupy.

While the issues cited here could seem to be daunting and complex, many policymakers working in public policy and legislation have often seen career development and career services as sociopolitical processes and have used elements of career development as tools to solve national goals. For the most part, career services in the United States have been put in place or enabled by some form of governmental policy, legislative enactment, or statute that defines what services are to be provided, by whom, to whom, and for what purposes. As such,

U.S. public policy related to career services reflects a values-based continuum of sorts, with one end of the continuum prizing social justice and the other end prioritizing national security. An example of the latter is legislation related to the NDEA of 1958. In response to the Soviet Union's launching of Sputnik in 1957, legislation containing $887 million over 4 years was enacted to bolster national security related to advances in science. The act contained ten titles designed to improve the nation's schools: Title I prohibited federal control over curriculum, administration, or personnel; Title II provided federal assistance for low-interest loans to college students ($295 million); Title III provided financial assistance for science, mathematics, and modern foreign language instruction ($300 million); Title IV created national defense fellowships for students entering teaching fields at universities or colleges; Title V established grants for state educational agencies for guidance testing services ($88 million); Title VI provided support for modern foreign language programs ($15.25 million); Title VII provided for research and experimentation in effective uses for television, radio, and other audiovisual mediums for educational purposes ($18 million); Title VIII authorized grants for occupations necessary for the national defense ($60 million); Title IX provided for the Science Information Service in the National Science Foundation; and Title X authorized federal grants for improving statistical services for state educational agencies.

Clearly, this legislation represented a major economic commitment on the part of the United States. Career guidance served as a primary mechanism for helping students talented in math and science pursue these career paths. As such, career guidance was viewed as an economic, educational, and defense-related imperative. It is not simply coincidental that career theories, career assessment instruments, and career practitioners grew in number during the decades immediately following the infusion of funding support via legislation like this. The NDEA was, for more than a decade, a public statement of the importance of career development programming for students in K–12 and community colleges. It also supported having counselors in schools and in community colleges to help teachers, administrators, parents, and students understand that career development was part of the mission of the school, not just a random, temporary process.

The NDEA and the more recent federal funding initiatives related to science, technology, engineering, and mathematics (STEM) occupations provide excellent examples of how funding streams link to the broader national context. In its simplest terms, NDEA funding emerged from the Cold War events (specifically Sputnik) in which the United States was attempting to keep pace with the Soviet Union's advances in developing satellite and space flight technologies that could eventually be used for military purposes. The fact that the Soviet Union was able to place a satellite in orbit before the United States stirred concern in the United States that it had fallen behind the Soviets relative to the capacity to bring about significant scientific and technological developments pertaining to the "race for space." The reaction in the United States was an enormous shift toward emphasizing science and technological research. Essentially, the government revamped military and educational systems throughout the nation. Moreover, the federal government began pouring unmatched amounts of money into science education, engineering, and mathematics at all levels of education. Public policy and legislative initiatives brought an intense emphasis on training in the STEM disciplines. These events transformed American education by creating a new emphasis on curricular development in STEM subject areas. Moreover, the infusion of funds to support strengthening the United States in STEM areas included providing increased support for counselors in the schools who would be able to guide the brightest students toward STEM careers.

The current landscape within the United States once again is focused on strengthening the nation in STEM-related competencies. Reports such as those from the Program for International Student Assessment (PISA) sponsored by the Organization for Economic Cooperation and Development (OECD) have given rise to another wave of consternation regarding how effectively the United States is preparing students in the STEM disciplines. Specifically, U.S. students (age 15) performed below average in mathematics and average in science and reading on the 2009 PISA assessment (OECD, 2010). Such reports have provided a catalyst for substantial educational reforms and related funding initiatives in the United States. For example, President Barack Obama's administration has provided more than $4 billion to advance reforms and innovations in education through its "Race to the Top" competition. A substantial proportion of this funding is allocated toward improving STEM education in the United States.

From a contemporary standpoint, connecting the current context of economic crisis and uncertainty to the federal and/or state values structure from which public policy emerges provides key indications as to potential public policy initiatives. When national security and/or substantial economic crises are prevalent (as during the 1950s and currently, respectively), public policy and related legislative initiatives focus on stimulating American competitiveness globally. As with NDEA and the Race to the Top initiatives, these policies attempt to increase academic rigor, stimulate educational reform, and improve educational achievement to position students, and the nation, to be more competitive globally. Such initiatives often include but do not necessarily emphasize social justice.

Public Policy and Career Development Realities

Public policy and the legislation that flow from it rarely identifies career development, career counseling, career guidance, or related interventions as the sole purpose of the public policy or the legislation at issue. Rather, in most cases, career counseling and career development are seen as part of a package of program elements created to solve the problems that gave rise to initiating consideration of the particular public policy. These processes might be linked with other elements included in a program of interventions being considered to address some form of need (e.g., unemployment, reintegration of veterans into the workforce, training for legal immigrants, career readiness for high school students). For example, such a program might include financial incentives, short-term job training, job shadowing, internships, career counseling, etc., in which these interventions are integrated to increase the program's odds of success. The basic premise here is that most people with career concerns have multiple career needs, not just one.

Concern about policy coherence in career services is often viewed in terms of the implementation of policy at the federal level (Herr & Pinson, 1982), although there are parallels in many state governments. In the United States, national policy, legislation, and funding are highly interactive. Policy directly spawns and gives rationale to specific legislative enactments and to the authorization of funding for specific purposes articulated in the policy. As noted previously, many separate power centers affect the content of the legislation that is ultimately passed. Federal departments (e.g., Education, Labor, Health and Human Services, Defense, etc.) are particularly important in recommending and shaping legislation as it moves through the political process. Each of these departments tends to have its own constituencies and the independent ability to recommend policies and levels of funding to the Congress for conversion into legislation.

One can also acknowledge other ways to frame legislation explicitly directed to the establishment and implementation of specific career services. As examples, in the midst of the Great Depression of the 1930s with widespread unemployment, the Wagner-Peyser Act (1933) established the U.S. Employment Service to provide vocational counseling for people with work adjustment problems, people experiencing difficulty in finding work, or people with disabilities. In 1998, the Workforce Investment Act subsumed the Wagner-Peyser Act and created one-stop centers for people falling into the following groups: (1) people seeking work, (2) people seeking information about the governmental benefits available to them, and (3) people who could benefit from computer-assisted information on available jobs and related topics and perhaps from limited time with a career practitioner.

In 1951, the Veterans Administration Vocational Rehabilitation and Education Service was created to provide career services for veterans. The Carl D. Perkins Vocational Education and Applied Technology Act (1985) has, through much of its history, provided the largest source of funding for career guidance in schools and other organizations. Thus, public policy and legislation over the decades have continued to address what are seen as national problems or national goals and have included the elements of career development as important evidence-based practices.

Career Development Public Policy at a Crossroads

The current context of public policy and career development raises serious concerns relative to continued funding for career services. For the multiple reasons identified above, the stage has not been set, the groundwork has not been laid, and the constituencies have not been adequately formed to convince policymakers of the need to invest money in career development services. As a result, the career services provided to students and adults are often uneven, varying across geographic settings, and a foundation for evidence-based best practices has not been established. A startling example of this truth is that even while experiencing record levels of unemployment, one-stop career shops funded by the Workforce Investment Act of 1998 are being substantially reduced in number. Furthermore, lawmakers question whether the continued funding of elementary and secondary school counselors to assist students with their career development is worthwhile. At best, the current context is at a crossroads relative to ongoing support for career services.

The need for organized and systematic public policy efforts among career development stakeholders is urgent and will continue to be so through the current economic challenges. The good news is that opportunities exist; the strategies seem obvious; practitioners are still in place; professional associations committed to career development thrive; and the need is demonstrated. Only what the eventual response will be is questionable. Unfortunately, this question looms large as roadblocks remain.

Despite the desperate condition of many workers and the fragile continuation of career development public policies and related legislation, stakeholders remain largely fragmented. Professional associations with career development investments rarely act collaboratively. Unions representing workers and practitioners providing career services to workers rarely interact. Training for career practitioners in one-stop career centers is low at best, by any standard, despite existing training standards. Data supporting the need for public policies supporting career development interventions remain minimal.

Opportunities for Public Policy Engagement

First, while it is important to note that the current economy stimulates a sense of crisis, the need for active engagement within the processes related to public policy and legislative action is ongoing. Ignoring the challenges in positive economic periods is just as dangerous as doing so during economic downturns. Indeed, from 1948 to 2010, the unemployment rate in the United States averaged 5.7%, a percentage that still represents millions of U.S. citizens. "Acceptable" levels of unemployment can be deceptive because they do not account for those who have simply given up searching for employment. Underemployment continues to be a structural challenge that reflects wasted talent within the labor force. Even in the best of times economically, many people are still occupationally and economically disenfranchised, so the need for active engagement in career development public policy is consistent and continual.

Most importantly, engagement in career development public policy needs to be comprehensive, wide-ranging, and systematic. Career development theorists, career practitioners, career development scholars, career development professional associations, business and industry leaders, educational

leaders, and others must commit to policy engagement. There are several basic ways that we can take concrete action:

1. Be sure that you understand the issues and what is at stake.

2. Be sure that members of Congress understand the issues and what is at stake.

3. Get in touch with your legislators and communicate clearly about the impact of career development interventions on the lives of their constituents.

4. Encourage career-related professional associations to engage in collaborative advocacy efforts to advance public policy and legislation in support of career development.

Many career development professionals are not engaged in policy issues. As noted previously, counselor training programs do little, if anything, to foster an awareness of the importance of career development and public policies (Niles & Nassar-McMillan, 2009). When this information is not taught to emerging professionals, then it is easy to conclude that such information is not important or relevant to one's subsequent work. Thus, acquiring an understanding of the issues and what is at stake can begin during training programs. Infusing information about public policy, legislation, advocacy, and social justice can link practice with policy and makes policy engagement part of career practitioners' work. Practitioners can also offer invitations to public officials to visit their workplace. Clients who are willing can offer testimonial statements as to how career development interventions have helped them manage their lives more effectively. Showing the impact of career services in such ways helps bring to life the importance of career development interventions for public officials.

That said, many trainers of career practitioners may themselves be unaware of public policy issues and processes. Arming oneself with data serves as an appropriate starting point for becoming aware of career development and public policy issues. Federal and state data available online include such resources as quarterly performance reports, salary information, and unemployment data. The International Centre for Career Development and Public Policy (http://www.iccdpp.org/) provides important resources related to public policy initiatives affecting career development services around the world. Reviews of career guidance policies in various national contexts, such as those conducted by Watts et al. (e.g., Watts, 2005), provide rich resources for identifying strategies being used to influence career service delivery. As noted above, personal stories regarding how career development interventions have made a difference in a person's life also communicate the real and potential impact of career development interventions. Career development scholars should look for opportunities to connect their research to public policy. Infusing an "Implications for Career Development Public Policy" section in manuscripts when it is appropriate to do so (as is being done in *The Career Development Quarterly*) will help elevate the importance of this topic in the professional literature. Sharing information, personal stories, and data with the press, online, and directly with governmental officials and others in positions to make decisions about career development public policies is essential and must fall within the realm of the career practitioner's responsibilities.

Collectively, these strategies can have an impact on Congress or on state legislatures. This is especially true when there is a substantial influx of new members of Congress, as happened recently in the United States. Career development stakeholders need to make their legislators' jobs easier by taking the initiative to raise legislative awareness related to the importance of career development interventions, especially in terms of how such interventions contribute to lower social and economic costs (Herr, Cramer, & Niles, 2004). Many legislators do not understand career development needs in general and within a developmental perspective in particular. Learning about career development is not likely to occur without systematic efforts on the part of career development stakeholders.

Summary

In this chapter we have emphasized reasons for engaging in public policy, the changing organization of work and the shifting skills requirements for employment, conflicts between work and family, the meaning of work, public policy defined, public policy in historical context, and other related themes. These themes give expression to public policy and career development. There are many other themes that arise in different venues, for different purposes, and with different levels of training of career practitioners. Suffice it to say that these themes change as the larger societies change and constantly create new practices, new policies, and new research and scholarship in career development services.

In large measure, many nations have participated in the collection, analysis, and reporting of the data that provide new understandings of career development and the effects of career interventions among different populations. The World Bank, the International Monetary Fund, National Funds, and other sources have funded much of this information. The articles or chapters we have cited represent a small proportion of the information now available on career development and public policy around the world. Those who have written about public policy in their own nation or globally are increasingly asking the following questions: How do we learn from other nations? How can we implement evidence-based practices as defined by scholars in the field? What are the major elements of public policy that must be compared across nations and within particular nations?

There is much to be proud of in our history, and given the increased awareness of the link between career services and public policy, the future can be even stronger. Whether the future is stronger, however, depends on the willingness of career development specialists to embrace the linkage between career practice, theory, and policy.

References

Arthur, N. (2008). Qualification standards for career practitioners. In J. A. Athanasou & R. Van Esbroeck (Eds.), *International handbook of career guidance* (pp. 303–332). Springer Science + Business Media B.V.

Bureau of Labor Statistics (2012). *International labor comparisons*. Washington, DC: Author.

Blustein, D. (1997). A context-rich perspective of career exploration across the life roles. *Career Development Quarterly*, 45, 260–274.

Bridges, W. (1994). *Job shift*. Reading, MA: Addison-Wesley.

Frone, M. R. (2000). Work-family conflict and employee psychiatric disorders: The National Co-morbidity Survey. *Journal of Applied Psychology*, 85, 888–895.

Grzyacz, J. G., Almeida, D. M., & McDonald, D. A. (2002). Work-family spillover and daily reports of work and family stress in the adult labor force. *Family Relations*, 51, 28–36.

Hall, D. T., & Mirvis, P. H. (1996). The new protean career: Psychological success and the path with a heart. In D. T. Hall & Associates (Eds.), *The career is dead—long live the career A relational approach to careers* (pp. 15–45). San Francisco, CA: Jossey-Bass.

Herr, E. L. (1974). *Vocational guidance and human development*, Boston, MA: Houghton Mifflin.

Herr, E. L. (1993). Multiple agendas in a changing society: Policy challenger confronting career guidance in the U.S.A. *British Journal of Guidance and Counseling*, 19, 267–282.

Herr, E. L. (1996). Trends in career guidance theory and practice and the effects of social context and individual reactions. *Educational and Vocational Guidance*, 58, 33–48.

Herr, E. L. (2002). Costs/benefits of career development. In L. Bezanson & E. O'Reilly (Eds.), *Making waves: connecting career development with public policy* (pp. 25–30). Ottawa, Canada: Canadian Career Development Foundation.

Herr, E. L. (2008). *The importance of career development for an uncertain world: Public policy, legislation, and professional advocacy.* Keynote address at the National Career Development Association annual conference, "Career Development, Public Policy, and Advocacy: Finding Our Voice and Making It Heard," Washington, DC.

Herr, E. L., Cramer, S. H., & Niles, S. G. (2004). *Career guidance and counseling through the lifespan* (6th ed.). Boston, MA: Allyn & Bacon.

Herr, E. L., & Pinson, N. (1982). *Foundations for policy in guidance and counseling.* Falls Church, VA: American Personal and Guidance Association.

Hoyt, K. B. (2005). *Career education: Its history and future.* Tulsa, OK: National Career Development Association.

Landy, F. J. (1989). *Psychology of work behavior* (4th ed.). Pacific Grove, CA: Brooks/Cole.

National Defense Education Act of 1958. Retrieved February 1, 2011, from Encyclopedia.com: http://www.encyclopedia.com/doc/1G2-3468301841.html

Niles, S. G., & Harris-Bowlsbey, J. (2009). *Career development interventions in the 21st century* (3rd ed.). Columbus, OH: Merrill Prentice Hall.

Niles, S. G., Herr, E. L., & Hartung, P. (2002). Emerging adult career concerns in contemporary society. Traditional career development theories. In S. G. Niles (Ed.), *Adult career development: Concepts, models, and practices* (3rd ed., pp. 3–20). Columbus, OH: National Career Development Association.

Niles, S. G., & Nassar-McMillan, S. (2009). *Public policy and social justice in career development training.* Paper presented at the International Association of Educational and Vocational Guidance conference, Jyvaskyla, Finland.

OECD (2010). *PISA 2009 Results: What students know and can do: Student performance in reading, mathematics, and science* (Vol. i).

President's Council of Advisors on Science and Technology. (2010, September). *Prepublication version.* Washington, DC: Author.

Raynor, J. O., & Entin, E. E. (1982). *Motivation, career striving, and aging.* New York: Hemisphere.

Reich, R. (1991). *The work of nations: Preparing ourselves for 21st century capitalism.* New York: Alfred Knopf.

Rifkin, J. (1995). *The end of work.* New York: Putnam.

Sampson, J. P. Jr., Dozier, V. C., & Colvin, G. P. (2011). Translating career theory to practice: The risk of unintentional social injustice. *Journal of Counseling & Development, 89,* 326–337.

Super, D. E. (1990). A life-span, life-space approach to career development. In D. Brown & L. Brooks (Eds.), *Career choice and development: Applying contemporary theories to practice* (pp. 197–261). San Francisco, CA: Jossey-Bass.

Watts, A. G. (2005). Career guidance policy: An international review. *Career Development Quarterly, 54,* 66–76.

INDEX

A
academic motivation, educational reform, 281–282
ACCESS program, 134
acculturation, career development, 77–78
Achieving Success Identity Pathways (ASIP), 285
ADFC. *See* Aid to Families with Dependent Children
adolescents, poverty and, 131–132
adult workers. *See also* older workers
  accessibility and acceptability, 303–304
  career coaching, 297
  case description, 301–303
  cultural context in career transition, 295–296
  entry and reentry transitions, 294
  faith-based programs, 297–298
  future directions, 306
  importance of finding a job, 304
  modifications to meet needs of, 303–306
  psychology of working, 301–303
  supporting interventions, 304–305
  training and employment services, 296–301
  vocational theory and employment, 305–306
  work transitions for, 293–296
African Americans. *See also* race
  age-related health status, 170–171
  American Dream, 274
  barriers, supports, and meaning of work, 236
  career transition, 295–296
  case of psychotherapy, 264–268
  counseling for work-based challenges, 236–237
  critical psychology, 22, 23
  demographics in United States, 73
  double jeopardy hypothesis, 75
  education and family support, 77
  education reform, 286
  harassment of employed women, 92

helping clients change, 237
history in U.S. labor force, 74
household economy model, 143
labor and education, 73
labor force projections, 165
new career paradigm, 259–260
racial group, 72
sexual identity management, 118, 119
sociopolitical development, 280
unpaid care work, 148
women to men's earnings ratios, 87
working, wages and poverty, 128–130
working women of color, 86
Age Discrimination in Employment Act (ADEA) (1967), 163, 176–177
agency, 43, 46
Age of Enlightenment, 38
Age of Reason, 38
aging and working, 11, 160–162. *See also* older workers
  age and training, 165–166
  age and work attitudes, 165
  age and work withdrawal, 166
  Age Discrimination in Employment Act (ADEA), 176–177
  age forms for work and retirement, 164–165
  Americans with Disabilities Act (ADA), 177
  assessing the older worker, 167–170
  defining the older worker, 162–164
  employment across lifespan, 161–162
  job analysis and job descriptions, 167–168
  low income and older workers, 162
  needs assessment, 168–170
  performance changes, 170–177
  prolonging productivity across lifespan, 178
  recommendations for future research, 179–181
  resilience of older worker, 161
  rethinking, 214
  retirement, 162, 164–165

self-management theory, 166–167, 168f, 169f
  unemployment, 161
Aid to Dependent Children legislation, 144
Aid to Families with Dependent Children (ADFC), 129
alienating approach, professional values, 25
American Dream, 129, 273, 274
American Psychological Association (APA), 256
American Psychologist, 228
Americans with Disabilities Act (ADA) (1990), 177, 187, 189, 190, 195
Asian Americans. *See also* race
  American Dream, 274
  career transition, 295
  demographics in United States, 73
  family changes, 152
  history in U.S. labor force, 74
  labor and education, 73
  labor force projections, 165
  racial group, 72
  unpaid care work, 148
  women to men's earnings ratios, 888
attachment theory, psychology of working and psychotherapy, 266–267
attitudes
  employers and disabilities, 189
  older workers, 165

B
backlash, resistance to change, 108
Bailey, Hugh A., 298–299
Bakhtin, Mikhail, 39
Baritz, Lorenz, 220
behavioral injustice, 27
behaviorism, psychometric psychology, 23
Best Buy, identity engagement, 208–209
Bingham, Walter Van Dyke, 219, 220
bisexual people. *See also* LGBT (lesbian, gay, bisexual and transgender)
  LGBT vocational psychology, 103–105